SCHOOL FINANCE
A Policy Perspective

SCHOOL FINANCE
A Policy Perspective

FOURTH EDITION

ALLAN R. ODDEN
University of Wisconsin–Madison

LAWRENCE O. PICUS
University of Southern California

Boston   Burr Ridge, IL   Dubuque, IA   New York
San Francisco   St. Louis   Bangkok   Bogotá   Caracas   Kuala Lumpur
Lisbon   London   Madrid   Mexico City   Milan   Montreal   New Delhi
Santiago   Seoul   Singapore   Sydney   Taipei   Toronto

The **McGraw·Hill** Companies

Mc
Graw
Hill

Published by McGraw-Hill, an imprint of The McGraw-Hill Companies, Inc., 1221 Avenue of the Americas, New York, NY 10020. Copyright © 2008. All rights reserved. No part of this publication may be reproduced or distributed in any form or by any means, or stored in a database or retrieval system, without the prior written consent of The McGraw-Hill Companies, Inc., including, but not limited to, in any network or other electronic storage or transmission, or broadcast for distance learning.

This book is printed on acid-free paper.

1 2 3 4 5 6 7 8 9 0 DOC/DOC 0 9 8 7

ISBN: 978-0-07-352592-1
MHID: 0-07-352592-8

Editor in Chief: *Emily Barrosse*
Publisher: *Beth Mejia*
Sponsoring Editor: *David Patterson*
Marketing Manager: *Sarah Martin*
Developmental Editor: *Jill Eccher, Van Brien & Associates*
Production Editor: *Holly Paulsen*
Manuscript Editor: *Thomas L. Briggs*
Design Manager: *Violeta Diaz*
Text Designer: *Sharon Spurlock*
Cover Designer: *Ayelet Arbel*
Production Supervisor: *Randy Hurst*
Composition: *10/12 Palatino by Laserwords*
Printing: *45# New Era Matte, R. R. Donnelley & Sons*
Cover: © Scott T. Baxter/Getty Images

Library of Congress Cataloging-in-Publication Data

Odden, Allan
    School finance : a policy perspective / Allan R. Odden, Lawrence
O. Picus.—4th ed.
      p. cm.
    Includes bibliographical references (p.) and indexes.
    ISBN-13: 978-0-07-352592-1
    ISBN-10: 0-07-352592-8
    1. Education—United States—Finance. 2. Education—United
States—Finance—Computer simulation. I. Picus, Larry. II. Title.

LB2825.0315 2007
379.1'21'0973—dc21

www.mhhe.com

About the Authors

Allan Odden is professor of educational leadership and policy analysis at the University of Wisconsin–Madison. He also is codirector of the Consortium for Policy Research in Education (CPRE), which is funded by the U.S. Department of Education; the director of the CPRE Education Finance Research Program; and principal investigator for the CPRE Teacher Compensation Project, funded by the Carnegie Corporation, the Joyce Foundation, and the Gates Foundation through the School Finance Redesign Project at the University of Washington. CPRE is a consortium of the University of Wisconsin–Madison and Pennsylvania, Harvard, Michigan, and Stanford Universities. He formerly was professor of Education Policy and Administration at the University of Southern California (USC) and director of Policy Analysis for California Education (PACE), an educational policy studies consortium of USC, Stanford University, and the University of California–Berkeley.

Odden is an international expert on education finance, school-based financing, resource allocation and use, educational policy, school-based management, teacher compensation, district and school decentralization, education incentives, and educational policy implementation. He worked with the Education Commission of the States for a decade, serving as assistant executive director, director of policy analysis and research, and director of its educational finance center. He was president of the American Educational Finance Association in 1979–80 and received its Distinguished Service Award in 1998. He has served as research director for special state educational finance projects in Connecticut (1974–75), Missouri (1975–77), South Dakota (1975–77), New York (1979–81), Texas (1988), New Jersey (1991), and Missouri (1992–93). Over the past five years, together with coauthor Lawrence Picus, he has conducted adequacy studies for Arkansas, Arizona, Kentucky, Washington, Wisconsin, and Wyoming. He also is directing research projects on school finance redesign, resource reallocation, the use of resources by educational strategy at the school level, the costs of professional development, and teacher compensation. He was appointed Special Court Master to the Remand Judge in the New Jersey *Abbott v. Burke* school finance court case for 1997 and 1998. He has written widely, publishing over 220 journal articles, book chapters, and research reports, and 30 books and monographs. He has consulted for governors, state legislators, chief state school officers, national and local unions, the National Alliance for Business, the Business Roundtable, New American Schools, the U.S. Congress, the U.S. Secretary of Education, many local school districts, the state departments of education in Victoria and Queensland, Australia, and the Department for Education and Employment in England.

Odden's books include *Reallocating Resources: How to Boost Student Achievement Without Spending More* (Corwin, 2001), with Sarah Archibald; *School-Based Financing* (Corwin, 1999), with Margaret Goertz; *Financing Schools for High Performance: Strategies for Improving the Use of Educational Resources* (Jossey-Bass, 1998), with Carolyn Busch; How to Create World Class Teacher Compensation (Freeload Press, 2007, downloadable at www.freeloadpress.com), with Marc Wallace; *Paying Teachers for What They Know and Do: New and Smarter Compensation Strategies to Improve Schools* (Corwin Press, 1997; 2nd edition, 2002), with Carolyn Kelley; *Educational Leadership for America's Schools* (McGraw-Hill, 1995); *Rethinking School Finance: An Agenda for the 1990s* (Jossey-Bass, 1992); *School Finance: A Policy Perspective* (McGraw Hill, 1992, 2000, 2004), coauthored with Lawrence Picus; *Education Policy Implementation* (State University of New York Press, 1991); and *School Finance and School Improvement: Linkages for the 1980s* (Ballinger, 1983).

Odden was a mathematics teacher and curriculum developer in New York City's East Harlem for five years. He received his Ph.D. and M.A. degrees from Columbia University, a masters of divinity from the Union Theological Seminary, and his B.S. from Brown University.

Lawrence O. Picus is a professor of school finance and educational administration at the University of Southern California's Rossier School of Education. He also serves as the director of the Center for Research in Education Finance (CREF), a school finance research center housed at the Rossier School of Education, that focuses on issues of school finance adequacy, equity, and productivity. His current research interests include adequacy and equity in school finance, as well as efficiency and productivity in the provision of educational programs for K–12 schoolchildren. He is past-president of the American Education Finance Association.

Picus's most recent books include *In Search of More Productive Schools: A Guide to Resource Allocation in Education*, published by the ERIC Clearinghouse on Educational Management in January 2001; *Leveraging Resources for Student Success: How School Leaders Build Equity*, co-authored with Mary Ann Burke, Reynaldo Baca, and Catherine Jones (Corwin Press, 2003); and *Developing Community Empowered Schools* (Corwin, 2001), co-authored with Mary Ann Burke. Picus is the co-author of *School Finance: A Policy Perspective* (McGraw-Hill, 1992, 2000, 2004) with Allan Odden, and *Principles of School Business Administration* (ASBO, 1995) with R. Craig Wood, David Thompson, and Don I. Tharpe. In addition, he is the senior editor of the 1995 yearbook of the American Education Finance Association, *Where Does the Money Go? Resource Allocation in Elementary and Secondary Schools* (Corwin, 1995). He has also published numerous articles in professional journals.

Picus has worked on the assessment and design of school funding systems in numerous states including Vermont, Washington, Oregon, California, Kansas, Texas, Massachusetts, and Wyoming. Together with Allan Odden, he has conducted adequacy studies for Arkansas, Arizona, Kentucky, Washington, Wisconsin, and Wyoming.

To my wife, Eleanor, still best friend, sharpest critic, and loving supporter.

Allan Odden

To Susan Pasternak and Matthew Picus, who still wake up at four in the morning to the smell of coffee and the tapping of my computer keys; your love and support make this work more meaningful.

Larry Picus

Contents

6 ALLOCATION AND USE OF THE EDUCATION DOLLAR *179*

7 USING EDUCATION RESOURCES MORE EFFECTIVELY *206*

8 SCHOOL DISTRICT BUDGETING *234*

9 SCHOOL FINANCE STRUCTURES: FORMULA OPTIONS *263*

10 THE PUBLIC FINANCE CONTEXT *322*

11 IMPROVING STATE SCHOOL FINANCE SYSTEMS *364*

Preface

Public school financing in the United States is a big business; it involved over $440.2 billion, 48.7 million public school students, over 3.5 million teachers, and an additional 1.5 million administrators and staff in 2005. School finance has been and continues to be a top-priority policy issue at the state and local levels, and one of the top issues the public identifies as needing attention at the national level as well. The adequacy of funding in general and productivity in the use of education dollars in particular are issues leading school finance policy deliberations today.

In this fourth edition of *School Finance: A Policy Perspective,* we continue the emphasis of the first three editions on the use of education dollars and the need to spend current and all new dollars on more effective programs and services—in short, to use the dollars in the education system to more effectively produce student learning. Our prime goal in the fourth edition is to strengthen the book's orientation to the issues that school principals and other site-based education leaders face on a daily basis, while maintaining our efforts to instill a deep understanding of the issues faced by those at the policy level in school districts and states. To do this, we have enhanced the chapters that we added in the third edition on budgeting at the district and school levels and on financing facilities, and we have added a new chapter that describes our evidence-based approach to school finance adequacy. That chapter addresses what resources, programs, and services are needed in prototypical elementary, middle, and high schools to provide every child an equal educational opportunity to achieve at a level that will meet any state's student proficiency standards. Following the introduction of our evidence-based model, we incorporate discussion of these resources in subsequent chapters on resource allocation and reallocation, budgeting, and reform of state school finance systems. This enables readers to compare and contrast the resources in their state, district, and school to at least one approach that could be deemed "adequate." We have continued to streamline several of the other chapters (sometimes even dividing them into two separate chapters) to concentrate on key issues in school finance litigation, definitions of equity and adequacy, revenue raising, and revenue distribution (both state-to-district and district-to-school). We also have updated all material from the third edition.

The fourth edition includes a revised simulation capacity that allows readers to input staffing and resource data from a school and to immediately receive a report indicating whether the school can, via resource reallocation, afford the strategies included in the adequacy model developed in Chapter 4. In addition, the book includes a revised and enhanced school finance simulation that enables students, professors, and researchers to use the web (www.mhhe.com/odden4e) to analyze the nature of school finance problems and to simulate the effects of different school finance structures on both a 20-district sample of districts and universe data sets for several states.

The fourth edition has five major sections:

1. Three introductory chapters, one providing an overview of key school finance issues, one on issues in school finance litigation, and one that develops an equity and adequacy framework for analyzing state school finance structures
2. Two chapters, one that identifies adequate resources for a prototypical elementary, middle, and high school using the evidence-based approach to school finance adequacy that the authors have developed and used with many state legislative commissions around the country, followed by a chapter that covers financing school facilities
3. Three chapters on allocating and budgeting resources: one on how resources are currently allocated; one on how resources could be more effectively allocated, emphasizing the allocation recommendations in the evidence-based model; and one on budgeting dollars to schools with an emphasis on moving to a school-based budgeting approach
4. Four final chapters that attempt to pull all of this together: an updated chapter on state-to-district formulas, a chapter on the tax issues related to school finance, a chapter on reforming a state's school finance system to make it fairer and more adequate, and a final chapter that describes a number of new approaches to enhancing teacher compensation
5. An appendix that provides instructions on the simulation in chapter 9

1. INTRODUCTION AND OVERVIEW

Chapter 1 serves as an introduction to the topic of school finance. It begins with information on the current status of funding for public K–12 education in the United States, showing how much is spent, where those funds come from, and how levels and sources of funding have changed over time. It shows that as a nation, we spend a great deal of money on K–12 education and that the amount we spend has grown considerably over time. Chapter 1 also discusses the manner in which school finance inequities have changed over the past 30 years. The chapter looks at the "traditional" school finance inequities in several states, where districts with lower property wealth per pupil tend to have lower expenditures per pupil—even with higher school tax rates—than do districts with higher per-pupil property wealth. These high-wealth districts tend to have higher per-pupil expenditures even with lower school tax rates.

The chapter then shows that several states today have what we call the "new" school finance problem: higher-property-wealth districts with higher expenditures per pupil but also higher tax rates, and lower-property-wealth per-pupil districts with lower expenditures per pupil but also lower school tax rates. The chapter suggests that remedying these different types of fiscal inequities might require very different school finance reform strategies. Finally, the chapter discusses how the issue of "adequacy" has entered the school finance policy agenda.

Chapter 2 reviews the evolution of school finance court cases, from the initial *Serrano v. Priest* decision to the adequacy cases of the late 1990s and early 2000s. The chapter shows how strongly litigation has shifted from equity to adequacy issues. This chapter has been almost completely rewritten to make the ideas and concepts more understandable and to update all the pertinent legal issues. A chart on the book's website (www.mhhe.com/odden4e) contains citations for the various school finance court decisions across the country, and their constitutional bases.

Chapter 3 begins with a short discussion of whether money "matters," arguing that this was more of an issue in the twentieth century, when attention was primarily focused on equity. We argue that today, the adequacy issue directly relates to the "does money matter" question, so it is not an "add-on" but a core issue in school finance. The chapter then develops an equity-and-adequacy framework for analyzing state school finance systems. It draws from the Berne and Stiefel (1984) equity framework that was used in the first edition of the text, and adds a discussion of such issues as ex ante versus ex post equity perspectives, the unit of analysis, and various elements of equity including the group, the object, and different measures of horizontal and vertical equity. The chapter also adds the concept of adequacy to the overall framework and presents an adequacy statistic, the Odden-Picus Adequacy Index. The chapter concludes by asserting that most analyses of the equity and adequacy of state school finance systems use state and local revenues per pupil, and focus on the degree of per-pupil revenue equality (using the coefficient of variation and the McLoone Index statistics) and the degree of "fiscal neutrality," or the linkage between revenues per pupil and property wealth per pupil.

2. AN APPROACH TO SCHOOL FINANCE ADEQUACY

This part includes two related chapters. Chapter 4 identifies an adequate level of school resources, and Chapter 5 addresses the facilities within which those resources would be used.

Chapter 4 uses the evidence-based approach to school finance adequacy. One of the four major methods used around the country to identify an adequate level of education resources, we created it to use in the conduct of adequacy studies in several states. The model identifies a set of resources for prototypical elementary, middle, and high schools, based on the best available research, that will have a strong chance of helping all or almost all students meet their state's performance standards. The material in this chapter draws heavily from the work we have done in Arkansas, Arizona, Kentucky, Washington, Wisconsin, and Wyoming. We are currently conducting research in schools that have used this level and type of resources to double student performance over the past several years, and we are increasingly confident that the resources identified represent a reliable approach to identifying the resources needed to ensure school finance adequacy. The precise cost of adequacy in any state will depend on the teacher salary and benefits levels used to estimate total costs. The issue of compensation is addressed in an updated and revised Chapter 12. We recommend a careful review of Chapter 12 as we make reference to the material contained in that chapter in several places throughout the rest of the text. These include our discussion of the effective use of resources in Chapter 7, the information regarding budgeting at the school and district level in Chapter 8, and the material in Chapter 11 on redesigning a state's school finance structure to make sure it is adequate.

Chapter 5 addresses state approaches to financing educational facilities. First it discusses the differences between financing current and capital expenditures, and describes how school districts raise funds to build new schools, renovate existing schools, and finance long-term capital improvements to their facilities and grounds. The chapter then examines the complexities of bond financing, the equity issues surrounding the use of property taxes to pay off the principal and interest on bonds levied by school systems, current court rulings on capital funding for schools, and alternative finance options available to states and school districts as they strive to build and maintain adequate school facilities. Chapter 5 also provides an overview of the comprehensive approach that Kentucky has taken in funding school facilities. The chapter concludes with a summary of research on the impact of school facilities on student learning.

3. ALLOCATING AND BUDGETING DOLLARS FOR EDUCATIONAL PURPOSES

This section includes three chapters: Chapter 6 on current allocation and use of educational dollars, Chapter 7 on resource reallocation at the site level, and Chapter 8 on budgeting.

Chapter 6 is completely rewritten. It provides a detailed analysis of the way states, districts, and schools allocate and use educational resources, summarizing research from national-, state-, and school-level databases. It uses 1994–95 Schools and Staffing Survey data to illustrate how a 500-student elementary school, a 1,000-student middle school, and a 1,500-student high school are typically staffed in different regions of the country. The chapter shows that there are surprisingly common patterns in the uses of the education dollar. It also shows that during the past 30 years the large bulk of new dollars has been used to expand services outside the regular, core instructional program (i.e., to provide extra services for numerous categories of special pupil needs). The chapter concludes that while these uses reflect good values—more money for many categories of special-needs students—the specific applications of those new dollars have not had much impact on student learning. The implication is that we need to retain these values but find more effective uses for these extra resources. The chapter concludes with a recommendation for reporting expenditures of education resources by educational strategy at the school level—a new financial reporting mechanism that would provide expenditure information, now lacking, by the categories of adequate resources developed in Chapter 4.

Chapter 7 addresses the challenge of using school resources more effectively. It discusses the issue of resource reallocation to school-level strategies that produce higher student performance. Drawing from the school staffing discussion in Chapter 4, it examines resource use and reallocation processes that could produce expenditures in line with the model. This chapter does not draw definitive conclusions about the impact of the adequacy model (though it is an approach we strongly support), but it does show how this model has a cost structure different from traditional schools, and thus uses dollar resources differently.

This chapter also shows that there may be sufficient resources in some regions to fund this evidence-based model, but insufficient resources in others, thus suggesting that cross-state differences in educational spending need to be considered at some point.

To use the school redesign computer simulation program, readers need to input staffing and discretionary dollar data (note that it is only staffing resources and not the school's actual budget), together with the average cost of teachers, administrators, and instructional aides. The simulation then provides a report analyzing whether, fiscally and via resource reallocation, the school could afford the evidence-based model developed in Chapter 4. For readers who have followed some of this history, this amount would be more than sufficient to fund any of the comprehensive school designs developed by the New American Schools (Stringfield, Ross, and Smith, 1996). The chapter suggests an activity a professor could use as a course paper using these simulation results.

Chapter 8 is a substantially revised chapter on budgeting educational resources. It focuses more on the nuts and bolts of budgeting and less on research about budgeting processes. The chapter starts with the traditional triangle that structures budgeting—revenues, expenditures, and educational programs—and then discusses how these play out as central issues in school district budgeting. It includes examples of what district budget documents look like and explanations of the general fund and restricted funds. It also includes descriptions of various ways that districts provide resources to school sites, from the more traditional staffing formulas to emerging needs-based, per-pupil funding formulas. In addition, the chapter examines how the recommendations in Chapter 4, which identify adequate resources for prototypical schools, could be used to budget resources to all schools in a district. It also raises the issue of how expenditures might be reported by the same budgeting categories in the future. It includes short summaries of the weighted-pupil budgeting programs used in Seattle and San Francisco. The goal is to illuminate the key ways in which districts allocate resources for schools.

4. PULLING IT ALL TOGETHER

This section contains four Chapters. Chapter 9 describes state school funding formulas. Next, Chapter 10 provides public finance context for the information found in this book, and Chapter 11 discusses school finance issues in three states. Finally, Chapter 12 addresses teacher pay.

Chapter 9 begins by noting that all levels of government (local, state, federal) in the United States play a role in funding schools; this system is called fiscal federalism. It then describes the core elements of state school finance formulas: base allocations provided through flat grant, foundation, guaranteed tax base (district-power-equalizing and percentage-equalizing), and combination formulas. The chapter discusses generally how they work, using a 20-district sample in an updated simulation program. The focus of this chapter is on how different school finance formulas work (i.e., their costs and their effects on horizontal and vertical equity, as well as adequacy). The chapter includes a discussion of four different methods for determining an "adequate" base spending level: the professional-judgment approach, the successful-district approach, the cost-function approach, and the evidence-based approach.

While the last part of Chapter 4 discusses the rationales and the types of adjustments for three categories of special-needs children (those from a low-income background, those with physical and mental disabilities, and those with limited English proficiency), Chapter 9 describes different ways states can adjust funding formulas for these categories of special pupil needs.

Chapter 10 reviews the public finance context for school finance, analyzing the base, yield, elasticity, equity, economic effects, and administrative costs of income, sales, and property taxes as revenue sources for public schools. It discusses mechanisms to improve the regressive incidence at lower income levels of both the sales and the property tax, and reviews various property tax limitations states have enacted on this primary public school revenue source. It also includes a short analysis of lotteries as a source of school revenues.

Chapter 11 uses the analytic tools outlined in Chapters 3, 4, and 6 to identify school finance problems in three states, and then, using district data from the three states representing different kinds of school finance situations, suggests reforms that would remedy the identified problems. This chapter uses the simulation program, available on the McGraw-Hill website (www.mhhe.com/odden4e), adapted for the individual states. Over time, this website should have data sets for more states; it has data for more recent years for the states discussed in the chapter, so professors could have students analyze the nature of the school finance problems with more recent data, as well as simulate and propose school finance reforms.

The Vermont data set discussed in Chapter 11 presents the traditional school finance problem of unequal distribution of funds due to the unequal distribution of wealth. The chapter shows how traditional school finance models can be used to increase horizontal equity, fiscal neutrality, and adequacy, and to make adjustments for different student needs. The Wisconsin data set presents the "new" finance problem. In this instance, the wealthiest districts are relatively high spending but also have relatively high tax rate districts, while the poorest districts tend to be low spending and exert low tax efforts. The chapter shows how guaranteed tax base (GTB) programs exacerbate fiscal equity for such states and identifies alternative school finance mechanisms to improve inequity and adequacy. The Illinois data present a finance situation that not only is tricky to resolve but also requires substantial additional resources on both adequacy and property tax reduction grounds.

The goal of Chapter 11 is to show how various elements of school finance structures can be used to resolve different types of school finance problems. For each state, the chapter includes an analysis of both the school finance problem and the effectiveness or ineffectiveness of different formulas in resolving the problem.

One of the problems often encountered in school finance is that either funding formulas are established in a vacuum or their parameters are the result of available dollars. In the context of these state cases, this chapter uses policy "targets" to help remedy the school finance problems identified. For example, a state might decide it wants to provide a certain minimum level of support for all schools equal to 90 percent of the average spending of a certain type of district. Alternatively, policymakers may feel that all districts should have access to funds equal to some fixed percentage of wealth. The simulation helps students understand and determine logical policy targets, and assess their impact on the school finance problems in the different states.

We encourage any reader or professor to send us data sets from their states that we could convert into a simulation that could be added to the website. The variables we would need are described at the end of Chapter 11.

Chapter 12 is based largely on a handbook designed by Odden and Wallace (2007b) for state and local policymakers interested in redesigning teacher compensation systems to make them both more effective and more efficient. It addresses the issue of teacher salary levels and benchmarks that could be used by states and districts to set teacher salary levels, potentially at an "adequate" level. It discusses the need to provide salary premiums for teachers in subject area shortages (e.g., mathematics and science) and in hard-to-staff schools in high-poverty areas. It identifies several new "knowledge- and skills-based" teacher salary structures that would link the key factors leading to teacher salary increases to student learning gains. Finally, the chapter discusses how to design performance bonus programs that would provide either individual teachers or all teachers (as well as administrators and classified staff) in a school with a salary bonus for meeting preset targets for improved student performance. More details on these ideas can be found in Odden and Wallace (2007a).

All chapters in this fourth edition include a set of study questions. Many of these study questions can be used as formal assignments in a school finance course.

5. APPENDIX: THE SIMULATION

An integral part of this book is the school finance simulation designed to accompany the text. We have made a number of improvements to the simulation that accompanied previous editions of this book. The original 10-district simulation has been expanded to include 20 districts. Additionally, two new school finance statistics are provided—the Verstegen Index and the Odden-Picus Adequacy Index. The 20-district simulation is designed to accompany Chapter 9. We have found that the simulation dramatically improves student understanding of the statistics used by the school finance profession and helps them understand the myriad complexities involved in making changes to a state's school-funding system. The 20-district simulation that accompanies this edition should continue that tradition.

The simulation is available on the book's website at www.mhhe.com/odden4e. The appendix describes the general use of the simulation and provides information on how to access it on the web. Additional documentation is available on the website.

In addition to the 20-district simulation, we include data sets for several years for Kentucky, Illinois, Vermont, New Jersey, Virginia, and Wisconsin for analysis and simulation of alternative school finance reforms. As noted, if professors send us an Excel file with their state's data, we will create a simulation for that state as well and put it up on the web.

At the end of the preface of the first edition, we said, "We hope this will help the country accomplish its goals of having all students learn to think, solve problems and communicate, graduate from high school, and be first in the world in mathematics and science." We continue this hope with this edition.

ACKNOWLEDGMENTS

Writing a book of this magnitude is almost always the result of activities far beyond those of the authors. We are responsible for the text and for any errors and omissions, but without the insights, assistance, support, and work of others, a book might never see the light of day. We would like to thank the people who played major roles in helping us produce the fourth edition of this book.

Sarah Archibald, a researcher in the University of Wisconsin–Madison offices of the Consortium for Policy Research in Education (CPRE), helped with the rewritten versions of Chapters 6 and 7 specifically, and with other portions of the entire text. We also thank Michael Goetz for his work over the years on both the 20-district simulation and the various state simulations. He is a genius at debugging the glitches that have emerged in the simulations over the years, and in tailoring new data sets to state simulations. Professor William Glenn of Virginia Tech University rewrote Chapter 2 on the law related to school finance and created the Virginia simulation on the book's website. All helped with proofreading and preparing the new appendix.

Lisa Armstrong, administrative assistant in the University of Wisconsin CPRE offices was, as usual, the preeminent citation sleuth, tracking down innumerable citations that either simply needed to be found or needed completion. Without her help, we would still be at the computer or in the library.

We also would like to thank Jing Li and Ronn Hallett at USC whose efforts in preparing data for the chapters on taxation and budgeting are very much appreciated. Their tenacity in finding the often obscure data needed to complete one of the many tables or to help make a point in the text is much appreciated.

We would also like to extend a special thank you to our reviewers:

Tak Cheung Chan, *Kennesaw State University*
David W. Haney, *North Dakota State University*
Peter R. Madonia, *Southern Connecticut State University*
Robert Sopko, *Rider University*

We also wish to acknowledge the many unnamed individuals at the national, state, district, and school levels who, over the past decade, have allowed the school finance community to conduct research on their allocation and use of education resources. Without this research, the chapters of this book focused on resource allocation and use could not have been written. The landscape of school finance has changed over the past years, and what we know and continue to learn about the nature of these changes depends on the continued cooperation of local school officials who give up their time and allow us to intrude into their domain, conduct research to better understand what they do, and even help us describe the results.

Finally, we would like to thank our families, who once again have endured our working on the computer rather than engaging in family activities. Their support and sustenance knows no bounds, and we are grateful for their understanding, love, and steadfast support.

Allan R. Odden   Lawrence O. Picus
Madison, Wisconsin   Los Angeles, California

Chapter 1

Introduction to and Overview of School Finance

School finance concerns the distribution and use of money for the purpose of providing educational services and producing student achievement. For most of the twentieth century, school finance policy focused on equity—issues related to widely varying education expenditures per pupil across districts within a state caused by the uneven distribution of the property tax base used to raise local education dollars. In the 1990s, new attention began to focus on education adequacy and productivity—the linkages among level and use of funds and to student achievement. As the twenty-first century began, policymakers increasingly wanted to know how much money was needed to educate students to high standards; how those dollars should be distributed effectively and fairly among districts, schools, programs, and students; and how both level and use of dollars affected student performance. These policy demands are pushing school finance beyond its traditional emphasis on fiscal equity.

This book traces these movements of school finance into new directions. It addresses traditional equity issues and also discusses adequacy and productivity issues, including what is known about the linkages among dollars, educational strategies, and student performance. The 1980s and the 1990s were remarkable not only for the intensity of the school reform movement but also for the duration of interest in educational reform. Today, standards-based education reform—from content standards, to charter schools, to new accountability structures—seeks to teach students to high levels. In most instances, the implications of these reforms for school finance have not been fully considered, though Odden and Clune (1998) have argued that traditional school finance systems were "aging structures in need of renovation." During the 2000s, states and their respective school districts will need to rethink school finance systems to ensure that they can adequately meet the productivity expectations and accountability requirements inspired by these reforms, and properly fund an education system that needs to prepare students for work in the knowledge- and information-based global economy.

This book takes a policy approach to school finance analysis. To that end, it emphasizes the actions schools, districts, and states can take—and the policies they can enact—to address the equity, adequacy, productivity, and performance issues raised herein. It is important for graduate students in education, as well as educators and education policymakers, to understand both the finance implications of school reform policies and, equally important, the ways in which decisions about the distribution of funds to local schools and school districts affect the implementation of those reforms. In a departure from previous editions, this book focuses on school finance policy issues related to adequacy. In this chapter, we begin with a discussion of the scope of education finance in the United States, including the nature of school finance disparities linked to local financing of schools. Chapter 2 focuses on legal issues surrounding school finance, and Chapter 3 examines equity and adequacy issues. Chapter 4 introduces an evidence-based approach to school finance adequacy, which the authors of this text have developed and used with policy groups in a number of states. That chapter shows how the evidence-based approach can be used to staff schools to include all necessary components of an adequate education, including strategies for students who are struggling with the current curriculum or who have special needs.

The book moves from there into a description of a number of school finance policy issues, first at the school level, and then at the district and state levels. Chapter 5 discusses school facilities and their related school finance implications. Chapter 6 examines the allocation and uses of resources for education in the twenty-first century. Chapter 7 describes how schools can allocate resources more effectively to meet the demands of today's standards-based policy environment. Chapter 8 shifts to the district level, addressing ways to fund schools for success, including a section on creating weighted student formulas to fund schools within a school district. Chapter 9 adds another layer to the discussion, focusing on the state and detailing the different methods states can use to provide funds to school districts. Each of these funding mechanisms can be assessed through the computer-based simulation program that accompanies this book. By designing their own school finance formulas and simulating the impact on a sample of school districts, students will develop a more realistic sense of how changes in funding formulas influence school districts across a state. The simulation helps students understand the technical and political complexities that result when one attempts to redesign school-funding programs. Chapter 10, which also focuses on the state, discusses the different taxes used to raise money for education. Each of these tax sources is a basic school finance issue that principals, superintendents, and other education leaders should understand to be more effective in their jobs.

Chapter 11 provides examples from three states, complete with a computer simulation and several state databases, available on the McGraw-Hill website (**www.mhhe .com/odden4e**), that can be analyzed and assessed using the school finance simulation. This chapter shows how these three states have solved their school finance problems, and provides data from several other states that students can use to simulate the effects, costs, and impacts of different approaches to school finance reform.

The final chapter covers a variety of new issues related to teacher compensation, which is the largest consumer of the education dollar.

This introductory chapter has three sections. The first outlines the scope of school finance within the United States. Funding public schools is big business, and this section outlines its fiscal magnitude. The second section provides a quick history of school finance developments, beginning in the seventeenth century. This section shows how schools evolved from privately funded, parent- and church-run entities to the large, publicly and governmentally controlled education systems of today. The final section gives several examples of the "school finance problem" and traces how it has evolved from the traditional fiscal disparities across districts to the new issue of education adequacy.

1. THE SCOPE OF EDUCATION FINANCE IN THE UNITED STATES

Education is an enormous enterprise in the United States. It accounts for the largest portion of most state and local governmental budgets; engages more than 100,000 local school board members in important policymaking activities; employs millions of individuals as teachers, administrators, and support staff; and educates tens of millions of children.

Enrollment

Table 1.1 provides detail on public school enrollment, including numbers of school districts and schools, in the twentieth century. Enrollment was relatively constant during the 1930s and 1940s but rose quickly after World War II as the postwar baby boomers reached school age. After 25 years of rapid growth, public school enrollment declined during the 1970s but began to grow again in the mid-1980s when the children of the baby boom generation started school. In 2004–05, public school enrollment was estimated to be 48.7 million students, almost 3 million more than the previous generation's peak of 45.6 million in 1970. The National Center for Education Statistics predicts that school enrollment will continue to grow annually until 2015 when it will peak at 51.6 million (U.S. Department of Education, 2006).

Schools and School Districts

One of the major stories of the twentieth century was the consolidation of school districts into larger entities. In 2004, there were 14,383 school districts; in 1940, by contrast, there were 117,108 school districts. The number of school districts dropped by over 33,000 between 1940 and 1950 (i.e., after World War II), and then dropped by another 43,000 districts between 1950 and 1960. By 1970, there were only 17,995 local school districts, and that number continued to fall to today's level of less than 14,400. The number of districts varies across the states, however. In 2002, Texas had 1,041 districts and California had 989, whereas Hawaii had only one statewide school district.

 Interestingly, as will be discussed here, although school district consolidation also entails consolidation of the local property tax base, remaining inequities in local school financing after the bulk of consolidation had occurred led courts during the late 1960s and early 1970s to declare finance structures unconstitutional (see Chapter 2).

 Table 1.1 also shows that the number of public schools has dropped over time while enrollments have risen, indicating that schools grew in size during the twentieth century.

TABLE 1.1 Historical Data on the Size of the Nation's School Systems, 1919–20 to 2003–04

Year	Public School Student Enrollment (in 1,000s)	Public School Districts	Public Elementary Schools	Public Secondary Schools	Private Elementary Schools	Private Secondary Schools	Private Schools as Percentage of Total
1919–20	21,578	—	—	—	—	—	—
1929–30	25,678	—	238,306	23,930	9,275	3,258	5%
1939–40	25,434	117,108	—	—	11,306	3,568	—
1949–50	25,111	83,718	128,225	24,542	10,375	3,331	9
1959–60	35,182	40,520	91,853	25,784	13,574	4,061	15
1969–70	45,550	17,995[a]	65,800[a]	25,352[a]	14,372[a]	3,770[a]	20[a]
1979–80	41,651	15,929[b]	61,069[b]	24,362[b]	16,792[b]	5,678[b]	26[b]
1989–90	40,543	15,367[c,d]	61,669[d]	23,461[d]	22,223[d]	8,989[d]	37[b]
1999–2000	46,857	14,928[c]	68,173	26,407	24,685	10,693	37
2001–02	47,672	14,559[c]	70,516	27,468	26,569	11,846	39
2002–03	48,202	14,465	71,270	28,151	—	—	—
2003–04	48,541	14,383	71,195	28,219	—	—	—

Source: National Center for Education Statistics, *Digest of Education Statistics,* 2005b.

[a]Data for 1970–71.
[b]Data for 1980–81.
[c]Because of expanded survey coverage, data are not directly comparable with figures for earlier years.
[d]Data for 1990–91; for private schools, these data are from sample surveys and should not be compared directly with the data for earlier years.

There were over 262,000 public schools in 1930, but that number had dropped by almost 60 percent to just over 99,400 schools in 2004. On the other hand, the number of private schools has risen since 1930, from a low of about 12,500 to over 38,000 in 2002.

The Impact on the Economy

Funding public schools requires large amounts of dollars. In 2003, public school revenues totaled $440.2 billion, an increase of $232 billion—more than double the 1990 total of $208.5 billion (Table 1.2).[1] Indeed, the data show that public school revenues more than doubled during each decade from 1940 to 1990, a remarkable fiscal record. By way of comparison, in 2004–05, Exxon Mobil, the number one company on the 2006 *Fortune* 500 list, had total sales of $339.9 billion (Fortune, 2006).

Table 1.2 also shows that during the twentieth century, public education accounted for an increasing portion of the country's total economic activity (as measured by the gross domestic product), growing steadily until 1970, dropping, slightly during the enrollment decline of the 1970s, and then approaching the high reached in 1970 in recent years. The same pattern emerges when total public school revenues are measured as a percent of personal income; revenues peaked at 4.8 percent in 1970 and today represent approximately 4.5 percent of personal income. The 4.5 percent of personal income devoted to education represents a considerable effort on behalf of schools considering all the other items that individuals could purchase or to which tax revenues could be channeled.

TABLE 1.2 Educational Revenues, GDP, and Personal Income (in Billions), 1929–2004

Year	Total Educational Revenues	Gross Domestic Product (GDP)	Revenues as Percentage of GDP	Personal Income (PI)	Revenues as Percentage of PI
1929	$ 2.1	$ 103.6	2.0%	$ 85.1	2.5%
1940	2.3	101.4	2.3	78.5	2.9
1950	5.4	293.8	1.8	229.0	2.4
1960	14.7	526.4	2.8	411.5	3.6
1970	40.3	1,038.5	3.9	838.8	4.8
1980	96.9	2,789.5	3.5	2,307.9	4.2
1990	208.5	5,803.1	3.6	4,878.6	4.3
2000	372.9	9,817.0	3.8	8,429.7	4.4
2002	419.5	10,487.0	4.0	8,878.9	4.7
2004	440.2[a]	11,734.3	3.8	9713.3	4.5

Source: National Center for Education Statistics, *Digest of Education Statistics*, 2005b.
[a]Data for 2002–03.

[1]For 2004–05, the National Education Association (2005b) estimated total public school revenues to be $508 billion.

School Revenues and Expenditures

The use of a sizable portion of personal income for education is supported by the data in Table 1.3. Column 2 shows that real expenditures per pupil (i.e., expenditures adjusted by the Consumer Price Index) have increased each decade at extraordinary rates: 100 percent between 1920 and 1930, 67 percent in the 1960s, and 35 percent in the 1970s. Even during the 1980s, a decade of government tax and expenditure limitations, expenditures per pupil increased by 36 percent to a total of $7,009 (in 2005 dollars) for current operating purposes in 1989–90. At the turn of the century, an average of $7,827 was spent on each public school student—an increase of 11.7 percent. Clearly, real resources for public school students are substantial, and rise substantially each decade, although the rise during the 1990s was the smallest of the twentieth century.

These facts certainly are at odds with popular perceptions that schools do not receive much more money each year. Though real resources might increase only 1–3 percent each year, over most 10-year periods, these amount to nearly a one-third increase in real resources. As discussed in later chapters, the current efforts to define adequacy suggest that this trend may well continue in the foreseeable future.

As the last three columns in Table 1.3 show, sources of school revenues have changed over the years. Earlier in the twentieth century, local districts provided the bulk of school revenues, and federal funds were almost nonexistent. Beginning in the 1960s, the federal government began to increase its financial role, which reached its maximum at 9.8 percent in 1980. Since then, the federal contribution has dropped to approximately 8.5 percent of the total. Today, the states are the primary providers of public

TABLE 1.3   Educational Expenditures per Pupil and Revenues by Source, 1920–2003

Year	Expenditures per Pupil Real (2004–05 dollars)	Nominal	Total Revenues (in Millions)	Percentage of Revenues by Source Federal	State	Local
1919–20	$ 401	$ 40	$ 970	0.3%	16.5%	83.2%
1929–30	804	72	2,089	0.4	16.9	82.7
1939–40	1,047	76	2,261	1.8	30.3	68.0
1949–50	1,511	187	5,437	2.9	39.8	57.3
1959–60	2,286	350	14,747	4.4	39.1	56.5
1969–70	3,812	751	40,267	8.0	39.9	52.1
1979–80	5,157	2,088	96,881	9.8	46.8	43.4
1989–90	7,009	4,643	208,548	6.1	47.1	46.8
1994–95	7,046	5,529	273,149	6.8	46.8	46.4
1999–00	7,827	6,912	372,944	7.3	49.5	43.2
2002–03	8,468	8,044	440,157	8.5	48.7	42.8

Source: National Center for Education Statistics, *Digest of Education Statistics*, 2005b.

school revenues, having outdistanced local school districts during the 1970s era of school finance reforms. During the 2002–03 school year, the states provided 48.7 percent of public school revenues, local districts (primarily through property taxes) 42.9 percent, and the federal government 8.5 percent.

These national patterns, however, are very different in each of the 50 states, as shown in Table 1.4. The national average expenditure per pupil was $8,600 in 2002–03, but expenditures ranged from a low of $5,247 in Utah to a high of $13,211 in New York. Note that some data in this table are different from those in Table 1.3 because of slightly different data sources.[2]

States also differ in the sources of public school revenues. In Hawaii, for example, 90.1 percent of revenues derive from the state, as compared to only 30.2 percent in Nevada. States provide over 60 percent of school revenues in 8 states, while local districts provide over 50 percent of school revenues in 11 states. This variation reflects differences in local perceptions of appropriate state and local roles, as well as differences in school finance formula structures (Sielke, Dayton, Holmes, and Jefferson, 2001). These data document one enduring characteristic of state school finance structures: though there are some similarities, the differences are dramatic. Students of school finance need to understand both the generic similarities and the factors causing the specific differences.

2. EARLY DEVELOPMENTS IN SCHOOL FINANCE

This country has not always had a system of free, tax-supported schools. Free public education only came into being in the United States during the nineteenth century, and the large network of public school systems was formed in a relatively short period, primarily during the latter part of the nineteenth and early part of the twentieth century.

The First Schools

American schools began as local entities, largely private and religious, during the seventeenth, eighteenth, and even early nineteenth centuries. As in England, educating children was considered a private rather than a public matter. Providing for education was a mandate for parents and masters, not governments. Eighteenth-century leaders of the new American republic viewed education as a means to enable citizens to participate as equals in affairs of government and thus essential to ensure the liberties guaranteed by the Constitution. Even though Thomas Jefferson proposed creation of free public elementary schools, his proposal was not adopted until the mid-1800s, largely through the efforts of Horace Mann and Henry Barnard, state superintendents of public instruction. Mann spearheaded the development of publicly supported "common schools" in Massachusetts, and Barnard did the same in Connecticut.

---

[2]For 2004–05, the National Education Association (2005b) estimated average current operating expenditures to be $9,102 per pupil in average daily attendance.

TABLE 1.4   Educational Expenditures per Pupil and Revenues by Source, by State, 2002–03

| State | Expenditures per Pupil | Percentage of Revenues by Source | | |
		Federal	State	Local
Alabama	$ 6,642	11.6%	57.6%	25.7%
Alaska	10,770	17.7	56.8	23.3
Arizona	6,783	11.4	48.4	37.1
Arkansas	6,981	11.7	55.2	28.8
California	7,601	9.9	58.9	30.3
Colorado	7,826	6.5	43.1	46.4
Connecticut	11,302	5.2	37.4	55.8
Delaware	10,257	8.6	63.4	26.8
District of Columbia	14,735	13.8	N/A	85.5
Florida	6,922	10.5	43.6	41.9
Georgia	8,308	8.1	48.2	42.0
Hawaii	8,770	8.2	90.1	0.8
Idaho	6,454	9.8	59.1	29.5
Illinois	9,309	8.5	33.0	56.4
Indiana	8,582	7.6	58.8	30.1
Iowa	7,943	7.4	46.6	40.9
Kansas	8,373	9.1	57.1	31.2
Kentucky	7,728	10.6	58.8	28.5
Louisiana	7,492	13.2	49.1	36.6
Maine	10,114	8.9	42.9	46.3
Maryland	9,801	6.7	38.3	52.0
Massachusetts	11,161	6.0	40.9	51.6
Michigan	9,847	7.8	63.3	26.6
Minnesota	8,440	5.9	73.8	17.1
Mississippi	6,186	15.4	53.8	27.8
Missouri	8,002	8.0	35.8	52.3
Montana	8,391	14.5	46.3	35.1
Nebraska	8,550	8.9	34.4	51.7
Nevada	6,496	7.0	30.2	59.1
New Hampshire	8,900	5.2	48.9	43.6
New Jersey	13,093	4.3	43.5	50.1
New Mexico	7,126	15.0	72.1	11.1
New York	13,211	7.0	45.6	46.6
North Carolina	7,057	9.6	63.7	24.2
North Dakota	7,315	15.3	36.8	42.8
Ohio	9,160	6.4	44.8	45.3
Oklahoma	6,540	12.7	54.7	27.6

TABLE 1.4 (*continued*)

State	Expenditures per Pupil	Percentage of Revenues by Source		
		Federal	State	Local
Oregon	8,486	9.1	50.9	37.2
Pennsylvania	9,648	7.7	36.6	53.7
Rhode Island	11,377	6.5	42.0	50.2
South Carolina	7,759	9.8	48.1	38.4
South Dakota	7,192	15.7	33.7	47.5
Tennessee	6,674	10.0	43.8	39.6
Texas	7,714	9.9	40.9	47.0
Utah	5,247	9.3	56.4	32.3
Vermont	10,903	7.0	67.8	23.7
Virginia	8,300	6.6	39.6	51.8
Washington	7,882	9.0	61.8	26.0
West Virginia	9,025	10.6	61.4	26.9
Wisconsin	9,538	6.1	53.4	38.2
Wyoming	9,906	8.8	50.9	38.9
United States	8,600	8.5	48.7	40.5

Source: National Center for Education Statistics, *Digest of Education Statistics*, 2005b.

In the nineteenth century, as education began to assume significance in economic terms, many compulsory attendance laws were passed. Despite these laws, when school attendance became compulsory beginning in the mid-1800s, government financing of schools was not uniformly required.

In 1647, the General Court of Massachusetts passed the famous Old Deluder Satan Act. The act required every town to set up a school, or pay a sum of money to a larger town to support education; required towns with at least 50 families to appoint a teacher of reading and writing, and required towns with more than 100 families to also establish a secondary school; and required that these schools be supported by masters, parents, or the inhabitants in general, thereby establishing one of the first systems of financing schools through local taxation. According to Pulliam (1987), the first tax on property to fund local schools was levied in Dedham, Massachusetts, in 1648. By 1693, New Hampshire also required towns to support elementary schools.

The Growing Importance of State Governments

Initially, one-room elementary common schools were established in local communities, often fully supported through a small local tax. Each town functioned, moreover, as an independent school district, indeed as an independent school system, since there were no state laws or regulations providing for a statewide public education system. At the same time, several large school systems evolved in the big cities of most states. Even at this early time, these different education systems reflected differences in local ability to support them. Big cities were usually quite wealthy, while the smaller, rural school districts were usually quite poor, with many having great difficulty financing even a one-room school.

As the number of these rural and big-city school systems grew, however, and the importance of education as a unifying force for a developing country became increasingly evident to civic and political leaders, new initiatives were undertaken to create statewide education systems. By 1820, 13 of the then 23 states had constitutional provisions, and 17 had statutory provisions pertaining to public education.

In the mid-eighteenth century, several states began to completely rewrite state constitutions, not only calling for creation of statewide systems of public education but also formally establishing government responsibility for financing schools. Today, all states have constitutional provisions related to free public education.

Creation of free common schools reflected the perceived importance of education in America. It also shifted control over education from individuals and the church to the state. Resolution of the problematic issue of crafting statewide education systems involved creation of local lay boards of education that, it was argued, would function in the place of parents and the church.

Local boards basically controlled public schools for the first century they existed, but the extent of local control has changed substantially in recent years. In the early twentieth century, in the Progressive Era of education, much school control was given to the new breed of educational professionals in an effort to take politics out of education (Tyack and Hansot, 1982). Beginning in the 1960s, both the states and the federal government began to exert more control over public schools. States continued this trend by taking the lead for education policy throughout the 1980s' education reform period (Doyle and Hartle, 1985; Odden, 1995a). Local boards were for the most part uninvolved in those reforms (Odden, 1995a). In the early 1990s, the president and the nation's governors established nationwide education goals; these were codified into law in 1994 by the U.S. Congress and continue in spirit if not in detail today.

The development of the state-controlled and governmentally financed "common school" also raised many fundamental issues about school finance. The key issues concerned the level of government (local or state) that would support public education and whether new constitutional phrases such as "general and uniform," "thorough and efficient," "basic," or "adequate" meant spending an equal amount of dollars for every student in the state or merely providing a basic education program for every student, with funding determined at the local level. As discussed in Chapter 2, this controversy persists today and is resolved in different ways by state legislatures and courts in the 50 states.

The Continuing Evolution of the State Role

While major differences exist in the specific approaches taken, most states finance public schools primarily through local property taxes. Indeed, in the mid- to late 1800s, most states required local districts to fully finance mandated public schools through local property taxation. In designing locally administered school systems, states generally gave local governments the authority to raise money for schools by levying property taxes. But when states determined school district boundaries, districts ended up with widely varying levels of property wealth per pupil, and thus large differences in the ability to raise local dollars to support public education. Districts with above-average property tax bases per pupil were traditionally able to spend at above-average levels with below-average tax rates, while districts with below-average tax bases spent at below-average levels even with above-average tax rates—inequities noted 100 years ago (Cubberly, 1906).

School finance policy debates throughout the twentieth century, including most school finance texts (see, e.g., Alexander and Salmon, 1995; Guthrie, Garms, and Pierce, 1988; Odden and Picus, 1992, 2000, Chapter 1; Swanson and King, 1997) and most court cases, focused on these types of fiscal inequities. To be sure, some individuals pointed to spending differences per se, regardless of whether they were related to varying tax bases, and argued that they should be impermissible in a state education system (Wise, 1968). But the bulk of discussion centered on the links between spending differences and local property wealth per pupil (see also Coons, Clune, and Sugarman, 1970).

As discussed at length in Chapter 9, states began to intervene in school financing first through small per-pupil "flat grant" programs in which the state distributed an equal amount of money per pupil to each local school district. The idea was for the state to provide at least some assistance in support of a local basic education program. Over the years, however, these flat grants came to be recognized as too small.

In the early 1920s, states began to implement "minimum foundation programs," which provided a much higher level of base financial support and were financed with a combination of state and local revenues (minimum foundation programs and other technical school finance terms used in this chapter are defined and explained in detail in Chapter 9). These programs were the first in which states explicitly recognized the wide variation in the local property tax base and so designed a state aid structure to distribute larger amounts to districts with a small property tax base per pupil and smaller amounts to districts with a large property tax base per pupil.

These "equalization formulas" were designed to equalize differences in local fiscal capacity (i.e., the unequal ability to finance education because of the variation in the size of the local property tax base). But over time, the level of the minimum foundation programs also proved to be inadequate, and additional revenues were raised solely through local taxation. As a result, local educational expenditures per pupil varied widely across local districts in most states, with the differences related primarily to the size of the local property tax base.

Beginning in the late 1960s, these fiscal disparities caused by unequal distribution of the local tax base and inadequate state equalization programs led to legal challenges to state school finance systems in which plaintiffs, usually from low-wealth and low-spending districts, argued that the disparities were not only unfair but also unconstitutional (Berke, 1974; Coons, Clune, and Sugarman, 1970). Chapter 2 traces the course of these lawsuits, which spawned a new political channel to improve the ways states financed public education. This evolved in the 1990s into an "adequacy" strategy to link the funding structure to an education system that could teach nearly all students to high performance levels.

3. EVOLUTION OF THE SCHOOL FINANCE PROBLEM

The school finance problem became much more complicated in the 1990s and early twenty-first century. Though many still define the major school finance problem as differences in spending across school districts caused by varying levels of property wealth per pupil, others (e.g., Odden and Clune, 1998) argue that linking finance to an adequate education is the core school finance issue today. Still others argue that educational productivity—determining how to produce higher levels of educational performance with current education resources—is the primary goal (Hanushek and Associates, 1994).

Traditional Fiscal Disparities

This section examines school finance inequities in several states and shows how these fiscal inequities have changed over time.

California.   There are many ways to depict the types of fiscal disparities among school districts created by the unequal distribution of the property tax. Table 1.5 shows 1968–69 data that were presented in the original *Serrano v. Priest* (Cal. 3d 584, 487 P.2d 1241, 96 Cal. Rptr. 601 [1971]) court case in California (see Chapter 2 for more on this case); at that time, California had a typical minimum foundation program, and most districts raised additional funds to spend at a higher level. These data represent property value per child, the local school tax rate, and resulting expenditures per pupil for pairs of property-rich and property-poor districts in several counties. In each county, the assessed valuation per pupil—the local tax base—varied substantially: by a factor of almost 14 to 1 in Los Angeles County and over 16 to 1 in Alameda County. In each case, moreover, the district with the higher assessed value per child had both the higher expenditures per pupil and the lower tax rate.

These counties were selected to show that the California school finance structure produced a situation—similar to most other states at that time—in which districts with a low property tax base usually spent less than the state average even with above-average tax rates, while districts with a high property tax base usually spent above the state average with below-average tax rates. The wealthy enjoyed the advantages of both high expenditures and low tax rates, while the poor were disadvantaged by both low expenditures and high tax rates. The shortcoming of the data in Table 1.5 is that school finance information for only a few districts is shown. While these districts statistically reflected the trends in the system, trends should be analyzed using all of the districts in a state, not selected pairs of districts from different counties.

Colorado.   Another potentially misleading approach in presenting school finance data is to show the extreme cases, as was often done in school finance equity analyses in the 1960s and 1970s. An example is shown in Table 1.6, which displays for Colorado the assessed valuation per pupil for the richest and poorest districts, districts at the 90th and 10th percentiles, and the district in the middle. These 1977 data show that the difference

TABLE 1.5   Comparison of Selected Tax Rates and Expenditure Levels in Selected California Counties, 1968–69

County	Pupils	Assessed Value per Pupil	Tax Rate	Expenditure per Pupil
Alameda				
Emery Unified	586	$100,187	$2.57	$2,223
Newark Unified	8,638	6,048	5.65	616
Fresno				
Colinga Unified	2,640	33,244	2.17	963
Clovis Unified	8,144	6,480	4.28	565
Kern				
Rio Bravo Elementary	121	136,271	1.05	1,545
Lamont Elementary	1,847	5,971	3.06	533
Los Angeles				
Beverly Hills Unified	5,542	50,885	2.38	1,232
Baldwin Park Unified	13,108	3,706	5.48	577

Source: California Supreme Court Opinion in *Serrano v. Priest*, August 1971.

TABLE 1.6   Assessed Valuation per Pupil in Colorado School Districts, 1977

Highest: Rio Blanco–Rangely	$326,269
90th percentile: Eagle-Eagle	57,516
Median: Mesa–Plauteau Valley	20,670
10th percentile: Montezuma-Dolores	10,764
Lowest: El Paso–Fountain	4,197
Ratio: Highest/Lowest	77.7:1
Ratio: 90th/10th Percentiles:	5.3:1

Source: Education Finance Center, Education Commission of the States, from official data of the Colorado Department of Education.

between the wealthiest and poorest districts was 77.7 to 1. This means that at a tax rate of one mill,[3] the wealthiest district could raise $325.27 per pupil, while the poorest district could raise only $4.20! To raise the amount that the wealthiest district produced at one mill, the poorest district would have had to levy a tax rate of 77.7 mills, which is prohibitively high. To blunt the criticism that the extreme cases might represent anomalies, the values for districts at the 90th and 10th percentiles are also presented in Table 1.6. The figures show that property wealth per child still varied substantially, from a high of $57,516 to a low of $10,764, a difference of 5.3 to 1. While these differences are smaller

[3]One will yields $1 in revenue for each $1000 of assessed value.

than the range between the very top and bottom, the data clearly indicate substantial differences in school district ability to raise school funds through local property taxes.

Table 1.6 also shows the emphasis on variation in the local tax base in many early school finance analyses. What really matters, of course, is the interaction between the local tax base, local tax rates, and state equalization aid on the final per-pupil spending figure for each district. But even in the first school finance case taken to the U.S. Supreme Court (see Chapter 2), more attention was given to the variation in the local tax base. The data in Table 1.6 implied that the Colorado school finance system would have substantial fiscal disparities.

Table 1.7 shows the magnitude of the actual disparities by displaying statistics calculated from a sample of all Colorado school districts in 1977. At that time, Colorado had a guaranteed tax base program (see Chapter 9) but had "frozen" all local expenditures and allowed only modest increases from year to year, letting lower-spending districts increase at a somewhat faster rate than higher-spending districts. This table organizes all data into groups (in this case, five groups, or quintiles) and presents averages for each quintile.[4] Note that each quintile includes approximately an equal percentage of students—not districts.[5] Interestingly, though property wealth per pupil varied substantially, both the authorized revenue base (ARB)[6] and current operating expenditures per pupil varied by a much smaller magnitude. Indeed, the ratio between the ARB of the top or wealthiest quintile and that for the bottom or poorest quintile is 1.4 to 1, much less than the 5.3 to 1 ratio of wealth at the 90th to that at the 10th percentile. Further, the ratio of current operating expenditures per pupil at the top quintile to that

TABLE 1.7   Authorized Revenue Base and Current Operating Expenditures per Pupil by Quintiles of Assessed Valuation per Pupil in Colorado, 1977

Assessed Valuation per Pupil	*Percentage of Districts*	*Number of Base*	*Authorized Revenue per Pupil*	*Current Operating Expenditures*
$ 4,197–12,800	19%	33	$1,196	$1,532
12,800–15,500	20	25	1,312	1,594
15,500–17,600	14	14	1,299	1,667
17,600–24,500	27	32	1,476	1,742
24,500–326,269	20	77	1,692	2,342

Source: Education Finance Center, Education Commission of the States, from official data of the Colorado Department of Education.

[4]Other studies organize districts into 7 groups (septiles) or 10 groups (deciles). The most common practice today is to use deciles.

[5]Several earlier studies grouped data into categories with equal number of districts, and that practice is still followed. However, the emerging practice is to have an equal number of students in each category, to assess the impact of the system on students. See Berne and Stiefel (1984) and Chapter 3 for a discussion of the unit of analysis.

[6]The ARB was a Colorado-specific, general-fund revenue-per-pupil limit that varied for each local school district. It included just revenues for the regular education program.

at the bottom quintile is slightly higher—1.5 to 1. Unfortunately, the local tax rate and state aid figures were not provided, so it is not possible to determine whether the more equal revenue and expenditure figures are produced by fiscal-capacity-equalizing state aid or by high tax rates in the low-wealth districts.

New Jersey.   New Jersey data for two time periods—1975–76 and 1978–79—are presented by septiles (seven groups) in Table 1.8. The purpose of these two charts is to

TABLE 1.8   New Jersey School Finance

Relationship between Property Wealth, Current Expenditures, and Tax Rates, 1975–76			
Equalized Valuation per Pupil	*Current Expenditures per Pupil*	*Current Expenditures per Weighted Pupil*	*Current School Tax Rate*
Group 1: Less than $33,599	$1,504	$1,372	$1.79
Group 2: $33,600–$45,499	1,414	1,324	2.12
Group 3: $45,500–$58,699	1,411	1,347	2.00
Group 4: $58,700–$67,199	1,460	1,401	1.99
Group 5: $67,200–$78,499	1,604	1,543	1.89
Group 6: $78,500–$95,499	1,689	1,628	1.74
Group 7: $95,500 and over	1,752	1,681	1.17
State average	1,550	1,473	1.69

Relationship between Property Wealth, Current Expenditures, and Tax Rates, 1978–79			
Equalized Valuation per Pupil	*Current Expenditures per Pupil*	*Current Expenditures per Weighted Pupil*	*Current School Tax Rate*
Group 1: Less than $37,000	$1,994	$1,760	$1.67
Group 2: $37,000–54,999	1,933	1,763	1.57
Group 3: $55,000–73,999	1,978	1,816	1.55
Group 4: $74,000–87,999	1,994	1,882	1.58
Group 5: $88,000–102,999	2,200	2,061	1.69
Group 6: $103,000–125,199	2,268	2,154	1.67
Group 7: $125,200 and over	2,390	2,262	1.11
State average	2,113	1,959	1.47

Source: Goertz, 1979.

show differences in the New Jersey school finance structure three years after the courts, responding to a 1973 court decision overturning the school finance structure, shut down that state's education finance system in 1976, forcing the legislature finally to enact major school finance reform (see Chapter 2). These tables are somewhat difficult to interpret because they do not include any typical univariate or relationship statistics (see Chapter 3). Nevertheless, several characteristics are clear from the data. First, in general, expenditures per pupil increased as property value per pupil increased; apparently, both before and after reform, expenditures were a function of local property wealth in New Jersey. But expenditures per pupil in 1978–79 were nearly the same for the first four groups, suggesting that some expenditure-per-pupil equality had been produced for the bottom half by the 1976 reform.

Second, the range[7] increased for both expenditures per pupil and expenditures per weighted pupil between 1976 and 1979; even the range divided by the statewide average increased, suggesting that overall spending disparities increased over those years.

Third, there seem to be wider expenditure-per-pupil disparities on a weighted-pupil basis, where the weights indicate special pupil needs (see Chapter 4). Indeed, the weighted-pupil count substantially reduces the expenditure-per-pupil figure for the lowest-wealth districts, indicating—correctly, it turns out for New Jersey—that these districts have large numbers of special-needs students.[8]

Finally, and quite interestingly, school property tax rates dropped over these three years, and school property tax rates were almost equal across all but the wealthiest group of districts in 1979.

The major impact of the 1976 New Jersey reform, then, was to equalize school tax rates for most districts and to increase unweighted expenditures per pupil in the bottom half to about the same level. On a weighted-pupil basis, however, spending was not equal in the bottom half, and overall spending disparities seemed to increase. This New Jersey system was overturned by a 1990 state supreme court decision (*Abbott v. Burke*), in a case filed in the mid-1980s, but not fully resolved until 1998 (again, see Chapter 2).

Texas.   In 1984, Texas enacted a major school finance reform as part of a comprehensive education reform (Odden and Dougherty, 1984), but that system was challenged in state court a few years later. The 1984 law provided for a minimum foundation program with a higher expenditure-per-pupil level than previously, a small-guaranteed-yield program on top of the foundation program, weights for several different categories of pupil need, and a price adjustment to account for the varying prices Texas districts faced in purchasing education commodities. In the fall of 1987, the court ruled the school finance system unconstitutional, and the state created an Education Finance Reform Commission in early 1988.

The data in Table 1.9 were presented to that commission. The data are organized into groups with approximately equal numbers of children; this time, 20 different groupings are provided, thus showing the impact of the finance structure on each 5 percent of students.

---

[7]The difference between the highest and lowest value.
[8]Many of these districts are large urban districts with large numbers and percentages of poor students, physically and mentally handicapped students, and low-achieving students.

TABLE 1.9 Selected Texas School Finance Variables, 1986–87

Number of Districts	Range of Property Wealth per Pupil	Average Property Wealth per Pupil	Local Revenue per Pupil	State Revenue per Pupil	State and Local Revenues per Pupil	Federal Revenue per Pupil
26	Under $56,150	$ 46,217	$ 508	$2,528	$3,036	$564
57	56,150–79,652	68,793	647	2,309	2,956	426
73	79,653–96,562	87,980	801	2,204	3,005	277
123	96,563–117,462	107,516	1,006	2,092	3,096	269
68	117,463–128,425	120,325	1,050	2,109	3,159	309
73	128,426–144,213	136,285	1,192	2,074	3,266	283
52	144,214–156,931	152,061	1,355	1,864	3,215	227
34	156,932–167,090	161,971	1,610	1,711	3,321	145
46	167,091–177,108	169,925	1,658	1,711	3,369	203
84	177,109–202,136	190,514	1,727	1,643	3,370	171
37	202,137–218,238	208,862	1,904	1,499	3,403	126
44	218,239–239,117	224,173	1,963	1,473	3,436	139
26	239,118–253,338	244,493	2,055	1,403	3,458	130
42	253,339–276,674	260,613	2,281	1,342	3,623	181
36	276,675–308,780	294,373	2,942	1,123	4,065	113
1	308,781–308,862	308,862	2,006	1,125	3,131	312
45	308,863–356,189	330,130	2,494	1,039	3,533	128
45	356,190–436,960	399,954	3,459	830	4,285	89
3	436,961–440,987	440,607	2,862	960	3,822	294
146	Over $440,987	799,896	4,764	418	5,182	143

Source: Texas State Board of Education, 1986.

The numbers show that, indeed, property wealth per pupil varied substantially in Texas, from under $56,150 to over $440,987, a difference of 7.9 to 1. In fact, the actual difference was greater, since several districts had assessed valuation per pupil from $800,000 to over $1 million. These very-high-wealth districts were not anomalies but actual districts that included several of Texas's largest cities and some very wealthy suburban districts. The bottom line in Texas was that the local property tax per pupil clearly was distributed unequally among local school districts.

The column displaying total state and local revenues per pupil shows, however, that while per-pupil revenues tend to increase with wealth, this trend is strongest primarily for the wealthiest districts, with 15 percent of the students. For the districts with revenues below that, revenues per pupil vary by about 10 percent above or below a figure of $3,300 per pupil—not a dramatic variation. Arguably, these data indicate that for the majority of students in the middle, revenues per pupil were basically equal. The problem with the system was the low spending of districts at the very bottom and the high spending of districts at the top. This problem definition requires a different policy response than if disparities are spread across the entire system. Nevertheless, the Texas lower court overturned the system, and that decision was unanimously upheld on appeal by the Texas Supreme Court in the fall of 1989. This pattern, where even modest variations in spending per pupil that are linked to local property wealth are likely to be overturned by a state court, continues to exist in some states today.

The resolution of these problems finally produced a formula that was focused largely on the top and bottom 50 districts. The top 50 districts were required to "voluntarily" give away some of the revenues from their high local property wealth, either to the state or to the bottom 50 districts. This "Robin Hood" clause has existed for over a decade, but in 2006, the Texas legislature began to ameliorate the structure. Many of the "wealthy" districts were high-need urban districts (e.g., Austin) that some believed should keep their education revenues; the revenues produced by the Robin Hood clause had reached into the multiple billions, which many thought too high; and more and more districts, including many suburban districts, had to pay under the clause and wanted a different system, with less money derived from local property taxes.

Solutions to School Finance Inequities

We should note that at these times, the underlying school finance problem was seen as the inequality of property wealth per pupil, and many believed that the way to remedy the problem was to make the ability to raise funds for schools more equal across districts. In school finance parlance, the solution was to enact a guaranteed tax base (GTB) or "district power equalizing" program (i.e., a program that guaranteed to all or nearly all districts—rich or poor—some high-level tax base; see Chapter 9). This kind of program allows local districts to tap the same size tax base and to have equal access to revenues at a given tax rate regardless of their actual property wealth per pupil—up to the tax base guaranteed by the state. This allows districts to determine for themselves the level of spending on local education programs, rather than constraining them because they are a low-wealth district.

Under a GTB, higher spending per pupil requires a higher tax rate, but all districts with the same tax rate should have the same revenues per pupil unless their property wealth per pupil exceeds the state guarantee—in which case they could generate more revenue per pupil. While differences in education spending per pupil might remain, these differences would be the result of different choices by local school districts and their voters, not the unequal distribution of the local tax base.

Early school finance reformers anticipated that GTB programs would reduce both spending differences across districts and the linkage between local property wealth per pupil and spending per pupil.

A Different Type of School Finance Problem

The school finance problems or fiscal inequities reflected in all of the previous examples—high property wealth per pupil associated with both high expenditures and low tax rates, together with low property wealth per pupil associated with both low expenditures and high tax rates—were preserved to be typical in every state. But even in the 1970s, this "typical" situation did not hold for all states. The New York school finance situation in 1978 is such an example, as the data in Table 1.10 show. At that time, New York state had a school finance system that functioned like a minimum foundation program but was actually a low-spending-level, percentage-equalizing formula (see Chapter 9). The data in Table 1.10 are for all districts except New York City, divided into 10 equal groups, or deciles. Each decile has approximately an equal number of students. New York City, with an enrollment of nearly 1 million in a state with a then total of 3 million, is shown separately, since if it were included with the other districts, it alone would comprise more than three of the deciles.

Several elements of the data should be noted. To begin, the data are grouped by deciles of spending per pupil; the idea in New York was that expenditure-per-pupil disparities were the key variable, and analysis of correlates of that variable should be the focus of the study. Columns 1 and 8 show that revenues per pupil from local and state sources varied widely in New York during the 1977–78 school year, from a low of $1,759 in the bottom-spending decile to a high of $3,443 in the highest-spending decile, a difference of about 2 to 1. Note that this is a much smaller disparity than the 5.8-to-1 difference in spending between the very top ($5,752) and the very bottom ($988) spending districts.

Second, both spending per pupil and revenues per pupil from local and state sources increase with property wealth, which is the traditional pattern in school finance. However, note that the school property tax rate also increases; in fact, the school tax rate for the top few deciles is between 50 and almost 100 percent higher than the tax rates in the lowest-spending districts. This reality distinguished New York school finance from that in most other states at that time. Indeed, one of the reasons the wealthier districts spent more per pupil was that they taxed local property at a higher rate. Yes, those districts had a larger property tax base, but they also taxed it more heavily.

It was also true that household income as measured by gross income per return on New York State income tax returns increased with property wealth, and thus with

TABLE 1.10　Selected New York School Finance Variables, 1977–78

Deciles of Approved Federal Operating Expenditures per Pupil	Assessed Value per Pupil	Gross Income per Return (1977)	Property Tax Rate (mills)	Property Tax Revenue per Pupil	Other Local Revenue per Pupil	Total State Aid per Pupil	Total Local and State Revenue per Pupil	Total Federal Aid per Pupil
First Decile ($988–1,389)	$ 37,957	$12,225	13.01	$ 485	$ 54	$1,220	$1,759	$ 35
Second Decile ($1,390–1,471)	41,924	12,446	15.34	634	56	1,176	1,866	37
Third Decile ($1,473–1,542)	46,902	12,422	17.11	770	62	1,107	1,939	58
Fourth Decile ($1,544–1,640)	50,968	13,527	17.61	862	67	1,081	2,010	40
Fifth Decile ($1,642–1,789)	57,916	14,190	19.63	1,086	68	1,006	2,160	63
Sixth Decile ($1,790–1,899)	58,986	13,311	21.68	1,178	72	998	2,248	117
Seventh Decile ($1,903–2,017)	64,323	15,274	23.48	1,430	81	953	2,464	44
Eighth Decile ($2,021–2,255)	66,469	16,157	23.69	1,526	178	896	2,600	74
Ninth Decile ($2,260–2,474)	78,069	16,778	25.26	1,896	102	866	2,864	57
Tenth Decile ($2,475–5,752)	115,535	21,639	23.84	2,583	154	706	3,443	36
New York City	81,506	13,607	22.52	1,760	41	864	2,665	217
Rest of state	61,732	14,762	20.05	1,240	89	1,002	2,331	57
Statewide average	67,715	14,412	20.79	1,397	75	960	2,432	105

Source: Odden, Palaich, and Augenblick, 1979.

spending and school tax rates. It turns out that higher-income families, not only in New York but also generally, choose to levy higher tax rates for schools. Thus, while higher spending in New York was due in part to higher local tax revenues, that higher tax effort in part was aided by higher household income. Further, household income and property wealth per pupil were highly and positively correlated in New York at that time.

In short, the New York data show that higher spending occurred in districts with higher property wealth, higher household income, and higher school tax rates, while lower spending occurred in property-poor and income-poor districts with low tax rates. In fact, the correlation between wealth and per-pupil spending was much stronger in New York than in Texas (see Table 1.9). In the 1970s, a Texas school finance case reached the U.S. Supreme Court (see Chapter 2 for details). That case was ultimately unsuccessful. New York, with a much clearer correlation between measures of wealth and per-pupil spending, might have made a better case that the state school finance system was inequitable at the federal level.

These variations from the traditional pattern (i.e., high tax/high spending and low tax/low spending rather than low tax/high spending and high tax/low spending) found in New York complicated the formulation of a school finance reform that could pass muster with both the courts and the legislature. When New York's highest court ruled in 1980 that the system, while unfair, was not unconstitutional, the push for reform abated, and school finance methods changed only incrementally over time.

New York is not the only state today that exhibits these school finance patterns. Three quite different states—Illinois, Missouri, and Wisconsin—provide additional examples of this "new" type of school finance problem. All three states enacted different versions of school finance reforms over the 1975–95 period. Illinois implemented a generous "reward for effort" GTB-type program in the late 1970s and early 1980s, but then changed it to a foundation-type program in the late 1980s and early 1990s.

In 1975, Missouri implemented a combination foundation-GTB program, that was continuously enhanced over 20 years so that in 1995, the GTB was set at the 95th percentile of property wealth per pupil,[9] with a minimum required tax rate that resulted in a minimum expenditure of just over $3,000 per pupil.

In 1993, Wisconsin created and implemented a fully funded GTB-type program. The program guaranteed that each district could raise property taxes as if it had the wealth of the district at the 93rd percentile of wealth, and guaranteed spending of at least the 60th percentile of expenditure per pupil.

To greater or lesser degrees, all three states deferred actual spending decisions to local districts, and their school finance structures represent the three major school finance systems: foundation, GTB, and combined foundation-GTB (see Chapter 9 for discussions of these structures). Tables 1.11 and 1.12, show the status of school finance in Missouri and Illinois in 1994–95, and Table 1.13 shows the status of school finance in Wisconsin in 2004-05,[10] with the data organized by decile of spending from state and local sources per

---

[9]This means that every district could levy property taxes and collect per-pupil revenues as if they had the same property wealth as the district at the 95th percentile of wealth.

[10]The numbers for Wisconsin were similar in the 1995 school year; the data in the table show that the situation had not changed in the succeeding 10 years, though all numbers are larger.

TABLE 1.11   School Finance in Missouri, K–12 Districts, 1994–95

Decile	Revenues per Pupil[a]	Assessed Value per Pupil (at Market Value)	Local Property Tax Rate
1	$2,987	$118,969	1.11%
2	3,221	90,120	1.17
3	3,288	103,279	1.17
4	3,426	140,218	1.18
5	3,562	157,524	1.26
6	3,665	150,897	1.34
7	3,829	200,460	1.31
8	4,049	217,998	1.36
9	4,411	254,362	1.44
10	5,973	523,521	1.24

Source: Odden, 1999.

[a]Each district also receives an additional $648 per-pupil flat grant from a state sales tax.

Horizontal equity
   Coefficient of variation: 19.5
     McLoone Index: 0.92
Fiscal neutrality
   Correlation: 0.90
   Wealth elasticity: 0.23

TABLE 1.12   School Finance in Illinois, K–12 Districts, 1994–95

Decile	Revenues per Pupil	Assessed Value per Pupil (at Market Value)	Local Property Tax Rate
1	$2,893	$103,238	0.60%
2	3,042	126,874	0.61
3	3,130	140,313	0.63
4	3,258	157,754	0.63
5	3,400	207,211	0.67
6	3,632	220,635	0.70
7	3,922	251,595	0.83
8	4,219	280,519	0.86
9	4,687	312,488	0.89
10	5,343	386,903	1.07

Source: Odden, 1999.

Horizontal equity
   Coefficient of variation: 20.4
     McLoone Index: 0.91
Fiscal neutrality
   Correlation: 0.75
   Wealth elasticity: 0.32

TABLE 1.13   School Finance in Wisconsin, K–12 Districts, 2004–05

Decile	Revenues per Pupil	Assessed Value per Pupil (at Market Value)	Local Property Tax Rate
1	$7,720	$409,766	7.07%
2	7,870	219,109	7.49
3	7,932	370,551	7.41
4	8,137	389,036	8.00
5	8,304	366,628	8.58
6	8,451	400,000	8.85
7	8,661	441,977	9.11
8	8,939	458,640	9.90
9	9,241	491,944	10.27
10	9,973	798,840	10.62

Source: Odden, Picus, et al., 2005.

Horizontal equity
    Coefficient of variation: 0.08
    McLoone Index: 0.95
Fiscal neutrality
    Correlation: 0.53
    Wealth elasticity: 0.05

pupil, again excluding spending for special-needs students.[11] The results indicate that the school finance reforms implemented in these states did not produce the anticipated equity effects. There are still wide spending disparities, and even with major school finance reforms, spending per pupil is still highly associated with property wealth per pupil—the higher the wealth, the higher the spending.

Further, the linkages between spending and tax rates are more like those in New York. In all three cases, although spending per pupil increases with property wealth per pupil, so too does the local tax rate for schools. In all three states, the higher the tax rate, the higher the spending. In all three states, higher-property-wealth-per-pupil districts have higher spending per pupil but also have the highest tax rates; conversely, lower-property-wealth-per-pupil districts still have lower spending per pupil but now also have the lowest tax rates.

What happened? First, overall spending per pupil increased in real terms in all three states (122 percent in Illinois, 144 percent in Missouri, and 144 percent in Wisconsin) from 1980 to 1995, using the consumer price index as the deflator. Indeed, school finance

[11]The data show only local property tax revenues and state equalization aid for these states, and exclude other sources of revenue, which in Missouri could have averaged $800 per student. The data also are only for K–12 districts in the three states. The figures are intended to show the final results of school finance reforms implemented over several years. The school finance structure did not change substantively in any of the states between 1995 and 2000, though in Wisconsin, substantial state revenues replaced local revenues, but because of spending controls, spending differences did not alter much. Readers are referred to Chapter 3 for definitions of the following terms in the tables: "horizontal equity" and "fiscal neutrality."

reform generally led to higher overall spending (Murray, Evans, and Schwab, 1998). But it seems that the school finance reforms, which would have allowed lower-property-wealth-per-pupil districts to increase their spending to average or higher levels while also lowering their tax rates, were not used for that purpose. Rather, at some point in that 15-year period, lower-wealth districts used the reform programs primarily to lower their tax rates from an above-average to a below-average level. The data show that while lower-wealth districts still tend to have below-average spending levels, they do so because they also have below-average tax rates. Although the high-level GTBs in both Missouri and Wisconsin would allow these lower-wealth-per-pupil districts to spend at substantially higher levels with only modestly higher tax rates, the districts have generally chosen not to do so. They have chosen low tax rates, which, in turn, have produced low expenditure levels. In short, many of the low-wealth districts did not behave as anticipated when provided a major school finance reform program.

The high-wealth districts also engaged in unpredictable behavior. As these states implemented their school finance reforms over the years, the higher-wealth districts, which had enjoyed both a spending and a tax rate advantage, decided to maintain their spending lead but could do so only by raising their local tax rates for schools. Yes, some of the exceedingly wealthy districts still can spend at a high level because of their wealth, but with the state guaranteeing to all the tax base of the districts at the 93rd–95th percentiles, a wealth advantage exists only for a small percentage of districts, and most of these have a wealth advantage just above what the state will guarantee. For the bulk of the districts in the top third of property wealth per pupil, therefore, the higher spending is primarily produced by their higher tax rates for school purposes, reflecting the desire of their taxpayers to provide a high-quality education system.

Overall, spending disparities did drop in states that had court cases, and the states responded with school finance reforms (Murray, Evans, and Schwab, 1998). But the decrease was modest, averaging between 16 and 25 percent, depending on the statistical measure used.

In sum, the school finance changes did not do as much to reduce fiscal inequities as expected. Instead, the programs led to overall increases in education spending, and in the process, lower-wealth districts reduced their tax rates to below the average and settled for below-average-spending-per-pupil levels, while higher-wealth districts maintained their spending advantage by raising their tax rates and thus their spending advantages. The result was continued spending disparities, although this time driven more rationally by local tax rate differences rather than by the accident of the distribution of the local property tax base. The outcome was at best only modest change in these states' fiscal equity statistics—both those measuring spending disparities and those measuring the connection between spending and property wealth.

The School Finance Problem as Fiscal Adequacy

Of course, improving fiscal equity might not be the most pressing school finance issue in these states, as it was for states in the 1970s and 1980s. In fact, delineating what the school finance "problem" is for New York, as well as for Illinois, Missouri, and Wisconsin, has become a major subject of debate. Some argue that the continued existence of spending disparities and their relationship to local property wealth, whatever the cause, remain a problem. But if the "old" problem was the unequal ability to raise revenues to support public schools, and that problem is resolved by a high-level GTB or other kind of school finance reform program, others say that any remaining spending differences are a matter of local taxpayer choice and reflect neither an inherent inequity nor a school-funding problem. Yet another group may argue that since education is a state function, spending differences per se (as a proxy for education quality) are a problem regardless of whether they are caused by the unequal distribution of the property tax base or local taxpayer choice. Still others focus on the spending of the bottom half of districts, arguing that it should be higher.

The problem with all of these arguments, however, is that they deal simply with money, focusing on whether base funding is equal, and are not related to any other substantive education goal, such as education quality or student achievement. Making this connection is the school finance challenge of today. The driving education issue is raising levels of student achievement (i.e., setting high and rigorous standards, and teaching students to those standards [Fuhrman, 1993; Massell, Hoppe, and Kirst, 1997; Smith and O'Day, 1991]). Research from cognitive science suggests that we know how to produce a much higher level of learning, or at least make substantial progress toward this goal (Bransford, Brown, and Cocking, 1999; Bruer, 1993; Siegler, 1998). Given this knowledge, Darling-Hammond (1997) argues that learning to high standards should be considered a right for all children. Moreover, school finance litigation in many states has begun to stress adequacy issues over equity issues (Enrich, 1995; Heise, 1995; Minorini and Sugarman, 1999a, 1999b; see also Chapter 2). The goals, which were created by state standards–based education reform, were reinforced with the federal government's No Child Left Behind Act of 2001.

Given this student achievement goal, and related education policy and program issues, what curriculum, instruction, incentive, capacity development, organization, and management strategies are required to achieve this higher level of student performance? And what level of funding is required for these programmatic strategies?

As both Odden and Clune (1998) and Reschovsky and Imazeki (1998, 2001) argue, the primary school finance problem today is to link school finance to the strategies needed to accomplish the goal of teaching students to higher standards. In new school finance parlance, the challenge is to determine an "adequate" level of spending. The task is to identify for each district/school the level of base spending needed to teach the average student to state standards, and then to identify how much extra each district/school requires to teach students with special needs—the learning disabled, those from impoverished and thus educationally deficient backgrounds, and those without English proficiency—to the same high and rigorous achievement standards. As Clune (1994a, 1994b) and Odden and Clune (1998) suggest, this requires a shift in school finance thinking from "equity" to "adequacy."

Interestingly, in each of the three sample states discussed earlier, educators and policymakers have begun to raise the issue of school finance **adequacy** in many ways. Some have questioned whether the spending levels of the bottom half of all districts (i.e., those districts with average or mostly below-average tax rates) were a "problem" (i.e., were too low) or whether those spending levels, even though below average, were "adequate" to teach their students to acceptable standards. Others have attempted to calculate a state-supported spending level that can be linked to a specified level of student performance (e.g., it will cost X dollars for 90 percent of students to meet or exceed state proficiency standards in core subjects). In a sense, this is a "back to the future" school finance objective, as many foundation programs have sought to make this linkage throughout this century. Still others have explored the degree to which any "adequate" spending level should be supplemented by additional funds to provide extra resources to teach students with special needs to high standards.

Chapter 3 discusses the complexities of determining an "adequate" spending level and the various methodologies that are being tapped to determine those levels (see also Guthrie and Rothstein, 1999). Chapter 4 summarizes the "evidence-based" approach the authors of this text have developed and used in several states (see, e.g., Odden, Picus, et al., 2005). Nevertheless, for many, the focus on adequacy constitutes a shift in defining the basic school finance problem—away from focusing solely on fiscal disparities across districts and toward linking spending to what could be construed as an adequate education program (i.e., a program designed to teach students to high levels of achievement).

The School Finance Problem as Productivity

Disparities or any other shortcomings in current state education finance systems notwithstanding, many analysts argue that the most prominent school finance problem is the low level of system performance and student achievement despite relatively large levels of funding (Hanushek and Associates, 1994). This is a significant part of the report of the National Research Council on school finance equity and productivity (Ladd and Hansen, 1999a, 1999b). These analysts are convinced that, on balance, there are substantial revenues in the American public school system and that the core problem is to determine how best to use those resources—particularly how to use the resources differently to support strategies that dramatically boost student performance. In one sense, much of this book addresses these productivity and adequacy issues. Nearly all chapters touch on the adequacy issue. Chapter 4 introduces the evidence-based adequacy model, and Chapter 7 details strategies for reallocating resources to produce higher student performance levels—how to use current dollars more effectively.

In any case, for the next several years, while equity will remain a topic of school finance, the issues of adequacy and productivity will probably dominate. Today, educators need to show how to transform current and new dollars into student achievement results, or the argument that education needs more—or even the current level of—money will be unlikely to attract public or political support.

4. SUMMARY

Public school funding is big business in the United States. Revenues for public schools are now over $500 billion—3.8 percent of the country's gross domestic product and 4.5 percent of all personal income. Moreover, revenues for public schools grew consistently during the twentieth century, so that by the end of that century and the first years of the twenty-first century, an average of $9,102 was being spent on each public school student. Unfortunately, those dollars were distributed unequally across states, districts, schools, and students. In too many instances, districts with higher property wealth per pupil and/or higher household income were able to raise and spend more money per pupil even at lower tax rates than were districts with lower per-pupil property tax bases and/or households with lower income. These fiscal disparities translated into differences in class size, teacher salaries, program offerings, and quality of buildings, with the wealthier districts having the advantage in each category, even with lower tax rates. As a result, the equity of the distribution of public school resources was the primary topic of school finance for over 100 years.

Although equity is still an issue, the adequacy of education revenues has assumed an even more prominent place on the school finance agenda. Today, the key school finance issue in most states is whether there is a sufficient—adequate—amount of dollars for districts and schools to teach students to new and rigorous performance standards that have been developed during the past 15–20 years of standards-based education reform, to meet both the goals of state standards–based education reform and the stiffer accountability requirements of the federal No Child Left Behind Act. Assuming student achievement goals are ambitious, many argue that if levels of school finance adequacy are met, remaining inequities are not as problematic, but not everyone agrees with this position. Thus, both the equity and the adequacy of school funding are central school finance issues today.

Study Questions

1. Create a local school district case study. Using the school district whose borders you live within or work in, identify the following characteristics:
    a. Locale: rural/suburban/urban
    b. Number of K–12, elementary, middle, and high schools
    c. Total number of students enrolled
    d. Description of students: percentage receiving free and reduced-price lunch (FRL), ethnicity make-up, percentage of students with individualized education programs (IEPs)
    e. Total school revenues
    f. Percentages of school revenues from local, state, and federal funding sources
    g. Expenditures per pupil
    h. Average property wealth per pupil
    i. School tax rate
    Create a one-page description of your district, comparing the demographic and fiscal characteristics to your state's averages in each category.
2. Building on the above case study, identify and describe the history of your district. When was it established? What did it consist of at that time (e.g., a one-room school house)? What laws was it established under? Who taught the first class(es)? How many students attended? What type of students

attended? Was this their first school experience, or had they been taught at home or in a private school? How was it financed? How did the school district evolve from its beginning to its current state? Analyze its evolution, commenting on the "progress" made from its inception. What are future plans for the district? Add this historical perspective to the case study from question 1.

3. Conduct a search of recent media coverage in your state concerning school finance. What is considered the most pressing "school finance problem"? Does it differ depending on the type of media outlet? Do state-level political party representatives have different answers? Identify whether they are speaking in terms of equity or adequacy, and compare the results with academic and legal analyses of the top school finance issue in your state. Finish your investigation with a search of local media coverage on your own school district, and identify what local opinions of equity/adequacy issues are in comparison to the state as a whole.

Chapter 2

Legal Issues in School Finance

The basic problem in school finance consists of providing sufficient resources to schools to enable them, in turn, to provide an equitable and adequate education to each child. Precise definitions of "equity" and "adequacy" will be given in Chapter 3, but simplified versions will suffice for the purposes of this chapter. Fiscal equity can be regarded as a situation in which each child receives substantially equal educational resources. Adequacy requires each child to receive an education that reaches a certain level of quality.

The inequities in education finance trace back to the use of local property taxes to fund the first public schools. American public schools began as a local enterprise, so using local property taxation to fund the schools was a natural choice. However, localities differed with regard to their property wealth, which meant that districts with greater property wealth per pupil could provide more resources per pupil to their schools. The variation in per-pupil educational expenditures across school districts was identified as a problem as early as 1905 (Cubberly, 1905), but it has become increasingly important as the role of education expanded beyond fulfilling local needs. States, and the federal government to a lesser extent, have taken steps to remedy the funding inequities, but the disparities remain problematic today, since some schools receive far more resources than others.

In addition to the equity issues, policy analysts are increasingly interested in whether schools receive an adequate supply of resources to provide a high-quality education to their students. A related issue concerns whether districts and schools effectively use the resources they receive. These types of resource-related issues continue to grow in importance with the escalation of the standards, the growth of accountability movements, and the passage of the federal No Child Left Behind Act.

State legislatures offer the best forum in which to address concerns of fiscal equity and adequacy. However, political factors sometimes limit the effectiveness of legislative solutions, especially because the children most often harmed by inequities and inadequacies are members of minority groups that lack clout in the legislature. In school finance, people who cannot achieve their goals in the legislature frequently seek relief through the courts. In nearly every state, parties have litigated over the distribution of educational resources.

School finance litigation initially involved rectifying funding disparities. The goal was to provide schools in areas with little property wealth a level of funding commensurate with that of wealthier districts. In the past 15–20 years, however, school finance litigation has evolved to place greater emphasis on whether each school receives adequate resources to educate all students to high standards. The shift in objectives brought to the forefront the relationship between educational inputs and student outcomes, as courts became less concerned with strict numerical equality and more interested in whether schools were receiving the necessary resources.

This chapter has four sections. The first sets forth the basic legal doctrines necessary to understand school finance legal cases. The second section discusses the early school finance cases, which dealt with equity issues related to the U.S. Constitution. The third section involves equity issues related to state constitutions, and the final section analyzes adequacy litigation.

1. THE LEGAL BACKGROUND OF SCHOOL FINANCE LITIGATION

This section provides an overview of the basic elements of school finance litigation. Keeping the fundamental points in mind will facilitate an understanding of the rest of the chapter.

School finance systems consist of a set of statutes passed by the state legislature that govern the distribution of educational resources within the state. The legislature possesses great discretion to fashion these systems in the manner it deems best. However, as with all other state legislation, the school finance statutes must not conflict with either the U.S. Constitution or the constitution of that state; if they do conflict, the system can be declared unconstitutional, in which case all or part of the system is void. Challenging the constitutionality of the legislation offers the only viable litigation strategy for school finance plaintiffs.

For that reason, the plaintiffs in school finance litigation argue that the school finance statutes conflict with various provisions of the federal and/or state constitutions. The state, of course, contends that its school finance system conforms to both constitutions. Therefore, any analysis of school finance litigation involves the considerations of (1) *which* constitutional provision(s) the plaintiffs claim has been violated and (2) *how* the school finance system allegedly violates the constitution(s).

School finance litigation involves a relatively small number of legal factors. The plaintiffs argue that three types of constitutional provisions have been violated. The three constitutional provisions are the Equal Protection Clause of the Fourteenth Amendment to the U.S. Constitution, the equal protection clause of the relevant state constitution, and the education clause of the state constitution. The plaintiffs raise two main arguments to advance their claims: (1) that the state failed to distribute resources equitably and (2) that it failed to provide an adequate amount of resources to some or all of the schools in the state.

A brief overview of the two types of arguments may provide a "big picture" perspective that will be helpful when the details of specific cases are discussed. *School finance equity cases* involve the claim that the school finance laws violate the state and/or federal constitutions by distributing educational resources unfairly. Each of the three constitutional provisions mentioned previously can provide the basis for a constitutional violation in an equity case. Generally, the plaintiffs argue that the unconstitutional inequity results from the system's reliance on local property taxes for a significant portion of the funding.

School finance adequacy cases involve the education clause in the applicable state constitution. The plaintiffs argue that the education clause requires the state to provide a certain standard of education, which the state has failed to supply because the school finance system provides insufficient resources to the schools. The U.S. Constitution lacks an education clause, so adequacy cases arise solely from the constitution of the relevant state.

The Three "Waves" of School Finance Litigation

Scholars categorize the history of school finance litigation into three "waves," based on the primary legal theory used in the cases. The waves should not be regarded as rigid divisions, because many cases involve arguments coming from each of the three waves. Instead, they serve as a conceptual device to synthesize the arguments made by the plaintiffs throughout the course of litigation.

The first wave of school finance litigation involved the argument that state school finance systems violated the Equal Protection Clause of the U.S. Constitution. The second wave concerned claims that the finance system violated provisions of state constitutions that guaranteed an equitable resource distribution. The most important constitutional provision in the second wave was the equal protection component of the state constitution, but the education clause was also prominent during the second wave. The third, and current, wave centers on issues related to educational adequacy, namely, that the finance structure does not provide enough resources to permit the schools to provide the level of education required under the state constitution.

2. THE FIRST WAVE: FEDERAL EQUAL PROTECTION LITIGATION

The first wave of school finance litigation primarily involved plaintiffs arguing that the challenged school finance system violated the Equal Protection Clause of the U.S. Constitution. They also made arguments based on state constitutional provisions, but the primary thrust was an attack based on the Fourteenth Amendment. This strategy provided the simplest option to remedy the funding inequities nationally, because a ruling based on the U.S. Constitution would have applied to the finance system of each state.

The ultimate arbiter of the federal equal protection litigation would be the U.S. Supreme Court, which has the responsibility and authority for defining the meaning of the rights identified in the U.S. Constitution and its amendments. The Supreme Court also determines whether the president, Congress, state governors, and state legislatures exercise their power in a manner consistent with the Constitution. Therefore, it was inevitable that cases from the first wave would reach the Supreme Court.

The Equal Protection Clause of the Fourteenth Amendment provides that no state shall "deny to any person within its jurisdiction the equal protection of the laws." This amendment was enacted after the Civil War for the primary purpose of barring states from treating African Americans differently from whites. The impact of the clause was not limited to that purpose, however, so equal protection issues soon arose in a broad spectrum of cases. Over time, the Supreme Court created tests for determining whether, and how, governmental actions might violate the Equal Protection Clause, as will be discussed shortly.

The Equal Protection Clause does not mean that states and localities must *always* pass laws that treat individuals equally. For example, perfectly valid laws specify that some individuals with a particular license can drive a car, practice medicine, or teach in public schools, while other people lacking the license cannot legally perform these functions. In each case, governments have determined that individuals need certain skills or expertise to engage in the activity. Therefore, the state provides a license only to those individuals who demonstrate that they have the requisite expertise. In contrast, a law that would limit voters to citizens from one racial group would lead to unacceptable differences in treatment, thereby rendering the law invalid.

The courts thus need to distinguish between those instances in which different treatment violates the U.S. Constitution and those that are acceptable. The Supreme Court uses three tests to make this determination, two of which apply to school finance cases. The two tests differ in terms of the amount of deference the courts give to the legislature that enacted the law.

The Strict Scrutiny Test

The first test involves "strict scrutiny," which means that the courts examine the challenged law extremely carefully when considering whether it is constitutional. Plaintiffs favor this test because the courts give little deference to the legislature when applying strict scrutiny. Instead, the courts hold the government to a very high standard in attempts to justify why the law is acceptable even though it treats people differently.

As one might expect, the courts apply the strict scrutiny test when the alleged constitutional violation involves very important issues. Specifically, the court will apply the strict scrutiny test when a *fundamental right* is involved or when the state law discriminates against people from a *suspect classification*. Thus, school finance plaintiffs argue that one or both of these categories have been impacted by the state's school finance system in order to convince the court to apply strict scrutiny.

Fundamental rights are those rights identified in the Constitution, either explicitly or implicitly. Examples of fundamental rights include the rights of free speech, a free press, assembly, and due process. These rights are valued by the courts because they involve protections at the heart of the republic.

Suspect classifications are groupings of people based on their religion, national origin, race, and/or alienage. Interestingly, certain classifications that are important from an educational perspective are not recognized by the courts as suspect classifications, including gender and wealth. The latter, in particular, has important implications for school finance litigation. The courts will apply strict scrutiny to laws that treat people differently due to their race or religion, because they are skeptical regarding the need for laws that treat individuals differently based on these distinctions.

The state must prove two things if a court applies the strict scrutiny test. First, it must show that the differences caused by the law resulted from the state's pursuit of a "compelling state interest." In other words, the state needs to prove that the discriminatory aspect of the law arose as a result of the state pursuing an extremely important objective, not merely-run-of-the-mill legislation. Second, the state must prove that it had "no less discriminatory" means by which it could achieve the compelling interest, meaning that the law was the very best way to achieve the vital objective. When a court invokes strict scrutiny, the state usually has difficulty proving either point, let alone both. Indeed, when strict scrutiny is invoked, the state nearly always loses the case, meaning all or part of the school finance system is ruled unconstitutional.

The Rational Basis Test

The rational basis test is applied when the litigation involves neither a fundamental right nor a suspect classification. The rational basis test simply requires the court to determine whether the government had any rational reason (not necessarily the best reason) for passing a law under which people are treated differently. The courts defer greatly to the legislature when the rational basis test is applied.

An everyday example will illustrate how the rational basis test operates. Each state restricts people from obtaining a driver's license until they reach a certain age. Since driving is not a fundamental right, and age is not a suspect classification, the rational basis test would apply. The state would merely have to show that the age requirement serves some state interest, such as roadway safety, in order to prevail against a legal challenge. States virtually always win when the rational basis test is applied because they can nearly always cite some sensible reason to support the law.

This brief treatment of equal protection law should facilitate understanding of the remainder of this section. The key point to remember is plaintiffs want the courts to apply strict scrutiny, while the states prefer the rational basis test.

The Early Cases

In the late 1960s, the first two modern school finance cases were filed in the federal courts: *McInnis v. Shapiro*[1] in Illinois and *Burruss v. Wilkerson*[2] in Virginia. These cases challenged the constitutionality of differences in educational expenditures across school districts that arose because of unequal property tax bases. The plaintiffs in each case argued

---

[1]*McInnis v. Shapiro*, 293 F. Supp. 327 (N.D. Ill. 1968), affirmed 394 U.S. 322 (1969).
[2]*Burruss v. Wilkerson*, 310 F. Supp. 572 (Virg. 1969), aff'd. 397 U.S. 44 (1970).

that strict scrutiny should apply because education was a fundamental right. They also claimed that the use of the property tax was not the least discriminatory means of funding education, since the wide discrepancies in expenditures and revenues per pupil across school districts were not related to the "educational need" of children. The plaintiffs conceded that differences in per-pupil expenditures were not always unconstitutional but contended that such differences had to be related to "educational need," not educationally irrelevant variables such as the local tax base.

The state prevailed in each case. In *McInnis*, the court applied the rational basis test (without saying why) and ruled that the state funding system, which was based on property taxes, furthered the legitimate state interest of ensuring local control over educational funding. The court also determined that the educational need standard proposed by the plaintiffs was *nonjusticiable*; that is, it failed to provide a standard by which the court could assess the plaintiffs' claims. The two justifications set forth by the court in support of its ruling have subsequently been used by many courts when denying the claims of school finance plaintiffs.

Burruss was decided on the novel ground that the finance system was constitutional because funding was provided according to a uniform and consistent plan, a portion of which required local contributions. In essence, the *Burruss* court found that the finance system was not discriminatory because it required a contribution from each district. The fact that some districts could raise less funds due to their lower property values was immaterial.

McInnis and *Burruss* shared the important similarity that the court in each case deferred to the legislature and subjected the legislation to the rational basis test. In nearly all subsequent school finance cases, one of the defendants' first tactics has been to file a motion asking the court to dismiss the case, citing *McInnis* and *Burruss* as precedents. Clearly, school finance plaintiffs could not prevail unless they could convince the courts that (1) judicially manageable standards exist in the cases (to get around the issue of nonjusticiability) and (2) the higher standard of strict scrutiny should be applied (see also Levin, 1977; Minorini and Sugarman, 1999a, 1999b; Sparkman, 1990; Underwood, 1995a, 1995b; Underwood and Sparkman, 1991).

Fiscal Neutrality

Plaintiffs' post-*McInnis/Burruss* challenge consisted of framing the equal protection argument in a way that persuaded the courts to subject the actions of legislature to strict scrutiny. The educational need concept devised by Arthur Wise (1968), then a doctoral student at the University of Chicago, relied upon the notions that (1) education was a fundamental right, (2) the Equal Protection Clause required that education be provided equally across all school districts, and (3) the variations in educational expenditures across districts in most states were not related to educational need. Although the first courts rejected the educational needs argument, the argument that education is a fundamental right remained viable.

At about the same time, John Coons, then a law professor at Northwestern University, and two law students, William Clune (now an emeritus law professor at the University of Wisconsin–Madison) and Stephen Sugarman (now a law professor at the

University of California–Berkeley), developed the argument that strict scrutiny should apply because education funding adversely impacted a suspect classification defined as students in low-property-wealth-per-pupil districts (Coons, Clune, and Sugarman, 1970). They contended that local school districts were creations of state governments, an important point that had been accepted nationally as a legal standard. They also claimed that school finance systems that relied upon local funding gave school districts unequal opportunities to raise educational revenues because property values per child varied widely. Thus, school financing systems needed to be "fiscally neutral," which means that expenditures per pupil could not be related to local district property wealth per pupil. A state could not be required to provide more money than it possessed, but each district should have an equal opportunity to share in the total resource pool, whatever the size of that pool.

Fiscal neutrality added two major arguments for school finance litigation plaintiffs. First, it suggested that district property wealth per pupil was a suspect classification, which supplemented the argument that education is a fundamental right. Second, it created the fiscal-neutrality standard, which required that there be no relationship between educational spending per pupil and local district property wealth per pupil. This standard enabled plaintiffs to avoid the nonjusticiability argument, because the two variables were collected by nearly all state school finance systems, and standard statistical measures could be used to identify the magnitude of their relationship. In addition, fiscal neutrality clearly identified boundaries that a school finance system could not cross, yet allowed for legislative discretion in designing school finance structures that could pass constitutional muster.

Even armed with the fiscal-neutrality arguments, plaintiffs still faced several challenges. First, they were asking the courts to recognize both the new fundamental right of education and the new suspect classification of property wealth per pupil. Second, the suspect class was different in kind from all previous suspect classes, which involved characteristics traceable to the individual, such as race and national origin. District property wealth per pupil related to a group characteristic—the wealth of the area in which people lived. Third, the Supreme Court had never indicated that even individual property wealth was a suspect classification. The court had appeared sympathetic to claims of discrimination based on individual income but had not (and still has not) recognized income as a suspect classification.

***Serrano v. Priest*, Part I.** The first case filed using the fiscal-neutrality concept was *Serrano v. Priest*[3] in California in 1968. The plaintiffs argued that strict scrutiny should apply because education is a fundamental right and because the plaintiffs were members of a suspect class. The state moved to dismiss the case immediately, in part because it argued that the case was nonjusticiable. The trial court immediately dismissed the case. This meant that the judge ruled that the plaintiffs could not prevail at trial no matter what facts they could prove, because the law was against them.

The California Supreme Court in August 1972 reversed that ruling and permitted the case to proceed to trial. The supreme court held that the trial court should have applied the

[3]*Serrano v. Priest,* 5 Cal. 3d 584, 96 Cal. Rptr. 601, 487 P.2d 1241 (1971).

strict scrutiny standard because education is a fundamental right under the U.S. Constitution and the plaintiffs were members of a suspect class under the Fourteenth Amendment.[4] The court also held that the case was justiciable, using the fiscal-neutrality standard. *Serrano I* was a vital opinion that gained nationwide media, policy, and legal attention. It immediately spawned a series of similar court cases in other states.[5]

It is important to understand that in *Serrano* (and in subsequent school finance court cases) the court did not find that the use of property taxes to finance schools is unconstitutional per se. States can use local property taxes to help finance schools within a constitutionally acceptable system. Finance systems that rely too heavily on local property taxation face an increased risk of being held unconstitutional, however, largely because such systems have greater inequities than do systems that *equalize* school resources.

Rodriguez v. San Antonio.   Eighteen months after the *Serrano* opinion, the U.S. Supreme Court decided *San Antonio School District v. Rodriguez,*[6] a case that originated in Texas. The trial court applied the strict scrutiny standard after determining that education is a fundamental right and that property wealth per pupil is a suspect classification. The court held that the Texas school finance system violated the Equal Protection Clause of the U.S. Constitution and ordered the legislature to devise a constitutional system.

The state of Texas appealed the case to the U.S. Supreme Court. In March 1973, the Supreme Court issued the definitive ruling with regard to the Equal Protection Clause and school finance litigation. The crucial decision in the case occurred when the court declined to apply the strict scrutiny test. The court determined that education is not a fundamental right under the U.S. Constitution because education is not mentioned in the Constitution, either implicitly or explicitly. It also determined that low property wealth is not a suspect class. Therefore, neither prong of the strict scrutiny analysis applied, so the court used the rational basis test. Texas argued that funding education by local property taxes reflected the principle of local control of education, a justification that the court accepted. Therefore, the court held that the Texas finance system did not violate the Constitution.

The *Rodriguez* decision eliminated the plaintiffs' ability to rely on the Equal Protection Clause of the Constitution because the court ruled that the rational basis test must be applied to school finance litigation under that provision. Recall that under the rational basis test, a state merely has to show a rational connection between funding schools via the property tax and some legitimate state interest. Every state followed the lead of Texas in arguing that their funding system promoted the goal of local control of

---

[4]The court stated that its ruling applied under the California Constitution as well, because it thought that the terms of those constitutions led to identical results. It analyzed the case using Fourteenth Amendment language, however.
[5]Arizona (*Shofstall v. Hollins,* 1973); Connecticut (*Horton v. Meskill,* 1977); Idaho (*Thompson v. Engleking,* 1975); Illinois (*Blase v. Illinois,* 1973); Kansas (*Knowles v. Kansas,* 1981); Minnesota (*Van Dusartz v. Hatfield,* 1971); New Jersey (*Robinson v. Cahill,* 1973); Oregon (*Olsen v. State,* 1976); Texas (*Rodriguez v. San Antonio,* 1972); Washington (*North Shore School District No. 417 v. Kinnear,* 1974); Wisconsin (*Buse v. Smith,* 1976).
[6]*San Antonio Independent School District v. Rodriguez,* 411 U.S. 1 (1973).

education. The *Rodriguez* decision, therefore, required plaintiffs to argue their cases by alleging violations of state constitutional provisions. This had the effect of requiring school finance litigation to be argued state-by-state on the basis of state equal protection and education clauses.

3. THE SECOND WAVE: STATE LAW EQUITY CASES

The *Rodriguez* decision led plaintiffs to turn to the state courts to seek school finance reform, in the so-called second wave of school finance litigation. Plaintiffs raised essentially the same arguments as in the first wave, except they argued that the inequities in school funding violated state constitutional provisions, rather than the Fourteenth Amendment. Fortunately for the plaintiffs, each state constitution contains an equal protection clause, some of which are identical in language to the federal provision (Minorini and Sugarman, 1999a, 1999b; Underwood, 1995a). In addition, the education clauses of some states have been interpreted as containing an equal protection component.

Before proceeding, it is important to understand why different results can be reached under different constitutions. The amendments to the U.S. Constitution grant certain rights to citizens that the states cannot take away. However, the states remain free to grant additional rights above and beyond those set forth by the federal government. For example, the U.S. Supreme Court ruled that education is not a fundamental right under the U.S. Constitution, but a state can determine that education is a fundamental right within that state. Therefore, school finance plaintiffs turned to the state courts to seek legal protections beyond those offered by the federal government.

Many cases arose during the second wave of school finance litigation, which lasted from 1973 until 1989. The states tended to be more successful than the plaintiffs in these cases, prevailing well over half the time. However, the two most important cases of the second wave involved victories for the plaintiffs.

Robinson v. Cahill. The New Jersey Supreme Court decided *Robinson v. Cahill*[7] in April 1973, just one month after *Rodriguez*. A loss in *Robinson,* while not eliminating litigation in other states, would have been a further blow for plaintiffs, especially following so closely in the wake of *Rodriguez*. The New Jersey court initially decided whether to invoke strict scrutiny or the rational basis test under the *state* equal protection clause. Although the court acknowledged that education was mentioned in the state constitution, it still ruled that education is not a fundamental right in New Jersey. Similarly, the court held that property wealth per pupil is not a suspect class even though rich and poor school districts had above- and below-average spending per pupil, respectively. Thus, the *Robinson* court applied the rational basis test and held that the New Jersey school finance system did not violate the New Jersey equal protection clause.

---

[7]*Robinson v. Cahill,* 303 A.2d 273 (N.J. 1973).

However, the court reached a different conclusion under the state constitution's education clause, which required the state to create a "thorough and efficient" public education system. The court held that a school finance structure that allowed for wide disparities in spending per pupil that were strongly linked to local property wealth per pupil was not a "thorough and efficient" system. The court ordered the state legislature to design a new system that would allow schools to provide "educational opportunities that will prepare [the student] for his role as citizen and as competitor in the labor market" (*Robinson I*, 1973, at 293), a statement that foreshadowed the subsequent adequacy cases that comprise the third wave of litigation. Nevertheless, the court ruled the system unconstitutional largely on the basis of spending differences, which were the only criteria available to determine whether the system was thorough and efficient.

The *Robinson* case was important for three reasons. First, it kept school finance litigation alive after *Rodriguez* seemed to doom it. Second, it paved the way for challenges to school finance systems on the basis of state education clauses, a substantively different strategy than invoking equal protection clauses. Third, it hinted at a new standard, which subsequently evolved into adequacy litigation.

As would be the case in many states, the New Jersey legislature procrastinated in response to *Robinson*. The *Robinson* decision required the state to play an enhanced role in education funding in New Jersey. The state did not have an income tax, so each year the state budget was short of the level of funds needed for a constitutionally permissible school finance structure. In July 1976, the New Jersey Supreme Court, in a dramatic but largely symbolic action, shut down the entire New Jersey school system.[8] In response, the legislature designed a new school finance structure, enacted a new tax system including a new state income tax to fund it, and provided local property tax relief as well.

Serrano v. Priest, Part II. A few years later, the *Serrano* case returned to the California Supreme Court after a trial in which the plaintiffs prevailed on state law equal protection grounds.[9] The state predictably argued that the verdict should be overturned because of the ruling in *Rodriguez*. The California Supreme Court ruled that the state constitution granted rights beyond those specified in the U.S. Constitution, which meant that the *Rodriguez* case was not determinative of the outcome in *Serrano II*. The court held that education was a fundamental right under the California Constitution and that per-pupil property wealth was a suspect classification. Therefore, the court applied strict scrutiny to the state's school finance system, determined that the system was unconstitutional, and ordered the state to create a new, fiscally neutral system in which per-pupil funding was nearly equal across California, although a relatively minor discrepancy would be deemed acceptable. The state restructured its funding system to accommodate the court's ruling, intending in part to "recapture" property taxes from wealthy districts and distribute them more equitably across the state. The voters of California,

---

[8]Since this occurred during the summer break, only summer schools were affected. The action, however, indicated the serious posture of the supreme court and was highly symbolic.
[9]*Serrano v. Priest*, 18 Cal. 3d 728, 135 Cal. Rptr. 345, 557 P.2d 929 (1976).

however, sent their own message by passing Proposition 13, which placed a constitutional limit on the property tax rate and the rate at which property taxes could increase. In the end, the state developed a fairly equitable, but relatively poorly funded, school finance system.

The second wave was moderately effective from the point of view of plaintiffs. In about half the cases, the state prevailed. However, both the successful suits and the threat of suits forced the state to focus on improvement in equity in funding the schools. The result was improved equity in many states—and in most, equity was accompanied by increases in funding for all schools (Evans, Murray, and Schwab, 1997; Ladd, Chalk, and Hansen, 1999). Perhaps more importantly, the reliance of the *Robinson* court on the New Jersey education clause paved the way for a new type of lawsuit.

4. THE THIRD WAVE: ADEQUACY

Challenging state school finance structures under the state education clause opened the way for legal strategies beyond those used in equal protection litigation. Some plaintiffs used the education clause to frame what is essentially an equal protection argument. Others used the education clause to buttress arguments about the fundamentality of education made under the equal protection clause. Cases in both Arkansas[10] and Wyoming[11] in the early 1980s were largely based on these arguments, as were the Texas[12] cases that were litigated between 1985 and 1995. In 1997, a suit in Vermont[13] relied on these arguments as well. Nevertheless, the most important use of the education clause consisted of arguing that it requires the state to provide a certain quality of education to children. This approach is at the heart of adequacy arguments.

Giving Meaning to the Education Clause

There are three important points that a court must consider when ruling on a challenge to the school finance system on the basis of the state education clause:

- Whether the education clause requires not just an education system but some level of quality
- The historical meaning of the education clause
- The substantive demands of the education clause—adequacy arguments

Each factor is discussed in more depth below.

---

[10]*Dupree v. Alma School District No. 30*, 651 S.W.2d 90 (Ark. 1983).
[11]*Washakie County School District No. 1 v. Herschler*, 606 P.2d 310 (Wyo. 1980).
[12]*Edgewood Independent School District v. Kirby*, 777 S.W.2d 391 (Tex. 1989); *Edgewood v. Meno*, 893 S.W.2d 450 (Tex. 1995).
[13]*Brigham v. State*, 692 A.2d 384 (Vt. 1997).

Education clauses requiring more than just an education system.   State supreme courts interpret state education clauses in terms of modern school finance structures. The state might argue that the constitution merely requires it to have some educational system in place, without regard to issues of equity and/or quality. The plaintiffs, conversely, might argue that the constitution mandates the state to provide a high-quality education to each child on a fair basis. The task for school finance litigants is to convince the court to accept their version of what the education clause requires.

Various courts have reached different conclusions regarding whether the education clause places an "affirmative duty" on the legislature to create an education system of a certain quality. For example, in *Robinson*, the court held that the "thorough and efficient" clause required an education system that allowed all students equal opportunities to compete in the labor market. The New Jersey Supreme Court later ruled in *Abbott v. Burke*[14] (discussed below) that the constitution ensured higher educational attainment for low-income and minority students in the state's property-poor and low-income central-city school districts. However, other state courts have concluded that the state education clause places no affirmative duty on the state to equalize educational opportunities[15] or that it is the prerogative of the legislature, not the court, to interpret the education clause.[16] The plaintiffs obviously cannot prevail if the court determines either that the state has no duty beyond providing some education or that the court cannot judge the decisions of the legislature with regard to the provision of education.

Ideally, these rulings would be based on the plain language of the relevant education clause. Each state constitution has some requirement for the state to create a system of public schools, with some calling for the creation of an education system and others calling for "thorough and efficient," "thorough and uniform," or "general and uniform" school systems. McUsic (1991) argued that the specific wording of the education clause can lead to stronger or weaker interpretations of the substantive meaning of the clause, which seems logical. However, both Sparkman (1994) and Underwood (1995a, 1995b) concluded that the specific constitutional language is unimportant. Instead, the courts will interpret an education clause based on the political history of both the state and the education clause, as well as on prior interpretations of that clause by the courts and the state's policymakers. In reality, the specific language of the state's education clause seems to have little impact on the results of adequacy cases.

The historical meaning of the education clause.   The historical meaning of the education clause can provide a court with insight into the proper interpretation of the clause. The intentions of the constitutional framers in different states vary with regard to the type of education systems they attempted to establish. Therefore, both the plaintiffs and the defendants must try to prove what the constitutional framers had in mind about a variety of issues, including the nature of the state education system, the type of

---

[14]*Abbott* I: *Abbott v. Burke,* 100 N.J. 269 (1985); *Abbott* II: *Abbott v. Burke,* 119 N.J. 287 (1990).
[15]*McDaniels v. Thomas,* 285 S.E.2d 156 (Ga. 1981); *Lujan v. Colorado State Board of Education,* 649 P.2d 1005 (Colo. 1982).
[16]*Thompson v. Engelking,* 537 P.2d 635 (Idaho 1975).

school finance structure that would support it, and whether those notions are relevant to current school finance issues.

Interpretation is rendered more difficult by the fact that most states did not have a statewide education system prior to their constitutional conventions, most of which occurred in the nineteenth century. Education was provided by local entities, with substantial differences existing from district to district. Sometimes there were local school districts or regional groupings of districts, but there was no statewide system.

States eventually began to consolidate these diverse systems into one statewide system, defined primarily by state laws, rules, and regulations, especially as they pertained to school accreditation and teacher licensure. In some states, education clauses had no apparent implications for the school finance system, which usually continued to rely heavily on local property taxes, with some state assistance provided via a flat per-pupil grant (see Chapter 5). In other states, records from the constitutional debates indicate that the framers envisaged a uniform statewide system, with equal spending per pupil, often fully financed with state funds. In these states, the education clause could reasonably be inferred to require something close to equal spending or equal access to core educational opportunities across all school districts. The early debates, therefore, remain an important consideration for the courts in their attempts to interpret education clauses.

Substantive demands of the education clause.   If the court determines that its constitution requires the state to provide some quality of education above the bare minimum, the court must determine precisely what the constitution requires. The historical debates can lend insight into this issue, but the courts must also apply modern concepts to interpret the substantive demands of the education clause. The analysis of these demands led courts to define "adequacy" and apply it in school finance litigation in the 1990s and early twenty-first century.

"Pre-Adequacy" Cases

Adequacy traces its roots back to decisions from the early second wave. The *Robinson* case was discussed earlier, but a 1978 case in Washington also contributed to the early development of the concept of adequacy.[17] In fact, as Minorini and Sugarman (1999a, 1999b) argue, these two cases were the precursors of the 1990s adequacy cases, though the courts never used the term "adequacy." These decisions began to expand the notion of school finance equity to include the delivery of an education program that would provide students a fair opportunity to learn to high standards. It took the New Jersey legislature more than two decades to define what that education program would be. Washington, however, defined its program in terms of the staffing that the average district had been providing to its schools, together with a statewide teacher salary schedule.

The 1982 case *Pauley v. Bailey*[18] in West Virginia furthered the development of a more specific definition of adequacy. Rejecting a motion to dismiss the case, the West

---

[17]*Seattle School District No. 1 of King City v. State,* 585 P.2d 71 (Wash. 1978).
[18]*Pauley v. Bailey,* C.A. No. 75-126 (Cir. Ct. Kanawha Cty., W. Va. 1982), initially decided as *Pauley v. Kelly,* 255 S.E.2d 859 (W. Va. 1979).

Virginia Supreme Court required the trial court first to determine what a "thorough and efficient" (the language from the state constitution) education system was and to assess the degree to which the existing system met that standard. The trial court concluded that the clause required equal programs and services across all school districts, and found that the existing finance system did not provide such equality. The state created numerous committees to define standards for education programs that would represent a thorough and efficient program. The standards became the basis of the state's master plan of standards for all operating programs and facilities. Funding this plan would have required the state to nearly double education resources in West Virginia, so it was only partially implemented. Finally in 1997, 15 years after the master plan was proposed, a court ordered the state to fully fund the plan. *Pauley* marked a step toward the adequacy era, but its impact was limited because the final ruling came from a trial court, rather than the high court of the state.

Adequacy Cases

School finance cases explicitly making the adequacy argument emerged in the late 1980s and early 1990s. The first to reach a state supreme court was *Rose v. Council for Better Education*.

Rose v. Council.   Adequacy fully blossomed in 1989 when the Kentucky Supreme Court[19] not only overturned the state's school finance system but also declared the entire state education system unconstitutional, including its curriculum, governance, and management. Although *Rose* began as a fiscal-neutrality case, the ruling turned it into an adequacy case. The court held that school finance equity required that all students have access to an adequate education program, one that provided the following:

- Sufficient oral and written communication skills to enable students to function in a complex and rapidly changing civilization
- Sufficient knowledge of economic, social, and political systems to enable students to make informed choices
- Sufficient understanding of governmental processes to enable students to understand the issues that affect their community, state, and nation
- Sufficient self-knowledge and knowledge of students' mental and physical wellness
- Sufficient grounding in the arts to enable students to appreciate their cultural and historical heritage
- Sufficient training or preparation for advanced training in either academic or vocational fields so as to enable students to choose and pursue life work intelligently
- Sufficient levels of academic or vocational skills to enable students to compete favorably with their counterparts in surrounding states, in academics or in the job market

[19]*Rose v. Council for Better Education, Inc.*, 790 S.W.2d 186 (Ky. 1989).

In response, Kentucky completely redesigned its education system, including the finance structure and the governance, management, and curriculum programs. The Kentucky redesign reflected the kind of education reform that was first known as "systemic reform" (Fuhrman, 1993; Odden, 1995a; Smith and O'Day, 1991) and later evolved into standards-based education reform (Massell, Hoppe, and Kirst, 1997). The reforms included a new three-tiered finance system accompanied by a large infusion of new money, content standards for the curriculum in all major subject areas, performance standards for students including a new testing system, changes in school governance and management including much more school-based decision making, and a new accountability system with rewards and sanctions at the school-site level (Adams, 1994, 1997).

At least five aspects of the overall Kentucky policy response were and continue to be significant:

- The system focused on student performance outcomes. The primary goal was not just increased dollars and education inputs but high levels of student achievement in a variety of educational areas. This link between inputs and outputs pointed the direction for future school finance research and policy.
- School sites gained substantial discretion for allocating and using dollars, with many finance decisions decentralized from the district to the school.
- Schools were rewarded financially (on an unequalized-wealth basis) for meeting performance improvement goals and sanctioned for consistently failing to meet goals (Kelley, 1998; Kelley and Protsik, 1997).
- Preschool was provided.
- The finance system included a substantially increased foundation program for base expenditures across all districts. And the state limited local add-ons to about an extra 50 percent, for which the first 15 percent was "equalized" by the state through a guaranteed tax base.

The *Rose* case set the agenda for school finance up to the present time. Many of the programmatic elements it mandated became the core of standards-based education reform and the basis for a definition of adequacy. The court emphasized the analysis of how resources related to student outcomes, a concept that has become perhaps the most important issue in education finance. Thus, school-funding policy moved beyond simply providing each school with the same resources to a consideration of how the resources were allocated and how such allocations impacted children.

Conflicts between the Courts and the Legislature

Not all cases produced the kind of reforms that derived from *Rose*. A common feature of some adequacy rulings involves the tendency of the court to defer to the legislature with regard to defining the specifics of the reforms. This policy can lead to conflicts between the courts and the legislature, as happened in Texas and Ohio.

Texas played an important role in the third wave, with the four decisions in *Edgewood v. Kirby* resulting in some fascinating interactions between the court and the legislature. Both the litigation and the resulting new finance structure proved unique. The court originally overturned the school finance system on fiscal-neutrality grounds, even though many analysts claimed that the Texas system was quite equal except for the bottom and top 50 districts. The legislature submitted plan after plan to create a new structure for the overall system, but the court kept rejecting these proposals. When the Texas legislature finally enacted a system that "recaptured" funds from the highest-wealth districts, the Texas Supreme Court ruled that the new system violated another section of the state constitution that prohibits the legislature from enacting ad valorem taxes, which removed meaningful discretion from localities with regard to making decisions about local taxes.

Eventually, the legislature created a two-tiered pupil-weighted system (Picus and Toenjes, 1994) that was similar to the original system but that required the wealthiest districts, with voter approval, to voluntarily give some of their annual revenues to lower-wealth districts as a condition for receiving any state aid. This system, which largely focused on the top and bottom 50 districts that the court identified as the core of the problem, finally passed muster with the court. Subsequently, however, the Texas Supreme Court again reconsidered the system. It ruled that the structure was constitutional with regard to education clause issues, but unconstitutional with regard to the ad valorem tax issue.[20] In addition, the court warned the state that the system was drifting toward unconstitutionality under the education clause as well. Texas will likely experience continued upheaval over the next several years.

Ohio's adequacy litigation evolved into a quagmire due to conflicts between the legislature and the court. The Ohio Supreme Court held the finance system to be unconstitutional in *DeRolph v. State*.[21] The legislature made a number of partial efforts to remedy the constitutional violations, but the court rejected these efforts as insufficient. Finally, the court approved of a plan in *DeRolph III*. Shortly thereafter, however, the court vacated its own ruling, declared the system unconstitutional by a 4–3 vote, ordered the legislature to dismiss the case, and released jurisdiction, meaning the plaintiffs would have to start from scratch if the legislature did not enact effective reforms. The court timed its decision in the final *DeRolph* case to occur shortly before two members of the court were replaced by conservative judges. Meanwhile, the inequities and inadequacies of school finance continue virtually unabated in parts of the state. *DeRolph* was a case in which neither body of government accounted itself well.

Rulings with More Explicit Remedies

Some high courts opted not to defer crafting the remedy to the legislature to such a great extent. This choice has had good and bad points, as will be seen in this section.

New Jersey.   New Jersey possesses one of the more interesting series of school finance decisions. As stated earlier, the 1973 *Robinson* case foreshadowed adequacy but focused

[20]*Neeley v. West Orange–Cove Consolidated Independent School District,* 176 S.W.3d 746 (Tex 2005).
[21]*DeRolph*, I: *DeRolph v. Ohio*, 78 Ohio St. 3d 193; 1997 Ohio 84; 677 N.E.2d 733 (1997). *DeRolph*, III: *DeRolph v. Ohio*, 93 Ohio St. 3d 309, 754 N.E.2d 1184 (2001). *DeRolph*, IV: *DeRolph v. Ohio*, 97 Ohio St. 3d 434; 2002 Ohio 6750; 780 N.E.2d 529 (2002).

largely on financial disparities. The 1976 legislative response to *Robinson* sought to address those disparities. In the first challenge to the new school finance law, the court actually upheld those financial elements of the new system (Minorini and Sugarman, 1999a, 1999b). However, beginning in 1989 and continuing to the present, the state supreme court focused more and more on the substantive meaning of education in the *Abbott v. Burke* decisions.[22]

The *Abbott* cases involved lawsuits brought by 28 poor, urban school districts, collectively referred to as the Abbott Districts. The court in the first *Abbott* case (*Abbott I*) required the state to increase the funding per pupil of the Abbott Districts so that it approached the average of the wealthiest suburban districts in New Jersey. The subsequent legislative response, the Quality Education Act of 1990, moved in that direction, but the state failed to raise sufficient funds to finance it. Thus, the plaintiffs returned to the courts in the early 1990s and obtained two additional decisions (*Abbott II* and *Abbott III*) that required a revised system that could raise sufficient funds. However, the court gave the state a late-1996 deadline by which to comply. In essence, the court wanted the state to define and then to fund an education program that would teach students in the Abbott Districts to high performance standards.

In response to both the court cases and the evolution of education reform, New Jersey began in 1996 to create curriculum content and student performance standards in six different subject areas, as well as a new state testing system that would measure performance under those standards. The legislature also designed a new finance system, through the Comprehensive Educational Improvement Finance Act (CEIFA), that was intended to be sufficient for districts and schools to implement the standards. In CEIFA, the state identified the staffing for an elementary, middle, and high school that it felt was sufficient to teach students to the new standards, and used statewide average costs to determine what amount it would provide for each of the 28 Abbott Districts. As a result funding was increased for the Abbott Districts, but not to the level specified by the court. Nevertheless, the state argued in court that the proposal was sufficient to accomplish the educational goals of the state's new program, which was the ultimate intention of the school finance court case.

In early 1997, however, the court in *Abbott IV* ruled that CEIFA was unconstitutional, largely because it did not provide for a program specific to the requirements of the special-needs districts. Instead, the CEIFA school models were patterned after practices in districts that had very few similarities to the education challenges faced by the special-needs districts, which enrolled large percentages of low-income and minority students. The court then noted that the highest-spending districts were successful in teaching their students to high standards. So the court used the funding level of the highest-spending districts as the base funding level (called the parity standard) for the Abbott Districts. The court mandated that the state raise the funding in each of the Abbott Districts to the average level of the most advantaged districts ($8,664 in 1997–98),

---

[22]*Abbott* I: *Abbott v. Burke,* 100 N.J. 269 (N.J. 1985); *Abbott* II: *Abbott v. Burke,* 119 N.J. 287 (N.J. 1990); *Abbott* III: *Abbott v. Burke,* 136 N.J. 444 (N.J. 1994); *Abbott* IV: *Abbott v. Burke,* 149 N.J. 149, 168 (N.J. 1997); *Abbott* V: *Abbott v. Burke,* 153 N.J. 480 (N.J. 1998), Appendix I; *Abbott* VI: *Abbott v. Burke,* 153 N.J. 480 (N.J. 1998).

because it concluded that this level of funding would provide a sufficient base for the Abbott Districts to devise a quality, core educational program. The court also required the state to identify the additional, supplemental programs that students in the Abbott Districts would need in order to offset the disadvantage caused by the poverty of their local urban neighborhoods. The court left open the possibility of adopting a different parity standard but stated that the state would have to prove the sufficiency of any proposed new standard. The court also asked a remand judge to hold hearings to identify the supplemental programs and their costs.

During those hearings, New Jersey retained the general CEIFA structure but replaced the staffing proposal with the staffing for a whole-school model that had been specifically designed for the needs of low-income and minority students in urban locations, including language minority students: the Roots and Wings/Success for All program (Slavin, Madden, Dolan, and Wasik, 1996). The state showed that this model could be funded at the parity standard. The New Jersey Supreme Court ruled in *Abbott VI* in May 1998 as follows:

- Parity funding would be retained until a different standard was proposed and accepted.
- The state proposal to use an urban-specific, whole-school program as the way to implement school finance reform and determine whether there was sufficient funding was now appropriate, and the state had made a substantive case with the Roots and Wings/Success for All program.
- Each school would offer both full-day kindergarten and a half-day preschool program for all children ages 3 and 4.
- The state was responsible for improving the physical facilities in all the Abbott Districts, at a cost of billions of dollars.
- If schools could still demonstrate a need for additional funds, they could make a request for more through the commissioner of education.

There are several important aspects of the New Jersey evolution from a fiscal-equity to an educational-adequacy case. First, the state focused only on the most disadvantaged districts. Second, its responses included a new and unique approach to defining "educational adequacy," namely, a comprehensive, whole-school design that could be made compatible with state content and performance standards (see Stringfield, Ross, and Smith, 1996, for descriptions of additional school designs; see Odden and Busch, 1998, and Odden, 2000b, for a discussion of their costs). Because the school design was quite specific in all of its strategies and elements, its cost could be determined and then used as the basis for calculating the amount of money each district and each school in it needed. In this way, New Jersey began a process of defining "adequacy" as the resources needed to implement an effective (or evidence-based), comprehensive set of school strategies that would provide all students with an equal opportunity to learn to state performance standards. Third, the court expanded the notion of "educational adequacy" by requiring the state to provide preschool services to children who fell outside the 5–17 age bracket specifically mentioned in the education clause. Finally, the New Jersey court required the state to confront the complexities of defining "educational adequacy," rather than avoiding the issues.

Although the language of the court decision was quite specific, New Jersey has experienced difficulties implementing the 1998 court decree. Erlichson, Goertz, and Turnbull (1999) and Erlichson and Goertz (2001) found that schools, districts, and the state faced several challenges in having schools select comprehensive school reforms and reallocate resources in order to fund them with the level of resources at their disposal.

North Carolina.   The *Leandro* case in North Carolina involved an even more specific remedy than in New Jersey.[23] One implementing decision required preschool for all low-income 4- and perhaps even 3-year-olds. Another required schools to allocate funds to the educational needs of students from low-income backgrounds before spending money for any other purpose. The court's objective was to ensure that the first draw on education dollars was for the base program, and the second for the extra services low-income students require in order to perform to state performance standards. The North Carolina court, like its counterpart in New Jersey, has been comfortable delving into the specifics of how education dollars are used, in attempts to link funding levels to student achievement outcomes.

Adequacy and Standards

One of the main challenges in adequacy litigation involves determining the level of education required by the education clause. In this age of standards and accountability, one might assume that the state standards would be the natural choice because they embody the knowledge and skills the legislature has deemed necessary for students to possess. Interestingly, the courts do not always use the state standards as the required level of education. The *CFE v. State* case from New York illustrates how courts grapple with this issue.

The *CFE* case involved the claim that schools in New York City received less funding than was necessary to educate students adequately. The highest court in New York had previously defined a "sound basic education" as one that would enable students to be knowledgeable voters and to serve on juries. This standard is quite vague, so one of the main issues in the case was to define the court's standard in a way that could be applied by a court. The trial judge equated the court's standard with the Regents Learning Standards, which are extremely high.[24] The judge ruled that the finance system was unconstitutional because it did not provide enough resources to New York City. In 2002, an appellate court[25] overturned the trial court's decision, largely because it determined that an eighth-grade education was all that the state constitution required.

The highest court eventually struck a middle position when it decided the case.[26] The court determined that the Regents Learning Standards went beyond the requirements of a

---

[23]*Leandro v. State*, 488 S.E.2d 249 (N.C. 1997).
[24]*Campaign for Fiscal Equity, Inc. v. State*, 719 N.Y.S.2d 475 (N.Y.Sup., 2001).
[25]*Campaign for Fiscal Equity, Inc. v. State*, 744 N.Y.S.2d 130 N.Y.A.D. (1 Dept., 2002).
[26]*Campaign for Fiscal Equity, Inc. v. State*, 100 N.Y.2d 893, 801 N.E.2d 106 (2003).

sound basic education. On the other hand, the court opined that effective citizens need more than just an eighth-grade education. The court set the standard as "a meaningful high school education," which it purposely did not tie to any particular grade level. The court ruled that the state failed to provide schools in New York City with the resources needed to meet that standard, so it directed the state to determine the cost of providing a sound basic education in New York City and provide the requisite funding to the schools.

Does Adequacy Require Equal Outcomes?

Another important issue is whether adequacy cases require equal education outcomes in addition to having all students actually achieve to some high minimum standards. Legal analysts claim that they do not (Clune, 1994a, 1994b; Minorini and Sugarman, 1999a, 1999b; Underwood, 1995a). They argue that adequacy means a level of resources for a district or school that would allow it to provide the type of program in which each student has an equal opportunity to achieve to high standards. In other words, it would demand some comprehensive set of educational programs and strategies designed to teach nearly all students to high-performance standards—such as the comprehensive education reforms enacted in Kentucky, Massachusetts, and Missouri in the early 1990s; the comprehensive school design approach of New Jersey; or the evidence-based reforms of Arkansas in 2004 and Wyoming in 2006. However, adequacy would not require equality, because high-spending districts could provide an education beyond the high minimum standard.

We suggest that it is entirely possible that some court in the future might require the high level of student achievement to be uniform across the state. This would be a natural evolution of the adequacy issue, and the ultimate test of whether a comprehensive education program actually can deliver student achievement results.

In any event, the third wave has spawned an enormous amount of litigation that shows no sign of abating. The plaintiffs have fared far better from 1989 until the present, with their winning percentage increasing to comfortably more than 50 percent.[27] The connection between resource usage and student outcomes that is at the foundation of adequacy litigation promises to be one of the most important issues of the coming years from a policy perspective.

5. SUMMARY

School finance litigation has evolved over time. Initially, plaintiffs used state and federal equal protection clauses to address inequities in resource distribution across school districts. Later, plaintiffs relied more heavily on state education clauses to argue substantive issues linking school finance to education programs and services. Today, almost all school finance litigation is based on state education clauses and is delving into complex issues of education programs and services.

[27]For a complete list of school finance cases, go to highered.mcgraw-hill.com/sites/0072823186/student_view0/table_of_school_finance_legal_.html

School finance litigation is moving away from the traditional cases involving fiscal disparities and toward the more complicated educational adequacy cases. This evolving nature of school finance litigation mirrors the changes occurring in school finance research as a whole (see, e.g., Odden, Borman, and Fermanich, 2004). Issues of equity remain important, but the relationship between educational resources and student outputs is becoming the primary concern (see, e.g., Archibald, 2006). Courts have been driving this trend to some extent, resulting in linkages between the new litigation strategies and cutting-edge research. More and better data have become available in recent years, so the courts can become involved in analyzing how school- and district-level resource allocations impact student achievement.

It is important not to overemphasize the trend to adequacy, however. As Minorini and Sugarman (1999a) conclude, the prominence of the adequacy cases does not mean courts have shifted away from the equity argument entirely. It means only that the courts have turned from equity defined only in dollar terms to equity defined in terms of programs and services to which a dollar figure can be attached. Though this is clearly an advance, it also harkens back to the "education needs" cases in the early days of school finance litigation. Indeed, it could be argued that the adequacy approach, together with standards-based education reform and the implied comprehensive set of school strategies needed to deliver those standards, is simply an updated version of the old education needs argument.

6. A SCHOOL FINANCE LEGAL SCORECARD

The following McGraw-Hill website (www.mhhc.com/odden4e) summarizes the key school finance court cases since 1968 and indicates whether the system was overturned or upheld and what the constitutional basis for court action was. The chart shows that school finance cases have been decided in 42 states, and existing school finance systems were upheld in about half the cases and overturned in the other half. Thus, school finance litigants are batting about .500 in their attempts to overturn state school finance structures that allow wide variations in educational expenditures linked to local property wealth per pupil or in education programs and services. In several states, moreover, second and third rounds of litigation have been filed or are under way, and many of these second-generation cases have been successful in making their claims. Arkansas, Arizona, Connecticut, Minnesota, Missouri, New Jersey, Texas, Washington, and Wyoming are just some of the states where second and third cases were filed that finally convinced a court to overturn the school finance system. In short, the court route to reforming state school finance systems is alive and active, and a guiding motto could well be "If at first you don't succeed, try, try again."

Study Questions

1. Find out if there has been or currently is a school finance lawsuit in your state. Determine the current legal status of the case—is it pending in a trial court, on appeal to a higher court, or resolved?

2. If there is or was a school finance case in your state, what were the constitutional issues or clauses on which the case was argued? Would you categorize the case as an equity case or an adequacy case? Explain why you reached that conclusion.
3. Regardless of the current status of the case, what legislative action on school funding has been taken in response to the lawsuit? Have more dollars been appropriated to schools as a result of the lawsuit, and has the distribution of funds changed in response to the lawsuit?
4. How did the subsequent litigation impact funding levels and education programs in your local school district?
5. Do you anticipate future litigation over school finance? If so, what do you think the outcome will be? If not, why not?

A Framework for Assessing Equity and Adequacy in School Finance

There are many ways to assess the equity and adequacy of a state's school finance system. Underlying this concern, of course, is a key question: Does money matter? Traditional assessments of school finance, particularly during most of the twentieth century, assumed that money did matter and focused largely on equity issues (i.e., whether money was distributed fairly across school districts and students). During the latter quarter of the previous century, however, questions were raised about whether money mattered. Indeed, many policy analysts, particularly a group of economists, raised questions about that assumption and, after reviewing large bodies of literature, concluded that there was little research support for the assumption that money mattered. Around the same time, policy interest and, as shown in Chapter 2, the course of litigation began to focus on the adequacy of school finance systems, directly addressing the issue of how money would matter and how much money would be required.

This chapter has three parts. The first reviews the literature on whether money matters. It concludes that money *does* matter, but it is the way money is used that determines the power of differential levels of education dollars linked to differential levels of student learning. Since equity in school finance is still a driving policy issue, the second section draws from the work of Berne and Stiefel (1984, 1999) and develops an equity framework that can be used to determine the degree of finance equity of a state's school finance structure. Although Berne and Stiefel are not the only scholars to outline a school finance equity framework (see also, e.g., Alexander, 1982; Garms, 1979; Wise, 1968, 1983), theirs is the most comprehensive and has been used by many analysts to conduct empirical studies of the equity of state school finance structures (see, e.g., Adams, 1997; Goertz, 1983;

51

Goldhaber and Callahan, 2001; Hickrod, Chaudhari, and Hubbard, 1981; Kearney, Chen, and Checkoway, 1988; Odden, 1978, 1995b; Picus and Hertert, 1993a, 1993b; Picus, Odden, and Fermanich, 2004; Rubenstein, Doering, and Gess, 2000).

The final section addresses the issue of school finance adequacy. This approach to assessing a state's school finance system expressly attempts to link the finance side of district and school operations more directly to the program, curriculum, and instruction side, as well as to the student achievement that results. Put a different way, it explicitly tries to show how money does matter and how these conclusions lead to the design of "adequate" state school finance structures.

1. DOES MONEY MATTER?

One question that always has surrounded school finance is this: Does money matter in terms of student performance? Most educators would say yes, but policy and research communities have been more skeptical. The fact is, there has been disagreement among researchers as to whether a statistical link can be found between student outcomes and money (or, what money buys, such as class size, teacher experience and degrees, etc.). Production function research constitutes the largest body of research evidence on this issue, but the conclusions from this research are mixed (Monk, 1992).

A production function is an economic tool used to measure the contribution of individual inputs to the output of some product. It is possible to estimate an educational production function with this form:

$$P = f(R, S, D)$$

where

       P = a measure of student performance
       R = a measure of resources available to students in the school or district
       S = a vector of student characteristics
       D = a vector of district and school characteristics

One possible measure of R would be the class size in a school or school district. In fact, actual class size is in many ways a good choice for this particular variable as it provides a proxy for the level of resources available for children (i.e., it is highly correlated with per-pupil spending). However, production function studies typically use a pupil–teacher ratio measure as a proxy for class size, even though that variable is a very poor measure of actual class size (Achilles, 1999).

Several other methodological problems are associated with production function research: (1) determining the correct measure of results, (2) controlling for sociodemographic variables, (3) statistically adjusting for variables measured at different levels in the system (student, classroom, school, and district), (4) conducting longitudinal rather than cross-sectional analyses, and (5) correctly specifying input factors (pupil–teacher ratios, for example, as noted above, are not good proxies for actual class sizes). Nevertheless, a large number of production function studies have been conducted, and they can be used to help answer the question of whether money or resources are related to improvements in student performance.

The most often cited research in this field is the synthesis work of Eric Hanushek (1981, 1986, 1989, 1997). Hanushek has consistently argued that there does not appear to be a systematic relationship between the level of funding and student outcomes (see also Hanushek, 2002, on the class size debate).

Hanushek has analyzed 90 different studies, with 377 separate production function equations, over a 20-year period. In his 1997 publication, he continued to argue that "these results have a simple interpretation: There is no strong or consistent relationship between school resources and student performance. In other words, there is little reason to be confident that simply adding more resources to schools as currently constituted will yield performance gains among students" (Hanushek, 1997, p. 148).

Hanushek essentially divided the 377 different findings into two major categories: those indicating a positive and those indicating a negative relationship. After comparing the numbers in each category, he found more negative than positive outcomes. He then concluded that the variation in findings was such that a systematic relationship between money and outcomes had not yet been identified. He stated:

> The concern from a policy viewpoint is that nobody can describe when resources will be used effectively and when they will not. In the absence of such a description, providing these general resources to a school implies that sometimes resources might be used effectively, other times they may be applied in ways that are actually damaging, and most of the time no measurable student outcome gains should be expected (Hanushek, 1997, pp. 148–49).

He suggested that what is needed is a change in the incentive structures facing schools so that schools and teachers are motivated to act in ways that use resources efficiently and that lead to improved student performance.

Others have analyzed the same studies as Hanushek and reached opposite conclusions. Hedges, Laine, and Greenwald (1994a, 1994b; see also Greenwald, Hedges, and Laine, 1996a, 1996b; Laine, Greenwald, and Hedges, 1996) concluded that, in fact, money *can* make a difference. They first calculated the effect size of the different studies and, rather than counting the number of positive and negative outcomes, then calculated an average effect size. Their analyses produced a significantly positive effect size, mainly because the larger effects of the "positive" studies were greater than the smaller effects of the "negative" studies. Relying on this and other evidence, Hedges, Laine, and Greenwald (1994a) concluded that school spending and achievement are positively correlated. In his rejoinder, Hanushek (1994) argued that while there is evidence that the relationship exists, there is not evidence of a strong or systematic relationship. We side more with Hedges, Laine, and Greenwald than with Hanushek, viewing "effect size" as the best way to summarize across studies.

Differences in analytic methods and conclusions also characterize some of the debate over class size (see Hanushek, 2002; Krueger, 2002). On this issue, we also side with those concluding that class size does make a difference, but note that the research shows only that class sizes of 15 students, and only for kindergarten through grade 3, boost student performance (Achilles, 1999; Finn, 2002; Grissmer, 1999; Kreuger, 2002).

Other economic research bolsters the conclusion that money matters. Ferguson (1991) analyzed spending and the use of educational resources in Texas. He concluded that "hiring teachers with stronger literacy skills, hiring more teachers (when students-per-teacher exceed 18), retaining experienced teachers, and attracting more teachers with advanced training are all measures that produce higher test scores in exchange for more money" (Ferguson, 1991, p. 485).

In another study, Wenglinsky (1997) used regression analysis with three large national databases to see if expenditures had an impact on student achievement of fourth- and eighth-graders. He found that the impact of spending was in steps or stages. For fourth-graders, Wenglinsky concluded that increased expenditures on instruction and on school district administration increased teacher–student ratios (more teachers per same number of students, smaller class sizes), which in turn, led to higher achievement in mathematics.

For the eighth-graders, the process was more complex. Specifically, Weglinsky found that increased expenditures on instruction and central administration increased teacher–student ratios (reduced class size). This increased teacher–student ratio led to an improved school environment or climate, and the improved climate and attendant reduction in behavior problems resulted in higher achievement in math.

Equally interesting was Wenglinsky's (1997) finding that capital outlay (spending on facility construction and maintenance), school-level administration, and teacher education levels could not be correlated with improved student achievement. More recently, economists have used the "cost function" approach to determine what an adequate spending-per-pupil level would be in various states (see section 3). This methodological approach is technically the "dual" of the production function method. Both methods use essentially the same variables. But the production function method uses student performance as the independent variable and expenditures per pupil as the independent variable, while the cost function method uses expenditures per pupil as the dependent variable and student performance as the dependent variable. Nearly all cost function studies find a linkage between student performance and spending per pupil, and argue that a higher performance level would require a higher level of per-pupil spending (see, e.g., Taylor, Baker, and Vedlitz, 2004). So today, economists are divided on the issue of whether spending more should lead to higher levels of student achievement.

One of the most sophisticated studies of this issue was conducted by Archibald (2006). Using data from a large district that linked student achievement scores to teachers, classrooms, and schools, and employing a three-level hierarchical linear modeling statistical approach, she found that expenditures per pupil did matter, even after accounting for differences in student learning produced by teachers (one of the largest sources of variation in student learning) and in demographics at the student, classroom, and school levels.

We agree with researchers who assert a positive connection between resources and student achievement. As a result, we argue that the distribution of educational resources, discussed in the remainder of this chapter, is important for both equity and effectiveness reasons. But we also conclude that the connections between money and results are not all that strong, and, as we show in Chapter 7, that there are many ways to use money more effectively. In addition to the strategies we discuss in Chapter 7, there are also ways to pay teachers differently that would lead to better instruction and higher levels of student learning (see Odden and Kelley, 2002; Odden and Wallace, 2007).

2. EQUITY IN SCHOOL FINANCE

Berne and Stiefel's (1984) original framework for assessing a state's school finance structure required answers to several key questions:

- *Who* is the group for whom school finance should be equitable? There are two major groups: (1) children who attend the public schools and (2) taxpayers who pay the costs of public education. The equity issues for each group are quite different. Equity for children was discussed largely within an educational opportunity framework. Equity for taxpayers was discussed largely in the public finance context of tax burden, as it is in Chapter 10 of this book.
- *What* resource objects or educational services should be distributed equitably among the group of concern? The traditional answer to this question for children is dollars or revenues per pupil. But educational processes such as curriculum and instruction are also key educational resources. Outcomes such as student achievement are also possible objects to analyze. Deciding on the specific object is important in assessing the degree of school finance equity. Some objects could be distributed equitably, and others inequitably.
- *How* is equity to be defined, or what are the specific equity principles used to determine whether a distribution is equitable? There are three equity principles: (1) horizontal equity, in which all members of the group were considered equal; (2) vertical equity, in which differences (for which unequal resource distributions are legitimate) among members of the group were recognized; and (3) equal opportunity, which identified variables such as property value per pupil that should not be related to resource distribution. Because the term "equal educational opportunity" has been used in several non–school finance contexts and has multiple meanings, the school finance version of this term has become known as **fiscal neutrality.**
- *How much* equity is in the system, or what is the specific status of equity? This component includes the specific statistics used to measure the degree of equity in the system.

As Berne and Stiefel (1984) demonstrated, different answers to these key questions could result in different conclusions about the equity of the system. One major objective in developing and using a school finance equity framework is to help clarify how one analyst could declare a system equitable while another, using the same data, could declare it inequitable. The reason could simply be that they had different answers to these key questions. Berne and Stiefel's framework provides "rigor" and substance to discussions of equity because it helps one sort out the issues and shows how these more complex conclusions can be drawn.

Solid as the framework was, it nevertheless became problematic as it was applied over the subsequent 20 years. First, because wealth or fiscal neutrality was such a central issue in both litigation and school finance policy deliberations, it was difficult to establish it as just one of four different equity concepts. Second, though the framework was amenable for use with any unit of analysis—district or school—it came to be too strongly associated with the district, and thus seemed out of date or inappropriate as attention shifted to school-level finance (Busch and Odden, 1997; Goertz and Odden, 1999; Ouchi, 2005). Third, as adequacy emerged as a preeminent issue in school finance litigation and education policy, the framework seemed obsolete, as it addressed only equity and not the outcome aspect of what was popularly perceived as being central to adequacy. In short, largely due to how the framework was applied and defined in practice, it needed some refurbishing in order to incorporate evolving school finance issues.

Thus, in the late 1990s, in assessing the history of equity in school finance, Berne and Stiefel (1999) updated the framework, recasting some of its elements and also explaining how it actually could incorporate nearly all of the salient new issues in both school finance litigation and policy deliberations. This chapter draws largely from their recent work. Berne and Stiefel suggested that school finance analysis address six key topics:

1. Ex ante versus ex post analyses
2. The unit of analysis in terms of state, district, school, or student
3. The objects of interest, whether they be input fiscal variables, educational process variables, or student achievement variables
4. The group of concern, children or taxpayers
5. Equity concepts, but now leading with fiscal neutrality, while also incorporating horizontal and vertical equity (This chapter will include measures of equity under this general heading.)
6. The concept of adequacy, even though nearly all of its elements could be incorporated into the preceding five issues (Adequacy is addressed in section 3.)

Ex Ante versus Ex Post

Ex ante versus ex post analysis addresses the issue of whether the assessment of the school finance system is done on the basic structure, concepts, variables, and parameters prior to or before (ex ante) they are actually applied in practice, or on data, numbers, and results that emerge after (ex post) a system is implemented. Few analysts make this somewhat arcane but important distinction, though it is critical. Indeed, nearly all empirical analyses of state school finance systems use actual data and thus are ex post analyses.

An example should help clarify the distinction. Take this key historical issue in school finance: the unequal distribution of the property tax base and the resultant linkage between spending levels and wealth levels. As Chapter 1 discussed, and as is discussed further in Chapter 9, a high-level guaranteed tax base (GTB) program, such as at the 95th percentile, would be highly equitable from an ex ante perspective. Such a program would eliminate the traditional problem of unequal access to a school tax base and make the tax base that could be tapped for education purposes the same, at least for 95 percent of districts and children.

At the same time, as Chapter 1 also showed, such programs over time tend neither to eliminate spending differences across districts nor to reduce all statistical links between spending and property wealth per pupil. Thus, from an ex post perspective, such a system could have inequity statistics only slightly better than found in the system before such a high-level GTB was put in place. In this example, then, the system could be deemed eminently fair from an ex ante, formula parameter analysis, but unfair from an ex post, empirical analysis. This is the dilemma that underlies assessments of the equity of the Missouri school finance system (Odden, 1995b) and the Wisconsin system (see Chapter 11).

A similar dilemma could arise under the emerging adequacy issues. For example, suppose this definition of "adequacy" is used: sufficient funds to allow provision of the set of programs, services, and instructional efforts deemed necessary to give each student an equal opportunity to perform to state standards. Then suppose that school districts did not translate these dollars into appropriate programs and services. Such a system could correctly be characterized as adequate from an ex ante fiscal perspective but inadequate from an ex post, programs, services, and student results perspective.

The point is that beforehand (ex ante) analyses are quite different from after-the-fact, empirical (ex post) analyses, and finance policy analysts should make the distinction explicit in any report or study. Particularly if an analysis is conducted using actual data after full implementation, it should be made clear that an ex post analysis is being presented (such as those in Chapter 11); indeed, the conclusions could be compared to an ex ante analysis, even if findings about the equity and adequacy of the system were different.

The Unit of Analysis

There are two aspects to the discussion of the unit of analysis. The first concerns the primary unit at which measures of the object are taken (i.e., whether the measure is at the state, district, school, or student level). The second is a statistical issue of how to appropriately calculate statistical measures.

What unit of measure.   As to the first issue, historically and traditionally, measures of school finance, such as revenues and expenditures, have been taken at the district level, making the district the unit of analysis. Moreover, the analysis was usually conducted across school districts within a state. Recently, however, analyses of school finance equity have been conducted at the district level but across the entire country, without respect to state boundaries (Hertert, Busch, and Odden, 1994; Liu, 2006; Murray, Evans, and Schwab, 1998; Odden and Busch, 1998). These analyses generally show that most fiscal disparities are due to cross-state rather than within-state differences. Since the No Child Left Behind Act of 2001 establishes a virtual national goal to teach students to high standards, and since the primary issues of both equity and adequacy concern cross-state differences, this national focus might gain more attention in the future.

In addition, as education policy increasingly focuses on the school site, more analysis using the school site as the primary unit will likely emerge, as in for distributing revenues (e.g., Odden, 1999; Odden and Busch, 1998; Ouchi, 2005), for analyzing fiscal equity (Hertert, 1996; Odden and Busch, 1997; Rubenstein, 1998), or for assessing the efficiency and effectiveness of resource use (Miles and Darling-Hammond, 1997; Odden, 1997b; Odden, Archibald, Fermanich, and Gross, 2003; Odden and Busch, 1998; Speakman et al., 1997).

Nevertheless, we expect that most analyses of school finance issues will continue to be conducted with measures taken at the district level but with increasing numbers of analyses at the school site level, even though gathering good school-level data is difficult (Berne, Stiefel, and Moser, 1997; Cohen, 1997; Farland, 1997; Goertz, 1997; Monk, 1997; Odden, Archibald, Fermanich, and Gallagher, 2002; Odden, Archibald, Fermanich, and Gross, 2003; Picus, 1997; Rubenstein, 1998).

But whatever the unit at which measurement occurs, most analyses of school finance systems, and most of the discussion in the remainder of this chapter, are concerned with the impact of the system on students. Thus, there is something of a mismatch between the unit at which measurement occurs (districts or schools) and the unit of primary concern (children).

How to calculate measures   The challenge, then, is how to assess the impact on children. A statistical solution is to "weight" the district or site measure by the number of students in order to give larger districts or schools more influence on the statistical results. If this statistical weighting is not done, each district, regardless of size, is treated as one observation. Thus, in New York State, for example, New York City, with a million students, about one-third of all students in the state, would affect the statistical findings exactly as much as would a small, rural district with only 100 students. That simply does not make sense, although for years, analyses of school finance systems used district data without statistical weighting by number of students.

Thus, to produce more accurate results, the usual and recommended approach is to statistically weight each district or school measure by the number of students in it, an option provided by nearly all statistical software packages. In the preceding example, this procedure gives New York City more impact on the analytic conclusions than the small district with only a few students; indeed, this procedure actually turns the number of observations into the total number of students, with New York City accounting for a million observations and the rural district only 100. This approach also indicates more accurately how the overall resource distribution system impacts students.

To be sure, this strategy assumes that all students within a district or school receive the level of resources indicated by the district or school measure. Though a bold assumption, it is also a reasonable one, given 35-plus years of experience with federal Title I and Chapter 1 regulations requiring districts to distribute base resources equally among all schools and students. But since districts also legitimately distribute categorical dollars differently to schools based on variations in student need, either the measures used for analysis should exclude these additional resources, or some other adjustment should be made to ensure that these legitimate differences do not cause statistical inaccuracies (see the subsequent discussion on vertical equity).

This statistical weight should not be confused with the pupil-need weight, discussed below and in Chapter 4, that reflects different student needs. Both the unit of analysis–statistical weight and the pupil-need weight must be considered and addressed separately in equity analyses.

Objects of Interest

Berne and Stiefel (1984) identified three categories of children's equity objects: (1) inputs, such as fiscal or physical objects; (2) outputs, such as student achievement; and (3) outcomes, such as lifetime incomes. This chapter uses these three categories but combines the last two and suggests additional variables such as the curriculum content taught and measures of teacher quality. In this way, children's school finance equity objects would include the key variables needed for determining educational adequacy.

We should note explicitly that equity analyses need not be confined to educational inputs, such as dollars per pupil or even the enacted curriculum. Outcome variables that include measures of student achievement could easily be the object of analysis—to determine, for example, the distribution of average levels of achievement or the percentage of districts or schools that have taught students achieving to new, high standards. Further, because objects can include measures of educational provision (curriculum, instruction, teacher quality), as well as results in terms of student performance, this framework can also be used to assess different definitions of educational adequacy.

Fiscal and physical inputs.   A wide variety of fiscal and physical inputs could be targeted for analysis as school finance equity objects. The traditional object of analysis has been some measure of education dollars. Dollars, however, can be categorized in several ways, each of which can lead to different conclusions about the equity of the system.

First, dollars can be divided into two categories: (1) dollars for *current operating expenses* and (2) dollars for *capital outlay* or *debt service.* Analysis of current and capital dollars is usually done separately. Current dollars are analyzed on an annual basis since education services need to be provided each year. Capital and debt service dollars are usually (or should be) analyzed on a multiple-year basis because schools are built only periodically, last for decades, and are paid for incrementally over several years. Other capital items, such as buses and computers, are purchased periodically and also can be used for several years.

Second, dollars can be divided into revenues or expenditures, which may seem similar but are technically quite different. Revenues are usually identified by (1) source—local, state, and federal—and (2) type—general/unrestricted aid (i.e., for any educational purpose) or categorical/restricted aid (i.e., for specific purposes such as special education for the handicapped or special services such as transportation). Many studies analyze current unrestricted revenues from local, state, and federal sources, and leave categorical or special-purpose dollars out of the analysis. Other studies use only state and local general revenues. These general revenues, it is argued, are the revenues that support the regular or core education program, which is one key issue of concern across districts. Further, since the focus is on the equity of the state school finance system, federal dollars should be excluded from the analysis. Other studies analyze total current revenues from all sources, arguing that dollars are partially fungible (i.e., are interchangeable) and that total dollars are what districts have to run the entire education program. Using different revenue figures can yield different conclusions about the equity of the system.

Expenditures, which usually include dollars from all three government sources, can be analyzed on a total basis (current operating expenditures per pupil), by function (expenditures on administration, instruction, operation and maintenance, transportation, etc.), or by program (regular, special-education, compensatory education, bilingual education, etc.). It is also desirable to analyze expenditures by level of education or school site level (i.e., elementary, middle/junior high school, and high school). Though there has been much discussion of the need to collect fiscal data at the site level (Busch and Odden, 1997; Goertz and Odden, 1999), only a few states (e.g., Florida, Kentucky, Ohio, Oregon, and Texas) provide such data.

Collecting resource data by school level is important for both state and nationwide education policy. Many argue that if the education system were successful in educating all students at the elementary and middle school levels, high school and college education could be much easier. Many states, mainly in the Midwest and East, still spend 25–33 percent more for high school students than elementary school students, and insufficient public money supports preschool services for poor children. Perhaps a shift of dollars already available toward the lower grades could improve overall student achievement. Knowing and being able to analyze educational expenditures by school site could help the country, states, districts, and schools decide how to allocate scarce dollar resources to realize ambitious student performance goals.

Most school finance equity studies that use an expenditure figure rely on total current operating expenditures per pupil or on instructional expenditures per pupil, largely because these figures are commonly available. But other, more detailed expenditure figures are preferred, especially expenditures by program and school level. The latter are the key policy issues.

At any rate, different choices of dollar input variables can lead to different conclusions about the equity of the system. For example, Park and Carroll (1979) found a much more equitable distribution of instructional expenditures per pupil in six school finance reform states than they did for either total revenues per pupil or total current operating expenditures per pupil. But Speakman and colleagues (1997) often found more inequality in expenditure when the data were analyzed at the school site level.

Physical objects traditionally include, for example, teacher–pupil ratios, administrator–teacher ratios, support staff–pupil ratios, numbers of books in the library, and square footage of instructional space or of total space. The most common figures used are teacher–pupil ratios. But care should be taken in defining the ratio used. The total professional staff–pupil ratio includes several professionals who do not teach in the classroom; ratios that include these professional resources imply not only a much smaller class size than actually exists but also more teachers providing for core instruction than may actually be the case. Nevertheless, the pupil–professional ratio indicates the level of professional staffing in a school, a very important overall measure of professional educational resources, as discussed in Chapter 7. A more accurate indicator of class size, and a good measure of core instructional services, is the classroom teacher–student ratio (i.e., the average or median number of students actually in a teacher's classroom).

A new variable that will become available in the future is the number and percentage of different types of teachers. Several districts are adopting Charlotte Danielson's (1996) Framework for Teaching, which can be used to identify teachers as at the basic, proficient, or advanced levels of performance. Other teachers are becoming board certified by the National Board for Professional Teaching Standards (Buday and Kelly, 1996; Rotberg, Futrell, and Lieberman, 1998). The board assesses individual teachers against high professional standards; a board-certified teacher has demonstrated expertise in classroom practice that reflects accomplished teaching. These and other such measures and identifiers indicate the quality of the faculty in a school or district.

Though any fiscal and physical input variable could be analyzed, these key variables in per-pupil terms are suggested:

- Total revenues from local, state, and federal sources
- Total revenues from local and state sources
- Total general revenues from local and state sources (i.e., total state and local revenues minus restricted revenues [categorical aids])
- Total current operating expenditures
- Total instructional expenditures
- Total expenditures for the core instructional program, if available
- Pupil–professional staff ratio
- Average actual class size
- Number or percentage of basic, proficient, advanced, and board-certified teachers

Any analysis of resources and their links to student learning gains should involve a variety of data at the student, classroom/teacher, school, and district levels in order to conduct both equity analyses as well as more detailed assessments of what resources matter in terms of learning gains (Odden, Borman, and Fermanich, 2004). Important variables at the student level include the courses students take, especially at the secondary level. At the teacher and classroom level, key variables include the quality of instruction (see Milanowski, Kimball, and Odden, 2005) and measures of the curriculum actually taught. And at the school level, key variables include school-level resources, extent of professional development, nature of principal instructional leadership, and teacher professional community (Odden, Borman, and Fermanich, 2004).

Achievement or outcome variables.   This category includes the results of the education process—student achievement or performance in the short run, and labor market, family, and civic performance in the long run. Though Berne and Stiefel (1984) discussed longer-term outcomes such as an individual's income, job, occupational status, and ability to compete in the labor market, the connections between these outcomes and K–12 schooling are somewhat tenuous (Burtless, 1996). In the long term, showing connections between K–12 schooling and longer-term outcomes should be a research topic. As the connections are developed, analysis of the outcomes and their link to the distribution of school resources could be included in school finance equity analyses.

Shorter-term education system outcome variables include student achievement. Variables could include student achievement in different content areas (mathematics, science, etc.) or more global achievement, such as the overall measure from a standardized, but not necessarily norm-referenced, achievement test. High school graduation rates are also an important output measure, as are the number of academic courses taken, which is closely linked to student learning (Madigan, 1997). Finally, postsecondary attendance rates are outcome measures that indicate behavior in the year immediately following high school graduation.

Several issues arise in deciding how to measure these variables. The most debated are those related to student achievement. Traditionally, norm-referenced measures of student achievement have been used. These measures can be developed at different grade levels and in different content areas, but they indicate how an individual compares to other individuals at the same age or grade. They do not indicate the degree to which a student knows a certain content area, or indicate knowledge and skills to a set standard.

Norm-referenced measures of student achievement are gradually being replaced by criterion-referenced measures, which indicate what a student knows in a certain content area. Nearly all states are creating or using new student testing systems covering numerous subject areas, and providing the data at both the district and school and sometimes even individual student level. In part because of the requirement of the federal No Child Left Behind legislation, more and more states are testing students every year and are beginning to link students to teachers to assess the impact of instruction on learning gains. Further, as tests expand from just multiple choice to include expanded multiple choice, short answer, writing, and actual student performance tasks, they will be able to indicate not only what students know but also what they can do (e.g., whether they can conduct a laboratory experiment, solve multiple-step mathematics problems, or write a persuasive paragraph). As these more sophisticated measures of student achievement become available, they should be the measures used in a school finance analysis for both equity and adequacy purposes.

Whether norm- or criterion-referenced, the most useful test scores are those that are "equated" across each grade level. Equated tests use the same scoring metrics, so a higher score on a grade-4 test, for example, as compared to a grade-3 test, would indicate that the student had advanced in his or her achievement—beyond a normal year's expected growth. Indeed, such tests will be more useful to district and school leaders in determining whether students make "adequate yearly learning progress" under No Child Left Behind (see Chapter 4 for more on No Child Left Behind).

A new way to present achievement data has been suggested as a part of monitoring nationwide and state progress toward achieving the country's educational goals. The new way involves identifying the percentage of students who are performing at different levels on criterion-referenced tests, such as basic, minimal, proficient, and advanced levels. The argument is that the nation needs a workforce with a certain level of skills and that measures of student performance should indicate the degree to which the educational system produces student achievement, on average, with that range of skill levels (Murnane and Levy, 1996). As states adopt this strategy, and several have moved in that direction, outcome measures for schools, districts, or states could be the percentage of students performing at basic, minimal, proficient, and advanced levels on criterion-referenced assessments of what students need to know and be able to do, although the more continuous scale scores on these tests could also be used. Wide variations in such achievement could reveal economic or other variations in student performance that could lead either to additional adjustments in district budgeting to compensate for different needs (see Chapter 4) or to reallocation of resources to ensure that all schools, districts, and states meet those targets. The main problem with such a presentation is that student growth can be substantial but not sufficient to move the student to the next-highest level of performance, particularly for low-achieving students not even at the basic level. In part as a result, gain scores or value-added methods are being developed to track student learning changes over time, but even this more sophisticated approach is fraught with challenges (see e.g., McCaffrey, Lockwood, Koretz, Louis, and Hamilton, 2004).

Key student achievement measures to analyze include the following:

- High school graduation rate
- Postsecondary attendance rate
- Percent correct or percent scoring at basic, minimal, proficient, and advanced levels on equated measures of student achievement in mathematics, science, language arts (including reading in elementary grades), writing, history, and geography at the elementary, middle, and high school levels
- Value-added or gain scores

The Group

Children are just one, but undoubtedly the most important, group for whom the equity of a state's school finance system is an important policy issue. Children are a group of primary concern because they are the "customers" of the education system; the system is designed to educate children. Further, the ability of children to compete in the labor market and, ultimately, their incomes are determined significantly by what they do—by what they learn—in schools and classrooms (Murnane and Levy, 1996; Odden, 1995a). Thus, school finance equity, particularly the emerging concern with adequacy, emphasizes equity for children, and so children are generally the primary group of focus in this book.

But children also differ, so equity analyses focused on children should make appropriate distinctions among categories of students: the "average" student, the disabled, students from low-income backgrounds, students with limited English ability, minorities versus nonminorities, gifted and talented, and so on. This book will focus on the first four categories of children.

However, children are not the only group for whom school finance equity can be an issue. Taxpayers—both those who have children in public schools and those who do not—pay for public education services, so school finance equity is an important policy issue for them too. Chapter 10 discusses taxpayer equity, in terms of the burden various taxes place on different taxpayers, within a public finance context. But as an element of fiscal neutrality, this chapter also discusses taxpayer equity in terms of the equal-yield-for-equal-effort concept. "Yield" could include not only dollars or expenditures but also programs, services, and student achievement.

Teachers increasingly are another group for whom the equity of a state's school finance system is important. The level and distribution of teacher salaries; the state role in supporting minimum teacher salaries; the distribution of teacher quality, knowledge, and skills, including the percentage of teachers certified by the National Board for Professional Teaching Standards; and other policies designed to promote teacher productivity and teacher professionalism—all are salient teacher policy issues (Darling-Hammond, 1997; National Commission on Teaching and America's Future, 1996; Odden and Kelley, 2002; Odden and Wallace, 2006, 2007) and possible issues around which to assess a state's overall school finance structure. As school finance unfolds in the twenty-first century, it is likely that the equity of the school finance system as it relates to evolving teacher policy will become a more salient issue.

The list could continue. Nevertheless, children are the dominant group and have received the most attention in terms of school finance. This chapter primarily discusses issues related to school finance as they apply to children and the three subcategories of disabled children, children from low-income backgrounds, and English-language learners.

Equity Concepts

Once an object has been selected, an approach to assessing equity needs to be determined. This entails defining and selecting an equity principle. There are three different but related children's equity principles: (1) fiscal neutrality, (2) horizontal equity, and (3) vertical equity. This section discusses several issues surrounding each of these principles.

Fiscal neutrality for children.   This principle targets the traditional school finance problem and states that resources, or educational objects, should not vary with local fiscal capacity, such as property wealth per pupil, property value per pupil, or household income. This equity principle derives from the standard fiscal disparities that plagued state school finance structures throughout the twentieth century and directly relates to the legal standard of fiscal neutrality typically, as discussed in Chapter 2, used in most school finance court cases.

Assessing the degree of fiscal neutrality entails analyzing the relationship between two variables: (1) the object chosen and (2) the variable identified as something that should not be linked to resource differences. Traditional fiscal neutrality analysis assesses the relationship between current operating expenditures per pupil and property wealth per pupil, or local-plus-state general revenues per pupil and property wealth per pupil. But analysis of the relationship between any object just discussed and any measure of fiscal capacity, such as household income or even the sales tax base per capita, reflects the fiscal neutrality principle. Analyzing fiscal neutrality is different from analyzing either horizontal or vertical equity, because the former requires at least two variables, whereas the latter require only one variable.

Fiscal neutrality statistics.   To measure the degree of fiscal neutrality, statistics that indicate the relationship between two variables are necessary. Two have become increasingly common in school finance: (1) the correlation coefficient and (2) the elasticity (i.e., the elasticity calculated from a simple one-variable regression). For both statistics, measures of two variables are needed: (1) a measure of the object of concern, such as current operating expenditures per pupil, and (2) a measure of fiscal capacity, such as property value per pupil. Both fiscal neutrality statistics indicate whether the educational object is a function of some variable to which it should not be related, such as the local tax base.

The correlation coefficient is a statistic that indicates the degree to which there is a linear relationship between two variables (i.e., whether as one variable increases the other increases as well). It ranges in value between −1.0 and 1.0. A value of +1.0 or close to +1.0 indicates a positive relationship (e.g., as property wealth increases, so does expenditures per pupil). A negative correlation indicates that as one variable increases, the other decreases; it indicates that there is an inverse relationship between the two variables. In school finance, there is usually a negative correlation between state aid per pupil and property wealth per pupil, indicating that state aid is inversely related to wealth, that the poorer the district, the greater the state aid. A correlation coefficient of zero indicates that there is no linear relationship between the two variables.

Where a correlation coefficient indicates whether there is a linear relationship between two variables, the elasticity indicates the magnitude or policy importance of that relationship. For example, expenditures and wealth could be strongly related, but if a tenfold increase in property wealth resulted in only a small increase in revenues, one could argue that the magnitude of the relationship was not significant or of little policy significance.

Technically, the elasticity indicates the percent change in one variable, say, expenditures per pupil, relative to a 1 percent change in another variable, say, property value per pupil. It is a statistic that usually ranges in value from zero to any positive number, although it can also be negative. In school finance, an elasticity equal to 1.0 or higher indicates that spending increases in percentage terms at the same rate as or a higher rate than property wealth. Elasticities below 1.0 indicate that spending does not increase at the same percentage rate as local property wealth.[1]

The simple elasticity between a dollar object, such as expenditures per pupil and property wealth per pupil, can be calculated using the slope of the simple linear regression of expenditures on wealth; the elasticity equals the slope (the regression coefficient for wealth) times the ratio of the mean value of property wealth per pupil and the mean value of expenditures per pupil.

It is often wise to assess the correlation coefficient and elasticity jointly. If the correlation is high and the elasticity is low, there is a relationship between the two variables—fiscal neutrality does not hold—but the relationship is not of policy importance. On the other hand, if the correlation is low and the elasticity is high, even the tenuous link might have policy significance. If both the correlation coefficient and elasticity are high, then fiscal neutrality clearly does not exist—the two variables are linked, and the magnitude of the link is strong.

A correlation of less than 0.5 with an elasticity of less than 0.1 could function as a standard to determine whether a state system met the fiscal-neutrality standard.

---

[1]This might be a somewhat different definition of elasticity than is the case in economics, but it has become the approach used in school finance circles.

Berne and Stiefel (1984) discuss other relationship statistics for fiscal neutrality. Further, more complex econometric methods can be used to quantify the relationship between educational objects such as revenues per pupil and property wealth, the composition of the local property tax base (residential, commercial, and industrial property), and household income (Adams and Odden, 1981; Feldstein, 1975; Ladd, 1975; Yinger, 2002).

Fiscal neutrality for taxpayers.   Fiscal neutrality for taxpayers indicates whether the funding system allowed districts to raise equal dollars (or any object) per pupil for a given tax rate (see also Berne and Stiefel, 1979). The measure is generally local-plus-state dollars per unit of tax effort, or the appropriate measure of the object per unit of tax effort. If this measure is the same across districts, it indicates that fiscal neutrality for taxpayers has been provided.

Since this is a single variable, the measures of dispersion discussed under "Horizontal Equity" are the statistics used to determine whether the system meets the test of fiscal neutrality for taxpayers, using the same standards for each statistical measure (see, e.g., Reschovsky, 2004).

Link to litigation and school finance structural remedies.   Recall that fiscal neutrality has been a focus of many school finance court cases, even though adequacy has recently taken the lead. For fiscal neutrality for both children and taxpayers, moreover, the implied school finance structural remedy is a guaranteed tax base (GTB), district-power-equalizing (DPE) or percentage-equalizing program, each of which is discussed more fully in Chapter 9. These programs attempt to make the ability of districts to raise per-pupil revenues at a given tax rate as close to equal as is practical. School finance equity analyses, at least most of those focusing on within-state equity, nearly always include measures of fiscal neutrality.

Horizontal equity.   This principle is similar to the horizontal principle in public finance; indeed, Berne and Stiefel (1984, 1999) used traditional public finance principles and concepts to construct their school finance equity framework. Horizontal equity holds that students who are alike should be treated the same: "Equal treatment of equals" reflects the horizontal equity principle. Horizontal equity requires that all students receive equal shares of an object, such as total local and state general revenues per pupil, total current operating expenditures per pupil, instructional expenditures per pupil, or minimum scores on student criterion-referenced assessments. Horizontal equity is embedded in the standards-based education reform goal of teaching all students to high standards.

When horizontal equity is used, one assumes that all students are alike. While this is a crude assumption at best, it is implied when it is argued that spending should be equal across school districts or schools. Thus, horizontal equity has been widely used in school finance, despite its assumption that all students are alike.

The principle of horizontal equity is best applied to subgroups of students (e.g., all elementary students in the regular program, all high school students in an academic track, or all students performing below the first quartile on a student achievement measure). For carefully selected subgroups of students, it is reasonable to require equal distribution of resources, or the object selected for equity analysis. Of course, care must be taken to create a legitimate subgroup of students, for which homogeneity claims are valid.

Assessing the degree of horizontal equity entails measuring inequality or dispersion. Such statistics measure aspects of the distribution of one variable—specifically, the object chosen for analysis.

Horizontal equity statistics.   Many statistics assess the degree of equality for one variable, such as expenditures per pupil in school finance. Berne and Stiefel (1984) identified several and analyzed their various properties. Five statistics are discussed here, although many more are discussed by Berne and Stiefel.

The first statistic is the range, which is the difference between the value of the largest and the smallest observation. The larger the range, the greater the degree of inequality. This statistic indicates the maximum difference in the distribution of this variable among students in a state. That also is a disadvantage. It indicates the difference between only two observations, the top and the bottom. The fact is that there are a few outlying districts in every state: some very poor, low-property-wealth and low-income rural districts, and some very wealthy districts that might have a nuclear power plant or oil wells and few students. These districts are anomalies and do not reflect common circumstances.

The range does not indicate the degree of equality or inequality for any of the other observations, and thus is a poor indicator for assessing the degree of equity of the *system*. Further, the range increases with inflation. As inflation occurs, and all other structural variables remain the same, the range will increase. Indeed, one reason the range statistic might be used in some school finance court cases is that each year the range generally increases. An increasing range is interpreted (incorrectly, we believe) to indicate a system with increasing inequality. In any case, although used extensively and routinely by many school finance analysts, and showing the maximum degree of inequality in a distribution, the range has several detracting features and is not a desired horizontal equity statistic.

The second horizontal equity statistic is the restricted range, which is the difference between an observation close to the top and an observation close to the bottom, such as the difference between the 5th and 95th percentile, or the 10th and 90th percentile. The restricted range generally avoids the problem of outliers that afflicts the range, but the restricted range still measures the degree of inequality between just two observations, and not the overall system. Further, just as with the range, the restricted range increases (i.e., worsens with inflation), even if all other characteristics of the finance system remain the same. If a range statistic is used, the restricted range is preferred to the unrestricted range, but neither are good indicators of the equality of the distribution of the object for the entire education system.

A variation of the restricted range is the federal range ratio, which is the restricted range divided by the observation at the 5th percentile. Though the federal range ratio shares most advantages and disadvantages of the restricted range, because it is a ratio, it eliminates the inflation problem (i.e., the federal range ratio does not increase with inflation). In addition, the federal range ratio has been used to determine whether states can include federal Impact Aid in calculating state equalization aid (Sherman, 1992).

The third horizontal equity statistic is the coefficient of variation (CV), which is the standard deviation divided by the mean (i.e., the average); it can be expressed in decimal or percent form. Its value usually varies between zero and one, or as a percentage, from zero to 100, although the values can be larger. A CV of zero indicates that the object is distributed uniformly among all children.

The CV indicates the percent variation about the mean. For example, a CV of 10 percent (or 0.1) indicates that two-thirds of the observations have a value within one standard deviation of the mean (i.e., 10 percent above or below the value of the average), and 95 percent of the observations have a value within two standard deviations of the average (i.e., 20 percent above or below the mean).[2] So if the average expenditure per pupil is $6,000, and the CV is 10 percent, it means that two-thirds of all districts have an expenditure per pupil between $5,400 ($6,000 minus 10 percent) and $6,600 ($6,000 plus 10 percent).

The CV is a statistic that includes all values of a data set, unlike the range, which includes only selected values. Also, the CV does not change with inflation, an attractive characteristic. Thus, if the structural properties of a school finance system remain constant, but all economic and dollar variables rise with inflation, the CV will remain the same, correctly indicating that the equity of the system has not changed. The CV is also easy to understand. Because of these attractive features, the CV is increasingly being used by analysts.

Another issue, however, is determining the value that indicates an equitable or fair distribution of school funds. Determining a standard for the CV is a value judgment. Berne and Stiefel (1984) suggested a variety of ways to determine what the standard should be. The key distinction is whether to use a relative standard, which would compare districts in the top, middle, and bottom quartiles, or an absolute standard, which would establish a cut-off point for determination of equity. The problem with a relative standard is that some observations are always at the bottom, no matter how small the degree of inequality. An absolute standard provides a cut-off point, which separates equitable from inequitable resource distribution patterns. It is difficult to determine an absolute standard. Nevertheless, an absolute standard of about 10 percent for the CV is generally used throughout this text. This is a high standard, because few states have a CV for revenue-per-pupil figures below 10 percent. It is worth remembering that standard setting is an issue of both values and politics; different states and different analysts might reasonably set different levels as an acceptable CV.

We encourage readers to consider a tougher CV standard of 5 percent. Since average spending is closing in on $10,000 per pupil in many states, a CV of 10 percent would allow spending per pupil to differ by plus or minus $1000, or an absolute amount of $2000, for the middle two-thirds of students, which is a larger number. A 5 percent standard would limit the variation of what would be called equal enough to just plus or minus $500 a student.

[2] These comments assume a normal distribution.

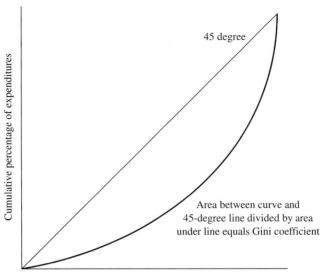

FIGURE 3.1   Example of a Graph Used to Determine a Gini Coefficient

A fourth horizontal equity measure is the Gini coefficient, a statistic taken from economists' measures of income inequality. To determine the Gini coefficient, a graph is made by plotting the cumulative value of the measure of the object as a percent of the total value on the vertical axis and the percent increments of the number of observations on the horizontal axis. The resulting graph indicates the degree to which the object is distributed equally to children at various percentiles; put differently, the graph indicates the degree to which children at different percentiles have the same amount of the object. If the object is perfectly distributed, the Gini graph would be a straight, 45-degree line. If the object is not perfectly distributed, the Gini graph would be a concave curve below that line. In school finance, the measure on the vertical axis is typically the cumulative percent of school district expenditures, and the measure on the horizontal axis is typically the percent of students enrolled in the state, as shown in Figure 3.1.

The Gini coefficient is the area between the Gini curve and the 45-degree line divided by the area under the 45-degree line. Its value ranges from zero to one, with a completely equitable distribution occurring when the Gini coefficient equals zero. Most values in school finance are in the 0.1–0.2 range. The Gini coefficient includes all observations and is insensitive to inflation (i.e., it remains the same when inflation is the only intervening variable).

The Gini coefficient is challenging to understand conceptually. What does it mean when the area between the Gini curve and the 45-degree line—even in a system with what most would call large differences in expenditures or revenues per pupil—is 0.1 or very close to zero? A value close to zero suggests equality, but the system may, in school finance terms, be quite unequal. Nevertheless, the Gini coefficient is a popular horizontal equity statistic in school finance. A standard for it has not been set, although a value less than 0.05 is probably desirable. The smaller the Gini coefficient, the more equal the distribution of the object.

A fifth measure of horizontal equity is the McLoone Index, which is a statistic unique to school finance, actually created by and named after Eugene McLoone, an economics professor emeritus at the University of Maryland. The McLoone Index provides a measure of the bottom half of a distribution, indicating the degree of equality only for observations below the 50th percentile. Since the American political culture often shows more interest in the condition of those at the bottom, the McLoone Index is a statistic that reflects that perspective.

Technically, the McLoone Index is the ratio of the sum of the values of all observations below the 50th percentile (or median) to the sum of these observations if they all had the value of the median. It ranges in value from zero to one, with a 1.0 indicating perfect equality.[3] The value of the McLoone Index for most school finance data sets is generally in the 0.7–0.9 range. Again, a standard has not been set for a "good" McLoone Index, but higher than 0.95 is desirable.

Though Berne and Stiefel (1984) analyzed other standard statistics that are sensitive to changes in the bottom half of the distribution, the more complex statistics are difficult for policymakers to understand. Because the McLoone Index is a measure of the equity of the distribution for the bottom half and is more straightforward, it has become popular in school finance and is included in many school finance equity analyses.

Another horizontal equity statistic is the Verstegen Index, which is the opposite of the McLoone Index in that it is a measure of disparity in the top half of the distribution. Nearly all analyses of school finance assess either characteristics of the entire distribution or characteristics of the bottom half of the distribution. But as discussed in Chapter 1, an issue that is gaining more attention is the behavior of the districts in the top half of the distribution. In some states, apparently, the differences in fiscal resources among these districts have increased over time, even while the disparities for those in the bottom half have diminished (Verstegen, 1996). The result is a McLoone Index closer to zero but a larger CV. Since the CV has become such a popular school finance equity statistic, a rising CV could indicate that fiscal disparities are increasing, but such an interpretation would not reflect the differences in the nature of the distribution among the top and bottom halves.

The Verstegen Index helps to show this phenomenon; it is the ratio of the sum of the values of all observations above the median to the sum of those observations if they were all at the median. It has a value of 1.0 or greater and, like the McLoone and CV, does not increase with inflation. It does increase as disparities in the top half increase. A careful analyst would calculate all three statistics—the CV, the McLoone, and the Verstegen—and determine whether overall disparities have improved (a lower CV), whether differences below the median have improved (a higher McLoone), and whether differences in the top half have improved (a lower Verstegen).

---

[3]A value of 1.0 for the McLoone Index indicates that per-pupil expenditures in the lowest-spending districts containing 50 percent of the state's children is equal. A value of less than 1.0 implies that among the low-spending districts with that 50 percent of schoolchildren, expenditures vary. The smaller the McLoone Index, the larger the spending differential among the low-spending districts.

Links to litigation and school finance structural remedies. Horizontal equity is most closely associated with two legal issues: (1) the equal protection argument that education is a fundamental interest, and (2) the adequacy argument as the intended meaning of a state's education clause. The general legal thrust is that the core or regular education program should be provided equally to all students, or that all students should have equal access at least to an "adequate" education program.

School finance structures that respond to these arguments are full-state funding, a very-high-foundation program, and an even broader federal role to ensure adequacy across all states. Full-state funding is the primary implication of the legal finding that education is a fundamental right, because if it is, it should be provided equally to all students and there would be no (or only an extraordinary) reason for allowing some students to have a better education than others. A high foundation is the primary implication of the adequacy argument, in that all students should have, at the minimum, a basic education sufficient to teach them to high standards. As Odden and Busch (1998) showed, and Liu (2006) recently argued, if the adequacy issue were considered nationwide, it might raise anew the need for a new federal role in education, as very preliminary analysis shows that many states are not providing, and might not be able to provide, any of their districts with sufficient resources to fund an adequate school program.

Studies of horizontal equity. There have been dozens of studies of the degree of horizontal equity within a state. Several studies have analyzed the status of school finance equity within the 50 states (Brown et al., 1977; Evans, Murray, and Schwab, 1997; Murray, Evans, and Schwab, 1998; Odden and Augenblick, 1981; Odden, Berne, and Stiefel, 1979; Schwartz and Moskowitz, 1988). Brown did one of the first studies that used a 50-state sample. He found that expenditure disparities actually increased nationwide from 1970 to 1975, a time of intensive school finance reform. Further analysis, however, showed that for states that underwent school finance reform in the early 1970s, expenditure disparities might have increased more than they did had the states not changed their school finance systems. Odden, Berne, and Stiefel, using data from only 35 states, showed that several school finance reform states improved both horizontal and fiscal neutrality over a multiple-year period during the mid-1970s. Odden and Augenblick, using 1977 National Center for Education Statistics (NCES) data for all 50 states, found that state school finance equity ratings changed depending on both the equity object selected and the statistic used. Schwartz and Moskowitz compared data from all 50 states for the years 1976–77 and 1984–85, and concluded that school finance fiscal equity had stayed, on average, about the same, for both horizontal equity and fiscal neutrality principles and for several different statistics (primarily the ones just discussed). Wyckoff (1992) then found that although fiscal neutrality was stable, horizontal equity improved modestly between 1980 and 1987. The 1997 General Accounting Office (GAO) study (1997) identified bigger improvements in fiscal equity, but Hertert, Busch, and Odden (1994) showed that substantial disparities remain.

The most comprehensive study of school finance disparities analyzed 20 years of data and concluded that fiscal disparities had been reduced over this period, but by only 16–25 percent and largely in those states with court cases (Evans, Murray, and Schwab, 1997; Murray, Evans, and Schwab, 1998). This study, together with others, (Odden and

Busch, 1998) makes a further advance in adjusting all dollar variables by a geographic price factor (Chambers, 1995; McMahon, 1994) to better compare differences in "real" resources across districts. Finally, Murray, Evans, and Schwab (1998) showed that the majority of fiscal differences, after adjusting for cost differences, are caused by inter- rather than intrastate disparities, so that even if all within-state disparities are elimi- nated, two-thirds of the disparities will remain, which supports Odden and Busch's (1998) conclusion that disparities across states exceed those within states.

Numerous authors have used the Berne and Stiefel (1984) framework, or varia- tions of it, to study the equity of the school finance structure within states (see, e.g., Goldhaber and Callahan, 2001; Hirth, 1994; Johnson and Pillianayagam, 1991; Porter, 1991; Prince, 1997; Rubenstein, Doering, and Gess, 2000; Sample and Hartman, 1990; Verstegen and Salmon, 1991; Wood, Honeyman, and Bryers, 1990). Picus, Odden, and Fermanich (2004) conducted a 10-year equity analysis of the Kentucky finance system enacted after a court decision overturned the system in 1989; they found that equity had indeed improved over the 1990s. These studies generally use a fiscal object, such as state-plus-local revenues per pupil. They also typically use two or three measures for horizontal equity, including the coefficient of variation, the McLoone Index, and the Gini coefficient, as well as two measures of fiscal neutrality, the correlation coefficient and wealth elasticity. The Picus, Odden, and Fermanich study also used pupil-need weights and a geographic price adjustment—two adjustments for vertical equity, dis- cussed next.

Vertical equity. Vertical equity specifically recognizes differences among children and addresses the education imperative that some students deserve or need more ser- vices than others.[4] "Unequal treatment of unequals" has been a traditional public fi- nance way to express the vertical equity principle. What this phrase means is that in some circumstances or for some reasons, it is acceptable to treat students differently or to provide more services to some students (or districts) than others. A key step in verti- cal equity is to identify the characteristics that can legitimately be used as a basis for dis- tributing more resources or more of the specific object selected. Three categories of characteristics have been identified: (1) characteristics of children, (2) characteristics of districts, and (3) characteristics of programs.

Characteristics of children that could lead to the provision of more resources in- clude physical or mental disabilities, low achievement perhaps caused by educational disadvantage from a low-income background, and limited English proficiency. It is gen- erally accepted in this country, and around the world, that students with these charac- teristics need additional educational services in order to perform better in school (see Chapter 4). More controversy surrounds the characteristic of gifted and talented. Some argue that these students learn more from regular instruction and do not need addi- tional resources; others argue that the best and brightest should be given some measure of extra services.

District characteristics that could lead to provision of more resources include is- sues such as price, scale economies, transportation, energy costs, and enrollment growth.

---

[4]Chapter 4 discusses how adjustments can be made in school finance formulas to recognize vertical equity issues.

As Chapter 4 shows, some districts face higher prices than others, and they need more money simply to purchase the same level of resources as other districts. Some districts also face higher costs either because of factors caused by very small size, such as a one-room school in a sparsely populated rural area, or factors caused by large size, such as most large-city school districts. While size adjustments can be controversial—some argue that small districts should be consolidated and that large districts should be divided into smaller entities—differential size can be a legitimate basis for allocating some districts more resources than others. Finally, transportation costs vary widely across most districts. Sparsely populated districts must transport students long distances and face higher per-pupil transportation costs, and big-city districts must often bus students to achieve racial desegregation. States often recognize these different district circumstances by allocating additional funds, usually to be used only for a specified purpose.

Some programs also cost more than others. For example, vocational education, laboratory sciences, small classes in specialized and advanced topics, and magnet schools tend to cost more than "regular" programs. State and district decisions to provide these programs can be a legitimate reason for allocating more resources for some students than others.

Although there is general agreement that additional funds should be provided in most of the circumstances discussed in the preceding paragraphs, controversy surrounds other school and student distinctions. For example, differential treatment on the basis of race or sex is generally viewed as illegitimate. The question remains, however, as to whether additional funds should be provided on the basis of race to foster desegregation (such as more money for magnet schools) or on the basis of sex to foster greater female participation in school athletics and in mathematics and science. Also controversial are issues about whether cost differences due to grade level should be continued.

In school finance, it is generally agreed that additional resources should not be available because of fiscal capacity, such as property value per pupil or household income. On the other hand, there is more controversy surrounding tax rates as a legitimate reason for resource variation. Those who support local control argue that higher local tax rates are a legitimate reason for having more resources; others argue that from a child perspective, educational resources should not vary because of local taxpayer preference for education.

In short, vertical equity, though seemingly simple on the surface, is difficult to implement. There is substantial agreement on some of the reasons for providing more resources to some students or districts than to others, but disagreement remains on several variables. Thus, implementing vertical equity entails making significant value and political judgments, with little widespread consensus as to what is "right."

Measuring and assessing vertical equity.   There are two main ways to assess vertical equity. The first is to assign a pupil-need weight to all students who need extra services (see Chapter 4) and then to conduct a horizontal equity analysis using the number of weighted pupils as the pupil measure. This approach combines vertical and horizontal equity in a joint analysis. Vertical equity is reflected in the weights; having recognized factors that can lead to different resource levels and made appropriate adjustments, equality of resources per weighted child indicates the degree of resource equality. This is the approach allowed by the computer simulation that accompanies Chapter 9.

This approach can be used only when there are good data to quantify the degree to which students with different needs require different levels of resources. This approach is strengthened if some independent analysis is done on the weights themselves, to assess whether they accurately represent the degree of extra services needed. It is more valid when the different weights have been calculated relative to the statewide average expenditure per pupil. The 1997 GAO and NCES studies used this approach, weighting each handicapped student an extra 1.3 and each low-income student an extra 0.2.

Alternately, categorical revenues for extra services and programs can be eliminated from the object, and analysis conducted for just general revenues or educational expenditures for the regular instructional program. This approach assesses the degree of equality of the base program for all students, but essentially skirts analysis of vertical equity.

If price differences are part of the state aid formula, the equity analysis should be conducted with price-adjusted dollars, not nominal dollars, which is the usual approach (Barro, 1989; Chambers, 1995; McMahon, 1994). Furthermore, all dollars should be price-adjusted, not just those that might be adjusted by a state formula price factor. This approach was taken by the GAO (1997), Odden and Busch (1998), Murray, Evans, and Schwab (1998), and Picus, Odden, and Fermanich (2004). Taylor and Fowler (2006) and Imazeki (2006) have developed a new approach to price adjustments, called the comparable wage index. This is in response to criticisms of the most common approach in the past, the hedonic index (Baker, 2005; Chambers, 1995).

Link to litigation and school finance structural remedies.   Vertical adjustments are integrally embedded in the adequacy approach to school finance litigation; in fact, Underwood (1995b) argued that vertical equity was educational adequacy. Although we would not limit educational adequacy to vertical equity, we certainly would agree that any comprehensive definition of educational adequacy should include a substantial degree of vertical equity adjustments, to ensure that students who could learn to high standards, but who need additional resources to do so, are provided those resources.

Vertical equity is not necessarily an integral part of fiscal neutrality. Further, the legal arguments about education as a fundamental right have not been the arguments that have led to the legal right to appropriate education programs for the disabled (i.e., provided by the federal Individuals with Disabilities in Education Act [IDEA]), and they certainly have not created a right to extra educational services for students from low-income backgrounds or students with limited English proficiency (again, provided by federal law and regulatory requirements).

As Chapter 9 shows, there are two primary ways to address vertical equity in school finance structures. The first is to weight by pupil need different categories of students in a way that quantifies, relative to the base level of expenditure, the additional resources needed. The second is to provide a separate program, like a categorical program, that provides revenues specifically for such services.

Studies of vertical equity.   Chapter 4 discusses the studies that pertain to vertical equity adjustments for students, districts, or programs, including the issues and controversies surrounding them.

3. ADEQUACY

This principle was not included in Berne and Stiefel's (1984) equity framework largely because adequacy had not appeared directly on the school finance agenda at that time. Today, however, as Chapter 2 showed, adequacy is the key focus of school finance litigation, and increasingly of school finance policy as well. Adequacy is thus an additional principle with which to judge a state's school finance system.

As we have suggested, the notion of adequacy involves the provision of a set of strategies, programs, curriculum, and instruction, with appropriate adjustments for special-needs students, districts, and schools, and their full financing, that is sufficient to provide all students an equal opportunity to learn to high performance standards. As Berne and Stiefel (1999) suggested, the notion of adequacy has its roots in the 1983 Nation at Risk report (National Commission on Excellence and Equity in Education), which added excellence to what had been a 20-year focus on equity. Adequacy could be viewed as having both an inputs and an outputs orientation—the inputs being the programs, curriculum, and instruction that are sufficient to teach students to high standards, and the outputs being the measurement of the results that are achieved. Indeed, as the education excellence reforms of the 1980s transformed into the systemic and standards-based education reform of the 1990s (Elmore, 1990; Fuhrman, 1993; Massell, Hoppe, and Kirst, 1997), the concept of educational adequacy matured. It continued with the Clinton administration's Goals 2000 programs and the Bush administration's No Child Left Behind (NCLB) legislation.

Links to Litigation and School Finance Formulas

A definition of "adequacy" as a high level of inputs—programs, services, curriculum, instruction, classroom, and school organization—certainly can be justified. This definition evolves from standards-based education reform, as well as what is needed to accomplish the general goals of NCLB. Standards-based education reform enhances the rigor of these inputs through curriculum content, student performance standards, and changes in school management, organization, finance, and accountability. These latter dimensions of educational adequacy appeared explicitly in most of the 1990s' adequacy cases discussed in Chapter 2. Moreover, as Minorini and Sugarman (1999a, 1999b) argued that from the legal perspective, adequacy pertains only to inputs. They claim that the courts are requiring neither equal outcomes nor outcomes for all students who are at or above some high, minimum level.

An input definition of "adequacy" would also include a range of appropriate adjustments for special-needs students, schools, and districts. Indeed, "adequacy" in the legal context certainly requires adjustments for low-wealth and low-spending districts. Further, since the cases include the phrase or notion of "all students" achieving to high standards, adjustments for special-needs students are required.

Once a set of programs and services and other adequate educational elements are identified, it is straightforward to price them and calculate a dollar amount that could be used for each district or school as the foundation, or "adequate" base, spending amount per pupil. In this way, the foundation school finance formula and educational adequacy seem to fit well with each other.

At the same time, the notion of adequacy as outputs can also be argued. Nearly all written discussion of adequacy includes the notion of students achieving to some set of performance standards, implying that "adequacy" could also be defined as a set of educational strategies and their funding, that teach students to some set of achievement standards. According to Odden and Clune (1998) and Verstegen (2002), this means that the school finance system needs some adequate high-foundation base, with appropriate supplements for special-needs students, as well as some performance-improvement mechanisms, such as more school authority over the use of resources to allow for site re-allocation to higher-performance programs, changes in teacher compensation to provide salary increases for more knowledge and skills, and school-based performance incentives to reward schools for improving student achievement. Economic analysts (e.g., Duncombe, Ruggiero, and Yinger, 1996; Reschovsky and Imazeki, 1998, 2001) have suggested that this means moving to a "performance-based funding system" that formally links spending levels and adjustments for special needs to a specified level of system output.

An adequacy approach can be applied to all districts and schools, as has been done in Kansas, Maryland (Augenblick and Meyers, 2001a, 2001b), Arkansas (Odden, Picus, and Fermanich, 2003), and Wyoming (Guthrie et al., 1997; Management Analysis and Planning, 2002; Odden, Picus, et al., 2005). But it could also be more focused on selected populations or places, such as low-income students (Clune, 1995) or special-needs districts in New Jersey.

One major difference between equity and adequacy is that equity implies something about a relative difference, while adequacy implies something about an absolute level. For example, a state system could have base resources distributed quite equally, as in California and Alabama, but still not be an adequate system. Similarly, one could conceive of a state or education system (perhaps New Jersey when its response to its 1998 court case is fully implemented) with substantial differences in resources, but with the lowest-spending districts still spending above some adequacy level.

Finally, given all these issues, adequacy requires some link between inputs and outputs, a set of inputs that should lead to certain outputs, or some level of spending that should be sufficient to produce some level of student achievement. This highlights the need to learn more about input–output linkages.

Measuring Adequacy

There has been little if any work on developing measures of educational adequacy in a statistical context. Thus, we propose an approach that we will call the Odden–Picus Adequacy Index (OPAI). Arithmetically, it draws from the McLoone Index but uses an "adequate" spending level rather than the median. The idea behind the OPAI is to calculate an index that roughly indicates the percent of students educated in schools or districts that are spending at an "adequate" level. If the calculation is conducted on the basis of weighted students, or if all expenditures are adjusted by an overall "cost function" index (see Chapter 4), then the OPAI includes vertical equity as well.

The OPAI is calculated as shown here:

1. Identify an "adequate" spending level.
2. Identify the percent of students/district spending above that level.

3. Calculate a McLoone-type ratio for those below that level, but using the "adequate" expenditure level rather than the median, and so calculating the ratio of all those spending below the adequate level to what it would be if they were spending at the adequate level.
4. Multiply this ratio by the percent of students/districts below the adequacy level.
5. Sum these two numbers.

Assume that an adequate expenditure level has been determined (step 1). Next, assume that 60 percent of students/districts are spending above that level, or 0.60 (step 2). Assume further that the McLoone-type calculation would produce a ratio of 0.8, which would mean the students/schools/districts below the adequacy level would have 80 percent of the revenues needed for full adequacy (step 3). This would then be multiplied by 40 percent, the percentage below adequacy, which would equal 0.32 in this example (step 4). Then the OPAI would be 0.92 (i.e., 0.60 plus 0.32) (step 5). It would indicate how close the system was to providing an adequate level of funding for all students.

Actually, the OPAI would show that if revenues were increased by 8 percent of the adequacy level, and given just to those students, schools, or districts spending below the adequacy level, everyone could be raised to that level. So it could be used in a very specific way to show how close the finance system was to providing an adequate base for all students.

If a weighted-pupil count were used, the adequacy index would include an assessment of vertical equity as well. Moreover, if the pupil-need weights themselves were adequate and calculated relative to the adequacy expenditure level, then the adequacy index could be used to indicate the degree to which the school finance system was adequate for all students, both "regular" students and those with special needs who needed more than the regular revenue level to learn to the proficiency standards set by the system for them.

The OPAI is about the same size as the McLoone but covers the entire distribution. It also is not subject to inflation, a positive characteristic of the CV and McLoone Index that was mentioned previously.

Setting the Adequacy Spending Level

There has been both conceptual and empirical research on educational adequacy. Clune (1994a, 1994b, 1995) produced some of the most thoughtful conceptual analyses of how educational adequacy and school finance can be linked. Although he emphasized the importance of adequacy for low-income students, conceptually, his work addresses the adequacy issue for all children.

But there has also been a segment within school finance that has always been concerned with adequacy (i.e., how high the foundation expenditure level should be, whether at a minimum, basic level, as was discussed years ago, or at an adequate level, as is discussed today). Four methodologies have been used to determine an adequate foundation expenditure level: (1) the input or professional-judgment approach, (2) the successful-district approach, (3) the cost function approach, and (4) the evidence-based approach (for longer discussions, see Guthrie and Rothstein, 1999; Odden and Picus, 2004).

The input approach was first applied nearly three decades ago when the Washington state school finance system was declared unconstitutional. When that state's top court required the state to identify and fund a "general and uniform" education program, the state essentially identified the average staffing (teachers, professional support staff, administration, etc.) in a typical district and, using statewide average costs, determined a spending level. Washington has used this approach to fund schools for nearly three decades. But in 2005, a new governor created an education reform commission called Washington Learns, which sponsored a new study of adequacy in Washington. That study, completed in 2006, found that substantial new resources were needed to fund schools at an adequate level for the needs of the more demanding global economy of the twenty-first century (Odden, Picus, and Goetz, 2006).

Another input approach is the Resource Cost Model (RCM), created by Jay Chambers and Thomas Parrish (1994). Using groups of professional educators, the RCM first identified base staffing levels for the regular education program and then identified effective program practices and their staffing and resource needs for compensatory, special, and bilingual education. All ingredients were priced using average price figures, but in determining the foundation-base dollar amount for each district, the totals were adjusted by an education price index. This method was used to propose a foundation spending level for both Illinois and Alaska, but the proposals were never implemented. This method is very similar to what has been termed "activity-led staffing" in England, which is an English version of the RCM approach to school financing (Levacic, 1999).

Guthrie et al. (1997) made a further advance in the professional input approach as part of a response to the Wyoming Supreme Court's finding that the state's finance system was unconstitutional. Guthrie and colleagues also used a panel of professional education experts. In identifying the base staffing level for typical elementary, middle, and high schools, however, they relied on the findings of the Tennessee STAR class-size-reduction study results to set a class size of 15 in elementary schools (Finn, 1996; Grissmer, 1999), and then used the panel to determine additional resources for compensatory, special, and bilingual education. They, too, adjusted the dollar figures by a constructed price factor. As previously noted, similar types of adequacy studies have been conducted recently for Kansas, Kentucky, Maryland, Massachusetts, New York, and South Carolina.

The advantage of all these input approaches is that they identify a set of elements that a certain amount of dollars would be able to purchase in each school district, including additional resources for three categories of special-needs students, all adjusted by a price factor. The disadvantage is that the resource levels are connected to student achievement results only indirectly through professional judgment and not directly to actual measures of student performance. Moreover, expert judgments can vary both across and within states (see Augenblick and Myers, 2001a, 2001b; Guthrie et al., 1997; Management, Analysis and Planning, 2001), depending on how the process is carried out.

The second approach to determining an adequate spending level attempts to remedy this key deficiency of the input approach by identifying a spending level directly linked to a specified level of student performance. The successful-district approach first determines a desired level of performance using state tests of student performance, identifies districts that produce that level of performance, from that group selects those districts with characteristics comparable or close to the state average, and then calculates average spending per pupil. Such studies have been conducted in Illinois (Augenblick and Myers, 2001b; Hinrichs and Laine, 1996), Maryland (Augenblick and Meyers, 2001a; Management, Analysis and Planning, 2001), Ohio (Alexander, Augenblick, Driscoll, Guthrie, and Levin, 1995; Augenblick, 1997), and, most recently, Washington (Fermanich, Picus, and Odden, 2006). Interestingly, in most of these studies, the level of spending identified was approximately the median spending per pupil in the state. In Washington, however, that level was substantially above the level supported by state funds.

A major advantage of this approach is that it identifies the spending level that is linked to a specified student performance level. A disadvantage is that the method does not indicate how the funds should be spent to produce the student achievement results. Further, atypical districts are often eliminated from successful-district analyses, which usually include the highest- and lowest-spending and highest-and lowest-wealth districts, as well as large urban districts. The result is that the districts identified are usually nonmetropolitan districts of average size and relatively homogeneous demographic characteristics, which generally spend below the state average. The criticism of this approach is that the adequate-expenditure level typically identified is difficult to relate to the fiscal adequacy needs of big-city and small rural districts, even with adjustments for pupil needs and geographic price differentials.

The third procedure uses the economic cost function approach. This approach seeks to identify a per-pupil spending level sufficient to produce a given level of performance, adjusting for characteristics of students and other socioeconomic status characteristics of districts. This method can also be used to calculate how much more money is required to produce the specified level of performance by factors such as special needs of students, scale economies or diseconomies, input prices, and even efficiency. The result is an adequate expenditure per pupil for the average district, and then, for all other districts, an adjusted figure to account for differences in pupil need and educational prices, as well as diseconomies of both large and small size. The expenditure level is higher (lower) as the performance level is higher (lower). This analysis usually produces an adjustment for city districts of two to three times the average expenditure level, which, when combined with the complex statistical analysis, makes its use problematic in the political context.

No state currently uses this approach, though cost function research has been conducted for several states, including New York, Wisconsin, Texas, and Illinois (Duncombe, Ruggiero, and Yinger, 1996; Reschovsky and Imazeki, 1998, 2001). Research showed that there was substantial variation in the average adequacy level due to student and district needs, ranging from a low of 49 percent to a high of 460 percent of the average in Wisconsin, and a low of 75 percent to a high of 158 percent of the average in Texas. In both states, the adequate expenditure figures for the large urban districts were at the highest levels. In 2005 in Texas, cost function studies were used in that state's school finance court case (see Gronberg, Jansen, Taylor, and Booker, 2004; Reschovsky and Imazeki, 2004).

Moreover, these studies used different methodologies and had different definitions of "adequate" performance levels. In Wisconsin, it was teaching students to the average on state tests, and in the other two states, it was teaching at least 70 percent of students to state proficiency standards. But all studies sought to identify a spending level that was associated with a desired, substantive education result—student achievement to a specified standard—and in general, that spending level was close to the respective state's median spending level (see also Baker, Taylor, and Vedlitz, 2004).

The fourth approach to determining an adequate expenditure level, one that we have developed, is to identify research- or other evidence-based educational strategies, price them out, and then aggregate them to identify adequate school site, district, and state expenditure levels. This approach more directly identifies educational strategies that produce desired results, so it also helps guide school sites in how to use dollars in the most effective ways. Initially, this strategy used the ingredients of "high performance" school models (Odden and Picus, 2000; Stringfield, Ross, and Smith, 1996) to determine an overall cost level, often "whole school" designs created by the New American Schools models (see Odden, 1997a). And the costs of these models did not generally exceed the revenues available to the average elementary, middle, and high school in the country (Odden and Busch, 1998).

More recently, the evidence-based approach has been used to calculate adequate spending levels in Kentucky (Odden, Fermanich, and Picus, 2003), Arkansas (Odden, Picus and Fermanich, 2003), Arizona (Odden, Picus, Fermanich, and Goetz, 2004), Wyoming (Odden, Picus, et al., 2005), and Washington (Odden, Picus, and Goetz, 2006). As detailed more fully in Chapter 4, this approach identifies the following resources for a school of 500 students, with the goal of having schools double the overall level of student performance:

- Preschool for 3- and 4-year-olds, at least for children from lower-income backgrounds, with a teacher and an educational assistant for every 15 students
- An extended teacher year to include 180 days on pupil instruction and at least 10 days for professional development
- One principal
- Two and a half instructional facilitators, coaches, or mentors
- Teachers for a full-day kindergarten program
- Teachers to provide for class sizes of 15 students in grades K–3, and 25 for all other grades
- An additional 20 percent of teachers (sometimes 33 percent in high schools) to provide for planning and preparation time for the above teachers and to teach art, music, physical education, and other noncore academic classes, with the requirement that a substantial portion of such time be used by regular classroom teachers for collaborative instructional improvement work
- Tutors (professionally licensed teachers) for struggling students, at a rate of one tutor for every 100 students from low-income backgrounds and one teacher for every 30 students from low-income backgrounds to provide an extended day program, and the same resources to provide a summer school for students who need it, so schools can vary the learning time while holding rigorous performance standards constant
- Sufficient funds for all students with disabilities
- An additional $100 per pupil for trainers for professional development
- About $250 per pupil for computer technologies (hardware and software) to cover purchase, upgrades, and repair

- One to five positions for a pupil support/family outreach strategy, with one position for every 100 students from a low-income background and one counselor position for every 250 students in secondary schools
- Other resources for materials, equipment, and supplies; operation and maintenance; central office administrative district and school clerical secretarial support

This level of funding would allow schools to deploy just about every strategy research has shown to have statistically significant impacts on student learning and, as discussed in Chapter 4, is adequate for the education system to provide the kind of school restructuring that results in a doubling of student performance, particularly for low-income and minority students. It is also sufficient to fund any comprehensive school reform program (Erlichson and Goertz, 2001; Erlichson, Goertz, and Turnbull, 1999; Odden, 2000). It was used as the basis for the 1998 final New Jersey Supreme Court decree in that state's 25-year-old school finance case.

To be sure, additional work is needed to identify "adequate" expenditure levels (see also Baker & Taylor, 2004). Each approach just discussed has strengths and weaknesses, and none has been perfected. Any state would need to select one of the previous approaches, or some other approach, and determine what their level of adequacy would be. But at their core, these new approaches to school finance seek to link spending with student achievement results.

4. SUMMARY

This chapter has two emphases: (1) to argue that money does matter in education, and (2) since money is provided in both unequal ways and insufficient amounts to districts and schools, to identify various ways to assess the degree of equity and adequacy of a state's school finance system. In terms of whether money makes a difference, we side with those analysts who conclude that it does, but we also side with the critics who argue that the way money is used makes the most important differences, and, as we discuss in Chapter 10, there are more effective ways to use money in most schools.

In general, as is shown in Chapter 11, equity and adequacy are most commonly assessed from an ex post perspective, and focused on the impact of the system on students. The most common fiscal variable analyzed is state and local revenues per pupil. Fiscal neutrality is assessed by calculating the correlation coefficient and simple elasticity between this revenue-per-pupil figure and property value per pupil. Horizontal equity is usually assessed with such measures as the coefficient of variation and the McLoone Index. Vertical equity is assessed by providing need-based pupil weights and then conducting horizontal equity analyses. Four different approaches can be used to determine an adequacy expenditure level, and the Odden–Picus Adequacy Index can be used to measure the degree of adequacy for the school finance system.

Table 3.1 summarizes the equity/adequacy framework, and Table 3.2 provides a summary of the statistics used to measure the degree of equity/adequacy. Both charts portray the key aspects of the framework and important statistics, but there are several related issues, many of which this chapter has discussed. These issues will be addressed

TABLE 3.1   School Finance Equity Framework—Summary and Examples of Variables

Factors	*Components*	*Variables and Statistics*
Group (who)	Children Taxpayers Teachers Parents	District value weighted by the number of students
Objects (what)	Inputs—Fiscal (per pupil)	• Total revenues from local, state, and federal sources • Total revenues from local and state sources • Total general revenues from local and state sources • Total current operating expenditures • Total instructional expenditures • Total expenditures for the regular programs
	—Physical outcome (student achievement)	• Average student/classroom teacher ratio • High school graduation rate • Postsecondary attendance rate • % correct on criterion-referenced measures • % scoring at basic, proficient and advanced levels by content area
Principles (how)	Horizontal equity	• Equal treatment of equals—equal distribution of resources
	Vertical equity	• Unequal treatment of unequals—legitimate needs for children (handicaps, low achievement, limited English), districts (price, size, transportation, enrollment growth), programs (voc ed, lab science, advanced topics)
	Fiscal neutrality	• Linear relationship between object and fiscal capacity variable • Magnitude of the relationship
Statistics (how much)	Horizontal equity	• Range • Restricted range • Federal range ratio • Coefficient of variation • Gini coefficient • McLoone Index • Verstegen Index
	Vertical equity	• Weighted pupils for needs • Elimination of categorical revenues in the analysis • Price-adjusted dollars
	Fiscal neutrality	• Correlation coefficient • Elasticity
	Adequacy	• Odden–Picus Adequacy Index

TABLE 3.2 Assessing Equity Statistics

Statistic	Calculation	Value	Other Attributes	Overall
Range	Difference between largest and smallest observations.	Maximum difference in observations. The larger the range, the greater the inequity.	Based on only two observations—highest and lowest. Can reflect anomalies. Sensitive to inflation.	Poor.
Federal range ratio	Difference between observations of 95th and 5th percentiles, divided by value of 5th percentile.	Ratio of range between 95th and 5th observations. Ranges from 0 to any positive number.	Based on only two observations. Not sensitive to inflation.	Good range statistic.
Coefficient of variation (CV)	Standard deviation divided by mean.	Ranges from 0 to 1.0, or 0% to 100%. Zero indicates equal distribution. Equitable if CV less than 0.1.	Includes all values; does not change with inflation.	Good.
McLoone Index	Ratio of sum of all observations below median (50th percentile) to sum if all observations had value of median.	Ranges from 0 to 1. One indicates perfect equality. Most school finance data sets are between 0.7 and 0.95; 0.9 desirable.	Compares bottom half of districts to median (50th percentile).	Good; sensitive to bottom half of distribution.
Verstegen Index	Ratio of sum of all observations above median (50th percentile) to sum if all observations had value of median.	Ranges from 1 and higher. One indicates perfect equality. Most school finance data sets are between 1.2 and 1.5.	Compares top half of districts to median (50th percentile).	Good at indicating variation in top half of distribution.
Gini coefficient	Area of graph between Gini curve and 45-degree line divided by area under 45-degree line.	Ranges from 0 to 1.0; value close to 0 suggests equality, but in school finance, values usually less than 0.5.	Indicates degree to which children at different percentiles have same amount of object. Includes all observations. Insensitive to inflation.	Complicated, but good statistic.

(continued)

TABLE 3.2 (*Continued*)

Statistic	Calculation	Value	Other Attributes	Overall
Correlation coefficient	Measure of linear relationship between two variables.	Ranges from −1.0 to +1.0. values close to 0 indicate no relationship; values closer to −1.0 or +1.0 indicate a strong positive or negative relationship.	Includes all observations. Insensitive to inflation. Not good for indicating nonlinear relationship.	Good for indicating existence of relationship, but not magnitude.
Elasticity	Ratio of percent increase in one variable to percent increase in another.	Ranges from 0 to a number above that; can exceed 1.0. Numbers greater than or equal to 1.0 indicate elastic relationship.	Includes all observations. Insensitive to inflation.	Good for indicating magnitude of relationship. If correlation is low and elasticity is high, there is important link between two variables.
Odden–Picus Adequacy Index	Percentage of sum of all observations below adequacy level to sum if all observations at adequacy level.	Ranges from 1.0 or 100% to percentage less than 100. Numbers close to 100 indicate more adequate system.	Includes virtually all observations, but focuses on those below adequacy. Insensitive to inflation.	Good for indicating how close or far system is to providing adequate spending level for all districts.

further in Chapters 9 and 11. Chapter 9 goes into more detail on formula options for school finance structures, and Chapter 11 examines how state finance systems can be improved.

Study Questions

1. Conduct five short interviews with a K–12 educator, a politician, an academic, a taxpayer, and a K–12 student, asking them one question: Does money matter in terms of student performance? Summarize and analyze their responses, and compare them to the research literature surrounding this topic.
2. Describe your thoughts on what equity means. What do you think constitutes equity, and how you would measure it?
3. In small groups, carry out a theoretical, ex ante assessment of the equity of your state's school finance system. Then share your group's ideas in a whole-class discussion.
4. Research equity studies for your state's school finance system, and discuss results with a classmate. Identify which objects you assessed, which statistical procedures you applied, and which equity principles you employed to reach your conclusions.
5. Find adequacy studies for your state or a state with a similar educational system. Identify the pros and cons of the studies. What do the results suggest for an adequate spending level in your state? How does this compare to the spending level in your local school district?

Adequate Staffing and Resources for America's Schools

Although not all states are under school finance adequacy court mandates, all are implementing ambitious versions of standards-based education reforms. Under those objectives, all states seek to allocate sufficient resources for all schools to provide a set of programs and strategies designed to give every student an equal opportunity to learn the state's curriculum content standards as measured by the state's student performance standards. With or without a court mandate, standards-based reforms have forced states to focus on student outcomes, and in resource terms, this means shifting the focus from equitable inputs to adequate inputs. The fact is, state standards–based education reform, the federal No Child Left Behind Act, and school finance adequacy court mandates are all generally focused on the same goal—designing, funding, and implementing an education system that is effective in educating students to proficiency standards, and above those levels for some students.

At the end of Chapter 3, we discussed four different methods the school finance community has developed to determine an adequate set of resources. These approaches are also summarized in Odden (2003), an article that identifies strengths and weaknesses of each approach.

We have developed and use in our work with states the evidence-based approach, which identifies a comprehensive set of school-level elements required to deliver a high-quality instructional program within a school, as well as evidence for their effectiveness, and then determine an adequate expenditure level by placing a price (e.g., an appropriate salary level for personnel) on each component and aggregating the components to a total cost (Odden, 2000; Odden, Picus, and Fermanich, 2003; Odden, Picus, Fermanich, and Goetz, 2005; Odden, Picus, Goetz, and Fermanich, 2006; Odden, Picus, Goetz, et al., 2005; Picus, Odden, and Fermanich, 2003). The evidence-based approach to determining school finance adequacy defers to evidence on the level of resources needed to meet predetermined performance goals much more strongly than to the professional judgment of educators, though professional educator input is solicited. This approach, which we use in this chapter to identify a set of adequate resources for the typical American school, is based on evidence from these sources:

- Research with randomized assignment to the treatment (the "gold standard" of evidence)
- Research with other types of controls or statistical procedures that can help break down the impact of a treatment
- Best practices either as codified in a comprehensive school design (e.g., Stringfield, Ross, and Smith, 1996) or as derived from studies of impact at the local district or school level

The chapter takes this approach, with which the coauthors have been associated for several years.

This chapter is divided into five sections. Section 1 defines "adequacy," and section 2 addresses general issues in determining school adequacy. The final three sections address class size and staffing for core and specialist teachers, extra services for struggling students, and professional development including instructional coaches, pupil support staff, school administration, and dollar resources for books, technology and computers, student activities, and so on. Some of the information found in versions of this chapter in previous editions is now located in Appendix A, including the history and current federal provisions for compensatory education (ESEA Title 1), English-language-learning students, and students with disabilities.

1. A DEFINITION OF ADEQUACY

We propose here a general definition of educational adequacy, and that definition serves as a basis for identifying the resources required for adequate funding. Educational **adequacy** has several components:

- The expectations included in a state's curriculum standards, which define what all the state's students are to be taught.
- The standards included in the state's testing system, which include a definition of what would be considered a proficient score for each test. The goal is to have all, or all but the most severely disabled, students perform at or above proficiency on these tests (with proficiency standards calibrated over time to those of the National Assessment of Educational Progress and to the knowledge needs of the emerging global economy), and to boost the percentage of those performing at the advanced levels—particularly in mathematics and science.
- The standards implied by a state's accountability system and the federal No Child Left Behind law, which require further improvement for students at all levels in the achievement range, for all income levels, for all ethnicities, and which also aspire to enhance the learning of the top-scoring students.

- Sufficient funding to provide the resources identified in the resource matrix contained in Table 4.5.

Full implementation of this definition of an adequate education program with the proposed resources would require that each school rethink, if not restructure, its entire educational program and reallocate all current and any new resources. Such a system also would work best if it were accompanied by a clear accountability and monitoring program.

2. GENERAL ISSUES FOR DETERMINING ADEQUATE SCHOOL RESOURCES

This section discusses several general issues related to adequate school resources—preschool, full-day kindergarten, student counts for funding purposes, and school size.

Preschool

Research has shown that high-quality preschool, particularly for students from lower-income backgrounds, significantly affects future student academic achievement, as well as promoting other desired social and community outcomes (Barnett, 1995, 1996, 1998, 2000; Barnett, Brown, and Shore, 2004; Karoly et al., 1998; Reynolds, Temple, Robertson, and Mann, 2001; Slavin, Karweit, and Wasik, 1994). Specifically, students from lower-income backgrounds who experience a high-quality, full-day preschool program perform better in basic skills in elementary school, score higher on academic goals in middle and high school, attend college at a greater rate, and as adults earn higher incomes and engage in less socially undesirable behavior. According to the research, there is a return over time of *8–10 dollars* for every one dollar invested in high-quality preschool programs.

A published study of state-financed preschool programs in six states—California, Georgia, Illinois, Kentucky, New York, and Ohio—found, similar to the above studies, that children from lower-income families started to catch up to their middle-income peers after they attended a preschool program (Jacobson, 2003).

For the High/Scope Perry Preschool Program, the most recent long-term study of preschool program impacts found that adults at age 40 who had the preschool program had higher earnings, were more likely to hold a job, had committed fewer crimes, and were more likely to have graduated from high school than adults who did not have preschool (Schweinhart et al., 2005).

Given these research findings, we propose that all states fully fund full-day preschool for 3- and 4-year-olds, at least for children from families with an income at or below 200 percent of the poverty level. According to the National Association for the Education of Young Children, preschool standards generally call for one teacher and one teacher assistant for each preschool group of 15 students.

Because preschool quality is linked to impact, and quality is largely a function of staff (Whitebrook, 2004), including preschool students in a district's pupil count for state aid purposes is the most straightforward way to fund preschool services and would require preschool providers to pay a salary according to the salary schedule in the district in which the preschool program was provided, or consistent with the state's average teacher salary. In this way, preschool providers would be able to recruit highly qualified teachers for all preschool programs. At the same time, if this funding and salary approach were followed, districts would be required to allow multiple institutions and organizations to provide preschool services, not just the public schools.

Further, there is increasing recognition that preschool should be provided for all students; research has shown that this strategy produces significant gains for children from middle-class backgrounds and even larger impacts for students from lower-income backgrounds (Barnett, Brown, and Shore, 2004). However, most states' school finance systems focus on students age 5–17, the target of most states' education clauses. This age focus does not include preschool, and thus, under a constitutionally structured adequacy framework, preschool might not be required. Nevertheless, we strongly encourage all states to include preschool in their education policies because of the strength and longevity of the impacts of the program for all children.

Student Count for Calculating State Aid

Most states count students on some type of full-time equivalency basis (FTE), as applied either to average **daily membership (ADM)** or to **average daily attendance (ADA)**. We suggest an FTE enrollment or ADM count so that the aid system provides funding for all students in the district, even if they have intermittent attendance, which may mean that they require additional rather than fewer services.

States need to address two additional issues in determining the pupil count: (1) whether to use a resident or attendance count of students, and (2) whether to use a multiple-year average student count to cushion the loss of aid when enrollments decline. With the expansion of choice programs including open-enrollment programs, which allow students to enroll in a school outside of their district, the use of a resident student count makes state aid calculations complex, particularly when an additional administrative system is then needed to move dollars across districts to cover the costs of students who do choose to attend a school in a district outside of their actual residence. The easiest way to address student choice of school and appropriate flow of funds is simply to count each student in the school (and district) that she or he attends. This ensures that dollars follow the student and eliminates the need for a separate administrative system for transferring funds across districts to accommodate student choice of school.

To cushion the fiscal impact of declining student numbers, the most common approach is to use a three-year rolling-average student count. This approach was recommended by Cavin, Murnane, and Brown (1985) in a study of the issue in Michigan. However, a rolling three-year average is generally not appropriate for use in all schools, especially those schools experiencing enrollment growth. Schools with rising enrollments should use their actual student count so they have the resources to expand educational services as they grow in student FTE.

We suggest that states use full-time ADM (or an FTE count) as the mechanism for counting students in each school and each district. It is important that states use the same pupil count for all elements of the funding system—determining property wealth per pupil, calculating state aid, counting the number of students in a school and a school district, and calculating other aid elements. In addition, to simplify the student-counting system, states should count each child in the school and district where they actually attend school, even if this differs from the school district or school attendance area of their residence. Finally, since it is more appropriate to use a three-year rolling-average pupil count when enrollments are declining, and the actual pupil count for schools with stable or rising student enrollments, we suggest using the average of the current and past two years' pupil count or the current year's enrollment (as counted by the particular state), whichever is larger.

Full-Day Kindergarten

Although some states allow all districts to provide a full-day kindergarten program, many do not, and these states count kindergarten students as just a half (0.5) pupil for state aid purposes. However, research has shown that full-day kindergarten, particularly for students from low-income backgrounds, has significant positive effects on student learning in the early elementary grades (Fusaro, 1997; Gullo, 2000; Slavin, Karweit, and Wasik, 1994). Children participating in such programs do better in learning the basic skills of reading, writing, and mathematics than do children who receive only a half-day program or no kindergarten at all. The most recent study of such effects was released in mid-2003 by the National Center for Education Research (Denton, West, and Walston, 2003). This nationally representative, longitudinal study showed that children who attended full-day kindergarten had a greater ability to demonstrate reading knowledge and skill than their peers in half-day programs, across the range of family backgrounds. This study also found that the more children were exposed to literacy activities in the home, the more likely they were to perform well in both kindergarten and first grade. Funding full-day kindergarten for 5-year-olds as well as for 4-year-olds is an increasingly common practice among the states (Kauerz, 2005).

Indeed, the effectiveness of full-day kindergarten on student achievement is well established. In the most recent meta-analysis of 23 studies comparing the achievement effect of full-day versus half-day kindergarten programs, Fusaro (1997) found an average effect size of 0.77, which is quite substantial.

Since recent research suggests that children from all backgrounds can benefit from full-day kindergarten programs, we suggest that states provide support for full-day programs for all students, at least for those parents who want their child to be in such a program. The most direct way to implement full-day kindergarten is to have the school finance system allow each district to count each student in a full-day kindergarten program as a full (1.0) student in the school-funding formula.

School Size

Few if any states have a specific policy on school size, and school sizes differ substantially across all states. Since our evidence-based approach to adequacy shows resources for prototypical elementary, middle, and high schools, we need to suggest a size in order for the prototypes to indicate the relative level of resources in the schools. Our proto-typical school sizes reflect research on the most effective school sizes. In most cases, our numbers can be proportionately reduced or increased for schools smaller or larger than the prototypes. Further, when actual school sizes are significantly larger than the proto-types, we suggest that schools divide themselves into schools-within-schools that oper-ate as semi-independent units. Our proposals should not be construed to imply that the state replace all school sites with smaller buildings.

Research on school size is clearer than research on class size. Most of the research on school size addresses the question of whether large schools—those with over 1,000 students—are both more efficient and more effective than smaller school schools—of 300–500 students—and whether cost savings and performance improvements can be identified after consolidating small schools or districts into larger entities. The research has generally shown that school units of roughly 400–600 elementary students and 500–1,000 secondary students are the most effective and efficient. Analysts, however, argue that the expected cost savings from massive school and district consolidation have not been realized (Guthrie, 1979; Ornstein, 1990), and that consolidation might actually harm student performance in rural schools (Sher and Tompkins, 1977), as well as having broad negative effects on rural communities (Coeyman, 1998; Seal and Harmon, 1995).

The research on diseconomies of small and large scale generally does not support a consolidation policy. From an economic perspective, the concept of diseconomies of scale includes both costs and outputs. The issue is whether costs per unit of output are higher in small schools or districts, or, put differently, whether costs can be reduced while maintaining output as size rises. In an extensive review of the literature, Fox (1981) concluded that little research had analyzed output in combination with input and size variables, and Monk (1990) concluded, after assessing the meager extant research, that there was little support for either school or district consolidation.

For elementary schools, research knowledge is thin, but the data suggest that size economies that reduce costs by more than one dollar per pupil exist up to but not be-yond 200 pupils (Riew, 1986). Thus, very small schools experience diseconomies of small scale and, except in isolated rural areas, could potentially be merged into larger ones. But the real opportunities for cost savings from school consolidation in these cases are not great, precisely because many such schools are located in isolated rural areas, and there are no other schools nearby with which to consolidate.

At the secondary level, the data are more mixed. Few studies exist that simultane-ously assess both size and output, so scale diseconomies have not been adequately stud-ied. Riew (1986) found that there were cost savings, below one dollar per pupil, for middle schools with enrollments above 500; again, many middle schools already enroll more than this number. In analyzing whether larger secondary schools actually provided more com-prehensive programs, an argument for larger size, Monk (1987) concluded in a study of New York that program comprehensiveness increased consistently in secondary schools only for size increases up to but not beyond about 400 students. In subsequent research, Haller, Monk, Spotted Bear, Griffith, and Moss (1990) found that while larger schools of-fered more comprehensive programs, there was wide variation among both smaller and larger schools, and there was no clear size that guaranteed program comprehensiveness. Further, Hamilton (1983) showed that social development is better in small high schools.

Studies of district size generally analyze expenditures per pupil as a function of size without an output variable such as student achievement (Fox, 1981). To document diseconomies of district size, however, expenditures, size, and output need to be analyzed simultaneously, since the goal is to determine if costs per unit of output decrease as the number of students in the district increases. Again, in reviewing the literature, Monk (1990) concluded that definitive statements could not be made about district consolidation.

In the most recent review of scale economies and diseconomies, Andrews, Duncombe, and Yinger (2002) assessed both cost function and production function research. The studies reviewed generally assessed costs in tandem with student achievement outputs. The authors concluded that potential but modest cost savings could be realized by consolidating districts smaller than 500 students into districts with 2,000–4,000 students; of course, this would be an option only for small districts a short distance from each other, and not for rural, isolated small districts. The authors also found that the optimum size for elementary schools was in the 300–500 pupil range, and for high schools was in the 600–900 range (see also Lee and Smith, 1997, on high school size). Both findings suggest that our large urban districts and schools are far beyond the optimum size and need somehow to be downsized.

In other words, research suggests that elementary school *units* be in the range of 400–500 students and that secondary school *units* be in the range of 500–1000 students (Lee and Smith, 1997; Raywid, 1997/1998). Evidence from comprehensive school designs, moreover, generally suggests school sizes of about 500 students for both elementary and secondary schools, which we would argue falls within the range of the above research findings (Odden, 1997a; Stringfield, Ross, and Smith, 1996). Such school designers also suggest that larger schools be divided into subschools and run as schools-within-schools. So a secondary school with 2,000 students would be organized into two 1,000-student or four 500-student subschools, each with a separate student body, separate principal, and separate entrance, if possible (see also Murphy, Beck, Crawford, Hodges, and McGaughy, 2001). Teaming within larger schools is another way to enhance personalization of the social and academic environment for students.

Though some of the research on "schools within a school" is mixed, the bulk of research shows that when such efforts are implemented well, student performance improves, as do other outcomes. The recent Borman, Hewes, Overman, and Brown (2003) meta-analysis of comprehensive school designs, many of which are implemented as schools-within-school, documented significant positive impacts for fully implemented programs. A policy brief by Wonacott (2002) from the Career and Technical Education National Dissemination Center provides an overview of the impacts of smaller learning communities generally, and of secondary career academies specifically. The small-school initiative of the Gates Foundation is another support for smaller schools; indeed, the foundation is providing tens of millions of dollars all around the country to enable large high schools to break themselves into smaller school units (see, e.g., Dobbs, 2003). Many states have been successful in creating schools-within-schools within their larger high school buildings, but this school restructuring is a complex and challenging process.

Astute readers will have noted that the above conclusions apply for school *units*, and not necessarily school buildings. And many districts and states have already built larger school buildings. Evidence on effectiveness would suggest that districts should build smaller school buildings in the future, but this could increase the cost of educational facilities. Moreover, some parents and students prefer large school buildings, believing that such schools offer a larger variety of courses and more extracurricular activities. At the same time, some states and districts have built school buildings of a variety of sizes, reflecting the above research findings. Finally, for those who want students to attend school in small buildings, an increasing number of states also offer charter schools.

Giving parents and children access to their school of choice—a large, comprehensive high school; a school within a larger school building; or a charter school—would allow a state and its districts to provide option's for the "size" of the educational environment in which students are educated. Although such options may not in fact exist in sparse, rural areas, and parents in lower-income areas often do not have the time or resources to avail themselves of choice were it to be provided, these conclusions about the issue of school size remain sound.

For secondary school effectiveness, curriculum offerings should emphasize a solid core of academics for all students (Bryk, Lee, and Holland, 1993; Lee, Croninger, and Smith, 1997; Newmann and associates, 1996). The most effective strategy for having all students perform to proficiency on state standards and to close the achievement gap between minorities and nonminorities is for high schools to offer a strong set of core academic courses in mathematics, science, language arts, history/social science, and foreign language, and to require all students to take the bulk of their courses from this core (Clune and White, 1992; Lee, Croninger, and Smith, 1997; Madigan, 1997; Public Agenda, 1997; Steinberg, 1997), excluding altogether such low-level classes as general and consumer math. Indeed, the Education Trust has argued that one of the top two strategies for closing the achievement gap between low-income students and students of color, and other adolescents is to have high schools prepare *all* students for college—that is, to offer a core of solid academics (American College Testing Service and Education Trust, 2004; Education Trust, 2003).[1] This is the kind of secondary education required for full participation in any and all post–high school activities, whether it is taking a job, enrolling in a two-year postsecondary institution, or attending a college or university.

Thus, to indicate the relative level of resources in schools, we will use prototypical school units of 432 elementary students (grades K–5), 450 middle school students (grades 6–8), and 600 high school students (grades 9–12). As discussed in the class size section below, this allows for a whole number of teachers (as opposed to partial teacher counts) and facilitates staffing discussions for schools with fewer students. Though these numbers are larger than many of the "small" high school programs that are developing across the county, they more accurately reflect the research on the most effective school sizes (Iatarola, 2005).

---

[1]The other strategy is to provide a quality teacher in every classroom, a topic addressed later in this book.

3. ADEQUATE STAFFING FOR THE CORE PROGRAMS IN PROTOTYPICAL SCHOOLS

This section covers personnel for the major elements of the regular education program: core teachers, specialist teachers, and instructional coaches. Section 4 addresses additional staff for students with extra needs. Section 5 addresses all other school-level resources, such as pupil support professionals, librarians, administrators, and secretaries, and dollar-per-pupil figures for instructional materials, computers and technology, student activities, and so on.

Core Teachers/Class Size

In staffing schools and classrooms, the most expensive decision superintendents and principals make has to do with class sizes for core teachers—the grade (or multigrade) teachers in elementary schools, and the core subject (e.g., mathematics, science, reading/English/language arts, and social studies) teachers in middle and high schools.

The research findings. Research on class size has shown that small classes of 15 (not a class of 30 with an instructional aide or two teachers) in kindergarten through grade 3 have significant positive impacts on student achievement in mathematics and reading (Achilles, 1999; Gerber, Finn, Achilles, and Boyd-Zaharias, 2001; Grissmer, 1999; Mishel & Rothstein, 2002; Molnar, 1999; Nye, Hedges, and Konstantopulous, 2002). It is commonly also concluded that the impact of small class size is even larger for students from low-income and minority backgrounds (Finn and Achilles, 1999; Krueger and Whitmore, 2001). The evidence thus supports a policy to provide class sizes of 15 in all of a state's K–3 classrooms.

Over time, different analysts have reached different conclusions on the role of resources generally and on the role of class size in student achievement specifically. In a late 1970s meta-analysis of the class size research, Glass and Smith (1979) concluded that class sizes needed to be reduced to at most 15 students before an impact on achievement could be produced. However, in a reanalysis of that research, Odden (1990) noted that Glass and Smith had no samples of class sizes of 14–17 students that actually improved student achievement, and that the class-size-of-15 finding was a statistical artifact of little if any impact until individual tutoring was provided. And Hanushek (2002) has always questioned the efficacy of small class sizes.

But research in the late 1980s and early 1990s provided new evidence of the impact of class size on achievement. The "gold standard" of educational research is randomized experiments, which provide scientific evidence on the impact of a certain treatment (Mosteller, 1995). Thus, the primary evidence for the impact of small classes today is the Tennessee STAR study, which was a large-scale, randomized experiment of class sizes of 15 for kindergarten through grade 3 (Finn and Achilles, 1999; Word et al., 1990). The study showed that students in the small classes achieved at a significantly higher level (effect size of about 0.25 standard deviations) than those in regular-size classes and that the impacts were even larger (effect size of about 0.50) for low-income and minority students (Achilles, 1999; Finn, 2002; Grissmer, 1999; Krueger, 2002). The same research study showed that a regular class of 24–25 with a teacher and an instructional aide did *not* produce a discernible positive impact on student achievement, a finding that undercuts proposals and widespread practices placing instructional aides in elementary classrooms (Gerber, Finn, Achilles, and Boyd-Zaharias, 2001).

Subsequent research showed that the positive impacts of small classes in the Tennessee study persisted into the middle and high school years, and even the years beyond high school (Finn, Gerber, Achilles, and Boyd-Zaharias, 2001; Krueger, 2002; Mishel & Rothstein, 2002; Nye, Hedges, and Konstantopulos, 2001a, 2001b). Thus, although differences in analytic methods and conclusions characterize some of the debate over class size (see Hanushek, 2002; Krueger, 2002), we side with those concluding that class size does make a difference. Specifically, we conclude that the research shows only that class sizes of 15 students, and only for kindergarten through grade 3, boost student performance (Achilles, 1999; Finn, 2002; Grissmer, 1999; Krueger, 2002).

Two main mechanisms have been proposed through which class size reduction effects may operate. Some have suggested that teachers may alter their instructional methods in smaller classes, making greater use of small groups, for example, or assigning more writing. However, several studies, including those tied to the STAR project, have failed to find consistent teaching differences related to class size (see, e.g., Betts and Shkolnik, 1999; Evertson and Randolph, 1989; Rice, 1999). A more likely operating mechanism is that students respond better to the same instruction in smaller classes. With fewer students per teacher, less time is needed for disciplinary matters, and students may be more engaged (Betts and Shkolnik, 1999; Finn and Achilles, 1999; Finn, Pannozzo, and Achilles, 2003). Particularly in the early elementary grades, smaller classes facilitate forming social relationships among teachers, students, and their families that may be essential for school success.

Evidence on the most effective class sizes in grades 4–12 is harder to find. Most of the research on class size reduction has been conducted at the elementary level. Thus, we turn to evidence on the most appropriate secondary class size from typical and best practices to determine class sizes for these grades. First, the national average class size in middle and high schools is about 25. Second, nearly all comprehensive school reform models are developed on the basis of a class size of 25 (Odden, 1997; Odden and Picus, 2000; Stringfield, Ross, and Smith, 1996), a conclusion on class size reached by the dozens of experts who created these whole-school design models. Although many professional judgment panels in other states have recommended secondary class sizes of 20, none cited research or best practices to support such a proposal.

Thus, we use evidence of best practices to build our prototypical schools with class sizes of 25[2] in grades 4–12 and class sizes of 15 for grades K–3. This means that a K–5 elementary school would have an average class size of 18. With this formula, an elementary school of 432 students would receive 24 core teachers (4 teachers for each of six grade levels), a middle school of 450 students would receive 18 core teachers, and a

---

[2]In many states, educators have argued not to bump class size from 15 in grade 3 to 25 in grade 4 and subsequent grades, and that class sizes in those grades should be closer to 20. We encourage all states to sponsor experiments with various class sizes in grades 4–12 to see if smaller sizes indeed impact student performance. Whatever the results, the conclusions could provide stronger evidence for what size classes should be at those grade levels.

high school of 600 students would receive 24 core teachers. Note that these core teachers would not be the only teaching staff in these schools. Several of the following sections include a variety of additional teachers for all school levels.

Fractional teacher units and grouping students for instruction.   An issue that often emerges in applying this general formula to schools of different sizes is how to calculate the number of teachers when the number of students in a school, grade level, or class is not so neatly divided by 15, 25, or 18, particularly at each grade level for a school. For example, if an elementary grade had 18 students, 1.0 FTE teacher position is provided. But what would happen if there were 19 students? Would that trigger an additional entire FTE teacher or just a small fraction of an additional teacher? The formula would likely trigger just the additional fraction, and so all teacher FTEs would need to be considered when organizing a school's instructional program. In other states, individuals have suggested a "rounding up" of each calculation so that any small fraction would produce an additional 1.0 FTE teacher position; this would allow an elementary grade with 19 students to trigger 2.0 FTE teacher positions. But many view such an approach as too generous, countering that the additional FTE teacher should be triggered at 22 or 24. That approach would create a "step" function, as the state would need to distinguish clearly between a grade with 21 students that triggered just 1.0 FTE positions and a grade with 22 students that triggered 2.0 FTE positions. A formula that simply calculated FTE teachers to the nearest tenth (or hundredth) by dividing the student count by 18 (or 25 for middle and high schools) would solve the "step" function problem but not the problem of the number of students in the class.

The issue here, as well as for very small elementary schools, is how students are grouped for instruction. If students are grouped by grade level, the fact that each grade level does not have a number of students evenly divided by 15, 18, or 25 raises an issue of student placement and numbers of teachers. On the other hand, if schools adopt a multiage approach and in elementary schools, for example, create K–1, 1–2, 2–3, 3–4, and 4–5 classes,[3] then it would be much easier to create classrooms of approximately 18 students, regardless of the specific number of students in each grade. This approach would also allow for differential placement of students according to their developmental progress, since there is great variability among elementary students in their academic development, even when they are of similar ages, a phenomenon that grade-level grouping of students ignores.

Furthermore, research has shown that multiaging of students in elementary classrooms is actually better for students; students in multiage classrooms achieve at least as much as students in age-grouped classes and usually learn more, with effect sizes ranging from 0.0 to 0.5 (Gutierrez and Slavin, 1992; Mason and Burns, 1996; Mason and Stimson, 1996; Pavan, 1992; Veenman, 1995). The reasons for increased student achievement are at least twofold. First, classes can be organized so that the academic development of children in each class is more homogeneous, thus allowing teachers to provide more whole-group instruction and so more instruction during each day. Second, if teachers stay with a student group over a two-year period, a process called "looping,"

---

[3]Or in the case of smaller schools, groupings such as K–1, 2–3 and 4–5.

then less time is lost in starting the school year, determining how to organize and manage the class, and learning the academic achievement status of each student. Moreover, a recent report from the Rural School and Community Trust on school finance adequacy (Malhoit, 2005) lists the prevalence of multiage classrooms in rural schools as one of several advantages that small, rural schools provide.

Multiaging, though, works best if the teacher instructs the entire class as a group and essentially has a two-year curriculum that all students are taught over a two-year period. Some multiage classrooms run as "combination" or "multigrade" classes, in which the teacher provides half a day of instruction for one grade and half a day of instruction for the other grade. However, this can be a detriment to student learning, in part because each student might receive only a half day instead of a full day of instruction, with effect sizes ranging from –0.1 to 0.0. In short, the way multiage classrooms are taught impacts whether they are more or less effective for students.

Specialist Teachers and Planning and Preparation Time/Collaborative Professional Development

Schools also need to teach art, music, library skills, and vocational and physical education. Teachers also need some time during the regular school day for collaborative planning, job-embedded professional development, and ongoing curriculum development and review. Providing each teacher with one period a day for collaborative planning and professional development focused on the school's curriculum requires an additional 20 percent allocation of specialist teachers to maintain the above class sizes. These teachers could teach the above or other specialist content classes.

The 20 percent additional staff is adequate for elementary and middle schools, but a different argument could be made for high schools. If the goal is to have more high school students take a core set of rigorous academic courses, and learn that material at a high level of thinking and problem solving, one could argue that a block schedule that allows for longer class periods would be a better way to organize instructional time. And typical block scheduling for high schools requires an additional 33 percent of specialist teachers, as the school creates a schedule of four 90-minute blocks, with teachers providing instruction for three of those blocks and having one block for planning and preparation each day. This type of block schedule could be operated with students taking four courses each semester and attending the same classes each day, or with students taking eight courses each semester while attending different classes every other day. Such a schedule could also entail some "skinny" blocks for some classes. Each of these specific ways of structuring a block schedule, however, would require an additional 33 percent of specialist teachers to provide the regular teacher with a "block" for planning and preparation each day.

Based on the findings from cognitive research on how children learn complex materials (Bransford, Brown, and Cocking, 1999; Donovan and Bransford, 2005a, 2005b, 2005c), which suggest longer, more concentrated times for learning, and the rigorous but needed performance expectations for high school students, we include resources for block scheduling for high schools, and thus more specialist teachers for high schools. Block schedules would also allow teachers of English and writing to give more writing assignments and to provide detailed feedback to students, which is very time consuming with large numbers of students. We should note that a school could provide 60 minutes of this preparation time for planning, preparation, and collaborative work with colleagues, and also require that teachers use 30 minutes of this time to provide additional help for struggling students, which could be organized in many different ways.

As we discuss in a later section on professional development, the best way to provide job-embedded professional development is to dedicate a significant portion of planning and preparation time within the normal school day for this purpose (see Odden and Archibald, 2001a, for examples). This means that the planning and preparation time needs to be provided as 45–60 minutes of uninterrupted time, not 15–30 minutes at different times during the day. Such professional development should involve 100–200 hours annually for each teacher, include extensive coaching in the teacher's classroom (provided by site-based instructional facilitators/coaches, discussed next), incorporate all faculty and administrators in a school, focus heavily on the content and curriculum that each teacher teaches, and be aligned with state/district content standards and student tests (Birman, Desimone, Porter, and Garet, 2000; Cohen and Hill, 2001; Desimone, Porter, Birman, Garet, and Yoon, 2002; Desimone, Porter, Garet, Yoon, and Birman, 2002; Garet, Birman, Porter, Desimone, and Herman, 1999). Again, we expand on the structure and costs of effective professional development below.

For our prototypical schools, elementary and middle schools receive an additional 20 percent of the number of core teachers for specialist teachers, and high schools receive an additional 33 percent, in order to teach specialist classes and also to provide time for teachers to engage in collaborative planning and preparation, as well as job-embedded professional development during the period when they do not teach. The 20 percent formula provides an additional 4.8 FTE positions in the prototypical 432-student elementary school and 3.6 FTE positions in the prototypical 450-student middle school, and the 33 percent formula provides an additional 8.0 positions in the prototypical 600-student high school.

In summing the core and the specialist teachers from above, the total teaching staff for prototypical schools is 28.8 for the 432-student elementary, 21.6 for the 450-student middle, and 32 for the prototypical 600-student high school. Again, we note these are not the only professional staff or the only teaching staff allocated to each school.

Instructional Facilitators/School-Based Coaches/Mentors

Few states—Arkansas and Wyoming are exceptions—explicitly provide resources for school- and classroom-based instructional coaches, yet they are key to making professional development work. Most comprehensive school designs, and the evidence-based studies conducted in Kentucky (Odden, Fermanich, and Picus, 2003), Arkansas (Odden, Picus, and Fermanich, 2003), Arizona (Odden, Picus, Fermanich, and Goetz, 2004), and Wyoming (Odden, Picus, et al., 2005), call for school-based instructional facilitators (sometimes called mentors, literacy or numeracy coaches, curriculum specialists, or lead teachers). The technology-intensive designs also require a technology coordinator (see Stringfield, Ross, and Smith, 1996). Further, several designs suggest that while one facilitator might be sufficient for the first year of implementation of a schoolwide program, in subsequent years, an additional 0.5–1.0 FTE facilitators are needed. Moreover, the technology designs include a full-time facilitator who spends at least half of his or her time as the site's technology expert. Thus, drawing from all programs, we conclude that about 2.5 FTE instructional facilitators/technology coordinators are needed for each school unit of 500 students. This resourcing strategy works for elementary as well as middle and high schools.

These individuals would coordinate the instructional program but, most importantly, would provide the critical ongoing instructional coaching and mentoring that the professional development literature shows is necessary for teachers to improve their instructional practice (Garet, Porter, Desimone, Birman, and Yoon, 2001; Joyce and Showers, 2002). This means that they would spend the bulk of their time in classrooms, modeling lessons, giving feedback to teachers, and helping improve the instructional program. We expand on the rationale for these individuals in the section on professional development but include them here as they represent teacher positions. The technology staff would provide the technological expertise to fix small problems with the computer system, install all software, connect computer equipment so it can be used for both instructional and management purposes, and provide professional development to embed computer technologies into the curriculum at the school site.

The impact of coaches as part of the professional development program is very large. Joyce and Calhoun (1996) and Joyce and Showers (2002) found that when teachers had sufficient time to engage in professional development that was embedded in classrooms with the aid of instructional coaches, teacher practices changed significantly, with effect sizes of 1.68 in the transfer of training to classrooms, 1.25 for skill-level objectives, and 2.71 for knowledge-level objectives. Effects were almost negligible without the classroom-based coaching.

The staffing formula for such positions is one instructional coach for every 200 students. This would translate into 2.2 FTE facilitators for the 432-student prototypical elementary school, 2.25 FTE facilitators for the 450-student middle school, and 3.0 FTE facilitators for the 600-student high school. This formula would produce 0.5 facilitators for a small 108-student elementary (one-fourth the size of the prototype) and 0.75 facilitators for a 150-student middle or high school (one-third the size of the middle school prototype and one-fourth the size of the high school prototype).

Although these positions are identified here as FTE positions, schools could divide the responsibilities across several individual teachers. For example, the 2.2 positions in elementary schools could be structured for four teacher/instructional facilitators providing instruction 50 percent of the time and functioning as curriculum coaches in reading, mathematics, or technology 50 percent of the time. The same allocation of functions across individuals could work for the middle and high schools.

4. STAFFING FOR EXTRA STUDENT NEEDS

Because not all students will learn to performance standards within the core instructional program, districts and schools should design a powerful sequence of additional effective strategies for struggling students, that is, students who must work harder and who need more time and help to achieve to the state standards. Rather than simply provide a pot of dollars, or a pupil weight, we identify a series of specific extra-help programs for struggling students, including these:

- Tutoring—immediate, intensive assistance to keep struggling students on track
- Sheltered English and ESL instruction for English-language-learning (ELL) students
- Extended-day programs
- Summer school for struggling students still needing extra help to achieve to state standards
- A new approach to providing resources for special education

These programs all extend the learning time for struggling students. The key concept is to implement the maxim of standards-based education reform: keep high standards for all students, but vary the instructional time so all can achieve at least to the proficiency performance level.

Indicators of Struggling Students

As an indicator of the potential presence of struggling students, most states collect and use the number of students who are eligible for free and reduced-price lunches, which nationally is the most available variable to indicate the number of struggling students in a school. We will use that student count to indicate the number of students who might need extra help to achieve to proficiency standards or above, in addition to counts of students with disabilities and students who are ELLs. However, it is well known that fewer high school students who are eligible for the federal free or reduced-price lunch program apply for such support than are eligible. Thus, we would encourage states to adjust the high school figures to more accurately reflect the number of such students (eligible but not participating) in each school, by comparing the free and reduced-price lunch count to the poverty count, from the last census, and using that relationship to adjust the count.

Tutors

The most powerful and effective strategy to help struggling students meet state standards is individual one-to-one tutoring provided by licensed teachers (Shanahan, 1998; Shanahan and Barr, 1995; Wasik and Slavin, 1993). Students who must work harder and need more assistance to achieve to proficiency levels (i.e., students who are ELL, are low income, or have minor disabilities) especially benefit from preventative tutoring (Cohen, Kulik, and Kulik, 1982). Tutoring-program-effect sizes vary by the components of the approach used, such as the nature and structure of the tutoring program, but effect sizes on student learning reported in meta-analyses range from 0.4 to 2.5 (Mathes and Fuchs, 1994; Shanahan, 1998; Shanahan and Barr, 1995; Wasik and Slavin, 1993), with an average of about 0.75 (Wasik and Slavin, 1993).

The impact of tutoring programs depends on how they are structured. The alignment between tutors' effects and the regular instructional program is important (Mantzicopoulos, Morrison, Stone, and Setrakian, 1992; Wheldall et al., 1995). Who conducts the tutoring matters, as does the intensity of the tutoring (Shanahan, 1998). Poorly organized programs in which students lose instructional time moving between classrooms can limit tutoring effects (Cunningham and Allington, 1994). Researchers (Cohen, Kulik, and Kulik, 1982; Farkas, 1998; Mathes and Fuchs, 1994; Shanahan, 1998; Shanahan and Barr, 1995; Wasik and Slavin, 1993) have found greater effects when the tutoring includes the following mechanisms:

- Professional teachers as tutors
- Tutoring initially provided to students on a one-to-one basis
- Tutors trained in specific tutoring strategies
- Tutoring tightly aligned to the regular curriculum and to the specific learning challenges, with appropriate, content-specific scaffolding and modeling
- Sufficient time provided for the tutoring
- Highly structured programming, both substantively and organizationally

An important issue is how many tutors to provide for schools with differing numbers of at-risk students. The standard of many comprehensive school designs is a ratio of one fully licensed teacher-tutor for every 100 students in poverty, with a minimum of one for every school. Using our prototypical schools, this standard would provide from one to four-plus professional teacher-tutor positions for the elementary and middle schools, and up to six for the high school.

We note several characteristics of an effective one-to-one tutoring strategy. First, each tutor should tutor one student every 20 minutes, or three students per hour. This would allow one tutor position to tutor 18 students a day. (Since tutoring is such an intensive activity, individual teachers might spend only half their time tutoring; but 1.0 FTE tutoring position would allow 18 students per day to receive one-to-one tutoring.). Four positions would allow 72 students to receive individual tutoring daily in the prototypical elementary and middle schools. Second, most students do not require tutoring all year long; tutoring programs generally assess students quarterly and change tutoring arrangements as warranted. With modest changes such as these, close to half the student body of a 400-pupil school unit could receive individual tutoring during the year. Third, not all students who are from a low-income background require individual tutoring, so a portion of the allocation could be used for students who might not be from a lower-income family but nevertheless might have a learning issue that could be remedied by tutoring.

Though the above discussion focused on *individual* tutoring, schools could deploy these resources provided for intensive intervention in other evidence-based ways. In a detailed review of the evidence on how to structure a variety of early-intervention supports to prevent reading failure, Torgeson (2004) showed how one-to-one tutoring, one-to-three tutoring, and one-to-five small-group sessions can be combined for different students to enhance their chances of learning to read successfully. One-to-one tutoring would be reserved for the students with the most severe reading difficulties, scoring, say, at or below the 20th or 25th percentile on a norm-referenced test. Intensive instruction for groups of three to five students would then be provided for students above that level but below the proficiency level.

The instruction for all tutoring groupings, though, needs to be more explicit and sequenced than that for other students. For example, young children with weaknesses in knowledge of letters, letter–sound relationships, and phonemic awareness need explicit and systematic instruction to help them first decode and then read and comprehend.

Meta-analyses consistently show the positive effects of reducing reading group size (Elbaum, Vaughn, Hughes, and Moody, 1999), and Torgeson (2004) identified experiments with both one-to-three and one-to-five teacher–student groupings. While one-to-one tutoring works with 20 minutes of tutoring per student, a one-to-three or one-to-five grouping requires a longer instructional time—up to 45 minutes. In the latter two groupings, with 45 minutes of instruction, students reduced their rate of reading failure to a minuscule percentage.

If the included numbers of tutors are used for such small groups, a one FTE tutoring position could teach 30 students a day in the one-to-three setting with 30 minutes of instruction per group, and 30+ students a day in the one-to-five setting with 45 minutes of instruction per group. Four FTE tutoring positions could then provide this type of intensive instruction for up to 120 students daily. In short, while we have emphasized one-to-one tutoring, and some students need this tutoring, other small-group practices can also work, with the length of instruction for the small group increasing as the size of the group increases. The interventions help students learn to read only if they provide the type of explicit instruction Torgeson (2004) described.

While Torgeson (2004) stated that similar interventions can work with middle and high school students, the effect, unfortunately, is smaller. It is simply much more difficult to undo the lasting damage of not learning to read when students enter middle and high schools with severe reading deficiencies.

Overall, tutoring-program-effect sizes vary by the components of the approach used (e.g. the nature and structure of the tutoring program), but effect sizes on student learning reported in meta-analyses range from 0.4 to 2.5 (Mathes and Fuchs, 1994; Shanahan, 1998; Shanahan and Barr, 1995; Wasik and Slavin, 1993), with an average of about 0.75 for one-to-one tutoring programs (Wasik and Slavin, 1993).

We staff each prototypical school with one FTE tutor for every 100 adjusted students eligible for free and reduced-price lunch, with a minimum of one in every prototypical school.

To review, the multiplicity of programmatic elements *so far* that are focused on getting students to read proficiently by the end of grade 3 and to perform at proficiency levels after that, which are then augmented by tutoring, include the following:

- Full-day kindergarten
- Classes of 15–18 students for the first four years of school, K–3—and perhaps even smaller classes if schools have all-licensed staff teach reading during 90-minute reading blocks

- At least 90 minutes of regular reading instruction daily
- An evidence-based reading curriculum, with a balance of phonics, phonemic development, writing, and comprehension
- More effective teachers with access to rigorous professional development
- Individual and small-group tutoring if all of the above still leave the student struggling.

English-Language-Learning (ELL) Students

Research has shown that ELL students from lower-income, and generally less educated, backgrounds tend to struggle in school and need extra help. Triggering tutoring resources, as described in the last section, on the basis of the economic background of students provide some extra help needed by struggling ELL students. However, research, best practices, and experience also suggest that when students both come from a low-income background and are English language learners, some additional assistance is needed. This includes some combination of small classes, ESL classes, professional development for teachers to help them teach "sheltered English" classes, and "reception" centers for districts with large numbers of ELL students who arrive at different times during the school year.

In addition to teachers who provide ESL instruction in to students for whom English is not their primary language, ELL students need a solid and rigorous core curriculum as the basis from which to receive any extra services. For example, a recent study of what is needed to help ELL students achieve to high performance standards (Gandara, Rumberger, Maxwell-Jolly, and Callahan, 2003) suggested that what is in the core or base program is critical. That study concluded that ELL students need several things:

- Qualified teachers—the key to student learning
- Adequate instructional materials and good school conditions
- Sound assessments of ELL students so teachers know in detail their English-language reading and other academic skills
- Less segregation of ELL students
- Rigorous curriculum and courses for all ELL students, and affirmative counseling of such students to take those courses
- Professional development for all teachers, focusing on sheltered-English-teaching skills.

In studying specific strategies to provide ESL instruction during the regular school day by having ELL students take such a course rather than an elective course, we have found that additional staff are needed. For example, for one middle school's seven-period daily schedule, the school was providing an ESL class to its ELL students instead of an alternative, elective class offering. Although we initially believed that that strategy would not require any additional resources—ELL students were simply taking an ESL class rather than another class—we came to understand that additional resources for this strategy were necessary. Because the district had determined that the ELL students were best served through three levels of ESL classes (each taught during a different period of the day), enrollment in any one of those classes was insufficient to enable the school to reduce the number of non-ESL classes in that time slot. Instead, between two and four ELL students were pulled from each class. ESL classes were organized to accommodate the number of students requiring service, and additional teacher resources were needed to meet this need.

Although there may be the potential to cancel some classes if sufficient numbers of the same class have sufficient numbers of ELL students pulled out, it was generally agreed that if the ELL formula triggered an additional 1.0 FTE positions for every 100 ELL students, the staffing resources would be sufficient to allow for the provision of the ESL classes. We should note that this school was providing structured English immersion for all ELL students, with ESL as an additional course, and not a bilingual education program. Thus, the pull-out class provided ELL students with an additional "dose" of English instruction, reinforcing the key program goal of having ELL students learn English so they could continue their schooling in English-language-instruction classrooms.

Other ELL programs also work. In a best-evidence synthesis of 17 studies on bilingual education, Slavin and Cheung (2005) found that ELL students in bilingual programs outperformed their nonbilingual program peers. Using studies focused primarily on reading achievement, the authors found an effect size of 0.45 for ELL students.

Our staffing strategy for ELL students provides each prototypical school with an additional 1.0 FTE teacher positions for every 100 ELL students.

It bears repeating that these are not the only resources provided for ELL students. All ELL students from lower-income backgrounds (most ELL students) are included in the free and reduced-price lunch counts, which trigger tutoring, extended-day, and summer school resources (see the discussion below), so all of these resources would also be available to ELL students. For example, if a 100-poverty-student count consisted of no ELL students, it would trigger 1.0 tutor position, plus the extended-day and summer school resources. But if the 100-poverty-student count consisted of ELL students, it would trigger the initial 1.0 tutor position, the extended-day and summer school resources *plus an additional 1.0 teacher position*.

Extended-Day Programs

Beginning in elementary school, and particularly in secondary schools, after-school or extended-day programs might be necessary for some students. Extended-day programs provide a safe environment for children and adolescents after the school day ends, as well as to provide academic support. In a review of the research, Vandell, Pierce, and Dadisman (2005) found that well-designed and -administered extended-day programs yield numerous improvements in academic and behavioral outcomes (see also Baker and Witt, 1996; Dishion, McCord, and Poulin, 1999; Mahoney, Stattin, and Magnusson, 2001; Posner and Vandell, 1994; Schinke, Cole, and Poulin, 2000; Tierney, Grossman, and Resch, 1995; White, Reisner, Welsh, and Russell, 2001).

Several recent experimental studies have documented the potential of extended-day programs. Cosden, Morrison, Albanese, and Macias (2001) found that the Gervitz

Homework Project improved sixth-grade SAT-9 math and reading scores for participants in the high-program-attendance group versus those in the low-program-attendance group, though a third of the control group participated in other after-school programs and over half the program students dropped out. Philliber, Kaye, and Herrling (2001) found that the Children's Aid Society Carrera-Model Teen Pregnancy Prevention Program produced significantly higher PSAT scores for program versus control youths. An evaluation of the Howard Street Tutoring Program (Morris, Shaw, and Perney, 1999) claimed significant differences between the treatment and control groups in gains on basal word recognition, basal passages, and two measures of spelling. Lastly, an evaluation of the Quantum Opportunities Program (Hahn, Leavitt, and Aaron, 1994; Lattimore, Grotpeter and Taggart, 1998) found that program members were much more likely than control group members to have graduated from high school and to be in a postsecondary school. The rate of four-year college attendance among members was more than three times higher than the control group rate, and the rate of two-year college attendance was more than twice as high. After two years, experimental group average scores for 5 of the 11 academic functional skills were significantly higher than control group scores. On the other hand, the 21st Century Community Learning Centers (CCLC) Program study evaluation (Dynarski et al., 2003), though hotly debated, indicated that for elementary students, programs did not appear to produce measurable academic improvement. However, critics of this study evaluation (Vandell, Pierce, and Dadisman, 2005) argued that the control groups had higher preexisting achievement, thus reducing the potential for finding a program impact, and that the small impacts had more to do with lack of full program implementation during the initial years than with the strength of the program.

Overall, these studies documented positive causal effects on the academic performance of students in select extended-day programs, but the evidence is mixed due to both inadequate research methods (few randomized trials) and poor program quality and implementation.

Researchers (e.g., Fashola, 1998; Vandell, Pierce, and Dadisman, 2005) have identified several structural and institutional supports necessary to make extended-day programs effective:

- Staff qualifications and support (staff training in child or adolescent development, after-school programming, elementary or secondary education, and content areas offered in the program; staff expertise; staff stability/turnover; compensation; institutional supports)
- Program/group size and configuration (enrollment size, ages served, group size, age groupings and child–staff ratio)
- Financial resources and budget (dedicated space and facilities that support skill development and mastery, equipment and materials to promote skill development and mastery, curricular resources in relevant content areas, locations that are accessible to youths and families)
- Program partnerships and connections (with schools to connect administrators, teachers, and programs, with larger networks of programs, with parents and community)

- Program sustainability strategies (institutional partners, networks, and linkages; community linkages that support enhanced services; long-term alliances to ensure long-term funding)

We include resources for an extended-day program in all school prototypes. The resources would be used to provide students in elementary and secondary school with additional help—during the school year but after the normal school day—to meet academic performance standards. Because not all poor students will need or attend such a program, we include resources for 50 percent of the adjusted free-and-reduced-price-lunch pupil count, a need and participation figure suggested by a recent study (Kleiner, Nolin, and Chapman, 2004). We suggest providing one teacher position for every 15 eligible students (defined as 50 percent of the adjusted free-and-reduced-price-lunch pupil count) and paid at the rate of 25 percent of the position's annual salary, to offer a $2\frac{1}{2}$-to 3-hour extended-day program five days per week. These resources could be used for a different mix of teachers and other noncertified staff, with teachers providing at least one hour of homework help or after-school tutoring.

Summer School

Because most states have set high standards for student achievement, and many students need extra instructional time to achieve to those standards, summer school programs should also be part of the set of programs giving struggling students the additional time and help to achieve to standards and earn academic promotion from grade to grade (Borman, 2001). Providing additional time to help all students master the same content is an initiative that is grounded in research (National Education Commission on Time and Learning, 1994).

Research dating back to 1906 has shown that students, *on average*, lose a little more than a month's worth of skill or knowledge over the summer break (Cooper, Nye, Charlton, Lindsay, and Greathouse, 1996). Summer breaks have a larger deleterious impact on poor children's reading and mathematics achievement, which falls further over the summer break than does that of middle-class students. This loss can reach as much as one-third of the learning during a regular nine-month school year (Cooper et al., 1996). A longitudinal study, moreover, showed that these family-income-based summer learning differences *accumulated* over the elementary school years, such that poor children's achievement scores—without summer school—fall further and further behind the scores of middle-class students as they progress through school grade by grade (Alexander and Entwisle, 1996). As a result of this research, there is emerging consensus that what happens during the summer can significantly impact the achievement of students from low-income and at-risk backgrounds, and thus influence achievement gaps in the United States (see also Heyns, 1978).

Evidence on the effectiveness of summer programs in attaining either of these goals, however, has typically been skimpy. Although past research linking student achievement to summer programs shows some promise, several studies suffer from methodological shortcomings and the low quality of the summer school programs themselves.

Two reviews (Ascher, 1988; Austin, Roger, and Walbesser, 1972) concluded that summer school programs in elementary mathematics and reading generally produced modest achievement gains, but noted the findings were tentative because none of the evaluations employed random assignment. Austin, Roger, and Walbesser (1972) also stated that few summer programs established clear academic goals that were easily evaluated, and in many cases, funding arrived too late for a full summer program, thus diminishing potential impact. On the other hand, a more recent meta-analysis of 93 summer school programs (Cooper, Charlton, Valentine, and Muhlenbruck, 2000) found that the average student in summer programs outperformed about 56–60 percent of similar students not in the programs. Again, however, the certainty of these conclusions is compromised because only a small number of studies (e.g., Borman, Rachuba, Hewes, Boulay, and Kaplan, 2001) used random assignment, and program quality varied substantially.

Nevertheless, research generally indicates that summer school is needed and can be effective for at-risk students. Studies suggest that the effects of summer school are largest for elementary students when the programs emphasize reading and mathematics, and for high school students when programs focus on courses students failed during the school year. The more modest effects frequently found in middle school programs can be partially explained by the emphasis in many such programs on adolescent development and self-efficacy, rather than academics.

Although Cooper and colleagues' (2000) meta-analysis found that students who participated in summer school outperformed other students, program effects varied significantly because the nature of the programs varied so widely. However, a random sample of 325 students who participated in the Voyager summer school program showed gains in reading achievement, with an effect size of 0.42 (Roberts, 2000). A summer school program that focuses on improving mathematics and reading achievement, and courses failed in high school, would help curtail the pace of achievement loss and help these students learn to state performance standards over time.

Ascher (1988), Austin and colleagues (1972), and Heyns (1978) identified several programmatic characteristics that undercut program impacts and thus produced the modest effects research has documented so far. They include short program duration (sometimes a result of funding delays and late program start dates), loose organization, lack of advanced planning, low *academic* expectations for either mathematics or reading, discontinuity between the summer curriculum and the regular-school-year curriculum, teacher fatigue, and poor student attendance. In their meta-analysis of summer program effects, Cooper and colleagues (2000) noted several program components that are related to improved achievement effects for summer program attendees. These are supported by the recommendations in the most recent book on summer school and ways to enhance its impacts (Borman and Boulay, 2004):

- Early intervention during elementary school
- A full 6- to 8-week summer program
- A clear focus on mathematics and reading achievement, or on failed courses for high school students
- Small-group or individualized instruction

- Parent involvement and participation
- Careful scrutiny for treatment fidelity, including monitoring to ensure good instruction in reading and mathematics
- Monitoring of student attendance

Summer programs that include these elements hold promise for improving the achievement of at-risk students and closing the achievement gap.

Because summer school can produce powerful impacts, all of our school prototypes include a summer school provision for 50 percent of all adjusted free-and-reduced-price-lunch students in grades K–12, an estimate of the number of students still struggling to meet academic requirements (Capizzano, Adelman, and Stagner, 2002). We provide resources for an eight-week, six-hour-a-day program, with class sizes of 15 students. This program allows for four hours of instruction in reading and mathematics, though the specific academic focus could be different for high school students. A six-hour day also allows for two hours of nonacademic activities. The cost of each FTE teacher position is estimated using a stipend equal to 25 percent of his or her annual salary. The 50 percent estimate of at-risk student need should be monitored over time to determine the degree to which it correctly estimates the number of at-risk students who need a summer school program.

In sum, for most at-risk students, the model includes a sequenced set of connected and structured programs that begin in the early elementary grades and continue through the upper elementary, middle, and high school grades. We propose that the most academically deficient at-risk students receive one-to-one tutoring, that the next group receive intensive and explicit instruction in groups of three or five, that students still struggling to meet proficiency standards then receive an extended-day program that includes an academic focus, and that children needing even more help then be offered a summer school program that is structured and focused on academics—reading and mathematics for elementary and middle school students, and failed courses for high school students.

Since the exact combination of services that will bring the vast proportion of at-risk students to a proficiency level is not known at this time, we also suggest that states add accountability and reporting requirements to the receipt of both extended-day and summer school funds. Schools should be required to identify the students who receive any and all of these interventions; data should be kept on their performance when they enter and when they exit the programs; and data on program structure and content should also be reported. In this way, over time, states will be better able to identify what features of each of these interventions is most effective, how much learning gains are produced by the various programs, and also perhaps what sequence of interventions works best for which types of struggling students. In this way, states can both provide resources to meet the needs of struggling students and simultaneously learn how to provide these services more effectively. Without such a reporting requirement, money will be spent, but knowledge about the programs, their design, and their effects will be lost.

Special Education

Providing appropriate special-education services, while containing costs and avoiding over identification of students, particularly minority students, presents several challenges. The chapter appendix provides an overview of the development of programs and funding for students with disabilities.

First, many mild and moderate disabilities, particularly those associated with students learning to read, are substantially correctable through strategic early intervention. For example, several studies (e.g., Landry, 1999) have documented how, through a series of intensive instructional interventions, nearly 75 percent of struggling readers identified in kindergarten and first grade can be brought up to grade level without the need for placement in special education. In many instances, this approach requires that school-level staff change their practice and cease to function in "silos" serving children in "pull-out" programs identified by the funding source of the staff member (e.g., General Fund, Special Education, Title I). Instead, all staff should team closely with the regular classroom teacher to identify deficits and work together to correct them as quickly as possible. This sounds like a commonsense approach that would be second nature to school personnel, but in many cases, they have heretofore been rooted in a "categorical culture" that must be corrected through staff development and strong leadership from the district office and the site principal. Allocating a fixed census amount (about 3.0 FTE positions for a school of about 432 students) would work for mild and moderate disabilities if such a functional, collaborative early-intervention model as outlined above could be implemented. We note that our staffing for the preceding programs for at-risk students meets this requirement—tutoring and ELL.

Second, for more severely handicapped students, large districts sometimes cluster them in specific schools to achieve economies of scale; this approach is often an effective strategy and provides the greatest opportunity to find ways to mainstream them (to the extent feasible) with regular-education students. In sparsely populated areas, this is often not feasible, but it is still at least worth exploring. Students in these categories generally include severely emotionally disturbed (ED), severely mentally and/or physically handicapped, and children within the spectrum of autism. The ED and autism populations have been growing dramatically across the country, and it is likely that this trend will continue. To make the provision of services to these children cost-effective, it makes sense to explore clustering of services where possible and to design cost parameters for clustered services in each category. In cases in which, due to geographic isolation, students need to be served individually or in groups of two or three, it is helpful to price service models for those configurations as well.

Particularly in the case of ED and autism, it is well worth building in the capacity to examine at the state level the service models, their effectiveness, and ways to make them more efficient and effective over time. Research on effective service models is growing in both areas and could provide helpful hints for districts on improving both quality and efficiency of services. For example, recent research on autism strongly indicates that very early intervention after the onset of the condition (usually between 18 months and 3 years) yields far better outcomes than simply starting services when the child enters school. Federal funding supports special-education infant/preschool programs, and the strategic application of these services, coupled with ongoing analysis of school programs, could avert costs down the road. If there is no state capacity to do this, it may be cost-effective for the states to contract for these research/advisory services.

One newer way states have begun to fund special-education services is the "census" approach. The census approach, which can be funded simply by providing additional teacher resources for prototypical schools, assumes that the incidence of these categories of disabilities is approximately equal across districts and schools, and includes resources for providing needed services at an equal rate for all schools and districts. The census approach has emerged across the country for several reasons:

- The continued rise in the numbers and percentages of "learning disabled," and continued questioning by some as to the validity of these numbers
- Underfunding of the costs of severely disabled students
- Overlabeling of poor, minority, and ELL students into special-education categories, which often leads to lower curriculum expectations and inappropriate instructional services
- Reduction of paperwork

Moreover, all current and future increases in federal funding for disabled students are to be distributed on a census basis. As a result, diverse states such as Arkansas, Arizona, California, and Vermont have moved to provide resources for students with mild disabilities through this strategy.

Often, the census approach for the high-incidence, lower-cost students with disabilities is combined with a different strategy for the low-incidence, high-need students, whose costs are funded separately and totally by the state, as these students are not found proportionately in all districts. California approved a census-funding system, in part because many felt that the old system created too many fiscal incentives to identify students as needing special education, and in part to improve the equity of the distribution of state aid for special education. Other reasons included the desire to give the local districts more flexibility while holding them accountable and to create a system that was easy to understand. Today, diverse states such as Alabama, Arkansas, California, Massachusetts, Montana, North Dakota, Pennsylvania, and Vermont all use census-based special-education funding systems.

As with all of the other state-local cost-sharing models, census-based funding has both advantages and disadvantages. The major advantages are all the reasons California decided to adopt it: simplicity, flexibility, equity, and built-in cost controls. The major disadvantage is that the equity depends on the distribution of special-education students across all the districts in a state; if they are concentrated in a few districts, those districts will have to make up the difference between the state aid distributed on the basis of total district enrollment and the actual count of students with special needs. This is an especially important issue with regard to the incidence of students with severe disabilities, who are sometimes extremely expensive to educate.

Another possible disadvantage involves the potential for districts to lose funding under a census-based system. In California, the phase-in process ensured that no district received less aid than under the previous system, but the possibility exists that in the future, some districts may receive less funding under a true census-based system. While this may not result in a true loss of equity, it may be difficult politically to convince school districts if they are receiving less money than the amount to which they were accustomed.

We argue for a census approach to funding special-education services for the high-incidence and lower-cost services for the disabled, and suggest that states reimburse districts for 100 percent of the costs for the severely disabled, minus federal Title VIb funds for such students. For the census funding of special-education teachers, we include three teacher positions for the prototypical 432-student elementary and 450-student middle school, and four positions for the 600-student prototypical high school.[4]

Gifted, Talented, Able, and Ambitious Students[5]

A complete analysis of educational adequacy should include gifted, talented, and able and ambitious students, most of whom perform above state proficiency standards. Indeed, this is important for all states whose citizens desire that all students improve performance at all levels of achievement, not just that they reach a proficiency standard. Research has shown that developing the potential of gifted and talented students requires the following:

- Efforts to discover the hidden talents of low-income and/or culturally diverse students
- Curriculum materials designed specifically to meet the needs of talented learners
- Acceleration of the curriculum
- Special training for teachers

Discovering hidden talents in low-income and/or culturally diverse high-ability learners.   Research studies on the use of performance assessments (Baum, Owen, and Oreck, 1996; VanTassel-Baska, Johnson, and Avery, 2002), nonverbal measures (Naglieri and Ford, 2003; Naglieri and Ronning, 2000), open-ended tasks (Scott, Deuel, Jean-Francois, and Urbano, 1996), extended try-out and transitional periods (Borland and Wright, 1994; Maker, 1996), and inclusive definitions and policies (Gallagher and Coleman, 1992) have documented increased and more equitable identification practices for high-ability culturally diverse and/or low-income learners. However, identification is not sufficient; it must be accompanied by services (Rito and Moller,

[4]Washington State, following research by Chambers, Parrish, and Harr (2002), provides to each district 93 percent of the state's base student funding. If that base amount were adequate, that state's approach would represent a similar way to fund special-education services.

[5]This section is based on an unpublished literature review written by Dr. Ann Robinson, professor, University of Arkansas–Little Rock.

1989). Access to specialized services for talented learners in the elementary years is especially important for increased achievement by at-risk or low-income students. For example, high-ability, culturally diverse learners who participated in three or more years of specialized elementary and/or middle school programming had higher achievement at high school graduation than did a comparable group of high-ability students who did not participate (Struck, 2003). Gains on other measures of school achievement were reported as well.

Access to curriculum.   Overall, research has shown that curriculum programs specifically designed for talented learners produce greater learning than do regular academic programs. Increased complexity in the curricular material is a key factor (Robinson and Clinkenbeard, 1998). Large-scale curriculum projects in science and mathematics in the 1960s, such as the Biological Sciences Curriculum Study (BCSC), the Physical Science Study Committee (PSSC), and the Chemical Bond Approach (CBA), benefited academically talented learners (Gallagher, 2002). Further, curriculum projects in the 1990s designed to increase the achievement of talented learners in core content areas such as language arts, science, and social studies produced academic gains in persuasive writing and literary analysis (VanTassel-Baska, Johnson, Hughes, and Boyce, 1996; VanTassell-Baska, Zuo, Avery, and Little, 2002), scientific understanding of variables (VanTassel-Baska, Bass, Ries, Poland, and Avery, 1998), and problem generation and social studies content acquisition (Gallagher and Stepien, 1996; Gallagher, Stepien, and Rosenthal, 1992).

Access to acceleration.   Because academically talented students learn quickly, one effective option for serving them is acceleration of the curriculum. Many educators and members of the general public believe that acceleration always means skipping a grade. However, there are at least 17 different types of acceleration ranging from curriculum compacting (which reduces the amount of time students spend on material they already know) to subject matter acceleration (going to a higher grade level for one class) to high school course options like advanced placement (AP) or concurrent credit (Southern, Jones, and Stanley, 1993). In some cases, acceleration means *content* acceleration, which brings more complex material to the student at his or her current grade level. In other cases, acceleration means *student* acceleration, which brings the student to the material by shifting placement. Reviews of the research on different forms of acceleration have been conducted across several decades and consistently report the positive effects of acceleration on student achievement (Kulik and Kulik, 1984; Southern, Jones, and Stanley, 1993), including AP classes (Bleske-Rechek, Lubinski, and Benbow, 2004). Other studies report participant satisfaction with acceleration (Swiatek, 2002) and benign effects on social and psychological development (Rogers, 2002).

Access to trained teachers.   Research and teacher reports indicate that general classroom teachers make very few, if any, modifications for academically talented learners (Archambault et al., 1993; Westberg, Archambault, Dobyns, and Salvin, 1993), even though talented students have mastered 40–50 percent of the elementary curriculum before the school year begins (Reis et al., 1993). In contrast, teachers who receive appropriate training are more likely to provide classroom instruction that meets the needs of talented learners; students report differences, and independent observers in the classroom document them (Hansen and Feldhusen, 1994). Curriculum and instructional adaptation requires the support of a specially trained coach at the building level, who could be embedded in the instructional facilities discussed above (Reis et al., 1993; Reis and Purcell, 1993). Overall, learning outcomes for high-ability learners are increased when they have access to programs whose staff have specialized training (Delcourt, Loyd, Cornell, and Golderberg, 1994), which could be accomplished with the professional development resources provided below.

Research on gifted programs has shown that the effects on student achievement vary by type of intervention. Enriched classes for gifted and talented students produce effect sizes of about 0.40, and accelerated classes for these learners produce somewhat larger effect sizes of 0.90 (Gallagher, 1995; Kulik and Kulik, 1984, 1992).

Program and policy implications.   In serving gifted and talented students at the elementary and middle school level, the best practice is to place them in special classes and to accelerate their instruction because such students can learn much more in a given time period than can other students. When the pull-out-and-acceleration approach is not possible, an alternative is to have these students skip grades in order to be exposed to accelerated instruction. Despite anecdotal claims to the contrary, research has shown that neither of these practices results in social adjustment problems; indeed, many gifted students become bored and restless in classrooms that do not have accelerated instruction. Both of these strategies have little or no cost, except for scheduling and training of teachers.

The primary approach to serving gifted students in high schools is to enroll them in advanced courses AP or IB [international baccalaureate], to participate in dual enrollment in postsecondary institutions, or to have them take courses through distance-learning mechanisms.

We have sought to confirm our understanding of best practices for the gifted and talented by contacting directors of three of the gifted and talented research centers in the United States: Dr. Elissa Brown, of the Center for Gifted Education, College of William and Mary; Dr. Joseph Renzulli, of the National Research Center on the Gifted and Talented at the University of Connecticut; and Dr. Ann Robinson, of the Center for Gifted Education at the University of Arkansas–Little Rock.

When contacted in late 2005, the College of William and Mary center was in the midst of developing a literature and best-practices review, together with an analysis of effect sizes of various approaches to serving the gifted and talented, and their relative costs. Their analysis, not yet published, showed that effect sizes for placing students into homogeneous classes of gifted students and accelerating instruction, as well as grade skipping, were between 0.5 and 1.0. Their analyses further showed that neither approach produced negative social or emotional impacts for students, and often actually enhanced social and emotional adjustment. In addition, they ranked these approaches in terms of impact and cost. Their analysis showed that enrichment programs, in which staff worked with gifted students in smaller groups, could have nearly the same high-level effects but were more costly. Thus, they ranked enrichment approaches as high-impact and medium-cost, while the accelerated-class and grade-skipping approaches were ranked as high-impact and low-cost.

Ann Robinson of the University of Arkansas center agreed with these findings, as did the University of Connecticut center. The latter has also developed a very powerful Internet-based platform, Renzulli Learning, which provides a wide range of programs and services for gifted and talented students. This system takes students through a 25- to 30-minute detailed assessment of their interests and abilities, which produces an individual profile. The student is then directed, via a search engine, to 14 different Internet data systems, including interactive websites and simulations that provide a wide range of opportunities to engage her or his interests. Such an approach may be the future for the very bright student.

Career and Technical Education

Vocational education, or in modern parlance, career and technical education, has been experiencing a shift in its focus for the past several years. Traditional vocational education focused on practical, applied skills such as those needed for wood- and metalworking, automobile mechanics, typing and other office assistance careers, and "home economics." Today, many argue that voc-tech is info-tech, nano-tech, bio-tech, and health-tech. The argument is that career-technical education should begin aggressively to incorporate courses that still teach applied skills, but for employment in the growing, higher-wage economy that includes information technologies (such as computer network management), engineering (such as computer-assisted design), health care, and bio-technology positions. All of these careers can be entered directly from high school. Indeed, the American College Testing company (2004) recently reported that the knowledge, skills, and competencies needed for college and for work in these higher-wage jobs in the evolving economy are quite similar.

In a paper prepared for a Wisconsin school finance adequacy task force, a national expert on career and technical education made the same argument (Phelps, 2006). Further, Phelps implied that designing such applied career–technical education courses would not require any additional funding; the major task would be to redesign a mathematics course so that it covered, for example, the knowledge and skills for an algebra trigonometry class but in an applied, engineering format. The same would be true for biology and health science courses for jobs in the bio-tech and health care areas.

Though these positions can be challenged—both the new focus of career–technical education and the claim for no extra costs—they are gaining currency across the country. Even in schools and districts that provide additional resources, the approach can be to weight FTE career–technical education students an additional 0.3 for smaller class sizes, and to provide a sum of money, approximately $7,000, for every teacher of career–technical education (Odden, Picus, Goetz et al., 2005).

5. ADDITIONAL STAFFING AND RESOURCE NEEDS

This section completes the identification of resources needed for the prototypical schools: substitute teachers, pupil support personnel, librarians, aides, and administrators, as well as professional development, technology and equipment, and instructional materials.

Substitute Teachers

Traditionally, specific provisions for substitute teachers have not been included in any state's school finance formula. States with new, adequacy-based systems, however, have begun to explicitly include these resources. Schools need some level of substitute teacher allocations in order to cover classrooms when teachers are sick for one or two days, absent for other reasons, or on long-term sick or pregnancy leave. A good approximation of the substitute teacher resources needed is to add 5 percent of teachers to all teacher positions discussed in previous sections, or 10 days for each teacher.

Student Support/Family Outreach

Schools need a student support and family outreach strategy. Various comprehensive school designs have suggested different ways to provide such a program strategy (Stringfield, Ross, and Smith, 1996; for further discussion, see Brabeck, Walsh, and Latta, 2003). In terms of level of resources, the more disadvantaged the student body, the more comprehensive the strategy needs to be. The general standard is one licensed professional for every 100 students from a low-income background, with a minimum of one for each prototypical school.

Although schools can provide outreach to parents or involve parents in school activities in many ways—from fund-raisers to governance—research has shown that school-sponsored activities that impact achievement address what parents can do *at home* to help their children learn. For example, if the education system has clear content and performance standards, helping parents and students understand both what needs to be learned and what constitutes acceptable standards for academic performance is helpful. Put succinctly, parent outreach that explicitly and directly addresses what parents can do to help their children learn and to understand the standards of performance that the school expects are the types of school-sponsored parent activities that produce discernible impacts on students' academic learning (Steinberg, 1997).

At the secondary level, the goal of such activities should be to have parents learn about what they should expect of their children in terms of their academic performance. For example, if a district or a state requires a minimum number of courses for graduation, that requirement should be made explicit. Further, if there are similar or more extensive course requirements for admission into state colleges and universities, those requirements should be addressed. Finally, if either average scores on end-of-course examinations or a passing score on a comprehensive high school test is required for graduation, they should be discussed as well. The key point is that secondary schools need to help many parents know how to more effectively assist their children in determining an academic pathway through middle and high school, standards for acceptable performance, and, at the high school level, an understanding of the coursework necessary for college entrance.

At the elementary school level, parent outreach and involvement programs should concentrate on what parents can do at home to help their children learn academic material. Too often, parent programs focus on fund-raising through the parent–teacher organization, involvement in decision making through school site councils, or other nonacademically focused activities at the school site. Although these school-sponsored parent activities might impact other goals—such as making parents feel more comfortable being at school or involving parents more in some school policies—they have little effect on student academic achievement. Parent actions that impact children's learning include (1) reading to them at young ages, (2) discussing stories and their meanings, (3) engaging in open-ended conversations, (4) setting aside a place where homework can be done, and (5) ensuring that homework assignments are completed.

In addition, middle and high schools need some level of guidance counselor resources. Our model uses the standards from the American School Counselor Association (ASCA), which is one counselor for every 250 secondary students.

Our model also provides one teacher-level position for every 100 students eligible for free or reduced-price lunch, with a minimum of one for each of the prototypical schools (432-student elementary, 450-student middle, and 600-student high school). In addition, we provide an additional 1.8 and 2.4 guidance counselor positions in the prototypical middle and high schools, respectively, based on the ASCA standards.

This model enables districts and schools to allocate FTE staff as guidance counselors, nurses, and social workers in a way that best addresses such needs from the perspective of each district and school.

Note that this model provides substantial resources for parental outreach and involvement, as well as counseling for students. For an all-poverty school, our model provides 4.3 staff positions for an elementary school of 432 students (so it can have a nurse, counselor, social worker, and parent liaison), and the same staff plus 1.8 additional counselors at the middle school level and 6.0 positions plus an additional 2.4 counselors for the high school.

These resources are adequate to create and deploy the ambitious and comprehensive parent involvement and outreach programs that are part of two comprehensive school designs: (1) Roots and Wings/Success for all and (2) the Comer School Development Program. The Roots and Wings program includes a family outreach coordinator, nurse, social worker, guidance counselor, and education diagnostician. This group functions as a parent outreach team for the school, serves as case managers for students who need nonacademic and social services, and usually also includes a clothing strategy to ensure that all students, especially in cold climates, have adequate clothes and coats.

The Comer program is based on the premise of integrating schools more fully in their communities. Its parent–school team has a somewhat different composition and is focused on training parents to raise expectations for their children's learning, to work with social service agencies and even to colocate social services on school site premises, and to work with faculty to raise their expectations for what students can learn.

All effective parent outreach programs should have several workshops training parents specifically on what they can do at home to help their children learn.

Aides

Elementary, middle, and high schools need staff for such responsibilities as lunch duty, before- and after-school playground supervision, and school bus monitoring. Covering these duties generally requires an allocation of *supervisory* aides at the rate of about 2.0 FTE positions for a school of 400–500 students.

But the research is not supportive of *instructional* aides. As noted above, the Tennessee STAR study, which produced solid evidence through field-based randomized trails that small classes work in elementary schools, also produced evidence that instructional aides in schools do *not* add value (i.e., do not positively impact student academic achievement (Achilles, 1999; Gerber, Finn, Achilles, and Boyd-Zaharias, 2001).

At the same time, districts may want to consider a possible use of instructional aides that is supported by research. Two studies suggest how instructional aides could be used effectively to tutor students. Farkas (1998) showed that if aides are selected according to clear and rigorous literacy criteria, are trained in a specific reading-tutoring program, provide individual tutoring to students in reading, and are supervised, they can have a significant impact on student reading attainment. Some districts have used Farkas-type tutors for students still struggling with reading in the upper elementary grades. A recent study by Miller (2003) showed that such aides could also have an impact on reading achievement if used to provide individual tutoring to struggling students in the first grade.

Evidence suggests that instructional aides can have an impact, but only if they are selected according to certain educational criteria, trained in a specific tutoring program, deployed to provide tutoring to struggling students, and closely supervised.

We include in our prototypical schools 2.0 FTE aide positions for the elementary and middle schools, and 3.0 FTE aide positions for the high school, to be used to relieve teachers from lunchroom, playground, and other nonteaching responsibilities.

A school or district could decide to use resources, including some of those targeted for at-risk students, for instructional aids. These resources are provided in the school finance equalization formula for Farkas-type reading tutors, but to be effective, they would need to follow his suggestions for training, focus, and supervision.

Librarians

Most schools have or should have a library, and the staff resources must be sufficient to operate the library and to incorporate appropriate technologies into the library system. Further, some elementary librarians could teach students for some of the day as part of special subject offerings.

Our staffing for each prototypical school includes a librarian, and, for the high school, a library media technician.

The Principal

Every school unit needs a principal. There is no research evidence on the performance of schools with or without a principal. The fact is that essentially all schools in America, if not the world, have a principal. All comprehensive school designs, and all prototypical school designs from all professional judgment studies around the country include a principal for every school unit. However, few if any comprehensive school designs include assistant principal positions. And very few school systems around the country provide assistant principals to schools with 500 students or less. Since the evidence suggests that instead of one school with a large number of students, school buildings with large numbers of students should be subdivided into multiple school units within the building, we provide each unit with a principal. Further, if the school finance system is based on school-by-school resources, we provide a full-time principal for every elementary school unit down to 108 students and a principal for every middle and high school unit down to 150 students. For schools larger than the 432-, 450-, and 600-student prototypes, we prorate up from the 1.0 position. For elementary schools with fewer than 108 students and middle and high schools with fewer than 150 students, principal positions are prorated down by pupil counts.

School buildings with two or more school unit principals could organize themselves so that there was one "superordinate" principal in charge. Larger schools with several schools-within-school could field combined athletic teams.

In our experience across the country, many districts and states argue that the high school should also have an assistant principal, responsible for discipline and sports activities. Our model provides more instructional coaches than are found in most schools, so it does not include this additional administrative position. But states and districts could certainly add the position.

In sum, the prototypical elementary and middle school leadership team consists of the principal and 2.3 instructional coach positions, and the high school leadership team consists of the principal and 3.0 instructional coaches. Schools could organize this leadership team differently, according to their needs and administrative philosophies.

The importance of instructional leadership.   The key role of a school's principal and the importance of instructional leadership are uniformly accepted, but the nature of principal leadership and its impact on instructional practice are only partially understood (Hallinger and Heck, 1996). Most researchers and policymakers agree that principals play important roles in schools' success (Hallinger and Heck, 1996). This is particularly true for restructuring schools, an assumed need for all schools applying this model, and for enabling and supporting teacher success (Murphy, 1994).

Although studies have found that principal leadership alone may account for a significant portion of the variation in student test scores among schools, principals generally have little or no *direct* effect on student achievement. Instead, principals influence school success through indirect means (Hallinger and Heck, 1996, 2002, 2003). In particular, it is the principal's influence on a school's instructional climate and organization that is crucial, especially for high schools (Murphy, Beck, Crawford, Hodges, and McGaughy,

2001). Principals influence the learning climate within which a school's teachers work in several ways:

- Establishing clear instructional goals
- Providing programmatic coherence
- Communicating relevant information, including best practices, to teaching staff
- Establishing accountability for student learning
- Fostering collaboration and building professional community
- Maintaining student discipline (Bossert, Dwyer, Rowan, and Lee, 1982)

They also support the professional growth of individual teachers through direct classroom supervision, including teacher observation and feedback, and creating professional development opportunities (Hallinger and Heck, 1996, 2002, 2003; Heck, Larsen, and Marcoulides, 1990).

One of the most important aspects of principal instructional leadership is creating a professional community within schools (Halverson, 2003). Establishing a professional community has been shown to increase both the intellectual quality of instruction and the overall level and distribution of student achievement by strengthening the instructional capacity and focus of schools (Louis and Marks, 1998; Newmann and Wehlage, 1995). Newmann and Wehlage (1995) describe a professional community as possessing three general traits, in which teachers do the following:

1. Pursue a shared sense of purpose for student learning
2. Engage in collaborative activities to achieve this purpose
3. Take collective responsibility for student learning

Others have identified deprivatization of practice and reflective dialogue as additional elements of a professional community (Louis, Kruse, and Marks, 1996; Louis and Marks, 1998; Louis, Marks, and Kruse, 1996).

A "shared sense of purpose" refers to a consensus among school staff as to the mission and principles by which the school operates. "Collaborative activity" describes the extent to which teachers engage in cooperative practices to achieve the school's goals. "Collective responsibility" refers to the degree to which all teachers share responsibility for the academic success of all students. "Deprivatization of practice" refers to the practice of teachers interacting professionally—for example, observing and providing feedback on each others' teaching. "Reflective dialogue" refers to the professional conversation teachers have about specific issues of instructional practice (Louis and Marks, 1998).

In short, a school's instructional team is critical to its success in producing high levels of student achievement. Principals provide instructional leadership by (1) creating professional communities in which teachers offer considerable instructional leadership (see also Spillane, Halverson, and Diamond, 2001), (2) creating professional development opportunities for teachers, (3) signaling that instructional improvement and student achievement are core goals, and (4) helping the school as a whole take responsibility for student achievement increases or decreases while also managing the noninstructional aspects of the school.

School Site Secretarial Staff

Every school site needs secretarial support to provide clerical and administrative assistance to administrators and teachers, answer the telephone, greet parents when they visit the school, help with paperwork, and perform other tasks essential to the operation of a school site.

The prototypical elementary and middle schools include two secretary positions, and the prototypical high school includes three secretary positions.[6]

Intensive Professional Development[7]

All school faculties need ongoing professional development. Indeed, improving teacher effectiveness through high-quality professional development is arguably as important as all of the other resource strategies identified; better instruction is the key to improving student learning (Rowan, Correnti, and Miller, 2002; Sanders and Horn, 1994; Sanders and Rivers, 1996; Webster, Mendro, Orsak, and Weerasinghe, 1998).

Moreover, all the resources included in this model need to be transformed into high-quality instruction in order to increase student learning (Cohen, Raudenbush, and Ball, 2002). And effective professional development is the primary way those resources get transformed into effective and productive instructional practices. Further, as we have stated many times, while the key focus of professional development is for better instruction in the core subjects of mathematics, reading/language arts, history, and science, the professional development resources are adequate to address the instructional needs of gifted and talented and ELL students, to embed technology in the curriculum, and to serve administrators as well. Finally, all beginning teachers need intensive professional development, first in classroom management, organization, and discipline, and then in instruction.

Fortunately, there is recent and substantial research on effective professional development and its costs (see, e.g., Elmore, 2002; Joyce and Showers, 2002; Miles, Odden, Fermanich, and Archibald, 2004). Effective professional development is defined as development that produces change in teachers' classroom-based instructional practice that can be linked to improvements in student learning. The practices and principles researchers and organizations use to characterize "high-quality" or "effective" professional development draw upon a series of empirical research studies that linked program strategies to changes in teachers' instructional practice and subsequent increases in student achievement. These studies include, among others, the long-term efforts

---

[6]The distinction between the senior secretary and clerk/typist is that a senior secretary would be a 12-month position, and the clerk/typist a 9-month position.
[7]This section draws from Odden, Archibald, Fermanich, and Gallagher, 2002.

of Bruce Joyce (Joyce and Calhoun, 1996; Joyce and Showers, 2002), research on the change process (Fullan, 2001), a longitudinal analysis of efforts to improve mathematics in California (Cohen and Hill, 2001), a study of District 2 in New York City (Elmore and Burney, 1999), the Consortium for Policy Research in Education's longitudinal study of sustained professional development provided by the Merck Institute for Science Education (Supovitz and Turner, 2000), studies of comprehensive professional development to improve science teaching and learning (Loucks-Horsley, Love, Stiles, Mundry, and Hewsen, 2003), and an evaluation of the federal Eisenhower mathematics and science professional development program (Garet, Birman, Porter, Desimone, and Herman, 1999).

Collectively, These studies identified several structural features of effective professional development:

- The *form* of the activity—that is, whether the activity is organized as a study group, teacher network, mentoring collaborative, committee, or curriculum development group. The above research suggests that effective professional development should be school-based, job-embedded, and focused on the curriculum taught rather than a one-day workshop.
- The *duration* of the activity, including the total number of contact hours that participants are expected to spend in the activity, and the span of time over which the activity takes place. The above research has shown the importance of continuous, ongoing, long-term professional development that totals at least 100 hours each year, and ideally closer to 200 hours.
- The degree to which the activity emphasizes the *collective participation* of teachers from the same school, department, or grade level. The above research suggests that effective professional development should be organized around groups of teachers from a school that over time includes the entire faculty (see, e.g., Garet, Birman, Porter, Desimone, and Herman, 1999).
- The degree to which the activity has a *content focus*—that is, the degree to which it is focused on improving and deepening teachers' content knowledge, as well as how students learn that content. The above research concludes that teachers need to have thorough knowledge of the content they teach and to be aware of common student miscues or problems students typically have learning that content, and effective instructional strategies linking the two (Bransford, Brown, and Cocking, 1999).
- The extent to which the activity offers opportunities for *active learning*, such as opportunities for teachers to become engaged in the meaningful analysis of teaching and learning—for example, by scoring student work or developing and refining a standards-based curriculum unit. The above research has shown that professional development is most effective when it includes opportunities for teachers to work directly on incorporating the new techniques into their instructional practice (see, e.g., Joyce and Showers, 2002).
- The degree to which the activity promotes *coherence* in teachers' professional development, by aligning professional development to other key parts of the

education system such as student content and performance standards, teacher evaluation, school and district goals, and the development of a professional community. The above research supports tying professional development to a comprehensive, interrelated change process focused on improving student learning.

Form, duration, and active learning together imply that effective professional development includes some initial learning (e.g., a two-week [10-day] summer training institute), as well as considerable longer-term work in which teachers incorporate the new methodologies into their classroom practices. Active learning implies some degree of coaching during regular school hours to help teaches incorporate new strategies in to their normal instructional practices. Clearly the longer the duration, and the more extensive the coaching, the more time is required of teachers and of professional development trainers and coaches. Content focus means that effective professional development focuses largely on subject matter knowledge, what is known about how students learn that subject, and the actual curriculum that is used in the school to teach this content. Collective participation implies that the best professional development includes groups of, and at some point all, teachers in a school, who then work together to implement the new strategies and, in the process, help build a professional school community. Coherence suggests that the professional development is more effective when the signals from the policy environment (federal, state, district, school) reinforce rather than contradict one another or send multiple, confusing messages. Coherence also implies that professional development opportunities should be a part of implementation of new curriculum and instructional approaches. Note that there is little support in this research for the development of individually oriented professional development plans; the research implies a much more systemic, all-teachers-in-the-school approach.

Each of these structural features has cost implications. Form, duration, collective participation, and active learning require various amounts of both teacher and trainer/coach/mentor time, during the regular school day and year and, depending on the specific strategies, outside of the regular day and year as well. This time costs money. Further, all professional development strategies require some amount of administration, materials and supplies, and miscellaneous financial support for travel and fees.

From this research on the features of effective professional development, we conclude that the resources needed to deploy this kind of professional development, which is key to transforming all the resources from the model into student learning, are as follows:

- *Time during the summer* for intensive training institutes. This training can most easily be accomplished by ensuring that approximately 10 days of the teacher's normal work year will be dedicated to professional development. Because these days exist in few teacher contracts, our pricing strategy augments the average teacher salary by an additional 10 days, calculated by dividing the initial average salary by 200 days to determine the daily rate, and then adding the product of that amount times 10 to the average. This ensures the minimum number of 10 days for intensive training.

- *On-site coaching* for all teachers to help them incorporate the practices into their instructional repertoire. The instructional facilitators described above provide this function.
- *Collaborative work* with teachers in their schools during planning and preparation periods to improve the curriculum and instructional program, thus reinforcing the strategic and instrumental need for planning and preparation time during the regular school day. This requires smart scheduling of teachers during the regular school day and week.
- *Funds* for training during the summer and for ongoing training during the school year, the cost of which is approximately $100 per pupil. This would provide $43,200 for the prototypical elementary school, $45,000 for the prototypical middle school, and $60,000 for the prototypical high school.

These resources should be adequate for all professional development needs of all teachers over time.

Technology and Equipment

Over time, schools need to embed technology in instructional programs and school management strategies. Although the use of technology in schools may seem vital to most, the effect it produces depends on how it is used and what training is provided for that use. Research has identified four areas in which education technology can benefit students: (1) student preparation to enter the workforce or higher education, (2) student motivation, (3) student learning or increased academic achievement, and (4) teacher/student/administrator access to resources (Earle, 2002).

Student preparation. Student preparation for higher education or the workforce includes technology literacy and the ability of students to find, sift, manipulate, and communicate information using the latest software. Government organizations, both within and outside education, view technology use in schools as workforce preparation. In 1991, the (Labor) Secretary's Commission on Achieving Necessary Skills (SCANS) issued a report that underscored the need for students to be able to select technical equipment and tools, apply technology to specific tasks, and maintain and troubleshoot computers. The 21st Century Workforce Commission (U.S. Department of Labor, 2000) called for students to have technological proficiency to compete in a "highly skilled" workforce. Dede (2000a, 2000b) echoed this view in an article written for the Council of Chief State School Officers emphasizing the importance of informational and technical literacy. Gilster (2000) argued that technology skills go beyond informational and technical literacy, encompassing what he calls "digital literacy." Most recently, the National Education Technology Plan released by the U.S. Department of Education (2004, p. 6) emphasized the need "to help secure our economic future by ensuring that our young people are adequately prepared to meet these challenges [competition in the global economy]."

Student motivation.   Aspects of increased student motivation include improvements in student attitudes toward schoolwork, time on task, quality of work, and/or attendance. Becker (2000) found that teachers who structure the right type of assignments using technology motivate students to spend more time on them. Teaching methods that encourage students to create their own learning path, a "natural" for good technology (think of the popularity of many complex computer games), produce more excitement than drill-and-practice types of activities (Becker, 2000; Lewis, 2002; Valdez et al., 2000).

Student achievement.   The third potential impact of technology is increased student achievement. There are mixed findings on the impact of technology on student achievement (Archer, 2000; Earle, 2002; Kulik, 1994, 2003). Many studies are based on small cases, evidence in several studies is anecdotal, too many programs are of short duration and not tested through replication, and many studies lack appropriate control groups. But several recent reviews of studies offer useful information. The Milken Family Foundation (1999) reviewed five large-scale studies of the impact of education technology on student achievement: (1) the 1994 Kulik study, (2) Sivin-Kachala's (1998) research review, (3) Apple Classrooms of Tomorrow (ACOT) (1994), (4) West Virginia's Basic Skills/Computer Education (BS/CE) Statewide Initiative (1999), and (5) Wenglinsky's National Study of Technology's Impact on Mathematics Achievement (1997). Positive effects were found in all of these studies, but all had caveats as well. For example, in the Wenglinsky study, eighth-grade students using computer simulations had measurable gains in mathematics scores, but only if the computers were used correctly and teachers had been trained in, and implemented correctly, proper teaching techniques. The ACOT study showed measurable gains in student *attitude* but no measurable increases in *learning*. And, in the West Virginia study, scores on the Stanford 9 for fifth-graders increased, but it is not clear if technology was the sole cause of the gains.

In one of the most recent meta-analyses of the impact of specific technology programs, Kulik (2003) found that "integrated learning systems" (i.e., programs tailored to individual students with ongoing diagnoses and feedback) had average effects of 0.38 in mathematics but much lower effects (0.06) in reading, although the effects were higher for the Jostens program (now known as Compass Learning)—0.37 in reading and 0.22 in mathematics. For all programs, the effect gets larger as the students spend more time on them and work in structured pairs. Word processing also has significant and positive effects on students' writing proficiency (Bangert-Drowns, 1993; Cochrane-Smith, 1991). Though more work is needed on designing strategies for integrating computer technologies into instruction, the emerging research suggests that, when used effectively, doing so can have significant positive impacts on student learning.

Other research has yielded more optimistic findings about the impact of technology on student achievement—specifically, a positive impact on student test scores in curriculum programs that embed technology into the instructional delivery system. The reviews documented effect sizes from 0.30 (Waxman, Connell, and Gray, 2002) to 0.38 of a standard deviation improvement in test scores (Murphy et al., 2002), thus approximating the effects of class size reduction in the early grades.

Student/teacher/administrator resources.   Finally, education technology has opened schools and their students to a world of resources that can be explored and manipulated. The Internet affords access to information, communication, opinions, simulations, current events, and academic coursework that were formerly inaccessible or delayed. Networks allow districts to communicate and share data with their schools with the purpose of increasing student achievement.

Computers and software also have increased importance as an administrative tool. As the demands of NCLB legislation intensify, schools have begun to rely on data as a means to achieving instructional excellence through gap analysis of student benchmark tests. Student administration systems and other programs that collect and analyze student data and assist administrators and teachers in interpreting the data more efficiently have become common. Edusoft, Renaissance Learning, Scantron, and other vendors provide such analytical tools. As these programs become more complex, their initial and ongoing direct and indirect costs will continue to increase.

In sum, although the evidence is somewhat mixed, technology, if used correctly, is important for preparing students for both postsecondary education and the workforce, can increase student motivation to learn, positively impacts student achievement, and opens a new world for schools and their students.

Associated costs.   In terms of identifying the costs of purchasing and embedding technology into the operation of schools, significant advances have been made in the past decade (COSN, 2004). One concept that has emerged is the total cost of ownership (TCO). TCO is a type of calculation designed to help policymakers and administrators assess both the direct and indirect costs of technology. The *direct* costs of technology include hardware, software, and direct labor costs. Direct labor refers to those individuals who are specifically hired by the district to repair, update, and maintain instructional technology. *Indirect* costs include the costs of users supporting each other, time spent in training classes, casual learning, self-support, user application development, and downtime costs (COSN, 2004).

TCO can vary greatly depending on the district context, including the age of equipment, and the level to which the district makes education technology an integral part of its instructional and management strategies. Eight case studies conducted by COSN and the Gartner Group (2004) in various states and in urban, suburban, and rural school districts found that total direct annual costs varied from a low of $385 per pupil in a rural district to a high of $1,242 per pupil in a suburban district, with a median of about $750. But these numbers included both direct and indirect costs.

Although a total per-pupil figure in the TCO model is useful, we separate direct labor costs from direct technology costs and have incorporated the training costs into our professional development provisions, so we mainly need to identify the direct costs of purchasing, upgrading, and maintaining computer technology hardware and software. In studies conducted by several states and several professional judgment studies of this narrower aspect of technology costs, the annual costs per student are about $250 for the purchase, update, and maintenance of hardware and software (Odden, 1997a; Odden, Fermanich, and Picus, 2003). This figure is almost exactly what the average direct costs would be for the eight TCO case studies (COSN, 2004) reported above and adjusted to provide a one-to-three student-to-computer ratio.

The $250-per-pupil figure would be sufficient to purchase, upgrade, and maintain computers, servers, operating systems and productivity software, network equipment, and student administrative system and financial systems software, as well as other equipment such as copiers. Systems software packages vary dramatically in price, but this figure would cover medium-priced student administrative and financial systems software packages.

The $250 per pupil would also allow a school to have an overall ratio of one computer for every two to three students. For clarity, a one-to-three ratio would be sufficient to provide every teacher, the principal, and other key school-level staff with a computer, and to have an actual ratio of about one computer for every four students in each classroom. This level of funding would also allow for the technology needed for schools to access distance-learning programs and for students to access the new and evolving local web-based testing programs. Fortunately, most states have developed a substantial technology infrastructure over the years, so nearly all schools in America are linked to the Internet and to district offices and/or a state network. This allocation would be sufficient for small schools as well, particularly today when schools begin with some technology.

Further, we suggest that districts either incorporate maintenance costs in lease agreements or, if purchasing the equipment, buy 24-hour maintenance plans, to eliminate the need for school or district staff to fix computers. For example, for a very modest amount, one can purchase a maintenance agreement from a number of computer manufacturers that guarantees computer repair on a next-business-day basis. Regarding educator concerns that it would be difficult for a manufacturer's contractors to serve remote communities, the maintenance agreement makes that the manufacturer's or contractor's problem, and not the district's. Indeed, these companies often bring a new computer with them, leave it, and take the broken computer to fix, which can be more cost-effective than sending technicians to fix broken computers.[8]

Instructional Materials

The need for current, up-to-date instructional materials is paramount. Newer materials contain more accurate information and incorporate the most contemporary pedagogical approaches. To ensure that materials are current, 20 states have instituted adoption cycles in which they specify or recommend texts that are aligned to state learning standards (Ravitch, 2004). Many states that adopt textbooks encourage districts to purchase recommended texts by requiring that funds specified for instructional materials be used only to purchase approved texts. Other states, like Washington, allow districts local control to purchase texts approved by the local school board.

Up-to-date instructional materials are expensive but vital to the learning process. Researchers estimate that up to 90 percent of classroom activities are driven

---

[8]A more detailed analysis of technology costs that reaches the same $250-per-pupil conclusion can be found in Odden, Picus, Goetz, and Fermanich, 2006.

by textbooks and textbook content (Ravitch, 2004). Adoption cycles with state funding attached force districts to upgrade their texts rather allow these expenditures to be postponed indefinitely.

The type and cost of textbooks and other instructional materials differ across elementary, middle, and high school levels. Textbooks are more complex and thus more expensive at the upper grades, and less expensive at the elementary level. Elementary grades, on the other hand, use more workbooks, worksheets, and other consumables than do the upper grades. Both elementary and upper grades require extensive pedagogical aides, such as math manipulatives and science supplies, that help teachers to demonstrate or present concepts. As school budgets for instructional supplies have tightened in the past, consumables and pedagogical aides have typically been the first items to be cut, with teachers forced to make do or to purchase materials out of their own pockets.

The price of textbooks ranges widely. In reviewing the price of adopted materials in California, Texas, and Florida, certain patterns emerge creating price bands (see Table 4.1). Although there are texts with prices that lie outside of these bands, most publishers seem to stay within or close to these constraints. The top end of the high school price band is notable at $120 per book. Ten to 15 years ago, such prices for textbooks at the high school level were uncommon, but as more students have taken AP courses, districts have been forced to purchase more college-level texts, at college-level prices.

The subtotal for textbooks and consumables does not need to be adjusted for the size of school or school district because it is assumed that costs for adopted textbooks are negotiated at the state level. Additionally, the total figure provides sufficient funds for adequate instructional materials and texts for most nonsevere special-education students. Modifications for severe special-education cases need to be funded from special-education funds.

Adoption cycle.   The assumption of the purchase of one textbook per student annually allows for a six-year adoption cycle (see Table 4.2). The six-year adoption cycle fits nicely with the assumption of a secondary pupil's schedule of six courses in a six-period day. It also comes close to matching the content areas covered at the elementary level.

At the elementary level, there are fewer subject areas to be covered, creating an opportunity for a sixth year in the cycle to be used for purchasing not only additional supplementary texts but also consumables/pedagogical aides (see Table 4.3.)

TABLE 4.1   Costs of Textbooks and Instructional Supplies by School Level (in annual dollars per pupil)

Item	Elementary School	Middle School	High School
Textbooks	$45–70 ($60)	$50–80 ($70)	$75–120 ($100)
Consumables and pedagogical aides	60	50	50
Total	120	120	150

TABLE 4.2   Potential Secondary Six-Year Adoption Cycle

	2006	*2007*	*2008*	*2009*	*2010*	*2011*
Content area	Science Health P.E.	Social studies	Foreign language	Fine arts	English language arts	Mathematics

TABLE 4.3   Potential Elementary Six-Year Adoption Cycle

	2006	*2007*	*2008*	*2009*	*2010*	*2011*
Content area	Language arts	Mathematics	Social studies	Science/ health	P.E. Visual and performing arts	Supplements Consumables Manipulatives

Library funds.   The average national per-pupil expenditure for library materials in the 1999–2000 school year was $15 (excluding library salaries). This average varied by region, with western states spending $14 per pupil annually, eastern states spending $19, and states in the north central region spending $16. About 40 percent of the total was used to purchase books and the remainder was spent on other instructional materials and/or services, such as subscriptions to electronic databases (Michie and Holton, 2005).

As the world shifts to more digital resources, libraries are purchasing or using electronic databases such as online catalogues, the Internet, reference and bibliography databases, general-article and news databases, college and career databases, academic subject databases, and electronic full-text books. In 2002, 25 percent of school libraries across the nation had no subscriptions, 44 percent had one to three subscriptions to electronic databases, 14 percent had four to seven subscriptions, and 17 percent had subscriptions to seven or more. Usually, larger high schools subscribed to the most services (Scott, 2004).

Electronic database services vary in price and scope and are usually charged to school districts on an annual per-pupil basis. Depending on the content of these databases, costs can range from $1 to $5 per database per year per pupil.

Thus, to adequately meet the needs of school libraries, we fund elementary, middle, and high schools at $20, $20, and $25 per pupil, respectively, for library text and electronic services. These figures modestly outstrip the national average, allowing librarians to strengthen print collections. At the same time, they allow schools to provide, and experiment with, the electronic database resources on which more and more students rely (Tenopir, 2003).

Total per-pupil apportionment for instructional materials.   Taking the apportionment for "library texts and electronic services" and adding it to the "textbook and

TABLE 4.4   Total Annual Costs Per Pupil for Instructional Materials and Library Resources

Item	Elementary School	Middle School	High School
Library texts and Electronic services	$ 20	$ 20	$ 25
Textbook and consumables subtotal	120	120	150
Total	140	140	175

consumables" figures gives the totals listed in Table 4.4. States could add to each of these figures $25 per pupil for formative assessments to enable data-based decision making on the part of teachers.

Student Activities

Elementary, middle, and high schools typically provide an array of after-school programs, from clubs, bands, and other activities to sports. Teachers supervising or coaching in these activities usually receive small stipends for these extra duties. Further, research has shown, particularly at the secondary level, that students engaged in these activities tend to perform better academically than students not so engaged (Feldman and Matjasko, 2005), though too much extracurricular activity can be a detriment to academic learning (Committee on Increasing High School Students' Engagement and Motivation to Learn, 2004; Steinberg, 1997).

In our earlier adequacy work in a variety of states, we recommended amounts in the range of $60 per pupil for middle school students and $120 per pupil for high school students. But subsequent research in additional states has found that these figures are far below what districts and schools actually spend. An amount in the range of $200–250 per pupil more accurately reflects an adequate level of student activities resources.

Size Adjustments

There is substantial controversy over size adjustments in state school finance systems. But because the above recommendations are for prototypical schools of a certain size, there has to be some set of policies to tailor the general recommendations to schools of different sizes.

Several possible conditions could produce higher costs that might qualify for a size adjustment in state aid programs: (1) small school size, (2) small district size, (3) large school size, and (4) large district size. The general policy issue is whether small (or large) schools or districts experience diseconomies of scale (i.e., whether it costs more per pupil to run a small [or large] school or district). If size affects school operational costs, the policy question is whether those costs should be recognized in the state aid formula through a special adjustment or whether the school or district should be urged or required to consolidate (or separate) into a larger (or smaller) entity, thereby reducing costs and avoiding the need to spend extra money.

The major focus for size adjustments has been on small schools and districts. The general perception in the policymaking community is that small schools or districts are inefficient and should consolidate into larger entities. Indeed, as the data in Chapter 1 showed, school and district consolidation has been a common occurrence over the past 50 years. Both districts and schools have consolidated into larger entities. Many states have had incentive programs that rewarded small districts that consolidated into larger ones (Salmon, Dawson, Lawton, and Johns, 1988).

Analysts, however, argue that the expected cost savings from the massive school and district consolidation were rarely realized (Guthrie, 1979; Ornstein, 1990), and that consolidation might actually harm student performance in rural schools (Sher and Tompkins, 1977), as well as having broad negative effects on rural communities (Coeyman, 1998; Seal and Harmon, 1995). Nevertheless, consolidation may be a smart policy in some places, especially where schools and districts are far smaller than the size the general research addresses, which is about 300–400 for a high school. Indeed, except for necessary small schools and districts in sparsely populated areas, districts and schools with fewer than 100–200 students will find it difficult to meet the requirements of either a state's standards-based education reform or the federal No Child Left Behind Act.

From an economic perspective, the concept of diseconomies of scale includes both costs and outputs. The issue is whether costs per unit of output are higher in small schools or districts or, put differently, whether costs can be reduced while maintaining output as size rises. In an extensive review of the literature, Fox (1981) concluded that little research had analyzed output in combination with input and size variables. After assessing the meager extant research, Monk (1990) concluded that there was little support for either school or district consolidation—again, not from extremely small size into "small" schools or districts but into much larger units.

For elementary schools, research findings are thin, but data suggest that size economies that reduce costs by more than one dollar per pupil exist up to but not beyond 200 pupils (Riew, 1986). Thus, very small schools experience diseconomies of small size and, except in isolated rural areas, potentially could be merged into larger ones. But the real opportunities for cost savings from school consolidation for these small schools are not great, precisely because many such schools are located in isolated rural areas and there are no other schools nearby with which to consolidate.

At the secondary level, the data are more mixed. Few studies exist that simultaneously assess both size and output, so scale diseconomies have not been adequately studied. Riew (1986) found that there were cost savings, below one dollar per pupil, for middle schools with enrollments above 500; again, many middle schools already enroll more than this number. In analyzing whether larger secondary schools actually provided more comprehensive programs, an argument for larger size, Monk (1987) concluded in a study of New York that program comprehensiveness increased consistently in secondary schools only for size increases up to but not beyond about 400 students. In subsequent research, Haller and colleagues (1990) found that while larger schools offered more comprehensive programs, there was wide variation among both smaller and larger schools, and there was no clear point that guaranteed program comprehensiveness. Further, Hamilton (1983) showed that social development is enhanced in small high schools.

Studies of district size generally analyze expenditures per pupil as a function of size without an output variable, such as student achievement (Fox, 1981). To document diseconomies of district size, however, expenditures, size, and output need to be analyzed simultaneously, since the goal is to determine if costs per unit of output decrease as the number of students in the district increases. Again, in reviewing the literature, Monk (1990) concluded that definitive statements could not be made about district consolidation—again, for consolidation into districts of more than 1,000 students.

In the most recent review of scale economies and diseconomies, Andrews, Duncombe, and Yinger (2002) assessed both cost function (an approach to determining educational adequacy discussed in Chapters 3 and 5) and production function research. The studies reviewed generally assessed costs in tandem with student achievement outputs. The authors concluded that potential but modest cost savings could be realized by consolidating districts smaller than 500 students into districts with 2,000–4,000 students; of course, this would be an option only for small districts a short distance from each other, and not for rural, isolated small districts. The authors also found that the optimum size for elementary schools was in the 300–500 pupil range and for high schools was in the 600–900 range (see also Lee and Smith, 1997, on high school size). Both findings suggest that our very large urban districts and schools are far beyond the optimum size and need to be somehow downsized.

6. SUMMARY

Tables 4.5 and 4.6 summarize all of the above elements included in the prototypical elementary, middle, and high school. Table 4.6 shows how the resources would be provided in schools smaller than the prototypes. Schools larger than the prototypes would simply have the resources prorated up based on the actual number of pupils and their demographics. We have identified a poverty level of 50 percent for the schools that reflects the growing incidence of such students in America's schools. However, if used, the elements would need to be tailored to the exact enrollment and demographic data for each school.

7. APPENDIX: A HISTORY OF SPECIAL-NEEDS PROGRAMS

There is a rich developmental history associated with the major special-needs programs: (1) compensatory education programs for low-income students (Borman, Stringfield, and Slavin, 2001), (2) language acquisition programs for ELL students (Hodge, 1981; Slavin and Calderon, 2001), and (3) special-education programs for students with physical and mental disabilities (Verstegen, 1999). Both the federal government and the states have been major actors in this history.

TABLE 4.5 Adequate Resources for Prototypical Elementary, Middle, and High Schools

School Element	Elementary Schools	Middle Schools	High Schools
School Characteristics			
School configuration	K–5	6–8	9–12
Prototypic school size	432	450	600
Class size	K–3: 15 4–5: 25	25	25
Full-day kindergarten	Yes	NA	NA
Number of teacher work days	200 teacher work days, including 10 days for intensive training	200 teacher work days, including 10 days for intensive training	200 teacher work days, including 10 days for intensive training
% disabled	12%	12%	12%
% poverty (free and reduced-price lunch)	50%	50%	50%
% ELL	10%	10%	10%
% minority	30%	30%	30%
Personnel Resources			
1. Core teachers	24	18	24
2. Specialist teachers	20% more: 4.8	20% more: 3.6	33% more: 8.0
3. Instructional facilitators/mentors	2.2	2.25	3.0
4. Tutors for struggling students	One for every 100 poverty students: 2.16	One for every 100 poverty students: 2.25	One for every 100 poverty students: 3.0
5. Teachers for ELL students	Additional 1.0 teachers for every 100 ELL students: 0.43	Additional 1.0 teachers for every 100 ELL students: 0.45	Additional 1.0 teachers for every 100 ELL students: 0.60
6. Extended-day	1.8	1.875	2.5
7. Summer school	1.8	1.875	2.5
8a. Learning and mildly disabled students	Additional 3 professional teacher positions	Additional 3 professional teacher positions	Additional 4 professional teacher positions
8b. Severely disabled students	100% state reimbursement minus federal funds	100% state reimbursement minus federal funds	100% state reimbursement minus federal funds
9. Teachers for gifted students	$25/student	$25/student	$25/student
10. Vocational education	NA	NA	No extra cost
11. Substitutes	5% of lines 1–11	5% of lines 1–11	5% of lines 1–11

(continued)

TABLE 4.5   (*continued*)

School Element	Elementary Schools	Middle Schools	High Schools
12. Pupil support staff	1 for every 100 poverty students: 2.16	1 for every 100 poverty students plus 1.0 guidance/250 students: 3.25	1 for every 100 poverty students plus 1.0 guidance/250 students: 5.4
13. Noninstructional aides	2.0	2.0	3.0
14. Librarians/media specialists	1.0	1.0	1.0 librarian 1.0 library technician
15. Principal	1	1	1
16. School site secretary	2.0	2.0	3.0
17. Professional development	Included above: Instructional facilitators Planning and prep time 10 summer days Additional: $100/pupil for other PD expenses—trainers, conferences, travel, etc.	Included above: Instructional facilitators Planning and prep time 10 summer days Additional: $100/pupil for other PD expenses—trainers, conferences, travel, etc.	Included above: Instructional coaches Planning and prep time 10 summer days Additional: $50/pupil for other PD expenses—trainers, conferences, travel, etc.
18. Technology	$250/pupil	$250/pupil	$250/pupil
19. Instructional materials	$140/pupil	$140/pupil	$175/pupil
20. Student activities	$200/pupil	$200/pupil	$250/pupil

Types of Programs

Compensatory education.   Federal government involvement in compensatory education began in 1965 with passage of the Elementary and Secondary Education Act (ESEA); Title I provided grants to local school districts on the basis of the number of students from families with incomes below the poverty level. Within districts, schools use the funds to provide extra educational services for low-achieving students. While there is a long history of implementation of this federal compensatory education program, by the early 1980s, the program was firmly in place across the country (Odden, 1991).

Further, while in the early years a substantial portion of Title I dollars supplanted, or replaced, local dollars, by the end of the 1970s, each Title I dollar produced a minimum of an extra dollar of expenditures on compensatory education programs (Odden, 1988). A series of rules and regulations developed during the 1970s, focused primarily

TABLE 4.6 Summary of Personnel by Prototype of Various Sizes

Personnel Resource Category	Elementary			Middle			High School		
	108	**216**	**432**	**150**	**300**	**450**	**150**	**300**	**600**
School enrollment	108	216	432	150	300	450	150	300	600
Core teachers	6.0	12.0	24.0	6.0	12.0	18.0	6.0	12.0	24.0
Specialist teachers	1.2	2.4	4.8	1.2	2.4	3.6	2.0	4.0	8.0
Instructional facilitators	0.55	1.1	2.2	0.75	1.5	2.25	0.75	1.5	3.0
Teacher tutors (state avg.)	0.54	1.08	2.16	0.75	1.5	2.25	0.75	1.5	3.0
ELL teachers	0.1	0.2	0.43	0.15	0.30	0.45	0.15	0.30	0.6
Extended day program	0.45	0.9	1.8	0.625	1.25	1.875	0.625	1.25	2.5
Summer school	0.45	0.9	1.8	0.625	1.25	1.875	0.625	1.25	2.5
Special education	0.75	1.5	3	1.0	2.0	3.0	1.0	2.0	4.0
Gifted	$25/pupil	$25/pupil	$25/pupil		$25/pupil			$25/pupil	
Vocational ed	NA	NA	NA		NA			No extra cost	
Substitutes				Additional 5% of above staff					
Aides	0.5	1.0	2.0	0.5	1.0	2.0	0.75	1.5	3.0
Pupil support	0.33	0.65	1.3	1.05	2.1	3.15	1.05	2.1	4.2
Librarian media technician	0.25	0.5	1.0	0.3	0.67	1.0	0.5	1.0	1.0
	0.0	0.0	0.0	0.0	0.5	0.0	0.25	0.5	1.0
School administration	1.0	1.0	1.0	1.0	1.0	1.0	1.0	1.0	1.0
Secretary/clerical	1.0	1.0	2.0	1.0	1.33	2.0	1.0	2.0	3.0
Special education	0.75	1.5	3.0	0.75	1.5	3.0	1.0	2.0	4.0

on allocation and use of funds, helped produce those fiscal outcomes. "Comparability" required districts to allocate district and state funds equally across schools before allocating Title I dollars. "Supplement and not supplant" required districts to ensure that Title I dollars provided extra educational services and did not merely replace local funds. And "children in greatest need" requirements ensured that only the students with the lowest achievement were eligible to receive extra educational services once Title I funds reached the school level.

In 1981, ESEA was replaced with the Education Consolidation and Improvement Act (ECIA), and Title I was replaced by Chapter 1. In 1988, the Hawkins-Stafford School Improvement Amendments made several changes to Chapter 1 with the intent of improving compensatory education programs across the country. During the 1990–91 school year, Chapter 1 provided approximately $5.4 billion to serve close to 5 million children. In 1994, the Improving America's Schools Act was passed, which reauthorized Title I of ESEA, and changed the name of the program back to Title I. This act represented a shift in federal aid to education, giving new responsibilities to states, districts, and the federal government to ensure quality education for low-income children.

In 2001, the program was again reauthorized by the U.S. Congress and named the No Child Left Behind (NCLB) Act. Though funding levels were increased to $13.5 billion for 2001–02, the distribution and funding requirements remained essentially the same. NCLB has become known largely for its new accountability requirements (Linn, Baker, and Betebenner, 2002). The legislation requires states to test all Title I students in grades 3–8 every year and to document that each child makes "adequate yearly progress" in academic achievement. Not doing so subjects failing schools to a series of intervention programs and ultimately allows students not making such progress to choose to attend another school or to use their Title I funds to seek private tutoring. Title II of NCLB also consolidated several other federal programs into a single "pot" to be used for a wide array of strategies to improve teacher quality, including professional development and performance pay.

Over the years, Title I stimulated many states to enact their own compensatory education programs. Most state programs were designed to complement the federal program. California and New York were among the first states to enact compensatory education programs. In the early 1980s, nearly 20 states had compensatory education programs in their general-aid formula, with about 10 states distributing the funds on the basis of pupil weights (McGuire, 1982). A mixture of poverty and student achievement measures determined student eligibility. In 1993–94, the number of states with compensatory education programs and/or compensatory education pupil weights increased to 28, and by 1998–99 to 34, and some type of such program exists in all states today. Previous editions of the book have identified the various ways states have provided funding for these programs (Odden and Picus, 1992, 2000, 2004).

It is important to keep in mind that while both federal and state compensatory programs provide opportunities for low-achieving students to receive additional educational services, the programs do not establish a legal right to such extra services, as does the law for students with disabilities. The services are available solely because the federal and state programs exist.

The federal government has provided funds to local school districts for compensatory programs since the 1965 passage of ESEA. The 1994 ESEA reauthorization made several changes to the Title I allocation formula, which were largely retained by the 2001 NCLB reauthorization as well. Before the reauthorization, the federal government allocated funds to states on the basis of the number of low-income children in each county and the state's per-pupil expenditures for elementary and secondary education (with an upper and lower limit on the amount that state expenditures could deviate from the national average). The funds were suballocated to counties and then to districts and schools within counties.

The reauthorized act made two major changes. The first involved the data by which the number of low-income children is counted. Previously, the number of low-income children was calculated using decennial census data. But because the numbers of children in need change more than once every 10 years, there was concern about using census data that are only updated once a decade. The reauthorized act required data on low-income children to be updated every two years using biennial census data that was collected beginning in 1996. In FY 1997, these data were used for the first time.

The second change involved the federal government's practice of distributing money to states on the basis of county-level poverty data. Under the old law, Title I dollars were distributed to states on the basis of county-level data and then suballocated to districts. If the county and school district boundaries were not coterminous (which is the case in most states), the state used a subcounty allocation formula to distribute funds to local school districts based on the number of low-income students in each district. Under the new law, allocations continued in this manner until FY 1999, when grants began to be calculated on the basis of the population of low-income children in each district.

Once the funds have been allocated to the district, districts must distribute them among the schools in that district. Initially, the idea was to concentrate the funds in the highest-poverty schools and then on the lowest-achieving students in those schools. Though districts had always had some discretion over school distribution, more restrictive requirements were added over the years. Today, in determining school allocations, districts must first rank all of their schools in terms of poverty levels. The poverty measure employed must be one of the five specified by Title I, including (1) children age 5–17 in poverty as counted by the most recent census, (2) children eligible for free and reduced-price lunches under the National Free School Lunch Act, (3) children in families receiving income assistance, (4) children eligible to receive medical assistance under the Medicaid program, and (5) a composite of any of the preceding measures.

Once all the schools in a given district are ranked according to poverty level, the district is required to serve all schools with 75 percent poverty and higher. After serving all of those areas, the district may serve the lower-poverty schools by using the rank that has already been determined or by creating grade-level groupings. Since the law does not specify what a service is, the districts still have considerable discretion in funds allocation. The lower cost a district specifies for a service, the more possible it is to distribute at least some dollars to more schools. Higher-cost programs direct most funds to the highest-poverty schools.

Bilingual education.   In 1967, Title VII was added to the federal ESEA program. Title VII provided funds for districts to design and implement bilingual education programs. Funds were available on a proposal basis only; districts wrote proposals, and a review process determined which received funding. Services for students with limited English proficiency emerged in the mid-1970s primarily after the 1974 *Lau v. Nichols*[9] case, which originated in California. This case was filed in San Francisco, where students who did not speak English were immersed in classes taught in English. Although filed as an equal protection case, it was decided on the basis of federal antidiscrimination laws. The court held that it was discriminatory to place non-English-speaking students in classes where the language of instruction was English. As a result, districts created bilingual programs that provided instruction in English as a second language and instruction in subject matter classes in the students' native language until they learned enough English to be instructed in English only.

Although debates have surrounded various approaches to bilingual education, the key finding of *Lau* was that the language capability of students must be considered in designing an appropriate instructional environment. Today, for example, when one class might have students with many different native languages, bilingual instruction is not possible, and a "sheltered English" instructional approach may be an acceptable option (Krashen and Biber, 1988; Slavin and Calderon, 2001). In all instructional approaches, lessons have dual objectives: development of English-language as well as content knowledge. The *Lau* decision made access to a language-appropriate classroom environment a legal right of all limited-English-proficient (LEP) students.

In 1990, the federal government provided about $189 million for bilingual education. In 1998, the amount of federal funds allocated to bilingual education in the form of instructional services, support services, professional development, and foreign language assistance was approximately $204 million.

The population of LEP students in this country continues to grow. According to some estimates, there are now 50 percent more LEP students than there were in 1990 (Pompa, 1998). Three states—New York, California, and Texas—continue to enroll the majority of LEP students, but populations are growing in Arizona, Florida, Illinois, New Mexico, Oklahoma, and Washington as well. States began to provide bilingual education programs in part as a response to *Lau*, and many more are finding them necessary due to the growing numbers just cited. In 1975, 13 states had bilingual education programs. By 1993–94, 30 states had bilingual education programs, many of which were allocated on the basis of pupil weights. In 1998–99, 34 states had programs for students whose native language was other than English, and the number is higher today, with more states prohibiting the use of bilingual strategies. Previous editions of this book identified the various ways states have provided funding for these programs (Odden and Picus, 1992, 2000, 2004).

In 2002, NCLB incorporated a reauthorization of Title VII of ESEA and the Bilingual Education Act into a new Title III with two grants, one of which is titled the "English

[9]414 U.S. 563 (1974).

Language Acquisition, Language Enhancement, and Academic Achievement Act." Eighty percent of the first grant is calculated from the number of LEP students, and the other 20 percent from the number of immigrant children enrollments in the state compared to all states. The other grant, titled "Improving Language Instruction Educational Programs," is federally administered and takes effect when Congress appropriates less than $650 million in a school year. NCLB authorized $750 million in FY 2002.

Special education.   For years, most states have supported special-education programs for students with physical and mental disabilities, at least to some degree (Verstegen, 1999). But during the late 1960s and early 1970s, it became apparent that many disabled students were being prohibited from attending local public schools. As a result of certain disabilities being so severe that they required very costly services, or because of blatant discrimination against individuals with disabilities, these exclusions were challenged on equal protection grounds. One of the first court decisions occurred in the *Pennsylvania Association for Retarded Children (PARC) v. Pennsylvania* case in 1972, in which a Pennsylvania court held that district actions prohibiting students with disabilities from attending local public schools violated the Equal Protection Clause of the U.S. Constitution. This decision spawned several other court cases, as well as a spate of new federal and state policy initiatives. A notable follow-up case, also in 1972, was *Mills v. Board of Education, DC,* which took legal precedents from *Brown v. Board of Education* to prove that exclusion by the District of Columbia of thousands of students with disabilities from education was unconstitutional.

In 1975, Congress enacted the federal Education for all Handicapped Children Act, P.L. 94-142, now known as the Individuals with Disabilities Education Act (IDEA). This sweeping new federal program made access to a free, appropriate, public education program in the least restrictive environment possible a legal right of all children. In order to receive any federal education dollars, states have to demonstrate that they are providing appropriate special-education services to all disabled children. The services have to meet a series of detailed federal requirements, including an individualized educational program for each eligible student. While several states initially responded negatively to the federal requirements, and some states refused all federal education aid for a few years, today all states comply with the mandates of this law.

IDEA authorized the federal government to fund up to 40 percent of nationwide average per-pupil expenditure (APPE) for special-education services. In the year it was enacted, Congress appropriated $300 million, or about $74 per disabled student, much less than the 40 percent that had been authorized. In 1990, federal outlays for special education were $2 billion (in constant FY 1998 dollars; National Center for Education Statistics, 1998b); and by 1999–2000, that figure had climbed to $3.7 billion (Chambers, Parrish, and Harr, 2002). Underfunding continues today. In 2004, only about 19 percent of costs were provided by the federal government (House Committee on Education and the Workforce, 2004). The most recent reauthorization, in 2004 (P.L. 108–446), added an adjustment that took effect in FY 2006, wherein the maximum state grant calculation was 40 percent of the APPE times the number of children with disabilities in the state in the 2004–05 school year adjusted by the annual rate of change of students with disabilities (85 percent) and change in students living in poverty (15 percent) (Apling and Jones, 2005).[10]

Federal funds are allocated on a per-pupil flat grant basis. The federal law requires that states identify students in these 10 special-education categories:

1. Mental retardation
2. Hearing impairments (including deafness)
3. Speech or language impairments
4. Visual impairments (including blindness)
5. Serious emotional disturbance
6. Orthopedic impairments
7. Autism
8. Traumatic brain injury
9. Other health impairments
10. Specific learning disabilities

According to the most recent data collected by the National Center for Education Statistics (2006), approximately 6.6 million children were served under the federal IDEA program in 2005, representing about 13.7 percent of the total enrollment. Studies have shown that the counts of students with disabilities range from 9 to 18 percent in various states (U.S. Department of Education, Office of Special Education Programs, 2002). As will be discussed, many states use the 10 federal categories to structure their state programs. Even though the per-pupil costs of providing services vary substantially by category, the federal program allocates the same flat grant amount for each identified student, regardless of category.

In the late 1980s, a regular-education initiative was launched by a diverse group of individuals who believed that a focus on pigeon-holing students with disabilities into a number of special categories and pulling them out of regular classrooms for instruction was doing more harm than good for many of these students. This initiative reinforced the earlier views of many that labeling these students was not the best approach to providing extra services for them. Instead, many argued that all students had particular needs and that schools should identify the different types of services necessary to serve their student population. The service levels needed could then guide funding decisions. States such as Iowa and Massachusetts, in fact, restructured their state programs for the disabled on this basis.

In the 1990s, the regular-education initiative transformed into a more "inclusive" initiative. The goal, generally consistent with the original intent of IDEA, was to include disabled students in regular-education classrooms as much as possible. Although there

---

[10]Under the 2004 Amendments to the Individuals with Disabilities Education Act, after FY 2006, states will receive a base level of funding in the amount of 40 percent of the national average per pupil expenditure (APPE) times the number of children with disabilities served in 2004–05 adjusted by the state's annual rate of change of school-age population (85 percent of adjustment) and low-income school-age population (15 percent of adjustment) (Apling and Jones, 2005).

has been controversy over how best to implement inclusive practices, this remains the dominant service delivery focus for disabled students today (McDonnell, McLaughlin, and Morison, 1997). All states now have programs to serve disabled students, though the funding and program and service strategies vary a great deal.

General Approaches to Formula Adjustments for Special-Needs Students

Previous editions of this text discussed the different ways states can provide grants for students with extra educational needs. The state can fully fund the extra costs or create a state and local cost-sharing program, which can take many different forms. There are two general approaches states can use to assist local districts in providing extra educational services for students with special-education needs: (1) full-state funding and (2) state-local cost sharing. The more popular approach is some form of state and local cost sharing. Of the many methods of sharing the cost with localities, **pupil-weighted programs** have become the most popular, with about 20 states using them. Pupil weights provide a way to directly identify the degree of additional services a state wants to provide, as well as a method of sharing the cost by allocating state aid through the general-aid formula using a weighted count of pupils. This strategy also links the level of extra aid received to local fiscal capacity; even if the number of special-needs students is the same, districts with low property values per pupil will receive more money for special education than districts with high property values per pupil.

Finally, the interaction of the specific funding formulas and the rules and regulations accompanying them provide incentives and disincentives for student identification, program placement, and dollar use. At the local level, districts sometimes identify students in higher-reimbursement categories and place them in lower-cost instructional programs to increase revenues and reduce costs. While some of these interactions are desired, the limits of such flexibility need to be understood and addressed (see Hartman, 1980).

As discussed previously, census-based funding addresses the incentive problem as well. Further, after years of experience, local educators have become quite sophisticated at "pooling" dollars for special-needs students and creatively providing services (McLaughlin, 1999). Today, the push for comprehensive school reform programs (see, e.g., Stringfield, Ross, and Smith, 1996), which was bolstered for several years by the federal Obey-Porter Comprehensive School Reform program, actively encourages schools to include special-needs students in all aspects of the regular-education program.

Readers are encouraged to read the previous versions of the text for more detailed descriptions of these alternatives (Odden and Picus, 1992, 2000, 2004). In the adequacy environment, programs for special-needs students are incorporated into the adequate-staffing models for each school.

Costs and formulas for financing compensatory education programs.   Because school districts have substantial latitude in the kinds of compensatory programs they offer, determining compensatory education program costs is a difficult task. In contrast, programs for other special-needs students are better defined. The law requires districts, for example, to provide appropriate services to all disabled children. Once a child's disability has been identified, and an appropriate level of service agreed upon, it is relatively straightforward to determine the costs of that service. While there may be variations in costs and instructional techniques across districts, it is possible to estimate an average cost for each special service provided within a region or state.

The problem of determining compensatory education program costs, however, is more complex. Although Title I and most state compensatory programs require that program funds be expended on low-income and/or low-achieving students, neither generally specifies the types or levels of services that should be provided. As a result, districts have considerable flexibility in determining the breadth and intensity of services provided. This flexibility was enhanced in the 1990s by allowing schools with 50 percent or more poverty students to use Title I funds for schoolwide programs serving all students.

As a result, one district may choose to offer intensive services to a subgroup of eligible low-income students (e.g., one-to-one tutoring for low-achieving students in grades 1–3), while another district may elect to serve all of the eligible student population with a less-intense program (e.g., pull-out, resource room, remedial services). In fact, a number of program options and thus program costs are possible, all of which can impact the final distribution of compensatory education dollars. In the late 1980s, Goertz (1988) found that among 17 large districts, allocation rules included the following:

- Uniform allocation to each eligible building
- Allocations based on the number of low-achieving students in a building
- Allocations based on the relative size and/or poverty of the building's student body

It is likely that these procedures increased in variability in the 1990s, with the trend toward more schoolwide programs.

In part as a result of these allocation and service variations, Goertz's (1988) study found considerable differences in instructional expenditures per pupil within and among Chapter 1 (Title I, as it was known in 1988) programs. In one district, the Chapter 1 expenditure range was $300–2,500 per pupil, while in another district, the range was $450–625. The lowest per-pupil Chapter 1 expenditures identified in the 17 districts was $175 (in a district with an expenditure range of $175–1,070), and the highest was the $2,500 per pupil. Similar program cost variations probably exist today.

At the state level, the Texas State Board of Education (1986) reviewed the costs of compensatory education and recommended an extra weight of 0.2 for all eligible compensatory education students—implying that compensatory education costs 20 percent more than the state's foundation expenditure level. Although subsequent studies suggested that many districts did not spend that much extra for compensatory education, in part because compensatory education services within the regular school day were provided in lieu of other services, the legislature retained the 0.2 extra weighting.

Another problem in identifying the costs of compensatory education programs today is the fact that many programs are schoolwide. This makes it extremely hard, if not impossible, to determine how much money is spent on low-income children in a school, since the compensatory education money is being used to fund programs for all children.

Further, because schools with high poverty levels are the ones that are eligible and therefore likely to apply their Title I allocation to schoolwide programs, it is no longer easy to discern where the more intensive services for low-income children are offered. Nor is it clear whether "intensive services" are the ones bringing the best results

A final challenge in identifying the costs of compensatory education programs has arisen in this era of standards-based reform. Many more states now fund programs, in addition to the Title I funds they receive, in order to raise the achievement of low-income students. A survey of the states conducted by the Center on Budget and Policy Priorities (Carey, 2002) found that 83 percent of existing programs for low-income students have been implemented in their current form only since 1990. Where states once had one overarching compensatory education program under Title I, many states now have several programs targeting students from disadvantaged backgrounds. In part as a result of this increase, programs for low-income students today are more diverse in terms of size, focus, and method of funding (Carey, 2002). The Center on Budget and Policy Priorities (Carey, 2002) reported that 13 states adjust their basic state aid formulas in order to fund additional programs for disadvantaged students, while 18 states have separate categorical grants for this purpose. This change in the breadth and nature of programs for low-income students makes it more difficult to estimate costs because the definition of a compensatory education program is evolving as additional programs are being funded by states and because the funding mechanisms for them vary by state and program.

Given all of the complications, finding the answer to the long-standing question of how much extra funding needs to be provided per pupil for compensatory programs is difficult. It requires specifying the level of achievement desired, the additional programmatic strategies needed to produce this achievement, and the costs of those strategies.

One program for which this type of analysis can be approximated is the Success for All/Roots and Wings program (Slavin, Madden, Dolan, and Wasik, 1996). It includes a core curriculum designed to teach students to proficiency standards in reading, writing, mathematics, science, and social studies. There is considerable evidence of the effectiveness of this program, and it has been shown to be replicable across a wide range of schools and education systems (Borman, Overman, and Hewes, Brown, 2002; Slavin and Fashola, 1998). For purposes of this discussion, let us assume that this program provides the types of additional services and strategies students from low-income backgrounds need to achieve to rigorous proficiency standards.

The costs of this program have been identified (Odden, 1997a). In addition to all of the elements associated with a traditional school, the minimum elements of this program for an elementary school of 500 students, with nearly all from poverty backgrounds, are these:

- One to two schoolwide instructional facilitator(s)
- Four to five reading tutors
- A family liaison professional
- $30,000 for instructional materials
- $30,000 for professional development provided by the national network associated with this school design

These elements thus include six to eight (an average of seven) professional staff positions and $60,000 for training and materials. Using national average prices, this would require the school to have an additional $410,000 (seven positions times $50,000 in salary and benefits for each, plus $60,000 for training and materials). This would be above the core staffing of one principal, one teacher for every 25 students, appropriate additional teachers for preparation time and for art, music, and physical education. Also, the program strongly recommends a full-day kindergarten program, which, if not already in place at the school implementing the design, would require two additional teachers, raising the costs to $510,000. Roots and Wings/Success for All also strongly suggests that each student receive a preschool education, which could further increase the costs. Finally, some schools find that an additional tutor or two enhances the ability of the program to teach all students to rigorous proficiency standards.

For illustrative purposes, assume that a program slightly above the minimum requirements is needed and that the additional costs of that version of the Roots and Wings/Success for All program is about $500,000. That would amount to $1,000 for every low-income student in the school, which in this case would be every student in the school. If the state average expenditure were $5,000, this would represent a 20 percent addition, or a 0.20 weight; the weight would rise (drop) as the expenditures were lower (higher). This would mean that in addition to the "adequate" foundation program, the state would need to provide an additional $1,000 for every low-income student, assuming that those extra dollars would be used to finance a strategy or set of strategies to teach all students to state-set proficiency standards (i.e., a schoolwide program such as Success for All/Roots and Wings). Districts should be able to pool the funds from both Title I and state compensatory education programs to provide this level of extra funding to each school.

As indicated above, our approach to compensatory education is to provide resources for tutoring, extended-day, and summer school programs. We calculate the appropriate pupil weights for this approach in Chapter 9.

In sum, compensatory education funds are distributed to school districts on the basis of the number of eligible pupils. For the federal Title I program, the number of low-income students in a district determines eligibility. Many state programs use income measures for eligibility, while others offer compensatory aid for low-achieving students. Compensatory education programs generally include requirements to ensure that districts do not use the money to replace local funds, but they do not delineate how services should be provided or how many of the eligible students must be served. Consequently, some districts attempt to provide compensatory services to all eligible schools and students, others focus their resources on specific populations, and still others use their Title I resources to fund schoolwide programs. This results in a tremendous range in the breadth and intensity of the compensatory education services provided across the United States.

Costs and formulas for financing bilingual education programs.   Studies of the costs of providing bilingual education have produced widely varying results, from less than an extra 5 percent (Carpenter-Huffman and Samulon, 1981; Gonzalez, 1996) to an extra 100 percent (Chambers and Parrish, 1983). There are several reasons for these variations, and they speak to what a bilingual education program is and how it should be structured.

Five specific issues determine the costs of bilingual education programs: (1) student eligibility, (2) the minimum number of LEP students required to trigger provision of a bilingual education program, (3) the instructional approach used, (4) the transition into the regular program, and (5) class size.

A score on some type of English-language proficiency test usually determines student eligibility. States use different tests and have selected different cut-off points for eligibility, from below the 23rd percentile in one state to much higher levels in other states. Clearly, the higher the threshold, the more students will be eligible, and the fewer the number of low-incidence programs.

Most states also require a school or district to have a minimum number of students in a grade level in order to provide a bilingual education program. Minimums have ranged widely, from 10 students in a grade in a school in California to 20 students in a district in Texas (Nelson, 1984). The lower the minimum number of children and the larger the unit for that minimum, the more students will qualify.

Class size in many states is also limited, sometimes to as low as 10 students. Other states do not set lower limits on class size for bilingual or ESL classes. Small class size requirements boost per-pupil costs.

The instructional approach and transition policies also affect the level of services provided. Most state bilingual education policy assumes that students classified as limited-English-proficient will be able to transition into regular classes, taught in English, within a three-year period. A longer transition period (i.e., providing extra services to students who need more than three years to transition and perform well in English-only classrooms) will boost per-pupil costs.

Finally, the instructional approach used is a major determinant of program costs. A few comments on bilingual education program goals and characteristics of instructional strategies that work will help provide some background for assessing the nature of the instructional approach and thus the results of cost studies based on different instructional approaches.

Students who are eligible for bilingual education programs usually live in families in which a language other than English is spoken, so that English is not the student's native language. The key issue is the degree to which the student is proficient in English as a language for learning. Literacy (i.e., the ability to read, write, do mathematics, and think) can be developed in any language; literacy is neutral with respect to language (Office of Bilingual Education, 1984). Once literacy is developed in one language, it is easily transferred to another language once the second language is learned. Students diagnosed as limited-English-proficient do not have sufficient English-language proficiency to learn in English. Research has shown that the most effective approach for such students is to teach them regular subjects in their native language, as well as in an ESL class (Krashen and Biber, 1988; Slavin and Calderon, 2001). The goal of such a program is to have the students learn English while simultaneously learning regular academic subject matter.

The same research has shown that students (including adults) learn conversational English first; this English proficiency is sufficient for conversing on the playground, playing with friends, talking about the weather, but it is not sufficient for academic learning (see also Cummins, 1980). When this conversational level of English proficiency is learned, students are ready for "sheltered English" instruction in subjects that have some language and terminology of their own, such as mathematics and science (Krashen and Biber, 1988), but they still need instruction in their native language for history and language arts, and continuation of ESL classes. This intermediate approach helps students gain the level of English proficiency needed to learn academic subjects. History/social science is the next subject for sheltered-English instruction; the last such class is language arts. In other words, the most effective approach is to begin instruction in the native language; transition sequentially to sheltered-English instruction in mathematics, science, history/social science, and language arts; and only then transition to regular classroom instruction. ESL instruction also should continue until the full transition to the regular classroom.[11]

The Krashen and Biber (1988) report did not make recommendations for major class size reductions. Nor did this report recommend the common school practice of having an English-only instructor assisted by a bilingual education aide. This configuration is quite common across the country because there are insufficient numbers of bilingual teachers to teach students in their native language. In this circumstance, Krashen and Biber recommend ESL with a sheltered-English instruction approach.

Thus, the major extra costs of bilingual education for the most effective instructional approach are threefold:

- An ESL teacher. If the class has a normal number of students, and is used for six periods a day, the extra cost is about one-sixth (i.e., the cost of the extra period of instruction).
- Intensive staff development in sheltered-English instruction. This is professional expertise that can and should be learned by all teachers. Knowledge of a second language is not required. Sheltered-English instruction is mediated by a variety of mechanisms and has a conscious English-language-development component.
- Additional materials both in the native language of the student and for mediating the sheltered-English instructional approach. These extras add up to a maximum of an extra 20–25 percent. Note that regular classes are taught either by bilingual teachers or teachers using a sheltered-English approach, or in a regular classroom; other than staff development, these classes entail no additional costs.[12]

[11]We are aware that bilingual programs are somewhat controversial, and indeed, California by initiative eliminated such programs. Nevertheless, schools need to adopt some strategy to ensure that students who do not have English proficiency learn English and other academic content as well.

[12]Some states and districts pay bilingual teachers a bonus of up to $5,000. This clearly is an extra cost. The bonus is rationalized on the basis that bilingual teachers are in short supply and have an area of expertise—proficiency in a second language—that other teachers do not have.

Most studies of bilingual education programs reflect these levels of costs. Garcia (1977) found the add-on costs for bilingual education in New Mexico to be about 27 percent. Three studies by the Intercultural Development Research Association found bilingual education to cost an extra 30–35 percent in Texas (Cardenas, Bernal, and Kean, 1976), an extra 17–25 percent in Utah (Guss-Zamora, Zarate, Robledo, and Cardenas, 1979), and an extra 15–22 percent in Colorado (Robledo, Zarate, Guss-Zamora, and Cardenas, 1978). An early 1990s study of such programs in California found the marginal cost of LEP services to be $361 in 1990–91 (Parrish, 1994); when compared with the total education revenues per pupil in California in the same year, the cost of LEP services amounted to an additional 8 percent. Parrish (1994) also found a broad range of costs depending on the instructional approach, which he attributed to the range in the resource teacher services needed for the different approaches. The costs in his study ranged from $131 per student in a sheltered-English program to $1,066 for an ESL program, or from 3 to 22 percent above regular-education costs.[13] While some of these studies analyzed program configurations quite different from that just described, the findings provide a range of cost estimates that are nevertheless comparable.

Finally, though districts have typically reported higher costs for bilingual education programs than most studies have found (Carpenter-Huffman and Samulon, 1981), studies have also reported considerably higher costs for bilingual education programs than those just cited. The Chambers and Parrish (1983) study in Illinois found that these additional costs ranged from $848 to $5,113 per pupil, or between 33 and 100 percent for different program structures in Illinois school districts. The highest cost figure assumed both a low incidence and a very low class size; the latter characteristic is absent from some of the other studies, including the Krashen and Biber (1988) studies of effective California programs.

Bilingual education continues to be controversial. In California, Proposition 227, which took effect in the summer of 1998, sharply curtailed bilingual classes, instead encouraging immersion for LEP students. In 2002, Massachusetts voters approved a similar initiative while Colorado voters turned one down. In spite of the controversy, the key ingredients for an effective program structure are an ESL program to teach English and regular teachers who teach either in the native language or in a sheltered-English format, neither of which entails extra costs, supplementary materials, and staff development. Moreover, as the diversity of the student's native language increases, as is increasingly the case, sheltered-English instruction inevitably becomes the dominant instructional mode in addition to ESL; the many languages within each classroom preclude a bilingual teaching strategy. Additional costs for this program structure, as well as those found in several research reports, range between 25 and 35 percent.

Costs and formulas for financing special-education programs. Identifying the costs of special-education programs for students with physical, mental, and learning

---

[13]If the base revenue limit ($3,331), rather than total revenues per pupil ($4,743), is used to calculate these percentages, the estimate for LEP services will be 11 percent above regular-education costs, sheltered English instruction will be 4 percent above, and the more expensive ESL program will be 32 percent above (Gold, Smith, Lawton, and Hyary, 1992).

disabilities has been a major focus of study for the past three decades. Initially, studies sought to identify different costs by disability, taking into account how that cost varied by the size of the district. Then special-education cost research focused more on excess costs as a function of educational placement (Moore, Strang, Schwartz, and Braddock, 1988; Rossmiller, Hale, and Frohreich, 1979).

Rossmiller conducted some of the earliest work under the auspices of the National Education Finance Project (NEFP) in the early 1970s (Johns, Alexander, and Jordan, 1971; Rossmiller et al., 1970). This work was probably the first analysis of special-education costs that produced results that could be used to create pupil-weighting programs. Indeed, in 1973, Florida enacted one of the first special-education pupil-weighting programs as a new approach to financing special education, a program that became a model for other states. Florida adopted these weights for 1976–77, based in large part on the Rossmiller and NEFP analyses:

Educable mentally retarded	2.3
Trainable mentally retarded	3.0
Physically handicapped	3.5
Physical/occupational therapy, part-time	6.0
Speech and hearing therapy, part-time	10.0
Deaf	4.0
Visually handicapped, part-time	10.0
Visually handicapped	3.5
Emotionally disturbed, part-time	7.5
Emotionally disturbed	3.7
Socially maladjusted	2.3
Specific learning disability, part-time	7.5
Specific learning disability	2.3
Hospital and homebound, part-time	15.0

In addition to the general points made previously on factors that determine program costs, there are three key issues related to determining special-education program costs. The first is the level of program quality. Most of the early studies sought to identify good special-education programs and based special-education cost estimates on the expenditure patterns of those programs. Few studies set a priori standards for program quality. Thus, studies have been plagued over the years by various definitions of program quality.

The second issue is identification of services included in the study. The most controversial aspect of this issue is whether to include administrative services, such as general district administration, as well as related noneducational services.

A third issue, especially for determining per-pupil costs, is how the number of students is determined—whether by head count or full-time equivalents. The importance of this issue, and resultant program structures, is shown by the high weights for students receiving part-time services in the early Florida program. Kakalik (1979) provided an overview of issues in determining special education costs. Parrish (1996) also discussed costs in his article on special-education finance.

Three large studies of nationwide special-education costs have been conducted: (1) by Kakalik, Furry, Thomas, and Carney (1981), using data from the mid-1970s; (2) by Moore and colleagues (1988), using data from the mid-1980s; and (3) by Chambers, Parrish, and Harr (2002), using data from the late 1990s. All three used a representative national sample, thus providing a picture of actual special-education expenditures across all programs in the country. The results in terms of excess costs for special-education programs for the first two studies were quite similar. Kakalik and colleagues (1981) presented results as ratios of special-education expenditures to regular-education expenditures in 1977–78 for 13 categories of disabling conditions; the weights ranged from 1.37 for speech-impaired children to 5.86 for the blind. The overall weight across all categories was 2.17. Kakalik and colleagues also presented data comparing special-education expenditures with regular-education expenditures by 10 categories of educational placement. For the in-school program, the ratios or weights ranged from 1.37 for regular-classroom plus related services to 3.24 for special all-day school. The regular-classroom-plus-part-time-special-classroom arrangement had a weight of 2.85.

Moore and colleagues (1988) presented no pupil weights or ratios in their report, tending rather to emphasize the linkage between type of educational program or placement and disabling condition. These figures are summary findings of 1985–86 special-education program costs:

Handicapping Condition	Preschool	Self-Contained	Resource Room
Speech impaired	$3,062	$ 7,140	$ 647
Mentally retarded	3,983	4,754	2,290
Orthopedically impaired	4,702	5,248	3,999
Multihandicapped	5,400	6,674	NA
Learning disabled	3,708	3,083	1,643
Seriously emotionally disturbed	4,297	4,857	2,620
Deaf	5,771	7,988	NA
Deaf-blind	NA	20,416	NA
Hard of hearing	4,583	6,058	3,372
Other health impaired	3,243	4,782	NA
Autistic	6,265	7,582	NA
Visually impaired	4,068	6,181	3,395

These results can be transformed into pupil weights by comparing these costs with 1985–86 expenditures per pupil for regular students, which was $2,780. Since these figures are costs just for the special-education services, the $2,780 figure would have to be added to them in order to calculate the weight. Moore and colleagues found that the overall average expenditure for special education across all programs and placements was $3,649. Thus, their study produced an overall weight of 2.3 ([$3,649 + $2,780]/$2,780), close to the Kakalik and colleagues (1981) finding of 2.17 (see also Chaikind, Danielson, and Braven, 1993).

As recently as 1996, Parrish (1996), a leading expert on special-education expenditures and costs, called 2.3 "the generally accepted cost figure" (i.e., on average, educating special-education students required 2.3 times the amount for "regular" students, or an additional 130 percent to provide appropriate additional educational services to all disabled students). Actual additional costs were difficult to capture because of a lack of uniform accounting for both expenditures and service strategies, demographic trends suggesting a higher rate of students with special needs and more complex disabilities, consolidation of funding sources, and inclusion. Nevertheless, the extra 1.3 figure was generally accepted with the caveat that it was increasingly difficult to sort out the costs of educating students with special needs (Chambers, Parrish, and Guarino, 1999; National Research Council, 1999).

In March 2002, however, Chambers and colleagues reported the results of the largest and most sophisticated study of special-education costs ever conducted. The Special Education Expenditure Project (SEEP) collected data for the 1999–2000 school year from more than 9,000 students with disabilities who attended more than 1,000 schools in over 300 local education agencies. The major new finding from the study was that the 1.3 extra weight had declined to 0.9. This amounts to $5,918 per pupil over the base expenditure of $6,556. This does not mean, however, that overall special-education expenditures dropped, because the actual number of students classified as disabled has been increasing for years. It simply means that because of changes in both service delivery (with considerable inclusion) and student demographics (with an increase in students identified with less intensive service needs, such as learning disabilities), the overall weight reflecting the need for extra revenues had dropped from 1.3 to 0.9. The state of Washington has taken this approach. The major issue with the Washington structure was whether the base funding level was adequate; a 2006 adequacy study found that it was not (Odden, Picus, Goetz, and Fermanich, 2006).

Study Questions

1. Log on to your state's Department of Education website.
   a. Can you find your state's curriculum standards? What subjects are covered? What grade span is incorporated into the standards?
   b. Next, search for your state's testing system. Is the test norm-referenced or criterion-referenced? Does it cover all of the subjects and grade levels that the curriculum standards lay out? If not, are there plans to expand the testing system to cover the untested subjects and grades? Locate the most recent test scores for your local school district. Can you view scores disaggregated by students with differing economic backgrounds, ethnicities, and disabilities? How do they compare to the state averages in each category?
   c. Finally, look for your state's accountability system. What actions, if any, are taken if student achievement scores at a school consistently fail to make progress?
2. Brainstorm about how to dramatically improve student achievement in your school or in a low-performing school. Outline what the key programs and strategies would be. Are the resources in the adequacy model sufficient to implement your strategy? Create a sales pitch to the teachers' union making a case for your improvement plan.

3. Instructional aides and assistant principals are not specifically funded in the adequacy model. Set up a mock school board meeting in which resources for these two positions are debated. Write up the results as if you were a local newspaper reporter who attended the meeting.

4. Playing the role of special-education director, determine the staffing resources sufficient to provide the educational services for all categories of students with disabilities in a middle school with an enrollment of 450 students. How did you determine your staffing allocations? Contact the special-education director for your local middle school, and compare your special-education teacher–student ratio to the one in that school. What are the differences? Are there any changes you would make to your resource allocations after speaking with the local special-education director?

Financing Educational Facilities

Most school finance texts focus on current revenues and expenditures—money raised and spent in a single year. The focus on current resources has been typical in most school finance activity and research over the past 30 or more years. However, there is another important finance issue that all states and school districts must deal with—the financing of school facilities. This has recently become more important as many of the school finance adequacy court rulings have required adequate school facilities as part of an adequate educational program. So we thought it appropriate to place this chapter immediately after the chapter that identifies adequate programs and services.

This chapter looks at the issue of capital funding for schools, discussing the differences between financing current and capital expenditures. It also describes how school districts raise funds to build new schools, renovate existing schools, and finance long-term capital improvements to their facilities and grounds. We will discuss the complexities of bond financing, the equity issues surrounding the use of property taxes to pay off the principal and interest on bonds levied by school systems, current court rulings on capital funding for schools, and the alternative finance options available to states and school districts as they strive to build and maintain adequate school facilities.

This chapter is divided into four sections. The first section discusses the condition of school facilities in the United States. In that section, we review current court rulings on facilities adequacy and discuss the actions some states have taken to meet the requirements of those court rulings. Section 2 considers how facilities are financed, and section 3 examines the literature on whether school facilities affect student performance. The chapter concludes with a summary of the current literature on the impact of school facilities on student learning.

1. THE CONDITION OF SCHOOL FACILITIES IN THE UNITED STATES

There has been a great deal of discussion since 1990 about the condition of school facilities in the United States. The Education Writers Association (Lewis et al., 1989) emphasized the need to consider the condition of school facilities. The existence of tremendous disparities in the condition of school buildings was highlighted by Jonathan Kozol in his book *Savage Inequalities* (1992). Since then, a number of organizations have attempted to better understand why many school buildings are substandard and what it might cost to upgrade them.

A number of difficulties are associated with determining the facility needs of our nation's schools, including these:

- An absence of good data on facilities and their conditions in many states
- Few clear standards on what constitutes an "adequate" school facility
- An inability to account for routine—but deferred—maintenance and repairs
- A lack of understanding of the costs of upgrading existing school facilities to meet the demands of schooling today—particularly an issue in relation to the growing demands of technology on the infrastructure of school buildings

While each of these represents an important issue in ascertaining what it will cost to bring all school facilities up to standard, the biggest problem is a lack of clear data on exactly what is needed.

The National Education Association (2000) has identified six specific components of school infrastructure needs:

1. New construction
2. Deferred maintenance
3. Renovation
4. Retrofitting
5. Additions
6. Major improvements to grounds

The costs of each of these can be substantial, and individual school and district needs vary depending on the age of existing school buildings and the current population needs of each school district and state.

The National Center for Education Statistics (Lewis et al., 2000) estimated that in 1999 one-quarter of school campuses in the United States had at least one building in less-than-adequate condition. These campuses enrolled some 11 million children, of whom 3.5 million attended school on a campus where at least one building was in poor condition or even nonoperational. Many other schools have adequate facilities but need upgrades to provide enough electricity for computers or infrastructure improvements for networks within the school and connections to the Internet. One of the problems with assessing school facility needs is the somewhat subjective issue of what constitutes an adequate facility.

The National Center for Education Statistics (NCES) survey of school facilities did not find substantial differences in the condition of school buildings related to school characteristics such as instructional level, school size (enrollment), or location in a city, suburb, or rural area. However, schools with more than 70 percent of students eligible for free and reduced-price lunches had more buildings that were reported to be in less-than-adequate condition. These schools were typically located in urban areas where the buildings tended to be older (Lewis et al., 2000).

This description of facility needs leads to the question of how much it might cost to upgrade or modernize school facilities today. Unfortunately, data about school facilities and construction needs are not kept uniformly by the states—and even many districts do not have accurate assessments of the conditions of their facilities. Thus, estimates have been hard to find. The U.S. General Accounting Office (GAO) has conducted a number of studies on the condition of school facilities in the early 1990s (General Accounting Office, 1995a, 1995b, 1995c, 1996, 2000). The GAO estimated the construction and deferred-maintenance needs of the public schools to be $112 billion (General Accounting Office, 1995a).

In 2000, the GAO issued a report indicating that between 1990 and 1997, there had been a considerable increase in school construction expenditures in most of the states. The National Education Association (NEA) also conducted an analysis of school modernization needs. In 2000, the NEA estimated that a total of $321.9 billion would be needed nationwide to fully modernize school facilities. It divided this figure into two major components: (1) $268.2 billion for school infrastructure and (2) $53.7 billion for educational technology (National Education Association, 2000). Moreover, it found considerable differences in facility needs by state. New York had the largest funding need among the 50 states, with modernization requiring over $50 billion ($47.6 billion for infrastructure and $3 billion for technology). California had the second-largest need, amounting to nearly $33 billion ($22 billion for infrastructure and $10.9 billion for technology). Seven states were estimated to need more than $10 billion to meet their school modernization needs, and more than 40 percent of the total need was accounted for by five states—New York, California, Ohio, New Jersey, and Texas (National Education Association, 2000).

Court Rulings on School Facilities

Many state school finance cases (see Chapter 2) have included some discussion of school facilities.[1] However, the pressure to resolve the general school-funding issues in these

---

[1]These include New Jersey (*Robinson v. Cahill*, 303 A.2d. 273 [1973]), California (*Serrano v. Priest*, Cal. 3d 584, 487 P.2d 1241, 96 Cal. Rptr. 601 [1971 or 1976]), Colorado (*Lujan v. Colorado State Board of Education*, 649 P.2d 1005 [1982]), Texas (*Edgewood Independent School District v. Kirby*, 777 S.W.2d 391 [1989]), and Montana (*Helena Elementary School District No. One v. Montana*, 236 Mont. 44, 769 P.2d 684 [1989]).

cases (whether successful or not) overshadowed facility issues, so, in most instances, little attention was paid to financing school facilities.[2]

In other states, facilities have played a greater role in court rulings. *Roosevelt Elementary School v. Bishop*,[3] in Arizona, focused primarily on school facilities, with the court requiring the state to implement a program to help school districts finance their school facilities. In recent adequacy cases,[4] courts have ruled that facilities are an essential component of an adequate education. In California, plaintiffs in a school finance adequacy suit took a somewhat different approach. In the complaint filed in *Williams v. California*,[5] the plaintiffs alleged that deteriorating and unsanitary facilities proved that school funding in California is inadequate. In an interesting development, the state of California in a cross complaint alleged that the districts had adequate funding, and the problem was poor management on the part of some school districts. The case was settled in 2004 with an agreement that the state would spend approximately $1 billion to identify and repair deteriorating, low-performing schools, and to provide additional instructional materials in those schools. The settlement also established a process for identifying facility problems and concerns that would be established in each school across the state.

Although this litigation trend has continued, no national source of data on school facilities construction is currently available. A number of states, including Arkansas, Wyoming, Kentucky, Texas, Arizona, California, and New Jersey have embarked on significant programs to better record the number and condition of school facilities in their states. In many of these states, the efforts to measure the condition of school facilities have resulted in the construction of new facilities or renovations to existing facilities. In the bulk of the cases where the most school construction has taken place, it has been in response to court rulings regarding facility adequacy. Facilities have been an important part of school finance litigation in Alaska, Arizona, Arkansas, Colorado, Idaho, Louisiana, New Jersey, New Mexico, and Wyoming. These cases tend to be argued from the perspective of adequacy, addressing the crucial issue of whether schools and school districts receive enough facilities funding to educate children to the applicable standard.[6]

Sciarra, Bell, and Kenyon (2006), in summarizing current adequacy litigation surrounding school facilities, suggested that there have been two approaches to filing facility adequacy suits across the United States. The comprehensive approach includes facilities in adequacy challenges of school funding systems. Sciarra and colleagues noted that courts facing stacks of statistical evidence regarding student performance and learning often look

---

[2]One exception to this was California. It was not the court ruling in *Serrano*, however, but rather passage of Proposition 13 in 1978 that forced the state to help with facility construction costs. Because Proposition 13 prohibited the levying of ad valorem property taxes in excess of 1 percent of assessed value for any purpose, property-tax-guaranteed bond issues could not be issued in that state for eight years, until another constitutional amendment was passed allowing bond measures for capital construction purposes.

[3]179 Ariz. 233, 877 P.2d 806 (1994).

[4]These include Ohio (*DeRolph v. State*, 78 Ohio St. 3d 193, 677 N.E.2d 733 [1997]), Wyoming (*Campbell County School District v. State*, 907 P.2d 1238 [1995]), and Arkansas (*Lakeview v. Huckabee*, 01-836, Ark. Sup. Ct. [2002]).

[5]312 236, dept. 16, Cal. Sup. Ct. City and County of San Francisco.

[6]*Roosevelt Elementary School District Number 66 v. Arizona*, 2003; *Lake View School District #25 v. Huckabee*, 2005; *Idaho Schools for Equal Educational Opportunity v. Idaho*, 2006; *Abbott v. Burke*, 2005; *Zuni Public School District v. New Mexico*, 2002; *DeRolph v. Ohio*, 1997; *Campbell County School District v. State*, 1995.

to the facilities data as being more accessible (i.e., it is hard to argue with photos of broken toilets, dirty floors, and leaking ceilings). Courts faced with this type of evidence in New Jersey, Ohio, Alabama, Arkansas, New York, and Wyoming have required that facility improvements be part of an adequate education.

Wyoming and Arkansas undertook comprehensive reviews of every school building in their states. Wyoming was able to place an index number between 1 and 100 on the condition of each building. Faced with these data, the court in Campbell III[7] ruled that schools with index numbers below 49 required immediate replacement or renovation, and all schools with index numbers below 90 needed to be brought to a standard of at least 90 as soon as possible. Between 2002 and 2008, the Wyoming School Facilities Commission estimates that it will spend $990 million on school renovation and construction (see sfc.state.wy.us/index.aspx for details). Arkansas has spent approximately $900 million on facilities construction since the court ruling in the *Lake View* case, which included a mandate for adequate school facilities.

Sciarra, Bell, and Kenyon (2006) noted that plaintiffs in Arizona, Idaho, and California took a more "focused" approach to facilities, choosing to center the challenge squarely on the issue of inadequate school facilities as a way to generate a ruling questioning the equity and/or adequacy of the funding system. In response, Arizona and California have, to date, spent more money on school facilities. However, Idaho has challenged the court's ruling regarding school facilities, and to date those challenges have not been resolved, and no additional facility funding has been appropriated for school renovation and construction.

What's clear from this discussion is that there is a tremendous need for more money to build and modernize school buildings. The need varies considerably from state to state, and within states there are vast differences in the condition of school facilities across school district boundaries and sometimes within districts. These disparities in the quality of school facilities stem from the federalist approach we use in this country to govern education (i.e., with a strong sense of local authority and control). In a number of states, the courts have recognized both that school facilities are important to the educational process and that there are substantial inequities in how new facilities, repairs, and facilities modernization efforts are funded. In some states, programs to mitigate the disequalizing effects of differing property wealth have been implemented. The next section discusses how facilities are funded and how one might measure the equity of facility distribution methods.

2. FINANCING SCHOOL FACILITY CONSTRUCTION AND REPAIR

The most commonly used tool in financing school facilities is general obligation bonds issues by the local school district. Because a number of important equity issues are associated with the use of local bond measures, many states have developed programs to reduce these inequities, either on their own or under pressure from the courts.

---

[7]*State v. Campbell County School District*, 32 P.3d 325,327 (2001).

General Obligation Bonds

Financing school facilities has traditionally been a local responsibility. The most common approach has been to use general-obligation bonds to pay for the costs of construction. In general, with voter approval, a school district is authorized to "borrow" a given sum of money through the sale of general-obligation bonds. This "loan" is then repaid through a property tax assessment in excess of the district's property taxes for general operations. Districts receive favorable interest rates both because, as a government, investors' income from the bonds (i.e., the interest paid to investors), is generally not subject to income taxation, and because repayment of the bonds is guaranteed by the district's property tax base and a legal commitment to raise property taxes to pay for the principal and interest on the bonds.

This approach makes sense for a number of reasons. Just like most purchases of a family home, districts rarely have enough cash to fully pay for the construction of a facility when it is built. Moreover, since the life span of a new school facility is usually 30 or more years, it makes sense to pay for its construction over some portion of its life—and the duration of most bond issues is 20 years. Interest paid on school district–issued bonds is tax-free to the purchaser of those bonds, enabling districts to take advantage of low interest rates.

An equity problem arises because of variations in the ability of school districts to raise funds through property taxes to make the payments on bonds they issue. This is precisely the issue we have discussed throughout this text—variations in the local tax base lead to considerable differences in how much a district can raise with a given tax rate. Just as in our discussion of current expenditures, high-wealth districts (those with a high property value per pupil) are able raise considerably more money through a given tax effort than are low-wealth districts. Therefore, low-wealth districts often have lower-quality facilities, overcrowded schools, and/or considerably higher tax rates than their wealthier neighbors. We will discuss models for correcting these inequities below.

The mechanics of school bond issues vary from state to state. In most states, voter approval is required, and in many, there is a limit to the amount of debt a district can incur. Alaska requires state approval of local district bond issues, while in other states, the bonds are issued by another taxing jurisdiction such as a municipality or county.

Voter approval.   As Table 5.1 shows, 41 of the 50 states require local districts to gain voter approval of local bond issues. Nine of these states (California, Idaho, Iowa, Mississippi, New Hampshire, Nebraska, North Dakota, Oklahoma, and Oregon) require a supermajority for passage of bonds. This supermajority is most commonly 60 percent, although California has two passage thresholds. Traditionally, in California, the requirement was a two-thirds majority. A voter-approved change, however, allows school districts to obtain passage of a bond measure with 55 percent of the vote provided (1) the election takes place during a regularly scheduled statewide primary or general election, (2) the district establishes an oversight committee to monitor the expenditure of the bond funds, and (3) the district meets certain other accountability standards. In Oregon, in addition to obtaining a majority vote, at least 50 percent of the registered voters must vote in the bond election.

TABLE 5.1   Bond Programs and State Aid for Debt Service

State	Bonds	Conditions	Debt Limits	State Aid for Debt
Alabama	X	Municipality may issue bonds	None reported	None
Alaska	X	Districts may issue revenue warrants State approval	None reported	Reimburses up to 70%
Arizona	X	Voter approved for projects that exceed state standards	10%—unified districts	None
Arkansas	X	Voter approved 2nd lien bonds	30% AV	None
California	X	Voter approved; supermajority	None reported	None
Colorado	X	Voter approved	None	Part of basic program
Connecticut	X	Issued by municipality not school district	None reported	Limited
Delaware	X	Voter approved	10% AV	None
Florida	X	Voter approved	Not reported	None
Georgia	X	Voter approved	10% AV	Yes—equalized funding to pay for bond issues, funds for new classrooms, and additional help for low-wealth districts
Hawaii		Full state funding		
Idaho	X	Voter approved; supermajority	10–20 years	Partial subsidy—interest
Illinois	X	Voter approved	None reported	10% principal × grant index
Indiana	X	No approval but subject to remonstration	2%	Flat grant—$40/ADA in 1–12
Iowa	X	Voter approved; 60% majority	5% AV, 20 years	None
Kansas	X	Voter approved	None reported	Equalized grants—AV/p
Kentucky	X	Districts sell bonds with state oversight	20 years	Yes—flat grant, equalized assessments and grants based on unmet needs
Louisiana	X	Voter approved	10–20% AV, 40 years	None
Maine	X	Voter approved	State approval	Yes—equalized based on local need

(Continued)

TABLE 5.1 (*continued*)

State	Bonds	Conditions	Debt Limits	State Aid for Debt
Maryland		Only state-issued bonds		Not reported
Massachusetts	X	Voter approved	2.5% AV	None
Michigan	X	Voter approved	15% AV; 30 years	Equalized
Minnesota	X	Voter approved	15% market value	Included in flat grant—$24/ADA
Mississippi	X	Voter approved; 60% majority	15% AV	None
Missouri	X	Voter approved	15% tax base; 20 years	Yes—equalized funding for debt service
Montana	X	Voter approved	45% AV	
Nebraska	X	Voter approved; 55% majority	None	None
Nevada	X	Voter approved	15% AV	None
New Hampshire	X	Voter approved; 60% majority	None reported	None
New Jersey	X	Voter approved	None reported	Formula that considers debt service, district basic aid percentage, eligible costs, and LEA fulfillment of maintenance requirements
New Mexico	X	Voter approved	6% AV	None
New York	X	Voter approved	Not reported	Equalized funding available
North Carolina	X	Voter approved	Not reported	Yes—funding based on wealth, and enrollment growth; also a flat grant based on corporate income tax receipts
North Dakota	X	Voter approved; 60% majority	10% AV	None
Ohio	X	Not reported	Not reported	None
Oklahoma	X	Voter approved; 60% majority	10% AV	None
Oregon	X	Voter approved; 50% voters with 50% majority	Based on AV and school grade level	None

(*Continued*)

State		Bond approval	Limit	Provisions
Pennsylvania	X	Voter approved	No limit	Reimbursement based on approved payment schedule
Rhode Island	X	Not reported	Not reported	State share calculated; minimum state funding is 30%
South Carolina	X	Voter approved	8% AV	Not reported
South Dakota	X	Voter approved	10% AV	None
Tennessee	X	Voter approved; issued by local municipalities, counties, etc.	None reported	Part of basic state aid
Texas	X	Voter approved	None reported	Part of Instructional Facility Allotment distributed as guaranteed yield program
Utah	X	Voter approved	40% market value	Equalized based on local effort
Vermont	X	Voter approved	None reported	Based on guaranteed yield provisions of basic aid formula
Virginia	X	Voter approved for county schools	None	Lottery allocation and maintenance supplement program
Washington	X	Voter approved	None reported	None; bonds are local required share
West Virginia	X	Voter approved	5% AV	Lottery proceeds dedicated to debt service
Wisconsin	X	Voter approved	10% AV; 20 years	Part of basic state aid formula
Wyoming	X	Voter approved	10% AV	Supplements mill levy if AV/ADM is <150% of state average

AV = assessed value
ADA = average daily attendance
ADM = average daily membership

Source: Sielke, 2002.

Debt limits. Many states impose a limit on the amount of bonded indebtedness a school district may incur. This is typically imposed as a percentage of a district's assessed valuation. While designed to protect school districts from incurring more debt than they can reasonably pay back, these limits again present equity problems. A district with a low assessed value per pupil cannot raise as much money through the bond process as a wealthier district. So, even if the voters of that poor district are willing to tax themselves at a high rate to build school facilities, they may be constrained by the state. As Table 5.1 shows, half the states impose limits of this type.

Other jurisdictions. As Table 5.1 also shows, in a number of states, jurisdictions other than local school districts actually issue the bonds. This process can make the approval and issuance of bonds more complex. However, to the extent that the greater resources of a county or municipality can equalize tax rates across school districts, or that the higher total assessed value of the government can provide a higher debt limit, it may be possible to reduce the inequities inherent in a property tax–based system. By the same token, dependent school districts may also have to compete with other service needs for bond financing.

In any case, when districts can rely only on school bonds to finance school facilities, substantial inequities exist. The courts have also noted this problem in some states.

State Assistance for School Facilities

On the surface, it would seem that funding for school facility construction could be equalized using the same formulas that are described in Chapter 9. There are a number of difficulties with this approach, however. These include variations in the timing of facility needs among school districts and the long-term costs of such programs.

District Facility Needs

Facility needs among school districts vary over time. While all school districts need at least a certain amount of funding each year to provide for ongoing expenditures, some districts have vastly greater facility needs than others. Factors that impact a district's facility needs include the school district's current enrollment and projected changes in that enrollment, the age of current school buildings, the physical condition of those buildings, and the need for major repairs and renovations to existing facilities, to either improve their condition or enable them to better accommodate today's instructional practices—in particular, the increasing power supply demands of technology.

School districts experiencing rapidly growing student enrollments need to build new schools to accommodate this growth. The need to avoid overcrowding in schools may require building new schools immediately. Many state formulas provide aid for district facilities on the basis of some figure, such as unhoused student need (i.e., the number of students exceeding the intended capacity of the schools in the district). Assuming a state has limited funds available to equalize school facility construction, how should it prioritize between districts that need to replace existing schools and ones that need to build new facilities to keep up with enrollment? Moreover, what impact does timing have on the state's decision?

Finding a fair way to distribute limited resources to schools on the basis of changes in enrollment is challenging, but even more difficult is making decisions about when funds should be made available for replacement of school buildings and for major repairs and renovations. Determination of what constitutes an "adequate" school facility is a subjective matter, though it can be guided by facilities standards, leading to the potential for heated arguments about which districts qualify for funding. Some states have established standards for school facilities that provide an objective set of measurements that can be used to assess the quality of a school facility. For example, North Carolina has established a number of standards for school construction, maintenance, and renovation that are frequently used as a model for other states. The information provided by the North Carolina Department of Public Instruction can be found on their website. The example of Wyoming's index number described above is one recent effort to resolve this issue. Information on the operation of Wyoming's construction program can be found on the Wyoming School Facilities Commission website.

Long-Term Costs of State Facility Programs

As previously mentioned, there are also substantial costs involved in equalizing the property tax levies used to pay for school facility bond issues. For example, if a state decides that it wants to devote $200 million a year to equalization of property taxes levied for school construction, it faces some difficult choices. First, assuming that an acceptable formula can be developed (which should be relatively easy to do using the models and principles discussed in Chapter 9), and that all of the $200 million is allocated to school districts in the state, the state will need to commit that amount of money to those recipient districts for the life of the bonds they issue. If the typical bond measure is paid for over 20 years, this means the state has committed something on the order of $200 million a year to the qualifying districts for 20 years.[8]

If the state wants to provide similar opportunities in the following years, it will need to find an additional $200 million in the second and each subsequent year until the first group of bonds is paid off in 20 years. If the state commits $200 million a year, after 20 years, the program will cost $4 billion a year. This hypothetical example is displayed in Table 5.2. The fundamental difference between equalizing current expenditures and facility expenditures is this "multiplicative" effect resulting from the 20-year life of a bond issue.

Other options for state assistance for school facilities are in use in some states. These include flat grants, categorical grants, equalization aid, support within the basic

---

[8]The estimate is approximate as the actual assistance to a school district will vary with variations in the district's assessed value each year.

TABLE 5.2   Hypothetical Costs of a State Facility Equalization Program

Year	State Annual Commitment to Equalization Program (in millions)	Total State Cost per Year (in millions)
1	$200	$ 200
2	200	400
3	200	600
4	200	800
5	200	1,000
6	200	1,200
7	200	1,400
8	200	1,600
9	200	1,800
10	200	2,000
11	200	2,200
12	200	2,400
13	200	2,600
14	200	2,800
15	200	3,000
16	200	3,200
17	200	3,400
18	200	3,600
19	200	3,800
20	200	4,000

Assumptions:
1. State commits $200 million in new funding annually.
2. All bond measures have 20-year payback period.

state support program for current expenditures, and full state funding. The use of each of these models in 2001–02 in each of the states is summarized in Table 5.3.

Flat grants.   Identical to the flat grants described in Chapter 9, flat grants are used in nine states to support school facilities. For example, Indiana provides $40 per pupil in funding for debt service to all school districts. Kentucky provides each district $100 per pupil, in addition to other facilities aid programs. Flat grants for facility construction suffer from the same problems as flat grants used for current operations: they are disequalizing in that they provide the same amount of money to all districts regardless of need and/or wealth. If districts receive this money regardless of wealth or existing debt, some clearly benefit more than others from the state program. Districts without facility construction needs would be advantaged as they could use the funds for maintenance and renovation. This method works best once it is agreed that all districts have adequate facilities.

TABLE 5.3 State School Infrastructure Funding Programs, 2001–02

State	State Funding Program	Flat Grant	Equalized	Basic Support	Full Funding	Categorical Grant	None
Alabama	Guaranteed tax yield for capital improvements.		X				
Alaska	Grants with required local contribution ranging from 5–35%.		X				
	Reimburses debt up to 70%. Debt must be preauthorized.		X				
Arizona	Full-state funding within required state standards. Per-pupil amount for "soft," short-term capital needs.				X		
Arkansas	Provided within basic state aid—ADM × wealth index × $39.	X					
California	State provides approximately 55–66% of costs.						
Colorado	Included in basic support program—$223–800 per pupil.			X		X	
Connecticut	Equalized funding for 20–80% of eligible costs. Magnet schools receive 100%.		X				
	Additional funding for initiatives such as early childhood, reduced class size, full-day kindergarten.				X		
Delaware	State pays 60–80% of costs. Equalized based on taxing ability.		X				
Florida	PECO funds projects based on need.					X	
Georgia	Equalized funding based on AV/p ranging from 75–90%. SPLOST funds also included in the formula.		X				
	Grants for new classrooms, reduced class-size initiatives.					X	
	Additional incentives available for low-wealth districts.					X	

(Continued)

TABLE 5.3 (Continued)

State	State Funding Program	Flat Grant	Equalized	Basic Support	Full Funding	Categorical Grant	None
Hawaii	Full state funding.				X		
Idaho	Subsidies for debt retirement based on mill rate, health and safety issues.	X				X	
Illinois	Equalized grants based on EAV/p at the 90th percentile.		X				
	Grants for debt service equaling 10% of principal × grant index.		X				
Indiana	Flat grant of $40 per pupil ADA in grades 1–12. Purpose—debt service.	X					
Iowa	Grants based on enrollment size and inverse relationship with sales tax proceeds. Required local equalized match based on district fiscal capacity. Minimum match is 20%.		X				
Kansas	Weighting per pupil in basic aid of 0.25 for costs of new facility.	X					
	Grants for debt service equalized inversely to AV per pupil.		X				
Kentucky	Flat grant of $100 per pupil.	X					
	District levy of 5¢/$100 AV equalized if property wealth is <150% of state average.		X				
	Grants for debt service based on percent of district unmet needs compared with state unmet needs.		X				
Louisiana	No state funding.						X

(Continued)

Maine	Funding for debt service based on local share for approved projects.				
Maryland	Funding based on state share of minimum foundation/pupil. Minimum is 50% of costs.		X		
Massachusetts	Reimbursement of 50–90% for approved projects. Funding based on calculation of property value, average income, district poverty level, and incentive points (type of construction, project manager, efficiency, maintenance history).		X		
Michigan	No state funding.		X		X
Minnesota	Funding by weighted ADM × ($173 + district average building age). Equalized debt service aid. Incentive grants such as $30 per year-round pupil served, health and safety issues.		X	X	
Mississippi	Flat grant of $24 per ADA. Other grants based on specific needs.	X		X	
Missouri	No state aid.				
Montana	Funding for debt service only. Based on ratio of district mill value per pupil enrollment and the state mill value per pupil.			X	X
Nebraska	Funding for accessibility and environmental issues: 0.052/$100 AV.		X	X	

(Continued)

TABLE 5.3 *(Continued)*

State	State Funding Program	Flat Grant	Equalized	Basic Support	Full Funding	Categorical Grant	None
Nevada	No state funding with exception of special appropriations for two districts due to extreme need.						X
New Hampshire	State funds 30–55% of building costs depending on number of towns. Funding not equalized.	X					
New Jersey	Abbott districts receive 100% funding.				X		
	Non-Abbott districts receive equalized funding (minimum of 40%) based on district wealth (personal income and property tax base).		X				
	Some districts may be eligible for debt service aid.						X
New Mexico	Equalized funding for voter-approved 2-mill levy.		X				
	Grants for critical needs if district bonded to 65% of capacity.						X
New York	Equalized funding based on building aid ratio and approved building expense.		X				
North Carolina	Funding provided based on ADM, growth, and low wealth.		X				
North Dakota	Additional flat grant from proceeds of corporate income tax.	X					
	No state funding.						X
Ohio	Funds Ohio School Facilities Commission.						
Oklahoma	Equity list developed based on 3-year average property wealth—local district must pass levies. State designs manual requirements.		X				
	No state funding.						X

(Continued)

Oregon	No state funding.		
Pennsylvania	Funding (reimbursement) based on the greater of district's market value aid ratio, capital account reimbursement fraction, or density.	X	
Rhode Island	Funding for debt service. State share ratio = $1 - ((\text{district wealth per pupil}/\text{state wealth per pupil}) \times 62\%)$. Minimum funding 30% of cost.		X
South Carolina	Funding allocated per pupil based on available funding divided by K–12 ADM.		X
South Dakota	No state funding.	X	
Tennessee	Funding through the basic education program. Based on cost per square foot/ADM +10% for equipment +5% for architect fees + debt service at state bond rate.	X	
Texas	Guaranteed yield funding through instructional facility allotment, which is based on size of district, property value, ADA, and amount of annual debt service.		X
Utah	Equalized funding based on local effort (.0024), AV/p, and need.		X
Vermont	Funds about 30% of cost of project based on prioritized needs. Debt service reimbursed based on guaranteed yield provisions of general-aid formula.	X	X

(Continued)

TABLE 5.3 (Continued)

State	State Funding Program	Flat Grant	Equalized	Basic Support	Full Funding	Categorical Grant	None
Virginia	Flat grant of $200,000 per district.	X					
	Remaining amount prorated based on enrollment and ability to pay.		X				
	Per-pupil supplement for maintenance and debt service.	X					
Washington	Funding based on eligible area, area cost allowance, and matching ratio. Required local effort (matching ratio) determined by comparing district AV/p to state AV/p.		X				
West Virginia	State funding based on need: efficiency, adequate space, educational improvement, educational innovations, health and safety, changing demographics. Lottery money dedicated to debt service.					X	
Wisconsin	Funding included in the basic support program.			X			
Wyoming	State supplements mill levy if AV/ADM below 150% of state average.		X				

Source: Sielke, 2002.

Equalization aid. This program, used by most states, provides funds generally in inverse relationship to a district's property wealth. The disadvantage of an equalization program was previously described and is shown in Table 5.2. This typically results in relatively low equalization efforts on the part of the state.

Basic support. Only two states, Colorado and Wisconsin, fund facilities within the basic school support funding program. In both cases, funding per pupil for facilities is provided to districts as part of the distribution of state money to schools.

Full-state support. In Hawaii, which is a state-operated school system, the state provides full funding for facilities.

Other approaches to facility funding. Table 5.4 displays for each of the states other approaches that have been used to finance school facilities. These include lease-purchase agreements, leases, and rentals of school space, as well as local option sales taxes, developer fees, and sinking funds.

Facilities Funding in Kentucky: A Comprehensive Approach

This section describes the Kentucky school facilities–funding system, which is one of the most comprehensive programs in the country. The basic elements of the current system were enacted as part of the Support Education Excellence in Kentucky (SEEK) legislation, which was passed in 1990. The funding scheme evolved over the next decade as the legislature attempted to address a variety of needs that arose in the state. Most of the changes have been systematic modifications designed to correct certain problems in the state, but some of the more recent legislation has been ad hoc in nature.

Capital Outlay program. The Kentucky funding system has contained three core elements since 1990–91. The first is the Capital Outlay program. This funding stream consists of $100 per pupil from the base SEEK outlay that each district is required to place in its Capital Outlay Fund. Therefore, the Capital Outlay program essentially functions as a flat grant to districts. The Capital Outlay funds can be used for the purposes of direct payment of construction costs, debt service on bonds, payment or lease-rental agreements that will lead to the ownership of a physical plant, deficit payments from overexpenditure for capital construction, and as a reserve for the above purposes (Kentucky Revised Statutes (KRS) 157.420(4)). The Capital Outlay program can be expected to share the typical characteristics of a flat grant program, namely, being very equitable, but not as cost-effective as other approaches.

The "First Nickel." The second element of the system is the Facilities Support Program of Kentucky (FSPK) or the so-called first nickel. The FSPK consists of a mandatory tax of $0.05, or a nickel, levied by districts on each $100 of "equivalent" value in their jurisdiction (KRS 157.440(1)(b)). The equivalent value of a district

TABLE 5.4   State School Infrastructure-Funding Programs, 2001–02

State	Additional Funding Availability
Alabama	Revenue warrants that do not exceed 80% of pledged revenue
Alaska	None
Arizona	None
Arkansas	State loan program
California	Developer fees
Colorado	Voter-approved mill levies up to 10 mills for 3 years
Connecticut	State loan program
Delaware	May assess tax rate without referenda for state matching requirements
Florida	Up to 2-mill levy without voter approval, voter-approved 1/2¢ sales tax
Georgia	Grants, voter-approved 1¢ local option sales tax up to 5 years
Hawaii	None
Idaho	2/3 majority–approved tax levies
Illinois	None
Indiana	Leases, rentals
Iowa	County local option sales tax, 1¢ up to 10 years
Kansas	Additional mill levies with approval of State Board of Tax Appeals
Kentucky	None
Louisiana	None
Maine	State revolving-loan fund
Maryland	None
Massachusetts	None
Michigan	State loan fund, sinking funds of 5 mills up to 20 years
Minnesota	State loans
Mississippi	3-mill levy up to 20 years without voter approval, state loan fund
Missouri	Lease purchase up to 20 years
Montana	Building reserves
Nebraska	Voter-approved mill levies
Nevada	Voter-approved mill levies, developer's fees
New Hampshire	None
New Jersey	Lease purchase
New Mexico	None
New York	None
North Carolina	Local option sales tax
North Dakota	Voter-approved building funds up to 20 mills annually
Ohio	None
Oklahoma	Mill levy up to 5 mills annually
Oregon	None
Pennsylvania	Some nonelected debt allowed
Rhode Island	Leases, reserve funds
South Carolina	Children's Education Endowment Fund; funding based on total revenue available, basic aid support formula, weighted pupils, and need

(Continued)

TABLE 5.4 (*continued*)

State	Additional Funding Availability
South Dakota	None
Tennessee	Lease purchase, capital outlay notes
Texas	Lease purchase
Utah	Revolving loan fund
Vermont	Sinking funds
Virginia	Revolving loan fund, pooled bond issues
Washington	Fund reserves, special levies
West Virginia	None
Wisconsin	State loan fund, sinking funds
Wyoming	None

Source: Sielke, 2002.

comprises its real property value, plus certain elements of personal property, such as automobile registration. The funds raised by the first nickel may be used for "debt service, new facilities, or major renovations of existing facilities" (KRS 157.440(1)(b)). The state equalizes the tax collection up to 150 percent of the average assessed per-pupil equivalent value in the state. The equalization funds are to be directed toward debt service as much as possible (KRS 157.440(1)(b)). The state does not recapture funds that wealthy districts collect in excess of the equalized amount, so it is possible for those districts to raise funds in excess of the equalization amount.

SFCC regular funding.   The third element of the system is the School Facilities Construction Committee (SFCC) regular offer. The SFCC funding is designed to provide extra debt service to districts that have unmet facilities needs. The SFCC offers are based on legislative appropriations, which in recent years have been approximately $100 million. The offer each district receives equals the percentage of the funding that is proportional to that district's percentage of the state's unmet facilities needs. Districts do not have to accept the offer. If the offer is declined, the SFCC retains the funds for the district for eight years. This permits the district to accumulate multiple offers and use them for one large-scale project. Once the district accepts an offer, the funds become "obligated" by the state. The amount of the obligated funds can, and often does, differ from the amount offered, so we have evaluated the systems equity twice in each year, first using the amount offered and second using the amount obligated.

The SFCC funding stream would appear to be a likely source of horizontal inequity in the system, since different districts would have different unmet needs. However, the program may contribute to vertical equity of facilities funding by providing additional funds to districts that possess the greatest need for improved facilities.

The First Growth Nickel.   The First Growth Nickel was added to the system as part of the 1994–96 biennial budget. This program applies only to growing districts, defined as those that have these features:

- Growth of at least 3 percent and 150 students or more over the past five years
- Bonded debt to their maximum capacity
- Student enrollment in excess of classroom space
- An approved facility plan (KRS 157.621(2))

The First Growth Nickel permitted growing districts to levy an additional $0.05 equivalent tax, which would raise an amount equal to that raised locally via the FSPK. This tax is not subject to voter recall, but it was not originally equalized by the state. This tax was expected to reduce the horizontal equity of the system, but it may increase its vertical equity by providing funds to districts that are experiencing rapid growth.

The Second Growth Nickel.   The legislature created two more local tax options as part of the 2002–04 biennial budget. The first of these was the creation of the Second Growth Nickel, which functions the same as the First Growth Nickel, with one important exception. Districts that levy the Second Growth Nickel are eligible to receive equalization of the First Growth Nickel, but the Second Growth Nickel itself is unequalized. This tax was expected to have the same impact on equity as the First Growth Nickel.

The Recallable Nickel.   The second tax option is the Recallable Nickel. All 176 Kentucky school districts are eligible to levy this tax, but the tax is subject to recall by the voters of the district. For the first several years, this tax also was not equalized by the state, but that changed in the 2005–06 school year when it was equalized. This program also seemed likely to reduce the horizontal equity of the system but unlikely to increase its vertical equity.

The Equalized Facility Funding program.   The Equalized Facility Funding (EFF) program provides equalization funding to districts that levied, or have debt service on, a $0.10 equivalent tax rate for building purposes and have not received growth equalization or another EFF. Like the Recallable Nickel, the EFF was expected to reduce the horizontal equity of the system without increasing its vertical equity.

Additional funding for category 5 buildings.   Finally, the state also provides funding to districts that have buildings that rate as "Category 5" on the Department of Education's building assessment. Category 5 buildings rate as being in "poor" condition and are generally more than 40 years old. Category 4 buildings are described as those that need renovation, which implies that Category 5 buildings need to be replaced or require even greater renovation. This funding comes outside of the normal funding formula and is administered by the SFCC.

Summary.   Very few states have this many facilities-funding components. As mentioned, some of the components are provided to all districts, and others are focused on special facilities needs for specific types of districts. In the next section, we briefly discuss the results of a study on the horizontal and vertical equity impacts of the overall system.

Assessing the Equity of School Facility Funding

As hinted at above, facilities equity can be an important equity concern, especially when facilities quality and funding are extremely unequal. For example, the fact that several rural Alaska school districts had facilities with collapsing roofs, no drinking water, sewage backup, and buildings filled to nearly double their capacity played an important role in the court declaring facilities financing unconstitutional in Alaska (*Kasayulie v. Alaska*, 1999). Alaska's position was further weakened because its capital improvement funding program went unfunded, and its bond program was restricted to incorporated cities and boroughs and called for a 30/70 percent split in funding between the locality and the state, which meant that poor and/or unincorporated rural districts could not participate in the bond program (*Kasayulie v. Alaska*, 1999).

States often overlook facilities equity issues, despite their importance (Vornberg and Andrews-Pool, 1998). In fact, very few studies of facility finance equity exist. Among those few studies, Arsen and colleagues (2005) assessed the equity of facilities funding in Michigan, where facilities are funded almost exclusively at the local level. They judged equity using four criteria: (1) the range of funding disparities between districts, (2) building quality differences, (3) unmet needs differences, and (4) different effective tax rates. They found that poor districts had access to less funding due to their lower capacity and had lower-quality buildings, greater unmet needs, and higher effective tax rates. Thus, the Michigan funding system produced a negative impact on poor districts in every possible way. The authors listed five possible reforms, including state financing of certain bonds, facilities grants, and facilities-funding equalization.

Small school districts are another group that can face facilities-funding shortfalls. Hughes (2000) showed that small districts in Arkansas faced several hurdles that impeded their ability to receive equitable funding. These factors included lower property values and less ability to sustain higher tax rates.

Lowe (1996) found inequities in the California facilities-funding system. Unlike the previously discussed studies, Lowe used a broad spectrum of the typical equity statistics, rather than focusing on just the range. Lowe found that the California system contained widespread inequity, especially at the bottom of its distribution.

The foregoing studies contain an important similarity: they apply the usual equity measures (or a subset thereof) to the study of facility equity. This usage of the statistics is consistent with the suggestions of other authors (see, e.g., Sielke, 1998).

An analysis of school facilities equity should follow the same logic and analysis tools described in Chapter 3, and should consider both horizontal and vertical equity. While the statistics described in Chapter 3 do an excellent job of estimating horizontal equity, measurement of vertical equity is more complex and can be accomplished either through pupil weights or by removing from the equation all the programs that address special needs and assessing the horizontal equity of the remaining programs. The pupil-weight measure of vertical equity does not seem useful in this situation because no valid weighting system exists to adjust for differing facilities needs, so any weights assigned would be purely arbitrary.

Thus, one approach to vertical equity assessment of facilities programs is to measure the equity of programs that were designed to promote horizontal equity, but go one step further by investigating the extent to which the funding that is designed to achieve vertical equity reaches the intended districts.

A pathbreaking study on school facility equalization was recently completed by Glenn, Picus, Odden, and Aportela (2006). Kentucky has a number of programs to provide financing for school facilities, some aimed at providing equalized aid to school districts that elect to renovate existing schools or build new ones, and some aimed at specific groups of districts—those with growing enrollments and with facilities in poor condition. Glenn and colleagues conducted a horizontal and vertical equity analysis of the Kentucky system, concluding that the flat grant and foundation program portions of the system, money available to all school districts, was equitably distributed. The authors also found that programs aimed at specific districts seemed to provide funds to those districts as well, offering some sense of vertical equity, although some of these programs did not seem to be as highly equalized as the flat grants and foundation aid to districts. Finally, it was recommended that Kentucky develop standards for adequate facilities and that it improve its measurement system for the condition of school buildings.

While funding for facilities will clearly continue to be an important issue in school finance, likely becoming more important as school finance adequacy issues move to the forefront in more states, a key question remains: What impact do school facilities have on student performance? We address this issue briefly in section 3.

3. THE IMPACT OF SCHOOL FACILITIES ON STUDENT PERFORMANCE[9]

Conventional wisdom suggests that a school's physical environment has an effect on student learning, but researchers have had difficulty demonstrating a statistically significant relationship. Despite the fact that several hundred studies have been conducted on how school buildings affect student achievement, there are no conclusive findings. Many of the studies were based on the open-schools movement of the 1970s and are no longer relevant to today's schools. Most of the rest are plagued with severe methodological problems and, not surprisingly, produce conflicting, ambiguous results.

It is difficult to study the relationship between school building quality and student achievement. To begin with, there are measurement problems. School building quality involves numerous factors, many of which are hard to separate and most of which are hard to measure objectively. Some studies have attempted to look at each factor separately, independently assessing how, say, paint color, carpeting, lighting, thermal control, and acoustics affect student learning. Other studies take one composite measure such as

---

[9]This section draws heavily on Picus, Marion, Calvo, and Glenn, 2005: and Glenn, Picus, Marion, and Calvo, 2006.

building age and use it as a proxy for general building condition. However, both approaches are problematic. When researchers attempt to independently assess each factor, they may run into difficulties controlling for the other factors and understanding how they relate to one another. On the other hand, using a composite variable like building age may create difficulties as well, since schools have different life spans. A 40-year-old building that was initially constructed to last 35 years will likely be in significantly worse condition than a similarly aged building designed to last 100 years. Also, the deferred-maintenance decisions made by school officials have a profound affect on building upkeep, further obscuring the relationship between building age and condition.

In addition to measurement difficulties, school building quality studies suffer from data availability problems. When examining how the building environment affects student learning, researchers ideally would like to control for a host of other factors, such as parents' education level and occupation, percent of the student body on free lunch, median family income, percent of single-parent families, number of student transfers, school size, length of school day, amount of instructional time, principals' experience, district allocation of operating funds, entry-level student achievement, school climate, motivation, class size, homework and attendance policies, and teacher experience and credentials. Unfortunately, these data, along with an objective measure of building quality and student achievement, are rarely all available for large-scale studies. The studies that have been completed so far control for only a tiny fraction of all these factors—they might take into account only the percent of students on free lunch, for instance—making it impossible to draw definitive conclusions about the effects of building quality alone on student learning. Given these problems, not surprisingly, researchers have not conclusively demonstrated a relationship between school building condition and student achievement.

Several attempts have been made to summarize the research in this field, most recently by Earthman and LeMasters (1996). They encapsulated the findings from two previous literature reviews—Weinstein (1979) and McGuffey and Brown (1978)—who together covered 232 separate studies on how buildings influence students. Their main conclusion was that "even with this large number of studies, it is difficult to determine any definite line of consistent findings" (p. 3). After cautioning that there were serious methodological problems and difficulties in interpreting the studies, McGuffey examined the "preponderance of the evidence" and drew two major conclusions: (1) old, obsolete buildings have a detrimental effect on student achievement, while modern buildings facilitate learning; and (2) building conditions have a differing impact across grades and subjects. Specifically, McGuffey found that the research supported school building age, thermal factors, lighting quality, color, acoustic factors, and school size as factors affecting student achievement, while no relationship was found for open space, amount of space, windowless facilities, and underground facilities.

McGuffey's finding that building conditions have a differing impact across grade levels and subjects is a difficult finding to explain, given that the underlying theory suggests that facilities affect behavior, which in turn affects learning. The theoretical base is best summarized by a 1989 Carnegie Foundation for the Advancement of Teachers report: "The report acknowledged that a good building does not necessarily make a good school, but points out that students' attitudes toward education and the prospect of educational success, are a reflection of their environment. The report notes that the tacit message of the physical indignities in many urban schools is not lost on students. It bespeaks neglect, and students' conduct seems simply an extension of the physical environment that surrounds them" (Berner, 1993, p. 9).

There is nothing in this theory to explain why some grade levels would be more affected by building condition than others. The more puzzling issue is why some subjects, such as math and social studies, would be affected differently. The theory runs into further difficulty because the link between facilities and student behavior is even more tenuous than the link between facilities and achievement. For example, some of the studies that claim to find a positive relationship between building condition and student learning also report finding a negative relationship between facility quality and student behavior.

McGuffey acknowledged that facilities have a very small potential impact on student learning, but they are still one of the variables over which school officials have complete control, unlike many of the other factors thought to influence student learning. Given this, shouldn't schools make every effort to ensure high-quality facilities? The answer may be no. It is extremely costly to build, maintain, and renovate facilities, and it is possible that it would be more cost-effective to use that money elsewhere. The amount of funding for education is limited, and school officials must choose how to best allocate their resources. Improved carpeting in a school may come at the expense of hiring more or better teachers. If future studies concentrate on specific elements of building structure and maintenance, and do so in a way that takes cost into consideration, schools may be able to assess whether installing air-conditioning, painting the walls certain colors, or adding better lighting will raise student scores, or whether they are better off buying new textbooks. Future studies would do well to take costs into consideration, and some type of cost-benefit analyses might be a productive line of research.

Researchers have obtained contradictory results on whether building age is related to student achievement. Because it is an objective measure with readily available data, researchers would like to be able to use building age as a proxy for building condition. While several early studies found a relationship between the two, some more recent studies have not. Building age is not necessarily a sound reflection of condition because buildings are built with different projected life spans and receive differing amounts of maintenance.

One solution that researchers should consider is using the percent of the life span attained rather than age itself as the independent variable, perhaps controlling for the level of maintenance funding. Another issue is that building age is not a particularly useful variable even if it does turn out to have a direct relationship to student achievement, because it would be impractical to replace schools every 10 years or so to ensure that they were constantly "modern." As already noted, it is more important to discover what aspects of building condition in particular are important to student achievement, and thus know what areas of maintenance (or levels of funding) are most crucial.

Finally, several studies have suggested that cosmetic building condition has a greater effect on student achievement than structural condition, for which the reported effect seems to range from weak to none at all. But the authors of these studies failed to discuss the implications of these findings, which appear to support routine maintenance efforts rather than the construction of state-of-the-art new schools. This approach is actually in line with the underlying theory, because while students would be expected to notice cosmetic features, they would be less likely to be affected by structural problems on a day-to-day level. This is not to say that structural factors are unimportant. Whether or not structural factors have a direct influence on student achievement, it is important to maintain buildings for safety reasons and for financial reasons—a little bit of maintenance funding goes a long way in forestalling major repairs down the road.

A recent study on the impact of school facilities on student achievement found virtually no linkage between the condition/quality of school facilities and student outcomes on standardized test scores (Picus, Marion, Calvo, and Glenn, 2005; Glenn, Picus, Marion, and Calvo, 2006). Using the results of standardized test scores from Wyoming students and a detailed assessment of every school building in the state of Wyoming, the study concluded that there is essentially no relationship between the quality of school facilities and student performance when other factors known to impact student performance are accounted for. This is not to suggest that investments in school facilities are not important—all children are entitled to attend school in safe, clean, and appropriate educational environments. But policymakers should be aware that investments in facilities by themselves are unlikely to improve student learning.

4. SUMMARY

Most of this book, as well as most studies of school finance, focuses on current expenditures—the ongoing expenditures of school systems to provide educational services to children. Despite this focus, considerable educational resources are devoted to the construction and renovation of school facilities each year. These expenditures occur on an irregular basis depending on a number of factors, including school enrollments, the age of existing facilities, and the capability of those buildings to meet today's educational standards and expectations. As a result, school districts typically resort to the use of long-term payment plans for their facility needs.

The most common approach to facility (and other capital) financing is the issuance of general-obligation bonds, guaranteed by the property tax wealth and tax-raising capacity of the school district. While this approach makes sense, reliance on local property taxes, and the willingness of local voters to approve the use of local property taxes to finance facilities, leads to disparities in the quality of local facilities.

The problems with property tax–based financing of school facilities are identical to those identified earlier in this book for financing the current operations of schools. It is made more complex by the long-term obligation created by the sale of bonds for school facilities and the fact that individual school district capital construction needs vary considerably. The result is that it is harder to develop programs that equalize these differences, and many of the solutions come with considerable costs.

This issue is made still more complex because there is relatively little data on the impact of school facilities on student learning. While clean, modern facilities would seem to be important to a quality education, evidence suggests that if such a relationship exists at all, it has a very small impact on student learning.

Study Questions

1. Find out how school facilities are funded in your state.
   a. What is the relative role or responsibilitiy of local school districts and of the state?
   b. What are the requirements for general-obligation bonds? Is local voter approval required? If so, what percentage of the vote is needed for passage?
   c. Are there limits on the level of bonds that can be issued by individual districts? If so, what are they?
   d. Do local school districts have alternatives to bonds for facility construction? What are those alternatives? (Examples might include such things as developer fees, special assessments, new tax districts, and alternative borrowing instruments.)
2. If the state has a facility construction program, determine how it operates. In addition, conduct an ex ante analysis of the potential equity of the program. You don't need to collect large amounts of data or do a formal equity analysis. Rather, given the nature of the programs in place in your state, assess the potential equity of the facility finance system.
3. Look into the school construction in your district. Does it currently have a building program in place? If so, how is it being funded? If not, is one needed, and what are the district's plans? Is the district's facility plan focused on renovation or replacement of aging facilities or on construction of new facilites to accommodate enrollment growth?

Allocation and Use of the Education Dollar

For more than a century, revenues per pupil for education, after adjusting for inflation, have consistently increased decade after decade, but over the past 50–60 years, most of the new dollars have not gone into the regular classroom. Instead, those dollars were used to pay for specialists in the school who provided services for noncore subjects or for extra student needs outside the regular classroom. This allocation of new education resources helps explain why pupil–staff ratios have declined substantially but actual class sizes have not. Most of these changes have occurred within the instructional function. However, because the percent of the education dollar spent on instruction has stayed about the same over this time, these changes have largely gone unnoticed. This chapter explores our increasing knowledge about how the education dollar is used and where new dollars have gone. We start with national averages and then move through the system, from the states and local school districts to schools, and use a new expenditure-reporting framework that identifies resource use at the school level by educational strategy. The latter is the type of information that is required to understand resource use and to make informed decisions about how to use resources even more effectively, an issue addressed in the next chapter.

This chapter has two sections. The first tells the story of how resources for education have changed over time, in terms of the total amount, expenditures by function, and the ways dollars are allocated. At the end of the first section, resources for K–12 education are summarized as being in one of three categories—core instruction, instructional support, or overhead—for ease of understanding. The second section uses one of the most detailed, existing sources of data from the school level, the 1999–2000 Schools and Staffing Survey (SASS), a National Center for Education Statistics (NCES) database, to analyze staffing patterns and resource use for core instruction and instructional support at the school level. However, even this database does not contain the level of detail needed to fully understand how educational expenditures are used in a programmatic sense. Therefore, this section concludes with examples of school-level spending for an elementary school and a high school using a newly created expenditure structure that arrays staffing resources by educational strategy.

1. CHANGES IN EDUCATIONAL RESOURCES OVER TIME

This section discusses several aspects of the level and use of education resources over the past several decades and describes how these changes have affected schools.

Changes in the Level of Resources

Despite the belief to the contrary of many educators as well as much of the public and even the policy community, real dollars per pupil for public schools rose consistently during the twentieth century and continue to rise in the twenty-first century. According to a hundred-year analysis by Hanushek and Rivkin (1997), real dollars per pupil (i.e., resources after inflation) increased by about 3.5 percent annually from 1890 to 1990. Resource increases slowed down substantially during the first half of the 1990s, but then picked up again and began rising in the beginning of the twenty-first century at about the same pace as prior to 1990. Since the figures are on a per-pupil basis, they indicate resource growth over and above enrollment growth, thus controlling for events such as the rapid expansion of high school education between 1925 and 1950, and rapid growth in enrollments during the baby boom following World War II. Moreover, we see that dollars per pupil adjusted for inflation grew essentially every decade, during good and bad economic times, although in good economic times the growth was larger. These changes can also be seen in Table 6.1, which uses NCES data.

Indeed, per-pupil expenditures averaged just under $9,000 for the 2003 school year, the latest year for which NCES reported data are available. The National Education Association (2005) estimates that per-pupil expenditures amounted to $9,102 for the 2004–05 school year. Although these figures are national averages, it is important to point out that while the level of per-pupil spending varies substantially across the 50 states, the overall growth pattern described above and in Table 6.1 is consistent for nearly all of the states.

This consistent and substantial increase in educational resources, after adjusting for enrollment growth and inflation, is one reason Hanushek and others began to ponder the dilemma of the relatively small improvements in performance among schoolchildren despite the large increases in spending. Resolving this dilemma, or more importantly, determining how to produce a more positive correlation between increases in spending and improved student performance, is one objective of Chapters 6 and 7.

Educational Expenditures by Function

The data on school expenditures presented above suggest some obvious questions: What happened to the new dollars? How were they used? Did resource use patterns change over time? And did resource use patterns reflect the most effective uses of those dollars?

TABLE 6.1   Total Expenditure per Pupil in Public Elementary and Secondary Schools in Nominal and Real Dollars, 1969–70 to 2002–03

School Year	Unadjusted Total Expenditures per Pupil	Total Expenditures in Constant 2004–05 Dollars[a]	Percentage Change from Previous Period
1969–70	$ 751	$3,812	
1979–80	2,088	5,157	35.28%
1980–81	2,307	5,106	(0.99)
1989–90	4,643	7,009	37.27
1990–91	4,902	7,017	0.11
1994–95	5,529	7,046	0.41
1995–96	5,689	7,059	0.18
1996–97	5,923	7,145	1.22
1997–98	6,189	7,335	2.66
1998–99	6,508	7,582	3.37
1999–2000	6,912	7,827	3.23
2000–01	7,380	8,080	3.23
2001–02	7,727	8,313	2.88
2002–03	8,044	8,468	1.86

[a]Based on the Consumer Price Index, prepared by the Bureau of Labor Statistics, U.S. Department of Labor, adjusted to a school-year basis.

Source: National Center for Education Statistics, 2006, Table 166. Retrieved from http://nces.ed.gov/programs/digest/d05/tables/dt05_166.asp on July 24, 2006.

Much of the information about the use of resources for education is available as expenditures by function. The primary functions are as follows:

- *Instruction.* This includes all resources dedicated to providing instruction to students, including teacher and instructional aide salaries, benefits, books, purchased services, tuition, and other instructional supplies. It also includes all teachers for core classes (e.g., grade-level classes in elementary schools and mathematics, science, reading, language arts, history, and foreign languages in secondary schools), for specialist classes (e.g., art, music, and physical education), and for special-needs students (e.g., students with disabilities, English-language learners, struggling students from poverty backgrounds, and gifted and talented students). Many times, it also includes instructional coaches in subjects such as literacy and math, who are being used more often by school districts to help improve instruction.
- *Instructional support.* This includes expenditures for curriculum development, staff training, libraries, and computer and media centers, including the salaries, benefits, purchased services, tuition, and supplies dedicated to this purpose.

- *Administration.* For both the site and the district level, this includes salaries and benefits of principals, assistant principals, other administrators, and secretarial staff, as well as purchased services, tuition, and supplies dedicated to this purpose at the district level.
- *Student support.* This includes salary, benefits, purchased services, and supplies dedicated to guidance, health, attendance, speech pathology services, social workers, family outreach, and other functions that support the instructional program or are focused on the well-being of students.
- *Operations and maintenance.* This includes the salaries, benefits, purchased services, and supplies for custodians, carpenters, plumbers, electricians, groundskeepers and other support personnel, and other expenditures for operating, maintaining, heating, cooling, and cleaning schools and grounds.
- *Transportation and food services.* Two separate categories, these include the salaries, benefits, purchased services, and supplies dedicated to those respective purposes.

Table 6.2 displays national data on expenditures by function in these categories for selected years between 1990 and 2002. The data show that expenditures for instruction accounted for between 60 and 62 percent of total expenditures. The data also show what have become typical expenditure distributional patterns: just over 60 percent for instruction, and then about 5 percent for instructional support, about 5 percent for student support, about 5 percent for site administration, about 5 percent for district administration, about 10 percent for operation and maintenance, and just less than 10 percent for transportation, food, and other services.

All 50 states collect fiscal data organized by function from their school districts. Staffing data usually include information on the number of employees, both licensed

TABLE 6.2   Expenditures by Function for the United States, 1991–2001

Function	*1990–91*	*1995–96*	*1998–99*	*1999–2000*	*2001–02*[a]
Instruction	60.5%	61.7%	61.7%	61.8%	61.5%
Instructional staff services	4.2	4.0	4.4	4.5	4.7
Student support	4.4	4.8	5.0	5.0	5.1
District administration	5.7	5.1	5.2	5.2	5.5
School administration	5.8	5.8	5.7	5.7	5.6
Operation and maintenance	10.5	10.1	9.7	9.6	9.5
Transportation	4.3	4.1	4.0	4.0	4.0
Food services	4.2	4.2	4.0	4.0	3.9
Other	0.5	0.3	0.3	0.3	0.2

Note: Totals may not equal 100 percent due to rounding.

[a]The most recent year data are available for these categories

Source: National Center for Education Statistics, 2006, Table 165. Retrieved from nces.ed.gov/programs/digest/d05/tables/dt05_165.asp, on July 25, 2006.

staff such as teachers, administrators, principals, librarians, and counselors, and classified staff such as maintenance and custodial personnel, truck drivers, data entry clerks, and secretaries. Although states often define functional expenditure categories somewhat differently, the NCES, which is the source of the data in Table 6.2, adjusts the data to common definitions. Thus, analyses of expenditure patterns at the state level generally conclude that the major portion of the education budget (approximately 60 percent) is spent on instruction and that the percent spent on instruction is close to the national average, differing by plus or minus approximately 5 percentage-points (Cooper, 1993; Monk, Roellke, and Brent, 1996; Nakib, 1995; Picus, Tetreault, and Murphy, 1996).

In a way, these findings are puzzling. If expenditures per pupil increased during many of the past decades, and if the portion of school budgets spent on each function—instruction, instructional support, administration, and so on—stayed essentially the same each year and even each decade, how were the new dollars spent? Did the use of education dollars stay the same, or were there changes in the patterns of resource use inside the different functional categories? Below, we begin to answer these questions.

Changes in the Use of Educational Resources over Time

In addition to documenting the rising levels of education spending in the twentieth century, Hanushek and Rivkin's study (1997) and others also examined the *use* of the increasing resources for education over time. Key findings include the following:

- Large portions of the real dollar increase were consumed by additional teaching staff, which could be used to provide instruction in classes of noncore subjects such as art and music, to lower class sizes, or to expand other education services.
- Although more teaching staff also were used to expand services for special-needs students, during the 1980s, special-education services accounted for a particularly large portion of increased education revenues, even as class size reduction and teacher salary increases continued (though at a slower pace).
- A portion of increased revenues were also used to increase teacher salaries, but this portion was substantially less than that used to hire the two categories of specialist teachers. Further, even substantial teacher salary increases did not keep teacher salaries on a par with wages in other occupations. This failure to maintain wage parity was particularly problematic for women in the last quarter of the twentieth century.

These conclusions are similar to those of three sets of other studies on the uses of educational resources at more specific time periods. One set was conducted in the 1970s (Alexander, 1974; Barro and Carroll, 1975; Kirst, 1977); a second set was conducted in the 1990s, on the use of school finance reform dollars (Adams, 1994; Firestone, Goertz, Nagle, and Smelkinson, 1994; Picus, 1994c); and a third set was conducted in the 1990s, on the use of new dollars over a decade and a half (Lankford and Wyckoff, 1995; Rothstein and Miles, 1995). All these studies showed that there were substantial changes in the use of the education dollar over the last quarter of the twentieth century but that the changes were primarily *within* the instructional function, even though the instructional portion of the budget remained around 60–61 percent. The changes in the use of education dollars inside the instructional category are described in the following paragraphs.

First, starting in the mid-1960s, school systems began to provide teachers with "planning and preparation" time during the regular school day by hiring art, music, physical education, library, and other teachers for noncore subjects. All of these new specialists were, and continue to be, tracked and expensed as part of the instructional function, mainly because they provide instruction to students. At the secondary level, the special classes proliferated far beyond art, music, and physical education to include such subjects as drama, family and consumer education, health, vocational education, and computer programming. Today, the percentage of teachers providing instruction in elective special classes in many high schools across the country is close to 50 percent or more of those providing instruction in the core subjects of mathematics, science, reading/English/language arts, history, and foreign language. Though these core subjects are desired by many students, teachers, parents, and policymakers, the reality is that increased investments have been made in special classes instead of the core subjects. This raises the question of whether some of the additional funds for electives could be reallocated to the core subjects, where student performance is not sufficiently high in the country, and which are the focus of most policymakers concerned about student performance levels.

A second, substantial portion of the new expenditures has been for students who need extra help—students with disabilities, students from lower-income backgrounds who often struggle to achieve to standards, students for whom English is not their primary language and must learn English as well as subject matter content, gifted and talented students, and other categories of students with special needs. All of these expenditures are accounted for in the instructional function.

As discussed in Chapter 4, the United States has a stellar history of identifying various categories of special student needs and developing programs and providing additional funding for their needs. Most of these resources began to be added to the education system in the mid-1960s and expanded in size and scope over the ensuing decades. These dollars should remain in state funding systems. Unfortunately, the programs and services for students with special needs that these dollars have supported have had at best modest long-lasting impacts on their achievement (Allington and Johnston, 1989; D'Agostino, 2000; Odden, 1991; Reynolds and Wolfe, 1999). The increasing numbers of schools across the country not meeting the adequate yearly progress requirements of the federal No Child Left Behind (NCLB) Act is the most recent indicator of the ineffective uses of many of these dollars. The children who were targeted to receive these services deserve extra help. Although the values that led the country to provide the extra dollars for these additional services remain important, these resources must be redirected to improve productivity and achievement.

As these first two uses of new dollars illustrate, growth by addition and specialization has characterized the education system for several decades (Odden and Massy, 1992). The three other major uses of new dollars expended within the instructional function were for (1) class size reductions, which occurred modestly, (2) increases in teacher salaries, which also increased modestly, and (3) instructional aides, which grew from virtually a zero base in 1960 to a substantial level by the close of the last century. But the bottom line is that the bulk of new dollars expended over the past four decades were for teachers providing instruction in subjects outside the core and providing a variety of extra help to students with an array of special-education needs. Very little of the new money was spent on the core instructional functions—the grade-level teachers in elementary schools and the mathematics, science, reading/English/language arts, history, and foreign language teachers in secondary schools.

As a result of the increase of specialist staff and programs, regular-classroom teachers—the primary service providers—represent a declining portion of professional staff in schools (see Table 6.3). The National Commission on Teaching and America's Future (1996) found that regular-classroom teachers as a proportion of all professional staff fell from 70 percent in 1950 to 52 percent in 1995, with 10 percent of the latter not engaged in classroom teaching. The fiscal implication is that a declining portion of the education dollar is being spent on the core activity in schools—teaching the regular instructional program. This is true, for the most part, in both high- and low-spending districts (Barro, 1992; Monk, Roellke, and Brent, 1996; Picus, 1993a, 1993b; Picus and Fazal, 1996).

The end result is a system in which the amount of money has increased, but only small portions of the additional dollars have been spent on the core subjects of mathematics, science, reading/English/language arts, history/social studies and foreign languages. In part, this could explain why the new dollars have not been overly productive, where "productive" is defined as increased student achievement in the core subjects.

Another Way to View the Allocation of Educational Resources

These realities about the use of new dollars in recent decades provide insight into what happened, but not necessarily into how the dollars might have been used to better impact student achievement. This issue is even more salient today as there is a movement across the country to increase the portion of the education dollar spent on instruction to 65 percent. The underlying assumption of this "65 percent solution" is that the inefficiencies in the system are

TABLE 6.3 Staff Employed in the Public Schools, 1960–2000

Staff	*1960*	*1970*	*1980*	*1990*	*1995*	*1999*	*2000*	*2002*[a]
District administrators	2.0%	1.9%	1.9%	1.7%	1.7%	1.7%	1.7%	1.9%
Instructional staff	69.8	68.0	68.6	67.9	67.1	67.8	67.9	67.5
Site administrators	3.0	2.7	2.6	2.8	2.4	2.4	2.5	2.8
Teachers	64.8	60.0	52.4	53.4	52.0	51.7	51.6	51.0
Teacher aides	—	1.7	7.8	8.8	9.9	11.1	11.2	11.1
Counselors	0.8	1.7	1.8	1.8	1.8	1.7	1.7	1.7
Librarians	0.8	1.3	1.2	1.1	1.0	1.0	0.9	0.9
Support staff	28.1	30.1	29.5	30.4	31.2	30.5	30.4	30.7

[a]The most recent year for which data are available in this form.

Source: National Center for Education Statistics, 2006, Table 80. Retrieved from nces.ed.gov/programs/digest/d05/tables/dt05_080.asp on July 25, 2006.

largely outside the instructional function and that if more were spent on instruction, greater education productivity (i.e., higher student achievement) would be attained. But as we just showed, the major "story" about the use of the education dollar over time is that there have been huge changes *within* the instructional function, but these changes have not bolstered spending on the core subjects, and thus have had little impact on student achievement.

Thus, the assumption of the 65 percent solution that it is the expenditures outside of instruction that are the problem, or that spending outside of instruction is wasteful or perhaps unneeded, is both off base and simplistic. The goal of the 65 percent solution is to improve the effectiveness of education spending, a goal with which we agree. But the focus of change needs to be reconceptualized to concentrate more on spending within the instructional function—perhaps enhancing spending on the core subjects, spending more directly on strategies that have proved successful (see Chapters 4 and 7), and improving the effectiveness of the use of the dollars for special student needs.

To improve the effectiveness of education spending, it is helpful to provide a framework focused on areas likely to impact student achievement. A useful way of thinking about a school's budget is as follows:

- About 30–40 percent is spent on regular-classroom teachers and their professional development, and a principal (i.e., the core function of schools and classrooms).
- About 30–40 percent is spent on specialist subjects (art, music, physical education, vocational education, etc.) and on extra services for struggling students (students with disabilities, English-language learning [ELL] students, students from poverty backgrounds, etc.), pupil support services (guidance counselors, social workers, psychologists, family liaisons, nurses, etc.), instructional aides, and other instructional supports.
- About 20–30 percent is spent on some level of necessary overhead (central office administration, superintendent, board support), business/fiscal/personnel services, operations (heating, cooling, electrifying, cleaning, grounds keeping), maintenance (plumbers, electricians, carpenters, etc.), transportation of students to and from school, food services, and short-term debt.

Let us call these categories the first, middle, and last portion of the education dollar. The *first portion* includes a teacher in every classroom and a principal in every building. The key issue here is how large or small the core class sizes should be; that decision is the one that has the most impact on how much money is spent and how the education dollar overall is spent. The effectiveness of core teachers could be dramatically improved by professional development to enhance their instructional expertise and to ensure that a high-quality teacher is found in every core classroom, issues that we discussed in Chapter 4. Unfortunately, most research has shown that the typical professional development dollar has little impact on classroom practices or student learning (Corcoran, 1995; Guskey, 1986; Little, 1993; Smylie, 1996), so even professional development expenditures must be restructured to have the desired impact. But until education delivery is totally restructured, perhaps with computer technologies, all schools will require core teachers—each of whom should be of high quality—and a principal. So, other than as it pertains to the most effective class sizes, this use of the education dollar is reasonably fixed.

The bulk of the *middle portion* of the education dollar has been added over the past 40 years or so with the intention of helping the "line staff"—core teachers—accomplish the core goals of the education system: having all students achieve at a higher level in mathematics, science, reading, writing, and history. As such, the middle portion of the dollar constitutes staff extension or help services. It is unlikely that additional instruction in specialist subjects such as art, music, and physical education will enhance student achievement in the core subjects, even though there is strong demand for instruction in these specialist subjects. Research has shown that although the extra dollars for specific student needs are spent on the appropriate students (disabled, ELL, and low-income students), the expenditures have usually been ineffective in boosting these students' learning (Borman and D'Agostino, 2001; Odden, 1991; Reynolds and Wolfe, 1999). Thus, huge potential exists to expend this middle portion of all education dollars more effectively—the focus of Chapter 7. Except for pupil support, this portion is virtually all tracked and expensed within the instructional function.

Note that we are not questioning the general allocation of dollars for specialist subjects, for students with special needs, or for professional development. All these issues need to be addressed, and the values that have underwritten the billions of dollars spent to address the special needs of many categories of students are to be lauded. The issue is whether there are more effective educational strategies than those on which these dollars have been used in the past.

Finally, although more efficient use could be made of the *last portion* of the education dollar, such overhead services are required simply to open, administer, govern, operate, heat, clean, and fix schools, and transport students to and from school. The bulk of these expenditures are needed, and we do not see where substantial efficiencies could be established to enable districts to shift significant sums of money to the first two portions of the education dollar.

In Chapter 7, we examine several ways that dollars in all three of these categories can be used more effectively and efficiently, although the major opportunities for better using the education dollar lie in rearrangement of the middle portion of expenditures, as well as improving the effectiveness and instructional expertise (better professional development) of all core teachers.

The next section shifts our analysis down to the school level and examines what is known about resource use of the first and second portions of the education dollar. We rely on the analysis of a national school-based data system for this assessment of resource use. However, as the analysis shows, even this school-based data system does not provide sufficient detail about spending by educational strategy to assess fully the effectiveness of educational resources. This suggests the need for a more detailed reporting framework to help address this problem.

2. SCHOOL-LEVEL EXPENDITURES IN AN ERA OF EDUCATIONAL ADEQUACY

Since schools and classrooms are the "production units" in education, gathering data on resource allocation and use at school sites is essential. In many states, particularly those under court order to provide an adequate education, it is primarily at the school level that the components of an adequate education can be specified. Ideally, for each level of schooling—elementary, middle, and high school—the following type of data on resources and resource use are needed:

- Staffing and expenditures by program—the regular-instruction program; programs for special-needs students such as compensatory, bilingual, and special education; administration; staff development; and instructional materials
- Staffing and expenditures by educational strategy—class size, professional development, tutoring, pull-out resource room, core versus elective subjects, and so on
- Staffing and expenditures by content area—mathematics, language arts (reading in elementary schools), science, history/social science, foreign language, art, music, and physical education
- Interrelationships among these staffing and expenditure patterns
- Relationships of these staffing and expenditure patterns to student performance

Although these types of data are not systematically collected at the school level (Busch and Odden, 1997), a number of states are beginning to do so, including California, Florida, Kentucky, Ohio, Oregon, Texas, and Wyoming.

Collecting and analyzing these data is a first step toward addressing the productivity questions that policymakers now ask. They want to know where money goes, what resources—especially instructional and curriculum resources—it buys, and what impact those resources have on student performance. As discussed in this chapter and in Chapter 7, altering resource use patterns at the school site may well be the most promising way to improve education system productivity in the near future.

By merging data from the Schools and Staffing Survey (SASS), which is a school-based national staffing data base, with Census Bureau data on district expenditures, Picus (1993a, 1993b) was able to estimate resource use patterns at the school level. Because detailed fiscal data were not specifically available at the site level, his analysis focused on the use of site staff, which constitutes the majority of the school site budget. What was particularly interesting in these analyses was the difference between the estimated pupil–teacher ratio and the teacher self-reported class size. He found that while the average pupil–teacher ratio reported in schools was in the vicinity of 16.5 or 17 to 1, similar to the Hanushek, Rivkin, and NCES results previously reported, self-reported class sizes ranged from 24 to 32 (Picus, 1994a; Picus and Bhimani, 1993) or from 50 to 100 percent higher than even school-level statistics indicated. A study by Miles (1995) confirmed this finding, showing that if all individuals classified as teachers in Boston public schools were placed in regular classrooms, class sizes could be reduced from an average of 22 to an average of 13.

Two important findings emerged from this work. First, many individuals classified as "teachers" in our public school systems had assignments other than spending the full day in a regular, core classroom. Second, as the size of the district increased, and as its wealth declined, the disparity between the calculated pupil–teacher ratio and the actual class size grew.

The bottom line, though, is that the percentage of regular-classroom teachers dropped nearly 33 percent in the latter half of the twentieth century, partially explained by the data in the previous section. They have been "augmented" by instructional aides, pupil support staff, and specialist teachers (for both special student needs and elective courses) working within schools but not teaching in regular classrooms. The policy and productivity issue is whether this use of resources is the most effective.

In an attempt to continue the analysis of school-level resources, we used data from a recent administration (1999–2000) of the SASS to determine the average staffing in elementary, middle, and high schools nationally, and in each major region of the country. Beginning with Table 6.4, which is based on national averages, we give the enrollment, staffing resources, and associated dollar values for the range of schools in the United States, the basis for showing how they could be used in ways to further improve student performance. The analysis uses a figure of $50,000 for salaries and benefits for each professional staff slot, and $15,000 for each instructional aide, values that reflect roughly a national average figure at the close of the twentieth century.

Although the data do not show secretarial and custodial staff expenditures, they do show the bulk of the use of the education dollar in the first two of the three categories of resource use (core teachers and specialist teachers and aides) and thus provide additional insights into how the education dollar is spent. For example, the resources dedicated to librarians and media aides tend to stay the same across all three education levels, whereas the resources for assistant principals rise with the level of schooling (and level of enrollment).

Many school principals think of their budget as being only $30,000–40,000; this may be partly because that is often the only amount over which the school has control. In fact, as Table 6.4 shows, the professional staffing resources in schools of these sizes reach into the millions (line 7); if the classified staff (secretaries, maintenance), operations, utilities, discretionary resources, and other funding were included, the totals

TABLE 6.4   School Resources in National Average Elementary, Middle, and High Schools

Ingredient	*Elementary School Grades K–5*	*Middle School Grades 6–8*	*High School Grades 9–12*
Average enrollment	**442**	**628**	**907**
1. Principal	1.0	1.0	1.0
2. Assistant principals	0.5	1.0	1.75
3. Teachers	30.0	43.5	58.5
4. Librarians and media aides	2.0	2.0	2.0
5. Counselors and psychologists	1.75	2.75	3.75
6. Teacher aides	5.75	2.5	2.5
7. Total staff resources	$2,101,250	$2,462,500	$3,352,500

Note: Average professional staff cost at $50,000; average teacher aide cost at $15,000.

Source: Staffing data from analysis of Schools and Staffing Survey, 1999–2000.

would be even higher. A number of other calculations can be made from the data in Table 6.4. For example, by dividing the number of students by the number of licensed teachers, we find that the elementary and middle schools have average pupil–staff ratios of 14.7 and 14.4 students, respectively. The high schools, on the other hand, have a slightly higher ratio of students to teachers, at 15.5. These ratios are not class size figures; they are simply ratios of students to licensed staff, many of whom do not teach a regular class. Actual class sizes would be larger, but data on actual class sizes are not provided in the SASS database. The national SASS data allow for these observations and calculations, but they do not provide further illumination—perhaps one plausible explanation for the higher high school ratios is that the small amount of extra money not being used to pay teachers in high schools may be used to purchase more administrators.

Table 6.5 illustrates the differing levels of enrollment by region by giving the average enrollment for schools in each of four regions of the country: (1) the Northeast (Connecticut, Maine, Massachusetts, New Hampshire, New Jersey, New York, Pennsylvania, Rhode Island, and Vermont), (2) the Midwest (Illinois, Indiana, Iowa, Kansas, Michigan, Minnesota, Missouri, Nebraska, North Dakota, Ohio, South Dakota, and Wisconsin), (3) the South (Alabama, Arkansas, Delaware, District of Columbia, Florida, Georgia, Kentucky, Louisiana, Maryland, Mississippi, North Carolina, Oklahoma, South Carolina, Tennessee, Texas, Virginia, and West Virginia), and (4) the West (Alaska, Arizona, California, Colorado, Hawaii, Idaho, Montana, Nevada, New Mexico, Oregon, Utah, Washington, and Wyoming). For purposes of comparison, it also reports the national average enrollment for each level from Table 6.4.

Table 6.5 reveals that school size differs considerably by region. Schools in the Midwest have the lowest enrollment for all three school levels. The largest schools at the elementary and middle school levels are in the South, but the largest high schools are in the Northeast. Perhaps the most striking difference between enrollments by region is at the high school level, with the Midwest having an average of 330 fewer students per high school than the Northeast.

For this reason, Tables 6.6–6.9 provide the same staffing information as Table 6.4, but the data are disaggregated into the four regions. Since prices of staff differ by region, to enhance comparability, we used national average-salary figures to calculate dollar levels for staff resources. We should note, though, that actual average salaries are quite low in the South and that one of the reasons the number of staffing in the South

TABLE 6.5   Average Enrollments for Elementary, Middle and High Schools by Region

Region	Elementary School	Middle School	High School
Northeast	426	654	1036
Midwest	354	500	706
South	490	708	946
West	467	619	998
National average	442	628	907

Source: National Center for Education Statistics, Schools and Staffing Survey, 1999–2000.

is higher than in some regions is because of the very low salary levels, making their expenditures per pupil the lowest of any region.

These tables document that school-level resources are quite different in the various regions of the country, and the national average might be accurate for only a few districts. The Northeast has more teachers than the national average, as does the South. Instructional aides are most prevalent in the South and West. Indeed, one southern state supports one instructional aide in every K–2 elementary classroom. With the exception of the average level of resources in elementary schools, for which the South has slightly more than the Northeast, the Northeast has the highest level of resources dedicated to education. This can be seen in terms of total dollars, number of teachers, and number

TABLE 6.6 Average School Resources in Elementary, Middle, and High Schools in the Northeast

Ingredient	Elementary School Grades K–5	Middle School Grades 6–8	High School Grades 9–12
Average enrollment	426	654	1036
1. Principal	1.0	1.0	1.0
2. Assistant principals	0.5	1.0	2.0
3. Teachers	32.0	53.75	78.5
4. Librarians and media aides	2.0	2.0	2.5
5. Counselors and psychologists	2.0	3.5	5.5
6. Teacher aides	5.5	3.25	3.0
7. Total staff resources	$1,922,500	$3,076,250	$4,476,250

Note: Average professional staff cost at $50,000; average teacher aide cost at $15,000.

Source: Staffing data from analysis of Schools and Staffing Survey, 1999–2000.

TABLE 6.7 Average School Resources in Elementary, Middle, and High Schools in the Midwest

Ingredient	Elementary School Grades K–5	Middle School Grades 6–8	High School Grades 9–12
Average enrollment	354	500	706
1. Principal	1.0	1.0	1.0
2. Assistant principals	0.25	0.75	1.0
3. Teachers	25.75	38.25	47.5
4. Librarians and media aides	2.0	2.0	2.0
5. Counselors and psychologists	1.75	3.0	3.0
6. Teacher aides	4.5	2.0	2.25
7. Total staff resources	$1,570,000	$2,245,000	$2,723,750

Note: Average professional staff cost at $50,000; average teacher aide cost at $15,000.

Source: Staffing data from analysis of Schools and Staffing Survey, 1999–2000.

TABLE 6.8   Average School Resources in Elementary, Middle, and High Schools in the South

Ingredient	Elementary School Grades K–5	Middle School Grades 6–8	High School Grades 9–12
Average enrollment	490	708	946
1. Principal	1.0	1.0	1.0
2. Assistant principals	0.5	1.5	2.0
3. Teachers	33.5	47.75	61.5
4. Librarians and media aides	1.75	2.0	2.25
5. Counselors and psychologists	1.75	2.75	3.5
6. Teacher aides	6.0	2.0	1.5
7. Total staff resources	$1,988,750	$2,675,000	$3,508,750

Note: Average professional staff cost at $50,000; average teacher aide cost at $15,000.

Source: Staffing data from analysis of Schools and Staffing Survey, 1999–2000.

TABLE 6.9   Average School Resources in Elementary, Middle, and High Schools in the West

Ingredient	Elementary School Grades K–5	Middle School Grades 6–8	High School Grades 9–12
Average Enrollment	467	619	998
1. Principal	1.0	1.0	1.0
2. Assistant principals	0.25	1.0	1.75
3. Teachers	27.75	35.75	53.75
4. Librarians and media aides	2.0	1.75	2.25
5. Counselors and psychologists	1.75	4.0	4.0
6. Teacher aides	6.5	3.75	3.5
7. Total staff resources	$1,987,500	$2,137,500	$3,146,250

Note: Average professional staff cost at $50,000; average teacher aide cost at $15,000.

Source: Staffing data from analysis of Schools and Staffing Survey, 1999–2000.

of student support staff, which are not all listed here, but for which the numbers of counselors and psychologists are representative.

The SASS is a rich database with information on many aspects of school-level resource allocation. However, it is limited in its use to the schools that are sampled and the years in which the surveys are conducted, and access to some of the data requires a license. In addition, some information is just not available from the survey, such as a distinction between core and specialist subject teachers, or between instructional facilitators, coaches, and tutors at the school level. To develop a more comprehensive understanding of resource use at the school level, even more detailed data are needed.

Frameworks for Collecting and Arraying School-Level Expenditures

To address this shortcoming of school-level databases, Odden, Archibald, Fermanich, and Gross (2003) created a school-level expenditure framework that would allow districts and schools to track resource use—staff and dollars—by educational strategy at the site level, thus providing much more detail on the specific use of educational resources. This expenditure structure is displayed in Table 6.10. The six instructional categories and three noninstructional categories array spending by category according to its educational strategy or purpose, enabling a study of the school's budget to reflect its educational programs and priorities at the same time. Since each decision about a school's educational program is tied to a decision about how to allocate resources, this framework facilitates thinking about school budgets in the context of trying to improve school effectiveness. As Table 6.10 illustrates, this framework also includes a set of resource indicators, or contextual information about the school, that gives further insight into nonfiscal measures of resource use practices, such as class size.

The main portion of the school expenditure structure consists of nine expenditure elements that reflect the core components of nearly all schoolwide educational strategies. The selection of the expenditure elements reflects a melding of existing "function" and "program" categories, together with specific service strategies, in an effort to provide a more explicit representation of the strategic allocation of resources within a school. The model includes nine expenditure elements that are broadly categorized as either instructional or noninstructional in nature. The six instructional elements are as follows:

1. *Core academic teachers.* The licensed classroom teacher is primarily responsible for teaching a school's core academic subjects of reading/English/language arts, mathematics, science, and history/social studies, and foreign languages. In elementary schools, core academic teachers consist of the teachers in the self-contained regular-education classrooms. Some elementary schools may also departmentalize certain core subjects such as math or science, especially in the upper grades. These teachers are also included as core teachers. In middle school, high school, or any other departmentalized school, core teachers consist of members of the English/language arts, mathematics, science, social studies, and world language departments, along with special-education or ESL/bilingual teachers who provide academic classes in these subjects.
   The cost of the core academic teachers, as well as staff costs in the other expenditure elements, is estimated by multiplying the number of full-time-equivalent (FTE) teachers in the expenditure element by the teacher's salary plus fringe benefits.
2. *Specialist and elective teachers.* This expenditure element consists of licensed teachers who teach noncore academic classes and usually provide planning and preparation time for core academic teachers:
   • Specialist teachers, such as art, music, and physical education teachers, who usually provide regular classroom teachers with planning and preparation time

TABLE 6.10   School Expenditure Structure and Resource Indicators

School Resource Indicators

Student enrollment	Length of class periods
Percent low-income	Length of reading class
Percent special-education	Length of mathematics class
Percent ESL/LEP	Reading class size
Expenditures per pupil	Mathematics class size
Professional development expenditures per teacher	Regular class size
Special academic focus of school/unit	Percent core[a] teachers
Length of instructional day	

School Expenditure Structure: Instructional

1. Core academic teachers
- Grade-level teachers
- English/reading/language arts
- History/social studies
- Math
- Science
- Foreign language

2. Specialist and elective teachers/planning and preparation
- Art, music, physical education, etc.
- Academic focus with or without special funding
- Vocational
- Driver education

3. Extra help
- Tutors
- Extra-help labs
- Resource rooms (Title I, special-education, or other part-day pull-out programs)
- Inclusion teachers
- English as a Second Language classes
- Special-education self-contained classes for severely disabled students (including aides)
- Extended-day
- Summer school
- District-initiated alternative programs

4. Professional development
- Teacher time—substitutes and stipends
- Trainers and coaches
- Administration
- Materials, equipment, and facilities
- Travel and transportation
- Tuition and conference fees

(continued)

TABLE 6.10 (*continued*)

5. Other nonclassroom instructional staff
- Coordinators and teachers on special assignment
- Librarians
- Instructional aides

6. Instructional materials and equipment
- Supplies, materials, and equipment
- Computers (hardware, software, peripherals)

School Expenditure Structure: Noninstructional

7. Student support services
- Counselors
- Nurses
- Psychologists
- Social workers
- Extracurricular and athletics

8. Administration
- Principal/assistant principal
- Clerical staff and supplies

9. Operations and maintenance
- Custodial
- Utilities
- Security
- Food service

Source: Revised version of framework in Odden, Archibald, Fermanich, and Gross, 2003.

[a]Math, English/language, arts, science, social studies, and world languages.

- Teachers who provide instruction in a subject area that represents the special academic focus of a school (e.g., foreign language teachers in a school offering a foreign language magnet program).
- Vocational/career education teachers, including business and keyboarding classes
- Driver education teachers

3. *Extra help.* This category consists mainly of licensed teachers from a wide variety of strategies designed to assist struggling students or students with special needs to learn a school's regular curriculum. The educational strategies that these teachers deploy are generally supplemental to the instruction of the regular classroom. Teachers deploying the following instructional strategies are included in this expenditure element:

- Tutors who are licensed teachers and provide one-on-one help to students. Tutoring is most often used in elementary schools.
- Extra-help laboratories, which generally provide extra help in reading and mathematics for students struggling to meet academic performance

standards. Such extra-help classes are used most often in secondary schools.

- Resource rooms that provide small groups of students with extra help, usually remedial reading or remedial mathematics that are or are not directly related to the school's regular curriculum or standards. Resource rooms have been the typical investment for compensatory, bilingual, and special-education funds.
- Inclusion teachers who assist regular-classroom teachers with mainstreamed students who have physical or mental disabilities, or some learning problem. These students generally have less severe disabling conditions.
- ESL teachers who work with non-English-speaking students to teach them English.
- Self-contained special-education classrooms in which teachers and instructional aides work with students with severe and profound disabilities for most or all of the school day. These teachers may teach a modified version of a school's curriculum or other learning goals required by their students' individualized learning programs.
- Extended-day and/or summer school programs. This strategy provides students with extra instructional time to achieve to the standards in the regular curriculum.
- District alternative programs located in a school. These alternative programs serve students who have trouble learning in traditional classrooms. These programs are often administratively and instructionally separate from the host school although they may be located in the school building or reported as part of the school's operating budget.

4. *Professional development*. This expenditure element includes spending on the professional development of a school's staff. The expenditures include the costs of teacher time for professional development; trainers and coaches; professional development administration; materials, equipment and facilities; travel and transportation; and tuition and conference fees (for more information on the details of the expenditure elements of professional development, see Odden, Archibald, Fermanich, and Gallagher, 2002).

5. *Other nonclassroom instructional staff*. Included here are licensed and nonlicensed staff who support a school's instructional program, such as program coordinators (e.g., curriculum or technology coordinators), substitutes, and instructional aides other than those working in self-contained special-education classrooms. This could also include librarians and library media specialists.

6. *Instructional materials and equipment*. This category includes books, instructional supplies, materials, equipment, and computer hardware and software for all instructional programs, including regular education and all extra-help programs.

The three remaining noninstructional expenditure elements are these:

1. *Student support.* This expenditure element consists of school-based student support staff such as counselors, nurses, social workers, psychologists, attendance monitors, or parent liaisons, and could include school expenditures for extracurricular activities and athletics, though often this is a separate expenditure category.
2. *Administration.* This expenditure element consists of all expenditures pertaining to the administration of a school, including the principal, assistant principal(s), clerical staff, administrative office, as well as supplies, equipment and technology, and school reserve funds.
3. *Operations and maintenance.* This expenditure element includes the costs of staff, supplies, and equipment for custodial services, food services, and security, as well as utilities and building and grounds maintenance charged to a school.

In addition, Table 6.10 includes a series of resource "indicators" to provide mainly non-dollar measures of important resource use practices. Indicators requiring more explanation are described below:

- *Professional development expenditures per teacher.* An indicator calculated by dividing a school's total expenditures for professional development by the total number of licensed teachers, which will usually include mentors and instructional facilitators.
- *Special academic focus.* The academic program focus, if any, of a school. Examples include science and technology, college preparatory, the arts, or a comprehensive school design.
- *Length of instructional day.* The number of hours per day that students are present for instruction.
- *Length of class periods.* The typical length of class periods in minutes. This indicator provides a benchmark of how much time is available for instruction in each subject.
- *Length of reading and mathematics class periods* (elementary schools). The length of math and reading class periods in minutes. These include periods when students are specially grouped for extended math or literacy instruction.
- *Reading and mathematics class size* (elementary schools). The average number of students per teacher in math and reading classes. Some educational strategies reduce class sizes only for reading or mathematics, not for all classes.
- *Regular class size* (elementary schools). The size of the regular-education, self-contained, classroom. This may be different from mathematics and reading classes if the school organizes those subjects differently, and it may also be different from "special" classes such as art, music, and physical education.

- *Length of core class periods* (secondary schools). The length of math, English/language arts, science, social studies, and world language class periods in minutes.
- *Core class size* (secondary schools). The average number of students per teacher in mathematics, English/language arts, science, social studies, and world language classes. This indicator gives the actual class size for core subjects and can be compared to noncore class sizes.
- *Noncore class size* (secondary schools). The average number of students per teacher of classes other than mathematics, English/language arts, science, social studies, and world language.
- *Percent core teachers*. For elementary schools, the percentage of all licensed school staff except the principal and assistant principal(s) who are regular classroom teachers. For secondary schools, the percentage of all licensed staff except the principal and assistant principal(s) who are mathematics, English/language arts, science, social studies, and world language teachers. This percentage provides a measure of core academic teachers compared to all licensed staff in the school.

Using data from a midwestern elementary school (see Odden, Archibald, Fermanich, and Gross, 2003), Table 6.11 displays what the expenditure structure can reveal about a school's educational strategies and priorities. Beginning with the resource indicators, we can see that this is a high-poverty school with a significant population of special-education students. Though each class period on average is 40 minutes long, reading is provided for an average of 90 minutes a day, reflecting a priority placed on reading instruction. The school's actual class sizes range from 13 to 24. Glancing at the expenditure portion, we see that the school dedicates the most resources to core classroom teachers (as is true in any conventional school), allocating very few resources to specialists and electives, perhaps reflecting a desire to focus more on core areas. The school does not employ certified teacher tutors, which is one strategy supported by research for helping struggling students. Instead, a large portion of expenditures are allocated in the nonclassroom instructional staff category, which could include program coordinators (e.g., curriculum or technology coordinators) and/or substitutes, but is likely to be largely made up of instructional aides.

Table 6.12 shows the resource indicators and expenditure elements of a traditional high school (see Odden, Archibald, Fermanich, and Gross, 2003). In terms of special-needs population, only 20 percent of the student population is poor, about 5 percent are English-language learners, and 15 percent require special-education services. The indicators show that the high school is quite large, far above the level of what research says is most effective (Lee and Smith, 1997). The resource indicators also show that noncore classes are actually smaller than core classes, an interesting anomaly. The table further shows that the school spends the largest portion of resources on core teachers, but also a substantial portion on specialists and electives, as well as on nonclassroom instructional staff. Though not a high-poverty school, a significant level of resources is dedicated to extra help, with 29 teachers, most of whom work in either resource rooms or self-contained classrooms. The school does not employ tutors, although research shows that this is an effective strategy to help struggling students.

TABLE 6.11   An Expenditure Structure for a Midwestern Elementary School

Resource Indicators

School building size	400
Percent low income	100%
Percent special education	15%
Percent ESL/bilingual	0%
Expenditures per pupil	$8,158
Professional development expenditures per teacher	$8,640
Special academic focus	Expeditionary learning—outward bound
Length of instructional day (minutes)	390
Length of class periods (minutes)	40
Length of reading class (minutes)	90
Length of mathematics class (minutes)	40
Class size	13–24
Percent core teachers	61%

Expenditure Elements	FTE	Total	Per Pupil	Percentage
1. Core academic teachers	19.0	$1,329,656	$3,324	40.7%
2. Specialist and elective teachers	2.6	191,743	479	5.9
3. Extra help				
Tutors				
Extra-help labs				
Resource rooms				
Extended-day and summer school				
English as second language				
Special education inclusion	1.0	69,982	175	
Special-education self-contained classes	4.0	279,982	700	
District alternative programs				
Total extra help	5.0	349,964	875	10.7
4. Professional development		229,833	575	7.0
5. Other Nonclassroom instructional staff	12.3	240,367	601	7.4
6. Instructional materials and equipment		49,859	125	1.5
7. Student support	4.4	364,421	911	11.2
8. Administration				
Principal/assistant principal	1.0	95,442	239	
Clerical	2.0	74,378	186	
Other administration		118,026	295	
Total administration	3.0	287,846	720	8.8
9. Operations and maintenance	4.0	219,410	548	6.7
Total School	**50.3**	**$3,263,099**	**$8,158**	**100.0%**

Source: Adapted from Odden, Archibald, Fermanich, and Gross, 2003.

TABLE 6.12   Expenditure Structure of a Traditional Comprehensive High School

Resource Indicators		
School building size	2,110	
Percent low income	20%	
Percent special ed	14.4%	
Percent ELL/ESL	5%	
Expenditures per pupil	$6,057	
Special academic focus	None	
Length of the school day	7.0 hours	
Length of class periods	49 minutes	
Length of core periods	49 minutes	
Core class size	23	
Noncore class size	21.1	
Percent core teachers	47%	
PD expenditures/teacher	$177	

Expenditure Elements	Total FTE	Total Dollars
1. Core academic teachers	66.4	$ 4,171,315
2. Specialists and electives	38.2	$ 2,417,895
3. Extra help	29.0	$ 1,650,751
Tutors	0	0
Extra-help labs	0	0
Resource room	10.2	$ 639,275
Extended-day/summer school	0	0
ESL/bilingual special education	4.8	$ 300,835
Inclusion special education	1.4	$ 87,744
Self-contained special education	9.0	$ 397,271
District alternative program	3.6	$ 225,626
4. Professional development	0.0	$ 14,684
5. Other nonclassroom instructional staff	25.2	$ 822,251
6. Instructional materials and equipment	—	$ 173,322
7. Student support	12.5	$ 1,028,620
8. Administration staff and supplies	18.5	$ 1,280,007
Principal/asstistant principal	5	$ 480,550
Clerical/nonleadership	13.5	$ 696,407
Other administrative	—	$ 103,050
9. Operations and maintenance	20.7	$ 1,221,670
Total school	**210.5**	**$12,780,515**

Source: Adapted from Odden, Archibald, Fermanich, and Gross, 2003.

To complement the overall expenditure framework and provide a tool for collecting even more comprehensive and detailed information on expenditures for professional development, Odden, Archibald, Fermanich, and Gallagher (2002) devised the professional development cost framework shown in Table 6.13. This framework is based on key features of effective professional development that researchers have traced to changes in teachers' instructional practices and improvements in student learning. As Table 6.13 details, the framework separates professional development costs into six categories, including teacher time, trainers and coaches, administration, materials and facilities, travel, and tuition and conference fees.

The same researchers used this professional development cost framework to evaluate spending on professional development at both the district and school levels. At the district level, the researchers joined forces with Karen Hawley Miles to study six districts' use of resources for professional development (Miles, Odden, Fermanich, and Archibald, 2004). These studies found that the actual level of district resources dedicated to professional development was much higher than the districts believed, partially because expenditures for professional development came from many different budgets, was called many different things, and was coded in various parts of the budget not labeled "professional development." The six-district study found that professional development spending ranged from about $2,740 to $5,000 per teacher or from $170 to $330 per student across the various districts. In part because of the fragmentation of professional development provision, these studies also found that very little money was being spent on professional development to improve instruction in core courses, which ties into the focus of the next chapter on how to use resources for education most effectively.

These researchers also studied the school-level use of professional development resources (Archibald and Gallagher, 2002; Fermanich, 2002; Gallagher, 2002), which added another sizable portion of funds that were dedicated to professional development but had not previously been counted by district-level studies of professional development. Indeed, the Fermanich analysis found that by including professional development funding at the school level, the total spent on professional development almost doubled, hiking the average amount spent per teacher in the district studied from $4,232 with just district dollars to $7,738 when site expenditures were added. This finding led to the conclusion that any study of professional development *should if at all possible* include an analysis of spending on professional learning at the school site, as well as the district, particularly because research-proven strategies such as instructional coaches are increasingly being employed by school sites. This is another example of the utility of our expenditure collection frameworks for both professional development and schools as a whole. The level of detail they provide is unmatched by other district-level studies or studies of schools relying solely on expenditures by function.

3. SUMMARY

The shift to adequacy is a considerable change from equity in that it involves not only ensuring that students have access to quality education but also that what is provided allows them to achieve according to the standards set out by their state of residence. In

TABLE 6.13   A Cost Structure for Professional Development

Cost Element	Ingredient	How Cost Is Calculated
Teacher time used for professional development	*Time within regular contract* • When students are not present before or after school or on scheduled in-service days, half days, or early-release days • Planning time	Teachers' hourly salary times number of student free hours used for professional development Cost of portion of salary of person used to cover teachers' class during planning time used for professional development
	Time outside regular day/year • Time after school, on weekends, or for summer institutes	Stipends or additional pay based on hourly rate that teachers receive to compensate them for their time
	Other time during the regular day/year • Release time provided by substitutes	Substitute wages
Training and coaching	*Training* • Salaries for district trainers • Outside consultants who provide training; may be part of CSRD	Sum of trainer salaries Consultant fees or comprehensive school design contract fees
	Coaching • Salaries for district coaches including on-site facilitators • Outside consultants who provide coaching; may be part of CSRD	Sum of coach and facilitator salaries Consultant fees or comprehensive school design contract fees
Administration of professional development	*Administration* • Salaries for district- or school-level administrators of professional development programs	Salary for administrators times the proportion of their time spent administering professional development programs
	Materials	Materials for professional development, including cost of classroom materials required for CSRDs

(continued)

TABLE 6.13 (*continued*)

Cost Element	Ingredient	How Cost Is Calculated
Materials, equipment, and facilities used for professional development	*Equipment*	Equipment needed for professional development activities
	Facilities	Rental or other costs for facilities used for professional development
Travel and transportation for professional development	*Travel*	Costs of travel to off-site professional development activities
	Transportation	Costs of transportation within district for professional development
Tuition and conference fees	*Tuition*	Tuition payments or reimbursement for university-based professional development
	Conference Fees	Fees for conferences related to professional development

Source: Adapted from Odden, Archibald, Fermanich, and Gallagher, 2002.

order to answer the question of whether a level of resources for education is adequate, we need to investigate not just whether schools are allocated enough money but also how that money is used. To do that, we need to employ a data collection instrument such as the expenditure structure presented in this chapter, which arrays spending according to education strategy.

This chapter identified eight key aspects about school-level resources and their use. First, real dollars per pupil rose by an average of 3.5 percent per year from 1890 to 1990, which represents substantial increases in real education resources over time. Real dollars per pupil are beginning to rise by about the same amounts in the first few years of the twenty-first century.

Second, it is helpful to think of three primary uses of the education dollar: (1) the 30–40 percent used for core classes, professional development, and a principal for each school; (2) the 30–40 percent used for extra, support services (e.g., instruction in specialist content classes; instruction for the additional needs of students who struggle to learn to standards; guidance, social work, family outreach, nursing, and other student support services); and (3) the 20–30 percent spent on central administration, operations and maintenance of schools, transportation of students to and from school, food services, and short-term debt service.

Third, the bulk of new dollars provided to public schools has been used to expand educational services inside the instructional function but usually outside the core or regular-education program, instead of raising teacher salaries or bolstering the core instructional program. One result of this practice has been that teacher salary levels have not kept pace with salaries for jobs that compete with education for worker talent.

Fourth, the largest portion of the new education dollars were used to expand education services in the second category, particularly during the past 40 years, and can be divided into three uses: (1) providing extra services for special-needs populations reflecting the best American values, (2) providing planning periods for regular teachers by hiring specialist teachers who provide instruction in noncore subjects (art, music, physical education, etc.), and (3) lowering class size.

Fifth, it is difficult to determine just which of these expanded services has been given the most attention, but class sizes of 25–30 along with pupil–staff ratios of 15 suggest that the first two, and particularly special education, have dominated over class size reduction. We should note, however, that several states enacted class size reduction policies—most often for the lower grades—during the late 1990s.

Sixth, despite the expansion of services for special-needs students, which represents a worthwhile allocation of extra dollars, research has shown that the students served in pull-out programs have not increased their learning all that much because of the extra services. This fact, combined with the stagnant nature of student achievement generally, suggests that it is reasonable to raise questions about the productivity of the use of those education dollars.

Seventh, a new professional development cost framework has shown that in several school districts, predominantly large, urban districts, professional development expenditures per pupil are much larger than the budget would suggest, totaling up to $5,000 per teacher in several districts.

Finally, there are some school-level data available to illustrate national and regional trends in the use of staffing resources at the school level. However, to get to the level of detail needed to answer many important school finance questions, even more detailed, microlevel staffing information is needed.

The next chapter addresses the important topic of how educational resources could be reallocated to maximize student learning and discusses the affordability of elements of an adequate education as it has been defined thus far in this book, according to the Odden-Picus evidence-based model.

Study Questions

For the questions in this chapter, obtain the budget of your school or of a school in your district. If you do not have access to one directly, perhaps another student could make copies or the instructor could provide a sample budget.

1. Identify the portion of your district budget that is for the major functions: instruction, instructional support, administration (school and district), pupil support, and so on. Make sure the budget numbers include all sources of revenues—local, state, and federal—but exclude capital outlays. Do the percentages spent on the various functions in your district match the averages

discussed in this book? If not, where are there differences, and what do you think are the causes?

2. Divide the items in the school budget into the three different parts as described in this chapter: (1) 30–40 percent used for core classes, professional development, and a principal; (2) 30–40 percent used for extra, support services such as instruction in specialist content classes or for the additional needs of students who struggle to learn to standards, and guidance, social work, family outreach, nursing, and other student support services; and (3) 20–30 percent for central administration, operations and maintenance of schools, transportation of students to and from school, food services, and short-term debt service. Does your school's budget match the percentage ranges for the three categories given in this chapter? If not, what are the differences and what are their causes?

3. Next, identify how the resources are being used in the school for which you have a budget by placing them into the categories of the Odden et al. expenditure framework, displayed in Table 6.10. Are the patterns described in this chapter also present in the school you are investigating? For example, calculate the percentage of teachers in core classrooms (or subjects) compared to the total number of teachers in the building. Does your school follow the pattern described in this chapter whereby many certified teachers are outside the regular classrooms?

4. Using the same budget and/or your own personal knowledge of the school or district, use the Odden et al. professional development framework displayed in Table 6.11 to estimate a per-teacher or per-student amount spent on professional development at your school or in your district. How does that amount compare to your perception, or others' perceptions, of how much is spent on professional development in your school or district? Are there any elements included in this framework that you did not previously associate with or count as professional development? Which ones?

5. Was the budget you used for these questions sufficient to enable you to answer the last three questions thoroughly? If not, what information did you lack? From this experience, are there ways that you believe school budgets could be arranged to facilitate access to school-level use of resources?

— *Chapter 7*————————————————————

Using Educational Resources More Effectively

As school finance adequacy court decisions in Arizona, Arkansas, New York, Wyoming, and other states indicate, some schools need more resources to teach all students to higher standards. These and many other states also argue that current resources need to be used more effectively, through resource reallocation. But in too many contexts, the reallocation claim is more a "throwaway line" than a specific promise. However, reallocating school resources to more effective strategies is a real possibility in most American schools. This chapter focuses on this issue—using educational resources more effectively—providing a number of examples of how schools have allocated and reallocated their resources to what they conclude are the most effective educational strategies. We maintain that using current resources differently and most effectively should be a starting point, *before* adding more resources to boost student achievement.

Many in education claim that because most of the education dollar is spent on salaries and benefits—on *people*—schools are unable to engage in the process of using resources differently. The argument is that use of labor in schools is like a string quartet, which always needs four musicians. But as this chapter shows, effective resource use in education today is not "fixed" like it is for a string quartet; rather, using resources most effectively is fundamentally about using teacher resources differently. To be sure, the examples discussed here are not exhaustive. In a very real sense, the nation's education system is just beginning to understand programmatically how to restructure and reallocate resources to achieve higher performance. But our knowledge base about more effective uses of resources, as well as insight into ineffective uses, is growing rapidly. With that in mind, this chapter identifies and analyzes some of the strategies that currently exist for using education dollars better. In the process, we note examples of ineffective *and* more effective uses of resources—both current and new. Understanding both can help leaders frame strategies to deploy the education dollar in more overall cost-effective ways.

Chapter 6 suggested thinking about a school's budget in terms of three parts:

1. *Core instruction*—resources dedicated to regular-classroom teachers, who provide instruction in core academic subjects, and their professional development, and to a principal in each school
2. *Other instruction and support for students*, including special- and elective-subject teachers (art, music, physical education, etc.), services for special-needs students (from poverty or English-language-learning [ELL] backgrounds, students with disabilities, etc.), and pupil support services (guidance counselors, social workers, family liaisons, etc.)
3. *Overhead* that includes central administration, business and personnel services, operations, maintenance, transportation, food, and short-term debt service

Grouping resources into these three categories can be helpful in providing examples of how education resources can be used more effectively via resource reallocation. For this reason, this chapter is organized into three sections based on these three categories. Section 1 describes examples of more efficient resource use within the area of core instruction, including class size strategies, resource use practices in small schools, and provision of high-quality teachers. Section 2 gives examples of reallocating categorical and specialist subject resources to a range of more effective strategies designed to improve the academic performance of those students who need extra help to learn to standards. Section 3 offers a few examples of more effective ways to structure the "overhead" functions of schools. Finally, section 4 gives examples of prototypical schools staffed according to the adequacy model described in Chapter 4 and introduces readers to a web-based simulation tool that can be used to determine how close a school is to (or how far from) being able to deploy the strategies of the evidence-based model discussed in Chapter 4.

1. CHANGES IN CATEGORY 1 RESOURCES: CORE INSTRUCTION

Resources in this category of expenditures include the core, "front-line" workers in education—teachers—and the managers of the organizational units where teaching and learning occur—principals. The teachers in this resource category are those who provide instruction in what we and most policymakers term the "core academic" subjects. These are the grade-level (or multiage) teacher in elementary schools and the mathematics, science, history, reading/language arts, and perhaps world language teachers in secondary schools. We include professional development in this category because it is so closely linked to teacher quality. Without ongoing, high-quality professional development, it is unlikely that instructional practices will change sufficiently to double or triple the performance of America's students, which we argue throughout the book is the performance challenge facing the nation.

The major policy issues for these resources involve class size and the quality of professional development.[1] We begin with examples from two Midwestern districts, discuss some high-cost but not necessarily more effective strategies in small high schools, examine the resource reallocation possibilities for current professional development expenditures, and end with an example of how to address all these issues.

Resource Reallocation

Madison, Wisconsin, is a medium-sized urban district in south central Wisconsin. For years, it was a relatively homogeneous community, with good schools and high levels of student achievement. In the late 1980s and early 1990s, however, its demographics and performance standards began to change. By the mid-1990s, it was moving from a 25 percent low-income and minority enrollment toward the 50 percent level, which it will reach sometime around 2010. And as its diversity grew, so did the achievement gap between its middle-class white students and the rising numbers of low-income and minority, particularly African American, students. A mid-1990s analysis of reading achievement showed that only about 30 percent of low-income and African American students met the state's third-grade reading benchmarks, and even worse, almost all such students who scored below the basic level in reading at grade 3 were below basic in grade 8 as well. In other words, if students did not read at or above the basic level by grade 3, they never caught up—at least not with the way the instructional program was then organized.

Something had to be done. There was a clear and urgent need to bolster the district's elementary reading program; actually, it was more the lack of a reading program because at that time the reading program varied by school, grade, and classroom! And it was not working for its new population of children.

Using a bottom-up approach that the culture in Madison required if a change were to be successful, the district created a new, districtwide, research-based reading program. Wanting to ensure that every teacher in grades K–3 had the skills to implement the program, the district expanded professional development, ultimately providing professional development in the new reading program for all elementary teachers, including an intensive summer induction program for all new teachers. The district provided instructional coaches for all of its highest-poverty schools to help all teachers incorporate the new reading strategies into their ongoing instructional practice. In those high-poverty schools, enrollment in K–3 classrooms was limited to 15 students. In addition, the district provided teacher tutors to help students who were still struggling after the regular reading instruction was provided. All these new resources—professional development, smaller class sizes, instructional coaches, and teacher tutors—were supported by reallocating the resources the district had been providing to its elementary schools; no new local funds were needed. The reallocation also helped the district tap a state program that provided some, but not all, funds to lower class sizes to 15 in grades K–3 for its high-poverty schools.

---

[1]We understand that in the private sector, computer technologies have replaced labor in the core work processes of many organizations. But that phenomenon is just beginning in public education and will take more time to "play out" as a substantively viable aspect of the restructuring of the core processes of schooling.

The result was that over a five-year period the percentage of low-income and African American students achieving at or above the proficiency level on the state's reading test doubled, while the number of third-grade students scoring below Basic was reduced to nearly zero. The district's success was based on two components:

1. Dramatic instructional change in the reading program
2. Reallocated resources focused on three evidence-based practices for the core instructional program:
   - Class sizes of 15 in grades K–3
   - Intensive and ongoing professional development including instructional coaches who helped teachers successfully implement new instructional approaches to reading
   - Teacher tutors to provide intensive, extra help to students who needed it to move toward proficiency

The results were impressive. Specifically, the percentage of low-income students scoring at or above proficiency grew from 50 percent in 1998 to 78 percent in 2005. The percentage of African American students scoring at or above proficiency grew from 31 percent in 1998, 62 percent in 2003, to 69 percent in 2005. Finally, the percentage of Hispanic third-graders scoring at or above proficiency increased from 60 percent in 1998 to 90 percent in 2005 at the same time that the number of Hispanic students in the district more than doubled. As of 2005, the percentage of all third-graders scoring at or above proficiency was 82.7 percent, compared to 58.9 percent in 1998.

Reducing Class Size in Grades K–3 and Expanding Half-Day Kindergarten to Full Day

Our second example is one of "surplus" resource allocation to some "high"-cost but effective strategies (Odden and Archibald, 2001b). It is taken from a mid-sized urban school district in Wisconsin that managed to extend kindergarten from a half- to a full-day program and significantly reduce class size in the majority of its elementary schools—without raising local revenues (Odden and Archibald, 2001b). The district had experienced an increase in the percentage of its students from lower-income and minority backgrounds, and sought to deploy what its leaders considered to be research-based strategies that could boost the achievement of those students—class sizes of 15 in grades K–3, and full-day, as compared to half-day, kindergarten. The district relied on the same research we cited in Chapter 4, where we also recommend these strategies.

The district knew that it could not raise more local funds to finance these interventions. The funding approach taken by the district was linked to the workings of its state's school finance system and an understanding of "marginal" versus "average" costs. *Marginal* costs are the extra costs of doing something additional, such as shifting from a half-day to a full-day kindergarten program. *Average* costs are the total current operating costs. The question to be answered was this: if it cost $X per pupil to run a half-day kindergarten program—the average cost—would it require $2X dollars to "double" the length of the program from a half to a full day? It turned out that the answer was no.

Once a district qualified for at least one dollar of state equalization aid, the district's school finance structure, like those in almost all states, provided the full expenditure amount for every new student. At the time of the study, that was about $7,000 per student. So, if the district expanded its kindergarten program from half to full day, it could count each kindergarten student as a full 1.0 student for state aid purposes. Thus, every two students who were shifted from a half-day to a full-day kindergarten program resulted in an increased student count of 1.0 (each producing an additional 0.5, which sums to 1.0). So every two additional students enrolled in a full-day kindergarten program generated an additional $7,000 in revenues.

What the district realized was that the additional, or marginal, cost of the full-day kindergarten program was only $3,000 for every new 1.0 student. Put differently, for every two students shifting from a half- to a full-day kindergarten program, the marginal cost of educating those students was only about $3,000. Meanwhile, the district received an extra $7,000 via the state school finance formula for the additional 1.0 student count this program expansion produced, or an excess of average over marginal costs of $4,000 per child. So, shifting from a half- to full-day kindergarten actually resulted in a revenue *gain* for the district. Thus, the district was able not only to "double" the length of its kindergarten program but also produce a fiscal surplus in the process—without raising any new local dollars. As we show below, this "surplus" was then used to reduce class sizes in grades K–3.

An additional phenomenon also helped the district—it was experiencing overall enrollment growth. As a result, the same approximate "surplus" revenue of marginal over average costs occurred in organizing instruction for these new students. Since the district already had considerable excess space in its buildings, it cost the district only about $3,000 per child to organize classrooms with 25 students each. But just as for the "additional" kindergarten students, each of these new students brought with them the full $7,000 from the state school finance system, again producing an excess of $4,000 per pupil when comparing marginal costs of running an additional class to the average new funds of $7,000 per pupil.

The total combined district enrollment growth from these two phenomena—natural growth and kindergarten expansion—was about 500 students a year. This produced excess revenues of nearly $2 million (500 students times $4,000 per student), which, it turned out, was sufficient to hire 40 additional teachers at an individual cost of $50,000 in salary and benefits. And this was the number of additional teachers needed to reduce class sizes from 25 to close to 15 students in grades K–3 in the district's highest-poverty schools. The small-class-size strategy was also aided, at that time, by a federal grant program to reduce class sizes in elementary schools, a similar state program, and some modest reallocation of federal Title I funding.

By deploying these "surplus" state resources to research-proven effective but "expensive" strategies, the district was able to expand its kindergarten programming from a half to a full day, as well as provide very small classes in its highest-poverty elementary schools, without asking taxpayers for any new revenues and while staying within the normal confines of the state's school finance system.

This case as an example of targeted resource deployment, and the practice is different from what we described in Chapter 6, where the vast bulk of resources were used to expand services outside of the core instructional program. We would argue that few districts would have used the "excess" revenues resulting from enrollment growth for such targeted, expensive but effective programs. More likely, they would have argued that more dollars were needed to expand kindergarten programming and to reduce class sizes by 40 percent. But in a student enrollment growth mode, the district was able to fund these initiatives without more than the normal revenue increases from the state's school finance structures.

This case shows how important it is for district leaders to fully understand the workings of the state school finance formula. They need to understand marginal versus average costs, find situations in which there are large differences between the two, and identify how those differences can be used to fund targeted and effective strategies. The leaders of this district were able to find "additional funding" because they understood the principle that "new" students, whether from natural enrollment growth or the shift from half-day to full-day kindergarten, produce "surplus" dollars when the marginal costs of providing education services are much less than the average-cost dollars received for every new student.

We will discuss other examples of reducing class sizes in the next section, where the prime funding source represented a different use of categorical dollars and reflected the belief of the schools' teachers and administrators that smaller classes were vital for boosting student academic achievement.

Class Sizes in Small Schools

One of the most common assumptions across the country is that expenditures need to be higher in small schools if they are to provide the same quality of educational services as more average-sized schools. Put differently, it is sort of an axiom that small schools suffer "diseconomies of small size" and so must spend more.

However, as we have worked in different states where this issue has arisen in many forms, we have come to realize that not all claims for scale diseconomies are necessarily valid. For example, assume that a state or a district provides funds to staff an elementary school with 20 students in each classroom. A school of 480 students, with 80 in each grade, would need 24 core teachers, or 4 teachers in each of grades K–5. A smaller school of 360 students, with 60 students in a grade, would need 18 teachers (3 for each grade); a school of 240 students would need 12 teachers (2 for each grade); a school of 120 students would need just 6 teachers (1 for each grade). The core teacher cost per pupil in these four schools would be exactly the same—no diseconomies of small size, at least for core teachers. Yes, the cost of providing the school with at least a principal, a secretary, and a librarian would rise on a per-pupil basis as the school got smaller, but the per-pupil *teacher cost* would be the same.

What about an even smaller school, with 60 students, 10 in each grade? Would the per-pupil teacher cost rise, becoming double that of the 120- (or 240- or 360- or 480-) student school because there were only 10 students in a grade? Yes, if the school organized itself by grade and employed one teacher per grade. But if the district and school decided to use multiage student groups, which research has shown is at least as effective and often more effective as a student organizational strategy than age grouping (Pavan, 1992; Slavin, 1992), then that district could organize into three nongraded classes, each with 20 students. With this organization, it would need to employ just three teachers, thus incurring the same per-pupil cost for teachers as in all of the above examples.

The point here is that while small schools often claim diseconomies of scale for teacher resources, it is not because of their small size that these diseconomies exist. Rather, it is the result of a specific and more expensive, but not more effective, way to organize instruction for students. Moreover, a "different" way to organize students—multiaging—reduces if not eliminates this higher cost while producing the same or higher levels of student achievement. So the claim that there are diseconomies of scale for teacher resources is not as straightforward as it might seem. We would argue that, depending on the class size policies directly or indirectly embedded in the school finance structure, such diseconomies for teachers do not really exist (and thus do not need to be accommodated in a school funding formula) until enrollments drop well below 100, and probably below 75, students in the school.

We should also note that existing "small" school research does not apply to very small schools of under 100 students, as most of the "small" school literature deals with schools in the 300- to 500-student range and compares them to much larger schools, often with enrollments in the range of 1,000–2,000 students (Odden and Picus, 2004, Chapter 6).

A parallel issue about the "necessity" of making adjustments for small schools due to diseconomies of scale can be raised for high schools. For example, Wyoming's school finance formula provides high schools with sufficient teachers for average class sizes of 21 students. But in many small high schools of 100–200 students, we observed that actual sizes for many classes, particularly core academic classes, were in the 8- to 12-student range, resulting in above-average costs per pupil. The reason for the small class sizes and higher per-pupil costs was that these high schools chose to provide all academic classes every year. For example, the school would offer physics, chemistry, biology, general science, and sometimes an advanced science every year. The result was classes with 8–12 students. The same was true for many other subject areas. Consequently, in these schools, the per-pupil cost for core teachers was very high. The school's version of equity and quality was that students needed to have these offerings *every year*.

A different way to organize the educational program in these small schools would be to alternate class offerings, with general science and chemistry one year, and biology and physics the next, with larger class sizes in each of the offerings. This strategy does restrict choice in any one year, but it still offers students the chance to take all four of these science courses during their four-year high school career, and at a lower per-pupil cost for teacher resources. Further, school systems could augment this approach by offering classes via the Internet and other distance-learning options, which the state—or other computer-based organizations—make available.[2] Again, most of the small high

---

[2]Research has shown that student achievement with distance-learning approaches in these science and math courses is at least as high as that in "regular" classes (Smith, Clark, and Blomeyer, 2005).

schools had many reasons, with local preference being a major reason, for not opting for these lower-cost ways to provide courses. But the result was a higher per-pupil cost to run the school and not much evidence of higher levels of achievement.

We raise these two examples to show that (1) sometimes higher costs result from specific ways education systems choose to organize the instructional program and (2) in many cases there are alternative ways to organize classrooms and provide courses that are less costly and, at least at first blush, just as effective. Although we recognize that individuals might have different views on these school and classroom organizational issues, and the alternative strategies we suggest that do not raise per-pupil costs for core teachers, we note them because higher costs and scale diseconomies for teachers do not have to be in the "DNA" of small high schools (down to a size of 150 or so students). To be sure, as noted above, if the goal is to provide a principal, secretary, and librarian in every school, the cost per-pupil is higher in schools with fewer students. But sometimes higher and lower per-pupil costs of teacher resources exist because of specific choices schools have made to organize the instructional program. We would argue that those selecting the higher-cost approach bear the weight of justifying that the higher costs are needed and that lower levels of student achievement would occur if alternative and less costly options—such as those identified above—were selected instead.

Indeed, Arkansas has taken a tougher stance toward these high-cost strategies for small schools. The legislature, with the support of the governor, has asserted that it wants each high school in the state to provide 38 different classes each year. It stipulates this requirement knowing that many of the state's very small high schools will have difficulty doing so because they receive the same level of revenue per pupil as do larger high schools, and often have difficulty providing the 38 units with that level of funding. The state's position is that if the high school and its district cannot provide the requisite courses—with the standard funding provided—then the district and its high school should consolidate with a neighboring district in order to do so. Although politically charged, the bulk of the state's districts can consolidate with districts that are geographically nearby. This has resulted in significant district consolidation, reducing the number of school districts in the state from 308 in 2003–04 to 245 in 2006–07.

District-Level Resource Reallocation: The Case of Professional Development

As policymakers and educators increasingly reach a consensus that the core classroom teacher is the most important element in the education system (see, e.g., Sanders and Rivers, 1996; Wright, Horn and Sanders, 1997), professional development has become a top policy concern. More and more educators and policymakers have concluded that significant resources are needed for intensive professional development designed to enhance teachers' instructional expertise. And the most typical clarion call is that more resources are needed to finance these professional development services. However, research is beginning to show that, at least in many large, urban districts, the issue is less the need for more money for professional development and more the need to recognize the extant large investment in professional development and reallocate those funds to more effective professional development strategies.

Our professional development recommendations in Chapter 4 can be translated into an amount per pupil of roughly $450.[3] This covers 10 days over the work year for intensive training, which costs approximately $42 per pupil;[4] the placement of instructional coaches in schools at the rate of 1 coach for every 200 students, which costs approximately $311 per pupil;[5] and $100 per-pupil for trainers. This is a substantial amount of money for school districts.

Research in several large, urban districts, however, showed that a large portion of this level of professional development funding was already being provided. In a five-district study, Miles, Odden, Fermanich, and Archibald (2004) found that the per-teacher amount varied from $2,100 to $7,900.[6] Translating these numbers into rough average per-pupil numbers, based on a staffing model of 30 teachers in a 500-student school, the amount spent on professional development ranged from $70 to $263 per pupil. In one district, moreover, professional development investment from school-level sources (separate from district sources) more than doubled the amount per-pupil, from $228 to $501 (Fermanich, 2003), sufficient to cover the ambitious professional development costs included in the adequacy model. The studies also showed that very little of the professional development spending was focused on improving instruction in the core academic subjects, further eroding the impacts of the expenditures on student achievement in the core academics.

The lesson from these studies is that large, urban districts should first do a professional development fiscal and program "audit" of their extant professional development strategies before deciding that additional funding is required. It could well be that what is required is a reallocation of their current professional development expenditures to strategies focused on improving teachers' instructional practice in teaching the core academics—math, science, reading/language arts, and history. This type of resource reallocation to fund new and ambitious professional development programs was the foundation of an effective program in New York City's District 2 (Elmore and Burney, 1999).

The superintendent of District 2, Anthony Alvarado, who successfully led the reform, was subsequently hired as a superintendent of instruction in San Diego. Hightower (2002) details the restructuring that took place in San Diego to refocus the district on teaching and learning, as well as the resource reallocation necessary to fund these changes. The main programmatic components were 300 peer coaches (at a cost of approximately $87,500 per coach), $5,000 for every first-grade classroom to purchase new materials, and additional learning experiences for students and staff after school and in the summer. A total of $62 million was reallocated for the 2000–01 school year, which was 6 percent of the operating budget. These funds came from a number of different sources, including $19 million from

---

[3]This amount will vary by class size, provision for planning and preparation, and other factors, but it is a good, median estimate of what an effective professional development program will cost.

[4]Based on the NEA average teacher salary rate for 2005 of $47,808, with 205 contract days per teacher or a daily rate of $233, we add here the cost of 5 additional days at $1166, and divide that by the average number of teachers in an average-sized school (500/18), for an additional $42 per pupil.

[5]Based on the NEA average teacher salary for 2005 and a benefit rate of 30 percent, for a school with 500 students, it would cost $155,376 to hire 2.5 coaches, or $311 per pupil.

[6]When expenditures for contracted professional development days are not included, the per-teacher amount ranges from $2,100 to $5,000.

Title I, $16.6 million from integration funds, and $15 million from state funds for school libraries and new teacher induction. An additional $6.2 million from a redesign of central administration was dedicated to the peer coaches. In the following school year, approximately $96 million was spent on this redesign strategy from similar sources of reallocated funds. The bottom line: This district was able to reallocate sizable funds to powerful instructional strategies.

However, suburban and rural districts might have more trouble finding enough money to reallocate, particularly if the district did not receive large amounts of categorical funding for students in poverty. We are aware that the research findings on professional development spending in large, urban districts should not be generalized to suburban or rural districts, and we do not know of such studies in suburban districts. But a study of one rural district in Wisconsin found that, other than a dual planning and preparation period for middle school teachers, similar levels of professional development spending did not exist, and any ambitious professional development program would require additional funds (Thayer, 2004).

Restructuring to Bolster Several Resources in the Core Program

Sometimes, schools seek to improve the core program by focusing simultaneously on class size, professional development, and related strategies. This was the case in five restructuring elementary and high schools (Miles and Darling-Hammond, 1997, 1998). In the early 1990s, Miles and Darling-Hammond studied three elementary and two high schools across the country that adopted or created a new school vision and reallocated their extant resources accordingly. All schools were in urban districts serving large numbers of low-income and, in some cases, disabled students. Three of the schools were "new starts," or schools created anew. Two schools restructured themselves from their previous to their new design. All five schools produced large increases in student achievement and other desired results such as greater attendance, higher graduation rates, and more student engagement.

To varying degrees, the schools implemented five different approaches to school and classroom organization through their resource reallocation efforts. They (1) increased the number of regular-classroom teachers, thereby reducing class sizes for the core academics; (2) provided varied class sizes for different subjects; (3) grouped students differently from the age/grade strategy of most schools; (4) expanded common planning time for teacher teams, part of which was used for professional development; and (5) increased teacher professional development. Each of these strategies involved using resources differently. All of these resource use strategies were designed to help strengthen the schools' core instructional program. And each school produced higher levels of student performance as a result.

None of the schools studied were given extra resources above those provided through normal district budgeting. Further, the schools were staffed with the same total number of professional positions and resourced the same as all other schools in their districts, with similar numbers and characteristics of students. But these schools used their professional teaching resources differently.

First, they all expanded the number of regular-classroom teachers. Two of the schools first traded administrative positions for more teachers and then involved more teachers in the management of the school. Most of the schools converted the bulk of their categorical specialist teacher positions, largely funded with categorical program dollars (federal Title I, state and local special education, bilingual education, etc.), into regular-classroom teacher positions, which allowed them to lower class sizes.

Second, all schools had different class sizes for different subject areas. They provided the lowest class sizes—sometimes as few as eight—for reading and language arts. One strategy was to have almost all teachers, including reading tutors and sometimes even music, art, physical education, and library teachers, teach a reading class during the reading period; this practice allowed schools to lower class size to 15 or fewer for reading. Other schools had some large, lecture-style classes that were supplemented by smaller discussion groups and individual student advising. Rather than have the same class size for all subjects, the schools varied class sizes. First, they required everyone in the school to teach reading, thus providing quite small class sizes. They then had less than half the staff teach larger classes such as music and physical education, thus freeing those not teaching for other activities, including both common planning time and professional development.

Third, most of the schools also grouped students differently from the traditional age/grade system. Several schools created multiage and multiyear student groupings, putting students of two or three different ages in the same classroom and having the same teachers work with those students over a two- to three-year period. This grouping strategy permitted teachers to build strong relationships and develop rapport with students, allowed them to provide a more personalized classroom atmosphere, and eliminated the need for the extended adjustment period at the beginning of each year when teachers must get to know a new class of students.

The high schools created block schedules with longer class periods, which let them reduce teachers' daily student load from over 150 to less than 100, and even to less than 60 in one case. This arrangement provided teachers with time to get to know a smaller number of students at a deeper level and thus to provide a more individualized instructional program. The high schools also assigned small groups of students to each teacher for ongoing advising and counseling, yet another strategy that enhanced the personal, caring nature of the school environment, which research shows helps to improve achievement (Bryk, Lee, and Holland, 1993; Newmann and Associates, 1996).

Fourth, all five schools created more planning time for teachers or simply rescheduled the planning time that existed to allow teams of teachers to work together during some portion of the regular school day. Many schools across the country already provide teachers with planning and preparation time. Too often, however, schools do not schedule this time for all members of a teacher team at the same time during the day. Although rearranging the school schedule to provide common planning time for teacher teams is not an easy task, it is a way to reallocate current resources to provide more paid time for professional development (for more examples, see Odden and Archibald, 2001a). The schools studied underwent this process and were able to make such changes to their schedules. But these schools also used the flexibility provided by their different class sizes for joint planning. During those times when students were in larger classes, and in the case of one high school, during those times when students were out of the school working on community service projects, the schools scheduled common teacher planning time. In this way, each school was able to provide more common planning time for their faculty by using both money and time differently.

Fifth, all schools increased investments in professional development. The additional professional development for the teachers in these schools was an important new way of using their resources.

How did they finance these new staffing and resource deployment strategies? First, they traded categorical program specialist positions for regular-classroom teachers, including many specialist teachers for students with mild disabilities, such as the learning disabled. As a result, each school had specific strategies for instructing low-achieving or learning-disabled students within the regular classroom or as part of the core features of the school design. For example, two schools not only taught reading in small classes of 15 but also provided one-on-one tutoring to any student, including learning-disabled students, not reading at grade level. One school mainstreamed all special-education students and trained the entire faculty to instruct students in this more inclusive environment. In order to make this approach to service provision for the disabled legal, each disabled student's Individual Education Plan (IEP) was modified, with parental consent, to reflect the instructional strategies of the school. The achievement data showed that these special-needs students also improved their performance, a result often not achieved by pull-out, resource room programs (Allington and Johnston, 1989; Reynolds and Wolfe, 1999), the typical service identified by individualized education programs. It should be noted that changing the way special-education students are served is a difficult task and one that benefits many, but not all, special-education students.[7]

The five schools implemented these restructuring and resource reallocation strategies over a number of years. In no case were teacher positions eliminated precipitously; in fact, many teachers assumed new roles, with training to give them the required new expertise. Miles and Darling-Hammond (1997, 1998) noted that the restructuring and reallocation processes would have been facilitated if the schools had had more authority over recruiting and selecting staff committed to the vision they were deploying.

In short, without any additional resources, these schools achieved the following:

- Reduced core class sizes
- Created even lower class sizes for reading
- Reduced the daily student–teacher contact numbers
- Personalized the teaching-learning environment
- Provided common planning time
- Expanded professional development.

---

[7]The schools also changed students' individual education plans (IEPs); if they had not done so, the restructuring strategies would have violated requirements of the federal IDEA program.

(Note that many of these changes are also recommended by the evidence-based adequacy model discussed in Chapter 4, and as such, they will appear in the prototypical schools detailed in section 4 of this chapter.)

Although all schools faced obstacles and challenges in implementing these different resource use strategies, they nevertheless made substantial progress and engaged in substantive resource reallocation. They also improved educational achievements for students, including those with special needs. In short, all five schools improved the productivity of their existing staffing resources through programmatic and organizational restructuring, accompanied by substantial resource reallocation.

A Final Word

We need to underscore that the possibilities for more effective uses of resources, via either resource reallocation or targeted deployment of new resources, depends largely on the approach to providing instructional services that schools select. Resource reallocation occurs when schools decide that previous uses of resources are not resulting in sufficient student performance and that a new instructional vision, funded by reallocation of extant resources, is needed. Many of the small-school scale "diseconomies" are also caused by a particular approach to organizing instructional services. And at least in some cases, we argue that different approaches can avoid the higher costs due to small school size. The key points here are twofold: (1) The instructional vision guides and drives schools' uses of resources, and (2) some visions are more programmatically and cost-effective than others.

2. CHANGES IN CATEGORY 2 RESOURCES: SPECIALISTS AND STUDENT SUPPORT

Resources in this category can be described generically as those that "help" accomplish the prime objective of schools: student performance in the core academic subjects. As such, this category consists of "staff" resources, provided by categorical programs for students who need extra help to learn to standards (students from lower-income backgrounds, students with disabilities, ELL students, etc.), resources to give students nonacademic help (guidance counselors, social workers, psychologists, family liaisons, etc.), specialist teachers in noncore subjects (art, music, physical education, vocational education, etc.), and other instructional and pupil support services outside the core, such as instructional aides. This section discusses the potential for reallocating these resources to more effective uses, particularly new uses that actually boost the performance of struggling students. We also provide an example of how schools around the country have increased spending, in ways that we conclude are inefficient, by expanding resources for elective classes at the expense of helping all students learn to standards in the core academic subjects.

Reallocating Categorical Staff Resources

As we learned in Chapter 6, although expenditures for instruction remained the same approximate percentage of overall school district spending over several decades, the pattern of spending within instruction changed. By the late 1980s, a smaller percentage of instructional expenditures was directed toward frontline education workers—regular-classroom teachers—and a larger percentage toward specialist staff (both teachers and instructional aides) working outside of the regular classroom and providing extra help for students with special needs. As we also discussed in the last chapter, allocating more resources to students who require more help to learn to standards (such as low-income students, students with disabilities, and ELL students) is necessary to give them opportunity to achieve to high standards; we do not dispute that fact. However, the addition of categorical program specialist staff outside the classroom, typically employed in a pull-out service model, has not helped these students learn significantly more (Borman, Stringfield, and Slavin, 2001; Odden, 1991; Reynolds and Wolfe, 1999).

We provide here a short summary of what Odden and Archibald (2000, 2001a) found about the specifics of the resource redeployment by schools that decided to reallocate categorical teacher resources to three "expensive" strategies: (1) smaller class sizes, (2) school-based instructional coaches, and (3) teacher tutors. Since the schools described here chose to retain a principal and all of their regular teachers, the research findings focus on reallocation of specialist staff in three categories—those in compensatory, bilingual or ELL, and special-education programs.

First, Odden and Archibald (2000, 2001a) found that the schools did not reallocate their regular-education specialists, such as art, music, and physical education teachers, and librarians. In all the cases they studied, schools eliminated none of these teacher positions, and in two cases, the number of these staff was actually increased. These staff positions were retained both because the schools valued the content these teachers taught and because collective bargaining required the schools to provide a daily planning and preparation period for all teachers. In some cases, this planning period was used to give teachers common time during the school day to enhance their instruction.

Second, Odden and Archibald (2000, 2001a) found that the schools made significant changes in the use of their categorical program specialist staff. These staff were primarily teachers and instructional aides supported by federal and state compensatory education money, bilingual education funds, and the learning disabilities portion of funds for students with disabilities. The vast majority of Title I remedial reading and math teacher positions were eliminated; many of these teachers were retrained as either instructional facilitators or reading tutors. In schools that reduced class size, these individuals became regular-classroom teachers. In some cases, the number of instructional aides was dramatically reduced; it took two to three aide positions to fund a fully certified teacher tutor position. But in some cases, the aides took on new roles, such as reading tutors, even though some research has suggested that they have less of a positive impact on student achievement than do professional teachers (Slavin, Karweit and Wasik, 1994).

Most schools traded a portion of their specialist teachers for the disabled (in most cases, learning disability [LD] teachers) either for regular-classroom teachers or for teacher tutors. But the general practice was to retain 60 percent or more of these positions. In several instances, the LD teachers were dually certified in special education and regular education; when assigned to a regular classroom, they were often given the lowest-level reading class (which tended to have the most students with a required IEP). Though this was not required, school staff nevertheless thought that it provided the best educational strategy for these students. Teachers at these schools reported that mainstreaming even the LD special-education students was quite challenging and that the changes were beneficial for some, but not all, such students.

Third, only a small number of pupil-support specialist staff at any of the schools were reallocated. Some of these staff were moved into new roles (e.g., to become a parental-outreach coordinator), but most were simply retained. They tended to represent staff positions that schools believed were necessary to serve their population of students.

All schools studied also had access to between $25,000 and $100,000 in additional funds from a variety of sources—state reading and school improvement grants, state compensatory education funds, federal Goals 2000 and Eisenhower training grants, and federal Obey-Porter comprehensive school restructuring funds—which they cobbled together to support their new school strategies.

Further, all schools rewrote the IEP for each student with a disability so that it conformed to the new service strategy of their restructured school. This task required extra effort in the first and second year of the school's restructuring process but was essential in the cases in which schools used a portion of their disability funds to finance their new school strategy. IEPs had to be changed, or the schools would have been out of compliance with state and federal requirements. Indeed, in the state where the schools reduced their class size, relying on both state and federal waivers to do so, another school that was not part of the study implemented the same strategies but did not seek the required waivers. Its strategies were found to be out of compliance, and the school was required to reverse its resource reallocation actions.

In sum, the schools studied by Odden and Archibald (2000, 2001a) found ways to finance expensive new school strategies through substantial reallocation of available resources. Federal Title I and state compensatory education funds were the largest sources of funds. But the schools also reallocated a portion of learning disabilities staff, a small portion of pupil support staff, and a large portion of other small grants they controlled. Nearly all regular-education specialist staff remained, as did the bulk of special-education staff and most pupil support staff. Finally, some schools shifted instructional aides into reading tutor roles rather than make the more difficult decision to redeploy these funds for more effective teacher tutors; this is often a difficult decision because of personal and contractual issues, but some schools did eliminate instructional aide positions. Additional specifics, in categorical resource reallocation for three different schools include the following:

- *Inclusive schooling for ELL and poverty students in small classes.* One school with 35 percent limited-English-proficient (LEP) students that had decided to reduce class size to 15, elected to trade all three pull-out ESL specialists for regular-classroom teachers. They also traded part-time gifted-and-talented and pupil support teacher positions for an additional regular teacher position to lower overall class size. In the first year, these and other teachers with dual certification in ESL had the classes with the highest percentage of LEP students, but the school also implemented a professional development strategy to dually certify all teachers as regular and ESL teachers. There were those in the school who questioned whether mainstreaming these students was the best option, but the majority of teachers believed it was in these students' best interests. The school also turned a federal Title I resource room teacher into a teacher tutor to provide intensive assistance to students struggling even after instruction in a small class. In this way, the school augmented the small-class-size strategy with some focused extra help. One sign that these students were learning more came in the same year that the changes were made—many more LEP students took standardized tests than had in the past, suggesting that they were more a part of the regular curriculum.

- *Inclusive schooling for students with disabilities in smaller classes.* At a 700-student K–8 school in the Midwest, both teachers and administrators believed that special-education students were being stigmatized rather than positively served by pull-out and resource room programming. In response, district and school leaders reallocated resources for eight additional regular-classroom teacher positions. Their resource reallocation process involved eliminating four special-education aide positions to hire 1.5 additional teachers; eliminating the half-time gifted-and-talented teacher position and reallocating those resources for a half-time regular-education classroom teacher; and reallocating six special-education teachers to regular classrooms (one worked with hearing-impaired students and five worked with students who had learning disabilities).

- *Class size reduction in urban schools.* In an urban elementary school in the Midwest, resources were reallocated to lower class sizes. The school served 300 students in grades K–8. Before reallocation, the school employed 12 teachers; the combination of resource reallocation and a flow of new money allowed them to hire 8 more teachers for a total of 20. To do this, the school first eliminated 12 instructional aide positions and converted them to 4 certified-teacher positions. Next, they converted a pull-out special-education teacher to a regular classroom position, and traded three Title I resource room aides and part of a counselor for another regular-classroom position. Thus, the school managed to fund six regular-classroom teachers by reallocating current resources. The two additional teacher positions were paid for with federal class-size-reduction money and extra resources from the district's redesign of the school finance funding formula.

These examples show the variety of ways schools in different parts of the country redeployed category 2 staff resources based on a new instructional vision each school thought would be better for its students. Smaller regular class sizes were a strong theme across the schools, but other elements were also the focus of their resource reallocation practices. Section 4 of this chapter provides another example of potential reallocation from this portion of the education budget by comparing how a middle school is currently staffed (Table 7.2) with how it would be staffed under the evidence-based adequacy model (Table 7.3) described in Chapter 4.

A Final Word

There are many possibilities for reallocating resources from the second portion of the budget, which includes other-than-core instructional expenses, both for students with special needs and for specials and electives. Although this is the largest potential source of funds for reallocation, the next section discusses the likelihood (or unlikelihood) that funds can be reallocated from the third portion—overhead.

3. CHANGES IN CATEGORY 3 RESOURCES: OVERHEAD

Relatively little is known about the possibilities for resource reallocation in this category, which includes central administration (superintendent, board support), business/fiscal/personnel services, operations (heating, cooling, electrifying, cleaning schools, caring for grounds), maintenance (plumbers, electricians, carpenters, etc.), transportation of students to and from school, food, and short-term debt. The next few sections give examples of possible ways to save money in these areas.

Transporting Pupils: The Foshay Bus

In many school districts, the number of field trips is limited to one or two per class per semester. The stated reason for this is often the high costs of pupil transportation. The principal at Foshay Middle School in Los Angeles realized that there was a cost-effective way to provide many more field trips for the students in his school by understanding how transportation costs operate.

Howard Lappin, the Foshay principal, learned that the bus contractor for the Los Angeles Unified School District has both variable costs (driver time, gasoline and oil, wear and tear on the buses, etc.) and fixed costs (rent on the school transportation garage, repair equipment, financing to purchase the buses, etc.). He also learned that the hourly cost of a school bus for to-and-from-school transportation needed to cover all of the contractor's fixed and variable costs, but that during the day—when buses were idle—the contractor could provide services at an hourly rate that covered only its variable costs.

By recognizing that the variable costs of school buses during the day were substantially lower than the hourly rate paid by the district for to-and-from transportation, and by entering into a long-term agreement to have a bus available to the school every day during school hours, Lappin was able to provide access to many more field trips and other extracurricular activities for the sixth-, seventh- and eighth-graders attending his school.

The "Foshay bus" was funded through the reallocation of resources for student activities and through specific fund-raising events and grant activities. Although Foshay spent more on pupil transportation than many other similar-sized schools in the district, teachers had regular access to transportation for field trips and could schedule bus time through the school office, rather than through the district's bureaucratic channels.

Because Foshay was located close to downtown Los Angeles and near a major university (the University of Southern California, where one of the authors of this book teaches), field trips to museums, libraries, and other cultural sites that supported the instructional program of the school could easily be scheduled. In fact, the near-downtown location made "deadheading" (the bus returning to the point of origin empty rather than with students) between drop-off and pick-up for most locations a minor issue, allowing the bus to transport children from multiple classes on a variety of field trips on the same day.

Although field trip costs at Foshay are higher than the average for schools in the district, the staff felt it was worthwhile to offer many more experiences to the children each semester. This would not have been possible if the principal had not had the financial knowledge to set up his own transportation arrangements, rather than letting the district take care of them.

Linking the Community through Food Services

Most schools across the United States serve lunch (and often breakfast) to their students. Generally, food service programs should be self-supporting. Because food services is one area in which there are real economies of scale—at least up to some point—many small schools have a hard time providing lunch for their children.

At the same time, many communities offer meal programs for the elderly. Nonprofit programs such as Meals on Wheels, and Loaves and Fishes ensure that community members in need receive a hot meal at least once or twice a week. These programs often operate with limited financial support.

Linking these two programs is one possible way to provide meals for more people at a lower per-meal cost. There are other potential benefits as well. For example, if local schools open their lunchrooms to retired community members on a weekly or biweekly basis, they can offer low-cost, nutritious meals to both students and the school's neighbors. In addition to making meals more affordable to local residents, the increased volume can lead to a reduced cost per meal and make it possible for the food service program to break even. As a side benefit, having community members visit the school and interact with the children can produce positive public relations benefits that translate into more local support for the school. Community members with unique skills might be more likely to volunteer to help the school, perhaps spending time reading to younger children on a regular basis. And when the time comes to vote on the next tax levy, local residents might be more willing to dig deeper into their pockets because they have a better understanding of what happens each day in the local school.

In a similar vein, Andrews (2004) showed how a district in Florida was able to develop a food service program that provided restaurant-style meals that were more appealing to high school students. As a result of this "Maxi-Meals" program, participation in the National School Lunch Program among middle and high school students—who traditionally are reluctant to participate in this program—increased. In turn, food service revenues increased by over half a million dollars a year.

Improving Energy Management

Dooley (2004) described how the public schools in Warwick, Rhode Island, reduced costs through improved energy management. The program included these components:

- Purchasing of heating oil futures to mitigate increases in the cost of heating oil over the school year

- Entering into cooperative agreements for the purchase of natural gas and electricity
- Retrofitting all school buildings with energy-efficient lighting
- Implementing solar energy at one of the high schools to power student projects and over time reduce dependence on electricity from the local utilities (As an additional benefit, the school was able to use the project to teach about renewable energy resources.)
- Shifting to biodiesel fuel for space heating

Dooley estimated that as a result of these actions, the district—which has over 12,000 students and a budget of over $113 million—was able to reduce heating and electricity costs by 25 percent and over two years save approximately $1 million.

A Final Word

While the efficiency of expenditures in all three categories can be examined and reallocations made as described above, the fact is that all categories of expenditures are needed. With regard to category 3 resources, some central administration is necessary, and 5–6 percent of the total budget is not a large figure. Students must be transported to school, and schools must be operated, heated or cooled, and maintained. Hayward (1988) showed that for many of these expenditures, the amount spent per item (such as per meal served, per student transported, or per square foot of physical plant) was below norms in the private sector, suggesting that school system expenditures were not profligate.

In short, nonteacher expenditures are not lost simply in some "administrative blob," though these expenditures are noninstructional. The route to improving school productivity does not lie in attacking administrative costs, although such costs may be too high in many districts. Instead, the reallocation of resources as described in the previous two sections will go further in improving student learning.

The following section uses the evidence-based adequacy model to show how school-level resources can be allocated according to the available evidence about what works.

4. ALLOCATING RESOURCES USING THE EVIDENCE-BASED ADEQUACY MODEL

In Chapter 4, we introduced the Odden-Picus evidence-based adequacy model. Table 7.1 displays the prototypical elementary, middle, and high schools staffed according to the evidence-based model; it represents the best possible allocation of resources using current evidence.

The following example uses the school finance redesign simulation, available on the CPRE-UW website (www.wcer.wisc.edu/cpre/), to illustrate how a middle school with 600 students, 50 percent of whom are eligible for free or reduced-price lunch and

TABLE 7.1 Recommendations for Adequate Resources for Prototypical Elementary, Middle, and High Schools

School Element	Elementary Schools	Middle Schools	High Schools
School Characteristics			
School configuration	K–5	6–8	9–12
Prototypical school size	432	450	600
Class size	K–3 : 15 4–5 : 25	6–8 : 25	9–12 : 25
Full-day kindergarten	Yes	NA	NA
Number of teacher work days	195 teacher work days: 180 for students, 5 to open/close schools, 10 for professional development	195 teacher work days: 180 for students, 5 to open/close schools, 10 for professional development	195 teacher work days: 180 for students, 5 to open/close schools, 10 for professional development
Percent disabled	14.5%	14.5%	14.5%
Percent poverty (free and reduced lunch)	30%	30%	30%
Percent ELL	~10%	~10%	~10%
Personnel Resources			
1. Teachers	24	18	24
2. Specialist teachers	20% more: 4.8	20% more: 3.6	33% more: 8.0
3. Instructional facilitators/mentors	2.2	2.25	3.0
4. Tutors for struggling students	1 for every 100 poverty students: 1.30	1 for every 100 poverty students: 1.35	1 for every 100 poverty students: 1.95

(continued)

225

TABLE 7.1   (*continued*)

5. Teachers for ELL students	Additional 1 for every 100 ELL students: 0.43	Additional 1 for every 100 ELL students: 0.45	Additional 1 for every 100 ELL students: 0.60
6. Extended day	1.2	1.5	3.0
7. Summer school	1.2	1.5	3.0
8. Learning- and mild-disabled students	Additional 3 professional teacher positions	Additional 3 professional teacher positions	Additional 4 professional teacher positions
9. Severely disabled students	100% state reimbursement minus federal funds	100% state reimbursement minus federal funds	100% state reimbursement minus federal funds
10. Teachers for gifted students	$25/student	$25/student	$25/student
11. Vocational education	NA	NA	Weight FTE voc ed students by 0.29 and provide $7000 per FTE voc ed teacher for equipment
12. Substitutes	10 days/teacher	10 days/teacher	10 days/teacher
13. Pupil support staff	1 for every 100 poverty students: 1.3	1 for every 100 poverty students plus 1.0 guidance /250 students; 3.15	1 for every 100 poverty students plus 1.0 guidance /250 students; 4.2
14. Noninstructional aides	2.0	2.0	3.0
15. Librarians/media specialists	1.0	1.0	1.0 librarian 1.0 library technician
16. Principal	1	1	1
17. School site secretary	1.0 secretary 1.0 clerical	1.0 secretary 1.0 clerical	1.0 secretary 2.0 clerical

(*continued*)

TABLE 7.1 (*continued*)

Dollar-per-Pupil Resources

18. Professional development	Included above: Instructional facilitators Planning and prep time 10 summer days Additional: $100/pupil for other PD expenses—trainers, conferences, travel, etc.	Included above: Instructional facilitators Planning and prep time 10 summer days Additional: $100/pupil for other PD expenses—trainers, conferences, travel, etc.	Included above: Instructional facilitators Planning and prep time 10 summer days Additional: $50/pupil for other PD expenses—trainers, conferences, travel, etc.
19. Technology	$250/pupil	$250/pupil	$250/pupil
20. Instructional materials, equipment, student activities, including textbooks	$140/pupil	$140/pupil	$175/pupil
21. Student activities	$250/pupil	$250/pupil	$250/pupil

25 percent of whom are ELL students, is currently (2005–06) staffed compared to how it would be staffed under the evidence-based model.[8] Table 7.2 shows how the current resources are allocated; Table 7.3 shows how a school with the same student population would be resourced under the evidence-based adequacy model. Note that in Table 7.3, the numbers are prorated from the prototypical middle school population of 450 students shown in Table 7.1.

Several differences between Tables 7.2 and 7.3 warrant discussion. First, note the changes in the school administration and leadership positions from the current to the adequacy model. The adequacy model provides 1.3 positions for a principal and assistant principal; the actual school had one principal and two assistant principals. Instead of using school leadership resources for multiple assistant principals, the adequacy model allocates three instructional facilitator positions that can be used to help the teachers improve their classroom practice.[9]

Second, the number of classroom teachers is approximately the same under both models—the adequacy model gives one additional teacher.

Third, and one of the biggest differences between the actual school and the adequacy model, is the number of specialist teachers in each. For elective classes, the actual school provides about twice as many specialist teachers as the adequacy model—11 to 5. Like many U.S. middle schools today, the actual school shown here uses a seven-period rather than a six-period structure. This approach requires a decrease in the number of minutes in each period, including fewer minutes of instruction in each core subject of reading, mathematics, science, world language, and history. It also allows for a 50 percent expansion in elective classes, from one per day to two. To finance those additional electives requires that the number of elective teachers be more than 40 percent above the number of core teachers rather than the additional 20 percent provided in the evidence-based adequacy model. The objective is to provide all core teachers with two periods a day for planning and preparation, one with their grade-level colleagues and one for their own use. But the strategy entails reducing the instructional minutes for all core subjects and hiking teacher staff costs by 20 percent. Though this is often recommended by those advocating for the middle school approach, there is little evidence that this resource deployment boosts academic achievement. And the resource deployment strategy undergirding this approach is hardly one that will boost student academic learning. It is difficult to argue that a strategy of *decreasing* instructional minutes for the core subjects and doubling the instructional minutes for nonacademic, elective classes will lead to improved student learning in mathematics, science, history, and reading/English.

The fourth notable difference is in the area of categorical program teachers. This middle school has substantial resources for its students with disabilities, which is about 18 percent of the total school population. This is the average percentage of special-education students identified at each school in this district, even though this is not an urban district with a particularly high special-needs population. However, the resources allocated to give

---

[8]This analysis does not address operations, maintenance, transportation, or central office resources, but rather focuses on the professional educational elements of a school.

[9]Note that the revenue per position is lower for the instructional facilitator than for the assistant principal since instructional facilitator positions are counted as teachers in terms of salary and benefits.

TABLE 7.2   Current Resources (600 students; 50% poverty, 25% ELL)

Title	Positions (FTE)	Revenue per Position	Total Revenues
Principal	1.0	$100,000	$ 100,000
Assistant principals	2.0	85,000	170,000
Instructional support staff	0.0	65,000	0
Classroom teachers	23.0	65,000	1,495,000
Specialist teachers	11.0	65,000	715,000
Categorical program teachers for mild special-education, compensatory education, ESL, gifted and talented, etc.	10.5	65,000	682,500
Counselors	0.4	65,000	26,000
Other pupil support staff	3.2	65,000	208,000
Instructional aides	13.5	20,000	270,000
Supervisory aides	0.0	17,500	0
Librarians	1.3	65,000	84,500
Secretary/clerk	2.7	30,000	81,000
Discretionary Funds			
Professional development			$ 10,000
Equipment and technology			50,000
Instructional materials			84,000
Gifted-and-talented education			15,000
Total of other discretionary			0
Total Actual School Revenues			**$3,991,000**

Note: Excludes all revenues for severely disabled, but includes revenues for such programs as desegregation, compensatory education (Title I or state), ESL and bilingual education, and the mild disabilities portion of state and federal handicapped funding.

extra help to students at this school are typical of those in this district and in this state. Education leaders report that in many cases the only way to get additional resources for students struggling with the curriculum is to label them as special-needs. As a result, the school ends up overidentifying students for special education rather than having the flexibility to instead allocate more resources to tutors who can intervene early, when the student begins to struggle with the curriculum. This is particularly true at the elementary level. Studies have shown that through a series of intensive instructional interventions, nearly 75 percent of struggling readers identified in kindergarten and grade 1 can be brought up to grade level without the need for placement in special education (see, e.g., Borman, Hewes, Overman, and Brown 2003; Landry, 1999; Slavin, 1996). While the same statistics may not apply

TABLE 7.3   Cost Feasibility of the Odden-Picus School-Based Adequacy Model (600 students; 50% poverty, 25% ELL)

Elements of Model	Number of Positions	Cost of Positions
Principal	1.3	$ 133,333
Instructional facilitators	3.0	195,000
Classroom teachers	24.0	1,560,000
Specialist teachers	4.8	312,000
Teacher-tutors	3.0	195,000
ELL/LEP teachers	1.5	97,500
Extended-day teachers	2.5	162,500
Summer school teachers	2.5	162,500
Special-education teachers (nonsevere)	4.0	260,000
Counselors	2.4	156,000
Other pupil support	3.0	195,000
Supervisory aides	2.7	53,333
Librarians	1.3	86,667
Secretary/clerk	2.7	80,000
Discretionary Funds		
Professional development		$ 60,000
Equipment and technology		150,000
Instructional materials		84,000
Gifted-and-talented education		15,000
Total Design Costs		**$3,957,833**

Note: The figures in the table use average salary and benefits for administration, teachers, and supervisory aides in this school, as listed in the "Revenue per Position" column of Table 7.2.

at the middle school level, early intervention through tutoring (and extended-day and summer school) would mean fewer students identified for special education at the elementary-level, and thus fewer students arriving at middle school classified as special-needs.

The adequacy model allocates less for special education but much more for intervention strategies that can be used to provide all struggling students with extra help *before* they need to be labeled as a student with a disability. The combined level of resources for extra help is about the same in the two models, but the adequacy model allocates the categorical program teachers separately while the actual school shows them in a single line. As discussed in Chapter 4, the adequacy model includes more resources for struggling students that can be tapped as soon as they need help, rather than relying on special education to provide the services some students need to meet standards. So, instead of the 10.5 categorical program teachers in the actual school, the adequacy model provides 4.0 special-education teachers (for students with nonsevere disabilities),

3.0 teacher tutors (in the current model there were none, but two aides were used to help students learn to read, which is not an evidence-based approach), 1.5 ELL teachers (the current model provided one), and 2.5 teachers to teach after school and in the summer.

The fifth difference is that the adequacy model provides two more counselors than the the actual school, but a fraction less of other pupil support (3.0 as compared to 3.2).

The sixth difference between the two models is in the use of instructional aides. The actual school has 13.5 instructional aides, none of which are classified as supervisory. The adequacy model allocates no instructional aides (as mentioned, there is no evidence to support their inclusion in classrooms), but it does include 2.7 supervisory aides to help monitor students when teachers are not present (at lunch, at the bus stop, etc.).

Seventh, significantly more resources are allocated to professional development ($60,000 as compared to $10,000) and equipment and technology ($120,000 as compared to $50,000) in the adequacy model than in the actual school.

Finally, the total amount of resources under the adequacy model in Table 7.3 is actually less than the amount currently provided (shown in Table 7.2), showing that significant changes can be made in the way resources are allocated without increasing (or even decreasing) the total amount provided.

In short, the actual school provides twice as many noncore subject electives but very little professional development. It also provides twice as much special-education services but little non-special-education intervention to ensure that students are learning and to decrease the number labeled as disabled. And the actual school provides fewer minutes of instruction in core subjects. Our perspective is that the resource deployment strategies in the evidence-based model have a higher potential for teaching more students to higher levels in the core subjects. The actual school has sufficient resources for all strategies in the evidence-based model but would need to undergo substantial program restructuring and resource reallocation to deploy them. To transform these resources into instructional practices that boost student learning, the school would need to adopt a specific curriculum program for each content area, create a professional development strategy, design a pupil support/family outreach program, and be led by principals who can provide the instructional leadership teachers need to succeed.

5. SUMMARY

Schools and districts have reallocated their resources in a number of ways to support higher levels of learning for their students. Resource reallocation is an important means of realizing a more efficient use of resources. It often involves rethinking the use of new dollars, making the best use of current dollars, and finding creative ways to finance the three categories of resources schools need to succeed.

As both this chapter and the previous one have shown, resources in the second part of the budget—teachers outside the core—are often not used as effectively as they could be. In the middle school discussed in section 4, twice as many specialists are present than are needed to provide teachers with one class period per day of planning time. As a result, time on core instruction is reduced, and time spent in electives is increased.

In this era of standards-based education, where the standards are focused on math, reading/language arts, science, and social studies, resources must be reallocated to strategies that help all students achieve in these core courses.

Study Questions

1. Conduct a case study of a local school or one in which you work. Interview the principal, asking about the current staff allocations in full-time equivalencies (a full-time staff member equals 1.0) for each of the following:

    a. Core teachers
    b. Specialist teachers
    c. Instructional facilitators/school-based coaches/mentors
    d. Tutors for struggling students
    e. ESL teachers
    f. Extended-day staff
    g. Summer school staff
    h. Special-education teachers
    i. Pupil support staff
    j. Noninstructional aides
    k. Librarians/media staff
    l. Principal(s)
    m. Secretarial staff

    Also ask the principal for the total student enrollment and the number of students who receive free and reduced-price lunch. Based on your own knowledge and what you have learned in this course so far (you may use the staffing tables in Chapter 4 as a reference), is the school adequately staffed? If not, what would you add, and what would you reallocate to pay for it? Compare your findings with the student achievement scores at this school, and discuss the implications of the current staff allocations on student performance. You can use the school-based resource reallocation tool discussed in this chapter to do the financial analysis for your school.

2. How would you justify the changes you suggested to the stakeholders most likely to be affected by this decision?

3. This chapter prices out the professional development recommendations from the adequacy model presented in Chapter 4. What elements of professional development might you want to add to your case study school, and how could you reallocate resources to pay for them? For example, assume your school is implementing a new math curriculum next fall, and the district has set aside two days of professional development to acquaint teachers with the new curriculum. However, after reviewing the research-based model, you believe at least a week (five full days) is needed. How would you propose to reallocate resources to pay for the three extra days?

4. Based on your interview or your own knowledge of your case study school, what aspects of the school might pose a challenge for resource reallocation? Can you suggest ways to overcome these challenges?

5. In your answer to question 4, you may have mentioned a lack of control over the school budget at the school level. Given what you have learned in this course so far, is it appropriate for school leaders to make decisions to reallocate resources like the decisions you were asked to make here? Why or why not?

Chapter 8

School District Budgeting

In Chapters 4, 6, and 7, we outlined an evidence-based approach to the allocation and use of educational resources in public schools. Notable about the models presented is that much of the focus is on schools and the use of resources in schools—not on school districts. In fact, the evidence-based model we describe in Chapter 4 builds from the school level. We took this approach because learning takes place at the school level, and, in fact, this is where most school district resources are actually spent—at individual schools. This is, however, very different from the way resources are typically budgeted by school districts. This increased importance of the school site in estimating the need for educational resources also reflects a growing trend that requires school site leaders to better understand what resources are generated to produce education at their school and how to use those resources to achieve the school's educational goals.

One essential tool in this process is the budget. Traditionally, the budget has been thought of as a district-level document, the contents of which are really only understood by the district's chief business officer and a few other analysts or accountants. In recent years, however, the trend has been to place more budget responsibility into the hands of individuals at the school site, or at least to make more transparent the kinds and levels of resources provided to schools. Unfortunately, this increased responsibility is often offset by a lack of training about what a budget is or what the district expectations for budgeting are—other than to make sure that there is a positive balance at the end of the year.

Most people think of a budget as a thick document full of complex formulas and numbers that they will never understand. But in truth, the budget of a school district—or a school—offers many insights into how that organization is translating resources into student learning. As a result, understanding what budgets are and how to use them is a critical component of school finance. Moreover, it is probably the type of finance information most school leaders will use most often.

This chapter provides an introduction to school budgets, describing what a budget is, how it is developed, and how it is used to manage a successful school—where success is defined as high student achievement. In this chapter, we will link the mechanics of budgeting to the material in earlier chapters. Our goal is for students to "think through" the resources (personnel, instructional materials, and other essential elements) needed to develop a successful school, estimate the costs associated with putting those resources in place, and then place the data in a budget format similar to those used in most school districts. Earlier chapters described the evidence-based model of school finance adequacy. In this chapter, we use that framework to build school budgets—the documents that are used to allocate dollars to purchase those resources.

This chapter has four sections. Section 1 discusses what a budget is and section 2 examines approaches to budgeting. Section 3 focuses on how revenues and expenditures are estimated and how budgets are prepared. The final section looks at budget implementation.

1. DEFINING BUDGETS

Hartman (1988, p. 2) defines a budget as "a document which specifies the planned expenditures and anticipated revenues of a school district in a given fiscal year, along with other data and information relating the fiscal elements to the educational philosophy, programs, and needs of the district."

There are three major components of a budget, which can be depicted as a triangle (Figure 8.1). These elements are (1) the educational program of the school district, (2) revenues that would support those programs, and (3) actual expenditures on those programs that occur over the school year. In our view, a description of the district's educational program should form the base of the triangle. This is because—absent a clear description of the district's educational priorities—there is no foundation on which to base decisions about the level of expenditures needed to operate the district. Expenditures and revenues are represented on the sides of the triangle to reflect the reality that expenditures must be less than or equal to revenues if the budget is to remain in balance.

Bennett, Hall, and Berg (2006) suggest that in its optimal form a budget has four major functions:

1. *It is a policy document* that reflects the philosophy of the school board, administration, and education community. As such, it expresses the district's philosophy in terms of resources. For example, it may emphasize certain grade levels through smaller class sizes or provide resources for instructional coaches in each school; define levels of support for positions such as tutors, counselors, librarians, nurses, and administrative staff; establish guidelines for additional resources for struggling students; determine the distance from home for which pupil transportation is provided; and provide standards for school maintenance and cleanliness.
2. *It is a financial plan* describing what has been done in the past and what is proposed for the future. It shows what was spent in previous years for each function and has the potential to estimate future expenditures as well.
3. *It is an operations guide* for administrative decisions, providing a guideline for fiscal, program, and personnel accountability.

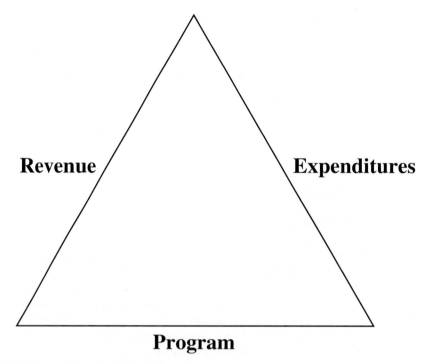

FIGURE 8.1   The Budget Triangle

4. *It is a communication tool* to share the strengths and challenges of the instructional program with the community by showing how educational dollars are spent and identifying the district's programs and priorities.

Budgeting is not a static activity. In fact, it is a continuous process that involves developing, approving, and implementing a spending plan for the district. Budget documents take many forms. Often, the format of a school district's budget is mandated by the state, leaving local districts with little opportunity to vary the information in or the look of the document. Where more local options are possible, budget documents themselves take on a variety of appearances. Throughout this chapter, we will argue that a budget document should be both comprehensible (easy to read and understand) and comprehensive in terms of describing the expenditure plan of the school district. This is, as we will see, a difficult task.

Developing a budget is a complex process. The first step is to determine what is needed and how much it will cost. Once determined, iterations and adjustments may be needed if revenues are insufficient to meet all identified needs. At that point, those responsible for the budget must either reduce the costs of providing services or find additional revenue sources.

2. APPROACHES TO BUDGETING

Given the large sums of money appropriated to school districts, it is not surprising that they play a central role in district management and are the focus of considerable attention. In fact, most school district budgets are remarkably similar in both appearance and content. There are six features common to any good budget (Wood et al., 1995):

1. *Unity.* The budget document should describe all of the programs and services of the school district. It should also include detailed revenue and expenditure forecasts for the general fund and for all other budgetary funds used by the school district federal revenues as well as capital funds.

2. *Regularity.* Budgets must be prepared on a regular basis. In the United States, virtually all government agencies, including school districts, prepare annual budgets. Some states use biennial budgets, but the norm is the 12-month or annual budget. More importantly, the budget should reflect the same 12-month period each year. Most school districts use a fiscal year that runs from July 1 of one year to June 30 of the next. The determination of a fiscal year is generally a state requirement. Several states rely on a calendar year, and at least one, Texas, requires school districts to use a fiscal year beginning on September 1 and ending on August 31.

3. *Clarity.* A well-designed budget document should clarify how the district's revenue is collected and spent. This means identifying all sources of revenue and indicating not only how much is spent but what those funds will be used to purchase. Particularly important are personnel counts by function or program and separate breakdowns of expenditures for supplies and materials, travel, and other goods and services. The budget should be displayed in a manner that is understandable to the average citizen and provides aids to its review, such as descriptions of the budget process and a comprehensive table of contents. We suggest that the budget show resources on a school-by-school as well as a district basis to enhance clarity and public understanding.

4. *Balance.* The budget must be balanced. This means that revenue should equal or exceed expenditures plus any amount budgeted for contingencies. If a district's end-of-year actual revenue exceeds expenditures, the difference can be added, where legally permissible, to the district's financial reserves. In years when revenue is tight, districts may choose to draw down these reserves rather than make larger reductions in the upcoming year's operational budget. If this is done, the budget document should make it clear that this year's expenditures are expected to exceed last year's revenues and indicate what plans exist to correct the imbalance before the reserves are exhausted.

5. *Publicity.* School district budgets are public documents that describe how the district plans to use the tax revenue it collects to provide educational services to the children in that district. As such, it is the right of every citizen in the district to review and comment on the budget. The budget

development process (described in this chapter) should provide ample opportunity for comment by the public, and all budget hearings should be open to the public. Often, state law prescribes the number and time of public hearings. Many school districts make copies of their budget publicly available through local libraries and district offices.

6. *Operational adequacy.* The expenditures detailed in the budget should be adequate to provide the services required to meet the district's mission and goals.

All budgets should have these six components. They ensure that the budget document will provide sufficient information on the programs of the school district. Within the context of these six components, however, there are still a number of different approaches to developing the budget and providing necessary information. At its core, the budget is a fiscal control document providing guidance to district and site personnel about what can and can't be allocated. Line-item budgets have typically been used for this purpose, often allocating resources—people, supplies, materials, and so on—to individual school sites and then serving as the measuring stick to make sure that sites or budget units don't overspend.

While line-item budgets are a powerful tool for management control, they offer little in the way of information about how resources are used to improve student learning. Moreover, they do little to help assess what should be done to help students learn. Two budgetary reforms have attempted to address these concerns.

Program budgeting was developed to help public officials deal with the evaluative concern identified above—that is, whether resources are being used in the best possible way. Program budgeting is a "top down" process that requires evaluation of alternatives, selection of the most cost-effective option, and extensive evaluaton of the implementation of that option. While successful in some levels of government, it has never really worked as a tool in education, possibly due to the large amount of work required to operationalize a true program budget. Moreover, program budgeting requires extensive budgetary staff, which could take away from resources devoted to the classroom. In districts where such progams were tried, it often led to conflict between budget analysts and program staff in the schools. The result was that program budgeting never really made strong inroads into public school budgeting.

A second reform that made few inroads into education was zero-based budgeting. Under this model, budget units establish priorities for each service and then fund them in order until funding is exausted. Zero-based budgeting also has a number of weaknesses when applied to public schools. For one thing, it is hard to rank programs with diverse goals. District managers need to establish the criteria on which decision packages will be ranked—choosing, for example, between the effectiveness, efficiency, equity, or extensiveness of each program. This is difficult in a situation in which goals are diverse and programs are provided because of legal requirements outside of the control of the local school board and superintendent. It is also improbable for a school district—or any public agency, for that matter—to use a cut-off point for decision packages. In a declining budgetary period, how could district decision makers decide, for example, to eliminate all science programs, or the twelfth grade, or special education? In each case, there are important and legal reasons why such actions would be impossible. As a result, when funds are limited, rather than eliminate departments or programs, each department is typically asked to make marginal reductions. For example, departments may be asked to indicate what they would do with reductions of 5, 10, and even 20 percent, and then reductions are made based on each program's individual priority resulting from the prioritization process. In other words, few programs are subject to a true "zero"-based analysis each year.

In fact, most school district budgeting has been—and remains—highly incremental in nature. That is, most budgets are developed by assessing what it will cost to purchase the same mix of goods and services in the next budget year, and then comparing that figure to available revenues. If inadequate revenues are available, and increasing taxes is not a viable option, reductions in anticipated expenditures are needed. On the other hand, if there are additional resources available, then it is possible to consider new or revised programs. The term *incrementalism* was first used by Aaron Wildavsky (1988) to describe how most public agency budgets are put together each year.

The first task facing school site leaders charged with developing a site-based budget is to move away from an incremental approach and look at all the resources available to the school site. They can then determine how to allocate those resources to focus on student achievement. That's easy to say, but hard to implement, as described in the next section.

3. BUDGET PREPARATION

The adequacy model described in Chapter 4 is school based. That is, it first determines resource needs at the school level and then adds to those resources funds to pay for district-level services such as central administration and instructional support, maintenance, and transportation. Although the adequacy model is based on prototypical schools of 432 elementary (K–5), 450 middle (6–8), and 600 high school (9–12) students, few schools will fit this profile exactly. Most will be a different size, and many will have different grade structures. Thus, the first step is to estimate district and school enrollment.

School Site Budgets

There are many methods for estimating school district enrollment. But to develop a school budget, it's essential to know how many students will enroll in the individual school. Moreover, in using our adequacy model to estimate the resources needed at any school, the budget maker needs a count of the students in the school by grade, the number of students who qualify for free and reduced-price lunch, the number of ELL students, and the number of children with disabilities who receive special-education services. Below we apply the resources summarized in Table 4.1 to an elementary school with the following characteristics:

- 576 elementary school children with 96 children in each of grades K–5
- 54 percent free and reduced-price lunch, or 312 children
- 8 percent ELL students, or 46 children
- 10 percent of the students with disabilities qualifying for special education

Table 8.1 uses the categories from Table 4.1 to estimate the resources needed to implement the adequacy model at this school. The first column of Table 8.1 identifies the resource categories from Table 4.1, while the second column repeats the evidence-based resource allocation formula. The third column applies this formula to the school described above.

From this table, it is possible to estimate the number of staff at the school and then develop a budget by taking the cost of compensation (salary and benefits) for each category of personnel and multiplying by the computed number of individuals in each position. To this would be added the per-pupil resources identified in many of the rows of Table 8.1. Table 8.2 displays those computations for our example school; the total estimated budget for the school would be $4,884,055. Some explanation of how this figure is derived follows.

For each of the personnel categories in Table 8.2, the number of full-time-equivalent (FTE) positions is identified in the second column. The unit cost of that position is assumed to be the district's average cost for this type of position and includes salary plus benefits. This is displayed in the third column. The fourth column computes the total cost of that row. For example, the model estimates a total of 33.3 core teachers at an average total compensation of $67,000 each, for a total of over $2.2 million. For simplicity, we have assumed that all nonadministrative but certificated personnel positions have the same average salary, which is unlikely to be the case in most districts. In any event, more detailed information may be available from the district office.

Clearly, as assumptions about class size and the number of tutors, facilitators, and pupil support personnel are varied, the total costs of these resources will also vary considerably. The key is that a total of 69.43 FTE personnel in various categories are needed to staff this school using the adequacy model as described in Chapter 4. In addition, another $502,000 needs to be budgeted for instructional materials, technology, and other resources generated on a per-pupil basis.

A concern often expressed when a budget like this is presented is how to deal with the fractional FTEs in each position. Rather than representing actual personnel positions in the school, these numbers are designed to provide an estimate of the number of staff needed at the school. In many cases, it is assumed that individuals combine multiple roles in their daily work. For example, this school would generate funds for 2.88 instructional coaches or facilitators. Rather than try to hire 2 full time and 0.88 part time coaches, the school might use 5 people to serve as half-time coaches and half-time teachers, and use the funds from the remaining 0.38 FTE to pay for additional work by mentor teachers or to hire an expert in an area where the school is having particular difficulty finding appropriate assistance for its teachers. These adjustments could be made through the staffing matrix.

This budget would be aggregated with the budgets from other schools in the district and combined with the central-office budget, which includes the costs for central administration, food services, transportation, special education for children with severe disabilities, and other district-wide functions, to get a total district budget. Armed with these figures, school site leaders can assist the district administration in developing a final budget.

TABLE 8.1 Estimated School-Level Resources Using the Evidence-Based Adequacy Model

Element	Adequacy Model	Example School
School Characteristics		
School configuration	K–5	K–5
Prototypic school size	432	576
Class size	K–3: 15	K–3: 15
	4–5: 25	4–5: 25
Full-day kindergarten	Yes	Yes
Percent disabled		10.0% (58 students)
Percent poverty (free and reduced-price lunch)		54% (312 students)
Percent ELL		8% (46 students)
Personnel Resources		
Core teachers	24	25.6 teachers in grades K–3 (96 students per grade divided by 15) 7.7 teachers in grades 4–5 (96 students per grade divided by 25) Total = 33.3 core teachers
Specialist teachers	20% of core teachers	6.7 (25.6 + 7.7)0.20
Instructional facilitators/mentors	1 for every 200 students	2.88 (576/200)
Tutors for struggling students	1 for every 100 poverty students	3.12 (312/100)
Teachers for ELL students	Additional 1 for every 100 ELL students	0.46 (46/100)
Extended day	½ poverty enrollment at ratio of 1:15 at 0.25 FTE	2.6 ((312/2)/15)0.25
Summer school	½ poverty enrollment at ratio of 1:15 at 0.25 FTE	2.6 ((312/2)/15)0.25
School Element		
Learning- and mild-disabled students	Additional 3 professional teacher positions	4.0 (576/432)3
Severely disabled students	100% state reimbursement minus federal funds	
Teachers for gifted students	$25/student	$14,440
Substitutes[a]	5% of all above teacher positions	$67,905
Pupil support staff	1 for every 100 poverty students: 2.16	3.12 (312/100)

(*continued*)

TABLE 8.1 *(continued)*

School Element		
Noninstructional Aides	2.0 for 432 students	2.66 (576/432)2
Librarians/media specialists	1.0	1.33
Principal	1	1.33
School site secretary	1.0 secretary 1.0 clerical	1.0 secretary 1.33 clerical
Professional development	Included above: Instructional facilitators Planning and prep time 10 summer days Additional: $100/pupil for other PD expenses—trainers, conferences, travel, etc.	$57,600 (576 × 100)
Technology	$250/pupil	$144,000 (250 × 576)
Instructional materials	$140/pupil	$80,640 (140 × 576)
Student activities	$200/pupil	$115,200 (200 × 576)

*aComputed as 5 percent of professional FTE staff identified in rows above Substitutes times $100 per day plus 22 percent benefits or $122 per day.

The District Budget Process

The preceding discussion provides an example of how a school-level budget could be developed using the evidence-based adequacy model. These data provide an estimate of the needed expenditures for the school and, when aggregated with central-office requirements, provide an expenditure estimate for the district. This section describes the process for developing that district budget, which would include individual school-level budgets.

The heart of the budget process is estimating revenues and expenditures and ensuring that the budget is in balance—that expenditures do not exceed revenues for the year.

Revenue projection.   Revenues include money the district receives from local property taxes, local fees and miscellaneous sources, state aid, and federal programs. The first step is to project student enrollments, followed by estimates of property tax receipts, levels of state funding, and revenues from categorical programs, both state and federal. Finally, other sources of revenue must also be estimated.

Enrollment projections.   As we describe in other chapters, most school district revenue is accumulated on the basis of student enrollment, and districts receive a large portion of their funds on a per-pupil basis. Thus, the first step in estimating revenues is to make an accurate enrollment projection for the school year. More importantly, as part

TABLE 8.2 **Budget Estimates of the Cost of Personnel and Resources at an Example School**

Category	Number	Unit Cost[a]	Total Cost
Core teachers	33.3	$ 67,000	$ 2,231,100
Specialist teachers	6.7	67,000	448,900
Instructional facilitators/coaches	2.88	67,000	192,960
Tutors for struggling students	3.12	67,000	209,040
Teachers for ELL students	0.46	67,000	30,820
Staff for extended day	2.6	67,000	174,200
Staff for summer school	2.6	67,000	174,200
Staff for students with mild and moderate disabilities	4.0	67,000	268,000
Gifted students	576	25	14,440
Substitutes[b]	556.6 days	122	67,905
Pupil support staff	3.12	67,000	209,040
Noninstructional aides	2.66	20,000	53,200
Library/media specialists	1.33	67,000	89,110
Principal	1.33	96,000	127,680
School site secretary	1.0	35,000	35,000
School site clerical	1.33	25,000	33,250
Professional development	576	100	57,600
Technology	576	250	144,000
Instructional materials	576	140	80,640
Student Activities	576	200	115,200
Custodians	3.0	35,000	105,000
Custodial supplies	576	20	11,520
Office supplies	576	20	11,250
Total			**$ 4,884,055**
Total per pupil			**8,479**

[a]Personnel cost estimates include salary plus benefits to represent total compensation.

[b]Computed as 5 percent of professional FTE staff at a cost per substitute of $100 per day plus 22 percent benefits or $122 per day.

of any long-range planning process, projections of enrollments into future years should be made as well. Methodologies for estimating enrollments are provided elsewhere (see, e.g., Hartman, 2002; Wood et al., 1995). It is essential, however, to recognize the importance of accurate estimates of student enrollment as the basis of any school district budget.

First, state funding is typically based on some measure of the number of students in each school district. Whether the enrollment number used in state computations is actual enrollment (head count) or some more limited measure, such as average daily membership (ADM) or average daily attendance (ADA), a district's basic revenue is determined by its number of students. Moreover, in state funding systems that equalize revenues on the basis of per-pupil property wealth, the student count is a critical component of the wealth calculation and determines how much state funding the district will receive. Indeed, Arkansas took a version of the adequacy model discussed in Chapter 4 and turned it into a $5,400-per-pupil figure that it used in a new foundation program.

In states with weighted-pupil funding systems, appropriate weights must be applied to each student before total "enrollment" for funding purposes is computed. For example, if a district has 1,000 students, and 10 percent of them are eligible for a special education weight of 0.9, then the enrollment of the district for state-funding purposes would be 1,090.

Local revenues.   Local revenues are generated primarily from property tax collections. The state finance formula may dictate the level of property taxation that is required. In many states, local districts have the authority to enact additional property taxes, with the approval of either the school board or the district's voters. In states with a guaranteed tax base (GTB) or combination formula, some portion of these property taxes will be equalized as described in Chapter 9. An important part of the budget process is to estimate total local revenues for general operating purposes.

Estimation of property taxes requires knowledge of the total assessed value of the property in the school district and the tax rate the district is legally allowed to apply to the taxable property. In some states, districts are granted authority to levy a tax rate, and revenues are dependent on the assessed value of the property in the district. In other states, districts have authority to raise a fixed sum of money through property taxes, making the tax rate dependent on the assessed value of the property in the district. In either case, the property tax collections are generally used as part of the computation of state aid to the district as well.

Each state has specific rules for levying property taxes that must be followed by school districts. An important component of estimating property tax revenues is to include a contingency for delinquent tax payments, which has the effect of reducing current-year tax receipts. Recall that districts not only must balance their budget but also are required to end the fiscal year with a balanced budget. Therefore, if revenues fall below projections, expenditures must also be reduced. Based on past experience, districts need to allow for the nonpayment of some property taxes in their budget estimates. Historical trends are generally the best way to make this estimate, although current economic conditions should be factored into the equation as well. The Arkansas school-funding formula adjusts estimated local property taxes that would be part of the formula as 98 percent of total collections, so it actually adjusts state aid to account for delinquent property tax payments.

State revenue.   Once enrollment has been estimated, this figure can be applied to state guidelines for funding. For example, the district can multiply its projected enrollment by the expected foundation level for the fiscal year to get an estimate of its general revenues funded through property taxes and state aid. This figure should represent the largest share of total revenues for the district. Wyoming, for example, builds up to the foundation level for each district by applying an adequacy model for each school and then adding the district functions at the end.

The different models of state aid are discussed in detail in Chapter 9. At the budget level, it is important for school administrators to estimate their state revenues as accurately as possible based on the mechanics of their individual state system. Understanding how the distribution formula works in a particular state is essential for managing a district's budget estimates.

In addition to general state aid, the district may be eligible for a number of categorical programs. Common programs include special education, compensatory education, and bilingual education—programs that may also be funded through the general-aid formula with a pupil-weighting program. In addition, many states provide aid for pupil transportation (both regular home-to-school and special education), capital for construction (see Chapter 5), and other priorities as established by the state legislature.

Successful school district business officers need to be aware of state categorical aid programs and how their district might qualify for funding to ensure that the children they serve receive all of the services for which they qualify. Moreover, once the funds are received, the business officers must be sure that they are expended in conjunction with any accompanying rules. Keeping track of large numbers of individual categorical grants can be a demanding and complex task, particularly in states with a large number of such programs. For example, researchers in California have identified as many as 100 different categorical programs in recent years (Finkelstein, Furry, and Huerta, 2000).

Federal funds.   The federal government provides resources for a number of categorical programs. The largest are Title I, which offers assistance to school districts with a high incidence of children from low-income families, and the school nutrition program, which subsidizes school food programs. There are many other federal programs for which school districts may qualify. Understanding the qualification requirements of federal programs and ensuring that the district receives funds for which it is eligible is a major undertaking in most school districts today.

Other revenues.   Following the estimation of general revenues, the district must also estimate revenue from special programs and grants. If the state system uses weighted pupils, much of this may be included in the general-aid system. If not, funding from programs for such things as special education, transportation, compensatory education, and bilingual education must also be estimated using state rules, regulations, and guidelines. Again, at the heart of this estimate is the number of pupils who qualify for each program.

Estimating Expenditures

In addition to revenues for the fiscal year, the district must estimate total expenditure needs. Earlier in this chapter, we provided an approach to estimating the expenditures needed to fund the resources identified in our adequacy model. This approach will, we argue, lead to spending strategies that improve student learning, and so it is this approach that we suggest districts and schools use.

Once the number of positions to be filled has been estimated, they are typically reported in terms of FTEs. FTEs provide a measure of the number of full-time employees needed by the district. While many individuals in a school district may work only part of a day, for budget purposes, the number of FTEs is computed. Thus, for example, if a district hires two individuals to work as librarians for a half day each, it has two employees but only one FTE. A district's budget may report that a school has 4.5 FTE custodians. If a typical work day is considered to be 8 hours, 4.5 FTE translates into 36 hours a day of custodial time (8 hours × 4.5 FTE = 36 hours). This does not necessarily mean that the school employs four fill-time custodians and one half-time custodian. It is just as likely that the school has one full-time head custodian, and seven individuals working half-time in that position. The school and the district would determine the exact distribution of personnel.

Budget documents should report the number of FTE personnel employed by program. Since personnel costs (salaries and benefits) often represent as much as 80–85 percent of a district's budget or more, accurate estimation of personnel requirements is essential to accurate budget development.

Once the number of employees has been determined, it is much easier to estimate the expenditures needed to carry out the district's educational plan. At this point, there are three general steps a district can take to estimate total expenditures:

1. Identify the specific programs and/or functions around which the budget is to be constructed.
2. Ascertain what resources are needed to operationalize the tasks essential to each of the programs or functions identified in the previous step.
3. Estimate the costs of the resources needed to implement each program or function.

Accounting for Expenditures and Revenues

After the budget is developed, districts need mechanisms for tracking expenditures. They do this through fiscal accounting systems that have various elements, including funds, objects, and functions.

Fund accounting. Like other public agencies, school district budgets rely on fund accounting. A fund is a self-balancing set of accounts related to a common topic. While the number of allowable funds varies across the 50 states, all school districts have a general fund. The general fund sometimes has a different name such as the operations and maintenance fund or the operating fund, but its purpose is the same: to account for the general revenues and expenditures of a school system. As such, the general fund accounts for 75–90 percent of total resources in the average school district, and expenditures made through the general fund include those for instructional services (salaries, benefits, supplies), general administration, maintenance of school buildings, utilities, and other expenses associated with day-to-day operations.

Additional funds are used by school districts as needed. Table 8.3 lists potential account funds as provided by the federal government (National Center for Education Statistics [NCES], 1990). Note that these descriptions may change, as the NCES was

TABLE 8.3   Federal Fund Classifications

Fund	Description
01	General fund
02	Special revenue funds (i.e., special education or federal projects)
03	Capital project funds
04	Debt service funds
05	Enterprise funds
06	Internal service funds
07	Trust and agency funds
08	General fixed assets
09	General long-term debt

considering revisions to its accounting handbook as this book went to press. Updated information is available at the NCES website.

Objects of expenditure.   The basic unit of accounting for a budget relies on objects of expenditure. Objects represent actual items that can be purchased. Object-oriented budget systems can be very basic or very specific. Table 8.4 provides a simplified hypothetical accounting code for expenditures by object for a school district. The table is not based on the actual accounting system of any particular state or school district; rather, it is representative of what an object-level accounting system might look like. In a large, complex organization, all four of the digits in the code column might be used to fully identify the objects of expenditure in more detail. Again, the particular code combinations displayed here are only an example and not necessarily reflective of how codes are actually assigned to expenditures and revenues. Most school systems would have a more sophisticated set of object codes to fully track their expenditures.

The problem with budgets that provide only object-level data is that they do not give the reviewer any sense of the purposes for which the resources are being used. For example, an object-level budget might contain a line item summarizing total certificated salaries for teachers (e.g., the 1100 category in Table 8.4). This would give the reviewer a concept of how much is spent on teacher salaries by the school district, but no sense of how those teachers are allocated among elementary, middle, or high schools, or of how much is paid to substitute versus regular teachers. Moreover, a line item for teacher salaries at an individual school provides little information as to how those teacher resources are used by educational programs. To answer these questions, budgets can also be aggregated by function or program.

Function classifications.   Functions describe general areas of expenditure such as instruction, administration, operations and maintenance, pupil transportation, and instructional support. Functional definitions vary across state accounting systems, but the federal government has attempted to standardize them. Table 8.4 also displays sample

TABLE 8.4   Hypothetical Object-Level Accounting Classifications

Code	Classification
1000	Professional certificated salaries
1100	Teachers' salaries
1200	School administrators' salaries
1300	Supervisors' salaries
1400	Central office salaries
1900	Other certificated salaries
2000	Classified salaries
2100	Instructional aides' salaries
2200	Administrators' salaries
2300	Clerical and office worker salaries
2400	Maintenance and operations salaries
2500	Food services salaries
2600	Transportation salaries
2900	Other classified salaries
3000	Employee benefits
3100	Retirement
3200	Health
3300	Workers' compensation
3400	Unemployment insurance
3900	Other benefits
4000	Books and supplies
4100	Textbooks
4200	Books other than textbooks
4300	Instructional materials and supplies
4400	Other supplies
4600	Pupil transportation supplies
4700	Food services supplies
5000	Services and other operating expenditures
5100	Consultants
5200	Travel
5300	Insurance
5400	Utilities
5500	Rentals and leases
5900	Other services
6000	Capital outlay
6100	Sites and improvement of sites
6200	Buildings and improvement of buildings
6300	Books and media for new school libraries or major expansions
6400	Equipment
6500	Equipment replacement

(continued)

TABLE 8.4 (*continued*)

7000		Other outgo
	7100	Tuition
	7200	Transfers out
	7300	Interfund transfers
8000		Revenue
	8100	Local revenue
	8200	State revenue
	8300	Federal revenue
1000		Instruction
2000		Support services
	2100	Students
	2200	Instructional staff
	2300	General administration
	2400	School administration
	2500	Business
	2600	Operations and maintenance of plant services
	2700	Student transportation services
	2800	Central
	2900	Other support services
3000		Operation of noninstructional services
	3100	Food services operations
	3200	Other enterprise operations
	3300	Community support operations
4000		Facilities acquisition and construction services
5000		Other uses
	5100	Debt services
	5200	Fund transfers

Note: Classifications displayed here are examples of codes that are typically found in object-level accounting systems for public schools. Individual states and districts may use different definitions and provide greater detail through the use of the 3rd and 4th digits in each code.

Source: National Center for Education Statistics, 1990.

school district function classifications as developed by the federal government in Handbook II, Revised, 2nd ed. (National Center for Education Statistics, 1990).

Program classifications. Expenditures can also be classified by programs. Table 8.5 lists the programs used in Florida's accounting system. The more detailed the programmatic distinctions, the more complex the budget process becomes, and the bigger the budget document. The advantage of a program budget is that it gives managers, as well as school board members and the general public, a better picture of what the funds are actually being used to purchase. One of the difficulties with program budgets is that

TABLE 8.5   Florida Program Classifications

Code	Program Description
Basic programs	
101	K–3 basic education
102	4–8 basic education
103	9–12 basic education
Special programs for at-risk students	
120	Dropout prevention
131	Intensive English/ESOL K–3
132	Intensive English/ESOL 4–8
133	Intensive English/ESOL 9–12
Special programs for exceptional children	
210	Educable mentally handicapped
202	Trainable mentally handicapped
203	Physically handicapped
204	Physical and occupational therapy (part-time)
205	Speech, language, and hearing (part-time)
206	Speech, language, and hearing
207	Visually handicapped (part-time)
208	Visually handicapped
209	Emotionally handicapped (part-time)
210	Emotionally handicapped
211	Specific learning disability (part-time)
212	Specific learning disability
213	Gifted (part-time)
214	Hospital and home-bed (part-time)
215	Profoundly handicapped
K–12 vocational programs	
301	Agriculture
302	Office
303	Distributive
304	Diversified
305	Health
306	Public service
307	Home economics
308	Technical trade and industry
309	Exploratory
316	Vocational education mainstream
Adult job preparatory vocational-education programs	
331	Agriculture
332	Office
333	Distributive
334	Diversified

(continued)

TABLE 8.5 (*continued*)

335	Health
336	Public service
337	Home economics
338	Technical trade and industry
Adult supplemental vocational programs	
361	Agriculture
362	Office
364	Health
365	Public service
366	Home economics
367	Technical trade and industry
Adult general education program	
401	Adult basic skills
402	Adult secondary education
403	Lifelong learning
404	Adult handicapped

many services are hard to assign to a single program. Custodial services, for example, serve all programs at the school. If classified separately as a function, a great deal of information can be obtained about custodial services. But how those costs could—or should—be allocated to individual programs is not always a simple task since some programs, such as science labs and home economics, require larger spaces and more cleaning resources than do, say, traditional language arts and math classes.

We are also encouraging states to begin reporting expenditures at the school level by the types of education strategies reflected in our adequacy model. Indeed, several states have committees discussing how such a new reporting system could be developed so that policymakers and the public would know not only how resources were budgeted by educational strategy at the school level, but also the degree to which they were spent that way.

Accounting codes.　In reality, it is helpful to be able to track an individual expenditure by all three of these methods—object, function, and program, and in the future perhaps by educational strategy at the school level. In addition, it is often helpful to track expenditures by the location where the expenditure is made. Locations usually include the schools in the district, the central office, and other areas and subareas as determined by the district. A generic accounting code might look something like that shown in Table 8.6.

Additional sets of digits could be added to this account code structure to provide additional detail about every expenditure. The important factor to keep in mind in designing accounting code structures is that the greater the level of detail (i.e., the more digits in the code), the greater the potential for error in coding expenditures. Thus, there is always a trade-off between the complexity of the code and the potential accuracy of the data entered into the code. In Oregon, when a new accounting system was instituted, the system designers realized early on that if decision makers were to have useful data at

TABLE 8.6   Sample Budget Presentation

Code	Actual 2002–03	Estimated 2003–04	Projected 2004–05
General fund			
1000 (certificated salaries)			
2000 (classified salaries)			
3000 (benefits)			
4000 (books and supplies)			
5000 (services and other operating expenditures)			
6000 (capital outlay)			
7000 (other outgo)			
8000 (revenue)			

the school level as promised, a significant portion of the resources for implementation of the system would need to go to training staff at all of the schools and school districts.

Budget Preparation Summary

Clearly, many steps are required to prepare a school and school district's budget. To recap, typically, a budget presents information on the expected revenues and expenditures of the school district, along with information on the number of students served and the number of FTE employees who will be employed in the provision of educational services for those students. This information can be displayed by object of expenditure, function, or program, and can be provided at an aggregate district level or disaggregated to specific locations such as school sites and other logical locations, including the central office, the transportation department, and others either as determined by the district or as mandated by state policy.

The typical budget provides all of this information for at least three years. The most common presentation is to show actual revenues and expenditures for the year most recently completed, estimated revenues for the current year, and projected revenues and expenditures for the budget year. For example, if a district used a July 1–June 30 fiscal year (FY), then as it prepared its budget for FY 2004–05, it would include actual expenditure and revenue data from 2002–03, estimated data for 2003–04, and projected data for 2004–05. An example of a highly simplified budget document is shown in Table 8.6. Obviously, a district's actual budget would have many more entries, and each fund would be displayed separately. In addition, this example focuses on objects of expenditure; other displays by function and program could be provided as well. Examples of budget documents can also be found in Bolton and Harmer (2000).

Budget Modification

If expenditure estimates exceed revenue projections, the district's administrators must make adjustments on one or both sides of the equation. Typically, it is easier to reduce expenditures than it is to increase revenue. Most state and federal programs have fixed revenue levels, and a school district is unlikely to be able to seek additional funding from these sources over the short term. Local property taxes offer somewhat more hope, depending on the tax statutes in the particular state. In many states, it is possible to seek voter approval for higher property taxes. However, tax limitations in many states have curtailed this option. Additionally, there are often state restrictions on how much property taxes can be raised to maintain the equity of the system, as discussed in Chapter 9.

Reductions in expenditures often mean limited compensation for employees or elimination of some positions or programs. Personnel reductions are never easy, and most districts attempt to make those cuts as far from instructional personnel as possible, although in times of severe budget reductions, reductions in the number of teachers—with the resultant increase in average class size—may be unavoidable.

Budget Approval

Once a balanced budget has been developed, the district's school board must approve it. The timing of this process, along with the required documents that must be submitted and the time in which the general public may comment on the budget, is generally prescribed by state law. In general, however, the superintendent submits the budget to the school board, makes copies available to the public, and helps the board schedule public hearings on the document. At this time, the board may further modify the budget to reflect its policies and goals (although superintendents typically work closely with either the board or a budget committee of the board to develop the budget, so generally there are few board-directed changes at this point).

Administering the Budget

The adopted budget serves as a guide for expenditure allocations throughout the year. Since it is impossible to estimate all expenditure needs perfectly during the budgeting process, it is important to continually monitor revenues and expenditures to make sure they are in line with budget projections. If there are changes either in the revenue available to the district or in its expenditure needs, modifications to the budget document must be approved by the school board. Such change may be the result of an unexpected influx of students, requiring more teachers and classroom space, or a drop in the revenue receipts for one or more programs. At all times, the district administration and school board must strive to keep the budget in balance, reducing expenditures if revenue projections fall short and increasing expenditures to meet the needs of a growing student population—provided the revenues to support those students are available. In short, the budget becomes an important management tool to help ensure that educational resources are focused on the priorities established at the beginning of the budget cycle.

4. BUDGET IMPLEMENTATION

In this section, we first discuss how school districts might consider developing a budget while attempting to give school sites more autonomy. Then we provide a brief description of budget implementation in two large cities, San Francisco and Seattle.

Distribution of Funds to the School Site

In the preceding discussion, we developed a school budget estimate using the adequacy model to determine the resources needed at a school with certain characteristics. If the school district were fully funded based on this model, then it would be practical and feasible to provide the estimated level of resources to that school in the form of the number of personnel in each category along with the per-pupil dollar figures. This would make distribution of funds to school sites straightforward and transparent. Unfortunately, most districts are not funded on the basis of such a model at this time, and there are often differences in the level of resources a district receives and the amount of resources the schools need under this model. Moreover, because most states do not use an adequacy model to fund schools at this time, alternative approaches to distributing funds to schools may be more common. Here, we outline some of the approaches used by school districts to distribute funds to schools.

School districts in the United States typically use a set of formulaic ratios to direct resources to school sites. For instructional personnel, teachers are usually provided to a school site based on the number of students at the school—for example, one teaching position for every 25 students. Other personnel are generated on a variety of similar formulaic ratios based on numbers of students, other staff, or school characteristics.

The problem with using formulaic ratios for staff is that they use numbers of personnel, not costs of the individual personnel assigned to the school site. Individual teacher salaries, for example, can vary by as much as two to one, depending on an individual's previous teaching experience and educational attainment. Thus, if a school site were to receive a dollar distribution (e.g., based on the number of students in the school), the composition of its teaching staff would affect how well it could stay within its budget.

As a result of the differential costs of staff, most districts allocate positions to schools on the basis of average cost. That is, a school site generates its staff positions without regard to the cost of the individuals employed at the site and essentially pays the average cost for each type of individual. Whether this model leads to school site control depends on the way it is implemented at the district level. For example, can a school site change its mix of personnel, perhaps trading an assistant principal for one-and-a-half or two teaching positions? If so, are there district employment rules that limit this flexibility, even if it is provided for in theory? More importantly, what flexibility does a school have to change the mix of professionals? If it is unlimited, the district must absorb the risk of suddenly having surplus teachers, assistant principals, or counselors, if different trade-offs are made by the school sites. If the district absorbs the risk, the effect is likely to be a higher average cost for each position and potentially fewer staff at each school site.

On the other hand, giving each school a fixed budget based on enrollments and letting the site allocate the funds across staff has its own problems. What happens to schools in which the average cost of a teacher is above the district average? With a fixed per-pupil budget, these schools will not be able to hire all the teachers they need, whereas a school with a relatively young teaching staff may be able to hire more teachers and reduce class size. Adding to this complexity is the effect of time: eventually, experienced and expensive teachers will retire, even as currently inexperienced teachers gain increases in pay. Thus, a school that is advantaged today may be at a disadvantage in a few years.

Districts that want to use dollar formulas to allocate funds to schools must take these factors into account. One possibility is to adopt a model similar to that used by the Los Angeles Unified School District (LAUSD) under its consent decree from the *Rodriguez v. LAUSD* lawsuit. Plaintiffs seeking to equalize general-fund per-pupil expenditures across all the district's schools sued the district. The court recognized that a large component of the differences in per-pupil expenditures are differential salaries of teachers due to variation in experience and education. The settlement called for equalizing per-pupil expenditures on teacher salaries over time by requiring school sites to hire teachers such that the average cost of a teacher is approximately the same as the average cost of teachers across the district. Thus, a school with a relatively expensive teaching staff must hire additional teachers with relatively low salaries (and consequently less education and experience), and a school with a relatively inexpensive teaching staff must hire new teachers who are relatively expensive (and thus have more education and experience). The goal is to equalize the educational and experiential characteristics of teachers at each school site.

Rather than provide school sites with more control over the characteristics of their teaching staff, the Los Angeles system seems to have put more constraints on school decision makers, forcing them to consider both the price of a teacher and his or her qualifications. Similar pressures would exist in any system that gave school sites a fixed-dollar amount per pupil for budget purposes. This may or may not be a good thing.

On one hand, principals and school-based decision-making councils feel that some of their hiring flexibility has been eliminated. On the other hand, forcing schools to have a teaching staff with mixed levels of education and experience may have long-term benefits in terms of consistent school leadership and instructional quality. In theory, there will always be a group of teachers at the school with knowledge and experience related to the school's goals and mission, and a broad view of what programs are most successful. Regardless of how a district resolves this issue, if school sites are held to total budget amounts, regardless of staff composition, then some kind of safety net will be needed to help schools deal with temporary highs and lows in teachers' salaries. The same applies to other certified and classified staff in schools. Differences in the unit cost of personnel, despite similar responsibilities, need to be taken into account if central districts are to continue to distribute funds to school sites.

Allocation of Nonstaff Resources

This section describes some of the difficulties school sites may encounter if they are given substantial responsibility for many of the fiscal management functions now handled at the district level. For more information on specific issues and how they are managed in today's school business office, see Wood and colleagues (1995).

Technology.   One of the most frequently discussed and most expensive items facing schools involves the purchase, maintenance, repair, and updating of tools for instructional technology, particularly computers. The cost of placing computers and Internet connections in classrooms or in computer labs is substantial. And once the investment in equipment has been made, the expense of maintaining that equipment is considerable. It is also expensive to provide technical training and support for teachers so that they make maximum use of the technology. Further, a plan must be established to keep both the hardware and the software up to date. Providing equity for schools in making these purchases and then maintaining their investment is complicated. Moreover, unless schools are able to carry over funds from one year to the next, it may never be possible to establish a fund large enough to purchase enough computers to equip an entire computer lab at one time. This could lead to nonstandardization of hardware, further complicating the management of a school's technology program.

Transportation.   The costs of transporting students to and from school vary with the distances children have to travel and the density of the population within the school's attendance boundaries. If school sites are held responsible for funding student transportation out of site funds, schools with fewer children to bus or shorter distances to travel will have more money for alternative programs. For this reason, districts typically keep transportation as a district-level function.

Maintenance and operations.   Although few have suggested that authority for transportation be given to school sites, Hentschke (1986) does suggest shifting authority for utilities to school sites, assuming they can keep all or part of any savings they generate. Again, this will not work well if each school receives a flat amount per pupil (or per classroom or per square foot) for utilities. Older and less energy-efficient buildings might require substantially higher expenditures per student for utilities than newer and more energy-efficient schools. Thus, formulas to distribute funds to school sites need to take site characteristics into account. Similar problems exist for the maintenance and repair of school facilities. Newer buildings require less maintenance and repairs and are less likely to require expensive rehabilitation, such as roof repairs or the replacement of a boiler. Either allocation rules must take these differences into account or school-site decision makers must have the foresight to establish reserves to pay for these items when they come due.

Risk management.   Another area critical to this discussion is risk management. For expenses such as insurance and medical benefits, large risk pools are helpful in keeping costs down. There are some advantages to cooperative purchasing programs, across schools or districts. The main advantage to letting school sites purchase their own benefits and insurance packages is that they can tailor their programs to meet the needs of their staff and students. The downside is that in smaller risk pools, the potential for one lengthy illness or catastrophic loss to make future insurance very expensive is much greater. Thus, programs that provide more autonomy at school sites need to be structured very carefully so that these functions do not take away from funds available for direct instruction.

Food services.   Virtually every school in the United States provides food services for its students. In many schools, federal assistance pays for meals of low-income children. Although it is possible to shift authority for operation of food services programs to school sites, there may be little reason to do so. This is one area that frequently benefits from substantial economies of scale, particularly in the purchase of food. Moreover, it is unlikely that a school principal, or his or her staff, will have the skill and expertise to operate a food services program efficiently. Although school sites could consider contracting out for food services, again, there may be benefits of scale in allowing the district to handle this.

Purchasing.   For years, districts have operated large purchasing operations, buying supplies in bulk and then distributing them to school sites. Although this yields substantial savings in the purchase price of materials, the costs of maintaining and distributing inventory are significant. Today, many districts have eliminated the cost of inventories and warehouses through the decentralized purchasing of many office supplies. Widely available office supply stores make it possible for local school sites to manage their supply needs more economically through arrangements with local providers, who are often willing to distribute purchased materials to the school for free. Thus, districts not only save inventory expenses but can reduce the costs of intradistrict shipping from a central warehouse to school sites.

Alternative approaches to resource allocation.   In recent years, two other alternatives for the allocation of resources to schools have received considerable attention. One is the weighted-pupil approach, and the other is the so-called 65 percent solution.

The weighted-pupil approach to resource allocation is similar to the weighted-pupil approach used by some states to allocate funds to school districts. Children with extra needs—low income, special education, and so on—are counted as more than one student when funds are distributed, thus focusing additonal resources on programs for those students. Recently, the Fordham Institute released a report titled "Fund the Child" calling for school districts to use weighted-pupil methods to distribute funds to schools across each district (Fordham Institute, 2006).

Arguing that there are substantial inequities in per-pupil funding within school districts, and that often the children with the greatest needs receive the lowest levels of funding because teachers with the most experience (and thus highest salaries) work to be assigned to schools with fewer problems and hard-to-educate children. "Fund the Child" recommends using a weighted-pupil approach whereby students with greater educational needs carry higher levels of funding than do children with fewer needs. The dollar amount associated with each weighted child follows that child to the school he or she attends, meaning that the additional resources needed to meet that child's needs should be available at whatever school he or she elects to attend.

While this model is attractive on the surface, Rubenstein, Schwartz, and Stiefel (2006) argue that it will really only work if the level of per-pupil funding is adequate to meet the needs of all students—and that simply redistributing inadequate funds won't meet the needs of any students. We would add that developing a school's budget using an adequacy model such as that postulated above would have the same effect, directing additional resources toward children with greater educational needs. They also point out that a weighted-pupil model won't alleviate large disparities across school districts within a state or across the 50 states. Finally, as hinted at above and discussed in more detail in Chapter 12, absent reform of teacher labor contracts, it may be impossible to fund schools on a weighted-pupil basis if teachers retain seniority rights that allow them to select the school where they teach, regardless of the impact of their salary on the school's budget.

A second popular movement in recent years has been the so-called 65 percent solution, requiring that at least 65 percent of a district's budget be spent on instruction at the school level. On the surface this seems attractive—particularly since in many locations only 60 percent or less goes to instruction. However, this rather inflexible standard does not take local factors into consideration and, more importantly, does not provide a rationale or method for using that 65 percent in ways that will lead to enhanced student learning.

As this discussion shows, there are a number of alternative ways budget resources can be directed to school sites. Here, we provide brief descriptions of the approaches used in two large, urban school districts.

Case Study: Seattle

The Seattle Public School District is widely recognized as having developed a successful approach to allocating budget resources to school sites. The weighted-student formula developed by the district was first implemented for the 1997–98 school year. As described in district materials (see the district's website), three basic principles guide the weighted-student methodology:

1. Resources follow the student.
2. Resources are denominated in dollars, not FTE staff.
3. The allocation of resources varies by the personal characteristics of each child.

For 2002–03, the district's budget totaled $423,083,787. Of this, $246,941,284, or about 58.4 percent, was distributed directly to the schools through the formula. The remaining funds were controlled centrally for these functions:

- Centrally held instructional support
- Logistics and other support
- Central administration
- General reserves

The funds distributed to the schools have two components. The first is a foundation allocation or allocation to each school based on the type of school. To be funded, a school must have a minimum enrollment. This figure ranged from $200,000 for elementary and nontraditional schools with a minimum enrollment of 250 students, to $425,000 for middle schools with a minimum of 600 students, to $544,000 for high schools with a minimum of 1,000 students. These funds are to ensure the minimum operational viability of each school.

The balance of a school's funds is distributed through the weighted-pupil formula. Each student receives a weight based on his or her characteristics. The formula provides different weights for regular-education students, plus additional weights for students based on special-education needs, bilingual-education eligibility, and eligibility for free and reduced-price lunch. The sum of the weighted pupils is multiplied by the base funding factor, which in 2002–03 was budgeted at $2,680 for each weighted student.

As Table 8.7 shows, the pupil weights for Seattle were quite different from those in Houston and Edmonton (Canada) in 2004. It is very difficult to compare student weights across districts. The size of the weight depends on both the set of services it is designed to support and the base spending to which it is applied. The weights in Table 8.7 are all higher than the weights we calculate for Wisconsin in Chapter 11, but the base in Wisconsin is $6,400 a child, compared to a base in Seattle of around $3,000 per pupil. The Wisconsin weight discussed in Chapter 11 would be over two times the suggested figure if it were to support the same program but be applied to just $3,000 per child.

A school's total allocation is the sum of the foundation allocation plus the funds generated through the weighted-student formula. Principals and the school community are responsible for managing the resources to provide the educational program. Because the district has an extensive system of school choice, supported in part through an excellent public transportation program that allows students to commute throughout the district, schools actually compete for students. Schools with enrollments falling below the minimum are eventually scheduled for closure. The system places substantial control for the educational program at a school in the hands of local school officials.

Case Study: San Francisco[1]

The San Francisco Unified School District has also made efforts to devolve more budget authority to the school sites. The district has established these components as part of a school program:

- Adequate administrative support
- Adequate secretarial/clerical support
- Library resources, including a skilled librarian
- Counseling resources, including a head counselor or dean in secondary schools
- Arts education and physical education programs
- Other services to meet the social, emotional, and psychological needs of students

[1]The primary source of this information is Leigh, Myong, Memorandum to Principals regarding Budget Information Packet for Planning School Year 2002–2003, April 3, 2002.

TABLE 8.7   Extra Pupil Weights in Three School Districts

Category of Special Need	Seattle	Houston	Edmonton
Student with disability (lowest)	0.95	1.10	0.99
Student with disability (highest)	7.76	6.00	4.46
Student from poverty background	0.10	0.20	None
English language learner (ELL)	0.27	0.10	0.26
Gifted and talented	None	0.12	0.26

Source: Fordham Institute, 2006.

- Supports for general-education enrichment
- Class sizes in various subject areas that are proportional to the goals set out in the district's negotiated contract with its teachers

Under district guidelines, each school must fund a principal, assistant principals if enrollment exceeds minimum levels, and teachers at various ratios depending on the grade level and the subject matter being taught. Unlike Seattle, funds are based on the average cost of staff, not actual dollars. Schools are allowed to allocate personnel funds in patterns different from those in the funding formulas as long as certain minimums are met. At least one middle school in the district with 300 students has elected to employ two assistant principals to focus attention on the needs of its students.

In addition, each school receives revenues based on the characteristics of individual children. Special education remains a central-office function, while other needs such as bilingual instruction (within the requirements of California's Proposition 227, which places limits on such programs), free and reduced-price lunches, and any other of the many categorical programs available to students, schools, and districts in California fall to school sites. Table 8.8 shows the division of responsibility between school sites and the central office in the district. Decisions about the allocation and use of resources that are the responsibility of the school site are under the control of the site administrators and their site councils.

5. SUMMARY

A school district's budget is a planning document that links programmatic decisions to financial information about the district's revenues and expenditures. As such, a budget document provides a description of the district's priorities and strategies along with a description of the resources to be used to meet those priorities. Budgets can also be used by school districts as a basis for long-range planning and as a management tool to ensure that resources are allocated and used on the basis of established policies and goals.

At the most basic level, a budget document should include an introduction describing the district's educational plans, the expected revenues and expenditures of the district, the number and type of personnel to be employed in carrying out those plans,

TABLE 8.8   Central vs. Site Based Responsibilities in San Francisco Unified School District

Site Budget Responsibility	Central Office Budget Responsibility
General-education teachers	Itinerant staff
Paraprofessionals	Boiler plant engineers
Librarians	Transportation
Counselors	Business services
Building administration—leadership	Human resources
Building administration—office support	Legal services
Parent liaisons	Athletic coaches
Noontime supervisors (elementary)	Food and nutrition services
Elementary advisors	Telecommunications/telephones
Substitutes for staff development absences	Substitutes—nonstaff development
Extra-duty pay for student activities	Professional development
Special-education supplies	Special-education teachers, aides, and related service providers
Special-education professional development	Furniture
ELL school-based teachers and aides	Equipment
School supplies	Utilities
Library books	Assistive technology for special education
Instructional materials and technology	Maintenance and groundskeeping staff and supplies
Extended-learning opportunities	
Optional test preparation	District-wide assessment
Replacement texts	Custodial staff supplies, salaries, and overtime
Benefits for all positions funded by site	Basic texts (new adoptions)
Security aides, other than those out	Language interpreters and translations
of general funds	Capital outlay
"Adjustment" teachers	Information technology and hardware
Specialty programs	General-fund security personnel
AP teachers	STAR schools staff
	Vocational education staff
	Administrative interns (elementary schools)

and a description of the way funds are allocated to school sites and programs within the district. In addition to providing revenue and expenditure estimates for the budget year, a budget document typically provides information for the previous year and the current operating year.

While there are many approaches to budgeting, most school districts rely on line-item budgets that provide information by object and often by program and function as well. All 50 states have established legal requirements for the format, timing, and publication of budgets. Many districts provide more information than the minimum required by their state, seeking ways to make the information more useful to administrators and the public. Two large urban districts, Seattle and San Francisco, provide examples of districts that have devolved a large amount of budgeting control to school sites.

Study Questions

1. Collect data on the number of students in your school (or a school of your choosing) according to these criteria:
   a. By grade
   b. Who qualify for free and reduced-price lunch
   c. Who are English-language learners
   d. Who receive special education
   Using the evidence-based adequacy approach described for budgeting in this chapter, determine the resources needed at this school to provide an adequate education. Compare the number of personnel and their positions/work assignments to the model. How do the two compare and contrast? What are the major differences in the way personnel are allocated?

2. Get data on the average salaries of personnel in the school district where this school is located, and compare the costs of personnel under the adequacy model with the personnel expenditures for the school today. If you can't get actual personnel expenditures for the school you are studying, use the average salary data you have to estimate the personnel costs at the school. How do they compare?

3. How do the level of nonpersonnel dollars at the school compare to the level generated by the model?

4. Using the budget you obtained from a school district to answer the questions in Chapter 6, look carefully over that document to see if it reflects the six features common to good budgets:
   a. Unity
   b. Clarity
   c. Regularity
   d. Balance
   e. Publicity
   f. Operational adequacy
   Whether or not you found those items, what additional information do you think should be available through the school district's budget? Why?

School Finance Structures: Formula Options

School finance is concerned not only with district budgeting and school allocation and use of resources but also with how states provide each of their districts with adequate revenues. State formulas for distributing revenues to local schools have been the major focus of school finance for over a century. This chapter comes after extensive discussion of how many resources are needed (Chapter 4), how resources have been used (Chapter 6) and could be used more effectively (Chapter 7), and how districts can budget those revenues to each of their schools (Chapter 8). The last issue in resource distribution concerns how states can provide for an adequate and equitable level of resources across all districts in the state. In public finance terms, this chapter focuses on state school finance equalization formulas.

The chapter has four sections. Section 1 discusses intergovernmental-grant theory because school finance equalization formulas represent one type of grant from one level of government—in this case, the state—to another level of government—local school districts. Section 2 analyzes four types of formulas that states have used and continue to use to distribute general-education aid to local school districts: (1) flat grants, (2) foundation programs, (3) guaranteed tax base[1] programs, and (4) combination foundation and guaranteed tax base programs. Full-state funding and other types of state-determined spending programs are also discussed briefly. Section 3 examines the issue of "adjusting" each of the formulas to account for the varying purchasing power of education dollars across school districts. The final section addresses the issue of adjusting the various formulas for the extra needs of various categories of students.

The school finance computer simulation that accompanies the text should be used when reading this chapter. The appendix describes how to access the simulation on the web, download it, and use it. The text includes some printouts from that simulation. However, developing a more in-depth understanding of what the different school finance

---

[1]Guaranteed tax base programs are algebraically equivalent to district power equalization, percentage equalization, and guaranteed yield programs. These latter programs are not discussed individually in this chapter.

formulas are, how they work, and what impacts they have requires using the simulation to experiment with design variations of the formulas.

1. INTERGOVERNMENTAL FISCAL RELATIONS

Chapter 1 showed that financing education in the United States is achieved through the efforts of three levels of governments: (1) local school districts, (2) each of the 50 states, and (3) the federal government. Indeed, financing for most public services in this country usually entails contributions from all three governments. This pattern of multiple levels of government finance is known as fiscal federalism.[2]

This section discusses two aspects of the fiscal-federalism approach to school financing: (1) the general advantages in financing K–12 educational services, and (2) intergovernmental-grant theory and its application to school financing. A full understanding of how school finance formulas work, which is the focus of section 2, entails knowledge of the more general theories of public finance and intergovernmental grants.[3]

Advantages of a Federal Approach to Financing Education

Financing educational services through three levels of government—local school districts, states, and the federal government—offers four general advantages to governments in meeting public responsibilities: (1) fiscal-capacity equalization, (2) equitable service distribution and adequate provision for education, (3) more economically efficient provision of the governmental service (education), and (4) decentralized decision making (Musgrave and Musgrave, 1989; Rosen, 2004).

Each of these advantages is discussed here in terms of the state role in financing local school districts. While the state is the focus, the policy issue is the state fiscal role in a function that historically was primarily financed at the local level. As discussed in Chapter 1, the main problem with local financing is the variation in the local ability to raise education funds. Ability to raise tax revenues is usually called a district's **fiscal capacity** and is usually measured by property value per pupil. Property value per pupil is used because, historically, most school districts have raised education revenues by taxing property. Other measures of fiscal capacity, such as personal income, sales, or combined measures, could be used instead of, or in addition to, property wealth per pupil. But our discussion focuses on the most common measure of school district fiscal capacity—property wealth per pupil.

Fiscal-capacity equalization.   The first and most important advantage of a fiscal-federalism approach to financing schools is that a state, and only a state, can equalize the fiscal capacity of its local school districts. As Chapter 1 showed, in most states, there are

---

[2]See also Musgrave and Musgrave (1989) and Rosen (2004) for a more comprehensive discussion of fiscal federalism within the broader context of public finance.

[3]This chapter refers often to various specific school finance formulas. You might first quickly read section 2 of the chapter to gain some familiarity with these formulas before reading this section.

substantial disparities among school districts in their ability to raise revenues through local property taxes. Some districts have a large per-pupil property tax base, and others a much smaller base. Consequently, the same tax rate produces widely varying amounts of revenue per pupil. Local districts cannot compensate for these varying levels of fiscal capacity—that is a role for a higher level of government, such as the state.

Indeed, school finance has a long tradition of states providing assistance to offset local disparities through what are known as fiscal-capacity or school finance equalization formulas (see Cubberly [1906] and the rest of this chapter). Fiscal-capacity equalization mitigates inequalities in the financial ability of school districts by offering relatively larger amounts of aid to districts with less fiscal capacity (i.e., those less able to raise funds from their own sources). Fiscal-capacity equalization has been the major focus of school finance for more than 150 years, and it is only possible because education is financed through a fiscal-federalism system.

Equity and adequacy in service distribution.   A second advantage of a fiscal-federalism approach to school financing is that states can create mandates or provide financial assistance to school districts to promote equity in service distribution and adequacy in service provision. Fiscal-equalization grants do not guarantee that districts will make the same decisions regarding the level of services they offer students. In fact, different approaches to providing the level and quality of education services (or any local government service for that matter) are one of the strengths of a fiscal-federalism system. However, if the state believes a minimum level of service must be provided, a federal structure offers a number of mechanisms (e.g., mandates, minimum expenditure levels, categorical programs) to ensure that minimum service levels—in today's terms, adequate service levels—are provided.

Efficiency in service production.   A third advantage to creating a multilevel school system concerns efficiency in producing educational services. Many schools or school districts can benefit from economies of scale. That is, as the size of the school grows, the unit costs of educating each child decline; a larger school or district organization thus might be more efficient than a very small one. The state may be able to use its influence to encourage very small school districts to consolidate and thereby promote efficiency in the local production of educational services. It is possible that if a school or school district grows beyond a certain size, it will no longer realize these efficiencies; in fact, the unit cost of providing educational services may begin to increase. Indeed, large statewide school systems, as well as large urban districts, may suffer from such diseconomies of large scale. Therefore, a decentralized system of schools helps avoid the diseconomies that would exist if each state were simply one large school system. Andrews, Duncombe, and Yinger (2002) provide an excellent summary of current research findings on scale economies in education.

Decentralized decision making.   The fourth advantage of a fiscal-federalism system is that decentralized decision making provides individuals with choices in selecting the mix of public services that match their personal preferences. Tiebout's (1956) classic theory of local expenditures described this phenomenon as "voting with your feet." He suggested that when a number of jurisdictions are located within close proximity, individuals choose to live in the area that offers a mix of public services most closely matching their preferences.

The nearly 15,000 school districts in the United States provide an example of Tiebout's theory. For example, realtors report that homebuyers frequently ask about the quality of local schools. Clearly, many people make decisions about where to live, at least in part, on the basis of their perception of the quality of local educational services. One would expect young families concerned about the education of their children to move into areas identified as having good schools, even if that required higher property tax payments. By contrast, a retired couple living on a fixed income might be less concerned with the quality of the local schools and more interested in an area with substantial senior citizen services and generally lower property taxes. This is not to imply that people without school-age children are not concerned about the quality of education, nor that good local schools are the only issue that matters to young families with school-age children. The example merely suggests how individuals can make decisions about where to live on the basis of a number of factors—the quality of the local schools, and resulting tax payments, being but two of those factors.

The emergence of adequacy in school finance, though, provides something of a "floor" for the mix of education services. As states—either through court orders, full understanding of standards-based education reform, or positive response to the performance demands of the federal No Child Left Behind Act—require each district to provide an adequate education program, districts have a rigorous constraint on the minimum level of education services they must provide.

Intergovernmental Grants and Their Objectives

In a fiscal-federalism system, there are two ways the central government can influence or coordinate the decisions of school districts in order to capitalize on these four advantages. The central government—states or the federal government—can mandate changes in the way local services are provided, or it can use intergovernmental grants to influence local behavior. While mandates offer the most direct way of achieving legislative goals, there are political and, in many states, financial problems with their use.

Thus, the most common approach taken by the states and the federal government to influence school district behavior is through intergovernmental grants. For example, when the federal government decided that more attention should be given to low-achieving students in districts with large numbers of students living in poverty, it created a program—the Elementary and Secondary Education Act of 1965 (now No Child Left Behind)—that provided funds to local school districts to design and implement additional education programs designed to help academically struggling students learn. Similarly, state general-education-aid grants are designed to assist local school districts in implementing overall K–12 education programs, which today in most states must be sufficiently ambitious and comprehensive to provide each child an equal opportunity to learn to the state's proficiency standards.

Different designs of state or federal grants can have quite different local fiscal impacts. Some grants simply replace local funds with state or federal funds. Other grants produce higher education expenditures than would occur if only local districts provided revenues. Still other grants both increase educational expenditures and focus the new spending on services for specific students or on specific areas within education. A key issue in designing school finance grants is to specify the objective(s) of the grant and then design it on the basis of intergovernmental grant principles to maximize that objective(s).

Intergovernmental grants from states or the federal government to local school districts can take one of two main forms: (1) general or block grants and (2) categorical aid. In addition, both of these mechanisms can include or not include requirements for matching expenditures on the part of local school districts. Decisions on these dimensions (i.e., the specific design of the grant formula, together with programmatic requirements) affect how local districts respond to the state or federal grant initiative. Break (1980), Musgrave and Musgrave (1989), and Rosen (2004) provide more discussion on the theory of intergovernmental grants, and Tsang and Levin (1983) apply this theory to school district behavior.

Unrestricted general aid.　Unrestricted general-aid or block grants, the primary form of school finance equalization grants, increase a school district's revenue but do not place restrictions on the use of that revenue. General grants are most effective when the state's goal is fiscal-capacity equalization (i.e., to provide districts with additional revenue to offset their varying ability to raise local education revenues). Flat grants are a school finance mechanism that provides an equal amount of per-pupil revenue to each school district based solely on the number of students. On the other hand, foundation and guaranteed tax base programs provide general aid to districts on the basis their level of revenues per pupil and their property wealth per pupil, providing more funds to districts lower in property wealth.[4]

General grants, however, are least effective in getting school districts to change their behavior in line with state expectations, precisely because such grants generally carry no restrictions. Districts can use general aid to supplant local revenues and thus reduce tax rates, or to increase overall education spending and thus provide more or better educational services. Without constraints, there will likely be no clear pattern to local district response. In particular, if the state provides general aid and hopes that the new funds will be used for specific purposes (e.g., to hire instructional coaches for teachers, to hire teacher tutors to give struggling students extra help, or to increase spending for mathematics and science education), the likelihood of such a uniform local response is low. This is because local governments attempt to maximize their local objectives, and in the process will likely make different spending decisions than the state might prefer.

Numerous studies of unrestricted or state general-aid grants to school districts have consistently found that school districts use a portion of the state equalization grant

---

[4]Section 2 provides a detailed description of how flat grants and foundation programs operate. It also gives examples of the effects of these programs using fiscal-capacity equalization criteria.

for tax reductions and a portion for increased education spending (Adams, 1980; Black, Lewis, and Link, 1979; Bowman, 1974; Cohn, 1974; Grubb and Osman, 1977; Ladd, 1975; Miner, 1963; Park and Carroll, 1979; Stern, 1973; Vincent and Adams, 1978). In reviewing these studies, Tsang and Levin (1983) found that, on average, local school districts spend about half of increases in state general-aid dollars on educational programs and about half to reduce local tax rates; this typical behavior is included in all simulations that accompany this text. However, as we discussed in Chapter 1, over the past decade and a half, many lower-wealth districts in several states appear to have used a larger portion for property tax relief.

Generally, though, if the state's goal for general-aid programs is fiscal-capacity equalization, unrestricted grants work quite well. Since districts low in property wealth per pupil generally have above-average tax rates and below-average expenditures per pupil, increases in general aid let them reduce their tax rates more to the average while also increasing education spending, thus addressing both disadvantages that exist with heavy reliance on local education financing.

If one accepts the notion that local districts are better able to determine the program needs of the local population (in this case, student educational needs), then unrestricted grants offer advantages in terms of economic efficiency. Unrestricted grants provide local districts with increased revenues and let each district decide how to use those revenues, drawing upon local needs and priorities. Unrestricted grants are also effective tools for maintaining an equitable but decentralized decision-making system.

As we indicated in Chapter 6, however, some states that provide substantial new revenues to local districts as a block grant (i.e., without any restrictions on their use) are beginning to question the effectiveness of local decisions about the use of those dollars. One year in Minnesota, for example, local educators requested more funds to reduce class size in early elementary grades. The legislature agreed and included such dollars but provided them through the general-equalization formula with no specific conditions on their use. Many districts used the bulk of the additional funds to hike teacher salaries and then, the next year, told the legislature they needed more money to reduce class size! The resulting conversations were a bit tense. Beginning in the 2004–05 school year, Arkansas pumped more than $1.5 billion into its schools in response to a school finance adequacy court mandate. Although the new revenues were rationalized generally on the basis of the recommendations in Chapter 4 (see Odden, Picus, and Fermanich, 2003), the state placed virtually no restrictions on the use of the funds, deferring to local educator judgment. But when a 2006 study (Mangan, Odden, and Picus, 2006) showed that few of the resources had been used for several of the high-impact strategies included in the fund model (e.g., instructional coaches to bolster professional development and teacher-tutors to provide struggling students with extra help to learn to standards), the state began to rethink how it could get districts to deploy those effective strategies.

Unrestricted general grants can be used to provide some equity in service distribution— either to establish some minimum level of service or to provide districts with at least some minimum level of funding. As section 2 of this chapter shows, flat grants and foundation school finance programs were designed to accomplish these objectives. And today, foundation programs are the primary way states implement an adequacy-focused approach to school funding. However, since unrestricted grants do not place limitations on district expenditures from local sources, there is no constraint on wealthy districts' ability to increase education spending substantially above the minimum. One way to address these problems is to link a district's general aid to its willingness to spend local resources for education through a matching requirement.

Matching general grants.   The most common way to tie state general aid to a district's own willingness to spend is to use a matching grant program. Matching grants link the level of state general-aid assistance at least in part to the level of effort made by the local school district, as well as to its fiscal capacity. In school finance, the most common general matching grant system is the guaranteed tax base (GTB) program.[5] Many state school finance programs are called percentage equalizing, guaranteed yield, or district power equalizing. Although the specific operating details of each of these systems vary, they are all designed to achieve the same goal, namely, to equalize the revenue-raising ability of each school district and to link the level of state aid to spending at the local level.

Intergovernmental-grant theory analyzes matching grants in terms of how they change the relative tax prices[6] districts pay for educational services. A GTB program, for example, lowers the tax price of educational services for districts low in property wealth per pupil, because with the GTB, they are able to levy a lower tax rate, and thus pay less, for a certain level of education services. Indeed, for the level of education services supported before a GTB program, property-poor districts are able to substantially lower their tax rates to provide the same level of services. In other words, the tax price to local citizens—taxpayers—is substantially decreased. Economic theory predicts that individuals faced with choices are price sensitive and will purchase more of lower-priced items, all other things being equal.

As it plays out in school finance, a GTB gives a district with low property value per pupil the ability to raise as much money at a given tax rate as the wealthier district that has a per-pupil property value equal to the tax base guarantee. Thus, with the same tax rate or tax effort, the poor district will be able to raise substantially more revenue than it could before the GTB. As predicted from the preceding discussion, a district would be expected to use part of this new money to increase expenditures and part of it to reduce its tax rate. Thus, the impact of a general matching grant is similar to that of an unrestricted general grant. Again, as Chapter 1 showed, over the longer term, many school districts in several states have taken advantage of the property tax relief element of GTB programs at the expense of raising spending levels.

GTB programs have another impact. With no restrictions on the level of spending, GTB programs actually serve as a stimulus to spending for education because they lower

[5]While a foundation program also requires a local match—the local required tax effort—it functions more like a flat grant than a more open-ended matching program, such as the GTB.

[6]The tax price generally is the tax rate a district must levy to purchase a given level and quality of school services. Poor districts generally have to levy a higher tax rate and thus pay a higher tax price to purchase a given bundle of school services than a wealthy district because, at a given tax rate, the poor district would raise less per pupil than the wealthier district.

the "price" of education services. All things being equal, districts in a state with a GTB school finance system spend more on education than they normally would. Wisconsin discovered this phenomenon during the 1970s, 1980s, and early 1990s. When its current system was initially designed and implemented in the mid-1970s, there was bipartisan agreement that the GTB approach to school finance was the best way to provide school finance equity *and* reduce local property taxes. In the first few years of the program, that indeed was the case. But since the GTB lowered the tax price for schools, and education was a desired commodity, districts wanted more and more of education, and so began to hike spending levels. Every few years, when citizens complained about high property taxes, the state responded by hiking the GTB level for schools. This provided tax relief in the short term but lowered once again the "price" of buying education. Over time, districts' spending for education grew, which increased demands for state equalization aid. This pattern was halted in the early 1990s when, for several reasons, the state placed controls on the annual increase in allowable school district revenues. Today, the cost controls are reviled by most local educators, but they are a predictable school finance element for a school finance system that, rather than producing property tax relief, actually over time was a stimulus to both increased local and state spending for schools (Reschovsky, 2004).

Categorical grants.   In contrast to general unrestricted grants, categorical grants have restrictions on how they can be used, as well as significant impacts on school district behavior. **Categorical grants** are provided to school districts for a specific reason or purpose, and often come with strict application, use, and reporting requirements. Categorical grants are used to ensure that school districts provide services deemed important by the state or federal government. These services are often provided more efficiently locally, but without the grant, school districts might not choose to provide them, at least not at the state- or federal-desired level for such services.

A variety of categorical-grant mechanisms are used by states and the federal government. Some categorical grants require local school districts to meet the needs of specified populations. For example, Title I assistance was created so districts would provide additional educational services to academically struggling children from low-income backgrounds. Other categorical-grant programs are designed to support specific district functions, such as pupil transportation. The manner in which a district receives categorical grant funds can also vary. Many categorical grant programs are designed so that funds are available to recipient districts automatically—dollars flow by formula. Others have application rules and procedures, and districts must write proposals in order to receive funds.

States can provide school districts with categorical grants using a variety of grant formula designs. Districts might receive categorical grants on the basis of some sociodemographic characteristic, such as incidence of poverty measured by the number of students eligible for the federal free and reduced-price lunch program, or degree of urbanization. Alternatively, districts might be eligible for categorical grants on the basis of the number of children meeting a specific criterion, such as a learning disability. Finally, districts could simply be reimbursed for expenditures devoted to a specific function, such as transportation. District fiscal response to a categorical program will depend on the specific nature of the grant's distribution mechanism.

Since one purpose of a categorical grant is to encourage specific actions on the part of local school districts, federal and most state categorical grants usually include rules and regulations that restrict district use of these resources to their intended purpose. A commonly used fiscal-enforcement tool is the maintenance-of-effort provision. This provision requires the district to prove that spending on the supported program from its own funds does not decline as a result of the grant. The early Title I "supplement not supplant" requirement is an example of a maintenance-of-effort provision. Other enforcement provisions include audits and evaluations to ensure that recipient districts establish programs designed to meet the purpose or goals of the grant program. Many categorical grants have specific reporting requirements that help the contributing government monitor use of the funds.

Numerous studies have shown that categorical grants usually stimulate educational expenditures by at least the amount of the grant, and sometimes by more (Grubb and Michelson, 1974; Ladd, 1975; Tsang and Levin, 1983; and Vincent and Adams, 1978). The primary explanation is that the strings attached to categorical grants make it difficult for districts to spend the funds elsewhere and virtually force districts to increase spending by at least the amount of the grant. Another explanation is that categorical grants are provided for specialized programs on which local districts would spend less, if anything at all, in the absence of the categorical grant.

Categorical grants present a different trade-off between equity and efficiency than do general grants. Categorical programs encourage districts to treat needy students differently by making additional resources available to produce similar, or hopefully similar, achievement outcomes. Anytime resources are devoted to a needy student, it implies a loss of what could have been produced if the resources were evenly distributed across all students (Monk, 1990). As a result, categorical grants trade economic efficiency for equity or adequacy in the provision of services.

By their nature, categorical programs are more centralized than general grants since it is the state or federal government that determines what population or function needs extra resources. Moreover, some federal programs, such as the program for children with disabilities (IDEA), include very specific requirements for identifying and serving eligible students. Although the final determination of what specific services to provide are left to district and parental discretion, there are very detailed identification and service procedures identified in the law and accompanying regulations.

Finally, since categorical grants are designed to provide assistance to groups of students or to districts on the basis of some characteristic (e.g., expensive transportation needs in a small, sparsely populated rural district), they are not generally designed to equalize fiscal capacity. Nevertheless, both special-service provision and fiscal-capacity equalization can be accomplished with well-designed grant schemes. These issues were discussed in more depth at the end of Chapter 4.

2. SCHOOL FINANCE FORMULAS

This section uses the equity and adequacy framework developed in Chapter 3 to analyze how different school finance formulas affect the equity and adequacy of a representative 20-district sample of school districts. The text shows how various school finance objectives can be in conflict, as well as how politics might intervene to constrain the amount of equity a state political system can produce. Thus, school finance formula design is both a technical and a political task that seeks to balance many objectives—equity, educational, fiscal, and political. "Perfect equity" is generally not possible.

This section has six parts: discussion of the characteristics of the illustrative sample of districts included in the simulation, and then a discussion of flat grant programs, foundation programs, guaranteed tax base (GTB) programs, combination foundation-GTB programs, and full-state funding.

Equity and Adequacy of the Simulation Sample Districts

In designing new school finance structures today, analysts and policymakers begin with state education finance systems that have evolved over several years. Local districts have real property tax rates, and state general aid has been distributed according to some mechanism, usually with the goal of reducing spending disparities caused by unequal distribution of the local per-pupil property tax base.

Figure 9.1 displays data for a representative sample of 20 districts that will be used throughout the chapter to demonstrate the impact of various new school finance structures (see www.mhhe.com/odden4e). The data are from a state with school finance circumstances typical of the rest of the country. The numbers indicate several characteristics of the extant school finance system in the state from which the sample was selected.

First, there are large differences in property value per pupil. The richest district has $278,052 in property value per pupil, which is almost 16 times the value ($17,456) in the poorest district. The weighted-average[7] property value per student is $97,831, which is about 5.6 times the value of the poorest district, and about half the value of the second-wealthiest district ($198,564).

The third column in Figure 9.1 shows that property tax rates also vary considerably, from a low of 25.5 mills to a high of 39.64 mills, a difference of over 50 percent. Notably, it is the lower-property-value districts that have the higher property tax rates and the higher-property-value districts that have the lower property tax rates, which reflects the "traditional" school finance problem as discussed in Chapter 1. Because of differences in the tax base, the second-wealthiest district raises $199 per pupil for each mill levied, and thus raises $5,445 per pupil in local revenues at its tax rate of 27.42 mills. On

---

[7] All statistics in the table and in the computer simulation are calculated in a manner that statistically weights each district value by the number of students in the district. Thus, the values for district 17, with 30,256 students, contribute more to the weighted average than the values for district 6, which has only 956 students. Using student-weighted statistics has become the more prominent way to present statistics in school finance analyses. The results, therefore, indicate the impact of the funding structure on students.

Adequacy Level	$5,350.00
Pupil Weights	**No**
Disabled	—
Limited English	—
Low income	—

District	Pupils	Property Value per Pupil ($)	Property Tax Rate (Mills)	Local Revenue per Pupil ($)	State Revenue per Pupil ($)	Total Revenue per Pupil ($)
1	1,290	17,456	39.64	692	2,788	3,480
2	5,648	25,879	38.50	996	2,623	3,620
3	1,678	31,569	37.15	1,173	2,535	3,708
4	256	35,698	36.20	1,292	2,460	3,752
5	10,256	40,258	35.91	1,446	2,401	3,847
6	956	43,621	35.74	1,559	2,393	3,952
7	4,689	49,875	34.89	1,740	2,358	4,099
8	1,656	55,556	34.17	1,898	2,273	4,171
9	8,954	61,254	33.73	2,066	2,218	4,284
10	1,488	70,569	33.44	2,360	2,091	4,450
11	2,416	78,952	33.23	2,624	2,081	4,704
12	5,891	86,321	32.89	2,839	2,031	4,870
13	2,600	94,387	32.10	3,030	1,969	4,999
14	15,489	102,687	31.32	3,216	1,937	5,154
15	2,308	112,358	30.85	3,466	1,908	5,374
16	2,712	125,897	30.50	3,840	1,724	5,564
17	30,256	136,527	30.05	4,102	1,527	5,630
18	2,056	156,325	28.63	4,476	1,424	5,899
19	3,121	198,564	27.42	5,445	1,130	6,575
20	1,523	278,052	25.50	7,090	437	7,527
Weighted average		97,831	32.34	3,028	1,925	4,953
Weighted std. dev.		48,514	2.91	1,269	433	841
Median		102,687	31.32	3,216	1,937	5,154

Totals		
Category	Amount	Percent
Local revenue	318,727,208	61.14
State revenue	202,540,166	38.86
Total revenue	521,267,374	
Pupils	105,243	

Equity Measures	
Horizontal Equity	
Range	$4,047
Restricted range	$2,955
Federal range ratio	0.816
Coef. of variation	0.170
Gini coefficient	0.094
McLoone index	0.810
Verstegen index	1.086
Fiscal neutrality	
Correlation	0.991
Elasticity	0.324
Adequacy	
Odden-Picus	0.895

FIGURE 9.1   Base Data for a Representative Sample of 20 School Districts

the other hand, the second-poorest district raises only $26 for each mill levied, and thus raises just $996 for its 38.5 mill tax rate. Thus, even though the poorer district exerts a higher tax effort, it produces a much lower level of revenues, because its tax base is so low. On the other hand, the wealthier district raises a much higher level of local revenues per pupil even though it exerts a lower tax effort, because its tax base is so much larger.

State aid is distributed in an inverse relationship to property value per pupil (i.e., the poorest districts receive the largest amount of per-pupil state aid), and state aid per pupil declines as property value per pupil rises. In fact, the poorest district receives about 6.4 times the state aid of the wealthiest district on a per-pupil basis. Thus, state aid is distributed in a fiscal-capacity-equalizing pattern. But even the wealthiest district receives some level of state general aid ($437 per pupil for this sample). This distribution of state aid is characteristic of most states. All states use some type of fiscal-capacity-equalizing school finance formula to distribute general aid, and all districts receive some minimum level of general aid.

But the difference in state aid allocations, while providing higher amounts to property-poor districts, is not sufficient to offset the 16-to-1 difference in property value per pupil among districts. Thus, the poorest district, receiving 6.4 times the aid of the wealthiest district and exerting 1.5 times the tax effort, still has revenues per child that total only 46 percent of those in the highest-spending district. The figures illustrate a consistent pattern—the lower the property value per child, the lower the total revenues per pupil, even though per-pupil state aid and property tax rates are higher.

Figure 9.1 also includes statistical measures of the fiscal equity of this school finance system. In terms of horizontal equity for students, the coefficient of variation for total revenues per pupil is 17 percent, which means that roughly two-thirds of these districts have total revenues per pupil that are within 17 percent of the weighted average ($841 in this case). If this were a normal distribution, 95 percent of districts would have total revenues per pupil within 34 percent of the average ($1,682 in this case). The value of the coefficient of variation indicates that the fiscal-capacity-equalizing distribution of state general aid is modest, offsetting just a portion of the differences in local ability to raise property taxes. To further understand the impact of state general aid, compare Figure 9.1 with the results of a "no-state-aid" situation, which can be determined by running a computer simulation and setting the "flat grant" equal to zero. Notice that the coefficient of variation more than doubles, showing that the state aid that was provided clearly helped to reduce, but not eliminate, differences in total revenues per pupil.

The McLoone Index in Figure 9.1 indicates that the average total revenue per pupil for the bottom 50 percent of students is just 81 percent that of the student at the median, or 19 percent below the median. Again, state aid has helped push this statistic toward 1.00, which would indicate full equity for the bottom 50 percent, as compared with the McLoone Index of 0.582 in the no-state-aid case (again, run a "flat grant" at zero in the simulation).

The Verstegen Index shows that the average total revenues per pupil in the top 50 percent is just 8.6 percent above the median. This figure shows that for this sample the revenue-per-pupil figures for the higher spenders are closer to the median than the revenues per pupil for the lower spenders, which are just 19 percent shy of the median.

In terms of fiscal neutrality, or the degree to which total revenues per pupil are linked to property wealth per pupil, Figure 9.1 shows a high correlation at 0.991, as well as a healthy elasticity at 0.324. This means that revenues are strongly related to property wealth and that increases in property wealth produce substantial increases in revenues—specifically, that a 10 percent increase in wealth produces a 3.2 percent increase in revenues. For example, as wealth increases about 100 percent, from about

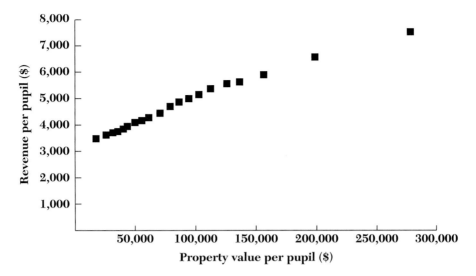

FIGURE 9.2   Scatter Plot of Total Revenue versus Wealth: Base Data

$50,000 to $100,000, revenues per pupil increase about 33 percent, which is slightly more than the actual total revenue per pupil increase from $4,099 to $5,154. To see this graphically, click on the "base chart" tab at the bottom of the simulation spreadsheet. It shows that as property wealth per pupil increases, so do revenues per pupil, reflecting the positive value for elasticity.

We have used $5,350 as the revenue-per-pupil figure that represents an "adequate" amount in all subsequent simulations. We simply selected a figure somewhat above the median, although this was an arbitrary selection. As discussed in Chapter 3 and later in this chapter, sophisticated analysis is needed to identify an "adequate" expenditure figure. But we had to select some figure, and we use $5,350 consistently in all simulations in this chapter. The Odden-Picus Adequacy Index shows that those districts spending below the "adequate level" spend on average just 89.5 percent of the "adequate" figure of $5,350.

Figure 9.2 shows graphically the relationship between revenues per pupil and property value per pupil for this sample, and Figure 9.3 shows the same data but with no state aid. For both, there is an almost linear relationship between the two variables, but the slope of the graph is much steeper for the no-state-aid case. Thus, state aid has reduced the magnitude but has not eliminated the role of property value per pupil in producing revenue-per-pupil disparities.

In sum, the sample of 20 districts in this state reflects the context of school finance in many states. There is wide disparity in the local per-pupil property tax base. State aid is distributed inversely to property wealth, and it is somewhat fiscal-capacity-equalizing, but not sufficiently to offset differences in property wealth, nor sufficiently to produce an "adequate" spending level for all districts. As a result, the equity statistics reflect a

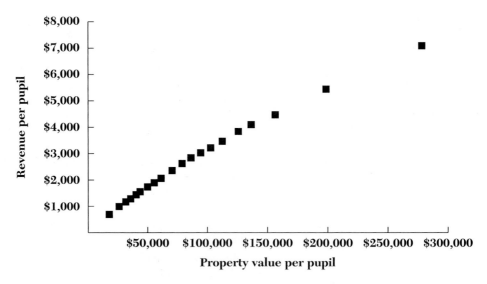

FIGURE 9.3   Scatter Plot of Revenue versus Wealth: Flat Grant

system that needs further improvements to meet horizontal equity, fiscal-neutrality equity, or adequacy standards. This chapter discusses how different types of school finance formulas for general school aid produce equity improvements in the distribution of fiscal resources for this sample of districts.

All school finance general-aid programs are education block grants. They provide unrestricted revenues to be used by local districts and schools for any education purpose. Sometimes they require districts to spend a minimum percentage on teacher salaries or a maximum on administration, but generally, they are completely unrestricted. Furthermore, they rarely carry restrictions for maintaining local efforts, so districts can even use large increases in general-aid revenues to help reduce local property tax rates. Indeed, as discussed previously, on average, half of each general-aid dollar is used to increase local education spending, and half is used to reduce local property tax rates.

Although the history of education block grants is associated with attempts to deregulate and consolidate categorical programs for special students such as the disabled or low achievers, the idea of a block grant is attractive to local educators. Block grants give local school districts more autonomy since the money can be spent as the districts wish. Indeed, the history of school finance general-aid programs is one of education block grants.

Flat Grant Programs

During the late eighteenth and early nineteenth centuries, there were few public schools in this country. Most schools were private, and many were run by churches. Only a small proportion of the population attended formal schooling. As the nation developed and became more interested not only in formally educating its citizens but also in forging a common culture, local governments began to create public schools.

As discussed in Chapter 1, these schools were not part of state systems of education as we know them today, but were independent creatures of local governments. Through various means, including taxation and "in kind" contributions, localities built schools (often one-room schools), hired teachers (who often lived in the schools and were paid in room and board rather than money), and educated increasing numbers of children.

By the middle of the nineteenth century, the inequities associated with this laissez faire approach to creating and financing schools were recognized. Indeed, some localities were too poor to create any type of public school, while larger, wealthier localities were able to levy local taxes to finance them.

Recognizing these different circumstances, states began to require each locality to have at least one public elementary school and often provided a lump sum—a **flat grant**, usually on a per-school basis—to help support the local elementary school program. This approach remedied the problem of the poorest localities being unable to create schools on their own; in these communities, state funds often became the only fiscal support for the school.

But the flat grant approach also provided funds to localities that had been able to create a school with their own resources, thus providing them with even more education dollars. Though the overall impact was to expand education and boost the average level of schooling, and even perhaps education quality, the flat grant program benefited poor and rich districts alike.

Over time, states increased the level of flat grants in part to reflect rising costs of education. Growing numbers of students meant that shifts in the formula structure were needed—from flat grants per school to flat grants per classroom or per teacher to finance schools and classrooms that had outgrown the one-room-school context. As the education system continued to grow, it became clear that the level of the flat grant, always quite low, would need to be increased to finance the type of education system needed for an emerging industrial society. The response to these growing needs is described in the next section on foundation programs.

Today, states do not use flat grants as the major formula to apportion general school aid. However, as recently as 1974, Connecticut's school aid formula was a flat grant of $250 per pupil. Nevertheless, flat grant programs have several intriguing characteristics, some of which may be quite attractive to some districts. For example, some states, such as California, have constitutional requirements to provide a minimum amount of per-pupil state aid to local districts. These minimums function as flat grant programs for the very wealthy districts. California must provide a minimum $120 per pupil in state aid for all districts even if the formula calculation would provide for no state aid.

From an intergovernmental-grant design perspective, flat grants provide general-purpose operating funds. They are based solely on some measure of local education need, such as the number of schools, classrooms, teachers, or students. Flat grants have no local matching requirements. Flat grants also flow to local districts in equal amounts per unit of educational need regardless of differences in local fiscal capacity (i.e., regardless of local property wealth per pupil or household income). As such, they are unlikely to have a major impact on improving the fiscal neutrality of a school finance system, because they are unlikely to reduce the connections between local fiscal capacity and expenditures per pupil. Moreover, flat grants are not the most effective tool for raising local education spending, since districts could use the state funds to reduce the level of local dollars and thus to reduce local property tax rates.

The flat grant formula. One appealing aspect of flat grants is that they are easy to calculate. Algebraically, state aid per pupil for a flat grant is:

$$SAPP = FG$$

and total state aid is defined as:

$$TSA = SAPP \times Pupils$$

where

$$SAPP = \text{state aid per pupil}$$
$$FG = \text{amount of flat grant}$$
$$TSA = \text{total state aid}$$
$$\text{Pupils} = \text{number of students in school district[8]}$$

Once the unit of need is identified (which most recently has been the number of pupils), a flat grant provides an equal number of dollars for each of those units of need in all districts. Such a program is appealing because all education policy leaders, at both the state and local level, can easily understand it. Furthermore, because a flat grant treats all districts equally, it seems fair on the surface. State education revenues are raised by taxing citizens across the state and then returning the money to localities in what appears to be a fair manner by providing an equal number of dollars for each unit of need.

Flat grants reflect the traditional American concern with the bottom half, or poorest segment, of the population. A flat grant implements the value of providing a bare-minimum level of support for those students and districts at the bottom in terms of relative spending or fiscal capacity. As the previous discussion indicates, education flat grants were created to ensure that even the poorest localities could offer some type of education program. And while they have been successful in doing so to some extent, the

---

[8]In this book, pupils are the unit of need. But there are other measures of local need, such as teachers, classrooms, and schools, that could also be used with these formulas.

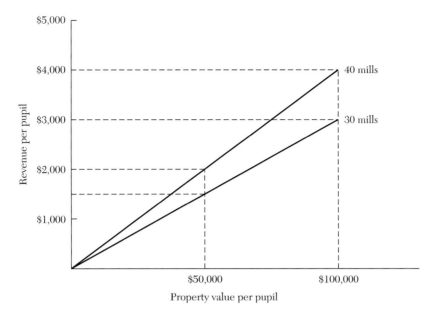

FIGURE 9.4 **Graphical Representation of the Impact of No State Aid**

fact that flat grants were typically quite low has meant that they fall short of ensuring a minimum level of quality—or, in today's terminology, adequacy.

Figures 9.4 and 9.5 graphically depict the impact of a flat grant program on the ability of school districts to raise funds for education. Figure 9.4 represents the situation prior to a flat grant program. The solid lines show the revenues per pupil raised at different tax rates—30 and 40 mills in this example—for districts with different levels of property value per pupil. For example, at 30 mills, the district with a property value per pupil of $50,000 raises just $1,500 per pupil, whereas the district with a property value per pupil of $100,000 raises $3,000. At 40 mills, the district with a property value per pupil of $50,000 raises more, $2,000 per pupil, and the district with a property value per pupil of $100,000 raises $4,000. The graph shows that revenues increase both as property value per pupil increases and as the local tax rate increases.

Figure 9.5 depicts the same districts under a flat grant program. The result is simply that the amount of the flat grant—$1,000 in this case—is added to local revenues per pupil. The slopes of the lines do not change. The district with a property value per pupil of $50,000 now has $3,000 ($2,000 of local revenues plus the $1,000 flat grant) at a 40 mill tax rate, and the district with a property value per pupil of $100,000 now has $5,000 ($4,000 of local money plus the $1,000 flat grant) at the same tax rate. Wealthier districts still raise more money, but with the flat grant, all districts have at least $1,000 per pupil.

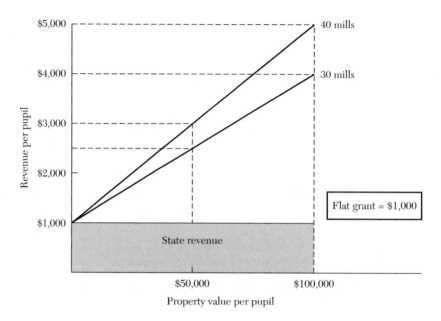

FIGURE 9.5   Graphical Representation of the Impact of a Flat Grant

Fiscal equity impacts of flat grant programs.   Figure 9.6 shows the result of replacing the extant state aid system for the sample of districts with a flat grant of $2,000 per child. We have programmed the simulation for the flat grant with no fiscal response in terms of using half the funding for increased spending and half for property tax relief; for just the flat grant, the simulation assumes all new dollars are used to increase district spending. That amount is slightly higher than the average state aid in the original sample and about 40 percent of average total revenues per pupil, although there is no magic in the $2,000 figure. This flat grant increases state aid by $7.9 million, from $202.5 million to $210.4 million. Note that there is no increase in local effort, and the total increase in funding from $521.3 million to $529.2 million is the result of the state's flat grant.

The flat grant completely erases the fiscal-capacity-equalizing impact of the original state aid, actually decreasing state aid in the poorest districts and increasing it in the wealthier ones. All the equity statistics indicate a less equal distribution: the range increases, the coefficient of variation increases, the McLoone Index decreases, the Verstegen Index rises, and the Adequacy Index falls. Further, both fiscal-neutrality statistics increase, thus showing a stronger and more significant relationship between total revenues per pupil and property value per pupil. Indeed, the graph of this flat grant (use the simulation to view the graph by clicking on the "flat grant" tab) is very similar to the graph of the no-state-aid case (see Figure 9.4). The difference is that revenues per pupil are about $2,000 higher with the flat grant; the graph has been shifted upward by the

Adequacy Level	$5,350.00
Pupil Weights	**No**
Disabled	—
Limited English	—
Low Income	—

Amount of Flat Grant	$2,000.00

District	Pupils	Property Value per Pupil ($)	Property Tax Rate (Mills)	Local Revenue per Pupil ($)	State Revenue per Pupil ($)	Change in State Revenue per Pupil ($)	Total Revenue per Pupil ($)	Change in Total Revenue per Pupil ($)
1	1,290	17,456	39.64	692	2000	(788)	2,692	(788)
2	5,648	25,879	38.50	996	2000	(623)	2,996	(623)
3	1,678	31,569	37.15	1,173	2000	(535)	3,173	(535)
4	256	35,698	36.20	1,292	2000	(460)	3,292	(460)
5	10,256	40,258	35.91	1,446	2000	(401)	3,446	(401)
6	956	43,621	35.74	1,559	2000	(393)	3,559	(393)
7	4,689	49,875	34.89	1,740	2000	(358)	3,740	(358)
8	1,656	55,556	34.17	1,898	2000	(273)	3,898	(273)
9	8,954	61,254	33.73	2,066	2000	(218)	4,066	(218)
10	1,488	70,569	33.44	2,360	2000	(91)	4,360	(91)
11	2,416	78,952	33.23	2,624	2000	(81)	4,624	(81)
12	5,891	86,321	32.89	2,839	2000	(31)	4,839	(31)
13	2,600	94,387	32.10	3,030	2000	31	5,030	31
14	15,489	102,687	31.32	3,216	2000	63	5,216	63
15	2,308	112,358	30.85	3,466	2000	92	5,466	92
16	2,712	125,897	30.50	3,840	2000	276	5,840	276
17	30,256	136,527	30.05	4,102	2000	473	6,102	473
18	2,056	156,325	28.63	4,476	2000	576	6,476	576
19	3,121	198,564	27.42	5,445	2000	870	7,445	870
20	1,523	278,052	25.50	7,090	2000	1563	9,090	1,563
Weighted average		97,831	32.34	3,028	2,000	75	5,028	75
Weighted std. dev.		48,514	2.91	1,269	0	433	1,269	433
Median		102,687	31.32	3,216	2,000	63	5,216	63

Totals			
Category	Amount	Percent	Change from Base Amount
Local revenue	318,727,208	60.23	(0)
State revenue	210,486,000	39.77	7,945,834
Total revenue	529,213,208		7,945,834
Pupils	105,243		

Winners and Losers			
Category	Winners	Losers	No Change
State aid	8	12	0
Total revenue	8	12	0

Equity Measures	
Horizontal Equity	
Range	$6,398
Restricted range	$4,448
Federal range ratio	1.485
Coef. of variation	0.252
Gini coefficient	0.140
McLoone Index	0.742
Verstegen Index	1.149
Fiscal Neutrality	
Correlation	0.995
Elasticity	0.485
Adequacy	
Odden-Picus	0.871

FIGURE 9.6   Flat Grant from the State

level of the flat grant. In short, at low levels, a flat grant is not a viable option for enhancing the fiscal equity of a state's school finance system.

As the size of the flat grant increases, though, it begins to have a positive impact on the fiscal equity of the school finance system. For example, a flat grant of $4,000 per pupil reduces the coefficient of variation from 0.252 to 0.181, and the fiscal-neutrality elasticity from 0.489 to 0.347. Use the simulation to confirm these figures. A flat grant of $5,000 further improves these statistics, lowering the coefficient of variation to 0.158 and the property wealth elasticity to 0.304. Again, use the simulation to confirm these figures. Note that when the flat grant is $5,000, no district spends less than the adequacy level of $5,350, so the Adequacy Index will be 1.0, as shown in the equity measures box.

If the flat grant were increased over time to $10,000, and local tax rates and property value per pupil stayed the same, the flat grant would be the major source of school revenues. At this level, both the coefficient of variation and the wealth elasticity would be negligible. Put a different way, though a low-level flat grant would have a deleterious impact on the fiscal equity of the sample districts, a very high flat grant would swamp the current inequities and produce a highly equalized system.[9]

Of course, as the level of the flat grant rises, so does the total or state cost of the program. The positive impacts on fiscal equity, in other words, are achieved only at significant cost. Nevertheless, the point of this example is that while low-level flat grants are unattractive except on simplicity grounds, higher-level flat grants can improve the fiscal inequities characteristic of most state school finance structures.

Finally, in reviewing the equity measures and the means and standard deviations of the major variables, we can make a few technical (statistical) points. First, the standard deviation ($433) stays the same irrespective of the level of the flat grant. Thus, adding a constant amount to all variables in a sample does change the standard deviation. This phenomenon helps explain why the coefficient of variation decreases as the flat grant increases. Since the coefficient of variation is the standard deviation divided by the mean, the numerator (standard deviation) remains constant while the denominator (mean or average revenues per pupil) increases, thus reducing the value of the statistic. Second, the correlation coefficient also stays the same irrespective of the level of the flat grant. Again, adding a constant amount to all variables in a sample does not change the correlation. This suggests that the equity gains are achieved with substantial state expenditures, and the wealthy districts still receive more than the poor districts. Equity is achieved because the differences caused by variation in property wealth per pupil are a smaller portion of total district revenue as the flat grant increases. Also note that the range and restricted range remain the same as you run increasingly larger flat grants.

Flat grants were early attempts to involve the state in redressing local differences in the ability to support public schools. Flat grants are easy-to-understand intergovernmental-aid programs that provide assistance to poor and rich districts alike. But they are expensive, even at relatively low values. And at the affordable low values, they tend to worsen measures of school finance equity. For these reasons, they are not used as general-aid school finance policy instruments today.

---

[9]We encourage you to run these flat grant amounts on the computer simulation and to review the results on the computer screen, as well as perhaps print them out. In addition, you should view the scatter plots for each run. The scatter plot for the flat grant at $10,000 shows that the graph of total revenues per pupil versus property wealth per pupil is almost a straight, horizontal line.

Foundation Programs

As the shortcomings of flat grant programs became increasingly obvious at the turn of the twentieth century, there was a search for a new and more powerful formula. At about that time, New York State created a commission to study its school finance system, with a specific charge to create a new school finance structure that went beyond the flat grant approach. George Strayer and Roger Haig, professors at Columbia University, were hired as consultants to this commission. Their new creation was a formula that would come to dominate school finance during the rest of the century. Even today, most states use some variation of the Strayer-Haig foundation, or minimum foundation program as it originally was called. Indeed, in many states, the synonym for "school finance formula" is "minimum foundation program"; the state role in school finance is defined, as it were, as providing a minimum foundation program.

Strayer and Haig ingeniously incorporated several school finance issues into their new **foundation program** school finance structure. First, the foundation program addressed the issue of a minimum quality-education program. Though flat grants provided financial assistance to localities to provide some level of school funding, the levels of the flat grant were rarely sufficient to finance what could be called even a minimum quality-education program. A goal of the minimum foundation program, however, was to set an expenditure per pupil—the foundation expenditure—at a level that would provide at least a minimum quality-education program. The idea was to put a fiscal "foundation" or floor under every local school program that was sufficient to provide an education program that met minimum standards. Thus, the foundation program was designed to remedy the first major defect of the low-level flat grant.

But what about the cost? The reason flat grants remained low was that to raise them to higher levels required more funds than states could afford. The foundation program resolved this dilemma by financing the foundation per-pupil revenue level with a combination of state *and* local revenues. A foundation program requires a minimum local tax effort as a condition of receiving state aid. The required local tax effort most typically is applied to the local property tax base. State aid per pupil is the difference between the foundation per-pupil revenue level and the local per-pupil revenues raised by the required local tax rate. State aid is also inversely related to local property wealth.

The foundation formula.   Algebraically, state aid per pupil for a foundation program is:

$$SAPP = FRPP - (RTR \times PVPP)$$

where

$$SAPP = \text{state aid per pupil}$$
$$FRPP = \text{foundation revenue per pupil}$$

$$RTR = \text{local required tax rate}$$

$$PVPP = \text{local property value per pupil}$$

A district's total state aid would be:

$$TSA = SAPP \times \text{Pupils}$$

where

$$TSA = \text{total state aid}$$

$$SAPP = \text{state aid per pupil}$$

$$\text{Pupils} = \text{number of students in school district[10]}$$

Thus, the state and local school district share the total cost of the foundation program. States can afford to enact such a program, and therefore substantially raise the minimum revenue per pupil, because local tax revenues finance a large portion of the increase. Indeed, the advent of foundation school-aid formulas formally underscored the joint and interrelated state and local roles in financing public elementary and secondary schools.

Foundation Policy Issues.   From an intergovernmental-aid design perspective, the foundation program has several attractive features. First, it links local school districts to the state in a sophisticated structure of intergovernmental fiscal relationships. Second, it continues to provide large sources of general aid to local school districts, but through a mechanism by which local and state revenues are formally combined in the general-aid "pot." Third, it formally requires a local match in order to receive state aid; the district must levy the required local tax rate as a condition of receiving state foundation aid.[11]

In addition, per-pupil state aid is related to fiscal capacity. Since the required local tax rate produces less money in a district with low property value than in a district with high property value, state aid increases in the poor district. In fact, there is nearly a linear relationship between the level of state aid per pupil and the level of local property

---

[10]Again, teachers, classrooms, or schools could be used as the need measure. Several states have used a foundation program with teachers as the need measure; Texas used such a program up to 1984.

[11]Historically, states have "hedged" on this requirement. Though most districts levy a tax rate above the minimum required local tax rate, a few do not. The policy issue for most states is whether to force these districts to raise their tax rate to the minimum level. The dilemma is that most of these low-tax-effort districts are districts lowest in property wealth and household income (i.e., the poorest of the poor). States usually have not ultimately required these districts to raise their tax rates. Sometimes, as in New York State, the districts received state aid as if they were levying that minimum tax rate. Other states, such as Texas, reduced state aid by a factor equal to the ratio of the actual local property tax rate to the foundation-required tax rate. In the school finance simulation, there is no option not to force districts to levy the required minimum tax rate or to have state aid reduced in the preceding proportionate manner. All simulations discussed in the text require districts to levy the minimum local tax rate in order to receive state general aid.

value per pupil: as property value decreases, state aid increases. Thus, a foundation program finances a minimum base education program in each school district, provides general aid in a manner that is fiscal-capacity-equalizing (i.e., increases as property value per pupil decreases), and requires a local contribution as well. These are all attractive features of intergovernmental-aid formulas.

The foundation program takes one or two steps beyond the flat grant, reflecting the American concern with the less well-off and the value of providing at least a minimum quality-education program. Initially, foundation programs were designed, in fact, to ensure that there would be sufficient revenues from state and local sources to provide a minimum quality-education program in each school district. In terms of today's education objectives, especially adequacy, which seek to have all students achieve to some high minimum level, this does not seem to be a very lofty goal. But compared to the situation in the early twentieth century, it was a bold step forward. The foundation program allowed states to implement an education finance structure that substantially upgraded the education systems in the lowest-spending schools, to a level that at least passed a standard of minimum adequacy. In 1986–87, 30 states had a foundation program as a component of their school aid program (Salmon, Dawson, Lawton, and Johns, 1988); by 1993–94, the number had increased to 40 (Gold, Smith, and Lawton, 1995), and it is about that number today (see Sielke, Dayton, Holmes, and Jefferson, 2001).

Three major shortcomings of foundation programs emerged over the years. The first is that a foundation program typically allows districts to spend above the minimum foundation expenditure level. This fiscal leeway, or local add-on, is generally financed entirely by local revenues, though sometimes it is aided by a GTB program (see page 303 for a discussion of combination foundation–GTB programs). Without the GTB, districts with a high property value per pupil can levy a small tax above the required local effort and take in large amounts of supplemental revenues, while districts with a low property value per pupil can levy a substantial extra tax and still see only a small amount of additional revenue per pupil. In fact, this feature of foundation programs ultimately led to the court cases discussed in Chapter 2. This is because, over time, the local add-on component of education revenues far surpassed the foundation program revenues, producing a system that, while more equitable than a system with no state aid, still left education revenues per pupil strongly linked to local property wealth per pupil. Further, this local add-on feature is viewed by some as the "Achilles heel" of the finance structure in all states that have a foundation program as their system for providing general school aid.

Second, though minimum foundation programs initially boosted the minimum level of local school spending, often the minimum revenue level increased very slowly over time and quickly ceased being sufficient to meet minimum standards. Put another way, after the initial years, minimum foundation programs often did not provide sufficient revenues per pupil for an education program that would meet even the lowest acceptable standards. The low foundation revenue level was due in part to technical problems (the law specified dollar amount as the foundation revenue and required legislative action each year for it to increase) and in part to fiscal constraints (the state could not afford to raise it significantly). Over time, the low level forced districts that wanted to provide a higher-quality program to expand their local add-on, which gradually moved the overall system into one based more and more on local add-ons, and thus on local property value per pupil.

More recently, either by choice or by court decree, states have been adjusting the foundation revenue level every year. For example, Wyoming's school finance structure receives an annual "external cost adjustment" that reflects an external inflation factor. In 2006, the Arkansas Supreme Court overturned that state's school finance system, enacted in 2004, in part because the legislature did not provide the system with an annual inflation adjustment. In a 2006 special session, the legislature remedied this problem and provided an inflator to both years of the education biennium budget for 2005–06 and 2006–07.

Third, while foundation programs usually increased total education revenues in property-poor districts, and thus helped them to enhance their education program, strict state aid formula calculations for wealthier districts yielded a negative number. This meant that these districts could raise more than the minimum foundation expenditure at the required tax rate. In a world of perfect fiscal equity, such districts would have been required to send a check in the amount of the negative aid to the state, which the state would then have deposited in the general fund for redistribution to poorer districts. But states generally did not enact this "recapture" or "Robin Hood" component. If state aid calculations produced a negative-aid figure, the state simply provided no aid to that district. One state that did have a recapture provision, Wyoming, recently capped the amount districts had to send back to the state and allowed them to keep any additional revenue they raised. But in November 2006, the electorate voted to restore the full recapture amount.

This meant that even under a minimum foundation program, districts high in property value per pupil were able to raise more funds at the given required tax rate just with local funds than other districts could with a combination of state and local funds. The fiscal advantage for districts high in property value per pupil was further enhanced by prior receipt of flat grant state aid, which had been distributed to all districts, irrespective of their level of property wealth per pupil. For these districts, the state faced a dual-policy dilemma: (1) whether under the foundation aid calculation to require them to send negative-aid checks to the state, which was rarely if ever invoked, and (2) whether to take away the flat grant aid and thereby reduce their state aid to zero. Most states took a political route to this dilemma and distributed an amount that was the larger of the new amount under the foundation formula or the previous level of aid (i.e., they did not take away the old flat grant aid). This "hold harmless" approach has typified school finance structures (as well as most other intergovernmental-aid structures) for years. So, not only were the wealthiest districts not forced to return negative aid to the state, but also they kept some minimum level of per-pupil state aid. Indeed, states often gradually increased the minimum amount over the years.[12]

Such policy dilemmas and ultimate policy decisions substantially blunted the ability of minimum foundation programs to impact the fiscal equity of a state's school finance structure. While new minimum foundation programs boosted the fiscal resources

---

[12]Nevertheless, a few states have "recapture" or "Robin Hood" mechanisms, including Montana, Texas, Utah, and, up to a point, Wyoming.

of the lowest-spending districts, which was a clear objective and a definite positive feature, their shortcomings, especially over time, severely limited their role as an adequate school finance mechanism.

The base sample of districts shows the residue of these incremental approaches to school finance (see Figure 9.1); even the districts highest in property value per pupil receive some state aid. Thus, the school finance policy question becomes: What type of foundation program can enhance the fiscal equity of the school finance condition of the sample districts? In addressing this question, two policy design decisions have to be made:

- The foundation expenditure level
- The required local tax rate

These policy impact issues then have to be considered:

- The impact on the fiscal equity of the sample
- The total costs (usually in state revenues but also potential changes in local revenues)
- The political impact, measured in the simulation results by the number of "winners" and "losers" (i.e., the number of districts with increases and decreases in *state* aid)

And a politically viable combination of these policy issues needs to be produced in order for a specific foundation formula to be enacted into law. Generally, equity must improve, the cost must be affordable, and there need to be more "winner" than "loser" districts. Accomplishing these goals simultaneously, however, can be difficult.

Setting the foundation level. There are no magic solutions to setting the foundation revenue level. Most commonly, at least before the adequacy era, states set a level that, combined with the amount raised locally by the required tax rate, equaled the amount of state appropriations available. This was a politically grounded but substantively vacuous approach since it was decided on an availability rather than a needs basis, but it was the norm. From 1950 to 2000, most states simply determined a particular spending level, deemed sufficiently high by the appropriate cross-section of political and education leaders, and sought to fund that spending level over time. To ensure that the level stayed "current" or increased with inflation, some states legislated mechanisms that automatically increased the foundation revenue per pupil each year. Inflating it by the increase in the consumer price index, or the deflator for state and local governmental services, was a common approach, even though most legislators are reluctant to build in automatic inflators to any program.

A second approach is to set a specific policy target, such as 50 or 100 percent of the statewide average expenditure. The policy target can even be to bring the foundation level up to the spending level in some district above the average. Whatever the level, this approach provides a clear policy target as to what the foundation base spending level will be. Odden and Clune (1998) recommend the use of such policy targets to give the school finance system a specific and clear equalization goal. Setting the foundation expenditure level at the median will eliminate all "savage" fiscal inequalities (Kozol, 1992) because it will raise the expenditures of all low-spending districts up to at least the median.

Determining an adequate foundation revenue level.   Today, the goal in identifying a foundation revenue level is to determine an "adequate" level (i.e., an amount of money per pupil sufficient to provide all students with an equal opportunity to achieve to some high proficiency standard). Odden and Clune (1998) and Verstegen (2002) argue that this is one of the most pressing, as well as complex, tasks for linking the school finance structure to the goals and strategies of standards-based education reform, as well as to the federal No Child Left Behind (NCLB) legislation.

Chapter 3 identified four methods that have been used to identify an adequate foundation level of expenditure: (1) the successful-district approach, (2) the professional-judgment approach, (3) the cost function approach, and (4) the evidence-based approach. Further research is needed for all of these methods, as the findings about the adequate revenue level vary both across as well as within states, depending on the method used (see, e.g., Augenblick and Myers, Inc., 2001a, 2001b; Odden, Picus, and Fermanich, 2003; Odden, Picus, et al., 2005; Picus, Odden, and Fermanich, 2004).

Chapter 4 shows how the "evidence-based" approach can be used to identify the programs and strategies that could be considered adequate and that, consistent with the nature and level of resources, enable schools to double student academic achievement. Chapter 11's discussion of Wisconsin shows how those recommendations can be used to set an "adequate" expenditure level for a state. But in this era of standards-based education reform, bolstered by the federal NCLB law, both of which seek to have the vast bulk of students learn to high standards, the foundation revenue level takes on heightened significance. It must be set at an "adequate" level in order for an education system to be adequately funded (see odden, et al., 2007).

We should note that in our work on adequacy around the country, our evidence-based model has produced an adequate revenue per pupil level in the $7,000–9,000 per-pupil range, depending on the teacher salary level and components included in the model, plus the additional resources for struggling students – tutors, extended day, summer school, and fully funded programs for students with disabilities.

Finally, when running simulations, a rationale needs to be provided for any specified adequate revenue level, or the results for the Odden-Picus Adequacy Index should be ignored. The figure that might be in the simulation when it is initially downloaded does not necessarily have any substantive rationale; it might simply be the figure used by the individual who last used the simulation program. A figure derived from an explicit adequacy study gives a much stronger meaning to the Adequacy Index.

Setting the foundation tax rate.   After the foundation expenditure level is determined, setting the required tax rate raises another set of interrelated issues. First, if the required tax rate is above the tax rate in any poor school district, it will require that district to raise its tax rate. That often is a politically difficult requirement to enact. Second, and related, the level of the required tax rate determines the state cost of the program: the higher the required local effort, the less the state cost (but the greater the local cost).

Third, the foundation expenditure level and required tax rate are connected in a way that determines which districts are eligible for at least some aid and which districts receive zero (or even negative) aid. The zero-aid district is defined as:

$$SAPP = FRPP - (RTR \times PVPP) = 0$$

Solving this equation for PVPP identifies the property value per pupil below which districts will receive some foundation aid and above which they will not. The solution becomes:

$$FRPP = RTR \times PVPP$$

or, transposing and dividing by RTR:

$$PVPP(\text{zero-aid district}) = FRPP/RTR$$

where

$$FRPP = \text{foundation revenue per pupil level}$$

$$RTR = \text{required tax rate}$$

$$PVPP = \text{property value of zero-aid district in thousands}$$
$$\text{of dollars of assessed valuation}$$

Thus, if the foundation level is $3,000, and the required tax rate is 30 mills, the zero-aid district has a property value per pupil of $100,000 (100,000 = 3,000/0.03).

The zero-aid district is an important policy variable to consider. Districts with property value above this level will not be eligible for any state aid (or at best be "held harmless" with their previous level of state aid), and their legislative representatives might vote against the proposal if self-interest is the only motivating variable. Another policy aspect of the zero-aid district is that it identifies a level up to which the state provides some fiscal-capacity equalization. The policy issue is the level to which the state wants to equalize fiscal capacity: to the statewide average, or the 75th percentile, or the 90th percentile, or the property value per pupil of the wealthiest district, or any other level it chooses.

In other words, setting the foundation expenditure level and the required tax rate simultaneously determines the level of education program that becomes the base, the state and local cost, the zero-aid district, the level up to which the state seeks to equalize fiscal capacity, and the numbers of state aid gainers and losers. In

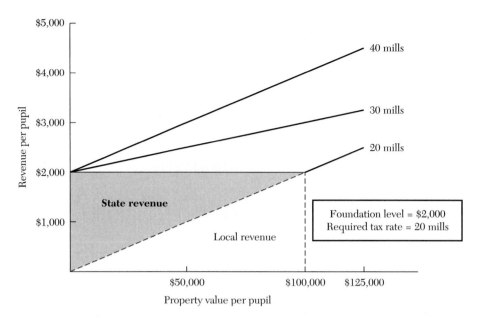

FIGURE 9.7 Graphical Representation of the Effect of a Foundation Program

short, it determines several key aspects of the political economy of the foundation program itself.

All of these characteristics of a foundation program are depicted in Figure 9.7 for a foundation program with a revenue per pupil of $2,000 and a required tax rate of 20 mills. For the first 20 mills, all districts with a property wealth less than $100,000 (the zero-aid district) receive a total of $2,000 per child; districts with a property value per pupil above $100,000 raise more than the foundation level, as the slope of the 20-mill line shows. If districts decide to levy a tax rate above the required rate, as most districts do, the additional funds are raised solely from the local property tax base. So, at 30 mills, the district with a property wealth per pupil of $50,000 would produce $2,000 per pupil for the first 20 mills but only $500 per pupil for the next 10 mills, or $2,500 per pupil in total. In contrast, the district with a property wealth per pupil of $100,000 also would produce $2,000 per pupil for the first 20 mills and another $1,000 for the next 10 mills, or $3,000 per pupil in total.

Fiscal equity impacts of foundation programs.   Setting these parameters determines how the new foundation program will impact the fiscal equity of the finance structure. Figure 9.8 shows several figures for a foundation program with the foundation revenue level set at $5,154, the median level for the base sample, and a required

Adequacy Level	$5,350.00
Pupil Weights	No
Disabled	—
Limited English	—
Low income	—

Foundation Level	$5,154.00
Required Tax Rate	31.32

District	Pupils	Property Value per Pupil ($)	Old Property Tax Rate (Mills)	New Property Tax Rate (Mills)	Change in Property Tax Rate (Mills)	Old Local Revenue per Pupil ($)	New Local Revenue per Pupil ($)	Change in Local Revenue per Pupil ($)	New State Revenue per Pupil ($)	Change in State Revenue per Pupil ($)	Total Revenue per Pupil ($)	Change in Total Revenue per Pupil ($)
1	1,290	17,456	39.64	35.48	(4.16)	692	619	(73)	4,607	1,819	5,227	1,747
2	5,648	25,879	38.50	34.91	(3.59)	996	903	(93)	4,343	1,720	5,247	1,627
3	1,678	31,569	37.15	34.23	(2.91)	1,173	1,081	(92)	4,165	1,630	5,246	1,538
4	256	35,698	36.20	33.76	(2.44)	1,292	1,205	(87)	4,036	1,576	5,241	1,489
5	10,256	40,258	35.91	33.62	(2.30)	1,446	1,353	(92)	3,893	1,492	5,246	1,400
6	956	43,621	35.74	33.53	(2.21)	1,559	1,463	(96)	3,788	1,395	5,250	1,298
7	4,689	49,875	34.89	33.11	(1.79)	1,740	1,651	(89)	3,592	1,233	5,243	1,144
8	1,656	55,556	34.17	32.75	(1.43)	1,898	1,819	(79)	3,414	1,141	5,233	1,062
9	8,954	61,254	33.73	32.53	(1.21)	2,066	1,992	(74)	3,236	1,017	5,228	944
10	1,488	70,569	33.44	32.38	(1.06)	2,360	2,285	(75)	2,944	853	5,229	778
11	2,416	78,952	33.23	32.28	(0.95)	2,624	2,548	(75)	2,681	601	5,229	525
12	5,891	86,321	32.89	32.11	(0.78)	2,839	2,771	(68)	2,450	419	5,222	352
13	2,600	94,387	32.10	31.71	(0.39)	3,030	2,993	(37)	2,198	228	5,191	192
14	15,489	102,687	31.32	31.32	0	3,216	3,216	0	1,938	0	5,154	0
15	2,308	112,358	30.85	33.28	2.43	3,466	3,739	273	1,635	(273)	5,374	0
16	2,712	125,897	30.50	34.57	4.07	3,840	4,353	513	1,211	(513)	5,564	0
17	30,256	136,527	30.05	34.80	4.76	4,102	4,752	650	878	(650)	5,630	0
18	2,056	156,325	28.63	36.09	7.46	4,476	5,641	1,166	258	(1,166)	5,899	0
19	3,121	198,564	27.42	33.11	5.69	5,445	6,575	1,130	0	(1,130)	6,575	0
20	1,523	278,052	25.50	27.07	1.57	7,090	7,527	437	0	(437)	7,527	0
Weighted average		97,831	32.34	33.37	1.03	3,028	3,261	232	2,173	248	5,434	481
Weighted std. dev.		48,514	2.91	1.56	3.17	1,269	1,598	382	1,318	907	384	610
Median		102,687	31.32	31.32	0	3,216	3,216	0	1,938	0	5,246	0

Totals

Category	Amount	Percent	Change from Base Amount
Local revenue	343,155,687	60.01	24,428,479
State revenue	228,688,560	39.99	26,148,394
Total revenue	571,844,247		50,576,873
Pupils	105,243		

Winners and Losers

Category	Winners	Losers	No Change
State aid	14	6	0
Total revenue	14	0	6

Equity Measures

Horizontal Equity	
Range	$2,373
Restricted range	$1,384
Federal range ratio	0.267
Coef. of variation	0.071
Gini coefficient	0.030
McLoone Index	0.992
Verstegen Index	1.070
Fiscal Neutrality	
Correlation	0.900
Elasticity	0.146
Adequacy	
Odden-Picus	0.985

FIGURE 9.8 Foundation Program

tax effort of 31.32 mills, also the median.[13] This means that the zero-aid district has a property value per pupil of $164,559, which is between districts 18 and 19 in the sample.

This also means that this program will provide fiscal-capacity equalization for districts that enroll 95.6 percent of the students (which is the cumulative enrollment of districts 1–18). The program increases state aid by 9.7 percent—$50.6 million. It also positively impacts fiscal equity, reducing the coefficient of variation from 17 percent for the base sample to 7.1 percent; reduces the wealth elasticity from 0.324 to 0.146; and raises the Adequacy Index from 0.895 to 0.985. It raises revenue above the foundation level in the poorest and lowest-spending 13 districts. This impact can be seen by using the simulation to view the graph of the results; the left-hand portion of the graph from Figure 9.2 (the base data) has been rotated up (clockwise) at about the wealth of the zero-aid district to form a horizontal line at the foundation revenue level of $5,154. But this foundation program also reduces aid to six districts; even districts 15–18, which receive some foundation aid, have a net loss of aid from their base context.

A foundation program with the revenue level set at $4,000 and the required tax rate at 39 mills, which thus provides for fiscal-capacity equalization up to just $102,500, the statewide average property value per pupil, produces a net drop in state aid and also a reduction in state aid for 15 of the 20 districts. (Use the simulation to assess the broader impacts of this set of parameters.) On the other hand, a foundation revenue level of $5,154 with a required tax rate of 25 mills, which provides for fiscal-capacity equalization up to $206,160, provides at least some state general aid for 19 of the 20 districts and further enhances fiscal equity (the coefficient of variation drops to 5.8 percent, the wealth elasticity declines to 0.131, and the Adequacy Index becomes 1), but the state cost rises by $64 million. (Again, use the simulation to assess the broader impacts of this set of parameters.)

These results indicate that the foundation revenue level, required tax effort, level of fiscal-capacity equalization, state costs, numbers of winners and losers, and school finance fiscal equity and adequacy are all interrelated. These interrelations suggest why getting legislatures to enact a complicated school finance reform is not an easy task; several variables—educational, political, and fiscal—need to be balanced simultaneously.

As found in some research (Odden and Busch, 1998), a school finance system that required all districts to spend at least at the median of state spending per pupil reflects a strategy that might begin to move the system toward adequacy (see also Rubenstein, 2002). Granted, research in every state would be needed to determine more explicitly what an adequate spending level might be. But ensuring that districts spent at least as much as the median would be a way for states to move immediately forward on the adequacy school finance agenda. Odden (1998) has shown the results of such a

---

[13]For the foundation, guaranteed tax base, and combination simulations, state aid has been set equal to zero if the calculation produces a negative figure, but districts are not held harmless (i.e., they lose state aid if the calculation produces a zero-aid figure). Further, a local tax response has been built into the simulation under which districts increase their local property tax rate to cover the lost aid. For these districts, the last column of the results shows no total revenue loss, but this is a result of a loss of state aid and an equal increase in local revenues. There is also a response model for districts that have state aid increases. These districts use half the state aid increase to raise spending, and half to reduce local property tax rates. For the foundation part of the program, though, spending and tax rates cannot be reduced below the required tax rate.

school finance system for the three states with the "new" school finance problem discussed in Chapter 1: Illinois, Missouri, and Wisconsin. He simulated a foundation program set at the median spending level in each state. Not only did such a program represent progress in providing an adequate level of funding, but the programs produced substantial improvements in fiscal equity. In all three states, both the statistical measures of spending disparities (coefficient of variation and McLoone Index) and the statistical measures of the linkage between spending and wealth (correlation and wealth elasticity) improved, as did the Adequacy Index. To work over time, the spending level would need to be inflation-adjusted each year to continue to provide an adequate spending base.

A final word. In summary, foundation programs have several attractive features. They began as programs designed to provide a minimum quality-education program but, today, can be used to guarantee a higher-quality program, perhaps one sufficient to meet the needs of an adequacy-based education system, one in which students learn to high performance standards. They are unique in having this base program guarantee as a critical variable. Second, they are funded by a combination of state and local funds that link states and school districts inextricably in a fiscal-federalism partnership for funding public schools. Third, they are fiscal-capacity equalizing (i.e., they provide state aid in an inverse relationship to local property value per pupil), and thus also address the key structural problem of school finance—the disparity in the local property tax base. Their key defect may be that they allow local spending above the foundation program, and if the base program is low, these local fiscal add-ons—financed entirely with local property tax revenues—increase the linkages between property wealth and education spending, the major weakness of previous school aid formulas and an issue targeted in school finance litigation.

On the other hand, it could be argued that if the state actually determined and fully funded an adequate foundation base, together with appropriate adjustments for special student, district, and school needs, then the state's interest in education and its funding contribution would have been fulfilled. Such a position would allow districts to spend more if they wished, but only by using local money. Although this position could be criticized, a state could defend it as well, assuming it truly had determined and funded an adequate spending base.

Guaranteed Tax Base Programs

Guaranteed tax base (GTB) programs are a late-twentieth-century phenomena in school finance structures. The first GTB programs were enacted in the early 1970s after the initial rounds of school finance litigation. The late arrival of GTB programs is perplexing because, as the name suggests, this type of school finance program addresses the primary structural flaw in traditional approaches to local financing of public schools, namely, the unequal distribution of the local property tax base. A GTB program simply erases this inequality by guaranteeing, through state aid allocations, that each local district can function as if it had an equal property tax base per pupil. The details of how this program works will be described here. Conceptually, it is simple, and in terms of school finance policy, it addresses a basic inequity in school finance: unequal access to a local property tax base.

This simple and straightforward program took a somewhat complicated course in evolving to its current state. The early forms of GTB programs, first introduced in the 1920s, were actually called *percentage-equalizing programs*. They were proposed for two major reasons. First, foundation program levels remained low, and most districts enacted local add-ons that were financed entirely from their local property tax base. Local add-ons came to dominate the level of total revenues, and there was a search for a school finance mechanism that went beyond foundation programs and provided state fiscal-capacity-equalizing aid for the overall spending levels in local school districts.

Second, because the state fiscal role remained small as the level of the minimum foundation programs remained low, policy pressure grew to increase the state role in the financing of education. Over time, in fact, many states sought to increase their role to some fixed target, at least 50 percent. Since most state aid was distributed in a fiscal-capacity-equalizing manner, the assumption was that the fiscal equity of the school finance system would improve as the state role approached, or even surpassed, 50 percent.

The percentage-equalizing formula was designed to address both of these policy concerns. First, the state share (in percentage terms) of total costs was directly included in the formula. The formula provided for a larger state role in low-property-wealth districts and a smaller state role in higher-property-wealth districts, thus lending a fiscal-capacity-equalizing thrust to the program. The formula calculated a state-aid ratio for each district. The ratio was higher in property-poor districts and lower in property-wealthy districts. The state role policy target—say, 50 percent of total dollars spent on education—was usually set for the district with a statewide average property value per pupil.[14]

To determine state aid, the state aid ratio was applied to the district spending level, which was a local policy decision of each district. The aid ratio multiplied by the spending level produced the amount of state aid per pupil for each district. State aid, therefore, varied with both the level of wealth and the level of locally determined spending. During 1986–87, five states had percentage-equalizing programs, a number that went down to four in 1993–94 (Gold, Smith, and Lawton, 1995); the number is also small today. The percentage-equalizing formula is more complicated than but algebraically

---

[14]State aid per pupil for a percentage-equalizing program is equal to:

$$SAPP = [1 - LR(PVPPd/PVPPk)]TREVPP$$

where

$$SAPP = \text{state aid per pupil}$$
$$LR = \text{local role in percent terms [the state role is } (1 - LR)]$$
$$PVPPd = \text{property value per pupil for each district}$$
$$PVPPk = \text{property wealth per pupil in comparative district, usually} \\ \text{but not necessarily the statewide average}$$
$$TREVPP = \text{total (state and local) revenue per pupil}$$

The zero-aid district is PVPPk/LR. The aid ratio is $1 - LR(PVPPd/PVPPk)$.

equivalent to a GTB program. Thus, the percentage-equalizing-approach was dropped and replaced by its simpler GTB incarnation.

As previously stated, GTB programs were enacted beginning in the early 1970s, at the time of the first successful school finance court cases. These court cases had directly challenged the relationship between expenditures and wealth caused by the unequal distribution of the local tax base per pupil. The book that developed the "fiscal neutrality" legal theory for these cases (Coons, Clune, and Sugarman, 1970) also discussed the design and operation of a new district power-equalizing school finance structure. Power equalizing was a system that would equalize the power of local districts to raise funds through the property tax. The mechanism was for the state to guarantee a tax base that all districts would use in deciding upon school tax rate and expenditure levels. Subsequently, these approaches became known as guaranteed tax base programs. GTB programs are also called *guaranteed yield* or *resource-equalizing programs* in some states.

The GTB formula. The formula for calculating state aid for a guaranteed tax base program is:

$$SAPP = DTR \times (GTB - PVPP)$$

where

$$SAPP = \text{state aid per pupil}$$

$$DTR = \text{local district property tax rate}$$

$$GTB = \text{tax base guaranteed by the state, in thousands}$$
$$\text{of dollars of property value per pupil}$$

$$PVPP = \text{local district property value per pupil}$$

Total GTB state aid, therefore, is:

$$TSA = SAPP \times \text{Pupils}$$

where

$$TSA = \text{total state aid}$$

$$SAPP = \text{state aid per pupil from the GTB formula}$$

$$\text{Pupils} = \text{number of students in school district}$$

Several interesting features of the GTB state aid formula should be mentioned. First, the amount of per-pupil state aid a district receives varies with the size of the local tax base; the greater the local tax base (PVPP), the smaller the factor (GTB − PVPP), and thus the smaller the amount of per-pupil state aid. In other words, as with the foundation program, state aid varies inversely with property wealth per child.

Second, total revenue per pupil is equal to the tax rate times the GTB. This can be shown algebraically:

$$\text{Local Revenue} = \text{DTR} \times \text{PVPP}$$

$$\text{State Aid} = \text{DTR}(\text{GTB} - \text{PVPP})$$

$$\text{Total Revenues} = \text{Local Revenue} + \text{State Aid}$$

$$= (\text{DTR} \times \text{PVPP}) + (\text{DTR}(\text{GTB} - \text{PVPP}))$$

Combining terms on the right-hand side and factoring out DTR:

$$\text{Total Revenues} = \text{DTR}(\text{PVPP} + \text{GTB} - \text{PVPP})$$

$$= \text{DTR} \times \text{GTB}$$

In other words, the GTB operates exactly as it is designed to.[15] Districts can function as if they have the GTB as their local tax base. Once they determine their desired spending level, they divide it by the GTB to determine the local tax rate they must levy. Or, conversely, by multiplying their local property tax rate by the GTB, they identify their per-pupil spending level. As a corollary, by multiplying their local property tax rate by the local property tax base, they also identify the amount of local revenues they must raise.

A final feature is that state aid is a function of the local school tax rate; the higher the tax rate, the greater the state aid. This feature has two implications. First, if local districts increase their property tax rate, they not only raise more funds locally but also become eligible for more state aid. This can be an attractive component in a campaign to increase the local school property tax rate. Second, and related, the total amount of revenues the state needs to appropriate is, in part, determined by local action. Put differently, the state is not in complete control of the level of revenues needed to finance the general-aid school finance formula; if districts increase local tax rates more than anticipated, additional state funds are needed to fully fund the GTB formula.

This feature has been troublesome when the GTB formula has been considered by many legislatures, which themselves want to be in complete control of the level of funding needed for the general-aid program. Many states reject the GTB because of this feature. But, over time, local tax rates usually settle into fairly predictable patterns, and states can fairly easily predict the level of appropriation needed to fund the formula. Michigan, for example, had a GTB program for over a decade in the 1970s and 1980s and had no more difficulty predicting the level of appropriations needed than did other states that used different school aid distribution mechanisms. Many other factors complicate estimation of state aid, including, for example, enrollment projections, property valuations, and estimates of state tax revenues. Many factors beyond the design of the

---

[15]Strictly speaking, this holds for all districts only if the state has a total recapture plan. In the absence of such recapture, this applies only to districts with property wealth at or below the GTB level.

general-aid formula itself make state aid predictions an imperfect art. States also can specify an appropriation but state that the Department of Education can alter the GTB if the appropriation is not at the level needed to fully fund the system after districts decide on their spending levels.

GTB policy issues. GTB programs have several attractive features as an intergovernmental-grant mechanism. First, a GTB requires a local match, which is equal to the district tax rate times its property value per pupil. Indeed, while GTB aid increases as the local tax rate increases, thus requiring more state funds, the local tax rate applied to the local tax base increases local revenues as well. In other words, more GTB aid does not come without a local cost; it also requires an increase in local revenues. Indeed, the local-match feature of the GTB formula structure helps keep both local tax rates and state aid at acceptable levels over time.

Second, the GTB program equalizes fiscal capacity. As local property wealth decreases, GTB aid as a percentage of local expenditure increases, and vice versa. This is generally a desired feature for school finance formulas. But the GTB program goes further by directly addressing the disparity in the local property tax base per child. The GTB program simply makes the GTB tax base equal for all districts—at least those districts with a property value per pupil less than the GTB. If the primary school finance problem is the unequal distribution of the property tax base, the GTB program is precisely the school finance structure that remedies the problem.

In terms of values, the GTB program reflects the American values of choice, local control, and equal education opportunity as defined by equal access to a tax base. For districts with a property value per pupil less than the GTB, it provides for equal dollars per pupil from state and local sources for equal school tax rates. A pure GTB program, moreover, implements the value of local control since it allows local districts to decide on the level of tax rate they want to levy for schools, and thus the level of per-pupil school spending. If localities want a higher-quality program, they are free to enact a higher school tax rate. The GTB ensures that all districts levying that tax rate will have the same spending per pupil from the general fund, and thus provides ex ante equity. If districts want a program that is funded at a level comparable to the average, they need only levy the average school tax rate.

Because a GTB program allows different local decisions on per-pupil spending levels, equality of spending is not its focus. Indeed, without a requirement for a minimum school tax rate, GTB programs do not even require a minimum education expenditure level per pupil. Still, in most situations in which GTB programs have been enacted, they increase expenditures in all but the lowest-tax-rate school districts. However, it should be emphasized that a GTB program is incompatible with the horizontal-equity principal for students because it does not require equal spending per child. Instead, it is a funding approach that offers better fiscal neutrality.

We should also note that GTB programs, because they reduce the local cost of buying education services, are also a stimulus for districts to "buy" more education than they would without the GTB. Indeed, Wisconsin discovered this fact over a 20-year period from about 1975 to 1995. Its GTB program had been seen as a property tax relief

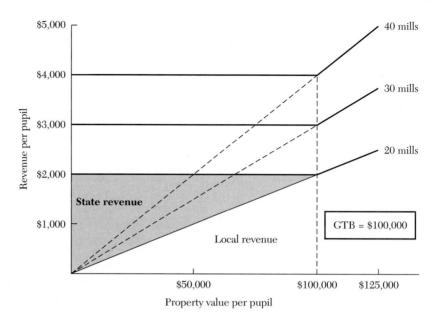

FIGURE 9.9   Graphical Representation of the Effect of a Guaranteed Tax Base Program

mechanism, which it was in the initial years. But then districts decided to buy more education, thus raising both local property taxes and the need for state revenues. In response, the state would hike the GTB level, which then, by lowering the price of education, encouraged districts to buy even more education, thereby both boosting local property taxes and increasing the need for state aid. Finally, by the mid-1990s, the legislature figured out this "stimulus" aspect of the system and placed revenue increase limits on local school districts.

Figure 9.9 depicts some of these characteristics of a GTB program, for a GTB set at $100,000. The graph shows that for districts with a property value per pupil below the GTB, revenues differ according to the tax rate, but that all districts have the same revenues per pupil (from state and local sources) if they levy the same tax rate. As the 20-mill line shows, the higher a district's property wealth per pupil, the greater the share of total revenue provided from local sources. If the tax rate is raised to 30 mills, all districts get $3,000 per pupil, and the proportion of state aid is inversely related to the district's property wealth. The graph also shows that districts above the GTB raise higher revenues per pupil at any given tax rate but receive no state aid.

In implementing a GTB program, there is one primary policy issue to resolve: the tax base level that the state wants to guarantee. While there are no absolute standards by which to assess this policy issue, there are several benchmarks. The state could seek to guarantee the tax base up to the 50th percentile of students, the statewide average, or a higher percentile, such as the 75th, 90th, or even higher. A GTB program in response to a typical fiscal-neutrality court case would need to hit at least the 75th percentile, and probably the 90th percentile or higher. The legal question would be: What constitutes substantive equal access to raising education dollars? The answer would be: at least the 75th percentile, and probably higher, but how much higher varies by state and court. Rather than just identifying a value for the GTB, Odden and Clune (1998) argue for selecting a specific target that provides a clear equalization goal, such as the wealth at some high level (e.g., the 90th percentile).

There are two secondary policy issues. One is whether a minimum tax rate is required. A minimum tax rate translates into a minimum revenue per pupil (which equals the minimum tax rate times the GTB). Requiring a minimum would mean a smoother transition from a minimum foundation program, for which the state policy goal includes a minimum base program, to a GTB program that in its pure form does not have a minimum expenditure requirement. Odden and Busch (1995) have shown that such a minimum tax rate would have eliminated all the very-low-spending-per-pupil districts in Wisconsin, which simultaneously would have provided all districts with sufficient dollars to fund the expensive, comprehensive, Modern Red Schoolhouse school design (Odden, Archibald, and Tychsen, 1998; Odden and Busch, 1998).

A minimum tax rate for a GTB program could also be set so that that tax rate times the GTB produces an adequate revenue level, thus giving the GTB an adequacy orientation as well. Of course, if the GTB produced an adequate revenue level at the minimum tax rate, the question could be raised as to why the state would support revenues above that level.

A second issue is whether to cap GTB aid at some tax rate, or whether to cap local school tax rates at some level. Under the first type of cap, GTB aid would be available only up to a set tax rate. As tax rates rose above the set level, the state would no longer participate, leaving the districts with only local funds from the extra tax effort. This would give the GTB an unequalized local add-on element, as exists for all foundation programs, but it would help to ameliorate the fiscal-stimulus aspect of an unfettered GTB. Over time, a tax rate cap could turn the GTB program into a structure in which non-fiscal-capacity-equalized add-ons dominate the structure and produce a system, as exists in many states, in which revenues per pupil are strongly related to the level of local property value per child.

The second type of cap is an absolute cap on the local tax rate. Not only would GTB aid not be available above this tax rate, but districts would not be allowed to levy a tax rate above the cap. This tax rate cap would have the effect of a revenue cap, since the maximum revenue would be the tax rate cap times the GTB. This type of cap certainly puts a major constraint on local control, but it also limits the variation in expenditures per pupil that would be allowed by a GTB program. The Kentucky school finance reform enacted in 1990 adopted both of these options (see the discussion on page 303 about the combination foundation–GTB program; see also Picus, Odden, and Fermanich, 2004).

Fiscal equity impacts of GTB programs. Figure 9.10 displays the simulation results for a GTB program in which the GTB is set at $138,000, which is about the 94th percentile for the sample of districts. Interestingly, this level of GTB would require a decrease in state aid and would leave the state role at a mere 29 percent ($155.8 million divided by $538.7 million).

Adequacy Level	$5,350.00		Guaranteed Tax Base	$138,000.00
Pupil Weights	No			
Disabled	—			
Limited English	—			
Low income	—			

District	Pupils	Property Value per Pupil ($)	Old Property Tax Rate (Mills)	New Property Tax Rate (Mills)	Change in Property Tax Rate (Mills)	Old Local Revenue per Pupil ($)	New Local Revenue per Pupil ($)	Change in Local Revenue per Pupil ($)	New State Revenue per Pupil ($)	Change in State Revenue per Pupil ($)	Total Revenue per Pupil ($)	Change in Total Revenue per Pupil ($)
1	1,290	17,456	39.64	32.43	(7.21)	692	566	(126)	3,909	1,121	4,475	995
2	5,648	25,879	38.50	32.37	(6.13)	996	838	(159)	3,629	1,005	4,466	847
3	1,678	31,569	37.15	32.01	(5.14)	1,173	1,010	(162)	3,407	871	4,417	709
4	256	35,698	36.20	31.69	(4.51)	1,292	1,131	(161)	3,242	783	4,374	622
5	10,256	40,258	35.91	31.89	(4.02)	1,446	1,284	(162)	3,117	716	4,401	554
6	956	43,621	35.74	32.19	(3.55)	1,559	1,404	(155)	3,038	645	4,442	490
7	4,689	49,875	34.89	32.29	(2.60)	1,740	1,611	(129)	2,846	488	4,457	358
8	1,656	55,556	34.17	32.20	(1.97)	1,898	1,789	(110)	2,655	382	4,443	272
9	8,954	61,254	33.73	32.39	(1.34)	2,066	1,984	(82)	2,486	267	4,470	185
10	1,488	70,569	33.44	32.84	(0.59)	2,360	2,318	(42)	2,215	124	4,532	82
11	2,416	78,952	33.23	34.09	0.86	2,624	2,691	68	2,013	(68)	4,704	0
12	5,891	86,321	32.89	35.29	2.40	2,839	3,046	207	1,824	(207)	4,870	0
13	2,600	94,387	32.10	36.23	4.13	3,030	3,419	390	1,580	(390)	4,999	0
14	15,489	102,687	31.32	37.34	6.02	3,216	3,835	619	1,319	(619)	5,154	0
15	2,308	112,358	30.85	38.94	8.09	3,466	4,375	909	999	(909)	5,374	0
16	2,712	125,897	30.50	40.32	9.82	3,840	5,076	1,236	488	(1,236)	5,564	0
17	30,256	136,527	30.05	40.79	10.75	4,102	5,570	1,467	60	(1,467)	5,630	0
18	2,056	156,325	28.63	37.74	9.11	4,476	5,899	1,424	0	(1,424)	5,899	0
19	3,121	198,564	27.42	33.11	5.69	5,445	6,575	1,130	0	(1,130)	6,575	0
20	1,523	278,052	25.50	27.07	1.57	7,090	7,527	437	0	(437)	7,527	0
Weighted average		97,831	32.34	36.17	3.83	3,028	3,638	610	1,481	(444)	5,119	166
Weighted std. dev.		48,514	2.91	3.76	6.04	1,269	1,871	674	1,279	882	638	272
Median		102,687	31.32	37.34	6.02	3,216	3,835	619	1,319	(619)	5,154	0

Totals

Category	Amount	Percent	Change from Base Amount
Local revenue	382,907,400	71.07	64,180,192
State revenue	155,839,458	28.93	(46,700,708)
Total revenue	538,746,858		17,479,484
Pupils	105,243		

Winners and Losers

Category	Winners	Losers	No Change
State aid	10	10	0
Total revenue	10	0	10

Equity Measures

Horizontal Equity	
Range	$3,153
Restricted range	$2,173
Federal range ratio	0.494
Coef. of variation	0.125
Gini coefficient	0.066
McLoone Index	0.866
Verstegen Index	1.086
Fiscal Neutrality	
Correlation	0.984
Elasticity	0.246
Adequacy	
Odden-Picus	0.926

FIGURE 9.10 Guaranteed Tax Base (GTB)

This level of GTB has positive impacts on fiscal equity and adequacy. It reduces revenue-per-pupil disparities. In terms of horizontal equity for students, the coefficient of variation drops to 12.5 percent, and the McLoone Index increases to 0.866. It also increases the Adequacy Index to 92.6.

In terms of fiscal neutrality, it reduces the correlation between total revenues per pupil and property value per pupil, but more importantly, it reduces the wealth elasticity to 0.246. The latter is to be expected since the GTB provides equal access to a tax base for districts with 94 percent of all students. This simulation shows the impact that a GTB at the 90th or so percentile can have on the equity of the school finance structure. (Use the simulation to view the graph of the GTB results.)

Although the GTB is focused on providing equal tax bases and not equal spending, it is nevertheless effective in helping to reduce overall revenue-per-pupil disparities, as the horizontal-equity statistics indicate. This impact on spending gaps occurs because the GTB raises the effective tax base in low-wealth districts that in the sample have above-average tax rates. Therefore, when a GTB program is implemented, these districts qualify for substantial new amounts of state aid—due both to their low wealth and high tax rates—which enables them to both increase their school spending (thus reducing expenditure-per-pupil disparities) and reduce their tax rates to more average levels. In short, while a GTB allows for differences in spending based on tax effort, when implemented in many states, it also reduces overall revenue-per-pupil disparities.

The data in Figure 9.10 reveal several other aspects of this GTB, as well as of the sample districts before application of the GTB. First, though the GTB covers 94 percent of the students, it increases aid for only 10 of the 20 districts (i.e., districts 1–10).[16] In the real world, a school finance program that at best would provide hold harmless aid for 50 percent of all districts would encounter serious political hurdles.

Put another way, even though 7 of the 10 districts are eligible for some state aid, only 10 districts would be eligible for greater amounts of state aid. Put differently, 7 of the districts eligible for at least some GTB aid would receive less state aid than under the old structure used by the sample state. Thus, fully half the districts would lose some or all of their state aid.

These realities would reduce the political chances of having such a program legislatively enacted. Though the old school finance program arguably allocated too much aid to districts high in property wealth per pupil, and a GTB at the 94th percentile would seemingly be good enough on an ex ante basis, these actual results suggest that the politics of enactment in the sample state would be difficult.

These potential effects of a relatively high GTB are not dissimilar to the actual impact of such GTBs in many states today. The reason is that most states allocate some general state aid in sufficiently large amounts to even the wealthiest districts, so that a transition to a GTB—even at a reasonably high level—becomes problematic politically. Though a hold harmless provision would blunt the loss of state aid, such an overall program would mean that for most districts, their general state aid would not increase in

---

[16]Recall that the fiscal-response model built into the simulation increases the local property tax rate to a level at which local funds replace lost state funds for state aid "losers" and increases expenditures and reduces the tax rate each by half the amount of the state aid increase for state aid "winners."

the short to medium run, an unappealing scenario. These realities also mean that unless states that want to enact a GTB program do so soon, the transition problems of the level of state general aid provided to the highest-wealth districts could worsen over time, making it more complicated to implement a high-level GTB program.

These dilemmas for a GTB are portrayed more drastically for a GTB at $98,000, roughly the statewide average property value per pupil and just above the wealth of district 13, and the wealth of the district that includes 45 percent of the students. (Again, run this GTB on the simulation and review the results.) Under this program, 18 of the 20 districts will lose state aid, and state aid itself will drop by almost two-thirds. This level of GTB, which is higher than the GTB component of the general-aid formula in most states,[17] would not likely be politically feasible in the sample state.

A GTB of $160,000, on the other hand, which guarantees a per-pupil property value higher than in 18 of the 20 districts, and districts that enroll over 95 percent of the students, would push the state role to 39 percent, would lower the coefficient of variation to just 0.094 and the wealth elasticity to only 0.194, and would increase the Adequacy Index to 0.955. These are substantial impacts.

For such a high-level GTB, however, the simulation probably indicates a higher-expenditure-per-pupil level for the lower-wealth districts than might occur in practice. It would be unlikely for districts to increase local spending by nearly 50 percent, as the current simulation response model assumes. With a GTB at this high a level, such districts would probably use more than half their state aid increase to reduce property tax rates. Moreover, as discussed in Chapter 1, some low-wealth districts might use most of their state aid increases for property tax relief rather than expenditure increases. (Again, run this GTB using the simulation, and review the results, as well as the scatter plot. Indeed, you should run GTB programs in between $98,000 and $160,000 to find a level that reduces some of the political minuses of the former, but is less costly than the latter.)

A final word.   In summary, GTB school finance formulas are relatively simple finance structures that address a primary structural problem of local financing of schools: unequal access to a school tax base. The GTB remedies this defect by making the tax base equal to the GTB for all districts with a property value per pupil below the GTB. The primary policy issue for a GTB is the level at which to set the GTB; courts would likely require the GTB to provide "substantial" equal access to a school property tax base. This would equal the level of the district for which the cumulative percentage of students in that district (and all districts with lower property value per pupil) was at or close to the 90th percentile.

GTB programs reflect the values of choice and local control. Thus, GTB programs allow for differences in per-pupil spending. While spending differences are allowed, they are caused not by differences in property value per pupil but by differences in tax effort: the higher the tax effort, the higher the expenditure per pupil. For policymakers and educators who hold the horizontal-equity principle for students above local choice, the GTB is not the appropriate school finance program.

---

[17]Most state GTB programs guarantee the wealth of the district for which the cumulative percentage of students is at some level below the 66th percentile

Further, although GTB programs are fiscal capacity equalizing, the level of state aid is determined both by the GTB level (set by state policy) and by local property tax rates (set by local policy). Thus, the amount of state aid is not under the complete control of state policymakers. This feature has made several states skittish about enacting a GTB program, even though they may prefer it as the general-aid structure. States that have enacted GTB programs, however, have devised several phase-in mechanisms that allow them to control the level of state aid. These states have found that, over time, local tax rates settle into a predictable pattern that makes forecasting the level of state-aid appropriations no more difficult than for other types of formulas, all of which have variables that require both art and science for predicting and thus determining state aid needs.

Finally, although GTB programs are the most straightforward form of school aid formulas designed to equalize the tax base, they often do not accomplish their objective of eliminating the link between spending and wealth, especially for the "new" type of school finance program. Because of the vagaries of local behavior, moreover, they often lead to overall rising education expenditures (because they lower the local cost of spending on education). They also lead to the "new" school finance problem: high expenditures, high tax rates, and high property wealth per pupil versus low expenditures, low tax rates, and low property wealth per pupil.

It should be noted that many economists predicted these impacts (Feldstein, 1975; Ladd, 1975; and, more recently, Reschovsky, 1994). As discussed previously in the example of Wisconsin, GTB programs lower the local cost, or "price," of spending on education. Rather than just tapping the local tax base at a high tax rate to spend an extra $100 per pupil, the district can tap the GTB and increase that amount of spending at a much lower tax rate. When prices are lowered for desired commodities, such as education, people usually buy more of that commodity. So, economic theory would predict higher overall education spending with a high-level GTB program. In addition, research has shown that the demand elasticity for education was often low in low-property-wealth districts, which were also typically low in average household income, and high in higher-property-wealth, higher-household-income districts, such as metropolitan suburban districts. Thus, these economists predicted that lower-wealth districts would decide not to raise relative spending very much while the higher-wealth districts would decide just the opposite.

To verify these ostensibly deleterious elements of GTB programs, Odden (1998) simulated pure forms of GTB programs for the three "new" school finance problem states discussed in Chapter 1—Illinois, Missouri, and Wisconsin—by setting the GTB at the 95th percentile of property wealth per pupil and providing GTB aid for all levels of spending. All of the equity statistics worsened, spending disparities widened, and the relationship between spending and property wealth strengthened. More generous GTB programs were not what these states needed to improve fiscal equity. We discuss this issue further in Chapter 11.

Combination Foundation and Guaranteed Tax Base Programs

States have also enacted combination school finance formulas. These two-tier plans usually include two different school finance formulas in the overall approach to providing general-education aid through a fiscal capacity–equalizing program. One type of formula is used for the base, or first tier, and another type for spending above the base — the second tier.

Missouri has had a two-tiered, combination foundation-GTB program since the late 1970s. Like many states, Missouri had a minimum foundation program before it underwent school finance reform in 1977. The program, which was enacted in 1977 and then updated in 1993, retained the foundation program to ensure a base revenue level, a key feature of a foundation approach. The 1993 bill set the foundation revenue level at just below the previous year's statewide average expenditure per pupil. For the second tier, the legislature put a GTB program on top, so that districts wanting to spend above the foundation level could have equal extra revenue for equal higher tax rates. The 1993 bill set the GTB at the level of wealth of the district for which, after rank ordering all districts on the basis of property value per pupil, the cumulative percentage of students was 95 percent (i.e., the 95th percentile). The bill was technically written as a GTB at the 95th percentile, with a minimum tax rate that determined the foundation expenditure base (i.e., the GTB was also the "zero-aid" district for the foundation portion of the formula). GTB aid was provided for spending up to the 95th percentile of expenditures per pupil.

The combination approach was used for other new school finance formulas established in early 1990. Both Texas and Kentucky, under court order to revise their school finance structures, enacted combination foundation-GTB programs. In Texas, the 1989–90 foundation program provided a base spending level of $1,477, equal to about 42 percent of the statewide average expenditure per pupil. The GTB program was set at $182,500, the wealth of the district just below the statewide average of $191,300. Texas placed a tax rate cap on the GTB component of the formula, providing GTB aid for just an extra 3.6 mills above the foundation-required tax rate, or an extra $657 per pupil. Districts were also allowed to levy higher tax rates, for which revenues were derived solely from the local tax base up to a maximum.

Kentucky enacted a similar type of combination program (see Picus, Odden, and Fermanich, 2004). The 1989–90 foundation base was set at $2,305, which was about 77 percent of the statewide average. Kentucky also put a GTB on top of the foundation program, setting it at about 150 percent of the statewide average. This GTB program, however, included two tiers, each with its own type of tax rate cap. The first tier limited the additional tax rate beyond which districts could not receive GTB aid, but it gave school boards the flexibility to increase spending (and thus the local tax rate) by 15 percent over the foundation base and still receive GTB aid. In addition, by a local vote, taxpayers could increase spending (and thus the local tax rate) by another 30 percent of the total amount generated by the foundation level and the first tier, but would not be eligible for GTB aid for this second 30 percent spending boost. Thus, expenditures above the foundation base are limited to an additional 49.5 percent, one-third of which is fiscal-capacity-equalized by a GTB.

This combination approach merges the best features of the foundation and GTB programs, and simultaneously remedies a major defect of each. The foundation portion of the combined program first ensures a base spending level, usually above what had been a minimum level. This base spending level, a key feature of foundation programs, is financed with a combination of local and state funds. The spending base remedies a possible shortcoming of pure GTB programs that do not require a minimum spending level.

The GTB portion of the combined program ensures equal education spending per pupil for equal tax rates above the foundation-required tax rate. This component remedies a defect of a minimum foundation program: unequalized spending above the foundation base.

The combination foundation-GTB formula. The formula for calculating the *foundation* portion of the combination program is the same as that for the regular foundation program:

$$SFAPP = FRPP - (RTR \times PVPP)$$

where

$$SFAPP = \text{state foundation aid per pupil}$$

$$FRPP = \text{foundation expenditure revenue per pupil}$$

$$RTR = \text{local required tax rate}$$

$$PVPP = \text{local property value per pupil}$$

Total foundation state aid, therefore, would be:

$$TFSA = SFAPP \times \text{Pupils}$$

where

$$TFSA = \text{total foundation state aid}$$

$$SFAPP = \text{state foundation aid per pupil}$$

$$\text{Pupils} = \text{the number of students in the school district.}$$

For the *GTB* portion, state aid would be:

$$SGTBAPP = (DTR - RTR)(GTB - PVPP)$$

where

$$SGTBAPP = \text{state-guaranteed tax base aid per pupil}$$

$$DTR = \text{local district property tax rate}$$

$$RTR = \text{required tax base for foundation program}[18]$$

---

[18]GTB aid is provided only for tax rates above the foundation-required tax rate.

GTB = tax base guaranteed by state, in thousand dollars of property value per pupil

PVPP = local district property value per pupil

Total GTB state aid, therefore, would be:

$$\text{TGTBSA} = \text{SGTBAPP} \times \text{Pupils}$$

where

TGTBSA = total guaranteed tax base state aid

SGTBAPP = state-guaranteed tax base aid per pupil from above formula

Pupils = number of students in school district

Total state general aid for the combination program, therefore, would be:

$$\text{TSA} = \text{TFSA} + \text{TGTBSA}$$

Combination foundation-GTB program policy issues. A combination foundation-GTB program can be a fairly attractive package. Both components of the program require local matching funds and provide for fiscal capacity equalization. A base spending level is guaranteed. The ability to spend above the base is possible on an equal basis for rich and poor districts alike, thus providing a fiscally neutral system, at least on an ex ante basis. And two American values—concern for the bottom half and local choice—are tied together in a single general aid program.

The downside of the GTB portion of the combination program is that it allows for different spending levels, and thus does not conform to the horizontal-equity principle for students. But the fact is that this value conflicts with the value of local choice; both values cannot be satisfied by any one formula. The combination foundation-GTB program is about the closest a school finance formula can come to adhering to both of these values. There is an expenditure equality dimension, in terms of a base program that is mandated for all students. But there is local choice to spend above this base. If a state enacted a cap on the level of extra revenues, such as the 30 percent cap in Kentucky, the program might be more appealing to those who champion horizontal equity for children.

At the same time, as just discussed, the second-tier GTB has turned out to function as an incentive to spend more, and primarily by above-average-wealth, suburban districts. As a result, the two-tier system, just like an unbridled GTB program, creates a system that generally leads to the "new" school finance problem: low-spending, low-tax-rate, and low-wealth districts versus high-spending, high-tax-rate, and high- (or above-average) wealth districts, which some would not consider to be a fair system.

Figure 9.11 depicts how a combination foundation–GTB program works. The lowest horizontal line shows that the minimum revenues per pupil are the foundation expenditure level of $2,000. The upper two horizontal lines reflect the impact of a GTB

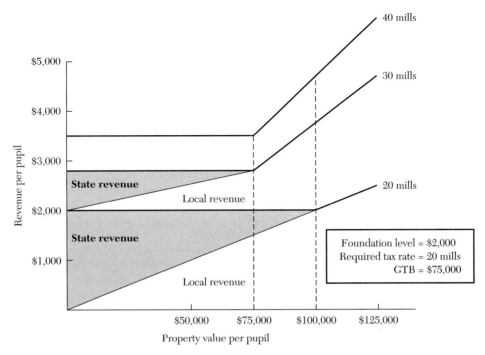

FIGURE 9.11   Graphical Representation of the Impact of a Combination Foundation and Guaranteed Tax Base Program

at $75,000 for total tax rates of 30 and 40 mills (with 20 mills being the required tax rate for the foundation portion of the program). Note that the zero-aid district level for the foundation portion of the program is $100,000 and, obviously, $75,000 for the GTB portion of the program. For each tax rate level, the revenue-per-pupil line is initially horizontal and then slopes upward only beyond the level of the zero-aid district, indicating that districts with a property value per pupil above this level will raise more per pupil than is provided even by the GTB.

Several issues need to be addressed with a combination foundation-GTB program. The first two are general policy targets:

- The level of base spending in the foundation program
- The level of the GTB

The same considerations raised here for each program individually can be applied to the combination program. States might set the base revenue at a level sufficiently high for districts, on average, to provide an adequate education program. This type of policy target could become a new rationale for how high the base revenue in state foundation programs should be in the future. Though not exactly stated in its new legislation, Kentucky sought to take this approach in its 1990 school finance reform.

For ex ante fiscal neutrality, the GTB also needs to be set at a relatively high level, such as the 90th percentile of property wealth per pupil. On the other hand, there may be some flexibility for the GTB level. For example, if the base spending level is set high enough for the average student to meet ambitious student achievement objectives, the state might want to limit local add-ons, as Kentucky has done. At this point, since all students on average have been funded for an education program designed to meet some new high-performance level, one could argue that local add-ons are merely an element of local choice about how to spend discretionary income. Thus, a GTB at just the statewide average, or the 50th percentile, which would focus the GTB on equal access to a tax base just for the bottom half, might be viewed as sufficient. This was the policy in Wisconsin for several years. How these policy dilemmas will play out in different states remains to be seen.

The key conceptual point in the preceding two paragraphs is that there is potentially an implicit trade-off between the level of the foundation base revenue and the level of the GTB. If the base revenue level is high enough to teach most students to bold new achievement levels, the base level will in itself require new education funds and substantially raise school spending for all students. Fewer districts will feel that they need to spend above the base. Thus, because GTB-aided spending becomes much more a matter of discretionary spending, the GTB level can be focused on districts with below-average spending. Extra revenue could even be capped, since revenue and spending levels would already be at much higher levels.

On the other hand, if the base revenue level is much lower, then the GTB component becomes a much larger portion of the overall program, and its level becomes much more critical to the fiscal-equity impact of the system. If the base revenue level is low, more districts—undoubtedly, more than half the districts—will want to spend more. Thus, local add-ons become a larger part of the overall system. To make the system fiscally neutral, the GTB would have to be set at a high level, such as the 90th percentile.

There is a plausible, substantive rationale for having a lower foundation base revenue level and a higher GTB level. This argument concerns differences in educational needs and costs between metropolitan (urban and suburban) and nonmetropolitan (rural) districts. In most states, foundation-revenue-per-pupil levels are too low for most districts to provide an adequate education program. But often, a modest increase in the foundation level would be sufficient to allow most nonmetropolitan school districts to provide an adequate education program.

However, raising the foundation revenue to a level that would be sufficient for metropolitan districts, which usually face educational prices that are 10–20 percent higher than those in nonmetropolitan districts, is usually too expensive for the state. Moreover, raising the foundation revenue to a level that would allow metropolitan districts to provide an adequate program could, then, also allow nonmetropolitan districts to provide a higher-level quality program than they need. Indeed, it might provide so much money for rural districts that some local education leaders and their legislatures would argue that excessive funds were being allocated to schools.

Though the divergence between the resource needs of urban and rural districts should not be overstated, this is an issue that arises in nearly all states that seek to raise the foundation base to a level sufficient to provide an adequate education program. In states with the most ambitious policymakers, the level usually becomes more than rural districts need for adequacy and less than urban districts need, a compromise that is not efficient for either.

However, this dilemma could be remedied by setting the base at an adequate level for the lowest-cost districts and then adjusting it by a price index (Chambers, 1981, 1995; Fowler and Monk, 2001; Imazeki, 2006; McMahon, 1994; Monk and Walker, 1991; Taylor and Fowler, 2006) for districts facing higher costs. But an education price index, though technically straightforward to develop, has been enacted in only a few states, including Texas, Ohio, and Wyoming. This issue is discussed in more detail in section 3.

Fiscal equity impacts of combination foundation-GTB programs. Figure 9.12 shows a combination program with the foundation set at the median, the required tax rate at the median, and the GTB add-on at about the 94th percentile. This is a fairly generous combination, two-tier school finance system.

For this simulated program, both local and state revenues increase. Local revenues increase in the wealthier districts and decrease in the poorer districts. The state role rises to nearly 41 percent. The impact on equity and adequacy is quite impressive: the coefficient of variation is below 10 percent, the McLoone Index is above 95 percent, the Verstegen Index is just 4.4 percent, and the Adequacy Index is 99 percent. These positive impacts are due in part to the generous parameters of the program and in part to the fact that the base data represent the typical school finance problem. You should run additional combination simulations that are somewhat less generous than the one depicted in Figure 9.12.

At the same time, combination foundation-GTB programs might not be a desired approach for states that face the "new" school finance problem, such as Illinois, Missouri, New York, and Wisconsin. Odden (1998) analyzed the results of adding a second-tier, 90/90 GTB to the adequate foundation program in these three states that was defined as the median expenditure level. The GTB was set at the 90th percentile of district wealth and provided aid to districts spending up to the 90th percentile of expenditures per pupil. He found that nearly all of the equity statistics worsen. Moreover, the extra state cost was considerable. Because these states exemplify the newer version of fiscal disparities (higher spending associated with higher tax rates, and both attributes associated with higher wealth), the equity results are not surprising.

For states with these types of problems, the results show that GTB programs, even on top of adequate foundation revenue levels, simply worsen fiscal equity. The results suggest that GTB school finance elements should probably not be a primary part of school finance systems for such states. Nevertheless, many school finance experts, including these authors in the first edition of this book (Odden and Picus, 1992), for years recommended second-tier GTB programs on top of foundation programs. Given the negative impact on fiscal equity as well as the considerable costs of such additions, such recommendations should be viewed skeptically in the future. Indeed, since a GTB simply assists districts in spending above an adequate level, one could argue that such a program, whatever its effects on fiscal equity, is beyond the state interest in school finance. The adequate spending base and the adjustments for special needs discussed in Chapter 11 largely fulfill the state interest.

Adequacy Level	$5,350.00
Pupil Weights	No
Disabled	—
Limited English	—
Low income	—

Foundation Level	$5,154.00
Required Tax Rate	31.32
GTB	$138,000.00
GTB Rate Cap above Foundation Tax Rate	99

District	Pupils	Property Value per Pupil ($)	Old Property Tax Rate (Mills)	New Property Tax Rate (Mills)	Change in Property Tax Rate (Mills)	Old Local Revenue per Pupil ($)	New Local Revenue per Pupil ($)	Change in Local Revenue per Pupil ($)	New State Foundation Revenue per Pupil ($)	New State GTB Revenue per Pupil ($)	Change in State Revenue per Pupil ($)	Total Revenue per Pupil ($)	Change in Total Revenue per Pupil ($)
1	1,290	17,456	39.64	35.48	(4.16)	692	619	(73)	4,607	501	2,321	5,728	2,248
2	5,648	25,879	38.50	34.91	(3.59)	996	903	(93)	4,343	403	2,123	5,649	2,030
3	1,678	31,569	37.15	34.23	(2.91)	1,173	1,081	(92)	4,165	310	1,940	5,556	1,848
4	256	35,698	36.20	33.76	(2.44)	1,292	1,205	(87)	4,036	250	1,826	5,491	1,739
5	10,256	40,258	35.91	33.62	(2.30)	1,446	1,353	(92)	3,893	224	1,716	5,471	1,624
6	956	43,621	35.74	33.53	(2.21)	1,559	1,463	(96)	3,788	209	1,603	5,459	1,507
7	4,689	49,875	34.89	33.11	(1.79)	1,740	1,651	(89)	3,592	157	1,391	5,400	1,302
8	1,656	55,556	34.17	32.75	(1.43)	1,898	1,819	(79)	3,414	118	1,259	5,351	1,179
9	8,954	61,254	33.73	32.53	(1.21)	2,066	1,992	(74)	3,236	92	1,110	5,320	1,036
10	1,488	70,569	33.44	32.38	(1.06)	2,360	2,285	(75)	2,944	71	924	5,300	850
11	2,416	78,952	33.23	32.28	(0.95)	2,624	2,548	(75)	2,681	56	657	5,286	582
12	5,891	86,321	32.89	32.11	(0.78)	2,839	2,771	(68)	2,450	41	460	5,262	392
13	2,600	94,387	32.10	31.71	(0.39)	3,030	2,993	(37)	2,198	17	245	5,208	209
14	15,489	102,687	31.32	31.32	0.00	3,216	3,216	0	1,938	0	0	5,154	0
15	2,308	112,358	30.85	32.91	2.06	3,466	3,698	232	1,635	41	(232)	5,374	0
16	2,712	125,897	30.50	34.29	3.79	3,840	4,317	477	1,211	36	(477)	5,564	0
17	30,256	136,527	30.05	34.77	4.72	4,102	4,747	644	878	5	(644)	5,630	0
18	2,056	156,325	28.63	36.09	7.46	4,476	5,641	1,166	258	0	(1,166)	5,899	0
19	3,121	198,564	27.42	33.11	5.69	5,445	6,575	1,130	0	0	(1,130)	6,575	0
20	1,523	278,052	25.50	27.07	1.57	7,090	7,527	437	0	0	(437)	7,527	0
Weighted average		97,831	32.34	33.34	1.00	3,028	3,257	229	2,173	82	331	5,512	559
Weighted std. dev.		48,514	2.91	1.55	3.15	1,269	1,596	380	1,318	120	1,011	363	478
Median		102,687	31.32	31.32	0.00	3,216	3,216	0	1,938	0	0	5,471	0

Totals

Category	Amount	Percent	Change from Base Amount
Local revenue	342,810,303	59.09	24,083,095
State revenue	237,324,515	40.91	34,784,349
Total revenue	580,134,818		58,867,444
Pupils	105,243		

Winners and Losers

Category	Winners	Losers	No Change
State aid	14	6	0
Total revenue	14	6	0

Equity Measures

Horizontal Equity	
Range	$2,373
Restricted range	$1,367
Federal range ratio	0.262
Coef. of variation	0.066
Gini coefficient	0.029
McLoone Index	0.962
Verstegen Index	1.044

Fiscal Neutrality	
Correlation	0.768
Elasticity	0.115

Adequacy	
Odden-Picus	0.992

FIGURE 9.12 Combination Program

Full-State-Funding and State-Determined Spending Programs

The final category of school-funding programs has generally been referred to as full state funding. A full-state-funding program implements the equality value, or horizontal equity, for students by setting an equal-expenditure-per-pupil level for all districts. Districts cannot spend less than this amount, nor can they spend more. For this reason, if a state wants to implement the horizontal-equity principle for students (i.e., a program that provides for equal spending), a full-state-funding program is the only choice.

As the name of the program connotes, in its pure form, it is fully funded by state revenues, which is the case in Hawaii. But that is not a necessary characteristic of such a program. The key characteristic is that a "full-state-funding" program requires equal or equitable spending per pupil in all districts and does not allow for any add-ons by local districts. The revenues, however, could be derived from a combination of state revenues and local property tax revenues. The state could require a uniform statewide property tax rate for schools and set state aid as the difference between that revenue and the total revenues needed to provide the equal-spending level. This has been the approach taken by New Mexico and Washington for years, and also the approach of the 1998 school finance reform in Vermont. California has a version of full state funding called a *revenue limit program.* The state sets a base spending level per pupil for each district and finances it with a combination of state and local property tax revenues. It is conceptually equivalent to a full-state-funding program.

Likewise, Florida has a different approach that makes the system function almost like a full-state-funding program, financed with a combination of state and local revenues. Florida has a combination foundation-GTB program, but the GTB program has an absolute maximum tax rate cap. Since most districts are at the cap, and since the GTB is higher than the wealth of most districts, the structure comes close to being the equivalent of a full-state-funding program.

In this book, full state funding is used to indicate a school finance program that requires equitable per-pupil spending across all school districts. The program can be financed solely with state funds, but it can also be financed with a combination of state and local funds, usually property tax revenues. For our purposes, the defining element of a full-state-funding program is that districts cannot spend less or more than the level set by the state, thereby satisfying the horizontal-equity principle.

Wyoming is an example of a state with a fully state-funded school finance structure. Using the evidence-based approach to adequacy, the state uses the same formulas to provide detailed school and central-office resources to each of its districts (Odden, Picus, et al., 2005). But because of variation in school size and the presence of many very small schools and many small districts and considerable price differences across the districts in the state, the final base spending per pupil varies considerably across each of its districts—even excluding the substantial additional categorical dollars for extra pupil needs. The result is that typical analyses of equity across its districts conclude that the system is very inequitable (see the various issues of *Quality Counts* by Education Week). And the federal government does not view the state as providing an equitable school-funding system. Yet there are absolutely no local add-ons. All spending differences are based on the characteristics of the schools, school districts, or students enrolled in those schools. The conclusion that the system is inequitable shows that even more sophisticated tools are needed to assess school finance equity in states.

3. ADJUSTMENTS FOR PRICE DIFFERENCES

An issue that gained prominence in school finance beginning in the 1970s and continuing today is the difference in prices that school districts face in purchasing educational resources. Districts not only purchase a different market basket of educational goods (just as individuals purchase a different market basket of goods), but they also pay different prices for the goods they purchase. Today, because some schools manage their budget on site and do all of their own purchasing, schools can also be included in this discussion. District (and/or school) expenditures determine quantity issues (numbers of different types of educational goods purchased, such as teachers, books, buildings, etc.), the level of quality of those goods, and the cost of or price paid for each good. The variety, number, quality, and price of all educational goods purchased determines school district (and/or school) expenditures. While "expenditures" are often referred to as "costs" in school finance parlance, there is a difference between these two economic terms. "Expenditure" refers to the money spent on school resources; "cost" refers to the money spent on school resources to receive a certain level of output or to provide a certain quality of service.

Prices that school districts (and/or schools) face in purchasing educational resources differ across school districts, and many states have taken an interest in trying to adjust school aid allocations to compensate for geographic cost or price differences. For example, a teacher of a certain quality will probably cost more in an urban area, where general costs of living are higher, than in nonurban areas, where general costs of living are lower. But prices or cost variations that districts must pay for teachers also differ among school districts because of variations in the nature of the work required, the quality of the working environment, and the characteristics of the local community. Teachers might accept marginally lower salaries if, for example, they teach four rather than five periods a day or have smaller classes, or if there are numerous opportunities for staff development (McLaughlin and Yee, 1988). Or teachers might want marginally higher salaries if there are few cultural opportunities in the surrounding community. The combination of differences in general cost of living, working conditions, and the amenities of the surrounding community produces differences in prices that districts must pay for teachers of a given quality.

Similarly, districts within the same state might have to allocate more or less general revenues for such noneducational activities as transportation and heating/cooling. Districts in sparsely populated rural areas face higher-than-average transportation costs because their students are spread over a wider geographic region and because fuel and repair costs may also be higher. Districts in especially cold or unusually warm environments must spend more for heating or air conditioning. These higher-than-average expenditures are beyond the control of the district and, holding quality constant and assuming similar technical efficiency, impose higher costs on district budgets.

These are just a few examples of factors that constrain the ability of school districts, even those with the same total general revenue per pupil, to provide the same level and quality of educational services to their students. States have recognized these price and cost variations but only recently have begun to make adjustments for them in state aid formulas.

While several different approaches can be taken in constructing cost-of-education indices (Berne and Stiefel, 1984; Brazer, 1974; Chambers, 1981; Kenny, Denslow, and

Goffmann, 1975), there is substantial correlation among price indices constructed with different methodologies (Chambers, 1981). Whatever methodology is used, price differences can vary substantially across districts. In earlier studies of California (Chambers, 1978, 1980), Florida (Kenny, Denslow, and Goffman, 1975), Missouri (Chambers, Odden, and Vincent, 1976), New York (Wendling, 1981b), and Texas (Augenblick and Adams, 1979; Monk and Walker, 1991), within-state price variations ranged from 20 percent (10 percent above and below the average) in California to 40 percent (20 percent above and below the average) in Texas. And price ranges remain about the same according to more recent studies of Wyoming and Texas (e.g., Baker, 2005; Taylor, 2004). These are substantial differences. These results mean that high-cost districts in California must pay 20 percent more for the same educational goods as low-cost districts; thus, with equal per-pupil revenues, high-cost districts are able to purchase only 75 percent of what low-cost districts can purchase. The differences in Texas are even greater. Such price differences, caused by circumstances and conditions essentially outside the control of district decision makers, qualify as a target for adjustments in some state aid formulas. For a primer on education price indices in education, see Fowler and Monk (2001).

After this primer was developed, however, a new approach to developing geographic adjustments for teacher salaries entered into school finance scholarly and policy debates. Rather than using the hedonic approach, which had been used for the preceding 30 years, the new method takes a "comparable wage" approach. Under this new approach, the adjustment for teachers is taken from salary variations in occupations other than teaching. Taylor and Fowler (2006) used all occupations requiring a bachelor's degree or greater while Imazeki (2006) used salaries only for occupations that were similar to teaching. Imazeki's analysis showed, moreover, that the indices produced for all occupations were different from those produced only for occupations similar to teachers.

States can take two different approaches in using a price or cost-of-education index. First, state aid can be multiplied by the price index, thus ensuring that equal amounts of state aid will purchase equal amounts of educational goods. But this approach leaves local revenues unadjusted by price indices. A better method is to multiply the major elements of a school aid formula by the price index to ensure that total education revenues can purchase the same level of resources. Thus, the price index is applied to the foundation expenditure level in a foundation program, the tax base guaranteed by the state in a GTB program, the state-determined spending level in a full-state-funding program, or total current operating expenditures for a percentage equalizing formula.

As such, including a price index in a school finance formula is relatively simple. In addition, the fact that price indices tend to remain stable over time (Chambers, 1981) suggests that states would need to develop price indices only periodically, perhaps every three to five years, if they were used as part of a state-aid formula. Further, the National Center of Education Statistics (NCES) has already developed different versions of such education price adjustments for all school districts in the country (Chambers, 1995; McMahon, 1994), which any state can use. And the NCES has recently produced comparative wage indices that can be used for all districts and all states (Taylor and Fowler, 2006) and should be available by the time this book goes to press (at nces.ed.gov/efin/) with documentation and a users' guide. States have been reluctant to add education price adjustments to their school aid formulas, in part because developing them requires some complex econometric analyses and manipulations, and in part because they have the potential of changing allocations considerably.

While the existence of the NCES price indices alleviates the need for analysis, price indices do alter the distribution of state aid. In general, education price indices are higher in urban and metropolitan areas than in rural areas. Thus, with a given amount of state aid, use of a price index shifts the shares of state aid at the margin from rural to urban school districts. This distributional characteristic injects an additional dimension to constructing a politically viable state aid mechanism. Nevertheless, prices vary across school districts and affect the real levels of education goods and services that can be purchased. Including an education price index in the school aid formula is a direct way to adjust for these circumstances that are outside the control of school district policymakers.

4. SIMULATION OF ADJUSTMENTS FOR SPECIAL-NEEDS STUDENTS

Adding adjustments for special-needs students to a state school finance structure clearly improves the vertical equity of the system, but it also improves both horizontal equity and fiscal neutrality. The improvements, however, require additional revenues. Figure 9.13 shows the base data simulated with the following weights representing additional student education needs:

- Compensatory education students (i.e., students from a low-income family, usually represented by the number of students eligible for free and reduced-price lunch) weighted an extra 0.20
- Limited-English-proficient (LEP) students weighted an extra 0.20
- Disabled students weighted an extra 0.9

It takes some analysis to fully understand the results in Figure 9.13, relative to those in Figure 9.1, the base data without pupil weights. First, as indicated near the bottom, left-hand side of Figure 9.13, these weights produce an additional 14,905 pupil units (120,148 – 105,243). The number of additional student units in each district can be determined by comparing the "Weighted Pupils" column in Figure 9.13 with those in Figure 9.1.

Second, the simulation shows that the 20-district sample needed an additional $103.5 million in revenues to fund these extra needs, which is shown as additional state revenue (again in comparison to Figure 9.1). This additional amount represents the full cost of the extra weights, and for the 20-district sample, it is assumed that the state provides all these additional dollars. In the state simulations that accompany Chapter 11, the additional amount would be the increment above what the state actually provides for special student needs, as most states already provide some level of assistance for low-income, LEP, and disabled students, but generally not a sufficient amount. Nevertheless, the $105.6 million figure identified in Figure 9.13 is the amount required to fully fund the identified pupil weights.

Note that the bulk of the extra costs is for students with disabilities. You should run a series of simulations, each time giving a weight to just one of the three categories

Adequacy Level	$5,350
Pupil Weights	**Yes**
Disabled	0.9
Limited English	0.2
Low income	0.2

District	Weighted Pupils	Property Value per Weighted Pupil ($)	Property Tax Rate (Mills)	Local Revenue per Weighted Pupil ($)	State Revenue per Weighted Pupil ($)	Total Revenue per Weighted Pupil ($)
1	1,703	13,224	39.64	524	3,173	3,697
2	7,286	20,061	38.50	772	3,145	3,918
3	2,098	25,255	37.15	938	3,091	4,029
4	312	29,261	36.20	1,059	3,014	4,073
5	12,205	33,830	35.91	1,215	2,943	4,158
6	1,128	36,967	35.74	1,321	2,946	4,267
7	5,458	42,848	34.89	1,495	2,915	4,410
8	1,911	48,142	34.17	1,645	2,834	4,480
9	10,243	53,544	33.73	1,806	2,776	4,582
10	1,702	61,686	33.44	2,063	2,728	4,791
11	2,764	69,014	33.23	2,293	2,789	5,083
12	6,669	76,255	32.89	2,508	2,703	5,211
13	2,933	83,676	32.10	2,686	2,651	5,337
14	17,317	91,849	31.32	2,877	2,560	5,437
15	2,576	100,679	30.85	3,106	2,556	5,662
16	3,010	113,421	30.50	3,459	2,364	5,823
17	33,463	123,442	30.05	3,709	2,153	5,862
18	2,266	141,856	28.63	4,061	2,041	6,102
19	3,433	180,513	27.42	4,950	1,840	6,790
20	1,672	253,235	25.50	6,457	1,308	7,765
Weighted average		85,694	32.46	2,653	2,548	5,201
Weighted std. dev.		45,280	2.97	1,199	388	821
Median district		83,676	32.10	2,686	2,651	5,337

Totals		
Category	Amount	Percent
Local revenue	318,727,208	51.01
State revenue	306,112,115	48.99
Total revenue	624,839,323	
Weighted pupils	120,148	

Categorical revenue included in state revenue calculation 103,571,949

Equity Measures	
Horizontal Equity	
Range	$4,068
Restricted range	$2,872
Federal range ratio	0.733
Coef. of variation	0.158
Gini coefficient	0.087
McLoone Index	0.838
Verstegen Index	1.095
Fiscal Neutrality	
Correlation	0.990
Elasticity	0.270
Adequacy	
Odden-Picus	0.923

FIGURE 9.13 Base Data with Pupil Need Weights

of special-needs students. The results will show that the incidence of bilingual students is quite low, which is the case in most states (with the notable exceptions of California, Arizona, New Mexico, Texas, Florida, and New York). Since the extra cost for each bilingual student is just 20 percent, the total additional costs for this group are minimal. Extra costs for compensatory education alone is higher because the incidence of low-income students is about 20 percent of all students. The incidence of disabled students is about 13 percent, which, when combined with an extra cost of 90 percent for each student, produces the largest extra cost for a special-needs student category.

The equity statistics for the base data with pupil weights (Figure 9.13) are also somewhat better than those for the same districts without the extra costs of special-needs students (see Figure 9.1). All equity and adequacy statistics for this simulation are based on the number of need-weighted pupils. The coefficient of variation and wealth elasticity are somewhat smaller, and the McLoone Index and Odden-Picus Adequacy Index are somewhat larger. Of course, costs also rise; horizontal, vertical, and fiscal-neutrality equity, as well as adequacy gains, emerge at a price—but this time the price of fully funding programs for special-needs students.

Figure 9.14 uses these weights for a foundation program simulated at the new median expenditure per weighted pupil of $5,337 and at a required tax rate of 32.10 mills, the new state median. All equity and adequacy statistics for this simulation are also based on the number of weighted pupils. First, the total state cost of the program increases by an additional $10.9 million, compared with the weighted-pupil base data. These increased costs should be expected because the foundation level raises spending in many of the low-expenditure districts. Local revenues rise too, largely because of state aid losses for the high-wealth districts.

Second, in part as a result, the equity statistics improve substantially, just as they did for a similar foundation program without weights. The coefficient of variation drops from 0.158 to 0.070, the McLoone Index rises from 0.838 to 0.991, the wealth elasticity drops from 0.285 to 0.141, and the Adequacy Index rises from 0.92 to 1.00. In short, vertical adjustments for special-needs students produce equity on all fronts, with this level of foundation program.

5. SUMMARY

School finance in the United States represents a fiscal-federalism approach; that is, all three levels of government fund schools—local school districts as well as states and the federal government. This approach to funding public K–12 education provides several advantages: fiscal-capacity equalization, equity in the provision of educational services, efficiency in producing educational results, and local choice for the level and quality of school services.

There are five different types of school funding formulas—flat grant, foundation, guaranteed tax base, combination foundation-GTB, and full-state-funding. For most formulas, educational, equity, fiscal, and political goals must be balanced in designing viable school finance formulas in order to get them enacted into law. Although equity and adequacy are prime goals, their costs and fiscal impacts play crucial roles in whether they will be accepted politically.

It's important to add a geographic price factor into school finance formulas to adjust for the varying purchasing power of the education dollar across school districts, adding another element to make the school finance structures even more equitable. In addition, all the basic school finance formulas must be augmented by adding "pupil weights" that trigger additional resources needed by districts to provide students with

Adequacy Level	$5,350
Pupil Weights	Yes
Disabled	0.90
Limited English	0.20
Low income	0.20

Foundation Level	$5,337
Required Tax Rate	32.10

District	Weighted Pupils	Property Value per Weighted Pupil ($)	Old Property Tax Rate (Mills)	New Property Tax Rate (Mills)	Change in Property Tax Rate (Mills)	Old Local Revenue per Weighted Pupil ($)	New Local Revenue per Weighted Pupil ($)	Change in Local Revenue per Weighted Pupil ($)	New State Revenue per Weighted Pupil ($)	Change in State Revenue per Weighted Pupil ($)	Total Revenue per Weighted Pupil ($)	Change in Total Revenue per Weighted Pupil ($)
1	1,703	13,224	39.64	35.87	(3.77)	524	474	(50)	4,913	1,740	5,387	1,690
2	7,286	20,061	38.50	35.30	(3.20)	772	708	(64)	4,693	1,548	5,401	1,484
3	2,098	25,255	37.15	34.62	(2.52)	938	874	(64)	4,526	1,435	5,401	1,372
4	312	29,261	36.20	34.15	(2.05)	1,059	999	(60)	4,398	1,384	5,397	1,324
5	12,205	33,830	35.91	34.01	(1.91)	1,215	1,150	(64)	4,251	1,308	5,401	1,243
6	1,128	36,967	35.74	33.92	(1.82)	1,321	1,254	(67)	4,150	1,204	5,404	1,137
7	5,458	42,848	34.89	33.50	(1.40)	1,495	1,435	(60)	3,962	1,047	5,397	987
8	1,911	48,142	34.17	33.14	(1.04)	1,645	1,595	(50)	3,792	957	5,387	907
9	10,243	53,544	33.73	32.92	(0.82)	1,806	1,762	(44)	3,618	842	5,381	798
10	1,702	61,686	33.44	32.77	(0.67)	2,063	2,021	(41)	3,357	629	5,378	588
11	2,764	69,014	33.23	32.67	(0.56)	2,293	2,254	(39)	3,122	332	5,376	293
12	6,669	76,255	32.89	32.50	(0.39)	2,508	2,478	(30)	2,889	186	5,367	156
13	2,933	83,676	32.10	32.10	0.00	2,686	2,686	0	2,651	0	5,337	0
14	17,317	91,849	31.32	33.18	1.86	2,877	3,048	171	2,389	(171)	5,437	—
15	2,576	100,679	30.85	35.33	4.48	3,106	3,557	451	2,105	(451)	5,662	—
16	3,010	113,421	30.50	36.39	5.89	3,459	4,127	668	1,696	(668)	5,823	—
17	33,463	123,442	30.05	36.35	6.31	3,709	4,488	779	1,375	(779)	5,862	—
18	2,266	141,856	28.63	37.49	8.86	4,061	5,319	1,257	783	(1,257)	6,102	—
19	3,433	180,513	27.42	37.61	10.19	4,950	6,790	1,840	0	(1,840)	6,790	—
20	1,672	253,235	25.50	30.66	5.16	6,457	7,765	1,308	0	(1,308)	7,765	—
Weighted average		85,694	32.46	34.56	2.10	2,653	2,992	339	2,638	90	5,630	429
Weighted std. dev.		45,280	2.97	1.68	3.85	1,199	1,635	475	1,314	939	394	562
Median		83,676	32.10	32.10	—	2,686	2,686	—	2,651	0	5,437	0

Totals				
Category	Amount	Percent	Change from Unweighted Pupil Base Amount	Change from Weighted Pupil Base Amount
Local revenue	359,459,562	53.14	40,732,355	40,732,355
State revenue	316,967,753	46.86	114,427,587	10,855,638
Total revenue	676,427,315		155,159,942	51,587,993
Weighted pupils	120,148			

Winners and Losers			
Category	Winners	Losers	No change
State aid	13	7	0
Total revenue	13	0	7

Equity Measures	
Horizontal Equity	
Range	$2,428
Restricted range	$1,423
Federal range ratio	0.265
Coef. of variation	0.070
Gini coefficient	0.030
McLoone Index	0.991
Verstegen Index	1.075
Fiscal Neutrality	
Correlation	0.916
Elasticity	0.141
Adequacy	
Odden-Picus	1.000

FIGURE 9.14 Foundation Program with Pupil Need Weights

disabilities, ELL and LEP students, and students from lower-income backgrounds with additional services to help them achieve to state performance standards. Of course, a major issue in most states is determining what the weights should be. One substantive way to calculate the weights is to identify the costs of specific extra-help programs, such as those identified in Chapter 4, and then calculate a weight as the ratio of the per-pupil cost of each program to, for example, the foundation-expenditure-per-pupil level in a foundation program. The book illustrates this approach in the Wisconsin section of Chapter 11.

Suggested Problems

Study Group Exercises

Problems 1, 2, and 3 should be considered as study group exercises using the 20-district simulation sample (see www.mhhe.com/odden4e). These problems raise the interrelated issues of school finance equity goals; state, local, and total costs; and the particular interests of districts with below-average and above-average property wealth per pupil.

1. Divide into groups of two or three so that each group represents one of the school districts in the 20-district sample. With your group, do the following:
    a. Design a foundation program with an increased state cost of $25 million that gives your district the greatest increase in state aid. Discuss why your plan should be the one proposed to the legislature, and argue on the basis of the impacts of your program on school finance equity and adequacy.
    b. Design a foundation program with an increased state cost of $25 million that you feel is best for your particular district and that you think would garner two-thirds support of your classmates, or of the legislature that would be deliberating such a proposed change.
    c. Compare the different foundation programs.
2. Divide into two groups. Members of group 1 represent superintendents from districts low in property value per pupil (i.e., districts 1–10). Members of group 2 represent superintendents from districts high in property value per pupil (i.e., districts 11–20). You could vary the districts in the different groups; there do not have to be 10 districts in each group. With your group, do the following:
    a. Simulate a combination foundation-GTB program with total extra costs at $45 million (i.e., the sum of increased state and local revenues).
    b. In terms of school finance equity and adequacy, as well as political feasibility, decide whether your interest is better served by a relatively low foundation program with a relatively high GTB or a relatively high foundation program and a modest GTB, or something in between. Explain why.
    c. Compare the different designs. Some should have large increases in state aid combined with large decreases in local revenues for a total revenue increase of $45 million. Others should have increased state costs much closer to the $45 million and much less property tax relief.
3. Again divide into groups—of two, three, or four depending on the size of the study group—representing different types of districts: below-average wealth, average wealth, and above-average wealth. With your group, do the following:

a. Design a school finance program—foundation, GTB, or combination foundation-GTB—that improves both horizontal equity and adequacy. Be sure to identify all the key formula and policy parameters, and have clear equity goals.

b. Argue the merits of your proposals on equity, adequacy, and cost grounds.

c. As a class, vote on the different proposals presented, keeping in mind that the collective group represents taxpayers as well as the education community. The vote should be on one proposal.

Individual Exercises

4. Assume that the base data for the 20-district sample on the school finance simulation represents the condition of school finance in your state. A taxpayer rights group has conducted an analysis of that system and, based on that analysis, has sued in state court arguing that school spending levels are a function of district wealth. The group has asked the court to invalidate the state's funding structure. You are the chief of staff of the state legislature's school finance committee. In analyzing a printout of the base data from the simulation, you see that per-pupil revenue ranges from \$3,480 to \$7,527, with a tax rate in the lowest-revenue district of 39.64 mills and in the highest-revenue district of 25.5 mills. The state share of total educational revenue is under 40 percent. Moreover, you note that the correlation of revenue and wealth per pupil is 0.991, and the wealth elasticity is far above 0.10. Looking carefully at a graph of revenue versus wealth per pupil for the base data, you conclude there is substantial likelihood the court will invalidate the state finance structure.

   Additionally, a number of years ago, the state's voters approved an expenditure limitation. As a result, the state is unlikely to have more than \$50 million in additional funds to devote to education next year.

   Using the school finance simulation, design a school finance foundation program that reduces the relationship between wealth and revenue, with increased state spending of \$50 million. Experiment with different combinations of foundation level and required tax rates. Also experiment with combinations of high and low foundation levels and high and low RTRs. Find more than one foundation level/RTR combination that costs the state \$50 million. Identify different foundation programs at this state cost that benefit poorer districts more than wealthy districts, and then identify foundation programs that spread the additional \$50 million to most districts. Once you have three or four possible options, answer these questions:

   a. How do each of these combinations meet the fiscal-neutrality criteria that might be used in the lawsuit?

   b. What impact does each of these options have on the horizontal equity of the system?

   c. How does total revenue for education change under each of these options? How does the state's share of total revenue change?

  d. Which foundation program option would you recommend to the legislature? Why?

  e. How will you address legislative questions about districts that gained and lost state aid?

  f. If the state suddenly found that it could devote $60 million to education next year rather than $50 million, how would you change your recommendations?

5. Using the same information as presented in problem 4, relax the restriction that you must use a foundation program to design a new school finance system. Experiment with the GTB option, and find a model that meets the $50-million state-spending-increase limitation. How does this model compare with the foundation program you recommended to the legislature in problem 4? Specifically:

  a. How does total state spending change under the GTB compared with the foundation program?

  b. How do local district tax rates compare?

  c. Are there more winners or losers under the GTB? How does the magnitude of each district's gain or loss in state aid vary between the two options?

  d. Which model—the GTB or the foundation program—does a better job of minimizing the relationship between wealth and revenue?

  e. Which of the two models better meets horizontal-equity standards?

  f. How does the state's share of total educational revenue compare between the two models?

  g. Which model would you recommend to the legislature? Describe the trade-offs that policymakers will have to make in choosing one option over the other.

  h. How does your analysis change if there is $60 million available for education instead of $50 million?

6. A number of states have opted to use a two-tier program, relying on a foundation program to provide a base level of revenue for all districts, and a GTB to equalize district decisions to supplement that base. Using the same $50-million limitation, design a combination (two-tier) school finance system for your state. How does this model compare to the two preceding models? What would you now recommend to the legislature? Why? What happens if the state is willing to increase its commitment to $60 million?

Summary Tables

For all proposals, create summary tables to display the results of your various simulations. For foundation programs, rank them from lowest to highest foundation level (or highest to lowest). The following indicates the type of data to include:

Simulation	Flat Grant	Foundation Level	Required Tax Rate	Zero-Aid District	GTB	Adequacy Expenditure Level	Number of State Aid Winners/Losers
Base data							
1	4,000	—	—	—	—	$5,350	20/0
2	—	$5,154	31.32	$164,559	—	5,350	14/6
3	—	—	—	138,000	$138,000	5,350	10/10
4	—	5,154	31.32	164,559	138,000	5,350	16/0

Simulation	Change in Local $ (in Millions)	Change in State $ (in Millions)	Change in Total $ (in Millions)	Coefficient of Variation	McLoone/Verstegen Index	Wealth Elasticity	Odden-Picus Adequacy Index
Base data	—	—	—	0.170	0.810/1.086	0.324	0.895
1	0	$218.4	$218.4	0.181	0.814/1.107	0.347	0.994
2	$24.4	26.1	50.6	0.030	0.992/1.070	0.146	0.985
3	64.2	−46.7	17.5	0.125	0.881/1.086	0.246	0.926
4	24.1	34.8	58.9	0.066	0.962/1.044	0.115	0.99

The Public Finance Context

Public K–12 education in the United States is a big business. As was shown in Table 1.2, revenue raised by all levels of government for K–12 education in 2003–04 amounted to nearly $450 billion (U.S. Department of Education, National Center for Education Statistics, 2006). These revenues are raised as part of the larger federal fiscal system in the United States. Under our federal system, governments at the local (city, school districts, etc.), state, and federal levels all raise and spend public tax dollars. In fiscal year (FY) 2004, total governmental receipts from all levels of government amounted to over $2.9 trillion (see Table 10.1). Revenues for K–12 education constitute only 15.5 percent of total governmental revenue.

Although responsibility for the education of our children almost always rests with the nearly 15,000 local school districts across the nation, nearly half the money spent on K–12 education is now provided by the governments of the 50 states. It is only in the past 30 or so years that the state has become an equal partner with local school districts in financing education.

States have taken a more prominent role in school finance for a number of reasons. In response to lawsuits across the nation, states either have been forced or have voluntarily agreed to use their financial resources to equalize differences in the property tax–raising capacity of their school districts. As local taxpayers have grown more reluctant to increase property taxes to finance local services, including education, states have filled in, either providing additional funds for schools or using their resources to provide property tax relief. Often, these two efforts go hand-in-hand, with increases in state revenues being used both to reduce local property tax burdens and to increase educational spending. In addition, movements for school finance adequacy, educational reform, and increased educational accountability have led to a growing state role in the provision of school services. In many instances, this growing state role is supported with additional funds.

Local school districts have traditionally provided almost all of their share of educational revenues through property taxes. This is because property is fixed in location, and values tend to change slowly, giving relatively small units of government—such

TABLE 10.1   Tax Revenue by Source and Level of Government, 1957–2004

Year	Total— All Governments	Federal Government	State Governments Own Source	Local Governments Own Source	School Districts[c]
Total Tax Revenue (in Billions)					
1957[a]	$ 108.6	$ 79.8	$ 14.5	$ 14.3	$ 4.5
1967[a]	209.8	148.8	31.9	29.1	10.8
1977[a]	531.6	355.6	101.1	74.9	27.1
1987[a]	1,159.5	854.4	246.9	158.2	51.8
1997[b]	2,307.9	1,579.3	444.2	284.4	93.4
2000[e]	2,893.2	2,025.2	539.7	328.3	106.5
2004[f]	2,900.6	1,880.1	610.4	410.1	116.1
Property Taxes (in Billions)					
1957[a]	$ 12.9	—	$ 0.5	$ 12.4	$ 4.4
1967[a]	26.0	—	0.9	25.2	10.6
1977[a]	62.5	—	2.3	60.3	26.4
1987[a]	121.2	—	4.6	116.6	50.5
1997[b]	218.8	—	10.3	208.5	90.4
2000[e]	246.2	—	11.0	235.2	102.0
2004[f]	314.5	—	11.8	292.4	116.1
Sales, Gross Receipts, and Customs (in Billions)					
1957[a]	$ 20.6	$ 11.1	$ 8.4	$ 1.0	$ —
1967[a]	36.3	15.8	18.6	2.0	—
1977[a]	83.8	23.2	52.4	8.3	0.2
1987[a]	192.7	48.4	119.9	24.5	0.5
1997[b]	254.4	74.8	147.8	31.8	[d]
2000[f]	311.6	88.8	178.6	44.2	[d]
2004[f]	349.4	96.5	202.3	50.6	[d]
Individual and Corporate Income Taxes (in Billions)					
1957[a]	$ 59.5	$ 56.8	$ 2.5	$ 0.2	$ —
1967[a]	103.5	95.5	7.1	0.1	—
1977[a]	250.0	211.6	34.7	3.8	0.2
1987[a]	582.8	476.5	96.7	9.7	0.4
1997[b]	1,112.7	919.8	175.7	17.2	[d]
2000[e]	1,459.5	1,211.8	227.1	20.6	[d]
2004[f]	1,463.9	1,205.5	239.0	19.4	[d]
Social Insurance (Federal Only)[e]					
1957	$ 10.0	$ 10.0	—	—	—
1967	32.6	32.6	—	—	—

(*continued*)

TABLE 10.1   (*continued*)

1977	106.5	106.5	—	—	—
1987	303.3	303.3	—	—	—
1997[b]	539.4	539.4	—	—	—
2000[e]	652.9	652.9	—	—	—
2004[e]	794.1	794.1	—	—	—

Other Sources of Revenue (in Billions)

1957[a]	$ 5.6	$ 1.9	$ 3.1	$ 0.7	$0.1
1967[a]	10.3	3.8	5.3	1.8	0.2
1977[a]	23.5	9.0	11.7	2.5	0.3
1987[a]	47.8	14.5	25.7	7.4	0.4
1997[b]	80.4	22.2	41.8	13.4	3.0
2000[e]	226.5	71.7	126.8	23.5	4.5
2004[f]	254.8	78.7	157.9	13.0	5.2

[a]*Source:* Advisory Commission on Intergovernmental Relations (1988), *Significant Features of Fiscal Federalism,* Volume II. Washington, DC: ACIR, p. 64. U.S. Bureau of the Census, *Government Finance in 1986–87.* Washington, DC: U.S. Bureau of the Census, p. 7.

[b]*Sources:* Office of Management and Budget (2003), Budget of the United States Government, Fiscal Year 2003: Historical Tables; w3.access.gpo.gov/usbudget/fy2003/pdf/hist.pdf. State and local data: U.S. Bureau of the Census (2000), *Compendium of Government Finances: 1997 Census of Governments,* Volume 4, *Government Finances;* www.census.gov/prod/gc97/gc974-5.pdf. School district data: U.S. Bureau of the Census (2000), *Public Education Finances: 1997 Census of Governments,* Volume 4, *Government Finances;* www.census.gov/prod/gc97/gc974-1.pdf.

[c]Figures for school districts are included in the state and local government totals. The Total—All Governments column represents the sum of the Federal, State, and Local columns and includes school districts.

[d]Data for all other tax sources are included in Other Sources of Revenue for 1997, 2000, and 2004.

[e]*Sources:* federal data for 2000 and social insurance data for all years: Office of Management and Budget (2003), Budget of the United States Government, Fiscal Year 2003: Historical Tables; w3.access.gpo.gov/usbudget/fy2003/pdf/hist.pdf. State data: U.S. Census Bureau (2002), State Government Tax Collections: 2000; www.census.gov/govs/statetax/0000usstax.html. Local government data: calculated from U.S. Census Bureau (2002), *Quarterly Summary of State and Local Government Tax Revenue,* Tables 1 and 2; www.census.gov/govs/www/qtax.html. School district data: U.S. Census Bureau (2000), Public Elementary–Secondary Education Finances, 1999–00; www.census.gov/govs/school/00fullreport.pdf.

[f]*Sources:* federal data for 2004: Budget of the U.S. (2006), *Historical Tables, Budget of the United States Government, Fiscal Year 2006;* frwebgate2.access.gpo.gov/cgi-bin/waisgate.cgi? WAISdocID = 05720239515 + 36 + 0 + 0&WAISaction = retrieve, retrieved, August 31, 2006. State and local: U.S. Census Bureau (2006), *Quarterly Summary of State and Local Government Tax Revenue,* Table 1, National Totals of State and Local Government Tax Revenue for Current and Prior Quarters, as well as 12-month calculations; www.census.gov/govs/www/qtax.html, retrieved August 31, 2006.

as school districts—a stable source of revenue (Monk and Brent, 1997). States, which have a larger base upon which taxes can be levied, have been able to use other taxes, in particular sales and income taxes, to finance their operations. Moreover, these broad-based statewide taxes make it possible for the state (through equalization grants, discussed in Chapter 9) to better ensure that educational spending in individual districts is more a function of the wealth of the entire state and not of the individual school district.

The purpose of this chapter is to set the context within which revenues for education are raised. The major reason for studying how governments raise revenue is that taxes are the primary source of dollars for public schools. While the focus of the chapter is on raising tax revenues, taxes can be used for other purposes as well. Taxes can be a means to redistribute income from the wealthy to the poor and can be used as a regulatory tool. For example, rather than regulate manufacturing plant emissions, pollution could be controlled by taxing those emissions or, alternatively, by providing tax breaks for companies that take steps to minimize pollution. However, this chapter focuses on taxes as a source of revenues for public schools.

This chapter has three sections. The first provides an overview of trends in federal, state, and local taxes from 1957 to 2004. Section 2 presents the public finance criteria commonly used to evaluate specific taxes, while section 3 uses those criteria to assess the individual income tax, sales taxes, and property taxes. The final section also contains a discussion of state lotteries, which are increasingly popular mechanisms for raising governmental revenues, and other alternative revenue options being considered.

1. TAXATION OVERVIEW

This section provides a short overview of the magnitude of local, state, and federal taxation, as well as changes in tax structures over time.

Trends in Federal, State, and Local Taxation

Over the past 40 years, there have been significant changes in the tax revenues raised by different levels of government. Table 10.1 exhibits tax revenues by type of tax for all levels of government, including school districts, from 1957 to 2004. Several trends in this table are worth noting. First, total tax revenues for all levels of government more than doubled in each of the first four decades presented in the table, and increased by over $600 billion between 1997 and 2004. These figures reflect government growth over that period. Second, nominal (not adjusted for inflation) state government revenues have increased at a faster rate than revenues for either the federal or local governments, rising by over 4,100 percent between 1957 and 2004. By contrast, total governmental revenues increased by 2,571 percent during that time: federal government revenues by 2,256 percent, local government revenues by 2,768 percent, and school district revenues from their own sources (not total school district revenue) by 2,480 percent.

Another trend displayed in this table is that property taxes are the primary source of tax revenues for local governments. The federal government does not collect any property taxes, and state governments collect only a small amount of property taxes. Further, nearly 40 percent of all property taxes were collected by school districts in 2004.

Table 10.1 also shows that most sales and gross receipt taxes are raised by state governments. Local sales taxes, though, have grown in importance as a revenue source since 1977. Sales taxes were the largest single source of tax revenues for state governments in 2004. Combined individual and corporate income taxes produced more state revenue, but sales taxes provided more revenue than either one separately. School districts raise very little revenue directly through sales taxes.

Finally, individual income taxes raise the largest amount of total governmental tax revenues, and the bulk of income taxes are raised by the federal government. But income taxes are rising at both the state and local levels. Federal individual and corporate income taxes grew from $56.8 billion in 1957 to just over $1.2 trillion in 2004, and represented 64 percent of total federal revenue in 2004. Income taxes have historically represented a minuscule amount of local school district revenues.

This discussion suggests that sources of tax revenue have been changing over the past 40 years. In 1957, governments at all levels collected a total of nearly $109 billion; by 2004, total tax collections were just over $2.9 trillion. Despite the changes, the individual income tax is the primary revenue source for the federal government, the sales tax the primary source for state governments, and the property tax the primary source for local governments, including school districts. It is important to remember these relationships as we discuss sources of revenue for schools later in this chapter.

Changes in Tax Structures

Federal, state, and local tax structures have experienced significant changes over time. At the federal level, there have been shifts in the proportion of taxes paid by individuals compared to business. There have also been changes in marginal tax rates and in the number of rate categories that are part of the tax system. The number and level of deductions, exemptions, and tax-sheltered items, as well as the treatment of capital gains, have also changed a number of times in the last 40 years. There have been a host of other modifications that alter the amount of money collected by the federal tax system and the way the taxes collected impact different individuals with different levels and sources of earnings. Most of these changes have affected federal, personal, and corporate income taxes, and the Social Security tax. The impact of the 2001 federal income tax reductions can be seen in Table 10.1: total federal individual and corporate income taxes produced approximately $6.3 billion less in 2004 than they did in 2000.

At the state level, tax structures have experienced even more changes. Over time, states have added new taxes, including on occasion a new income or sales tax. They have also changed tax rates, enacted a variety of mechanisms to alleviate tax burdens on low-income families, conformed their income tax structure to the ever-changing federal tax structure, and modified their tax systems to buffer increases and decreases in federal intergovernmental grants. In addition, during recent periods of economic growth, many states took steps to reduce taxes and/or curtail the growth of tax revenues. On the other hand, during the bleaker fiscal times of the early 2000s, many states raised tax rates slightly to close budget gaps. Although public finance economists urge governments to create stability in the tax structure so households and the business community can make decisions in a more stable fiscal environment, political leaders have difficulty heeding this advice. Change seems to be a hallmark of state and federal tax structures, catalyzed by both economic and political variables.

In the past two decades, states have become more dependent on income (and to some extent sales) taxes than in the past. At the same time, because measures of individual household income seem to be changing—with more households owning and trading stocks and bonds—state revenues seem to fluctuate with changes in the economy more than in the past. The result during the 1990s was substantial state revenue deficits during the recession at the beginning of the decade, followed by considerable state revenue surpluses later in the decade, when the economy was strong and growing. During this time, many states cut tax rates, which has resulted in even larger state revenue deficits early in the 2000s as the economy has weakened. As this is written at the end of 2006, most state economies seem to have rebounded, and state tax revenues appear to be increasing again.

At the same time, as pointed out previously and in Chapter 1, states continue to expand their share of public school revenues, making local school districts more dependent on swings in the economy, and hence swings in state revenues, than in the past. Although school districts have always had to cope with some variation in revenue over time, the recent swings have been proportionally much larger and have complicated the task of long-term planning at the same time that districts face increased calls for greater accountability. One of the challenges facing public finance today is finding ways to smooth out the gyrations in state revenue—a new factor to consider in raising and spending government resources.

2. ASSESSING AND UNDERSTANDING TAXATION

Raising taxes is not a simple endeavor. Not only are actions to increase tax revenues—or institute new taxes—unpopular politically, but new taxes often have side effects that may create economic inefficiencies (Musgrave and Musgrave, 1989; Rosen, 2004). In looking at the revenue potential of any tax, policymakers consider both the tax rate and the tax base.

The tax rate is simply the rate of taxation; the tax base is the entity to which the tax rate is applied. The yield is the amount of revenues raised. The relationship between tax rate and tax base is crucial to understanding the yield of any tax and can be captured in a simple equation:

$$\text{Tax Yield} = \text{Tax Rate} \times \text{Tax Base}$$

Policymakers seeking to increase revenue can increase either the rate or the base, or both. The decision they make will have differential impacts on individuals in different circumstances. It is important to understand what those impacts might be before recommending that changes in tax rates or tax bases be implemented. In general, economists argue that the most efficient taxes, those that create the fewest inefficiences in the economy, are those with low rates and broad bases (see, e.g., Musgrave and Musgrave, 1989; Rosen, 2004).

Public Finance Criteria for Evaluating Taxes

Public finance economists use several analytic criteria to evaluate taxes. These criteria are commonly accepted as both the economic and policy assessments needed when analyzing a tax (see Musgrave and Musgrave, 1989, or Rosen, 2004, for an example). These criteria include:

- The tax base
- Yield
- Equity
- The economic effects of the tax
- Administration and compliance issues

This section discusses each of these in detail.

Tax base.   Again, the tax base is the entity to which a tax rate is applied. For example, a tax could be based on the number of cars or television sets a person owned. The rate, then, could be a fixed dollar amount per car or television. Usually, tax bases are related to some economic category, such as income, property, or consumption. Broad-based taxes, such as property, income, and sales taxes, are taxes with broad or comprehensive bases. There are four major tax bases: wealth, income, consumption, and privilege.

Wealth.   There are many forms of wealth, some typically taxed and others not taxed. In economic terms, wealth represents an accumulation of value, or a stock of value, at any one point in time. Net worth—the sum of all economic assets minus all economic liabilities at some fixed point in time—is one measure of wealth. A wealth tax, then, could be levied on an individual's net worth. Proposals for net worth taxes have been made over the years but have never been enacted into law, in part because, although net worth is straightforward conceptually, it is complicated to calculate for each individual.

Another common measure of wealth is property. Property can be divided into two general categories: real and personal. Real property includes land and buildings. For individuals, personal property includes assets with a shorter life span, such as automobiles and other vehicles, and household items, such as furniture, video equipment, computers, rugs, and appliances. For businesses, personal property includes machinery and equipment, furniture and other office supplies, and inventories. Stocks, bonds, and other financial instruments (certificates of deposit, notes, bank accounts, etc.) are other forms of wealth that could theoretically be taxed. The value of an inheritance is yet another form of wealth that is often taxed.

A pure tax on wealth would tax all of these different categories. The United States does not have, and has never had, a wealth tax. Financial instruments such as stocks and bonds have rarely been taxed. Further, large portions of real property owned by the government and religious organizations are not taxed. And there has been an increasing tendency on the part of states to exempt some types of real and many forms of personal property from taxation.

The property tax comes closest to a wealth tax in this country. But the property tax generally covers only real property. The trend over the past three decades has been to eliminate both individual and business personal property from the property tax (Monk and Brent, 1997).

Income. Income represents another tax base. Compared with wealth, which is a measure of economic worth at one point in time, income is a measure of an economic flow over time. The net value of income minus expenses over time represents the change in net worth over that period. Income includes salaries, interest from financial instruments (savings and money market accounts, loans, etc.), dividends from stocks, gifts, and money from the sale of an item of wealth, including both property and a financial instrument. Earned income is typically money earned through work, such as wages and salaries. Unearned income represents money received from the returns on financial assets and investments, such as stocks, bonds, and mutual funds.

While income from salaries is rather easy to identify, income from business activities is more complicated, since net income is determined by subtracting legitimate expenses from gross receipts or sales. While conceptually straightforward, defining "gross receipts," "sales," and "legitimate expenses" is technically complex, and income can vary substantially depending on the specifics of the definition.

Regardless of how income is defined, it is generally viewed as the measure of ability to pay. This measure refers to all forms of taxation, not just income taxes. For example, if the value of a person's wealth is fixed, such as the value of a home, some current income is needed to pay a tax on that element of wealth. If current income is insufficient to pay the tax, the element of wealth would need to be sold, or partially sold, to meet the tax liability. Alternatively, the individual would need to borrow funds to pay the tax or alter his or her consumption patterns to be able to pay the taxes. This would likely result in a reduced ability to purchase other goods and services. The same is true for a sales or consumption tax; that tax is paid from an individual's current income, so the greater the tax, the fewer other things the individual can purchase with current income sources.

An important factor in using income as a measure of ability to pay is the period over which income is measured. Typically, income is measured in annual amounts, and most tax structures assume yearly income to be both the tax base and the measure of ability to pay. But individuals and businesses purchase capital items, such as homes, cars, manufacturing plants, factories, and equipment, on a longer-term basis, often with the assumption that average income will increase over time. For example, assuming their income would rise over the next decade, a family might purchase an expensive home with a mortgage that consumes a high proportion of their current income. Their assumption that income will grow over time means that in a few years the cost of the mortgage (monthly payments) will be less burdensome, eventually being a smaller portion of their monthly expenses. This suggests to many economists that some measure of long-term, or lifetime, income, might be a better measure of ability to pay, rather than annual income, which is generally used in such analyses today (see, e.g., Musgrave and Musgrave, 1989; Rosen, 2004).

Consumption.   Theoretically, a tax on consumption would include taxation of all goods and services purchased by individuals and businesses—including, for example, legal services and accounting services. A consumption tax is usually called a sales tax if it applies to a broad range of items that can be purchased. Most state and local sales taxes fall into this category. A consumption tax is usually called an excise tax if it applies to specific items, such as beer, alcohol, cigarettes, furs, jewelry, and luxury cars.

A broad-based consumption tax would tax income less savings—all income spent on purchases for current consumption. The United States does not have a broad-based consumption tax at the present time although there have been a number of calls for such a tax to be implemented. While most state sales taxes come the closest to this definition, they generally exclude *services,* which are an increasing component of current consumption, and they include both small and large products, such as food, prescription medicine, and cars. Thus, sales taxes in this country are more aptly described as broad-based selective sales taxes.

Privilege.   A small portion of revenues for federal, state, and local government services are raised by granting individuals or businesses a privilege and charging a fee for that privilege. A driver's license fee is paid for the privilege of driving a car; a car license plate fee is paid for the privilege of owning a car. Privilege fees are paid for a variety of other purposes, such as for running certain businesses, using park facilities, operating a taxicab, and using port facilities. A privilege tax is similar to an excise tax, the major difference being that the privilege tax is paid for the privilege of engaging in some activity, while an excise tax is paid for the privilege of purchasing and owning or using some product.

Yield.   Again, the yield is the amount of revenues a tax produces. Yield is equal to the tax rate times the tax base. Rates are usually—but not always—given in percentage terms. Examples include a 5 percent sales tax, a 10 percent gasoline tax, a 33 percent marginal federal income tax rate, and a 4 percent state income tax rate. Given a defined tax base, it is straightforward to determine the yield for each percent of tax rate on that tax base. Knowing the revenue-raising or yield potential of a tax (given a defined tax base) is important information for policymakers. Economists argue that it is preferable to be able to raise substantial revenues at low or modest rates, arguing for broad-based taxes rather than taxes with narrowly defined bases.

Broad-based taxes by definition can produce high yields even at modest rates, whereas selective taxes, such as a cigarette tax, are limited in the amount of revenue they can produce. A tax that produces a large amount of revenue, such as a property tax, is difficult to eliminate (a proposal often made for the unpopular property tax). This is because doing so would require either large cuts in governmental services or substantial increases in other tax rates. Neither option is politically popular—or viable in most cases. Indeed, broad-based taxes may make it easier to raise new revenues since it would require only a small tax rate increase.

Other aspects of tax yield include revenue stability and tax elasticity. Stability is the degree to which the yield rises or falls with national or state economic cycles. Stable tax revenues decrease less in economic downturns but also increase less during economic upturns.

The property tax historically has been a stable tax since property values consistently increase over time and fall only in deep, major recessions. Sales taxes on products tend to rise and fall more in line with economic cycles, as do taxes on income. Corporate income taxes follow economic cycles even more closely and thus tend to be an even more volatile revenue source. In the current economic environment, both income and sales tax receipts appear to have become less stable.

Elasticity measures the degree to which tax revenues keep pace with changes in either their base or, more commonly, in personal income. To measure the income elasticity of a tax, one compares the ratio of the percentage change in the tax yield to the percentage change in personal income. An elasticity less than one indicates that tax revenues do not keep pace with income growth; an elasticity equal to one indicates that tax revenues grow at the same rate as incomes; and an elasticity greater than one indicates that tax revenues increase faster than income growth. Since prices and demands for government services (including schools) tend to at least keep pace with income growth, an income elasticity of at least one is a highly desirable feature of any tax for schools. Individual income taxes, especially if marginal rates are higher for higher incomes, tend to be elastic, while sales tax revenues generally track income growth. Over time, property taxes have exhibited elasticities of approximately one.

To some degree, a trade-off exists between stability and elasticity. Elastic taxes tend to be less stable since their yield falls in economic downturns, when personal income also tends to fall or at least to grow more slowly. Stable taxes are less elastic. As a result, their yields remain steadier during economic fluctuations.

Tax equity.   Tax equity addresses the issue of whether the tax is fair, treating individuals or businesses equitably. Although conceptually simple, it is difficult to determine precisely the degree to which a tax treats all fairly. There are two primary aspects of tax equity: horizontal equity and vertical equity.

Horizontal equity concerns equal tax treatment of individuals in the same, or equal, circumstance, such as annual income. For example, if an income tax met the horizontal-equity test, individuals with the same taxable income (e.g., $40,000), would pay the same amount of tax (e.g., $4,000). Or two families with a home with the same market value would pay the same amount of property tax. But as will be discussed later, these two simple examples mask a variety of technical issues. In the income tax case, the issue is determining taxable income. At both the federal and state level, gross income is subject to a variety of exemptions, deductions, and adjustments—adjustments intended to recognize differences in individual circumstances and adjust tax liabilities accordingly—in determining taxable income. If there is disagreement about any of those modifications, the preceding conclusion about horizontal equity could be challenged. As a result, even horizontal tax equity is difficult to attain.

Most individuals are not equally situated. Vertical equity is the principle used to describe how a tax treats individuals in different economic situations. Determining vertical equity is more complex than estimating horizontal equity. The first issue is to decide on the criterion for differentiating tax treatment. That is, if taxes are to burden some individuals more than others, what variable should determine those differences?

The degree to which the tax would vary is a value judgment. But determining on what basis a tax should vary is an important tax policy decision.

One possible criterion would be benefits received—that is, taxes should vary with the benefits received—where the greater the benefits, the higher the tax paid. For example, a gasoline tax burdens drivers but meets the benefits-received criterion since individuals who drive benefit from use of public roads and highways. Moreover, the more they drive, the more they benefit from the roads, and the more they pay in gasoline taxes as they consume more gasoline.

By definition, a fee-for-service tax meets the benefits principle—the fee is simply the tax for the service (or benefit) received. Appealing as the benefits-received criterion is, it is difficult, if not impossible, to measure the individual benefits received for a broader array of services. For example, police and fire services generally benefit all individuals within the locality where those services are provided. But education, which is another locally provided service, benefits not only individuals in the form of higher incomes but also society in general in the form of economic growth and lower needs for social services (Cohn and Geske, 1990). Even if education benefits accrued only to individuals, today most individuals move from the district where they were educated, making it difficult to have anything other than a national tax related to those benefits.

At broader levels, the benefits principle becomes more problematic. For example, how do we measure the individual benefits from spending on national defense, public transportation systems, interstate highway systems, a statewide higher education system, or an interstate system of waterways for transit and agriculture? It would seem foolish to increase the taxes for individuals receiving public assistance (welfare) benefits since taxation of their benefits would defeat the purpose of providing the assistance in the first place. For these reasons, a benefits principle, though appealing to economists, has not been implemented as a basis for differential tax treatment, at least for broad-based income, sales, and property taxes.

Instead, ability to pay has been adopted in this country as the criterion for vertical tax equity. Ability to pay is generally measured by income. If taxes differ among individuals, they should differ because of differences in their ability to pay—that is, because they have different income levels.

Vertical tax equity can be measured by comparing taxes expressed as a percentage of income. Vertical equity is broadly defined by the terms "progressive," "proportional," or "regressive." **Progressive tax** burdens increase with income—as income rises, so does the tax liability as a percentage of income. Proportional tax burdens would impose the same percentage tax burden regardless of the level of income. Regressive taxes are the opposite of progressive taxes in that individuals with lower incomes pay a higher percentage of their income in taxes than do those with higher incomes. They may not pay more in total taxes, but as a portion of their income, more goes to taxes. For example, if an individual with $10,000 in income paid a 12 percent income tax and an individual with an income of $100,000 paid a 10 percent income tax, the tax would be regressive. However, the total dollar tax burden would be $1,200 for the low-income individual and $10,000 for the individual with the higher income.

In this country, it is generally agreed that **regressive tax** burdens should be avoided. It is widely felt that the poor, or low-income individuals or households, should not pay a larger percentage of income in taxes than average or above-average individuals. It is also generally agreed that the tax system should be at least proportional, and probably progressive, although support for progressive tax burdens has waned in recent years as initiatives at both federal and state levels have reduced the degree of progressivity of many taxes. For example, in the 1990s, there was considerable interest in a flat tax rate for federal income taxes. While a progressive tax burden has generally been sanctioned in the past, there is less consensus for that position today.

Measuring vertical tax equity entails an additional series of technical problems. First, one needs to distinguish tax impact from tax incidence or tax burden. Put differently, one needs to differentiate between who actually pays the tax to the tax collector from who actually bears the burden of the tax. The latter is commonly referred to as the *tax incidence*. For example, merchants actually submit sales tax payments to governments, but individuals who purchase products almost always bear the burden or incidence of the sales tax. Likewise, companies or organizations usually remit income tax payments to state and federal governments, but working individuals almost always bear the burden of that tax since income taxes are withheld from periodic salary payments. The issue of tax incidence or tax burden for other taxes is not as clear-cut.

Tax incidence for the property tax is the most complex. Four different types of property are taxed: owner-occupied homes, residential rental property, business and industry property, and commercial property. Not only is the property tax on individuals who own homes paid by homeowners, but they also bear the full burden of the tax. But property taxes on the other components can be shifted. For example, property taxes on rental property might be shifted to renters in the form of higher rents. The extent to which the apartment owner can shift the tax burden to the renter depends on such things as the competition for rental units in the area and the relative condition of the building in question. Depending on competitive conditions, property taxes on industries and corporations could be shifted forward to consumers in the form of higher prices or backward to workers in the form of lower wages, or could be borne by stockholders in the form of lower dividends and stock prices.

A similar issue exists for corporate income taxes: Are they shifted forward to consumers, in the term of higher prices, or backward to stockholders and/or workers? Likewise, depending on competitive conditions, property taxes on local commercial activities could be shifted forward to consumers or backward to owners. It turns out that shifting assumptions and patterns result in widely varying conclusions about property tax and corporate income tax incidence, from steeply regressive to steeply progressive.

Another issue to consider in assessing tax equity is income transfers. The federal government and many state governments have programs that transfer income from the broader group of taxpayers to the poor. Earned-income tax credits, food stamps, rent subsidies, and child-care supports are just some examples of income transfer programs. Thus, a comprehensive assessment of tax equity would consider taxes as well as income transfers. This is because, although the poor might pay a large percentage of their incomes in sales taxes and in assumed shifted property taxes, that regressivity could be counterbalanced by receipt of income from a variety of transfer programs. Likewise, average- and above-average-income individuals pay more taxes to support income transfer programs but receive none or few income transfer benefits.

Economic effects.   Although taxes are imposed by governments, and thus by definition distort the free functioning of the competitive market, some taxes and specific tax designs distort economic decision making more than others. The general goal is for taxes to have a neutral impact on the economy. So another criterion for assessing a specific tax structure is the degree to which it has neutral economic impacts.

Most taxes have some elements that are not economically neutral. The federal income tax is not neutral with respect to owning a home because it allows homeowners to deduct interest on home mortgages, thus encouraging housing consumption over other kinds of consumption. Since interest from savings is taxed at both the federal and state levels, consumption is encouraged over saving. Since most sales taxes cover only products, consumption of services (getting a hair cut, having legal or accounting services, etc.) is favored over consumption of products. Since business purchases, even of equipment and items that will be put into products for resale, are frequently (but not always, depending on the individual state sales tax structure) subject to the sales tax, vertical integration is somewhat encouraged if those costs are less than the costs of paying the tax. In California, for example, property taxes are based on market value at the time of purchase rather than current market value. As a consequence, purchase of a new home entails a high cost and is discouraged, while remaining in one's home is encouraged.

Differences in taxes across state borders can also encourage business investment and individual location. In metropolitan areas near state borders, individuals are economically encouraged to live in the state with the lowest sales and/or income tax rates in order to minimize their tax liability.

In short, almost all tax structures have elements that encourage or discourage a variety of economic behaviors. The goal is to structure the tax to neutralize its economic incentives as much as possible, or at least to minimize its economic distortions.

Administration and compliance.   Finally, both the administration of the tax and individual or business compliance with tax requirements should be simple and as low cost as possible. Often, simplicity is gained at the cost of some tax equity, and vice versa. Further, the more complex the tax, the greater the costs of both administration and compliance. Mikesell (1986) and others (e.g., Rosen, 2004) identify several factors in tax administration and compliance:

- Maintaining and gathering of records
- Computation of the tax liability
- Remittance of the tax liability
- Collection
- Audits
- Appeals
- Enforcement

Depending on the tax in question, responsibility for each of these steps falls on individual taxpayers or governmental agencies. Ideally, both administration of and ability to comply with the tax requirements should be simple. Monk and Brent (1997) point out that the more complicated the tax system, the greater the costs of administration and compliance.

An example of a revenue source with high administrative costs is a lottery, which is increasingly popular across the country. Lotteries are poor sources of revenue because of the high costs of administration. To sell lottery tickets, a wide variety of prizes must be offered to individuals who purchase tickets. In most states, the prize payouts account for 50 percent of all lottery sales. Put differently, for every $1 raised through lottery sales, 50 cents is allocated to prizes. Further, most merchants who sell lottery tickets earn a commission, which takes more away from other governmental uses. Other administrative costs also add to expenses. For example, in California, prizes are required to be 50 percent of sales, and administrative costs (which include commissions to sales agents) are capped at 16 percent of lottery ticket sales. Assuming that state lottery administration costs are equal to the full 16 percent of ticket sales, only 34 percent of each lottery dollar is available for other uses.

All other broad-based taxes, such as the income, sales, and property taxes, while requiring administrative costs for both the government and individuals, provide a much higher net yield, somewhere in the high 90 percent range. To be sure, there are ways of increasing and decreasing administration costs of these taxes, but in all cases, they are dramatically lower than those of a lottery.

States could nearly eliminate income tax administrative costs if they simply made the state income tax a fixed percentage of federal tax liability. States could eliminate sales taxes altogether, and thus sales tax administrative costs, by adopting a general consumption tax that could be administered entirely through the income tax. Short of these more dramatic choices, streamlining federal and state tax administration remains an important objective for any specific tax structure and any change in tax structure.

3. ANALYSIS OF INDIVIDUAL TAXES

This section uses the previous framework to analyze the key features of each of the following taxes: income, sales, property, and lotteries. The basis, yield, equity, economic effects, and administration of each is discussed.

The Income Tax

The individual income tax is the largest revenue producer for the federal government and is also used by 41 states. Another three states apply the income tax only to interest, dividends, and/or capital gains (i.e., on income from capital assets but not on earned income). Eleven states allow local governments to levy income taxes. As shown in Table 10.1, in 2004, individual and corporate income taxes produced $1.20 trillion for the federal government, $239.0 billion for state governments, and $19.4 billion for local governments. In the following analysis, we focus primarily on the federal income tax. The discussion of income taxes ends with comments on trends in state income taxes and needed changes for the future.

Tax basis.   Income is the base for both federal and state income taxes. But defining "income" and determining taxable income is a complex activity driven by federal and state tax codes that are revised frequently and run to thousands of pages. Defining "gross income" and determining taxable income requires a series of modifications, including income adjustments, standard and itemized deductions, and exemptions. While an income tax generally meets the horizontal-equity standard, since individuals with the same taxable income pay the same amount of tax, horizontal equity would be violated if any of the income modifications are deemed unjustified. In addition, both the federal and state governments have different tax schedules for individuals and for families (individuals generally paying higher tax rates than families under the assumption that it costs less for one individual to maintain a household than it does for a family). Horizontal equity is violated if there is disagreement over the particular mechanism for differential treatment of individuals and families in either the federal or state income tax structures.

Income adjustments, standard and itemized deductions, and various exemptions at first blush seem reasonable modifications to make to determine taxable income. Most would agree that two families with, for example, an income of $50,000 should pay a different amount of tax if one family consists of just husband and wife with few medical expenditures and the other consists of husband and wife, four children, a live-in parent, and high medical costs. But a reasonable deduction or adjustment for one person can seem unreasonable or unfair to another. For example, in the past, several types of investments provided large deductions for taxpayers, often exceeding the dollar amount of investment made. While such tax shelters encouraged investment in those activities, some having social values like low-income housing, the proliferation of tax shelters and their use primarily by higher-income individuals led to the perception over time that they were simply unfair.

Yield.   Individual and corporate income taxes are the largest source of revenue for the federal government. Table 10.1 shows that both federal and state income taxes have grown considerably over time. However, Table 10.2 shows that as a percentage of personal income, total individual and corporate income taxes have remained relatively stable—actually dropping from 16.6 percent of personal income in 1957 to a low of 13.6 percent 1994, and then increasing to 15.0 percent in 2004. This suggests that income taxes take approximately the same "bite" out of household income today as they did in the 1950s. However, inspection of the last column in Table 10.2 shows that individual income taxes as a percentage of personal income have increased slightly over time, reaching a total of 13.7 percent of personal income in 2001 and, following the federal tax reductions of 2001, declining to 11.8 percent in 2004. This suggests that over time, individual income taxes have dropped somewhat.

The income tax is an elastic tax: as income rises, income tax collections generally rise faster. Table 10.3 shows that the individual income tax elasticity exceeded one (i.e., tax collections grew at a faster rate than personal income) in each decade between 1957 and 1987. That pattern was reversed between 1987 and 1994, when the elasticity of the income tax amounted to only 0.73. This is due largely to the income

TABLE 10.2   Income Taxes as a Percentage of Personal Income, 1957–2004

Fiscal Year	Total Individual and Corporate Income Taxes (in Billions)	Total Individual Income Taxes (in Billions)	Personal Income (in Billions)	Total Individual and Corporate Income Taxes as a Percentage of Personal Income	Total Individual Income Taxes as a Percentage of Personal Income
1957	$ 59.5	$ 37.4	$ 359.3	16.6%	10.4%
1967	103.5	68.3	650.4	15.9	10.5
1977	250.0	189.5	1,637.1	15.3	11.6
1987	582.8	476.5	3,962.5	14.7	12.0
1994	840.6	671.9	6,200.9	13.6	10.8
2001	1,290.8	1,188.9	8,685.3	14.9	13.7
2004	1,463.8	1,147.6	9,731.4	15.0	11.8

Sources: Advisory Commission on Intergovernmental Relations (1988), *Significant Features of Fiscal Federalism,* 1988 ed. Volume II. Washington, DC: ACIR, p. 64, Table 59. U.S. Bureau of the Census (1988), *Government Finance in 1986–87.* Washington, DC: U.S. Bureau of the Census, p. 7. *Economic Report of the President,* January 1989, p. 333. Scott Moody, ed. (1998), *Facts and Figures on Government Finance,* 32nd ed. Washington, DC: Tax Foundation, Tables C23 and D22. Bureau of Economic Analysis (1998), *Survey of Current Business.* Washington, DC: U.S. Department of Commerce; www.bea.doc.gov/bea/ARTICLES/NATIONAL/NIPA/ 1998/0898nip3.pdf/, Table 1, p. 147. U.S. Bureau of the Census (2002), United States State Government Tax Collections: 2001. Washington, DC: U.S. Bureau of the Census; www.census.gov/govs/statetax/0100usstax.html. Bureau of Economic Analysis (2002), Regional Accounts Data: Annual State Personal Income. Washington, DC: U.S. Department of Commerce; www.bea.gov/bea/regional/spi/. Bureau of Economic Analysis (2002), Personal Income and Its Distribution: Table 2.1, and National Income and Product Accounts Tables: Table 3.2. Federal Government Current Receipts and Expenditures. Washington, DC: U.S. Department of Commerce; www.bea.gov/bea/dn/nipaweb/selecttable.asp?SelectedTable (select table, then select annual and "Refresh Table"). Personal income data for 2004 from www.bea.gov/bea/dn/home/personalincome.htm. State and local from U.S. Census Bureau (2006), *Quarterly Summary of State and Local Government Tax Revenue,* Table 1, National Totals of State and Local Government Tax Revenue for Current and Prior Quarters, as well as 12-month calculations; www.census.gov/govs/www/qtax.html, retrieved August 31, 2006.

tax revisions of 1986, which substantially flattened the tax brackets and left the highest bracket at 31 percent during the recession of the early 1990s, and to the indexing of income tax brackets so that increased marginal tax rates impacted only taxpayers whose incomes grew at a rate faster than the rate of inflation. The table shows that between 1994 and 2001 elasticity increased dramatically. This is the result of increases in the top marginal tax rate to 39 percent and the dramatic growth in personal income attributable to the large number of individuals who received stock options as part of their compensation package. The federal tax reductions in

TABLE 10.3   Income Tax Yield Elasticity, 1957–2004

Year	Individual Income Taxes (in Billions)	Personal Income (in Billions)	Percent Change Individual Income Taxes	Percent Change Personal Income	Elasticity: Ratio of Percentage Change in Tax Collections to Percentage Change in Income
1957	$ 37.4	$ 359.3	—	—	—
1967	68.3	650.4	82.6%	81.0%	1.02
1977	189.5	1,637.1	177.5	151.7	1.17
1987	476.2	3,962.5	151.3	142.0	1.07
1994	671.9	6,200.9	41.1	56.5	0.73
2001	1,188.9	8,685.3	76.9	40.1	1.92
2004	1,147.6	9,731.4	−3.5	12.0	−0.17

Sources: Advisory Commission on Intergovernmental Relations (1988), *Significant Features of Fiscal Federalism*, 1988 ed., Volume II. Washington, DC: ACIR. p. 64, Table 59. U.S. Bureau of the Census (1988), *Government Finance in 1986–87.* Washington, DC: U.S. Bureau of the Census, p. 7. Economic Report of the President, January 1989, p. 333. Scott. Moody, ed. (1998), *Facts and Figures on Government Finance*, 32nd ed. Washington, DC: Tax Foundation, Tables C23 and D22. Bureau of Economic Analysis (1998), *Survey of Current Business.* Washington, DC: U.S. Department of Commerce; www.bea.doc.gov/bea/ARTICLES/ NATIONAL/NIPA/1998/0898nip3.pdf/, Table 1, p. 147. U.S. Bureau of the Census (2002), United States State Government Tax Collections: 2001. Washington, DC: U.S. Bureau of the Census; www.census.gov/govs/statetax/0100usstax.html Bureau of Economic Analysis (2002), Personal Income and Its Distribution, Table 2.1, and National Income and Product Accounts Tables, Table 3.2, Federal Government Current Receipts and Expenditures. Washington, DC: U.S. Department of Commerce; www.bea.gov/bea/dn/nipaweb/selecttable.asp?SelectedTable (select table, then select annual and "Refresh Table"). State and local from U.S. Census Bureau. (2006), *Quarterly Summary of State and Local Government Tax Revenue,* Table 1, National Totals of State and Local Government Tax Revenue for Current and Prior Quarters, as well as 12-month calculations; www.census.gov/govs/www/qtax.html, retrieved August 31, 2006.

2001 were substantial enough to suggest a negative elasticity. That is, income grew and tax collections shrunk, resulting in lower tax collections despite higher personal income. As the recession of the early 2000s recedes further, personal income growth is likely to be substantial enough to see growth in tax collections and a positive elasticity again. In fact, it is likely that the data displayed in Table 10.2 are simply an artifact of the two years chosen as, over time, income taxes have generally been highly elastic.[1]

[1]Some might argue that the elasticity of a tax should be calculated after adjusting for any tax rate changes so the elasticity measures the growth in taxes as just a function of growth in personal income. The comments in the paragraph refer to an elasticity that did not adjust for changes in tax rates and thus show the link between actual revenue changes and actual income changes.

Income taxes, even though they are elastic, have historically been quite stable. Even in past economic downturns, personal income did not drop tremendously across the nation. As a result, individual income taxes have tended to drop little, if at all. As just described briefly, this pattern seems to have changed during the 1990s, such that the combination of income tax cuts during high-growth periods and changes in the structure of personal income have altered the realities of both federal and state revenue generation, at least in the years just before the tax rate changes and the years just after.

Since corporate profits fluctuate much more in recessions and economic growth periods, corporate income taxes tend to be less stable than individual income taxes. Thus, the trend toward making individual income taxes a larger portion of the total of individual and corporate income taxes works to make the income tax a more stable revenue source.

Equity.   Horizontal equity was discussed previously. In terms of vertical equity, the federal individual income tax is clearly progressive due to the use of marginal income tax rates that increase with income. Most state individual income tax structures are also progressive, although they tend not to be as progressive as the federal income tax, since many states have targeted income-tax-relief programs for low-income families (Johnson, 2000). Since individuals cannot shift the income tax, tax impact and tax burden are identical (i.e., those who pay the tax also bear its burden or economic incidence).

In addition to the marginal tax rate brackets, progressivity in the federal income tax system is increased through the use of exemptions and standard deductions. The personal exemption spares a portion of income from taxation under the theory that individuals need some income to pay their living costs and thus should be able to do so without the burden of taxation. Vertical equity among households is achieved to some degree by allowing an exemption for each individual in the household. The standard deduction also reduces taxable income using the same logic; however, it applies to an entire household. Families with high-deductible expenses, such as mortgage interest costs or medical bills, generally choose to itemize their deductions to further reduce their taxable income.

State income tax rates are not nearly as progressive as the federal rates. However, Monk and Brent (1997) have shown that they are generally progressive. Only 10 states have indexed income brackets, and the relatively low level of income subject to the highest tax rates in many states further reduces progressivity (Gold, 1994). States that use the federal tax liability as the basis for their own income taxes tend to have more progressive tax structures—in line with the progressivity of the federal system. Another way to look at the progressivity of the federal income tax is to consider who pays the taxes. Data from the Tax Foundation (www.taxfoundation.org/research/show/250.html [September 1, 2006]) show the percentage of total federal individual income taxes paid by different numbers of taxpayers in 1999 and 2003. For 1999, the top 5 percent of taxpayers (i.e., the 5 percent of tax returns with the highest incomes) paid 55.5 percent of the total federal individual income tax and earned 34.0 percent of total income. In 2003, they paid 54.4 percent of the total federal individual income tax and earned 31.2 percent of total income. This shows that the highest earners in the country pay a substantially higher portion of the taxes than their share of total income. On the other side, the bottom 50 percent of tax returns (those with the lowest incomes) paid 4 percent of the federal individual income tax despite earning 13.3 percent of total income in 1999, and 3.5 percent of the federal individual income tax with 14.0 percent of total income in 2003. This pattern suggests a strongly progressive tax structure. The Tax Foundation data show that the average tax rate declines steadily as income declines.

State tax burden studies have not been as detailed as those at the national level in large part because gathering such data for all 50 states is very costly. Nevertheless, Phares (1980) calculated indices of progressivity for state individual income taxes for 1977 and found state individual income taxes to be the most progressive state tax. Indeed, Phares found that only state tax structures with a major individual income tax were progressive overall. We would expect this conclusion to be true for today's state tax structures as well.

Economic effects.   To the degree that deductions and income adjustments are limited, the income tax can be quite neutral in its economic effects. Nevertheless, there are several economic impacts created by both the federal and most state income taxes. First, as stated previously, the deduction of home mortgage interest, though quite popular, encourages home purchases more than would be the case if the deduction were eliminated. Second, including interest earned from savings as well as returns from investments in taxable income is in some ways a deterrent to savings. While there is reasonable debate over these tax provisions, if neither were taxed, savings and investments would probably increase and arguably would help improve the productivity of the country's economic system.

Administration and compliance.   The federal income tax is complex and costly to administer for businesses and most individuals. And continual changes to the tax code make the system more, not less, complex. Large percentages of individuals use accountants and other services to complete income tax forms, and businesses have large accounting departments that spend considerable time keeping tax records and filing returns. Often, tax requirements are different from good accounting requirements. The costs borne by individuals and corporations reduce the economic efficiency of the income tax.

Income tax trends and issues at the state level.   While state sales tax increases received the most attention during the mid-1980s, the state income tax increased both as a percentage of personal income and as a percentage of total state taxes, as shown by the data in Table 10.4. Between 1957 and 2001, state income taxes rose from 0.7 percent to 2.8 percent of personal income, declining slightly to 2.4 percent in 2004. Income taxes represented 17.2 percent of total state taxes in 1957, growing to 42.8 percent of total state taxes in 2001 and again declining slightly in 2004 to 39.2 percent.

These trends emerged in part because few states reformed their income tax structures. Maximum tax rates were reached in nearly half the states when taxable income peaked at only $10,000, and the value of personal exemptions was low. Thus, inflation in the late 1970s, together with general wage increases, pushed individuals into the top income tax brackets. These realities interacted with rate increases in the

TABLE 10.4   State Individual Income Taxes as a Percentage of Personal Income and as a Percentage of Total State Taxes, 1957–2004

Fiscal Year	State Individual Income Taxes as a Percentage of Personal Income	State Individual Income Taxes as a Percentage of Total State Taxes
1957	0.7%	17.2%
1967	1.1	22.2
1977	2.2	34.3
1987	2.6	39.2
1994	2.7	38.2
2001	2.8	42.8
2004	2.4	39.2

Sources: Advisory Commission on Intergovernmental Relations (1988), *Significant Features of Fiscal Federalism*, 1988 ed., Volume II. Washington, DC: ACIR, p. 64, Table 59. U.S. Bureau of the Census (1988). *Government Finance in 1986–87*. Washington, DC: U.S. Bureau of the Census, p. 7. Economic Report of the President, January 1989, p. 333. Scott. Moody, ed. (1998), *Facts and Figures on Government Finance*, 32nd ed. Washington, DC: Tax Foundation, Tables C23 and D22. Bureau of Economic Analysis (1998), Survey of Current Business. Washington, DC: U.S. Department of Commerce; www.bea.doc.gov/bea/ARTICLES/NATIONAL/ NIPA/1998/0898nip3.pdf/, Table 1, p. 147. U.S. Bureau of the Census (2002), United States State Government Tax Collections: 2001. Washington, DC: U.S. Bureau of the Census; www.census.gov/govs/statetax/0100usstax.html. Bureau of Economic Analysis (2002a), Regional Accounts Data: Annual State Personal Income. Washington, DC: U.S. Department of Commerce; www.bea.gov/bea/regional.spi/.

early 1980s to combat revenue losses caused by recession and federal aid cuts, and income tax revenues rose. An unanticipated result, in part also due to unchanged income tax structures, was that increasing numbers of low-income households faced income tax burdens for the first time. Although several states began to reform their income tax in 1987, the strength of the economy in the late 1990s led to a number of state tax reductions.

Despite the changes that have occurred over time in the structure of the state income tax, it should continue to provide a stable source of revenue. Potential state income tax reforms include the following:

1. Broaden the base to improve horizontal equity, increase political and popular perceptions about the fairness of the tax, and negate the trend to narrow the base through exclusions.
2. Reduce rates in both numbers and levels to increase public perception of the tax and help improve the business climate.
3. Increase the values of personal exemptions, standard deductions, and earned income credits to eliminate the poor from income tax rolls.
4. Index the entire structure to require political votes to increase revenues rather than have tax revenue increases occur as a by-product of inflation.

Conclusions about the income tax. The income tax was historically perceived in the public finance community as a fair tax and as the nation's and most states' most progressive tax. During the 1970s and 1980s, however, it was increasingly viewed as unfair. Many saw the income tax as proliferating exclusions; special tax shelters, inflation, and privileged treatment drove most individuals into higher tax brackets, put the poor on the income tax rolls for the first time, and allowed many rich individuals and corporations to completely avoid paying any income taxes. Federal tax reform efforts in the 1980s and 1990s began to reverse those trends and to restore the income tax as a fair, high-revenue-producing tax. States began to reform state income taxes in 1987. In the 1990s, the federal income tax became slightly more progressive than it was in the late 1980s. States are relying on it for more of their revenue as well.

The Sales Tax

The general or retail sales tax is the single largest source of state revenue today. In FY 2004, states and local governments collected $252.9 billion in sales, gross receipts, and customs taxes (see Table 10.1). The sales tax is the most common state tax, currently in use by 45 states. Only one of the five states that does not have a state sales tax, Alaska, allows for local sales tax levies (Due and Mikesell, 1994). In FY 2004, general sales taxes and selective sales taxes represented 35.7 percent of total state revenue (Federation of Tax Administrators, www.taxadmin.org/fta/rate/slsource.html [September 1, 2006]).

Historical context. Mississippi was the first state to enact a sales tax. In 1932, it introduced a 2 percent sales tax designed to replace a low-rate business tax (Due and Mikesell, 1994). Initially a desperation measure designed to help states fund essential services during the Great Depression, the sales tax has become the single largest source of revenue for states. At the same time, states have typically transferred authority for property taxes to local governments (Monk and Brent, 1997).

Despite protests by retailers, sales taxes spread rapidly. Between 1933 and 1938, 26 more states, plus Hawaii (which was not yet a state), imposed a state sales tax (Due and Mikesell, 1994). Five states allowed the taxes to expire after one or two years, although they eventually reimposed them. The sales tax was particularly favored during the Great Depression when income tax yields fell due to declining incomes, local governments needed the revenues from property taxes, and the major tax available to the states was the sales tax.

Following the Depression and World War II, there was a slow trend toward renewed adoption of sales taxes. By 1963, 10 additional states had imposed sales taxes, and 3 of the 5 that allowed it to expire had renewed them, bringing the total to 37. The mid-1960s was a period of growth in state use of sales taxes, with 8 more states either introducing or reimposing a state sales tax. In 1969, Vermont was the 45th and last state to introduce a sales tax. Today, only Oregon, Montana, Delaware, New Hampshire, and Alaska do not have state general sales taxes, and in Alaska, there is substantial use of the sales tax at the local level. In many cases, local sales tax rates in Alaska are comparable to state sales tax rates in other states. Local sales taxes are feasible in Alaska because communities are fairly widely separated. This limits the possibility of avoiding the tax by making purchases in an adjoining no- or low-sales-tax community. This is generally not the case in most of the other 49 states.

Basis and yield.   State sales tax rates and revenue levels vary considerably (see www.taxadmin.org/fta/rate/sl_sales.html for current information). In 2004, state tax rates ranged from a low of 2.9 percent in Colorado to a high of 7 percent in Mississippi, Tennessee, and Rhode Island. In addition, local sales tax authority varies considerably from state to state, with sales tax rates as high as 11 percent in a few local jurisdictions in some states.

All general sales taxes are not alike. Many states offer exemptions for food and prescription (and nonprescription) drugs in an effort to reduce the regressive characteristics of the sales tax. The most common exemption is for prescription drugs. With the exception of New Mexico, all of the 44 states that levy a general sales tax exempt prescription drugs; 10 states exempt nonprescription drugs as well. Food is exempt from sales taxation in 27 states.

All 50 states levy one or more of a variety of additional sales and excise taxes. These are not general sales taxes, but represent additional levies on specific items. The exact nature and level of the taxes vary considerably. For example, gasoline taxes range from a low of 8 cents a gallon in Alaska to a high of 38 cents a gallon in Connecticut, while cigarette taxes vary from 3 cents a pack in Kentucky to $2.57 a pack in New Jersey. Even the five states without general sales taxes—Alaska, Delaware, Montana, New Hampshire, and Oregon—tax gasoline, cigarettes, and alcohol (Moody, 2002). Current information on state tax rates can be found at the Federation of Tax Administrators website.

Thirty-four states allow local jurisdictions to levy sales taxes as well. Local taxing authority varies substantially among the states, but cities and counties are typically granted some leeway in levying local sales taxes. In some states, other jurisdictions, such as transit agencies or special districts, are also allowed to levy sales taxes. Frequently, there is a limit on the tax rate any jurisdiction may levy, and in a number of states, there is a cap on the total local sales tax that may be levied.

The elasticity of the sales tax is considerably lower than that of the income tax (Gold, 1994). This means that as the economy of a state grows, and the more dependent the state is on income taxes compared to sales taxes, the faster state revenues will grow. The actual elasticity of a sales tax depends on the composition of its tax base. If food is taxed, elasticity tends to be relatively low since food consumption is not responsive to income growth (Gold, 1994). On the other hand, if services are taxed, the sales tax will be more elastic since demand for services is increasing more rapidly (Dye and McGuire, 1991).

Table 10.5 shows that in 1957, general sales taxes represented 2.4 percent of personal income. This figure grew to 4.0 percent by 1977 and remained at that level until the late 1990s when it began to decline slightly. In 2001, general sales taxes represented 3.7 percent of personal income, and by 2004, it had further declined to 3.6 percent of personal income.

TABLE 10.5   General Sales Taxes as a Percentage of Personal Income, 1957–2000

Fiscal Year	Total General Sales Taxes (in Billions)	Personal Income (in Billions)	Sales Taxes as a Percentage of Personal Income
1957	$ 8.6	$ 356.3	2.4%
1967	21.4	650.4	3.3
1977	64.0	1,637.5	4.0
1987	150.3	3,962.5	4.0
1995	243.6	6,200.9	4.0
2001	321.2	8,685.3	3.7
2004	349.4	9,731.4	3.6

Sources: Advisory Commission on Intergovernmental Relations (1988), *Significant Features of Fiscal Federalism,* 1988 ed., Volume II. Washington, DC: ACIR, p. 64, Table 59. U.S. Bureau of the Census (1988), *Government Finance in 1986–87.* Washington, DC: U.S. Bureau of the Census, p. 7. Economic Report of the President, January 1989, p. 333. Scott Moody, ed. (1998), *Facts and Figures on Government Finance,* 32nd ed. Washington, DC: Tax Foundation, Tables C23 and D22. Bureau of Economic Analysis (1998), Survey of Current Business. Washington, DC: U.S. Department of Commerce. Federation of Tax Administrators, www.taxadmin.org/fta/rate/00stl_pi.html/.

Stability.   A desirable characteristic of any tax is for it to produce revenue steadily, without large fluctuations from year to year. If revenue is unstable, the taxing jurisdiction will have more trouble balancing its budget (Gold, 1994). Sales taxes are clearly affected by changes in the economy. In times of recession, consumers have fewer dollars to spend, and businesses are less likely to purchase new equipment. On the other hand, when the economy is growing, consumer purchases tend to increase as well. Consequently, sales tax revenues may not be as stable as property tax receipts, but they are impacted less by changes in personal income than are income taxes (see Musgrave and Musgrave, 1989; Rosen, 2004).

The tax base for an individual state's sales tax also impacts how revenues respond to changes in the economy. For example, sales taxes in states that exempt food are more sensitive to economic downturns because individuals will continue to purchase food, and in many cases will shift purchases from prepared meals (e.g., restaurant meals, which are taxed) to grocery store purchases (which are not taxed). In times of economic growth, sales tax receipts may grow more slowly than income tax receipts since individuals with higher personal incomes may consume more services, which, as is discussed below, are taxed less often under state sales tax systems.

Equity.   Horizontal equity—the equal treatment of individuals in the same situation—is generally not a substantial problem with sales taxes since tax rates tend to be uniform across a state. Where local sales taxes are permitted, there may be differences, but they are relatively small and are uniform across a taxing jurisdiction.

Vertical equity is a problem for the sales tax. There is considerable evidence that sales taxes are modestly regressive. Since states generally obtain more income from taxes on consumption (sales taxes) than from taxes on income, most state tax systems are regressive (Gold, 1994), and the sales tax is a major source of that regressivity. While this regressivity may be lessened by the progressive, or less regressive, nature of other parts of the tax system, the sales tax places a greater burden on those in low-income categories. At the same time, the sales tax is not egregiously regressive. It is regressive more because familes with higher incomes spend less on items subject to the sales tax, so their sales tax burden declines with income, than because families with lower incomes spend significantly more on items subject to the sales tax.

Reducing sales tax regressivity.   Three approaches can be considered, either alone or together, in attempting to mitigate the regressive tendencies of a sales tax: (1) reduce the tax rate, (2) expand the tax base to include more items consumed by those with high incomes, or (3) tax services, which will also increase the yield.

Reducing the tax rate.   Since individuals in low-income categories consume a higher portion of their income and are less likely to consume items not currently subject to sales taxation (e.g., professional services), they tend to pay a higher proportion of their income in taxes. This makes the tax regressive (see, e.g., Pechman, 1985, 1986). Lower tax rates would mean a smaller percentage of household income devoted to sales taxes generally, reducing the regressivity of the tax overall. While this would have some impact on the vertical equity of the sales tax, it comes at the expense of lower revenues as well, unless the tax base is increased. As the discussion will show, the tax base can also be used to moderate the potential regressivity of the sales tax.

Changing the tax base.   A number of tax exemptions have been implemented by states over the years to reduce the level of sales tax regressivity. The most frequently discussed, and largest in terms of revenue impact, is the exemption of food. On the other hand, efforts to tax services that are consumed in greater proportion by those with high incomes, and that would thus improve the vertical equity of the sales tax, have generally met with little or no success. This discussion focuses first on ways to broaden the tax base through taxation on services to improve vertical equity and then on alternatives that tend to narrow the sales tax base to achieve greater vertical equity.

Taxing services.   A number of alternative services can be, and often are, taxed by states. Services that are taxed can include custom-written computer programs, the billable hours of an accountant or lawyer, and the costs of utilities such as phone or electricity service. The Federation of Tax Administrators has conducted a number of studies of the taxation of services and has identified 164 different services that are taxed by one or more states.

As the number of services taxed increases, the tax base is broadened, leading to greater levels of revenue per penny of sales tax rate. In Florida, early-1990s efforts to broaden the sales tax to include virtually all services ended in failure and repeal of the law. As Gold (1994) pointed out, one of the services subject to taxation was advertising. Not surprisingly, the advertisers, not wanting to see the costs of their services increase (or alternatively, their profits diminish), devoted considerable advertising resources toward defeating the tax measure. California's experience with a more limited tax on snack foods, which was also repealed in a campaign focused on the complexity of defining snack foods, shows that changes in what is and is not subject to sales taxation can be highly controversial. As the role of services in the economy expands, taxation of those services will yield greater revenues for states.

One problem with broadening the tax base is that, without careful redesign, the sales tax becomes more regressive (Gold, 1994). Taxation of food and utilities increases regressivity. However, if the tax is expanded to include services used more often as income increases, the regressivity is reduced. Regardless of how reliant a state is on sales tax revenues, any attempt to increase sales taxes must address the regressive tendencies of the tax. Broad exemptions for food and other items are one approach, but the downside of these alternatives is a substantial reduction in revenue. States would be better off using some form of tax refund based on income, or in the case of states that do not have income taxes, direct payments to low-income individuals, as in Wyoming, or some form of property tax relief, such as that used in Kansas.

Economic effects.   A routine argument against any tax is that it makes an area less competitive in attracting new business and thus promoting economic growth. To the extent that sales taxes are levied on products that are highly mobile, it can make an area less attractive for new business to locate. If the item taxed is highly mobile (e.g., items that can be procured via mail order), an individual can avoid paying sales tax by purchasing the item from a provider not subject to the local jurisdiction's sales tax. In this case, the local business must bear the burden of the tax to remain competitive—if the business tries to pass the sales tax on to consumers, they will purchase the item from another provider.

On the other hand, if a sales tax is levied on products that require close proximity of customers and providers, those products can be taxed with little concern that the producers will relocate. Such taxes, however, do add to the cost of doing business in that jurisdiction, making it somewhat less attractive for the business to relocate or expand in the future. Even if the seller of the product is able to shift the entire tax burden to purchasers of the product, there are still costs of collecting the sales tax and remitting the tax receipts to the state (see the next section on administrative costs).

Administration and compliance.   The administrative cost of a tax is the amount of money expended by the taxing jurisdiction to collect the tax from taxpayers. Administrative costs of a sales tax are generally lower than for income and property taxes (Due and Mikesell, 1994). Income taxes require filings by all individual taxpayers, and property taxes require accurate assessments of real, and in some states personal, property. On the other hand, many of the collection costs of a sales tax are borne by retailers, and the state has fewer tax returns to audit. Moreover, total sales are generally easier to measure than income and property value.

Many studies have suggested that compliance with sales tax laws is quite high due to the relatively low cost of compliance and the relative ease with which sales can be audited. Because sales tax rates are generally quite low (ranging from 3 to 7 percent), many argue there is little incentive to avoid compliance. If tax rates or the costs of compliance were to increase, avoidance activities would also likely increase.

Political acceptability. If additional revenue is needed for schools, policymakers need to find a way to generate support for raising those additional funds. In today's political climate, no tax is viewed as a "good" tax. Increasing taxes to generate additional state and/or local revenue continues to be a political challenge.

When faced with using income taxes or sales taxes to replace property taxes for schools in 1994, Michigan's voters elected to increase the state sales tax from 4 to 6 percent rather than pay higher income taxes. Although this action does not appear to be in the best interest of those with the lowest incomes, as sales taxes tend to be more regressive than income taxes (see the previous discussion of fairness), support for the sales tax over the income tax was widespread in Michigan. In Ohio, voters turned down a one-cent increase in sales taxes in 1998. The tax increase was to be split—half a cent for schools and half a cent for property tax relief.

Broadening the sales tax base through the taxation of more goods, and in particular, more services, does not appear to be particularly popular with taxpayers either. Recall California's effort to increase the sales tax base by subjecting snack goods to taxation, which resulted in failure.

On the other hand, increasing the sales tax has been the most popular way to fund quantum increases in state aid for education. Several states hiked sales tax rates in the 1980s and 1990s as part of education reforms, Arkansas increased the sales tax to fund its adequacy court mandate in 2004, and other states seeking to hike state education aid often look first to a sales tax rate increase.

Exportability. Taxes are exportable to people outside of the taxing jurisdiction to the extent that someone else has to pay them. Taxes can be exported either to the federal government or to nonresidents of the taxing jurisdiction. Exporting a tax to the federal government is possible if it is deductible on corporate or individual income tax returns. The federal government does not actually pay the taxes; rather, the deduction reduces federal revenues, meaning it must either borrow more money, spend less, or increase other tax sources. Since the elimination of the sales tax deduction for federal income taxes, it is no longer possible to export a portion of sales taxes to the federal government.

Sales taxes are ideal for export to other individuals. Tourists, business travelers, and other visitors to an area will purchase goods and services during their visit. To the extent that these goods and services are taxed, someone other than those in the taxing jurisdiction pays the tax. This same principle accounts for the popularity of hotel taxes, parking taxes, and taxes on automobile rentals. If others can be forced to pay taxes to support local services, local taxpayers will have to pay less themselves. The downside to this type of taxation is that it is more sensitive to economic fluctuations than are many other sales taxes, as travel is one of the first things that is cut back in a declining economy, whether it is travel for business or for leisure.

Conclusions about sales taxes. This discussion shows that a number of important issues must be carefully considered before relying on an increase in the sales tax rate or an expansion of the base to provide additional funds for education. Moreover, as tax rates increase, issues of fairness or equity, exportability, and compliance become more problematic. States often enact politically motivated, broad-based exemptions, reducing the potential yield of the new tax. An alternative is to broaden the base subject to sales taxation. One way to do this is to establish a sales tax on services as well as on products. To the extent that there is a trend away from consumption of goods and toward purchase of more services, this will also make the tax more elastic (see Dye and McGuire, 1991).

The Property Tax

The property tax has been and remains the mainstay of local government financing. In 2004, property tax collections represented 31.5 percent of total state and local tax collections (www.taxadmin.org/fta/rate/slsource.html [September 1, 2006]).

For years, the property tax produced the largest percentage of revenues for schools, but that role was ceded to state governments during the flurry of school finance reforms enacted in the 1970s and 1980s. The property tax still produces large amounts of steady local revenue, and except for the few local governments that can levy sales and income taxes, it is the only broad-based tax that most local governments, including school districts, can use to raise tax dollars. This section analyzes the property tax in terms of its base, yield, equity, economic effects, and administration and compliance costs. It ends with a summary of state approaches to property tax relief for the poor and a brief discussion of the impact of California's Proposition 13, enacted in 1978.

Basis. The basis of the property tax generally is wealth. Except for the inheritance tax, which is being lowered and even eliminated in many states, as well as at the federal level, the property tax is the closest approximation to a wealth tax in this country. But because so many elements of wealth are not included in the property tax, and because the elements of wealth that are included are primarily property, the tax has historically been called a property tax.

There are three categories of wealth or property: (1) real or land, (2) tangible, and (3) intangible. Referring to land as real property derives from medieval times, when all land was owned by royalty; "real" is actually a derivative of "royal." Tangible property includes improvements on land, such as buildings, homes, business establishments, factories, and office buildings, as well as personal property, such as automobiles, furniture, other household items, and business inventories. A value can be placed on all tangible property. Intangible property refers to items that represent a value but have no value in themselves, such as bank deposits, certificates of deposit, stock certificates, and bonds. The property tax base usually includes the bulk of real property or land, portions of tangible property (primarily land improvements but usually not personal property), and little if any intangible property.

In terms of horizontal equity, the property tax does not treat all wealth holdings equally. An individual with greater amounts of financial investments as compared to real estate would pay less property tax than an individual with a portfolio mostly in real estate. Similarly, individuals with larger portions of their wealth in personal property exempt from the property tax base will likely pay less in property taxes than will those with larger portions of their holdings in land and buildings. In short, the property tax treats holders of wealth differently primarily based on the composition of their wealth across real, tangible, and intangible property.

These generalizations mask other aspects of the property tax. A considerable amount of real property and land improvements escapes property taxation, driving up the property tax rate for the remainder that is taxed. Property and buildings owned by the government—federal, state, or local—are exempt from the property tax, as are land and buildings owned by religious and some charitable organizations. And there are substantial numbers of additional exemptions. Many states provide a homestead exemption that eliminates a certain amount of a home's value from the property tax altogether when that property is the taxpayer's primary home. There are exemptions for certain kinds of business activities. Several localities, especially cities, have enacted property tax abatements under which new business buildings are exempt from the property tax rolls for a fixed time, often as long as 20 years. These exemptions or exclusions add up to large totals over time. Thus, while all property that is on the tax rolls is taxed equally (except for that subsequently described), the large portions of property not on the tax rolls avoid the property tax altogether, further violating horizontal equity.

The assessment process.   Additional issues enter the picture because property is taxed on the basis of what is called **assessed valuation**, and the assessment process is riddled with technical challenges and problems. The assessment process basically has three steps:

1. All parcels of land across the country are identified, plotted, and recorded by local taxing jurisdictions, usually city or county government agencies.
2. Those parcels subject to the property tax are given a value, usually a value approximating the market value; both land and their improvements (buildings) are included in assigning a value.
3. An assessed valuation is assigned, which is some percentage of true or market value.

The sum of the assessed valuation of each parcel in a taxing jurisdiction is the local property tax base. The process seems simple, but actually determining assessed valuation is a complex technical and political process.

Determining market or true value.   Conceptually, determining a true value for a piece of land and its improvements is straightforward. True value is the market value; true value is what an individual would have to pay to buy the piece of property. That process is fairly straightforward for homes. The market value of a home is the value for which it would sell. Since records are kept of home sales, determining the market value of homes that sell is relatively straightforward.

But what about placing market values on homes that are not sold? The use of comparable homes that have sold in recent months provides an excellent way to estimate the value of a house in a given neighborhood and is frequently used to estimate the market value of all houses in an area. While technically this is fairly simple, as most real estate agents would attest, keeping up-to-date market values on the tax rolls requires that the figures be continually updated. Computer programs exist to provide such updating, but political pressures frequently mitigate against full record updating. Some feel it is unfair to tax a homeowner on unrealized home value gains, as happens when updating of tax files occurs regularly. That leads to the question of how often tax rolls should be updated— every year, every other year, once a decade, or some other time frame? If annual updates do not occur, horizontal equity may be violated as homeowners who do not move pay a decreasing portion of the local property tax. But annual updating costs money and creates some public displeasure.

Valuing homes is simple compared to placing values on other properties. Consider small commercial buildings or small businesses that use land and buildings that are rarely sold. Since a market value does not exist, a process called *capitalizing income* or *capitalizing rents* is often used. If net income or profits are 10 percent, the value then becomes total profits divided by 10 percent (which would be total profits multiplied by 10). That is, the value is linked to the profits that are earned by using the land and buildings. Another somewhat different method links the value of commercial buildings to the rents that can be charged for using the building. Rents are divided by an average rate of return to determine true or market value; indeed, this process often determines the building's market price if the owner decides to sell. Capitalized values are determined by two critical variables: sales and net profit, or rents and assumed rate of return. Values can be increased or decreased by changing either of these two figures.

Determining market value for factories or plants provides more complex challenges. While capitalized valuation is one possible approach, it is difficult to allocate profits and sales just to one plant for a business with multiple plants. So an alternative process, replacement costs less depreciation, is often used. Replacement costs are an estimate of what it would cost to completely rebuild the plant. In many respects, just replacement costs updated each year would indicate the true value of that type of property. But unlike homeowners, businesses are allowed to depreciate plants and factories in order to reinvest in and improve properties over time. So true values for a plant or factory would be replacement costs minus accumulated depreciation.

Utilities, such as gas and electrical lines, represent yet an additional technical challenge. While such lines have little worth in themselves, they represent a distribution network allocated by governments to utility companies. And these distribution networks have substantial value, just as plane routes and airport gates in the airline industry have a value that far exceeds the value of the item itself. States have taken a variety of approaches to valuing utilities and often use a combination of capitalized valuation and replacement costs less depreciation.

Farmland presents still another set of issues. While a market usually exists for farmland, often the actual selling price exceeds the farming value of the land, even for farms far from urban areas. In addition, even if the market value of farmland equals the farming capitalized price, a drought or other natural disaster can reduce a farmer's income to zero in any one year, making it very difficult to pay property taxes on farmland that still retains a value. Further, for farmland that does not turn over, if the selling price of nearby farmland is used as the basis for identifying a value, care must be taken to compare similar types of land. Land that can only be used for grazing should not be compared with land used for agriculture; and different types of agriculture, which often depend on the specific characteristics of the soil, produce different net returns for farmers. All of these factors must be considered in valuing farmland. Several states use some type of market value, and several also use the lower of market value or actual use value.

In short, determining property values is conceptually straightforward but technically, socially, and politically complex. In many cases, there are no "right" processes; technical approaches interact with value judgments. As a result, the question of whether horizontal equity is met has both a technical and a sociopolitical dimension.

Determining assessed valuation.   Once a value is given to a piece of property, an assessed value must be ascribed, because that is the value that officially becomes part of the tax base. In the best of all worlds, this step would be eliminated, and the determined value would be the measure that becomes part of the property tax base. But for a variety of reasons, fractional assessment practices exist across the country. That is, property is assessed at some fraction or percentage of actual value; percentages can range from as low as 10 percent to as high as 100 percent, which is the actual market or true value. Public finance economists argue for 100 percent valuations, and that should be the goal for most state property tax systems as well.

Fractional assessments have no inherent economic justification; they are simply a complicating factor, and often a factor fraught with substantial inequities. Fractional assessments have been used primarily to hide some of the realities of the property tax, since most individuals are not aware of the details of the local assessment process. For example, if the practice is to assess property at 25 percent of market value, a homeowner with a $100,000 home receives a tax notice showing the assessed value to be just $25,000. Most homeowners think their house is undervalued since it is assessed so far below market value when, in fact, the home is assessed at the correct level. While the tax rate applied to assessed valuation to raise a fixed amount of revenue would need to be four times the rate if it were applied to full or market value, the homeowner usually takes more comfort in a perceived valuation below market levels than the actual level of the tax rate. In addition, tax rates are often limited to some maximum level. So, if assessment levels are artificially low, the government reaches the maximum tax rate more quickly, and local taxes are kept artificially low. But this gives political decision making to the local assessor and not the local policymaking bodies, where tax rate decisions should be made.

This problem is clear in California, where Proposition 13 limits assessed value to the value of the property in 1975–76, with increases limited to no more than 2 percent a year. Property can only be reassessed at market value when it is sold. As a result, the assessed value of most property is substantially below its market value. Since property taxes are limited to percent of assessed value, there is a substantial difference between the taxes actually collected and the potential tax collections if all property were assessed at its true market value. Since homes and other properties sell at different times, it is possible for individuals living in identical houses next door to each other to pay substantially different amounts of property taxes based on the length of time they have owned the house. Additionally, since residential property is sold more frequently than commercial and industrial property, and thus reassessed more frequently, a growing proportion of the property tax base in California is shifting to residential property. This means that a greater share of the property taxes paid in California are paid by homeowners.

Fractional valuations can mask a host of related inequities. If the popular assumption is that most homes are assessed far below market value, two individuals with the same $100,000 home, one with an assessed value of $25,000 and another with an assessed value of $20,000, might both feel that they are being given a "deal" when, in fact, the latter is being unfairly assessed 20 percent less than legal requirements. This situation happens as homes grow older and families do not move, and these kinds of differences are often popularly accepted as fair.

Differential assessment practices create significant problems for state school finance systems that are designed to provide relatively more state education aid to districts low in assessed value of property per pupil than to districts with average or above-average levels of local property tax wealth per pupil. If two districts are alike in all characteristics, the district that is assessed at the lowest fraction of market value will look poorer and thus be eligible for more state aid. That is unfair, and state school finance systems need to adjust for such inequitable differences.

Consider two districts, A and B, with assessed valuations of $34,500,000 and $50,000,000, respectively. Just looking at these numbers would suggest that district B is wealthier in terms of total valuation. But further assume that district A assesses property at 25 percent of true value, and district B assesses at 50 percent. To determine the true or market value, or **assessed value, adjusted or equalized,** as it is called in school finance circles, the assessed valuation figures must be divided by the assessment ratios. Thus, the true valuation in district A is $138,000,000 ($34,500,000/0.25), and the true valuation in district B is $100,000,000 ($50,000,000/0.50), which shows that district A actually has more wealth than district B. In other words, the unadjusted assessed valuations do not give an accurate picture of relative total wealth between these two districts.

For school finance purposes, the property tax base is divided by the number of students to determine relative ability to raise property tax dollars for school purposes. Assume that district A has 2,500 students, and district B has 1,500 students. If the state uses just assessed valuation per pupil, district A will have a value of $13,800 ($34,500,000/2,500), and district B will have a value of $33,333 ($50,000,000/1,500). District B appears to be nearly three times as wealthy as district A. But if equalized or adjusted assessed valuations are used, as they should be, district B will appear just slightly more wealthy than district A, at $66,667 (district B) compared with $55,200 (district A).

Thus, it is important for the state to recognize that local assessing practices can vary from required state practice, to collect data to identify the variations, and to make necessary adjustments in school finance formulas. Usually, this adjustment is accomplished through a State Equalization Board, which monitors local assessing performance. The monitoring usually consists of gathering sales data, comparing them with assessed valuations, and calculating assessment/sales ratios to determine the degree to which local assessment practices reflect state requirements. Since assessment/sales ratios are available, the state legislature can and usually does use them to adjust local assessed valuations in determining state aid calculations.

In summary, numerous issues are associated with determining the local property tax base. The property tax base is primarily land and improvements on the land, although land owned by the government and by religious and charitable organizations is exempt. Further, tax abatements and homestead exemptions further erode the local property tax base. Determining true or market value of many types of property is a technically complex undertaking that raises social and political issues as well. Fractional assessments are widely practiced but serve only to mask the actual functioning of the property tax. Actual property assessments tend to differ within and across classes of property, as well as across areas within local taxing jurisdictions, leading to horizontal inequities. And differential fractional assessments across local taxing jurisdictions require state adjustments in order to allocate state education aid in an equitable manner.

Yield. The property tax is a stalwart revenue producer, providing $314.5 billion in revenues for state and local governments in 2004 (see Table 10.1). Table 10.6 shows total property taxes and property taxes as a percentage of personal income between 1957 and 2004. Total property tax yields rose from $12.9 billion in 1957 to $314.5 billion in 2004.

TABLE 10.6   Property Taxes as a Percentage of Personal Income, 1957–2004

Fiscal Year	Total Property Taxes (in Billions)	Personal Income (in Billions)	Property Taxes as a Percentage of Personal Income
1957	$ 12.9	$ 359.3	3.6%
1967	26.0	650.4	4.0
1977	62.5	1,637.1	3.8
1987	121.2	3,962.5	3.1
1995	193.9	6,200.9	3.1
2001	261.2	8,685.3	3.1
2004	314.5	9,731.4	3.2

Sources: Advisory Commission on Intergovernmental Relations (1988), *Significant Features of Fiscal Federalism*, 1988 ed., Volume II. Washington, DC: ACIR, p. 64, Table 59. U.S. Bureau of the Census (1988), *Government Finance in 1986–87.* Washington, DC: U.S. Bureau of the Census, p. 7. Economic Report of the President, January 1989, p. 333; Scott Moody, ed. (1998), *Facts and Figures on Government Finance*, 32nd ed. Washington, DC: Tax Foundation, Tables C23 and D22. Bureau of Economic Analysis (1998), *Survey of Current Business.* Washington, DC. U.S. Department of Commerce; www.bea.doc.gov/bea/ARTICLES/NATIONAL/NIPA/1998/0898nip3.pdf/, Table 1, p. 147. Bureau of Economic Analysis (2002), Personal Income and Its Distribution: Table 2.1, and National Income and Product Accounts Tables, Table 3.2, Federal Government Current Receipts and Expenditures. Washington, DC: U.S. Department of Commerce; www.bea.gov/bea/dn/nipaweb/selecttable.asp?SelectedTable (select table, then select annual and "Refresh Table").

Interestingly, property taxes represent a lower portion of personal income today than they did 30 years ago. While property taxes as a percentage of personal income rose from 3.6 percent in 1957 to 4.0 percent in 1967, during the next decade, when property taxes more than doubled, they dropped slightly to 3.8 percent. By 1987, property taxes consumed only 3.1 percent of personal income, and that figure remained the same in 2001. By 2004, if had risen slightly, to 3.2 percent of personal income. The drop since 1977 probably reflects the tax- and expenditure-limitation fever after 1978.

Property tax rates.   Expressed as a percentage, a property tax rate is easy to use to determine the property tax yield. If the tax rate were 1.5 percent, and assessed valuation were $50,000, the yield would be 1.5 percent times $50,000, or expressing a percentage as a decimal, 0.015 times $50,000, or $750.

Unfortunately, the property tax rate is not always given as a percentage of assessed valuation. Property tax rates are usually stated in "mills" and "dollars per hundred" dollars of assessed valuation. These rate units further add to the complexity surrounding the property tax. A tax rate in mills indicates the rate applied to each $1,000 of assessed valuation. Thus, if the tax rate is 15 mills, and assessed valuation is $50,000, the yield is 15 times $50, or $750. In many respects, the mill rate is useful because it can be multiplied by the assessed valuation with a decimal point replacing the comma that indicates the thousands. Technically, a mill is "one-thousandth," so a tax rate in mills, say, 15 mills, expressed as a decimal would be 15 × 1/1,000, or 15/1,000, or 0.015 (note this is the same as the decimal expression for 1.5 percent). If that representation of the rate is used, the yield would be just the rate times the base, or 0.015 × $50,000, or still $750.

The same tax rate given in units of dollars per hundred would be $1.50. Thus, the yield would be the rate, $1.50, times the number of hundreds of dollars of assessed valuation ($50,000/100 = $500), or again, $750. Notice that this rate is similar to the rate given as a percentage; for both, the number 1.5 is used.

This may seem confusing, even though the end result is the same regardless of which method is used. Table 10.7 is designed to help clarify matters by showing how tax rates are expressed in different formats. The first column of Table 10.7 displays the tax rate expressed as a percentage of assessed value. The next three columns display the same tax rate in mills, dollars per $100 of assessed value, and dollars per $1,000 of assessed value. The fifth column shows the decimal value to use when multiplying the tax rate by the assessed value to determine the property tax yield or revenue.

TABLE 10.7   Tax Rate Equivalents for Determining Tax Yield

Tax Rate	*Mills*	*$/100 of Assessed Value*	*$/1,000 of Assessed Value*	*Value to Use in Calculations*
1.0%	10	$ 1.00	$ 10.00	0.010
1.5	15	1.50	15.00	0.015
2.0	20	2.00	20.00	0.020
2.5	25	2.50	25.00	0.025
3.0	30	3.00	30.00	0.030
100.0	1,000	100.00	1,000.00	1.000

Mills and dollars per 100 were used in part because assessed valuation figures were so large. Such a rate helped reduce the number of figures needed to calculate results. But these two rates are confusing, especially in comparing rates across jurisdictions and across states and specific taxes. If it were possible, shifting to a simple percentage rate, as was done in California, would simplify matters. Then all tax rates—income, sales, and property—would be given in the same units and could easily be compared.

Property tax elasticity.   One of the major criticisms of the property tax has been that it is not responsive to economic growth. Mikesell (1986) estimated that the elasticity of the property tax is substantially less than one, meaning that as income increases, revenue from property taxes rises more slowly. This means that governments that are heavily dependent on property taxes (most school districts) need to raise their rates to meet increases in the demand for their services, such as education (Monk and Brent, 1997).

Property tax stability.   In terms of stability, the property tax has some ideal characteristics. In times of economic slowdowns, it produces a steady revenue stream, largely because property values maintain their levels except in very deep recessions. On the other hand, in times of economic growth and/or inflation, property values rise, so property tax revenues rise as well. In other words, property tax revenues relative to the business or economic cycle are stable on the downside and increase on the upside.

Property tax equity.   For years, the property tax was considered a regressive—actually, a steeply regressive—tax (Netzer, 1966). In the 1970s, a new view of property tax incidence held that it had a progressive incidence pattern (Aaron, 1975; Mieszkowski, 1972). Since the mid-1970s, analysts have essentially divided into two camps: those claiming an overall progressive incidence pattern and those claiming a regressive incidence pattern. More recently, Zodrow (2001) published an article describing three views of the incidence of the property tax that readers can consult for more information on this issue. There is, however, general consensus that at very low household income levels, generally less than $20,000, the property tax is regressive.

Economic and social effects.   For homeowners, the property tax is a tax on housing consumption. As such, it raises the price of housing and thus discourages housing investments. On the other hand, the property tax, which consumed 3.2 percent of personal income in 2004, is a smaller burden than the sales tax, and thus a much smaller burden than if housing consumption were simply rolled into the sales tax base, a policy for which good arguments could be made. Further, property tax payments can be deducted from federal income tax returns, thus offsetting the property tax impact. At the present time, sales taxes are not deductible for federal tax purposes. In addition, states have enacted a wide-ranging array of adjustments designed to reduce the property tax impact on homeowners and to encourage housing consumption. While all of these mechanisms might not fully offset the regressive effect of the tax, they certainly help.

Further, the costs of property taxes are offset by the benefits in local services that they support. Indeed, both taxes and services are capitalized into the price of property, with taxes decreasing the price and services increasing them. Research has shown that the capitalized impact of services is substantial (Wendling, 1981a).

Property taxes on the business sector raise a series of additional economic issues. One general issue is that businesses that rely more heavily on physical capital (land, buildings, equipment, machinery, including inventories) than human capital (lawyers, accountants, computer service vendors, etc.) bear the impact of higher costs from property taxation and thus have some economic disadvantages in the marketplace. This reality raises the overall issue of how businesses should be taxed. In recent years, states have generally exempted business inventories, as well as machinery and equipment, from the property tax rolls, thus including only land and buildings owned by businesses.

Administration and compliance.   The administrative burdens of the property tax consist of recording all property parcels, maintaining a record of changing ownership, and assessing property, which is fraught with technical and political challenges. Technically, tools exist to keep up-to-date values on just about any kind of property, and thus to maintain assessed values reasonably close to current market values. But, as noted, reality is generally otherwise. Appointed, rather than elected, local assessors, with clear requirements for the skills needed to qualify for appointment; some degree of funding for the local assessment process, with computer facilities to store, maintain, and update records; and a State Equalization Board to conduct periodic assessment-sales studies and provide equalization ratios for state school aid purposes—these are the minimal requirements for good property tax administration.

Individual compliance is probably the most straightforward for any tax. A tax bill is submitted once a year, and property owners pay, sometimes in annual and sometimes in semiannual payments. Some homeowners have the bank collect property tax liabilities monthly with their mortgage payment; in these cases, the bank pays the bill annually. The annual nature of property tax bills contributes to the unpopularity of this tax. Individuals would rather pay taxes in smaller amounts, as they do with the sales tax. That said, Monk and Brent (1997) pointed out that between 1987 and 1997, missed payments of school property taxes increased dramatically in a number of states—for example, by as much as 40 percent in New York State.

Property tax relief programs.   For years, states have enacted a variety of programs that ostensibly provide property tax relief for some if not all homeowners, but often only to low-income homeowners, the elderly, veterans, or the disabled. Public finance economists generally criticize these programs on a variety of grounds, but the programs remain and actually proliferate. Ebel and Ortbal (1989) summarized these programs from a detailed update by the Advisory Commission on Intergovernmental Relations (1989). Johnson (2000) also discusses a number of income tax relief programs targeted to low-income families.

Generally, property tax relief includes a variety of programs designed to reduce reliance on the property tax to raise local revenues. As such, the programs are designed to benefit all local property taxpayers, but they target additional relief to low-income households to reduce property tax regressivity. There are two categories of property tax relief programs: direct and indirect. Direct programs include homestead exemptions or credits, circuit breakers, tax deferral plans, and classification of the property tax base. These programs reduce property tax bills directly. Indirect programs include intergovernmental aid programs (which include school finance equalization programs at the state level), tax and spending limitations (for a review, see Gold, 1994), and local option sales and income taxes.

Homestead exemptions and credits. Reflecting the value this nation places on home-ownership, 48 states have some type of homestead exemption or homestead credit that simply reduces the property tax for an individual who owns his or her home. Homestead exemptions or credits are one of the oldest property tax relief programs. With the homestead exemption, the assessed valuation is reduced by a fixed amount, often several thousand dollars. This reduces the property tax bill, with the cost borne by local governments. Several states reimburse local governments for these revenue losses through a homestead credit, whereby the local government reduces the homeowner's property tax bill by the amount of the homestead exemption times the tax rate and then bills the state for the total amount for all local taxpayers. Since several of the programs are financed locally, a total cost of these programs has not been calculated.

Interestingly, a number of the states that provide this type of property tax relief do not link it to income (i.e., do not have a "needs" test—all homeowners, rich or poor, benefit from the homestead exemption or credit). Further, only 17 of the 48 states extend the program to all homesteads; others limit the program to the elderly (again, rich and poor), the disabled, the poor, and/or veterans or disabled veterans (Monk and Brent, 1997).

Circuit breaker programs. As the name suggests, a **property tax circuit breaker program** is designed to protect homeowners from property tax overload, which could happen if current income falls in a year due to illness or unemployment or drops for several years due to retirement. Circuit breakers typically relate property tax bills to a taxpayer's income; circuit breaker relief, then, is some portion of the property tax bill that exceeds a given percentage of income. Such programs can help reduce regressive residential property tax burdens.

Most states link the circuit breaker program to the state income tax through a separate schedule, but several states administer the circuit breaker program separately and send cash refunds to those who qualify. Still other states have local governments provide the property tax relief and then reimburse them for the total amount.

By 1994, 36 states had enacted some type of circuit breaker program. That number remained constant in 2001. Wisconsin enacted the first program in 1964; Michigan currently has the most comprehensive program. All 36 states make all homeowners eligible, and 21 states make renters eligible (based on the assumption that landlords shift property tax burdens to renters). Some states target relief to the elderly or disabled. Monk and Brent (1997) found that the average level of benefits granted in the states that reported such figures ranged from a high of $593 in Maryland to a low of $80 in California, with a median of $257 in Pennsylvania (Monk and Brent, 1997).

Tax deferrals. A tax deferral program extends the period over which property taxes can be paid. The taxpayer is given the option of paying the current tax bill or deferring the payment to some future time, usually when the property is sold. At that time, past property tax payments plus interest come due. Legally, these deferred property tax payments are liens on the property. Another way tax deferrals are used is to continue to assess property based on its current use as long as the qualifying use continues. If there is a change in use, the property owner is responsible for deferred taxes on the property. For example, if a farmer or parking lot owner sells the property for development, the taxing jurisdiction will collect back taxes, based on the highest- and best-use valuation of the property prior to the sale (Monk and Brent, 1997).

Tax deferrals are the most recently enacted property tax relief program. In 1979, only 9 states had such programs; the number had increased to 31 by 1991 (Monk and Brent, 1997). Tax-deferral programs have the "best" economic characteristics of all the property tax relief programs because they entail minimal governmental interference in housing consumption, reflect the social goals of owning a home and staying in one's home even when income drops, and maintain governmental revenues, at least over time.

Unfortunately, as with most tax relief programs that have the best economic features, they are not so popular. Deferral programs have few participants; apparently, the negative feature of placing a lien on one's home for deferred tax payments is not outweighed by the positive features of location stability and continued homeownership.

Property tax limitations. A commonly used indirect form of property tax relief is a limitation on property taxes. Many states impose a variety of limits on property taxes and taxing jurisdictions. According to the Advisory Commission on Intergovernmental Relations (1995), the most common types of limits are these:

- Overall property tax rate limits that set a ceiling that cannot be exceeded without a popular vote. These limits apply to the aggregate rate of tax of all local governments.
- Specific property tax rate limits that set a ceiling that cannot be exceeded without a popular vote. These limits apply to specific types of local jurisdictions (e.g., school districts or counties).
- Property tax levy limits that constrain the total revenue that can be raised from the property tax.
- Assessment increase limits that control the ability of local governments to raise revenue by reassessment of property or through natural or administrative escalation of property values.
- Full Disclosure or Truth in Taxation provisions that require public discussion and specific legislative vote before enactment of tax rate or levy increases.

Classification of the property tax base. The basic goal of a property tax classification program is to tax different elements of the property tax base—residential, commercial, industrial, farm, utilities, and so on—at different effective rates. Typically, the goal is to tax residential property at lower rates or, put differently, to tax nonresidential elements (i.e., business property) at higher effective tax rates. A classification system is often called a "split roll" system. In many states, this is prohibited constitutionally. However, 19 states and the District of Columbia use some kind of classification scheme.

The number of classifications of property varies substantially, from a low of 2 to what used to be a high of 34 in Minnesota. Minnesota's system was so complex that some analysts suggested the state had actually created 70 property classifications (Bell and Bowman, 1986). In 1989, Minnesota changed its classification system, reducing the number of classes to about 10.

Summary of property tax relief programs.   As this discussion suggests, property tax relief programs for all homeowners, as well as programs targeted to the elderly, the poor, veterans, or the disabled, are popular and are increasing in number. Several major policies are associated with these programs. The first is that most provide aid or relief to all homeowners, regardless of income level. Put differently, in these classification systems, all residential property is taxed less than nonresidential property, and general homestead exemptions and credits provide aid to the rich and poor alike. Other programs target certain groups (the elderly, veterans, the disabled) for protection, usually without needs tests (i.e., income tests), and exclude other groups with low property tax burdens and low incomes from assistance. On economic grounds, such programs can be challenged; they clearly weight the social goals of homeownership over the economic goals of a good tax system. A public finance economist would argue that all of these programs should be linked to income (i.e., that the overall policy objective should be to reduce regressivity, with relief targeted in increasing amounts to low-income property tax payers). Most public finance economists, however, go beyond this recommendation and argue that housing goals should be excluded completely from property tax adjustments and handled through other public policies (Musgrave and Musgrave, 1989).

Further, many of these programs, especially circuit breaker programs, make it easier for local governments to raise property taxes; the circuit breaker effectively cuts in for all taxpayers if residential property tax payments exceed the fixed percent of income. Thus, the programs become indirect state support for local choices for either more services or higher-quality services.

Another example of an attempt to bring property tax relief, different from those previously discussed, is California's Proposition 13. As noted previously, in 1978, Proposition 13 rolled back assessed valuations to the 1975–76 market value. Growth in assessed value was limited to 2 percent a year, with reappraisal to market value occurring only when property was sold. The tax rate was fixed at 1 percent of assessed evaluation. In passing this proposition, California shifted to an acquisition-based assessment system, under which property is assessed at market value only when it changes ownership.

Drawing on data over 10 years, Phillips (1988) analyzed the effects of this approach. Phillips' research showed that by 1981 the tax base relative to market value had dropped by nearly 50 percent. By 1986, the effective tax for a long-term owner was just 0.31 percent of market value, while a recent buyer faced a burden more than three times higher at 1.0 percent. Further, assessment/market values were inversely related to property value, meaning that individuals with the higher-valued homes had lower relative assessed valuations, so that the rich benefited more than the middle- or lower-income household. We would expect similar—if not worse—findings if this study were conducted today. Therefore, a consequence of California's switch to an acquisition-based system of property tax assessment was to significantly lower the tax base over time and to violate horizontal equity in directions that make the property tax even more regressive overall.

In sum, except for state-financed circuit breakers, most of the programs discussed in this section reduce the local property tax base. Thus, they make it more difficult to raise local tax revenues for schools and other functions.

Conclusions about the property tax.   The property tax has never been a popular tax; for most of the twentieth century, it was the most unpopular tax. Yet it has been and continues to be the pillar of local government and school finance. It produces large amounts of revenues, maintains those revenue levels in economic downturns, and then produces revenue increases during economic growth periods. Its burden is proportional in the middle-income ranges, and its regressivity can be reduced by circuit breaker and other income tax credit programs. While its unpopularity engendered property tax relief and reform during the 1970s, it also contributed to tax and spending limitations in the late 1970s. But, as the federal government cut real federal aid during the 1980s, and education improvement became a national imperative, states tapped the property tax for substantial new revenues. Property taxes are crucial for funding local government services, but they are rarely popular taxes. They are needed even though they are not liked.

Lotteries

First introduced in 1964 in New Hampshire, lotteries have grown in popularity and importance in terms of state revenue since that time. Indeed, many lotteries earmark their receipts to education funding. Although they represent a relatively small portion of total educational revenues (generally no more than 4 percent in any given state), many think that their implementation will solve (or has solved) education's funding problems. This is not so.

Monk and Brent (1997) argue persuasively that lotteries are a tax. They point out that the voluntary nature of the game does not make a difference and is no different than paying the sales tax on a meal consumed in a restaurant. That is, an individual voluntarily chooses to play the game or eat the meal, and in doing so, agrees to pay the tax.

Lotteries have changed dramatically from New Hampshire's first effort, which was designed to slow down increasing property tax–rate growth in that state. In New Hampshire and New York (which was the second state to introduce a lottery in 1968), participants had to register to play, tickets were expensive, and drawings took place only a few times a year. The result was they were relatively unpopular and raised little money.

In 1971, New Jersey introduced a number of changes, which made lotteries more successful. Among the new features were lower-priced tickets, instant winners, and aggressive promotional campaigns. By 1998, 37 states and the District of Columbia had introduced lotteries. According to Monk and Brent (1997), 12 of those states earmark the proceeds of the lottery to education, but the form of that earmarking varies. California, for example, provides the funds to school districts and institutions of higher education on a per-pupil basis. Georgia, on the other hand, uses the proceeds of the state lottery to provide Hope scholarships to students to attend Georgia public institutions of higher education.

Today, lottery proceeds are derived not from a single lottery but from a variety of games, each designed to attract different groups of players. Lotto games in which participants select (or have a computer randomly select for them) six numbers are the most popular. If there are no winners for several cycles of the game, for which drawings are generally held twice a week, the size of the jackpot grows. In some instances, lotto prizes have topped $100 million. A new version of lotto, called Powerball, has combined 20 states for one drawing. In 1998, one group of 13 individuals won a Powerball payout of over $250 million.

Other lottery games involve tickets on which players scratch off numbers to see if they have won an "instant" prize; numbers games, in which three to five numbers are drawn daily for prizes; and video lottery terminals (VLTs), which have recently been introduced. These machines allow lottery players to participate "online." These machines may be the fastest-growing sector of the lottery industry, and the states with the largest growth in lottery proceeds between 1990 and 1994 were apparently those with VLTs.

According to most research, lotteries are regressive. It is generally argued that poorer individuals are more likely to play and to spend a greater portion of their income on lotteries as compared to wealthier individuals. Borg and colleagues (1991) indicated that as lottery prizes grow, more higher-income individuals play, lessening the regressivity of the lottery. Monk and Brent (1997) suggested this makes sense intuitively since the appeal of a lottery is that if you win, you get rich. Rich people have less incentive to play than do poor people. As the size of the winnings grow, more and more individuals find the prize attractive and begin to play. In a recent analysis of Georgia's lottery, Rubenstein (2002) found that lower-income and nonwhite households tend to purchase more lottery products, yet receive lower benefits from the lottery, in large part because higher-income and white households are better able to take advantage of the Hope scholarships that pay for a student's tuition at a public Georgia university.

The stability of lottery proceeds is also problematic. In general, following the initial introduction, when interest is high, revenues from lotteries tend to taper off. Between 1990 and 1994, state lottery revenues (adjusted for inflation) increased 24.2 percent. However, the share of revenues retained as proceeds declined 1.7 percent. Total sales were down more than 15 percent in eight states. Total revenue grew by substantial amounts in Minnesota, Oregon, and South Dakota, but only 11 states saw increases in net proceeds between 1990 and 1994. In California, lottery proceeds at one time amounted to 4 percent of school district expenditures. Today, that figure is approximately 2 percent.

Lotteries are expensive to administer from the states' point of view, although for individuals, there is virtually no compliance cost—you either buy a ticket or you do not. As just suggested, the lottery is very inefficient given the substantial sums of money that must be returned in the form of prizes and the high costs of administration. These administrative costs include commissions paid to vendors, usually on the order of 5 percent of sales, as well as printing tickets, holding drawings, and promoting the games. Combined, between 30 and 35 percent of total sales are available to the government agencies benefiting from the revenue sales.

In summary, many states have enacted lotteries to help fund public services, often earmarking funds for education. As a form of taxation, lotteries are highly inefficient since over half of the revenues are used either for prizes or for administrative costs. In California, only 34 cents of each dollar collected finds it way to schools. In addition, after an initial burst of excitement, most lottery sales decline somewhat. Combined with higher administrative costs for new and more complex games and higher advertising costs to attract players, the amount of revenue available for government services may decline farther. Finally, lotteries appear to be generally regressive.

4. SUMMARY

Governmental, tax-financed activity in the United States represents a large share of our gross domestic product and consumes some 12–15 percent of personal income. This investment includes spending over $350 billion a year on public K–12 education. Raising the revenue to finance governmental operations is an important and complex issue.

There are five criteria on which taxes can be measured and compared: (1) the tax base, (2) yield, (3) equity, (4) the economic effects of the tax, and (5) administration and compliance issues. Each is important in terms of assessing the impact of taxes on individuals and on the jurisdictions that rely on the revenues they generate.

In general, the federal government relies heavily on income (corporate and individual) taxes, while state revenues are composed approximately equally of sales and income taxes. Local school districts, like other local governments, are heavily dependent on the property tax.

Economists generally agree that the "best" taxes are those that have a broad base and low rate. In addition, most analysts support the notion that taxes should be progressive, consuming a larger proportion of wealthy individuals' income than of poor individuals' income. Income taxes tend to be the most progressive while sales taxes are generally the opposite, or regressive. Although states have enacted many exemptions to the sales tax to make it less regressive, it remains a modestly regressive form of taxation. Property taxes also tend to be regressive at the lowest income levels. There are two ways to think about the regressivity of the property tax. One makes the tax appear less regressive than the other, but both show substantial regressivity at the lowest income classes.

But for any individual or family unit, the ultimate impact or burden of taxes is the sum of all taxes at the local, state, and federal levels. Table 10.8 indicates the total tax burden by quintiles of income for 2001. And the results are quite interesting. First, the taxes include all federal, state, and local income, sales, and property taxes; Social Security taxes; and federal and state tobacco, alcohol, and gasoline taxes. Thus, they provide a fairly good estimate of total tax burden. What the numbers show is that the total tax burden is approximately equal across the five income classes! It is 18 percent for the

TABLE 10.8 Tax Burden by Income Class, 2001

Income Quintile	Income	Total Taxes[a]	Percentage of Income[b]
First—bottom	$ 7,946	$ 1,449	18%
Second	20,319	2,847	14
Third—middle	35,536	5,622	16
Fourth	56,891	9,835	17
Fifth—top	116,666	21,623	19

Source: Altman, 2003.
[a]Income includes income from all sources, including pensions and Social Security.
[b]Taxes include all federal and state income taxes; employee share of Social Security; property taxes; federal and state tobacco, alcohol, and gasoline taxes; and state sales taxes.

lowest-income quintile, reflecting the regressivity mentioned above, then drops to 14 percent for the second quintile, and rises to 19 percent for the top quintile. So, although the federal income tax is very progressive, and most state income taxes are somewhat progressive, and while sales and property taxes are moderately regressive for the low-income categories, and the employee share of Social Security taxes is the same for incomes up to the cut-off point in the mid-$80,000s, the sum total average tax burden is between 14 and 19 percent of income, roughly more or less the same for all income categories.

Because different levels of government can collect different taxes more efficiently, and with fewer economic inefficiencies, a system of intergovernmental transfers, or grants, has developed in the United States. Intergovernmental grants are used by states and the federal government to provide incentives for local taxing jurisdictions (including school districts) to implement programs that are a high priority for the granting government. Intergovernmental grants have also been used to reduce property tax burdens.

The major problem in school finance is the differential ability of school districts to gain equal access to property tax revenues. State and federal funding can help equalize tax burdens and ensure that a school district's spending level is based on the wealth of the state where it is located, and not on the basis of its individual property wealth. This important issue of finance equalization and the tools states use to meet district needs was the focus of Chapter 9.

Study Questions

1. Find the website for a state agency (governor's office, state legislature, or the state Department of Finance). Locate the most recent state budget document or summary, and answer the following:
   a. What is the total state budget?
   b. What proportion of that budget is allocated to K–12 education?
   c. Summarize state revenues by source—income, sales, property, and other taxes
2. Are there any major categories of taxes that are not levied in your state? For example, some states do not levy sales taxes, others don't levy state income taxes, and one has neither. If one is not used in your state, what are the implications for overall state revenue and for funding for schools?
3. If all major taxes are levied in your state, do you think the relative proportions of total revenue derived from each tax are appropriate? Why or why not? What would be an appropriate distribution of tax resources?
4. School districts rely heavily on property taxes for their "own source" revenues. Is there a better way for school districts to raise local funds? Why or why not?
5. Is there a property tax limitation in your state? If so, determine how it works and what its impact is on potential revenues for schools. Has the limitation resulted in downward pressure on school revenues? Would you recommend any changes in the tax limitation? If so, what changes would you recommend? If there is not a property tax limitation in your state, are there discussions to implement one? What form would that take, and what are the potential implications for funding schools should it pass?

Improving State School Finance Systems

Chapter 9 described a variety of formulas and strategies for improving state school finance systems. In this chapter, we use those formulas and strategies to "fix" the school finance systems in four different states. The states present different types of school finance problems, so this chapter shows how to tailor a school finance formula or structural change to the specific nature of the school finance problem being addressed. As the chapter will demonstrate, a school finance structure that improves the equity or adequacy of a school finance system in one state might exacerbate it in another, and vice versa. We provide these cases as examples of how to analyze state school finance systems for equity and adequacy problems, and how to "fix" them in ways that are fiscally and politically reasonable but that also attain solid equity and adequacy policy goals. You can use additional data sets on the website to conduct similar analyses and propose changes.

The chapter has five sections. Section 1 describes the overall framework that will be used to determine the nature of the school finance problem in each state, as well as to identify the goals to be attained by any proposed improvement. Sections 2–5 then use the framework to analyze the school finance systems in Wisconsin, Illinois, Kentucky, and Vermont, respectively. In today's school finance adequacy environment, nearly all proposed school finance changes have to address the adequacy issue at least to some degree.

1. A FRAMEWORK FOR ANALYSIS

When assessing the degree of equity or adequacy in a state's school finance system, a framework is needed to structure the analysis. We provided a useful framework in Chapter 3. Here we start by using the concepts developed in Chapter 3 to structure our analysis of the finance systems in each of four states.

In the analyses that follow, students are the group of concern. Our discussions will assess equity and adequacy from the perspective of students.

The unit of analysis will be the district, because the data available on the website that accompanies this text is on a district-by-district basis. (The files can be accessed at www.mhhe.com/odden4e.) When computing the equity and fiscal-neutrality statistics, each district's values will be weighted by the number of students in the district. This means that the values of large districts will affect the statistical results more than the values of smaller districts, which is appropriate since the group of concern is students, and this approach assures that all students are treated equally in all of the analyses presented in the simulations. In Wisconsin and Illinois, the data include information only for the K–12 districts. This excludes a small number of districts in Wisconsin, but a larger number in Illinois. In these two states, there are both elementary-only and high school–only districts, in addition to districts that serve all grades. But we analyze only the data for the K–12 districts. Vermont is more complex. Many "districts" in Vermont are individual schools with locally elected boards. These schools are generally part of a supervisory union, which provides many district-level services to the school. The taxing authority for the schools, however, remain in the local community, and for the purposes of this analysis, they are treated as individual districts. All districts in Kentucky are K–12 districts.

In most cases, the analysis will use an ex post versus an ex ante perspective (i.e., will assess results using fiscal data on actual behavior). In some instances, though, there will be ex ante comments on the nature of the current state formula. As this discussion will show, sometimes when systems appear highly equitable from an ex ante perspective, they produce a system that is quite inequitable from an ex post perspective.

The object of analysis will be state plus local revenues per pupil. This fiscal object essentially includes all local revenues as well as state equalization aid, which is often called *state general aid*. This revenue total comprises the fiscal resources for the "regular" education program. Although the state data on this text's website for the state simulation exercises also contain categorical program data for state compensatory education, bilingual education, and handicapped programs, those revenues enter the analyses only when the pupil weights option in the simulation is used. For most of these states, this chapter addresses only issues related to the regular-education program, and not any programs for extra student needs. Such analyses ignore the issue of vertical equity, or adjustments for special student (or district) needs. We urge you to address vertical equity and to identify differences in results when issues of special-needs students are included in the analyses. We provide one example in our extended analysis of Wisconsin

Each state case will address the issue of adequacy, with the Odden-Picus Adequacy Index used to draw conclusions about the adequacy of each state's school finance system. For two states, this part of the analysis will reference studies that have addressed adequacy and include a proposed adequate revenue-per-pupil figure for the regular-education program. But for the other two states, the specification of the adequate amount per pupil has less research support, and those cases will comment only on the adequacy issue. We provide a more extended discussion of adequacy for Wisconsin, referencing the costs in Wisconsin of the adequacy proposals in Chapter 4. Again, see Baker, Taylor, and Vedlitz (2004) for an analysis of the results obtained from different adequacy research methodologies. Our standard will be an Adequacy Index of 1.0 on the assumption that there either are or are not "adequate" revenues per pupil in all districts.

Each analysis will also assess issues of both horizontal- and fiscal-neutrality equity. For horizontal equity, the coefficient of variation will be the key disparity statistic, but the analyses will also incorporate the McLoone Index, to make comments on the equity of the bottom half of the distribution. The analysis will use a 0.10 standard for the coefficient of variation; those less than or equal to 0.10 will indicate an equitable distribution. The analysis will use a 0.95 standard for the McLoone Index, labeling a distribution with a McLoone Index equal to or higher than 0.95 as providing equity for the bottom half of the distribution.

For fiscal neutrality, the analyses will focus on the wealth elasticity, using a standard of 0.10, thus concluding that a wealth elasticity less than or equal to 0.10 would indicate a negligible link between the resource variable and property wealth per pupil. The discussion will mention the correlation coefficient, particularly noting when it is below 0.5, but will use the elasticity statistic to draw conclusions about the connection between state and local revenues per pupil and property wealth per pupil.

Following the Odden and Clune (1998) call to set "policy targets" for improving state school finance structures, we will assess the impact of two general strategies in all states for improving the equity and adequacy of their school finance structure. First, we will simulate a guaranteed tax base (GTB) at or above the 90th percentile, a level that provides ex ante fiscal neutrality. Second, we will simulate a foundation at least at the median.

Before beginning the analysis, we want to note several aspects of decision rules programmed within the simulation. First, "winners" and "losers" are defined as those gaining or losing *state* aid. Second, politically, we assume that representatives of winner districts would vote for the program, with the reverse true for representatives of loser districts. Another political assumption is that more than 50 percent of districts, and closer to 65 percent of districts, must be winner districts in order for the recommendation to have a chance of being enacted by a state's legislature. Third, as discussed elsewhere, we assume a "50-50" use of new state aid dollars for increased spending and local property tax relief (i.e., the simulation has districts using half of state aid increases to hike spending and half to lower local property tax rates). This latter assumption, however, is constrained by foundation program parameters that first require a district to spend at least at the foundation expenditure level and, if below the zero-aid district, to tax at least at the required foundation tax rate.

2. SCHOOL FINANCE IN WISCONSIN

The data analyzed in this section are for the 1995–96 school year; the system has not changed structurally since then, and more recent data sets on the website allow students to analyze for themselves more current data. Property wealth is equalized to 100 percent of market value. For 1995–96, Wisconsin had a three-tiered, GTB school finance structure, which was enacted in 1995. The formula did not change over the next 10 years, and so was the same structurally in 2005–06, though the formula parameters changed each year. For tier one, the state guaranteed a tax base of $2 million per pupil, up to the first $1,000 of spending. This tier can also be considered a foundation program with an expenditure level of $1,000 per pupil and a required tax rate of 0.5 mills. Since the GTB for this tier exceeded that of all school districts, tier one provided some state aid to all school districts. There were two reasons for this "generous" nature of tier one. First, it transformed what had been termed "minimum" or "hold harmless" aid for the wealthy districts into a "bona fide" state aid allotment. To be sure, this shift was in part simply political, but it did eliminate the use of "minimum aid," a phrase that indicated an inequitable allocation of state support. Second, because this state aid formula was enacted primarily to provide property tax relief, the provision of at least some aid ensured that even the wealthiest districts would experience some property tax relief (see the subsequent discussion of revenue limits). Although many Wisconsin policymakers and education leaders criticized this element of the formula, it nevertheless was enacted as a part of the new structure.

Tier two provided the bulk of state aid. The GTB for tier two was $406,592, which covered districts that enrolled 95 percent of all students. Tier-two GTB aid was provided for spending from $1,000 up to $5,786, which was the expenditure per pupil of the district that enrolled the 56th percentile student.

Tier three had a straightforward and a unique element. The GTB was set at the statewide average. Districts with property wealth below that level could use tier three for any amount of spending above the tier-two ceiling of $5,786. This was the straightforward element of tier three.

The unique element of tier three pertained to those districts with a property wealth per pupil above the state average, or the tier-three GTB. For these districts, there was a "negative-aid" calculation. When these districts decided to spend above the tier-two expenditure ceiling of $5,786, a negative value for tier-three aid was determined. This negative amount was then subtracted from the tier-two aid, but only until and if it reduced tier-two aid to zero. Since a previous court decision in Wisconsin had determined that it was unconstitutional for the state actually to "recapture" local property tax revenue through a negative-aid calculation, the tier-three factor never required districts to send funds to the state for redistribution to other districts. But tier-three calculations could potentially reduce tier-two aid amounts to zero. Tier-three negative calculations primarily affected higher-spending metropolitan school districts, those surrounding Milwaukee and Madison. Districts also always retained their tier-one aid, which politically was intended as an amount that all districts would receive.

Finally, when the state enacted this program, it also imposed "cost controls" or "revenue limits" on local school districts. Previously, school boards had the power to raise local property tax rates to increase school spending. The cost controls continued that authority but only for an inflationary expenditure increase, which has been a little above $250 per pupil for several years. Districts could exceed this expenditure-per-pupil increase limit, but they needed voter approval to do so. When enacted in 1995, the $250-per-pupil cost increase limit combined with the $1,000 per pupil of aid for tier one meant that the bulk of that additional revenue, even for the wealthiest districts, had to be used for decreasing the property tax rate, absent a local vote to use it for increased spending.[1]

The overall goal of the Wisconsin school finance structure was to set the state role in financing schools at two-thirds of all revenues. The school finance structure remained essentially the same through the 2005–06 school year, though all the specific variables in the structure have been updated (see Odden et al., 2007). The Legislative Fiscal Bureau updates the detailed description of the state's school finance system every two years (www.legis.state.wi.us/lfb). But over time, the state has had difficulty maintaining the two-thirds state funding, and in 2005, the issue of adequacy took center stage on the state's school finance agenda (see www.wcer.wisc.edu/cpre and follow the links to the Wisconsin School Finance Adequacy Task Force).

The Wisconsin School Finance Problem

Figure 11.1 shows the base data for Wisconsin for 1995–96. The data are grouped into deciles ranked by total revenues per pupil; the simulation attempts to have approximately the same number of students in each decile. Since the data are ranked by total revenues per pupil, the averages in all columns show the average of that variable for their decile of spending. So the average property wealth per pupil in the first decile is the average of property wealth per pupil for the first decile of spending, not the first decile of property wealth. Nevertheless, in our discussion, we will refer to the property wealth figure as a rough indicator of the average of the respective decile as if the data had been ranked by property wealth per pupil. But be aware that this is a rough approximation.

The data show that there was a wide variation in property wealth per pupil: the average was $218,605, but it was only $165,734 in the lowest decile and fully $331,347 in the wealthiest decile. Without substantial state equalization aid, districts would have great difficulty raising equivalent amounts of money per child at the same tax rate. Note, however, that the GTB in Wisconsin's second tier ($406,592) exceeded the average property wealth per pupil of the tenth and wealthiest decile, so it was above the 90th percentile. This shows that the second tier of the Wisconsin system provided property wealth equalization up to a very high level (i.e., provided substantial ex ante fiscal-neutrality equity).

Tax rates also varied but within a small range, with an average tax rate of 12.56 mills in decile 1 and 17.73 mills in decile 10.

The table also shows that revenues per pupil varied, but by a much smaller percentage than property wealth per pupil. Spending per pupil from state, general, and local sources varied from $5,108 in the lowest-spending decile, to just $5,678 in decile 5, and then to $7,154 in the decile 10.

---

[1]The Wisconsin system also includes limits on teacher salary increases to help districts keep overall spending increases within the expenditure cap. If, during collective bargaining, districts provide a "qualified economic offer (QEO)," that offer can be imposed for a negotiation settlement, and teachers are prohibited from going to arbitration or on strike. Further, a QEO is defined as at least a 3.8 percent increase in salaries and benefits. As benefits have increased at far above that rate, the effect of the QEO over the years has been to hold teacher salaries to insignificant increases.

Adequacy Level	$6,030.00
Pupil Weights	**No**
Disabled	—
Limited English	—
Low income	—

Decile	Average Number of Pupils per District in Decile	Average Property Value per Pupil ($)	Average Property Tax Rate (Mills)	Average Local Revenue per Pupil ($)	Average State Revenue per Pupil ($)	Average Total Revenue per Pupil ($)	Number of Districts in Decile
1	1,701	165,734	12.56	2,084	3,025	5,108	47
2	1,959	168,277	13.23	2,228	3,153	5,381	41
3	2,697	186,804	13.53	2,528	2,975	5,502	30
4	1,811	167,573	13.78	2,309	3,294	5,602	32
5	34,060	151,904	13.96	2,121	3,557	5,678	3
6	2,911	183,485	14.15	2,598	3,153	5,751	28
7	1,476	169,609	14.84	2,514	3,415	5,929	54
8	1,919	188,730	15.72	2,971	3,173	6,145	38
9	1,904	204,424	17.03	3,444	3,016	6,460	47
10	1,723	331,347	17.73	5,146	2,008	7,154	47
Weighted average		211,438	14.67	3,137	2,726	5,862	
Weighted std. dev.		93,728	1.85	1,487	1,154	547	
Median		218,605	13.97	3,054	2,627	5,681	

Totals		
Category	Amount	Percent
Local revenue	2,527,836,576	53.50
State revenue	2,196,748,542	46.50
Total revenue	4,724,585,118	
Pupils	805,908	

Equity Measures	
Horizontal Equity	
Range	$4,694
Restricted range	$1,715
Federal range ratio	0.331
Coef. of variation	0.093
Gini coefficient	0.050
McLoone Index	0.961
Verstegen Index	1.033
Fiscal Neutrality	
Correlation	0.454
Elasticity	0.090
Adequacy	
Odden-Picus	0.947

FIGURE 11.1   Base Data, Wisconsin

One of the most interesting features of Figure 11.1 is that it reveals a state with the "new" school finance problem. As property wealth per pupil rises, so does spending per pupil. But local property tax rates also rise with property wealth. So Figure 11.1 shows that in Wisconsin, lower-wealth districts have lower tax rates and also lower spending levels, while higher-wealth districts have higher tax rates and thus higher spending levels. Apparently, it is the link between tax rates and property wealth that drives the spending–property wealth connection in Wisconsin. Further, recall that for a GTB, the higher the tax rate, the higher the spending-per-pupil level. In Wisconsin, most districts applied their tax rate to the GTB for spending at least up to $5,786; since the GTB was higher than the average for even the tenth decile, tax rates were more a determinant of spending levels than were property values.

Despite this phenomenon, the equity statistics show a fairly equitable distribution of education revenues. The coefficient of variation is 0.093 and thus meets the equity standard for that statistic. The McLoone Index is 0.961, which also meets the standard of 0.95 for this statistic. Thus, in terms of horizontal equity, the Wisconsin school finance system in 1995–96 for K–12 districts met tough standards for an equitable distribution.

This finding is important for two reasons. First, the Wisconsin constitution requires a school finance system that is as uniform as "practical," which these statistics show was accomplished—at least in 1995–96. The distribution was not perfectly equal, and even the wealthiest districts received some amount of state general aid. But the system nevertheless meets our horizontal-equity standards. Second, though, Wisconsin used a GTB-type school finance structure, which defers spending levels to local districts and thus was not focused on providing equality of spending per pupil, the structure nevertheless provided a high degree of spending-per-pupil equality.

In terms of fiscal neutrality, the Wisconsin system also received good but not superlative marks. The correlation coefficient was just 0.454, and the wealth elasticity was 0.090, both just meeting the equity standard for this statistic. Though some improvements could be made in reducing the linkage between spending and property wealth, the data already showed a remarkable degree of fiscal-neutrality equity. The problem in making improvements on this front will be the tax rate–property wealth link. Because higher-wealth districts have higher tax rates, they also have higher spending levels; the spending differences are caused mainly by tax effort differences, not tax base differences.

Finally, the Odden-Picus Adequacy Index is 0.947, with the adequacy expenditure level set at $6,030; this is the 1997 adequacy figure of $6,333 found by Reschovsky and Imazeki (1998), but deflated by 5 percent to a 1995–96 figure. The relatively high Adequacy Index suggests that Wisconsin may not be far from providing an "adequate" amount of money for the average child in all districts. It would need to increase the funding for those districts below the adequate level by an average of 0.053 percent relative to the adequacy level, or by an average of about $320, to produce adequacy for all K–12 districts for the average student.

Improving the Wisconsin School Finance System

A key question for Wisconsin school finance is: What needs to be improved? From an ex ante perspective, those who filed a court case in the late 1990s argued that districts with a wealth above that in the second-tier GTB should not receive any state support. They proposed eliminating tier one, which provided some aid to all districts, and either reducing state aid to zero for any district with a wealth above the tier-two GTB level or actually changing the constitution to allow for recapture. Others might take issue with that perspective, but it would produce a school finance structure with a "purer" version of ex ante fiscal equity.

In the summer of 2000, the Wisconsin Supreme Court[2] ruled that Wisconsin's school finance system was "as uniform as practicable," and found the system constitutional

---

[2]*Vincent v. Voight*, 614 N.W.2d 388 (Wis., 2000).

on equity grounds. However, the court suggested that an adequacy case could be brought and even identified an adequacy standard—the funding would need to be adequate for all students to achieve to proficiency standards in core subjects tested (reading and writing, mathematics, science, geography, and history) and to receive instruction in the arts, music, vocational training, physical education, social sciences, health, and foreign languages, in accordance with their age and aptitude. An adequacy case has not yet been brought, but a proposal for what would constitute adequate funding was made in 2002 using a professional judgment approach (Norman, 2002). In addition, Odden and colleagues at the University of Wisconsin–Madison launched a major adequacy initiative in the summer of 2005 using the evidence-based approach (see www.wcer.wisc.edu/cpre and follow the links for the adequacy study for copies of their analyses).

A second approach is to determine whether a high-level GTB program, which provides ex ante fiscal neutrality, can in fact reduce the link between spending and property wealth per pupil. This task is difficult because of the tax rate–property wealth link. To assess the efficacy of this strategy, we ran simulations of a one-tier GTB set at $350,000, $400,000, and $500,000, all guaranteeing property wealth per pupil greater than the 90th percentile. The horizontal equity statistics worsened under each of these programs, though the simulation results portray a "rosier" picture because all state aid losses are made up with greater local taxes to ensure that spending does not decline if aid is lost. And the lower of these GTB levels also produced many state aid losers, which diminished their political viability as well.

This result occurs because this state represents the "new" school finance situation. Since tax rates rise with property wealth per pupil, a higher GTB simply widens the spending-per-pupil difference between lower-wealth and higher-wealth districts. This result increases the coefficient of variation, reduces the McLoone Index, and increases the wealth elasticity between total revenues per pupil and property wealth per pupil. A GTB program, even a combination foundation-GTB program, with the GTB set at a high level, simply worsens fiscal-equity statistics in a state like Wisconsin with the "new" school finance problem. You can simulate these programs on your own and view the results to confirm these statements.

As an alternative, Figure 11.2 shows the results of simulating a foundation program at $6,000 per pupil with a required tax rate of 14 mills. Even though it is above the median, the $6,000 foundation expenditure figure was chosen because it had been suggested by many education and political leaders as an expenditure level and a school finance structure that might be more suitable for the state. The 14-mill tax rate was the median tax rate for this simulated program, and just above the median in the base data. Further, these two figures produce a "zero-aid" district of $428,571, which is slightly above the extant tier-two GTB level. Another way of interpreting this program is that it turns the extant system at that time from a GTB of around $428,571 with local decision making on the tax rate, to one with a required tax rate of 14 mills; this requirement raises the spending in all districts now spending below $6,000 to the $6,000 per-pupil level.

As just mentioned, the Wisconsin simulations we have discussed up to this point use $6,030 as the adequacy level, a figure slightly above the foundation level and the median, because that was the figure determined by Reschovsky and Imazeki (1998) to be

Adequacy Level	$6,030.00		Foundation Level	$6,000.00
Pupil Weights	No		Required Tax Rate	14.00
Disabled	—			
Limited English	—			
Low income	—			

Decile	Pupils	Property Value per Pupil ($)	Old Property Tax Rate (Mills)	New Property Tax Rate (Mills)	Change In Property Tax Rate (Mills)	Old Local Revenue per Pupil ($)	New Local Revenue per Pupil ($)	Change in Local Revenue per Pupil ($)	New State Revenue per Pupil ($)	Change in State Revenue per Pupil ($)	Total Revenue per Pupil ($)	Change in Total Revenue per Pupil ($)	Number of Districts in Decile
1	1,741	163,524	13.12	14.00	0.88	2,146	2,289	143	3,711	522	6,000	665	46
2	2,447	165,838	13.24	14.00	0.76	2,197	2,322	125	3,678	490	6,000	615	32
3	3,197	180,497	13.63	14.00	0.37	2,452	2,527	75	3,473	381	6,000	456	3
4	4,621	172,210	13.26	14.00	0.74	2,290	2,411	121	3,589	487	6,000	608	33
5	2,196	183,647	13.23	14.00	0.77	2,431	2,571	141	3,429	481	6,000	622	37
6	2,043	168,550	14.35	14.10	(0.25)	2,413	2,374	(39)	3,640	258	6,014	218	40
7	1,660	170,404	14.90	14.35	(0.55)	2,537	2,442	(95)	3,614	211	6,056	116	48
8	2,126	200,279	15.66	14.90	(0.76)	3,134	2,969	(166)	3,196	197	6,165	31	34
9	1,904	204,424	17.03	16.71	(0.33)	3,444	3,298	(146)	3,162	146	6,460	0	47
10	1,723	331,347	17.73	17.95	0.21	5,146	5,062	(84)	2,092	84	7,154	0	47
Weighted average		211,438	14.67	14.61	(0.06)	3,137	3,086	(50)	3,085	359	6,171	309	
Weighted std. dev.		93,728	1.85	1.39	1.01	1,487	1,326	254	1,105	209	334	291	
Median		115,363	13.48	14.00	0.52	1,555	1,615	60	4,385	460	6,000	520	

Totals

Category	Amount	Percent	Change From Base Amount
Local revenue	2,487,224,527	50.01	(40,612,049)
State revenue	2,486,126,518	49.99	289,377,976
Total revenue	4,973,351,045		248,765,927
Pupils	805,908		

Winners and Losers

Category	Winners	Losers	No Change
State aid	322	32	13
Total revenue	224	0	143

Equity Measures

Horizontal Equity	
Range	$3,032
Restricted range	$902
Federal range ratio	0.150
Coef. of variation	0.054
Gini coefficient	0.022
McLoone Index	1.000
Verstegen Index	1.057
Fiscal Neutrality	
Correlation	0.529
Elasticity	0.065
Adequacy	
Odden-Picus	0.997

FIGURE 11.2 Foundation Program, Wisconsin

sufficient for the average district to teach the average student to the average-performance level on Wisconsin standards. Actually, Reschovsky and Imazeki identified a figure of $6,333 but for the 1996–97 school year; we deflated that figure by 5 percent to $6,030 for 1995–96. Although we could have set the foundation level at the adequacy level, we decided to set it just below that level simply to show that it produces an Adequacy Index less than 1. If adequacy were the primary goal, we would have set the foundation expenditure level at the adequacy figure.

Figure 11.2 shows that the simulated foundation program improves equity on both fronts, as well as improves the adequacy of the Wisconsin school finance system. The CV drops from 0.093 to 0.054, the McLoone Index increases to a perfect 1.0, the wealth elasticity drops to 0.065, and the Adequacy Index improves to 0.997.

The cost is modest—about a 13 percent increase in state funds but a decline of about 3.5 percent in local funds. At the required tax rate of 14 mills, local school districts previously levying a school tax rate below 14 mills (mostly lower-wealth districts) increased their local effort, while the middle-wealth districts previously levying above 14 mills had modest local tax rate declines. The highest-wealth districts also had modest tax rate hikes. This foundation program could be simulated with a lower required tax rate; the equity statistics would remain about the same, and the total increased cost would be about the same, but the local portion of the increase would drop and the state portion would rise. Where to set the required tax rate would need to be determined through the political process. At the 14-mill rate, the program increased aid to 322 districts and, not surprisingly, reduced aid to 32 districts, largely those that had received some aid from the first tier.

In sum, a school finance system such as that in Wisconsin, which already produces a fairly equitable school finance system, but with differences in spending and wealth reflecting the "new" school finance problem, can be enhanced with high-level foundation programs. The simulations showed that GTB programs simply worsened equity measures. Further, in a state such as Wisconsin, which already spends far above the national average, the simulations show that adequacy can be approached with only modest increases in spending, however split between local districts and the state.

We should note, however, that the above equity results and simulation analyses do not address the issue of providing extra funds for special student needs, particularly those students who have disabilities, speak a native language other than English, or come from low-income families and thus need additional education supports. And in the mid-1990s, Busch, Kucharz, and Odden (1996) showed that insufficient aid for special-needs students was a shortcoming of the Wisconsin finance system. Moreover, the equity analyses produced as part of the 2005–06 adequacy initiative in Wisconsin showed that all equity figures worsened when student weights (0.9 for students with disabilities, and 0.25 for ELL students and students eligible for free and reduced-price lunch) were used. This is also true for the 1995–96 school year when the simulation is run with those same pupil weights. Indeed, for this year, the pupil weights add an additional 142,230 students to the system, which will increase the cost of any new program. Indeed, the $6000-per-pupil foundation program cost rises by over $1 billion with these additional students also funded at the $6000-per-pupil level. Nevertheless, improving the Wisconsin school finance system means addressing issues of vertical equity as well.

Further, given the results of the various adequacy studies that have been conducted, adequacy should also be addressed. We first ran a simulation with a foundation expenditure per pupil of $6400, which is the adequacy level set in the 2007 adequacy study (about $8,550) deflated by 1.33, equivalent to the cost-of-living change over those 10 years (again, for details, see www.wcer.wisc.edu/cpre and follow the links to the Wisconsin School Finance Adequacy Task Force). This figure is slightly above the Reschovsky and Imazeki figure discussed above, and we used the same pupil weights as above. All equity statistics improved, and both the McLoone Index and the Odden-Picus Adequacy Index, of course, were 1.0. But the cost was also high.

Figure 11.3 presents a simulation for Wisconsin using the adequacy foundation level of $6,400 but a different set of pupil weights. The weights of 0.9 and 0.25 are taken from the literature and are roughly the average weights for special education (0.9) and programs for ELL and students from low-income backgrounds (0.25). But a better way to determine extra weights for additional student needs is to identify specific programs and their costs, and then construct the weight from the actual system being simulated. Indeed, in Wisconsin, the adequacy study proposed a census approach for special education that, on average, provided three additional teachers for a school of 500 students, for services for the high-incidence but lower-cost students with disabilities. This approach cost about $197,550 for about 50 such students in the prototypical school in 2005–06 dollars, or about $3,000 per special-education student in 1995–96 dollars. The lower-incidence, higher-cost special-education student would be fully funded by the state, as discussed in Chapter 4. This cost of $3,000 for special education becomes an extra weight of 0.47 on a base spending of $6,400, ($3,000 divided by $6,400), which we will round up to 0.50. The program proposals in Chapter 4 for students from low-income backgrounds involved tutors and extended-day and summer school. Turning the proposals into specific dollar amounts produced a 2005–06 figure of $660 per free- and reduced-price-lunch student for tutoring, $660 for each ELL student, and $550 for each free- and reduced-price-lunch student for each of extended-day and summer school programs. These deflated figures for each free- and reduced-price-lunch student are approximately $500 for tutoring and $415 for each of extended-day and summer school, or a total of $1,330 for each students; this equates to an extra weight of 0.21 ($1,330 divided by $6,400). The ELL weight would be 0.10 ($660 divided by $6,400). Recall, however, that since most ELL students are from families with lower incomes, most of them first trigger the 0.21 weight on a poverty basis and then trigger the 0.10 weight for ELL, for a total weight of 0.31.

Several aspects of Figure 11.3 should be noted. First, note the odd results for decile 4. Occasionally, this happens in specific simulations; the numbers in the simulation are correct. The oddity is due to a ranking of all districts and a district in the state—in this case, Milwaukee—that has more students than exist in one decile. All the numbers in the other deciles are correct, as are the adequacy and equity statistics. The simulation simply does not produce accurate numbers for the "odd" decile. Second, as also noted above, the cost of this simulation is quite high, mainly because the foundation expenditure level is now applied to each additional weighted student, which increased the student count by over 142,000. Third, the equity statistics are excellent: the coefficient of variation is just 2.3 percent, the McLoone Index is 1.0, the restricted range

Adequacy Level	$6,400	
Pupil Weights	Yes	
Disabled	0.500	
Limited English	0.100	
Low income	0.210	

Foundation Level	$6,400.00
Required Tax Rate	15.00

Decile	Weighted Pupils	Property Value per Weighted Pupil ($)	Old Property Tax Rate (Mills)	New Property Tax Rate (Mills)	Change in Property Tax Rate (Mills)	Old Local Revenue per Weighted Pupil ($)	New Local Revenue per Weighted Pupil ($)	Change in Local Revenue per Weighted Pupil ($)	New State Revenue per Weighted Pupil ($)	Change in State Revenue per Weighted Pupil ($)	Total Revenue per Weighted Pupil ($)	Change in Total Revenue per Weighted Pupil ($)
1	1,736	146,095	13.50	14.96	1.45	1,961	2,170	209	4,229	1,081	6,399	1,290
2	2,551	157,033	13.64	15.00	1.36	2,138	2,355	218	4,045	974	6,400	1,192
3	2,626	161,182	13.51	15.00	1.49	2,174	2,418	244	3,982	944	6,400	1,188
4	#DIV/0!	#DIV/0!	#DIV/0!	#DIV/0!	#DIV/0!	#DIV/0!	#DIV/0!	#DIV/0!	#DIV/0!	#DIV/0!	#DIV/0!	#DIV/0!
5	4,769	156,307	13.50	15.00	1.50	2,112	2,345	233	4,055	997	6,400	1,230
6	2,734	153,109	13.57	15.00	1.43	2,087	2,297	210	4,103	1,020	6,400	1,230
7	1,838	165,972	14.28	15.04	0.76	2,352	2,495	142	3,910	923	6,405	1,065
8	1,748	163,036	16.34	15.46	(0.88)	2,659	2,510	(149)	3,954	766	6,465	617
9	2,613	179,609	17.16	16.00	(1.16)	3,045	2,851	(194)	3,706	694	6,557	500
10	2,089	313,258	17.54	16.14	(1.41)	4,858	4,559	(299)	2,311	611	6,869	312
Weighted average		190,047	14.67	15.22	0.55	2,819	2,886	67	3,580	837	6,466	904
Weighted std. dev.		84,515	1.85	0.64	1.41	1,339	1,199	318	1,106	288	147	433
Median		178,406	14.05	15.00	0.95	2,507	2,676	169	3,724	701	6,400	871

Totals

Category	Amount	Percent	Change from Unweighted Pupil Base Amount	Change from Weighted Pupil Base Amount
Local revenue	2,587,482,173	44.63	59,645,597	59,645,597
State revenue	3,210,092,046	55.37	1,013,343,504	750,910,868
Total revenue	5,797,574,219		1,072,989,101	810,556,465
Pupils	896,619			

Winners and Losers

Category	Winners	Losers	No change
State aid	356	11	0
Total revenue	333	0	34

Equity Measures

Horizontal Equity	
Range	$1,984
Restricted range	$298
Federal range ratio	0.047
Coef. of variation	0.023
Gini coefficient	0.008
McLoone Index	1.000
Verstegen Index	1.021
Fiscal Neutrality	
Correlation	0.548
Elasticity	0.028
Adequacy	
Odden-Picus	1.000

FIGURE 11.3 Foundation Program, with Adequate Foundation Expenditure and Adequate Pupil Weights, Wisconsin

375

is just $298 per pupil, and the Adequacy Index is 1.0. The major issue for Wisconsin, at least in 1995–96, was an insufficient amount of assistance for the extra needs of struggling students; that is also the bulk of the proposed increased funding that emerged from the 2007 adequacy studies (again, for details, see www.wcer.wisc.edu/cpre and follow the links to the Wisconsin School Finance Adequacy Task Force). Fourth, the vast bulk of districts receive additional state dollars, so assuming the additional dollars could be found, this system would pass political muster.

The text's website includes Wisconsin data for several more recent school years so you can analyze equity and adequacy impacts over several years, as well as select a more recent year to simulate alternative ways to make even more improvements in equity and adequacy.

3. SCHOOL FINANCE IN ILLINOIS

The Illinois data are for the 1994–95 school year and again include only the "unit districts" (i.e., the districts that serve all grades, K–12). Property wealth per pupil in Illinois is equalized to only about 33.3 percent of market value (i.e., lower than in Wisconsin). Thus, to compare the property wealth and tax rates in Illinois with those in Wisconsin, one would need to multiply the Illinois wealth figures by 3 and divide the tax rates by 3 to provide information relative to full market value.

In 1994–95, Illinois had a two-pronged school finance structure. Most districts operated under a typical foundation-type school finance formula. The foundation expenditure level was set at $2,900 with a required local property tax rate of 19 mills. You might conclude that the foundation level was quite low—and you would be correct. For that year, the average expenditure per pupil for operating purposes in Illinois was $6,136 (National Center for Education Statistics, 1998a), so the foundation expenditure level was just 47 percent of the average. The zero-aid district had a property wealth per pupil of $105,072, which was below that of many districts.

On the other hand, the state also used a weighted-pupil count to determine and allocate state aid; weights were provided by education level, counting students in kindergarten through grade 6 as 1.0, in grades 7–8 as 1.05, and grades 9–12 as 1.25. Using a weighted-pupil count as the denominator generally decreases the expenditure figure when compared with a figure without weighted-pupil counts. The database in the simulation includes weighted-pupil counts.

The data also exclude the Chicago school district; this large, urban district actually enrolls about one-third of all students in K–12 districts and thus would cover three deciles in a simulation. Such a district is usually identified separately in a school finance analysis, but the simulation data used exclude this district altogether.

The Illinois School Finance Problem

For more than a decade, Illinois has struggled with proposals to enhance the state role in public school financing. As Figure 11.4 shows, the state role in 1994–95 for these K–12

Adequacy Level	$4,500
Pupil Weights	**No**
Disabled	—
Limited English	—
Low income	—

Decile	Average Number of Pupils per District in Decile	Average Property Value per Pupil ($)	Average Property Tax Rate (Mills)	Average Local Revenue per Pupil ($)	Average State Revenue per Pupil ($)	Average Total Revenue per Pupil ($)	Number of Districts in Decile
1	1,834	51,825	22.79	1,056	1,552	2,607	45
2	1,645	31,555	28.88	905	1,992	2,897	51
3	1,919	31,120	30.87	942	2,004	2,946	43
4	1,261	31,768	32.53	1,020	1,986	3,007	62
5	2,161	42,664	33.63	1,412	1,685	3,098	41
6	1,940	44,988	35.24	1,565	1,621	3,187	43
7	2,427	50,658	36.71	1,832	1,465	3,296	34
8	2,269	54,741	38.57	2,077	1,352	3,429	37
9	2,392	63,644	41.15	2,564	1,129	3,693	32
10	4,304	182,744	35.21	4,994	359	5,353	21
Weighted average		57,107	33.45	1,881	1,450	3,330	
Weighted std. dev.		51,377	5.38	1,260	634	763	
Median		43,365	34.02	1,475	1,665	3,140	

Totals		
Category	Amount	Percent
Local revenue	1,565,784,916	56.47
State revenue	1,206,982,693	43.53
Total revenue	2,772,767,609	
Pupils	832,553	

Equity Measures	
Horizontal Equity	
Range	$10,883
Restricted range	$1,806
Federal range ratio	0.646
Coef. of variation	0.229
Gini coefficient	0.094
McLoone Index	0.931
Verstegen Index	1.161
Fiscal Neutrality	
Correlation	0.821
Elasticity	0.190
Adequacy	
Odden-Picus	0.726

FIGURE 11.4   Base Data, Illinois, 1994–95

districts was just 43.5 percent; when Chicago is included, the state role for K–12 districts was below 40 percent. For the decade prior to and even after 1994–95, the state experienced school finance legal challenges, referendums on constitutional changes to increase the state role, and proposals for school reform from both the governor and the legislature.

Figure 11.4 shows that there was a good case to be made for shortcomings in the Illinois school finance system. The data are grouped into deciles ranked by total revenues per pupil; the simulation attempts to have approximately the same number of students in each decile.

The data show there was a wide variation in property wealth per pupil: the average was $57,107, but it was close to $30,000 in the lowest deciles as compared to

$182,744 in the wealthiest decile. The wealthiest decile had just over six times the property wealth per pupil, and thus six times the ability to raise local revenues for public schools, as the poorest deciles. Even the average district had about twice the wealth as the poorest deciles. Without substantial state equalization aid, districts would have great difficulty raising equivalent amounts of money per child at the same tax rate. Though not shown, the property wealth per pupil in Chicago was substantially above the state average.

Tax rates also varied but within a smaller range, with an average tax rate of 33.45 mills, and ranging from at or below 22.79 mills in the lowest-spending decile to 35.21 mills in the highest-spending decile and 41.15 in the ninth decile.

The figure also shows that revenues per pupil varied, but by a much smaller percentage than property wealth per pupil. Spending per pupil from state general and local sources varied from $2,607 in the lowest-spending decile, to just $3,098 in the fifth decile, and then to $5,353 in the tenth decile. The average was just $3,330, far below the Wisconsin average of close to $6,000 (see section 2), though the Wisconsin data use un-weighted-pupil counts compared with the weighted counts in the Illinois database.

The data in Figure 11.4 also show that Illinois was a state with the "new" school finance problem. As property wealth per pupil rose, so did spending per pupil. But local property tax rates also rose with property wealth. Lower-wealth districts in Illinois had lower tax rates and also lower spending levels, while higher-wealth districts had higher tax rates and thus higher spending levels. This characteristic of the system holds today as well. Apparently, it is the link between tax rates and property wealth, as well as a wealth advantage, that drove the spending–property wealth connection in Illinois. The result is that wealth, tax rates, and spending levels rose in tandem.

The data also show that there are anomalies in the connections among property wealth, tax rates, and spending in Illinois. For example, the lowest-spending decile actually had a wealth of $51,825, close to the state average, but a very low tax rate of 22.79 mills. These are mainly rural and agricultural districts in southern Illinois. If these districts had levied just average tax rates, their expenditures per pupil would have been significantly higher. They simply did not tap their wealth advantage. Conversely, the property wealth per pupil of the tenth decile was over double that of the nearest (ninth) decile. This dramatic wealth advantage allowed these districts to enjoy very high spending with tax rates just a bit above the state average. Thus, although there was a general positive connection between wealth, tax rates, and spending, the bottom- and top-spending deciles represented differences from the overall pattern.

The larger role of local wealth in driving spending disparities in Illinois is reflected in the equity and adequacy statistics, all of which are "worse" than those in Wisconsin (see section 2). The coefficient of variation is 0.229, far above the standard of 0.10. The McLoone Index is below 0.95 at 0.931. The wealth elasticity is a high 0.190, and the correlation between spending per pupil and property wealth per pupil is high at 0.821. But again, since the state presents the "new" type of school finance problem, a high-level GTB, which provides ex ante fiscal-neutrality equity, will unlikely improve these equity statistics by much.

Finally, the low level of spending is reflected in the Odden-Picus Adequacy Index, which is just 72.6 percent. As is indicated in the figure, we set the adequacy spending level at $4,500. This was a level somewhat higher than that identified by an Illinois study of the level of state and local revenues per pupil needed to have 70 percent or more of students achieve at or above state standards on the Illinois state testing system (Hinrichs and Laine, 1996).

In sum, these Illinois data for 1994–95 present several types of school finance problems. They showed wide disparities in spending per pupil, a large local role in financing schools, a "new" school finance problem in which higher-wealth districts have higher spending but also higher tax rates, and a system that fell far short of providing adequate revenues. As you will see, the data for more recent years in Illinois reveal similar issues; school finance in Illinois has not been "fixed."

Improving the Illinois School Finance System

Though a state could focus on simply reducing expenditure-per-pupil disparities, or decreasing the link between spending and wealth, or providing more adequate levels of revenues, this analysis will assess the progress various new school finance strategies made on all three of these fronts.

We simulated a GTB program at $100,000, a figure that is at the lower-end approximation of the 90th percentile and close to the zero-aid district in the extant foundation program (check out the results using the Illinois 1994–95 data file). We can somewhat predict the effect of this program. For a $100,000 GTB, a tax rate of 30 mills is needed to produce spending at the $3,000-per-pupil level. Higher tax rates are needed to produce higher spending levels. Because of this, even this relatively high-level GTB might require most districts to increase tax rates just to maintain former spending levels.

That is precisely what we found. A GTB of $100,000 required both local and state revenues to rise. Local revenues rose in the lower-decile districts because even this high-level GTB provided less state aid. State revenues rose in the mid-wealth deciles because the GTB provided more money for both higher spending and local property tax relief. Local revenues also rose for the highest-wealth districts.

Perhaps not surprisingly, this GTB did not make significant gains on equity and adequacy statistics. The coefficient of variation was still high at 0.22, the McLoone Index dropped to 0.90, the fiscal-neutrality statistics improved modestly, and the Adequacy Index rose from 0.726 to 0.747. Though this program costs only an extra $79.5 million, it had almost no positive equity or adequacy impact on the system. The program also produced over 100 state aid losers, rendering the program politically problematic as well.

We ran a GTB at a much higher level—$150,000—thus ensuring some substantial property tax relief at the risk of not making sufficient equity gains in this state with the "new" school finance problem. Figure 11.5 presents the results. First, state costs rose substantially, which might make such a program unaffordable. There was some local tax relief, which was one of the goals, but it was not very high.

Though the equity and adequacy statistics improve, there is not sufficient progress to declare the system sound. The coefficient of variation at 0.178 is still far above the standard of 0.10. The McLoone Index is just 0.885. But both the fiscal-neutrality and the adequacy statistics are much better, with the wealth elasticity at 0.121 and the Adequacy Index at 90.2 percent.

Adequacy Level	$4,500
Pupil Weights	No
Disabled	—
Limited English	—
Low income	—

Guaranteed Tax Base	$150,000.00

Decile	Average No. Of Pupils	Average Property Value per Pupil ($)	Average Old Property Tax Rate (Mills)	Average New Property Tax Rate (Mills)	Average Change in Property Tax Rate (Mills)	Average Old Local Revenue per Pupil ($)	Average New Local Revenue per Pupil ($)	Average Change in Local Revenue per Pupil ($)	Average New State Revenue per Pupil ($)	Average Change in State Revenue per Pupil ($)	Average Total Revenue per Pupil ($)	Average Change in Total Revenue per Pupil ($)	Number of Districts in Decile
1	1,844	52,702	22.78	20.08	(2.70)	1,080	968	(112)	2,054	527	3,022	415	45
2	1,678	35,774	28.67	24.00	(4.66)	1,025	859	(166)	2,741	866	3,600	700	49
3	1,731	34,331	30.33	25.01	(5.32)	1,039	859	(180)	2,893	977	3,752	797	44
4	1,733	33,926	32.02	26.04	(5.98)	1,082	884	(198)	3,022	1,095	3,906	897	52
5	1,390	41,204	33.50	27.08	(6.42)	1,374	1,117	(257)	2,945	1,220	4,062	963	53
6	2,764	43,183	35.16	28.19	(6.97)	1,511	1,217	(294)	3,012	1,340	4,228	1,046	34
7	2,657	50,237	36.11	28.99	(7.12)	1,789	1,456	(332)	2,893	1,400	4,349	1,068	31
8	2,343	56,761	37.34	29.98	(7.37)	2,041	1,668	(373)	2,864	1,482	4,532	1,109	36
9	2,515	54,468	40.16	31.91	(8.26)	2,153	1,740	(413)	3,046	1,652	4,786	1,239	31
10	2,608	123,955	39.98	33.51	(6.47)	3,766	3,404	(361)	2,246	1,352	5,650	991	34
Weighted average		57,107	33.45	27.66	(5.79)	1,881	1,599	(282)	2,604	1,155	4,203	872	
Weighted std. dev.		51,377	5.38	4.18	2.06	1,260	1,219	165	768	408	749	298	
Median		51,477	34.22	27.79	(6.43)	1,762	1,431	(331)	2,738	1,296	4,168	965	

Totals

Category	Amount	Percent	Change from Base Amount
Local revenue	1,330,981,501	38.04	(234,803,415)
State revenue	2,168,176,978	61.96	961,194,285
Total revenue	3,499,158,479		726,390,871
Pupils	832,553		

Winners and Losers

Category	Winners	Losers	No Change
State aid	398	11	0
Total revenue	398	0	11

Equity Measures

Horizontal Equity	
Range	$10,883
Restricted range	$1,895
Federal range ratio	0.564
Coef. of variation	0.178
Gini coefficient	0.087
McLoone Index	0.885
Verstegen Index	1.125
Fiscal Neutrality	
Correlation	0.612
Elasticity	0.121
Adequacy	
Odden-Picus	0.902

FIGURE 11.5 Guaranteed Tax Base (GTB), Illinois

The problem with a GTB program for a state with the "new" school finance problem is that a very high, and thus very expensive, GTB must be used, and even then only modest gains on some equity and adequacy fronts are produced. Thus, we tried a foundation program to ensure that the lower-spending districts actually had to raise spending, which allowed spending above the foundation level but only with local wealth. Figure 11.6 shows a foundation program with a foundation expenditure of $4,300 and a required tax rate of 35 mills, which is 1 mill above the median. We simulated foundation programs at lower tax rate levels, but the costs seemed too high, though as Figure 11.6 shows, this program is not low-cost either.

Such a foundation program, which is similar to the reform enacted by Illinois in late 1997, does accomplish the goal of raising the state role and lowering the local role in financing schools, as a percentage. And it also makes larger gains on all equity and adequacy fronts. The coefficient of variation, at 0.110, is just above the 0.10 standard, and the McLoone Index is 0.997, which indicates that nearly all districts are spending at the median. The wealth elasticity is below 0.10 at 0.098, and the Adequacy Index is 0.964. But the program required an extra $825 million in state revenues and $66 million more in local revenues, the latter produced by setting the required minimum local tax effort at 35 mills.

The dilemma in "fixing" the Illinois school finance system was that lower foundation levels produced less progress on equity and adequacy. Higher foundation levels could not be accompanied by a required local tax effort that exceeded 35 mills, which is still quite high, and thus required large infusions of state dollars. The bottom line was that the only way significant equity and adequacy gains could be realized was by raising the foundation level, as the state ultimately did. But the "cost" of doing so was a substantially enhanced state fiscal role, close to an increase of $1 billion, which represented a 68 percent increase from the base of $1.2 billion.

The high state cost is one reason the state has struggled for years—and still struggles—to enact a school finance reform. The only option is a much larger state role; that requires either a state tax hike, which has not been politically feasible, or a very healthy economy that produced increased in-state revenues that could be devoted to school finance. Neither scenario has really occurred.

This text's website now includes data for the 2000–01, 2001–02, and 2005–06 school years. You are encouraged to analyze the equity and adequacy impacts of this system, as compared with that in 1994–95. Visit the website for links to more information about the Illinois school finance system.

4. SCHOOL FINANCE IN KENTUCKY

In response to the landmark ruling of the Kentucky Supreme Court in *Rose v. Council for Better Education*[3] in June 1989, the Kentucky General Assembly dramatically changed the school finance system of public K–12 education in that state. Among the many components of that ruling, the Kentucky Supreme Court upheld an earlier circuit

[3]*Rose v. Council for Better Education, Inc.*, 88-SC-804-TG (Ky., 1989).

Adequacy Level	$4,500.00
Pupil Weights	No
Disabled	—
Limited English	—
Low Income	—

Foundation Level	$4,300.00
Required Tax Rate	35.00

Decile	Pupils	Property Value per Pupil ($)	Old Property Tax Rate (Mills)	New Property Tax Rate (Mills)	Change in Property Tax Rate (Mills)	Old Local Revenue per Pupil ($)	New Local Revenue per Pupil ($)	Change in Local Revenue per Pupil ($)	New State Revenue per Pupil ($)	Change in State Revenue per Pupil ($)	Total Revenue per Pupil ($)	Change in Total Revenue per Pupil ($)	Number of Districts in Decile
1	1,665	38,308	25.85	34.07	8.22	869	1,176	308	3,033	1,139	4,209	1,447	49
2	1,587	28,626	29.42	35.00	5.58	824	1,002	177	3,298	1,225	4,300	1,402	53
3	1,265	36,557	30.63	35.00	4.37	1,078	1,279	201	3,021	1,160	4,300	1,361	63
4	1,941	44,736	31.52	35.00	3.48	1,372	1,566	194	2,734	1,094	4,300	1,288	45
5	2,294	57,029	31.59	35.00	3.41	1,782	1,996	214	2,304	1,013	4,300	1,226	30
6	3,355	55,841	33.92	35.04	1.12	1,879	1,956	77	2,346	1,006	4,301	1,083	29
7	2,009	43,754	36.30	35.59	(0.71)	1,585	1,552	(33)	2,769	1,095	4,321	1,063	40
8	1,951	51,579	38.18	36.55	(1.63)	1,951	1,874	(77)	2,495	1,039	4,369	963	40
9	3,384	51,440	40.32	37.66	(2.66)	2,055	1,928	(127)	2,500	1,049	4,427	922	25
10	2,591	126,140	39.30	36.53	(2.77)	3,771	3,647	(124)	1,468	601	5,115	477	35
Weighted average		57,107	33.45	35.48	2.02	1,881	1,960	79	2,440	990	4,400	1,070	
Weighted std. dev.		51,377	5.38	2.53	4.14	1,260	1,218	233	946	342	482	424	
Median		63,337	34.00	35.00	1.00	2,153	2,217	63	2,083	968	4,300	1,032	

Totals

Category	Amount	Percent	Change from Base Amount
Local revenue	1,631,873,444	44.55	66,088,528
State revenue	2,031,483,579	55.45	824,500,886
Total revenue	3,663,357,023		890,589,414
Pupils	728,146		

Winners and Losers

Category	Winners	Losers	No Change
State aid	397	12	0
Total revenue	393	0	16

Equity Measures

Horizontal Equity	
Range	$10,883
Restricted range	$359
Federal range ratio	0.083
Coef. of variation	0.110
Gini coefficient	0.023
McLoone Index	0.997
Verstegen Index	1.048

Fiscal Neutrality	
Correlation	0.785
Elasticity	0.098

Adequacy	
Odden-Picus	0.964

FIGURE 11.6 Foundation Program, Illinois

court ruling[4] holding that the state's school finance system violated the Kentucky constitution's education clause, which requires the General Assembly "to provide an efficient system of common schools throughout the Commonwealth."[5] In assessing the constitutionality of the Kentucky school finance system, the circuit court had found that (1) there was marked variation in property wealth of school districts, (2) the allocation of state aid did not compensate for the variation in wealth, (3) there was a wide disparity in the per-pupil revenue of school districts, and (4) the quality of education was contingent on available revenue (Augenblick, 1991). The circuit court concluded that an efficient school finance system required substantial uniformity and equality of financial resources.

In response to the ruling in *Rose*, the Kentucky General Assembly completely overhauled the organization and structure of K–12 education and created a new school finance system. The new system, called Support Education Excellence in Kentucky (SEEK), was designed to dramatically improve the equity of Kentucky's school finance system.

Various analyses of the SEEK formula concluded that the equity of the system improved substantially between 1989–90 and the implementation of SEEK in 1990–91 (see Adams, 1994; Augenblick, 1991). Further, Picus, Odden, and Fermanich (2004) concluded that equity had consistently improved throughout the 1990s, using a common equity framework (see Chapter 3) and data over a 10-year period from 1991 to 2000. Picus, Odden, and Fermanich also used pupil weights and a geographic price adjustment, finding that need- and price-adjusted dollars showed the most equity for the system. A March 2006 analysis by Augenblick and DeCesare (2006) concluded that the SEEK formula continues to provide an equitable funding model for Kentucky.

Developed a decade and a half ago as part of Kentucky's wide-ranging school reform, the SEEK formula has not been substantially revised since its inception. For 2005–06, the SEEK formula relied on three levels of funding for school districts, as described next.

Adjusted Base Guarantee

This foundation program provided each district with $3,445 per pupil in 2005–06 through a combination of local taxes and state aid. The number of pupils is adjusted by a series of factors or "add-ons" that affect the cost of providing services to students, including the following:

- A pupil-weighting system for exceptional children with special needs. This includes weights of 2.35 for severely handicapped children, 1.17 for moderately handicapped children, 0.24 for children requiring speech programs, and 0.075 for LEP children. In addition, home and hospital students are multiplied by the base guarantee less the capital outlay allotment of $100.

---

[4]*Council for Better Education, Inc. v. Wilkinson*, 85-CI-1759 (Franklin Cir. Ct., Div. I, Ky., May 31, 1933).
[5]Kentucky Constitution Sec. 183: Improving State School Finance Systems.

- A transportation adjustment based on the population density of a school district.
- A weight of 0.15 for students participating in the free-lunch program.
- An adjustment for students unable to attend regular school due to short-term health problems.

Each district levies a property tax of 30 cents per $100 of assessed value, or an equivalent amount through a combination of taxes for school purposes on utilities, motor vehicles, and occupational license receipts, or as an excise tax on income. The difference between the foundation guarantee and the district's locally raised revenue is provided by the state. The amount of the unadjusted per-pupil basic allotment for each of the 16 years from 1991–2006 is displayed in Table 11.1.

The other two levels of funding are these:

- *Tier I:* This is an optional component that allows a district to raise up to an additional 15 percent of the adjusted base guarantee ($3,445 for 2005–06) through an equalized property tax or property tax equivalent. Districts with property wealth less than 150 percent of the state average receive state equalization aid that makes up for the difference between the local tax base and equalization level. For 1999–00, the Tier I equalization level was $410,000, and it grew to $587,000 for 2005–06. Table 11.1 shows the equalization level for Tier I for each

TABLE 11.1   Adjusted Base Guarantee and Tier I Equalization Level in Kentucky, 1990–91 through 2005–06

Year	Adjusted Base Guarantee ($ per ADA)	Tier I Equalization Level ($ per ADA)
1990–91	$2,305	$225,000
1991–92	2,420	225,000
1992–93	2,420	280,000
1993–94	2,495	280,000
1994–95	2,517	295,000
1995–96	2,593	295,000
1996–97	2,673	365,000
1997–98	2,756	365,000
1998–99	2,839	410,000
1999–00	2,924	410,000
2000–01	2,994	470,000
2001–02	3,066	470,000
2002–03	3,081	545,000
2003–04	3,191	545,000
2004–05	3,240	587,000
2005–06	3,445	587,000

year from 1991 to 2006. It should be noted that FY 1994–95 was the first year in which a uniform system of valuing property at 100 percent of real value was required across Kentucky.

- *Tier II:* Another optional component of the system allows school districts to generate additional revenue up to 30 percent of the total of the adjusted base guarantee plus the revenue generated in Tier I. This revenue is not equalized by the state. Thus, a district taking full advantage of both Tier I and Tier II authority could raise a total of $5,150 per ADA before the add-ons are computed. This is 49.5 percent higher than the adjusted base guarantee. Obviously, the add-ons for special education, compensatory education, transportation, and home/hospital children establish a unique (and slightly higher) adjusted base guarantee for each individual district. However, the formula still allows each district to raise nearly half again as much as the adjusted base guarantee.

In addition to the funding in the SEEK formula, the state provides limited funding to school districts through a number of categorical programs, including programs for state agency children, gifted and talented, early childhood education, vocational education, textbooks, teacher testing and internships, staff development, family resource/youth service centers, and regional service centers. These programs are relatively small and, according to Murray (2001), represented less than 9 percent of total state aid in 1998–99. (Visit the text website for links to fairly recent and more detailed descriptions of the Kentucky school finance system.)

The Kentucky School Finance Problem and Simulated Improvements

Kentucky data for three school years—1990–91, 1995–96, and 1999–00—are available on this text's website. You are encouraged to select one, two, or all three years of these data; analyze the nature of the school finance problem in that year; and then simulate alternative school finance systems to make improvements beyond that which the SEEK program has produced. You can also use the data to assess the degree to which Kentucky school finance equity changed over that 10-year period. You can search for the several Kentucky adequacy studies that have been conducted over the past five years and use their results in your analyses (Odden, Fermanich, and Picus, 2003; Picus, Odden, and Fermanich, 2004; Verstegen, 2003).

5. SCHOOL FINANCE IN VERMONT

The Vermont data are for the 1996–97 school year, the year Vermont's school finance system was declared unconstitutional in *Brigham v. Vermont*.[6] The data were downloaded from the Vermont Department of Education's website and adjusted to include only public school districts that raised and spent public tax dollars. There were a total of 201 districts, with some 73,000 students and regular-education expenditures of

---

[6]*Brigham v. State of Vermont*, No. 96-502 (Vt., 1997).

$450.2 million that year from state and local sources. Property wealth is equalized to 100 percent of market value.

Prior to the enactment of Act 60, the 1997 school-funding law passed in response to the Vermont Supreme Court's ruling in *Brigham*, the Vermont school finance system relied primarily on a foundation program. The major problem with the foundation program, as pointed out in the court decision, was that average school-funding levels substantially exceeded the foundation level. Moreover, most funds raised and spent above the foundation level were raised through unequalized property tax levies. This led to the "traditional" school finance problem previously identified—low-wealth districts with high tax rates and low per-pupil revenues.

To address the problems identified by the court, the Vermont legislature passed Act 60, which established a block grant program guaranteeing each district essentially $5,000 per pupil at a uniform statewide tax rate of $1.10 per $100 of assessed valuation, or 11.1 mills. Although called a block grant, it is clearly a foundation program.

A second-tier GTB was also included in Act 60. Rather than provide state funding to help districts reach their revenue goals, however, tier two was funded entirely through property taxes in the districts that elected to participate in the second tier. The system, referred to as the "shark tank" by the Vermont media, created a system in which districts that elected to raise revenues beyond the $5,000 level did not know what their tax rate would be until all districts had determined how much revenue they would collect through the guaranteed yield. A uniform tax rate was then established across the state. Chapter 9 pointed out that one of the potential problems with a GTB is that the cost to the state can't be predicted with certainty. In Vermont, the state shifted that risk to school districts, with wealthy districts absorbing higher levels of risk—if they choose to participate in the second tier.

To mitigate against high property taxes, homeowner property taxes in the first tier were limited to a maximum of 2 percent of income for taxpayers with incomes below $75,000. Total property taxes, including the second tier and other municipal property taxes, were limited to no more than 5 percent of household income for those earning less than $75,000 a year (there is a sliding scale based on income). The impact of this was to shift more of the property tax burden to out-of-state property owners (who constituted a substantial proportion of taxpayers) and to nonresidential property.

The system was changed in 2003 through Act 63, which revised some of the property tax issues. For the 2005–06 school year, the tax rate was split between residential and nonresidential property, and the tax rate was set at $1.10 for a foundation level of $6,800 per pupil. Districts that elected to spend above the foundation level had their tax rate adjusted upward proportionally based on the percentage their spending is above the foundation level. Actual tax rates are determined by the state each year after all towns have approved the school budgets. The state equalizes the spending levels above $6,800 and recaptures funds from districts that raise more through property taxes than they voted to spend.

The Vermont School Finance Problem

Figure 11.7 displays the base data for Vermont from the 201 districts, displayed by deciles. Each decile has approximately 10 percent of the students in the state. Consequently, the number of districts in each decile (reported in the last column of the figure)

Adequacy Level	$5,000
Pupil Weights	**No**
Disabled	—
Limited English	—
Low income	—

Decile	Average Number of Pupils per District in Decile	Average Property Value per Pupil ($)	Average Property Tax Rate (Mills)	Average Local Revenue per Pupil ($)	Average State Revenue per Pupil ($)	Average Total Revenue per Pupil ($)	Number of Districts in Decile
1	252	239,362	11.51	2,719	1,940	4,659	29
2	385	242,444	12.79	3,107	2,177	5,284	18
3	368	249,748	14.02	3,475	2,056	5,531	21
4	432	236,776	14.33	3,402	2,342	5,744	17
5	371	507,437	12.86	4,392	1,536	5,928	19
6	821	317,844	13.73	4,269	1,831	6,100	9
7	391	350,994	14.60	4,805	1,540	6,345	18
8	214	432,737	14.05	5,517	1,160	6,677	27
9	466	509,522	15.09	5,699	1,436	7,136	18
10	335	777,284	13.09	7,392	800	8,191	25
Weighted average		338,713	14.05	4,452	1,691	6,142	
Weighted std. dev.		223,080	2.88	1,645	1,059	905	
Median		214,200	10.91	2,337	3,699	6,037	

Totals		
Category	Amount	Percent
Local revenue	326,279,231	72.48
State revenue	123,906,094	27.52
Total revenue	450,185,325	
Pupils	73,294	

Equity Measures	
Horizontal Equity	
Range	$6,712
Restricted range	$2,851
Federal range ratio	0.597
Coef. of variation	0.147
Gini coefficient	0.082
McLoone Index	0.900
Verstegen Index	1.016
Fiscal Neutrality	
Correlation	0.482
Elasticity	0.072
Adequacy	
Odden-Picus	0.994

FIGURE 11.7   Base Data, Vermont, 1996–97

varies from a low of 9 in the sixth decile to a high of 29 in the lowest-revenue decile. The figure shows total state plus local spending of about $450.2 million with local districts raising over 72 percent of this total.

Across the deciles, average total revenue per pupil ranges from $4,659 to $8,191, a ratio of 1 to 1.75. Property wealth generally increases as spending increases. Across the deciles, property wealth per pupil ranges from a low of $236,776 per pupil to a high of $777,284 per pupil, a factor of 3.25 to 1. State aid per pupil declines as revenues and wealth increase, while locally raised revenues climb with wealth and spending level.

The coefficient of variation is 0.147, above the 0.10 standard identified in Chapter 3. The McLoone Index is estimated at 0.90, below the 0.95 standard also established in Chapter 3. The Verstegen Index stands at 1.016, showing that there is some, but not substantial, variation in spending per pupil for districts above the median.

Determining a reasonable revenue level for the adequacy calculation was difficult. For Vermont, we have used a very low figure—$5,000 per pupil, the block grant level established by the legislature in Act 60. With that figure, the Odden-Picus Adequacy Index is 0.994. This means that to bring those districts with revenues per pupil below $5,000 to that spending level, revenues would have to increase by 0.006 percent relative to $5,000, or only by about $30 per pupil. Others might choose to set the adequacy level higher, in which case the Adequacy Index would be lower.

The adequacy calculation was a predictor of the problems Vermont encountered as Act 60 was implemented. Recall that the second tier is equalized entirely by local property taxes levied on districts that participate in that pool. Since most districts chose to spend above the level of the $5,000 block grant, a large number opted to participate in the second-tier GTB. In this case, property taxes on the wealthy districts went up relatively dramatically. The alternative was substantial declines in the level of per-pupil revenue, and hence spending. But if $5,000 was an appropriate adequacy level, then the argument for higher spending would have been less forceful. However, even in the late 1990s, $5,000 per pupil was a low adequacy figure. On the other hand, if $5,000 was below an adequate expenditure level, then there would have been pressures to increase the $5,000 base to a higher level and reduce "forced" spending above the base. Those pressures certainly emerged, but there were equally strong pressures to get rid of the "shark tank" aspect of the second tier, which was done in 2003, as discussed previously.

In terms of fiscal neutrality, Figure 11.7 shows that the correlation between revenue and wealth is 0.482, and the elasticity is a relatively low 0.072. However, if you download the simulation from this text's website and analyze the Vermont data, you will see that the graph of the base data shows the presence of a few high-wealth, medium-revenue districts. These outliers have the effect of lowering the elasticity. Eliminate those outliers from the model, and there is a very strong relationship between wealth and revenue.

Improving the Vermont School Finance System

Since the Vermont legislature in the late 1990s took steps to improve the equity of the state school finance system, we will begin our analysis with the changes made in Act 60. First, we will consider a simple foundation program using the parameters of the state's block grant. That will be followed by the promised GTB at the 90th percentile of wealth and then by a combination program with similar characteristics.

First, we simulated a foundation program with a foundation level of $5,000 and a required local effort (RLE) of 11.1 mills, which reflects the first tier of the reform Vermont enacted. The result increased total spending by just $3.1 million, with the state share falling by just over $3.2 million, and local taxes increasing by $6.3 million. A total of 108 districts experienced a loss of state aid and were forced to make it up through increased property taxes, which occurred in all but the second and third deciles. Only districts in the two lowest-revenue deciles experienced increases in revenue. Both the horizontal-equity and fiscal-neutrality measures showed very small improvements, while the Odden-Picus Adequacy Index improved to 1.0, meaning all of the districts received at least $5,000 per pupil in total revenue. Again, if a higher adequacy level were set, the Adequacy Index would have been less than 1.0.

Figure 11.8 shows the results of a GTB program using a per-pupil property wealth level of $510,800, representing the district at the 90th percentile of wealth. The data show immediately why the legislature was unwilling to fund a high-level GTB program. A GTB at this level would raise an additional $48.5 million for schools, provide taxpayers with $19.7 million in property tax relief, and cost the state an additional $68.2 million. Finding those revenues would have been difficult. Recall that additional revenues would be collected from a statewide property tax under Act 60. If this simulation is indicative of what would have happened after Act 60 was implemented, at an average property wealth of $338,713, property tax rates would have to increase an average of 2.75 mills across the state, thus offsetting the modest property tax relief shown in Figure 11.7.

Interestingly, although the GTB increased spending dramatically, it did little to change the horizontal-equity statistics, which remain roughly the same as in the base data. Correlation and elasticity do decline, however.

Figure 11.9 displays the results of a combination program using the block grant parameters and a GTB level of $510,800. This compromise appears to be the best option of those presented, but it is more generous than the program Vermont enacted. Total revenue increased by just over $31.3 million, with a drop of $4.9 million in local taxes and an increase in state funding of $36.2 million. While the horizontal-equity figures show very small improvements, the elasticity declined to 0.050. The correlation is higher than under the GTB, but this is in large part due to the very low elasticity observed and highlights the policy problem identified in Chapter 9 when using both figures. The state share of total revenue increases to 33 percent, and while 71 districts lose state revenue, all districts have as much total revenue, or more than before. Nevertheless, the number of loser districts represents about one-third of all districts, which diminishes the political attractiveness of even this program.

In short, the Vermont school finance system was difficult to improve without spending more state money. The reform that was enacted, Act 60, was controversial because of its burden on out-of-state property owners and the redistributive nature of the second tier. And this program was changed significantly in 2003.

Data for the recent school years are now on the text website, so you can analyze the impact of Act 60 for that school year, as well as simulate the impact of different types of school finance formulas to perhaps improve equity and adequacy even more than Act 60. For such simulations, the adequacy level of $5,000 should be substantially hiked. Data for 2005–06 are also on the website, enabling you to simulate the impact of the new foundation level and new tax rates.

6. SUMMARY

Fixing state school finance problems is no easy task. It requires balancing equity and adequacy goals with the political economy of education—producing sufficient winners at a cost the state can afford. Though not discussed at length here, all of the simulations produced many more school districts that had their state aid amounts increased than those that did not.

These examples also show that the nature of the school finance problem varied dramatically across the four states, thus requiring different kinds of solutions. The Vermont system was somewhat easier to improve as it represented a more "traditional"

Adequacy Level	$5,000.00
Pupil Weights	No
Disabled	—
Limited English	—
Low income	—

Guaranteed Tax Base	$510,800.00

Decile	Average No. of Pupils	Average Property Value per Pupil ($)	Average Old Property Tax Rate (Mills)	Average New Property Tax Rate (Mills)	Average Change in Property Tax Rate (Mills)	Average Old Local Revenue per Pupil ($)	Average New Local Revenue per Pupil ($)	Average Change in Local Revenue per Pupil ($)	Average New State Revenue per Pupil ($)	Average Change in State Revenue per pupil ($)	Average Total Revenue per Pupil ($)	Average Change in Total Revenue per Pupil ($)	Number of Districts in Decile
1	252	247,425	10.70	10.15	(0.54)	2,624	2,494	(130)	2,693	539	5,187	409	28
2	328	433,400	11.80	10.88	(0.92)	3,572	3,388	(184)	2,482	696	5,870	511	23
3	329	330,077	12.40	11.88	(0.52)	3,922	3,873	(49)	2,312	514	6,185	466	22
4	382	305,800	13.70	12.51	(1.19)	4,036	3,759	(277)	2,749	917	6,507	640	18
5	338	361,016	13.53	12.44	(1.08)	4,456	4,242	(213)	2,428	831	6,671	618	19
6	616	370,771	14.02	12.89	(1.12)	4,752	4,466	(285)	2,419	886	6,886	601	14
7	593	293,217	15.26	13.82	(1.44)	4,453	4,052	(402)	3,006	1,207	7,058	805	12
8	423	488,250	14.26	12.85	(1.41)	5,069	4,727	(342)	2,554	1,095	7,282	753	16
9	390	461,014	14.56	13.53	(1.03)	5,965	5,738	(226)	1,920	846	7,658	620	21
10	266	605,657	16.08	14.49	(1.59)	6,598	6,230	(368)	2,517	1,239	8,747	871	28
Weighted average		338,713	14.05	12.90	(1.14)	4,452	4,183	(269)	2,621	931	6,804	662	
Weighted std. dev.		223,080	2.88	2.07	1.26	1,645	1,734	407	1,417	862	923	489	
Median		347,600	15.27	13.28	(1.99)	5,306	4,616	(690)	2,167	1,705	6,783	1,014	

Totals

	Amount	Percent	Change from Base Amount
Local revenue	306,579,415	61.48	(19,699,816)
State revenue	192,126,350	38.52	68,220,255
Total revenue	498,705,765		48,520,440
Pupils	73,294		

Winners and Losers

Category	Winners	Losers	No Change
State aid	155	46	0
Total revenue	155	0	46

Equity Measures

Horizontal Equity	
Range	$6,407
Restricted range	$3,416
Federal range ratio	0.639
Coef. of variation	0.136
Gini coefficient	0.075
McLoone Index	0.897
Verstegen Index	1.101
Fiscal Neutrality	
Correlation	0.292
Elasticity	0.040
Adequacy	
Odden-Picus	0.999

FIGURE 11.8 Guaranteed Tax Base (GTB), Vermont

Adequacy Level	$5,000.00

Foundation Level	$5,000.00
Required Tax Rate	11.10

Pupil Weights	No
Disabled	—
Limited English	—
Low income	—

GTB	$510,800.00
GTB Rate Cap above Foundation Tax Rate	99.00

Decile	Pupils	Property Value per Pupil ($)	Old Property Tax Rate (Mills)	New Property Tax Rate (Mills)	Change In Property Tax Rate (Mills)	Old Local Revenue per Pupil ($)	New Local Revenue per Pupil ($)	Change in Local Revenue per Pupil ($)	New State Foundation Revenue per Pupil ($)	New State GTB Revenue per Pupil ($)	Change in State Revenue per Pupil ($)	Total Revenue per Pupil ($)	Change in Total Revenue per Pupil ($)	Number of Districts in Decile
1	251	235,630	10.82	11.45	0.62	2,518	2,688	170	2,385	102	212	5,175	425	27
2	408	247,653	12.87	12.18	(0.69)	3,154	3,004	(150)	2,268	296	623	5,567	473	19
3	297	447,444	11.65	12.04	0.40	3,779	3,974	195	1,609	344	15	5,927	500	25
4	367	289,842	14.06	13.29	(0.77)	3,961	3,785	(176)	1,893	540	615	6,218	539	19
5	471	323,380	14.24	13.37	(0.87)	4,385	4,204	(181)	1,655	545	693	6,404	466	15
6	445	391,318	13.45	13.20	(0.25)	4,819	4,814	(5)	1,285	506	254	6,605	258	17
7	491	389,057	14.37	13.63	(0.74)	5,002	4,887	(115)	1,312	574	619	6,772	446	14
8	546	331,433	15.17	14.69	(0.48)	4,939	4,798	(141)	1,446	720	560	6,964	269	12
9	302	515,566	14.34	13.74	(0.59)	5,848	5,761	(87)	1,069	646	510	7,476	359	29
10	315	668,483	15.62	14.58	(1.03)	6,918	6,735	(183)	1,031	891	795	8,658	390	24
Weighted average		338,713	14.05	13.60	(0.45)	4,452	4,385	(66)	1,647	538	494	6,570	428	
Weighted std. dev.		223,080	2.88	2.13	1.32	1,645	1,750	443	1,080	431	790	906	410	
Median		516,700	12.24	12.60	0.37	6,324	6,513	189	—	—	(189)	6,513	271	

Totals

Category	Amount	Percent	Change from Base Amount
Local revenue	321,417,276	66.75	(4,861,955)
State revenue	160,102,996	33.25	36,196,902
Total revenue	481,520,271		31,334,946
Pupils	73,294		

Winners and Losers

Category	Winners	Losers	No Change
State aid	130	71	0
Total revenue	106	9	58

Equity Measures

Horizontal Equity	
Range	$5,365
Restricted range	$3,235
Federal range ratio	0.623
Coef. of variation	0.138
Gini coefficient	0.076
McLoone Index	0.901
Verstegen Index	1.112
Fiscal Neutrality	
Correlation	0.365
Elasticity	0.050
Adequacy	
Odden-Picus	1.000

FIGURE 11.9   Combination Program, Vermont

391

school finance situation; a high GTB worked in this state, though the best structure was a two-tier system. But high GTBs did not work in either Wisconsin or Illinois, as both states represented "new" school finance problems. In these states, high-level GTBs were expensive and produced only modest equity and adequacy gains. The resolution in both states required a higher-level foundation program; such a program could be funded with quite small increases in state aid in Wisconsin but required large increases in Illinois. On the other hand, when the issue of providing adequate resources for extra student needs was added to the Wisconsin reform agenda, the required costs increased significantly. And the SEEK program in Kentucky was a high-foundation program.

Other states will require still other solutions, some perhaps requiring more of a two-tiered school finance structure as in Vermont, which we favored more in the first edition (Odden and Picus, 1992). Others will require still different mixes of state and local revenues. The bottom line in improving state school finance systems requires some combination of these:

- Getting a clear understanding of the nature of the problems—too much local revenue, inadequate spending, wide spending disparities, significant connections between spending and wealth, and so on
- Determining which type of school finance structure—GTB, foundation, or two-tiered, foundation-GTB programs—likely will work
- Determining an adequate level of spending
- Simulating alternative forms of the formula structures that might resolve the problems and then assessing the gains in equity and adequacy in light of both local and state costs, and political impacts (state aid winners and losers, and numbers of districts that have to raise local taxes)

Judging which program might be the one to try in a state will depend on answers to these school finance, public finance, and political effects questions, answers that will vary by state, and probably vary over time within any individual state.

Study Questions

1. From this text's website, select a state with newer data. Analyze the degree of equity and adequacy of that state's school finance system. Compare what you find with that for earlier years discussed in this chapter.
    a. Use the simulation to find alternative school finance programs that improve both equity and adequacy. Require viable programs to have at least 60 percent of districts be "winner" districts, and limit state aid increases to 20 percent.
    b. Discuss the cost and the impacts on equity and adequacy.
    c. Use the preferred program in part a to address vertical equity as well, by including pupil weights for students from low-income backgrounds, ESL students, and disabled students. What is the additional cost? What is the impact on equity?
2. Select a second state and conduct the same analyses as for Problem 1.
3. Briefly compare and contrast the following:
    a. The nature of the school finance problem in the two states

  b. The nature of the school finance reform to remedy the problem
  c. The effect that pupil weights have on the preferred school finance reform in terms of cost and impacts on equity

Essay Assignment

Pick two states and data sets on the McGraw-Hill website that are not discussed in Chapter 11. The objective of the paper is to identify the equity and adequacy problems for the states and to "fix" them. Specifically, do the following:

1. Provide a succinct conceptual framework for assessing equity and adequacy of a state school finance system (see Chapter 3). Include a discussion of legal issues if there has been a court case in the states you have selected.
2. For each state:
    a. Describe the state's school finance system.
    b. From the base data, identify the key equity and adequacy problems you seek to fix. Include the base table in the paper. Do *not* use the adequacy figure in the simulation; you need to do a literature review for each state to identify an appropriate adequacy number.
    c. Fix the problems with a GTB- or foundation-type school finance formula, or perhaps a two-tier school finance formula. Include the final table from the program you run.
    d. Discuss costs, winners and losers, the degree to which you fixed the problems you identified, and the special issues that emerged in that analysis.
3. Compare and contrast the problems and the solutions for the two states.

This could also be a class exercise: students could be divided into two groups, each with the same state. The groups could independently identify the problems and formulate remedies and then compare and contrast both in a class discussion.

Note: If data for your state are not on the web, we would be happy to tailor a simulation for your state. To do that, we would need an Excel file with the following data for each district in the state:

1. Number of students
2. Number of students eligible for free and reduced-price lunch, or an official poverty count of students
3. Number of students with disabilities
4. Number of ELL students
5. Equalized assessed valuation
6. Total local revenues for current operating purposes
7. Total state general-aid revenues
8. State aid for students with disabilities
9. State aid for ELL students
10. State aid for students eligible for free and reduced-price lunch

Send the file to either Allan Odden at arodden@wisc.edu or Larry Picus at lpicus@usc.edu.

— *Chapter 12* ————————————————————————

Redesigning Teacher Salary Structures[1]

Few school finance textbooks address the issue of teacher compensation. But in order to "cost out" the adequacy model developed in Chapter 4, a price needs to be placed on *all* resources—and teachers are the largest resource. This means identifying an appropriate or adequate teacher salary. It should also mean using those salary dollars in a teacher salary structure that is more productive than the current single-salary approach. This chapter addresses these teacher salary structure redesign issues.

The quest to change the way teachers are paid is not something new to this first decade of the twenty-first century. During the last half of the twentieth century, teacher pay structure changes were tried at least once a decade. And nearly all of the 1980s *Nation at Risk* reform recommendations included proposals for changing teacher pay structures to some sort of merit or performance basis (e.g., National Commission on Excellence and Equity in Education, 1983). But most failed, and only a handful survived more than a few years (Murnane and Cohan, 1986; Odden and Kelley, 2002). Today, the single-salary schedule that pays teachers on the basis of their years of experience and number of education credits and degrees is used by almost all states and districts across the country.

This chapter has six sections. Section 1 covers the reason for making teacher compensation change today and offers goals for a new teacher compensation system. Section 2 provides a short primer on how to think of the various elements of teacher compensation. Section 3 addresses beginning and average pay levels, section 4 discusses wage premiums, and section 5 examines base pay progression elements. The final section describes a new salary structure emphasizing teachers' instructional practice, including the design of a variable pay element for teachers.

---

[1]This chapter draws heavily from Odden and Wallace, 2007b.

394

1. CHANGING THE WAY TEACHERS ARE PAID

Although this chapter focuses on redesigning teacher compensation, there are several reasons for the resilience of the single-salary structure. First, it is easy to administer. Second, it is objective and not subject to administrative whim. Third, it provides for equity in pay for teachers—elementary and secondary teachers are paid according to the same schedule, male and female teachers are paid according to the same schedule, and minorities and nonminorities are paid according to the same schedule. Fourth, at least when initially adopted in the 1920s, when few teachers had a full college education, it encouraged all teachers to obtain at least a bachelor's degree, and over time even a master's degree. These features were prime goals for the single-salary schedule when it was created in the early decades of the twentieth century (Odden and Kelley, 2002), and the schedule has implemented these goals for nearly 100 years. So why change the teacher salary schedule now?

Why Change the Teacher Salary Schedule?

How people are paid, and how much they are paid, is serious business. Individuals and their families are substantially impacted by structural pay changes. Pay changes must be considered carefully, but there are certain conditions under which they are necessary.

First, pay structure changes should be considered when they reinforce attaining the strategic goals of the organization. When the current, single-salary structure for teachers was adopted in the early twentieth century, it was done to eliminate the inequities of paying women less than men, minorities less than nonminorities, and elementary teachers less than secondary teachers—substantial strategic goals. Those goals have been attained, but that structure no longer reinforces the current strategic goals of the education system.

Since changes in teacher pay structures generally follow changes in pay structures in the private sector (Odden and Kelley, 2002), it is useful to understand recent pay structure changes in the latter arena. When the private sector began paying workers differently in the last two decades of the twentieth century, it did so for strategic reasons (Lawler, 1990, 2000). Buffeted by pressures to dramatically increase performance, cut costs, and move new services and products more quickly into the marketplace, many private sector companies shifted to paying workers for knowledge and skills, rather than just years of experience, augmented with group-based performance bonuses. The knowledge and skills pay element was designed to encourage workers to acquire and apply new expertise to work more effectively in restructured work organizations. Performance bonuses, most often for groups of workers rather than individuals, were adopted to keep everyone focused on core organizational goals and to enable employees, including front-line workers, to share in the organization's financial success when performance targets were met and profits rose (Lawler, 2000).

Second, proposals to pay teachers for performance or merit seem innovative and are generally supported by the public. So those who propose paying teachers on something other than, say, age and useless university credits, seem to be on the right track, appear progressive, and have public support. Put another way, those who propose teacher pay changes seem to be forward, not backward, looking.

Finally, proposals to change the way teachers are paid create headlines and are good politics for both state and local policymakers. When California governor Arnold Schwarzenegger, made reference to paying teachers on the basis of merit in his 2005 state of the state address, the comments were broadcast nationally for several weeks. Although the governor at that point did not have, and never did make, a specific proposal, simply the statement of interest in creating merit or performance pay systems for teachers caught reporters' attention and filled newspaper columns across the country. The same was true when Minnesota governor Tim Pawlenty proposed merit pay for teachers, with the goal of creating the $100,000 teacher. Indeed, at least 15 governors made such proposals for performance pay for teachers in their 2005 state of the state speeches, and similar themes were present in the 2006 speeches as well. In short, teacher pay change is also good politics.

Linking Teacher Pay Changes to Core Educational Goals[2]

Today, education is being buffeted by intense performance pressures. State-initiated and-designed standards-based reforms seek to dramatically increase the performance of the education system. Indeed, when the data are closely scrutinized, the goal is to double and triple education performance—student achievement—over the next 10–20 years.[3] The federal No Child Left Behind (NCLB) Act gives further impetus to these goals, requiring more specific time frames for attaining the goals for all students, including students from poverty backgrounds and from families whose primary language is not English, and students with disabilities.

Moreover, the country has reached a strong consensus that the classroom teacher is the critical educational factor linked to accomplishing these lofty student achievement objectives (see, e.g., Wright, Horn, and Sanders, 1997). Thus, to accomplish the goals of dramatically improving the achievement of all students, most agree that the country must do three things:

1. Put a high-quality teacher in every classroom in the nation.
2. Ensure that each teacher covers the state and district's curriculum standards.
3. Enhance the actual instructional practices used so that students learn the content in ways that let them think, problem solve, and communicate about the content.

---

[2]These issues are covered in more detail in Odden and Wallace (2007a), Chapter 2.

[3]According to the National Assessment of Educational Progress (NAEP) test results, only about one-third of American students perform at or above the NAEP proficiency standard (Perie, Moran, Lutkus, and Tirre, 2005). Thus, the reform mantra of "teaching all students to high standards" means doubling and then tripling the current one-third of students who meet this standard.

Setting New Goals and Objectives for Teacher Compensation

These educational goals lead to clear and specific teacher labor market goals, which can be assimilated into a teacher compensation strategy (see Chapter 2 of Odden and Wallace, 2007, for a draft compensation strategy)—that is, a set of goals and redesign principles for a new teacher compensation structure. Such a teacher compensation strategy would have the specific objectives that could then be incorporated into revised teacher salary structures.

The first objective is to identify an overall average teacher salary level that would allow the state and each of its districts to compete for needed talent in the broader labor market. This would require the state to identify the noneducation professions and their salary levels with which the education system competes for teacher talent. It would also require the state to identify other states—if any—with which it competes for teachers in the education-specific labor market and to establish an appropriate or adequate teacher salary level to make the state competitive in those markets.[4]

Local districts would need to identify similar competitive salary levels, both for the broader labor market and for school districts with which they compete for teachers.

Such salary benchmarks would then allow the state's education system to compete in both the broader and the education-specific labor markets for the educator talent it needs to accomplish the ambitious student achievement goals.

The second objective is to identify the higher salary levels that would be needed to enable both large urban and geographically isolated rural districts to compete for teacher talent. The same applies for high-poverty and low-performing schools, as well as for subject areas in which there are teacher shortages.

It is a known fact that most large urban districts and many isolated rural districts across the country have teacher shortages, have been forced to hire less-qualified teachers, and have difficulty competing in their markets for good teachers (Lankford, Loeb, and Wyckoff, 2002). Addressing these teacher recruitment and retention problems will require, at least in part, that urban and many rural districts provide a wage premium in order to recruit and retain a high-quality teacher in every classroom.

Wage premiums are also needed to allow states and districts to fill certain subject area classrooms with quality teachers where there are obvious shortages (e.g., mathematics, science, and technology), mainly in large urban and small rural districts (Goldhaber, 2002). States and districts need to specify the criteria that would qualify a subject area as a shortage area and establish a wage incentive that would be sufficient to fill those classrooms with expert teachers.

The third objective is to set clear, ambitious, but attainable student achievement goals—specifically, for *improved* student performance, on both an individual classroom and a schoolwide basis. This means targeting the major student subgroups—those from lower-income backgrounds, those struggling to learn English, and those with disabilities—who should still be able to learn the regular, core curriculum. These improvement targets should be incorporated as an element of teacher compensation.

---

[4]The U.S. Bureau of Labor Statistics has created a new O*NET data system that allows such comparisons of teacher salaries to occupations with similar skills and competencies as teachers, as well as to other jobs that on their face compete with the education system for talent.

This would constitute a new element for teacher pay structures because the single-salary schedule does not include anything that directly rewards teachers, individually or as a group, for improving student academic achievement.

The final objective is to identify an instructional vision that would serve as a focus for teacher professional development and a target for enhancing a teacher's instructional practice over time. This means creating a performance assessment system that measures each teacher's instructional practice to various levels of performance to the new instructional vision. The results could be used to enact a knowledge- and skills-based pay structure. Rather than rewarding teachers merely for another year of experience and for university degrees and credits that are at best loosely linked to needed expertise, a knowledge- and skills-based pay structure can more directly reward teachers for acquiring and then applying instructional expertise that is linked to student-learning gains (Milanowski, Kimball, and Odden, 2005).

But setting these objectives is just the first step. The next step is to incorporate these important objectives into the appropriate elements of redesigned teacher salary structures so that the new structures indeed implement them. This design challenge requires an understanding of the various elements of teacher compensation structures and the ways in which they should be changed to incorporate the objectives. The new salary structure must not only implement these objectives but also simultaneously reinforce the education system's goal of doubling or tripling student academic achievement. The next section discusses the central elements of teacher salary structures.

2. THE ELEMENTS OF TEACHER SALARY STRUCTURES[5]

As in most occupations, there are several elements of total compensation for teachers. In the redesign process, it is important to understand the various elements of total compensation for teachers and then to identify which element is the best for implementing each of the teacher compensation objectives.

To begin, there are five critical elements of total compensation for teachers: (1) base pay, (2) variable pay, (3) benefits, (4) career opportunity, and (5) working conditions. Base pay is simply the monthly or biweekly check. For most workers, including teachers, base pay is the most important pay element and entails the largest amount of compensation dollars. This is not to say that the other elements of compensation are unimportant; it is only to say that base pay is critical to a teacher's decision to work in a school/district and to remain in that instructional position over time.

Base pay has three important components: (1) beginning or starting pay, (2) base pay progression over time, mainly annual pay increases, and (3) top pay. Beginning or starting pay is the salary offered to the brand-new teacher. Research has shown that beginning pay is critical for recruiting individuals into the teaching profession (Goldhaber and Player, 2005). Base pay progression refers to how a teacher earns or receives a pay

[5]This issue is addressed more comprehensively in Odden and Wallace, 2007a, Chapter 2.

increase year after year. Currently, base pay progression is determined largely by years of experience and education degrees and credits. However, research has shown that neither of these variables is strongly related to student achievement gains. So the pay elements that today allow teachers to earn more over time do not reinforce the critical education goals of improving teachers' instructional practice or boosting student achievement.

Most redesigned teacher salary structures include different variables that serve as the basis for pay progression, such as a direct measure of knowledge, skills, and instructional expertise. The objective is to use pay elements that are linked to student achievement gains in the mechanisms that determine teacher pay increases over time, so that teachers have an incentive (a base pay increase) to change their instructional practice in ways that contribute more to the bottom line of the education system—more student learning.

Top pay is the highest salary a teacher can earn, given the other elements of the salary schedule. In most occupations, there is usually a top pay level for nearly all jobs.

Compensation experts agree that base pay is the key element in recruiting and retaining employees. If it is difficult to either recruit or retain sufficient numbers of qualified and skilled individuals, it probably means that, among other things, base pay levels need to be increased. This is why we propose wage premiums for teachers in large urban districts, in high-poverty/low-achievement schools, and in subject areas experiencing shortages, such as mathematics and science.

Although paying some teachers more because of higher demand for their subject area content knowledge may seem to violate an aspect of the pay equity created by the single-salary schedule, it is necessary because teachers in those "hot" subject areas simply are in a different labor market. Not paying a wage premium leads to shortages of teachers or to lower-quality teachers in those subjects. The same is true for schools that provide more educational challenges. Similar pay equity issues have also been faced by private sector organizations, which have been forced to pay appropriate wage premiums for individuals in "hot" areas such as computer and information technologies. Companies that do not pay a wage premium have worker shortages in these areas or employ individuals in these areas who are less qualified—that is, they experience problems similar to schools.

Variable pay is an additional aspect of pay. Variable pay is almost always provided as a bonus to an employee or a teacher—for example, when the individual teacher or all teachers on a faculty produce some predetermined increase in student achievement. It is conditional: if achievement improves, the variable pay bonus is provided; if not, no bonus. It is called variable pay because it varies each year depending on whether the performance improvement target is met. Most compensation experts strongly urge organizations, including school systems, to provide variable pay as a bonus rather than as an increase in base pay. If a performance bonus is added to base pay, then the teacher is rewarded for producing that one-time, annual performance improvement every year thereafter. If provided as an annual bonus, that pay element must be re-earned each year.

Variable pay bonuses are appropriate when performance improvements are important and when organizations transform themselves into a continuous improvement mode. As most organizational experts know, continuous improvement is hard work and somewhat stressful; each year, the performance improvement target must be attained, the bonus paid out, and the worker or work team (faculty) is given a higher performance target. But that is what continuous improvement means—annually improving results until the performance goal is met—which in education means having higher and higher percentages of students achieve to a rigorous performance standard.

Base pay plus variable pay equals total cash compensation—money that teachers can spend. This chapter addresses only cash compensation—the monthly check and the annual bonus.

Benefits, including health and retirement benefits, are also very important, as are career opportunities and working conditions. And structuring each of these elements so that they help to accomplish the education system's strategic goals takes resources. Analyzing teacher benefit structures is beyond the scope of this chapter. But it should be noted that, on average, teacher benefits are better than those for the average worker and similar to what large corporations provide; most teachers have adequate health insurance and pension benefits (Allegretto, Corcoran, and Mishel, 2004)

Working conditions are also important, especially for teachers. Research has shown that most teachers require both a salary premium and good working conditions—strong principal leadership, decent class sizes, and appropriate instructional materials—in order to be attracted to and remain in urban schools and classrooms. But this chapter focuses on redesigning cash compensation for teachers—base pay, or the monthly check, and variable pay, or bonuses for improving student academic performance. The next section of this chapter describes how states and districts can determine beginning and average teacher pay levels that allow them to recruit and retain high-quality teachers.

3. DETERMINING ADEQUATE BEGINNING AND AVERAGE TEACHER PAY LEVELS[6]

An important step in restructuring teacher salary schedules is to identify the salary benchmarks that would allow the state and local districts to compete for quality teacher talent in the broad labor market. This first requires states and districts to identify salary benchmarks for both beginning and average salaries. Paying adequate overall salaries is critical to each district's ability to recruit and retain a quality teacher in every classroom, despite the school's location, education challenges it presents, or subjects that must be taught.

Beginning salaries should be set at a level that allows the education community to compete for beginning-teaching talent from among new college graduates. Beginning salary is one of the most important factors in any individual's decision to choose a profession; of course, other factors, such as interests and skills, also matter. But a low beginning salary can deter many individuals from choosing to enter a profession, especially teaching.

Average salaries are critical for retention and should be set at a competitive level to enable the education system to retain teachers who at some point must decide

---

[6]These issues are discussed in more depth in Odden and Wallace, 2007a, Chapter 3.

whether they want to remain in the profession. Two types of labor markets can be used to determine appropriate beginning and average salaries: (1) the education labor market and (2) the broader, total labor market.

Competition in the Education Labor Market

Many states identify surrounding states as their education competitors for teachers and set a benchmark with respect to those states. Another approach is to identify a region of states, such as the Southern Regional Education Board (SREB) states. A third approach is to identify the national average teacher salary as the education benchmark. But the fact is that for most states, there is not enough movement of teachers across state borders to fully justify these interstate or national comparisons, if the purpose for setting a benchmark is to retain teachers once they have chosen education as their profession.

Most local districts can identify other districts with which they compete for teacher talent; usually, but not always, it is surrounding districts. Steamboat Springs, a resort community, identifies other resort communities in Colorado (e.g., Vail, Breckenridge, and Telluride) as its primary competitors.

Competition in the Broader Labor Market

A second labor market, which is siphoning more and more teaching talent away from education, is the broader market that includes all government and private sector jobs. As the U.S. economy has shifted to a knowledge and service orientation, many jobs now require knowledge, skills, and competencies quite similar to those for teachers. So education competes for teacher talent in the broader labor market as well. The competition is even stiffer for math, science, and technology teachers, and thus their competitive wage is higher.

States and districts need to define what they mean by "market competitive." One approach is to be "at the market" (i.e., in the middle—average, mean, or median—of the market); another approach is to be "leading the market," (i.e., someplace in the top half or quarter, or even the top jurisdiction, in the market). Of course, the latter is more expensive, but if a state or district now leads a market, it might want to remain a market leader.

Each state and district, or region within a state, should look at teacher salaries with respect to these other occupations and set benchmarks for average and beginning salaries.

Beginning Salary Benchmarks

The most difficult decision for most states and districts is to determine where in the market it wants to compete. In years past, a market benchmark has been to have beginning salaries set at least at the average of college graduates with liberal arts degrees; in 2005, both were about $31,000 though the figures differed significantly in each state. Given the changing nature of the economy and the fact that the vast bulk of jobs have service and knowledge work embodied in them to some degree, a more appropriate target today might be the average salary for all college graduates, which is closer to $40,000. In early 2006, Arizona Governor Janet Napolitano and Maine Governor John Baldacci, both states with low teacher salaries, proposed raising beginning salaries to $30,000.

Average Salary Benchmarks

During its 2003 school finance adequacy study, Arkansas set its teacher salary benchmark at the average of the SREB states. In 2006, Iowa Governor Tom Vilsak and Virginia Governor Timothy Kaine proposed to bring their teacher's salaries up to the national average, and Kentucky Governor Ernie Fletcher proposed a hike to the average of the surrounding states. Our recommended benchmark is the salaries of jobs comparable to teaching, using data specific to each state. In 2004–05, for example, that figure would have been $46,800 for the state of Washington (Imazeki, 2006), about what the national average figure was as well.

Adjustments to Salaries

A final issue in making salary comparisons is whether teacher salaries should be "adjusted" to account for the fact that the typical teacher "works" only 9–10 months of the year, or even just 5–6 hours a day. This is a hotly debated issue within the education policy community, with many arguing for an adjustment and others arguing just as vociferously against it. But as Allegretto, Corcoran, and Mishel (2004) learned from the U.S. Bureau of Labor Statistics (BLS), such an adjustment is not warranted because it is difficult to determine how many hours or even weeks teachers work. Teachers prepare lessons and correct papers outside of the regular school day, and they often engage in training or curriculum development over the summer months. In comparing salaries among professions, the BLS makes no adjustments when "work" hours are difficult to determine, such as the number of hours airplane pilots or college professors work. Rather, it suggests that salary comparisons for such jobs, including teachers, be made on an annual salary basis. The next section discusses the special circumstances that require a wage premium above the general teacher salary schedule and how large those premiums should be.

4. PAYING WAGE PREMIUMS

Paying teachers who have the same characteristics the same salary has been a salary "equity" goal in education for almost a century; this type of pay equity has also been a strong value in the private sector. But when special circumstances arise that lead to substantial teacher shortages, then pay equity for all must be put aside.

When Are Wage Premiums Necessary?

One situation that warrants a wage premium is working in high-poverty and/or low-performing schools. It is increasingly common knowledge that many schools with large percentages of students from lower-income or poverty backgrounds and/or students performing at low levels on tests of academic achievement have large numbers of un- or underqualified teachers (Lankford, Loeb, and Wyckoff, 2002). This is probably the most important reason students in those classrooms achieve at unacceptably low levels. It is hard for students to learn if their teacher does not know the subject very well, cannot manage the classroom, and lacks pedagogical expertise. Thus, placing knowledgeable and expert teachers in those classrooms is critical.

Paying a wage premium for teachers in these schools will be required if these classrooms are to be staffed by a knowledgeable and expert teacher. Since the largest percentage of students not performing at an acceptable level attend schools with high concentrations of poverty, creating wage premiums for teachers in these schools should be a high priority on each state's teacher compensation change agenda.

Wage premiums are also needed for subject area shortages. Many districts across the country—again, large urban districts in particular—have difficulty recruiting teachers in subjects such as mathematics, science, and technology, as well as special-education teachers and teachers for ELL students. When shortages emerge, one part of the solution is a wage premium.

How Large Should Wage Premiums Be?

Of course, the key pay issue is to identify how large the wage premium should be. There is not a great deal of research on this topic. Some researchers have suggested that a 40 percent pay premium might be needed for teachers in high-poverty urban schools (Hanushek, Kain, and Rivkin, 2004; Imazeki, 2005). Other research has suggested that the premium might be in the 15–20 percent range, as compared to the state average. The bottom line is that it will take more than an extra thousand or two dollars to recruit and retain teachers in such schools. Wage premiums of at least $5,000–6,000 are likely needed, over whatever the state average salary benchmarks might be.

In 2006, Fairfax County (VA) provided a wage premium of 7 percent for teachers in their lowest-performing schools, and Miami provided a 20 percent premium; each district also required those teachers to work approximately an hour longer each day. After the premium program was implemented in Fairfax, all the schools met adequate yearly progress (AYP) standards.

It should be understood that a higher pay level *alone* will not solve the problem of recruiting and retaining high-quality teachers in high-poverty schools. Strong principals, decent class sizes, and ample instructional materials and supplies are also needed, issues addressed by the adequacy model developed in Chapter 4. But a substantial wage premium is also necessary.

The premiums currently offered across the country for subject area shortages are quite small, ranging from about $1,000 to $2,000 per year, amounts probably not large enough to make a real difference. Indeed, Clotfelter and Ladd (1996) investigated the impacts of a $1,600 mathematics and science premium offered by North Carolina, and found that the program had quite modest effects.

Milanowski (2003a) conducted focus groups in a midwestern research university, seeking to determine what undergraduates in engineering, mathematics, and science would identify as premiums that might make them consider altering their career paths to enter teaching. Although many students stated that no premium would alter their desire to become an engineer, mathematician, or scientist, a significant portion said that if the difference between what they could earn in a technical field and in education were reduced by half, they would seriously consider teaching. That difference equaled about $5,000 at the time of the study.

Though more analysis is needed, states and districts would be wise to think in terms of wage premiums for teachers in subject area shortages—particularly math, science, and technology—of at least $5,000 per teacher per year, and then track the impacts on both recruitment and retention of teachers in those areas to see if the premium is sufficiently high.

In most cases, a wage premium that is a one-time bonus is not sufficient. Teachers not only must be initially motivated to teach in a high-poverty school or in a subject area that is experiencing a shortage but also must decide to stay teaching in that school or subject area. One-time bonus payments are not effective strategies for reducing (if not eliminating) these types of teacher shortages.

The reality is that to recruit and retain teachers in high-poverty schools and in "hot" subject areas, the premium needs to be permanent, or at least provided as long as there are shortages of qualified teachers. But even if at some time there is an adequate number of teachers, the wage premium will probably need to be maintained in order for the education system to continue to recruit and retain teachers as natural turnover occurs. At some point, though, the labor market could change, and the premium may no longer be needed. However, for education, that will probably take several years, at least for teachers in many high-poverty schools or teachers in mathematics, science, and related areas.

Should the Wage Premium Be Coupled with an Effectiveness Criterion?

The short answer is yes. The goal is not to have just anyone teach in a high-poverty classroom or in a mathematics or science class; the goal is to have someone who knows math or science and is an effective teacher covering those classes. Thus, schools, districts, and states should provide wage premiums only to effective or trained teachers in high-poverty schools or subjects in which there are shortages. Each teacher qualifying for the wage premium should have to meet an effectiveness criterion. Requiring a major or a minor, or at least a certain number of academic credits, in the subject area shortage could be another criterion for qualifying for the incentive. And for individuals already in education, creating some measure of instructional effectiveness could be a third criterion. If the state or district had a performance assessment of teachers, an issue discussed later, the education system could require a certain score on the performance assessment to qualify for the subject area wage premium; a score of 2 or 3 on a 1–4 (low–high) scale would be a reasonable standard.

Chattanooga used Tennessee's value-added system for assessing student learning gains to identify those teachers who would qualify for a wage premium for teaching in its high-poverty schools. That wage premium, coupled with stronger principals and other school improvement efforts, turned around the student learning in several high-poverty schools in a short period of time.

Are Wage Premiums Needed for Urban and Rural Districts?

Wage premiums are also needed for urban and rural districts. In addition to schools and subjects that experience teacher shortages and thus warrant a wage premium, higher salary levels are also required generally for teachers in large urban districts and sometimes also in geographically sparse districts. It is hard for large urban districts to compete for teacher talent in the metropolitan labor market if all the surrounding districts pay higher salaries. Most suburban districts also offer less challenging education environments; which means, urban districts are doubly outgunned in that metropolitan labor market.

Emerging research is showing that big urban districts (e.g., Chicago, Los Angeles, Milwaukee, and New York City) probably need to pay average teacher salaries that are 15–40 percent above the state average. Although it will be difficult financially and politically to meet the upper levels of that kind of wage premium, hitting the lower levels of the range is very important. Otherwise, large urban districts, which enroll the bulk of low-performing students across the country, will be forced to staff their schools with underqualified, and thus less effective, teachers. The next section identifies the elements of base pay that help reinforce instruction.

5. BASE PAY PROGRESSION ELEMENTS THAT REINFORCE BETTER INSTRUCTION[7]

Of course, the major aspect of pay—for teachers or any worker—is starting pay and earned increases over time. As is well known, pay progression for most teachers today is based on years of experience and education units and degrees. Although these pay elements may have been associated with strategic goals in the past, they do not do so today. Research has shown that after three years, a teacher's years of experience are not linked to student learning gains. Research has also shown that neither education units nor degrees are linked to student learning gains, except for credits and courses in mathematics and science for those who teach those subjects (Monk, 1994).

Redesigned teacher compensation structures often include factors that are used to provide base pay increases. These factors can include the following:

- A major, minor, or master's degree in the subject taught, on the assumption that knowledge of one's subject is important to teaching it well
- Engagement in professional development, on the assumption that such activities will lead to better instructional practice
- Years of experience, on the assumption that a state or district might want some element of pay for loyalty for staying in the system

[7]See Odden and Wallace, 2007a, for more detail on these issues.

- Implementation of a project designed to improve student performance, on the assumption that the effort to design and implement such a program over time should lead to better instructional practice
- Knowledge and skills, or a high score on a performance assessment of teachers

Indeed, the new Denver pay plan includes all of these pay elements (see Odden and Wallace, 2007a, and www.denverprocomp.org).

Note that only the last option is not based on an *assumption* that the activity is effective; it actually measures a teacher's instructional performance to a set of teaching standards, which research has shown is linked to student learning gains (Milanowski, 2004; Milanowski and Kimball, 2005; Milanowski, Kimball, and Odden, 2005). Although there are many ways that knowledge- and skills-based salary structures can be designed, the following example uses a performance measurement of a teacher's actual instructional practice and can provide the long-term vision for how such a program could work (see also Odden and Wallace, 2007a, Chapter 4; Milanowski, 2003b)

A variation of an ambitious knowledge- and skills-based teacher salary schedule is displayed in Table 12.1.[8] The three-lane model shown illustrates that there are still financial incentives for some degrees. The schedule has four performance categories, but it has the "look" of a single salary schedule, as there are several rows and three columns. But the proposed schedule represents substantial change. For most states and districts, this schedule would replace a 20-plus-step and 6-plus-lane traditional schedule. The smaller number of columns sends the signal that miscellaneous units will no longer be rewarded. The units must earn a master's degree, and then a doctorate or specialist certificate. Though the number of rows was reduced, the key aspect of this schedule is that it includes four performance and pay categories that are determined by a teacher's performance on a newly designed performance-based evaluation system.

The schedule works the following way. Pay increases would be large for movement across categories and much smaller for step movements within categories. In the example given, the step increases are just 1.5 percent while the performance category increases are 10 percent. The message is that teacher instructional performance is the main way to earn salary increases.

First, teachers would be screened for "Entry"; this would usually be the preliminary license provided after a postsecondary training program, or perhaps some type of alternative training program. During the time in "Entry," teachers would be involved in an intense and focused new-teacher induction program.

Next, teachers would go through a performance assessment at the end of year 3, depending on the state or district. Teachers would need to meet the performance standards for the "Emerging career" level to move into that category. If that performance level were not met by the end of year 3, the teacher would lose his or her job in the district. So there is an "up-or-out" element, but based on performance.

---

[8]All the specific salary numbers and percentages are "plug" numbers and can be set at appropriate levels by any state or local school district.

TABLE 12.1 A Knowledge- and Skills-Based Pay Plan

Performance Category	Step within Level	Salary Schedule		
		BA	MA	MA + 30 Units/Doctorate Degree
Entry	1	$30,663	$31,890	$33,165
	2	31,123	32,368	33,663
	3	31,590	32,853	34,168
Emerging career	1	34,749	36,139	37,584
	2	35,270	36,681	38,148
	3	35,799	37,231	38,720
	4	36,336	37,789	39,301
	5	36,881	38,356	39,891
	6	37,434	38,932	40,489
Career	1	41,178	42,825	44,538
	2	41,795	43,467	45,206
	3	42,422	44,119	45,884
	4	43,059	44,781	46,572
	5	43,705	45,453	47,271
	6	44,360	46,135	47,980
Master	1	48,796	50,748	52,778
	2	49,528	51,509	53,570
	3	50,271	52,282	54,373
	4	51,025	53,066	55,189
	5	51,790	53,862	56,017
	6	52,567	54,670	56,857

Percent increase for step: 1.5%
Percent increase for performance category: 10.0%
MA, MA60/doctorate: 4.0%

In many states that have a two-tiered licensing system (Youngs, Odden, and Porter, 2003), moving into "Emerging career" could coincide with earning the professional license, which is usually done through a performance assessment of the individual's instructional practice. (This level of performance is equal to an overall score of 2 on the TEC standards and rubrics discussed in Chapter 5 of Odden and Wallace, 2007a and a 2 for the Connecticut and Indiana systems.)

Next, after earning the standard license and being in "Emerging career," teachers would continue with ongoing professional development and undergo a periodic performance assessment. Toward the end of year 3 in that category, teachers could request such an assessment, and if their performance met the standards for the next category, they could jump to "Career," step 1. Their salary would be capped at "Emerging career," step 6, if their performance never reached the "Career" level.

The system could require that teachers meet the "Career" standard in order to stay in the system—a new tenure standard, if you will. Indeed, if the professional license is granted after a teacher has been working for two to four years and meets the standard for "Emerging career" (the time period varies by state), it might make sense to postpone the tenure decision until a later time.

Finally, once in "Career," teachers would undergo a periodic performance assessment. Toward the end of year 3 in that category, teachers could request such an assessment and if their performance met the standards for the next category, they could jump to "Master," step 1. However, the standards for "Master" would be rigorous. Although not all teachers would be expected to perform at this level, a large percentage should reach it, and there would be no quota for the level. Thus, the schedule provides a fast track to the top for teachers who enhance their instructional practice and caps the salaries of those who do not.

Districts need a performance assessment system to operate such a salary structure. It is very difficult for districts to design a system from scratch, as some across the country have discovered. The lesson one can draw from these experiences is that adapting operant performance evaluation systems, like the Connecticut system (see www.state.ct.us/sde/dtl/t-a/best/handbooks/portfolio_forms2.htm),[9] the TEC system (see Odden and Wallace, 2007a, Chapter 5), or the Danielson system, will likely produce a framework that can be used to set pay categories.

The salary structure in Table 12.1 can be enhanced with additional incentives for the following:

- Subject area shortages, such as mathematics and science: districts should consider incentives in the range of $5,000 for such content areas.
- Hard-to-staff, high-poverty, low-performing schools: again, incentives in the $5,000-plus range are appropriate.
- Incentives for certification by the National Board for Professional Teaching Standards: incentives in the 10–20 percent range ($4,000–$8,000 annually), rather than just a one-time bonus, will motivate teachers to enhance their practices to the high and rigorous standards set by the National Board.

A new structure like that depicted in Table 12.1 represents one of the most strategic ways to redesign the teacher salary structure. It pays for the type of teacher expertise school systems need (i.e., powerful and effective instructional strategies), it signals that enhancing one's knowledge and skills is the way to higher pay levels, and it links the highest pay to the most effective teachers. Long term, a structure that resembles that in Table 12.1 could be a strategic goal for many states and local districts.

---

[9]Though the Connecticut system is now used only for conferring the professional license, if the novice teacher earns a score of 2 on the 1–4 scale of the performance assessment, the system could be used to assess the instructional practice of all teachers, and the scores of 1, 2, 3, and 4 could be used to place teachers in a knowledge- and skills-based salary structure.

Since a schedule such as that depicted in Table 12.1 is such a dramatic change from current teacher salary schedules, states and districts likely would need to transition into it over time. A first step would be to create a performance assessment system; Chapter 5 of Odden and Wallace (2007a) identifies and describes a system that could be used. As mentioned previously, systems developed and used by Connecticut and Indiana, as well as Charlotte Danielson's (1996) framework for teaching, could also be used.

In the first several years, the score on the evaluation system could be used to trigger a salary incentive on top of the state or district's single-salary structure. This would entail grafting a new element onto the old structure. After the performance evaluation system was up and running, more dollars could be directed to the incentive element of the system; indeed, at some point, all new dollars could be put into the incentive element based on the evaluation score. Then a transition to the structure depicted in Table 12.1 could occur. In this way, some portion of pay would initially be contingent on the level of a teacher's instructional expertise, then a bit more, and finally, the level of the teacher's performance on the performance assessment/evaluation would be the major determinant of the teacher's pay.

Two states, Iowa and New Mexico, have already adopted this approach. And both linked their pay system to their teacher licensing system. Iowa's program has four levels, each with a minimum salary, and New Mexico's program has three performance and pay categories, each with a minimum salary. Instead of specifying steps within each pay category, like the schedule in Table 12.1, the state programs simply required minimum salaries in each of the three categories. But each state has large differences between the minimums in each category, sufficient to allow local districts to provide step increases within the category if they want to do so.

The final section describes how bonus programs based on improvements in student learning can be structured.

6. STRUCTURING BONUSES BASED ON IMPROVEMENTS IN STUDENT LEARNING

Since improving student academic achievement, overall and for various subgroups of students, is a preeminent educational goal, the time has come to create a variable pay element for teachers, that is, a pay element that provides bonuses to teachers for improving student achievement. Although this type of pay element can be controversial, and factors outside the educational system impact student achievement, creating a pay element based on student learning gains is seen by many policymakers—and by many within education as well—as critical to any viable, relevant effort to redesign how teachers are paid.

Because the educational system has been experimenting with such bonus programs for over a decade, the country has developed extensive knowledge on how to design and implement effective programs (see, e.g., Odden, Kellor, et al., 1999; Odden and Kelley, 2002). Such programs enhance teacher motivation to improve student performance and, when provided to everyone in a school, do not cause competition among teachers (Kelley, Heneman, and Milanowski, 2002).

Kentucky was the first state with such a program; it was based on improvements in the performance of cohorts of students over time (this year's grade 4, 8, or 10 students versus last year's grade 4, 8, or 10 grade students). North Carolina has also operated a statewide program for years, based on a value-added model that provides schools with bonuses if they produce greater than historical annual increases in student performance. Charlotte-Mecklenburg began a bonus program on its own before the state acted, and then modified its program to conform to the state program; both continue to operate today. Dallas has operated a performance bonus program for over a decade.

There are several key questions that must be answered in creating bonus programs that reward teachers for improving student performance: (1) What performance elements will the program include? (2) How will each performance element be measured? (3) How are annual improvement targets set? (4) How can a level playing field be created to provide every school with a fair opportunity to produce targeted learning gains? (5) Should the awards be one-time bonuses or be added to base pay? (6) How large should the bonuses be, and should there be multiple bonuses? (7) Should the awards be provided on an individual-teacher or whole-school basis? and (8) How should the program costs be estimated?

Performance Elements

Selecting the performance elements to include in a variable-pay bonus plan is essential. The elements that are included become the most important performance factors for the educational system and school. The idea is to have teachers focus their professional expertise and energies first on the elements in the performance measure. As such, selecting the performance factors is a value judgment.

It could take up to a year to work through all the issues related to selecting the key performance factors. The goal is to have the large bulk of teachers, administrators, and policymakers agree that the factors selected are the most important educational goals.

Performance Measures

Most such programs across the country ultimately identify student academic achievement in the core academic subjects—mathematics, science, reading and writing, and sometimes history—as the core performance factors. Usually these factors constitute 50–100 percent of the set of performance measures, averaging 80 percent. Often, nonacademic factors are also included, such as the four-year graduation rate, the percentage of high school students taking advanced courses, the decline in the percentage of elementary students scoring at or below basic level, or the percentage of eighth-grade students taking algebra. The assumption is that these other performance factors are a means to accomplishing the achievement goals.

Today, most programs have some measure of average yearly progress (AYP), as this is an important NCLB accountability factor. Also, because schools are required to report test scores by subgroup, it is a means of ensuring that learning gains are produced by students from poverty backgrounds, ELL students, and students with mild disabilities.

Since AYP is such a stringent performance improvement goal, however, it often represents only one of many performance factors in a variable pay plan.

Although there is great debate on how best to measure student academic achievement for a bonus program, most states and districts use some combination of state and local tests that are currently being administered. Because the tests that states and districts currently use ipso facto are the key measures of student performance, they become the default measures for nearly all variable-pay programs.

The critical criterion for any performance measure is that it be valid and reliable. Most standardized achievement tests, created either by private companies or by state departments of education, meet these psychometric requirements. Few district- or teacher-developed tests meet validity and reliability criteria because developing valid and reliable tests is a complex and expensive undertaking, and few local districts devote either the resources or the time to develop tests that meet these psychometric standards.

Thus, most state and local variable-pay plans will be based heavily on state and local standardized test scores that are currently in use, or are being put into use as a result of the requirements of NCLB to test students in grades 3–8 and grade 10 in mathematics, reading, and science.

Any nonacademic achievement performance factor must also be measured in a reliable and valid manner in order for it to be used fairly in a variable-pay program. So, if a graduation rate is used, it must be defined carefully, and data must be collected the same way from every school and district.

Some performance factors considered important by many people are often left out of variable-pay programs because they cannot be measured in valid and reliable ways. One district that tried to include a measure of student virtues and responsibilities finally gave that factor up after teachers complained that it was not measured fairly across schools. Those who want to enhance student "character" rarely have a good measure of particular characteristics. Hard as it might be, it is better to exclude factors that cannot be validly and reliably measured than to include them in variable-pay programs.

Performance Improvement Targets

After selecting and measuring the key performance factors, the next step is to set improvement targets. This is a critical step. The general principle is that the improvement targets should be a "stretch" but attainable. The goal is to produce larger annual gains than have been produced in the past, so that student performance begins to rise year after year. But the improvement targets must be attainable, or they will not motivate teachers and administrators to change their behaviors in ways that boost system performance.

Another principle is that the improvement targets must be larger than the "measurement error" for the performance measures used. Those who have been engaged in setting AYP targets for NCLB have been embroiled in this issue for the past several years. Those who argue for a "value added" measure of improvement have also been cognizant of the measurement error issue (see, e.g., McCaffrey, Lockwood, Koretz, Louis, and Hamilton, 2004), as have variable-pay designers who use simpler gain scores or gain to a standard score (Milanowski, 1999). Dealing with measurement error is much more complex when the bonus is targeted to individual teachers. Such programs usually need two to three years of data to create stable improvement estimates.

Another issue in setting performance improvement targets is the methodology to use. Some argue for simple gain scores—this year's score minus last year's score. As long as gains are set above historical gain movements, this can be an easily understood approach.

Another approach, embedded in the 1990s Kentucky program as well as NCLB, is gain to a standard. The notion here is that over some time period, the goal is to have all or, more realistically, a large portion (85, 90, or 95 percent) of students achieving at or above some standard, such as proficiency. Setting the improvement target as increasing the percentage of students at or above the performance standard requires schools currently farther below the target to produce larger annual improvements than schools closer to the target. If the time frame for such improvements is too ambitious, as many claim with NCLB AYP targets, the local response can be frustration and anger rather than resolve to produce the attainable, but more than historical average, annual improvements.

A third approach is the value-added method. In this approach, the current year's test score is regressed on the previous year's score, sometimes with demographic data as control variables. The result allows the state or district to calculate a historical "expected gain" score. Schools that produce gains above this expected level then meet the performance improvement target. North Carolina has operated a program like this for over five years. It does not control for demographic factors under the argument that to do so would inherently require lower levels of performance for students characterized by the controls, such as low-income, minority, or ELL students. As schools and districts begin to meet these more aggressive improvement targets, the initial regression analysis should be redone to set an even higher expected-gain target. A reasonable time frame for such a recalibration is probably once every five years.

Another issue is on what group of students the improvement target is calculated. Kentucky used a cohort approach (e.g., for elementary schools, this year's fourth-graders versus last year's fourth-grades). By setting the target at a proficiency level, AYP counts mainly the students who achieve over the proficiency bar each year. The value-added approach uses data from all students, at least all students who are tested, and aggregates gains over them.

None of these approaches is the single best approach, and different policy analysts argue strongly for their preferred method. For example, if transparency were important, the value-added approach would not be the one to select because it is the most difficult to understand. The most important aspect of setting improvement targets is to set them above measurement error, to set them above historical improvement trends, and to make them "stretch" but attainable goals.

It should also be clear that using some type of gain scores is the smartest way to create bonus programs; the goal is to create incentives for improved performance. A program that counted only students already at an achievement level would simply reward the best schools, not those that were improving over time.

Bonus Payout Structures: Balanced Scorecards

One of the most straightforward ways to design a bonus payout structure is to use a balanced scorecard. The balanced scorecard makes the variable-pay structure transparent and easier to explain. An example of such a scorecard is provided in Table 12.2.

The scorecard shows that a small number of performance objectives and measures are included in the program. The general rule is to have three to six objectives. This scorecard has five different performance measures, three focusing on student achievement in core subjects—mathematics, reading/writing, and science—one on making AYP under the federal NCLB requirements, and one for reducing grade-level retention in third grade, a key grade for having all students be proficient readers.[10] The scorecard shows how AYP can be included in, but not be the sole determinant of, a state or locally designed school-based incentive program. AYP is also a proxy for closing the achievement gap because meeting AYP requires improvement for all key subgroups of students—ELL students, those from poverty backgrounds, each minority group, and females as well as males.

Column 3 shows that the balanced scorecard does not value all performance goals at the same level. The balanced scorecard allows the organization to assign a specific weight to each performance measure; the weights need to sum to a total of 100 percent. In this example, the achievement scores in the three core subjects are each weighted equally at 20 percent. AYP, the proxy for closing the achievement gap, is valued higher, at 30 percent. And the third-grade retention rate is valued at 10 percent. These weights are value and policy judgments; different states and districts could decide on weights that differ from these figures.

The scorecard identifies a target performance improvement goal for each measure in column 8 but, as will be shown, also provides partial rewards for partial progress toward the target (columns 5–7), as well as "extra credit" for beating the target (column 9). Indeed, column 6 indicates a minimum threshold that will qualify the school for at least some reward for achieving each objective. Note that the way this scorecard is designed, maintaining level of performance is defined as the threshold amount. That might or might not be appropriate in all schools. But as this scorecard shows, meeting the 25 percent threshold would earn the school 25 percent of the award, producing 50 percent of the target improvement would earn the school 50 percent, and producing the full targeted improvement would earn the full award. Column 9 indicates that beating the target by 25 percent or more will produce an incentive amount that is 125 percent of the target award.

To calculate the amount of the award, the percentage of target improvement attained (0, 25, 50, 100, or 125 percent) is determined by the actual score for each objective; this is shown in the column heading for each boldface item in the table. This percentage, then, is multiplied by the weight for that objective, and the result is included

---

[10]A middle school measure could be the percentage of students taking algebra in grade 8, and a high school measure could be the four-year graduation rate, that is, the percentage of students who begin grade 9 and graduate four years later.

TABLE 12.2   Balanced Scorecard for a Bonus Payout Structure

1 Objective	2 Measure	3 Weight	4 Prior Year Actual	5 Below Threshold (0%)	6 Threshold (25%)	7 50% of Target	8 100% of Target	9 125% of Target	10 Percent Accomplishment
Achievement	Mathematics	20%	60		60	**62.5**	65	66.25	10%
Achievement	Reading/ writing	20	70		70	72	**74**	75	20
Achievement	Science	20	50		50	**53**	56	57.5	10
Achievement									
Gap	Meets AYP	30		No	—		Yes		0
Retention rate	Third-grade retention	10	20		20	**18**	16	15	5
Totals		100							**45**

One approach:
  Target incentive: $2,500
  Percent accomplished: 45%
  Award: 45% × $2,500 × $1,125

A different approach:
  Target incentive: 6% of base salary
  Percent accomplished: 45%
  Award: 45% × 6% × base salary
  Award at base salary of $45,000 = 2.7% of 45,000 = $1215
  Award at base salary of $30,000 = 2.7% of 30,000 = $810

in column 10. So, for example, this school scored at 50 percent of target in mathematics, which, given the 20 percent weight for this objective, produced a percent accomplishment of 10 percent. The total earned accomplishment is the sum of each row in column 10, which in this case is 45 percent. In other words, for this scorecard, the school earned 45 percent of the target award.

The target award could be set as a percentage of salary or a fixed amount. The example shows both. Odden and Wallace (2006) provide more detail on the operation of such a balanced scorecard.

The balanced scorecard succinctly shows several things:

- The performance objectives in the award program
- The weights given to each objective, showing which ones are weighted the highest
- The improvement targets
- The way the school will earn its percentage of the target award.

The balanced scorecard is a powerful but simple way to communicate both the most valued objectives of the school and the key features of the incentive program.

Individual versus Whole-School Bonuses

It is important to specify up front who is eligible for the performance award. In education today, the big debate is whether to design a program for individual teachers or for groups of teachers, such as all faculty in a school. The balanced scorecard was designed for all teachers in a school. It could also be used for individual teachers, but measurement error would be more problematic unless multiple years of data were used, such as a rolling three-year average. Though bonus programs based on improvements in student achievement are somewhat controversial in education, programs that provide awards for all teachers (as well as administrators and classified staff) in a school are less controversial than programs that reward individual teachers.

We suggest that it may be time for states and districts to consider designing bonus programs for individual teachers as well as groups of teachers. Our reason is political as much as substantive. One aspect of the genius of the new Denver teacher compensation plan is that it includes an element that rewards teachers for the achievement gains of the students in their own classrooms. This element has given the program tremendous political credibility, and many in the media characterize the Denver plan as one that finally links pay to the achievement gains of each teacher's individual students. In fact, that element of the program accounts for a very small portion of the new dollars in the program (see Chapter 4 of Odden and Wallace, 2007a). Only about 35 percent of all teachers are eligible for this element (only teachers for whom student gain scores can be calculated over time), and only a small portion of those teachers are expected to earn that compensation bonus. But this program element has really "carried" the program among policymakers and the public. So whatever objections teachers might have to such a compensation element, they would be wise to consider the trade-offs between having such a program element (which will impact only a small number of teachers) and the political support it provides, and their opposition to it. Simply opposing such a compensation element, which seems so "natural" to most individuals outside of education, has the effect of making teachers seem opposed to attaining the prime goal of schools—student achievement.

On the other hand, if teachers strongly oppose such a individual-teacher bonus program, as was the case in Colonial, Pennsylvania, and seems to be the case in the recently adopted programs in Florida and Houston, imposing such a program can lead to organizational strife and political turmoil, hardly the context for having teachers work hard to boost student learning. Indeed, when such a program was "forced" on teachers in Colonial, the following year was characterized by anger and unsettledness. Further, many teachers who received the bonus checks at the end of the year actually turned them back in to the district in protest. The district dropped the program after one year of operation.

Cost Estimates and Overruns

Costs of such programs can be estimated with a few assumptions. If the average teacher salary is $50,000, and the target bonus is 6 percent, or $3,000 per teacher, and it is assumed that half the schools (or schools with half the teachers) qualify for the bonus, then a good "guesstimate" of the cost is $1,500 per teacher. Total costs are $1,500 times the number of teachers (licensed individuals paid on the teacher salary schedule) in the system. Clearly, costs will vary if the bonus is larger (or smaller), if the average salary is larger (or smaller), if a higher (or lower) percentage of teachers qualify, and if the bonus awards between threshold, target, and above target are not evenly distributed. But the above rule can still be used to make a decent estimate of costs, given the assumptions. Costs will also be higher if administrators and classified staff in schools are included in the program; those added costs can be estimated using the same simple formula.

What happens if program costs exceed budgets? Teachers are highly skeptical about whether states or districts will actually pay out performance awards that have been earned. This was true in the fifth year of the Kentucky program, even though appropriations for the program were made and put in a "lock box" *before* each academic year began. And, indeed, California dropped its program when the budget became tight. There are three options for providing the awards when actual costs exceed estimated or budgeted revenues.

The first, and best, approach is to increase the budget. Indeed, during the first year of North Carolina's program, many more schools qualified than had been anticipated. In response, the legislature added tens of millions to the program and paid the full award to each teacher in every school that qualified, thereby solidifying teacher trust in the program.

A second, and acceptable but second-best, approach is to reduce the award levels. This maintains the budget and provides at least a partial award to everyone who earned it. But lowering the award level creates some skepticism about the program for the next year.

A third, but not recommended, approach is, after the fact, to hike the bar for award qualification to a level that keeps the award payments within budget. However, this changes the rules of the game and "stiffs" teachers in schools that meet initial performance improvement targets but do meet the higher, after-the-fact targets. This approach would also likely create more skepticism across the education system, rather than bolster everyone's efforts to improve student performance.

Whatever approach is taken, it is probably best to identify the policy for budget overruns at the beginning of each year. Then at least everyone will know what happens when the cost of paying all who qualify for the award exceeds the initial budget. But the best policy is to adjust the budget to what it would take to pay everyone the full award for producing improvement. After all, producing more improvement than expected should be celebrated, even if it costs money, rather than dampened by reducing the award level or not giving anything to those who meet rigorous performance improvement targets.

7. EFFECTIVE PROCESSES FOR DESIGNING AND IMPLEMENTING TEACHER PAY CHANGES

The process of designing and implementing teacher salary structure changes is very important. There are four major process steps: (1) design, (2) implementation, (3) evaluation and change, and (4) funding. Odden and Wallace (2007a) cover these issues in depth, and you are encouraged to read those chapters in that book. This chapter addresses only the funding issue.

There are no magic new sources of funds to finance new approaches to teacher compensation. Raising beginning and average salaries, providing wage premiums in certain circumstances, and creating performance award programs will cost more money. New state or local appropriations will be needed to fund these new teacher salary elements, either through natural growth in general-fund revenues or through tax increases.

For example, in 2001, Arizona passed a half-penny sales tax increase, mandating that a major portion of the new revenues could be used only if local districts designed new "performance pay" structures. Unfortunately, a wide variety of such programs were created, many not rigorously performance-oriented, and many state policymakers have been disappointed with the results. In 2006, Minnesota provided about $385 per pupil for local school districts that design new performance pay programs meeting certain criteria. In both states, the criteria are quite broad and allow for rigorous as well as less rigorous programs. And both states provide districts with money "up front" to design and implement new forms of teacher compensation.

Denver passed a multimillion-dollar increase to fund its ProComp program through a special tax increase referendum, but after elements of the program were piloted over several years.

As with other school reforms, the long-lasting forms of new compensation are bound to be those that reallocate substantial dollars in the current salary structure. If all new pay elements are contingent on special categorical dollars, the likelihood of their demise in hard fiscal times is high, and local districts and teachers might not see them as a permanent part of the new pay structure. But if the new pay system is funded with substantial funds already in the system, then teachers might see them as more permanent structures, unlikely to vanish when the budget is tight.

Having said that, it is difficult politically to get teachers to agree to reallocate substantial portions of dollars in the current salary schedule into a new one that makes it more difficult to earn pay increases and sometimes merely to get bonuses. But funding new salary systems via salary dollar reallocation is likely to be the best route to solidifying the new salary structure in the future. Otherwise, what states and districts will create are salary add-ons, which, given past history, will be jettisoned when the economy slumps and public dollars dwindle.

8. SUMMARY

A key issue in redesigning teacher salary structures is setting "adequate" average salary levels; this is the key "price" variable in costing out the adequacy model developed in Chapter 4. There are several reasons for changing the way teachers are paid. The main argument is that the single-salary schedule designed in the early twentieth century has accomplished the equity goals it was created to attain, but is not appropriate to reinforce the performance goals of the education system in the twenty-first century. The base salary schedule for teachers should be redesigned to have the primary elements that trigger pay increases be variables linked to student learning gains, such as a score on a performance assessment of teachers' instructional practice. Also, several wage "premiums" should be added to teacher salary systems, including premiums for teaching in urban schools; in schools with high concentrations of low-achieving, poverty, or minority students; and in subject areas experiencing shortages, such as mathematics and science. Finally, states and districts should consider adding a variable-pay element to teacher compensation, such as an annual bonus for improving student achievement beyond historical benchmarks, either for all faculty in a school or for individual teachers. The purpose of these new approaches to teacher compensation is to get a high-quality teacher in every classroom, with sufficient instructional expertise to teach all, or nearly all, of the nation's children to new, rigorous performance standards, so that when they leave school they are ready for college, work in the global economy, and their responsibilities as citizens.

Study Questions

1. Compile a list of districts, or states, with which your district, or state, competes for teachers, and collect as much of the following data as possible to compare your salary levels to your competitors:
   a. Average salary
   b. Beginning salary with a BA
   c. Beginning salary with an MA
   d. Beginning salary with an MA plus 30 units
   e. Salary at step 5 for a BA, MA, and MA plus 30 units
   f. Salary at step 10 for a BA, MA, and MA plus 30 units
   g. Salary at step 15 for a BA, MA, and MA plus 30 units
   h. Top salary for a BA, MA, and MA plus 30 units

2. Is your district or state experiencing shortages of teachers in certain subject areas, such as mathematics, science, technology, and special education? If so, do you think it would be possible to provide a salary premium for those teachers? And if yes, how large would the premium need to be in order for it to function as an incentive to recruit and retain teachers in those areas? Should the incentive be provided to the teachers in these subjects who already work in the district or state?

3. Find a set of teaching standards and scoring rubrics. Such systems can be found in Danielson (1996), in the Appendix to Chapter 5 of Odden and Wallace (2007a), and on the Connecticut State Department of Education's website (www.sde.ct.gov) under the BEST program. Review the standards, and comment on how they do or do not conform to what is considered good instruction in your district or state.

4. Discuss the pros and cons of having your state or district adopt a new salary structure as depicted in Table 12.1.

5. Discuss the pros and cons of having your district or state adopt an incentive bonus program based on improvements in student test scores.

   a. Do you think the balanced scorecard or value-added approach would be the better way to calculate whether the bonus could be earned?

   b. What about the AYP approach of NCLB? Could that serve as a basis for the bonus?

   c. Do you think it would be best to base the bonus on schoolwide improvements in student performance, or should the bonuses be provided for the improved performance of each teacher's students? Give rationales for the approach you recommend.

Appendix: Using the Simulation

This appendix provides initial documentation for the use of the finance simulations that accompany this book. Students are encouraged to download the simulation from this text's website (www.mhhe.com/odden4e) and use it in conjunction with the material in Chapters 9 and 11. The simulation requires that you have Microsoft Excel Professional available and running on your computer. To take advantage of all the tools available in the simulation, you need to have Excel 2000 or 2003 in a Windows environment, or Excel 2004 in a Macintosh environment. Earlier versions of Excel do not have the functionality to run simulations. You do not need to be familiar with Excel to run the simulation, but the program itself must be installed for the simulation to operate correctly.

Additionally, the state-level simulations can be used to estimate the impact of school finance proposals on your own state in the future. Because we view the simulation as a dynamic product that will continue to change as school finance in the 50 states changes, it is important that you continue to download newer versions of the simulations. The balance of this appendix describes the system requirements for using the simulation and provides an introduction to its use.

SYSTEM REQUIREMENTS

The program relies on the Visual Basic Application (VBA) language that is part of Excel. Microsoft made a number of changes to that language with the introduction of Excel 2000. As a result, the macros written for this simulation in (VBA) will not run on older versions of Excel. Morover, with other changes in the simulation, versions of Excel older than Excel 2000 are likely to experience difficulties running the simulation. The simulation will run on any Windows-based computer that has the professional version of Microsoft Excel 2000 or higher installed. The simulation will operate in Excel 2004 for the Macintosh. It will also operate in earlier versions of Excel for the Macintosh, but the computations for correlation and elasticity will not function properly. Versions of Excel for the Macintosh before Excel 2004 do not support computation of the regression equations required for computing those statistics.

RUNNING THE SIMULATION THE FIRST TIME

Before you run the simulation the first time, you will need to install two of Excel's built-in add-ins. These two add-ins provide Excel with substantial data analysis capabilities that the simulation uses to calculate the equity statistics displayed in the printouts.

To install the add-ins, start Excel on your computer. When you have an empty file, do this:

1. Click on the **Tools** menu.
2. From the menu that appears below **Tools,** select the **Add-Ins** option.
3. You will see a dialogue box with the title "Add-Ins" in the bar across the top. The dialogue box contains a list of add-ins available to Excel. Place a check mark in two of them—**Analysis ToolPak** and **Analysis ToolPak–VBA**. You can place these check marks simply by clicking in the box to the left of each title.
4. Click on the box marked **OK**.

This will install the **Analysis ToolPak** on your version of Excel. Note that on versions of Excel for the Macintosh earlier than Excel 2004, you will only see the **Analysis Tool-Pak** option; the **Analysis ToolPak–VBA** is not available. On the Macintosh, just install that one option.

You only need to do this the first time you run the simulation. After that, Excel will automatically include these functions when it starts. Note that if you are using the simulation from a computer on a network installation at your institution, you will have to make sure the **Analysis ToolPak** and **Analysis ToolPak–VBA** are installed on each computer you use. You should be able to do this following the previous instructions. If that does not work, contact your network administrator for instructions on how to use these two Excel add-ins.

An Important Note on Security

Because macros (which are used extensively in the simulation) are a common source of computer viruses, Excel offers a number of security protections. Unfortunately, at the highest level of security, Excel will not allow macros in the simulation to load and run, so you need to change the security settings in Excel. To do this, click on the **Tools** menu and highlight **macro**. From the menu that appears to the side, select **security**. In the security dialog box, select the **medium level of security**. This allows you to choose whether to enable macros in Excel spreadsheets when they are started. When you double click on the icon for the simulation, and the simulation loads, you will be prompted as to whether you want to enable the macros. Choose the option **enable macros**, and the simulation will continue to load. Note that if you don't choose to enable the macros at this point, the simulation will not operate correctly.

The authors and McGraw-Hill have gone to great lengths to ensure that the simulations are virus-free. Moreover, your own virus check program should test the files for viruses as they download from the web . With these protections, there should not be a virus problem. If you don't have a virus protection program, we recommend that you install one on your computer, as we cannot be responsible for computer viruses that are resident on your computer.

Once the **Analysis ToolPak** is installed and the security level set, you can start the simulation. Follow the instructions on the website to download the simulation you want to run. Once the file has been downloaded, double click on the file's icon and it will start. Because the files are relatively large, if you are given the option, be sure to save the simulation to your local computer's hard drive, as the simulation will not function properly if you try to launch it within a web browser.

RUNNING THE SIMULATION

Once the simulation has loaded, you will see the greeting screen, which tells you which version of the simulation is running. Simulation options are chosen by using control commands. You access these by hitting the **<ctrl>** key plus one of the letter keys. Thus, if told to press **<ctrl> B**, you would hold down the **<ctrl>** key and press **B**. The commands you will need are very simple.

Base data **<ctrl> B**: this displays the base data for the simulation.
Flat grant **<ctrl> L**: this gives you a dialog box for simulating a flat grant.
Foundation **<ctrl> F**: this gives you a dialog box for simulating a foundation program.
Guaranteed tax base **<ctrl> G**: this gives you a dialog box for simulating a GTB.
Combination **<ctrl> K**: this gives you a dialog box for simulating a combination program.
Results **<ctrl> Q**: this runs the simulation and computes the results.

Note: It is essential to run **<ctrl> Q** after every change in the simulation parameters. Even if you see some of the output on your screen change when you enter new simulation parameters, it is no guarantee that all of them were property computed. The only way to ensure the computations are accurate is to type **<ctrl> Q** before reviewing any results.

After making a simulation selection using one of the control key combinations just outlined, you will see a box with the simulation parameters displayed. Simply replace the numbers in that box with the values you want to use in your simulation, and press **<ctrl> Q**. This will run the simulation. You will be returned to the **Base Data** view. To see the results of your simulation, press the **<ctrl>** and a letter for the relevant simulation option again, and the results will be displayed. You may need to scroll around the screen to see all of the results depending on the size of your display and the resolution the display is using.

Note: When running the simulation on a Macintosh with a version of Excel earlier than Excel 2004, you will get a macro run-time error because the **Analysis ToolPak–VBA** is not available. When you get this error box, simply choose the "continue" option. The simulation will complete its calculations, but the data presented for the correlation and elasticity will be wrong. Unfortunately, we cannot fix this bug. If you want to compute the correlation and elasticity, you need Excel 2004 for the Macintosh or the professional version of Excel 2000 or an earlier version for Windows.

Printing Your Results

To obtain a printout of your results, do this:

1. Pull down the **View** menu.
2. Highlight **Page Break Preview**. Your screen will change.
3. Highlight the portion of the spreadsheet you want to print, and click on the print button.

Viewing the Graphs

Across the bottom of the screen, there are a series of tabs with labels identifying the various graphs (charts) that are available through the simulation. To view one of the graphs, click on one of the tabs. To return to the simulation, click on the tab labeled **sim20** (or the tab related to the state simulation you are using).

Note: Before pressing **<ctrl> Q** to make calculations, it is important that you click on the **sim20** (or state simulation) tab. If you fail to do so, errors will occur and the simulation will be corrupted. If this happens, delete the simulation from your computer and download a new copy. Be sure to check for update notices as well.

PUPIL WEIGHTS

If you want to use the pupil-weight feature of the simulation, click on the **pupil-weights** tab. You will see a new worksheet. At the top is a question: "Do you want to use pupil weights?" Replace **no** with **yes**.

In viewing the 20 district simulation, you will see two boxes. In the first, you can determine the weight for each student category. These are "extra" student weights over and above the 1.0 that all students are counted. In the second box, you can assign the percentage of students in each weighting category for each district. If you want to make changes to the values presented, simply type them in the respective cells on the worksheet. On the state simulations, you will only want to alter the weights, as the percentages of district enrollment that are disabled, limited English, or low income are actual state values.

When you have finished making your weighting selections, click on the **sim20** (or state simulation) tab, and then press **<ctrl> Q**. If you fail to click on the **sim20** (or state simulation) tab before pressing **<ctrl> Q**, errors will occur and the simulation will be corrupted. If this happens, delete the simulation from your computer and download a new copy. Be sure to check for updated notices as well.

EXITING FROM THE SIMULATION

To exit from the simulation, either click the **X** box in the upper-right-hand corner of the screen, or go to the **File** menu and choose **Exit**. You will be asked if you want to save your changes. If you select **yes**, the most recent simulation options you selected will be saved. If you select **no**, you will have the data as it was downloaded from the website. Since more than one simulation option cannot be saved, either choice is fine. To re-create a simulation, all you have to do is use the command key for the simulation you want to run (i.e., **<ctrl> F** for a foundation program simulation), enter the parameters you want to simulate, and press the **<ctrl> Q**.

SUMMARY OF STEPS FOR OPERATING THE SIMULATION

1. Make sure the professional-version Microsoft Excel for Office 2000 or higher for Windows, or Excel 2004 for Macintosh or higher is installed on your computer.
2. Be sure that the **Analysis ToolPak** and **Analysis ToolPak–VBA** add-ins have been installed on Excel, and that macro security level is set to **medium**.
3. Log onto the text's website (www.mcgraw-hill.com/odden4e).
4. Read the documentation available on the website.
5. Download the simulation you want to run and save it on your hard drive. You might want to have two copies, one that you never use but can be used to make a second, working copy if, while running the simulation, you corrupt it somehow. We suggest you start with the 20-district simulation to become familiar with the operation of this program.
6. Run the simulations you want to analyze.
7. Exit from Excel.

Enjoy the simulation. If you have comments or suggestions, please send an e-mail to Lawrence O. Picus at the address listed on the text's website.

Glossary

This glossary contains a number of tax, education, and statistical terms that are used in school finance research and policy analysis. In order to make comparisons of tax and expenditure data among school districts, adjustments must be made in many measures. The purpose of these adjustments is to create a set of comparable numbers and a set of common terms. Standard procedures are used to make these adjustments, and the glossary indicates how some of the adjustments are made.

ADA, ADM   ADA is an abbreviation for student average daily attendance, and ADM is an abbreviation for student average daily membership. ADA and ADM are the official measures that most states use to represent the number of students in a school district for the purpose of calculating state aid. ADA is always less than ADM.

adequacy   Adequacy entered the educational arena primarily in the 1990s. For school finance, it means providing sufficient funds for the average district/school to teach the average child to state standards, plus sufficient additional revenues for students with special needs to allow them to meet performance standards as well. Many school finance court cases have shifted from challenging fiscal disparities to challenging the adequacy of the funding system.

assessment ratios   The assessed valuation of property in most states is usually less than the market value of the property. In other words, owners are able to sell property for a price higher than the assessed valuation of that property. Although most states have a legal standard at which all property should be assessed, assessed valuations are usually below even the legal level and may vary widely among jurisdictions in a state. The actual assessment level or assessment ratio is determined by comparing actual assessed valuations to market values.

assessed valuation   The assessed valuation is the total value of property subject to the property tax in a school district. Usually, it is established by a local government officer and is only a percentage of the market value of the property.

assessed valuation, adjusted or equalized   Because local assessing jurisdictions in a state usually have different actual assessment ratios, the reported assessed valuations need to be adjusted or equalized in order to compare them among school districts. The best way to make such adjustments is to convert the assessed valuations to what they would be if all counties assessed at 100 percent of market value and then adjust them to the legal standard (e.g., 33.3 percent). The mathematical way to make the adjustment is to divide the assessed valuation by the assessment ratio and multiply the result by 0.333. The result is called the *adjusted* or *equalized assessed valuation*. The following is an example:

Consider two school districts, A and B.

District A has an assessed valuation of $200,000.

District B has an assessed valuation of $250,000.

Focusing just on assessed valuations, district A would appear to be poorer in property wealth than district B. However, assume that the actual assessment ratio is 20 percent in district A and 25 percent in district B.

Assuming that the legal ratio is 33.3 percent, the computation of the adjusted assessed valuation for district A is as follows:

$$\text{Adjusted Assessed Valuation} = \frac{\$200,000}{0.20} \times 0.333 = \$333,333$$

The computation of the adjusted assessed valuation for District B is:

$$\text{Adjusted Assessed Valuation} = \frac{\$250,000}{0.25} \times 0.333 = \$333,333$$

Both school districts have the same adjusted assessed valuation. That is, both school districts effectively have the same total tax base, despite the differences in the reported assessed valuation.

Adjusted assessed valuations must be used to compare property wealth among school districts and should be the basis on which state equalization aid is calculated.

assessed valuation per pupil, adjusted   The adjusted or equalized assessed valuation per pupil is the adjusted assessed valuation for a school district divided by the district's total ADA or ADM, or whatever is the state's official pupil count.

categorical grants   Categorical grants refer to state aid that is designated for specific programs. Examples would be transportation aid, special-education aid, and aid for vocational education. Equalization formula aid is not an example of categorical aid. Formula funds provide general aid that can be used for any purpose.

correlation   Correlation is a statistical term indicating the relationship between two variables. When two variables are said to be positively correlated, as one variable increases, the other variable also tends to increase. When two variables are said to be negatively correlated, as one variable increases, the other variable tends to decrease.

correlation coefficient   The correlation coefficient is a number indicating the degree of relationship between two variables. Because of the way a correlation coefficient is calculated, it will always have a value between −1.0 and +1.0. When the correlation coefficient is around +0.5 to +1.0, the two variables have a positive relationship or are positively correlated—when one variable gets larger, the other tends to get larger. When the correlation coefficient is around zero, the two variables do not appear to have any relationship. When the correlation coefficient is around −0.5 to −1.0, the variables have a negative relationship or are negatively correlated—as one gets larger, the other tends to get smaller.

current operating expenditures   Current operating expenditures include education expenditures for the daily operation of the school program, such as expenditures for administration, instruction, attendance and health services, transportation, operation and maintenance of plant, and fixed charges.

district power equalization (DPE)   See *guaranteed tax base program.*

elasticity of tax revenues   The elasticity of tax revenues refers to the responsiveness of the revenues from a tax to changes in various economic factors in the state or nation. In particular, policymakers may want to know whether tax revenues will increase more rapidly than as rapidly as, or less rapidly than changes in personal income. The revenues from an elastic tax will increase by more than 1 percent for each percent change in personal income. Income taxes are usually elastic tax sources. In general, elastic tax sources have progressive patterns of incidence, and inelastic tax sources have regressive patterns of incidence. Expenditure elasticity may be defined similarly.

equalization formula aid   Equalization formula aid is financial assistance given by a higher-level government—the state—to a lower-level government—school districts—to equalize the fiscal situation of the lower-level government. Because school districts vary in their abilities to raise property tax dollars, equalization formula aid is allocated to make the ability to raise such local funds more nearly equal. In general, equalization formula aid increases as the property wealth per pupil of a school district decreases.

expenditure uniformity   Expenditure uniformity is part of the horizontal-equity standard in school finance requiring equal expenditures per pupil or per weighted pupil for all students in the state. See also *fiscal neutrality*.

fiscal capacity   Fiscal capacity is the ability of a local governmental entity, such as a school district, to raise tax revenues. It is usually measured by the size of the local tax base, usually property wealth per pupil in education.

fiscal neutrality   Fiscal neutrality is a court-defined equity standard in school finance. It is a negative standard stating that current operating expenditures per pupil, or some object, cannot be related to a school district's adjusted assessed valuation per pupil, or some fiscal capacity measure. It simply means that differences in expenditures per pupil cannot be related to local school district wealth. See also *expenditure uniformity*.

flat grant program   A flat grant program simply allocates an equal sum of dollars to each public school pupil in the state. A flat grant is not an equalization aid program because it allocates the same dollars per pupil regardless of the property or income wealth of the local school districts. However, if no local dollars are raised for education and all school dollars come from the state, a flat grant program becomes equivalent to full-state assumption.

foundation program   A foundation program is a state equalization aid program that typically guarantees a certain foundation level of expenditure for each student, together with a minimum tax rate that each school district must levy for education purposes. The difference between what a local school district raises at the minimum tax rate and the foundation expenditure is made up in state aid. In the past, foundation programs were referred to as *minimum foundation programs,* and the foundation level of expenditure was quite low. Today, most newly enacted foundation programs usually require an expenditure per pupil at or above the previous year's state average. Foundation programs focus on the per-pupil expenditure level and thus enhance the state government's fiscal role in education.

full-state assumption   Full-state assumption (FSA) is a school finance program in which the state pays for all education costs and sets equal per-pupil expenditures in all school districts. FSA would satisfy the expenditure per-pupil "uniformity" standard of equity. Only in Hawaii has the state government fully assumed the costs of education, except for federal aid.

guaranteed tax base program (GTB)   Guaranteed tax base (GTB) refers to a state equalization aid program that "equalizes" the ability of each school district to raise dollars for education. In a pure GTB program, the state guarantees to both property-poor and property-rich school districts the same dollar yield for the same property tax rate. In short, equal tax rates produce equal per-pupil expenditures. In the property-poor school districts, the state makes up the difference between what is raised locally and what the state guarantees. In property-rich school districts, excess funds may or may not be "recaptured" by the state and distributed to the property-poor districts. Most GTB state laws do not include recapture provisions.

However, Montana and Utah included recapture mechanisms in their school finance laws. GTB programs are given different names in many states, including *district power equalizing programs (DPE), guaranteed yield programs,* and *percentage equalizing programs.* GTB programs focus on the ability to support education and, thus, enhance the local fiscal role in education decision making. GTB would satisfy the 'fiscal-neutrality' standard without achieving "uniformity" of expenditures among school districts.

guaranteed yield program   See *guaranteed tax base program.*

median family income   Median family income is usually reported in the decennial U.S. census. It reflects income for the year before the census was taken (e.g., 1989 income for the 1990 census, or 1999 income for the 2000 census). If the income of all families in a school district were rank ordered, the median income would be the income of the family midway between the lowest- and the highest-income families.

municipal overburden   Municipal overburden refers to the fiscal position of large cities. Municipal overburden includes the large burden of noneducation services that central cities must provide and that most other jurisdictions do not have to provide (or at least not in the same quantity). These noneducation services may include above-average welfare, health and hospitalization, public housing, police, fire, and sanitation services. These high noneducation fiscal burdens mean that education must compete with many other functional areas for each local tax dollar raised, thus reducing the ability of large-city school districts to raise education dollars. The fiscal squeeze caused by the service overburden, together with the concentration of the educationally disadvantaged and children in need of special-education services in city schools, puts central-city school districts at a fiscal disadvantage in supporting school services.

percentage equalizing programs   See *guaranteed tax base program.*

progressive tax   A progressive tax is a tax that increases proportionately more than income as the income level of the taxpayer increases. Under a progressive tax, high-income taxpayers will pay a larger percentage of their income toward this tax than low-income taxpayers.

property tax circuit breaker program   A property tax circuit breaker program is a tax relief program, usually financed by the state, that focuses property tax relief on particular households presumed to be overburdened by property taxes. That is, it is intended to reduce presumed regressivity of the property tax. A typical circuit breaker attempts to limit the property tax burden to a percentage of household income and applies only to residential property taxes. The percentage usually rises as income rises in an attempt to make the overall burden progressive. Initially, most states enacted circuit breaker programs just for senior citizens, but a few states have extended circuit breaker benefits to all low-income households, regardless of the age of the head of the household. The circuit breaker is based on actual or estimated taxes paid on residential property and generally takes the form of a credit on state income taxes.

property tax incidence or **burden-traditional and new views**   The traditional view of property tax incidence divided the tax into two components: that which fell on land and that which fell on improvements (i.e., structures). Property taxes on land were assumed to fall on landowners. The part on improvements was assumed to fall on homeowners in the case of owned homes, to be shifted forward to tenants in the case of rented residences, and to be shifted forward to consumers in the case of taxes on business property. Nearly all empirical studies based on the traditional view found the incidence pattern to result in a regressive burden distribution, markedly regressive in lower-income ranges. The new view of property tax incidence considers the tax to be, basically, a uniform tax on all property in the country. Such a tax is borne by owners of capital, and so the burden distribution pattern is progressive. Although the new view allows for modifications caused by admitted tax rate differentials across the country, adherents of the new view hold that even with the modifications, the tax would exhibit a progressive pattern of incidence over much of the range of family incomes.

proportional tax   A proportional tax is a tax that consumes the same percent of family income at all income levels.

pupil-weighted system or **weighted-pupil programs**   A pupil-weighted system is a state aid system in which pupils are given different weights based on the estimated or assumed costs of their education program; aid is allocated on the basis of the total number of weighted students. Usually, the cost of the education program for grades 4–6 is considered the standard program and weighted at 1.0. For states, such as Florida, that choose to invest more dollars in the early school years, pupils in grades K–3 are given a weight greater than 1.0, typically around 1.3. In other states, high school students are weighted about 1.25, although these secondary weightings are slowly being eliminated. The two major programmatic areas where numerous weightings have been used are special and vocational education. Weighted-pupil programs, therefore, recognize that it costs more to provide an education program for some students than for others and includes the extra costs via a higher weighting. State aid is then calculated and distributed on the basis of the total number of weighted students in each school district. Determining the appropriate weight is a difficult matter.

regressive tax   A regressive tax is a tax that increases proportionately less than income as the income level of the taxpayer increases. Under a regressive tax, low-income taxpayers will pay a larger percentage of their income toward this tax than high-income taxpayers.

revenue gap   A revenue gap exists when projected expenditures exceed projected tax revenues. Although revenue gaps are usually not allowed to exist in fact for current fiscal years, of importance are the projected values. If revenue gaps are projected, tax rate increases or expenditure cuts, both politically difficult, will be required. Revenue gaps usually occur when the elasticity of expenditures exceeds the elasticity of revenues. This often happens at the state and local level because state and local taxes are, in most instances, less elastic than expenditures. If states want to eliminate the occurrence of revenue gaps and the constant need to increase tax rates or decrease projected expenditure levels, attention must be given to ways to increase the elasticity of state tax systems, usually by increasing reliance on income taxes. See also *elasticity of tax revenues*.

school district tax rate   School district tax rate is the term states use to indicate the local school property tax rate. The tax rate is often stated as the amount of property tax dollars to be paid for each $100 of assessed valuation. Or, if given in mills, the rate indicates how much is raised for each $1,000 of assessed valuation. For example, a tax rate of $1.60 per $100 of assessed valuation means that taxpayers pay $1.60 for each $100 of their total assessed valuation: a tax rate of 16 mills indicates that $16 must be paid for each $1,000 of assessed valuation. The tax rate can also be expressed as a percentage, so a tax rate of 1.6 percent would be the same as a tax rate of 16 mills or $1.60 per $100 of assessed valuation.

state aid for current operating expense   State aid for current operating expenses is the sum of the equalization formula aid and categorical aid for vocational education, special-education, bilingual education, transportation, and other categorical aid programs. See also *categorical programs*.

tax burden (or sometimes **tax incidence**)   Tax burden typically refers to the percentage of an individual's or family's income that is consumed by a tax or by a tax system. Usually, one wants to know whether a tax or tax system's burden is distributed in a progressive, proportional, or regressive manner. In the United States, a tax system that is progressive overall seems to be the most acceptable to a majority of people. Tax burden analysis takes into account the extent of tax shifting.

tax incidence   See *tax shifting* and *tax burden*.

tax price   The tax price generally is the tax rate a district must levy to purchase a given level and quality of school services. Poor districts generally have to levy a higher tax rate, and thus pay a higher tax price, to purchase a given bundle of school services than do wealthy districts, because, at a given tax rate, a poor district would raise less dollars per pupil than a wealthy district.

tax shifting or tax incidence Tax shifting refers to the phenomenon whereby the party that must legally pay a tax (e.g., a store owner) does not in fact bear the burden of the tax but shifts the tax to another party (e.g., the consumer of an item that is sold in the store). Taxes can be shifted either forward or backward. For example, landlords might be able to shift their property taxes forward to tenants in the form of higher rents, and a business might be able to shift property or corporate income taxes backward to employees in the form of lower salaries. The ability to shift taxes depends on a variety of economic factors, and there is great debate among economists over the extent to which some taxes are shifted. It is usually agreed, however, that individual income taxes are not shifted and rest on the individual taxpayer. It is also generally agreed that sales taxes are shifted to the consumer. There is argument over the extent to which corporate income taxes are shifted to consumers in the form of higher prices or to employees in the form of lower wages versus falling on the stockholders in the form of lower dividends. There is also debate about who effectively pays the property tax. Tax incidence analysis examines how various taxes may or may not be shifted.

References

Note: Visit the text's website at www.mhhe.com/odden4e for updates to any URLs included in the References.

Aaron, Henry J. (1975). *Who Pays the Property Tax? A New View*. Washington, DC: Brookings Institution.

Achilles, Charles. (1999). *Let's Put Kids First, Finally: Getting Class Size Right*. Thousand Oaks, CA: Corwin Press.

Adams, E. Kathleen. (December 1980). *Fiscal Response and School Finance Simulations: A Policy Perspective* (Report No. F80-3). Denver: Education Commission of the States.

Adams, E. Kathleen, & Odden, Allan. (1981). "Alternative Wealth Measures." In K. Forbis Jordan & Nelda H. Cambron-McCabe (eds.), *Perspectives in State School Support Programs* (pp. 143–165). Cambridge, MA: Ballinger.

Adams, Jacob E. (1994). Spending School Reform Dollars in Kentucky: Familiar Patterns and New Programs, But Is This Reform? *Educational Evaluation and Policy Analysis* 16(4), 375–390.

Adams, Jacob. (1997). School Finance Policy and Students' Opportunities to Learn: Kentucky's Experience. *The Future of Children: Financing Schools* 7(3), 79–95.

Advisory Commission on Intergovernmental Relations. (1989). *Local Property Taxes Called Worst Tax. News Release of 18th Annual ACIRPoll*. Washington, DC: Author.

Advisory Commission on Intergovernmental Relations. (1995). *Tax and Expenditure Limits on Local Governments*. Washington, DC: Author.

Alexander, Arthur J. (1974). *Teachers, Salaries and School District Expenditures*. Santa Monica, CA: RAND Corporation.

Alexander, Kern. (1982). Concepts of Equity. In Walter McMahon & Terry Geske (eds.), *Financing Education*. Urbana: University of Illinois Press.

Alexander, Kern; Augenblick, John; Driscoll, William; Guthrie, James; & Levin, R. (1995). *Proposals for the Elimination of Wealth-Based Disparities in Public Education*. Columbus, OH: Department of Education.

Alexander, Kern, & Salmon, Richard. (1995). *Public School Finance*. Boston: Allyn and Bacon.

Allegretto, Sylvia A.; Corcoran, Sean P.; & Mishel, Lawrence. (2004). *How Does Teacher Pay Compare? Methodological Challenges and Answers*. Washington, DC: Economic Policy Institute.

Allington, Richard. L., & Johnston, Peter (1989). Coordination, Collaboration, and Consistency: The Redesign of Compensatory and Special Education Interventions. In Robert E. Slavin, Nancy L. Karwcit, & Nancy A. Madden (eds.), *Effective Programs for Students at Risk* (pp. 320–354). Needham Heights, MA: Allyn and Bacon.

Altman, Daniel. (2003, January 21). Doubling Up of Taxation Isn't Limited to Dividends. *New York Times*, C1, C8.

American College Testing Service and Education Trust. (2004). *On Course for Success: A Close Look at Selected High School Courses That Prepare All Students for College*. ACT and Education Trust. Downloaded from www.act.org or www.edtrust.org.

Andrews, Daniel J. (2004). Redesign of Secondary School Reimbursable Meals Program: "Maxi-Meals." In David A. Ritchey (ed.,). *Innovative Ideas for School Business Officials: Best Practices from ASBO's Pinnacle Awards* (pp. 55–59). Lanham, MD: Scarecrow Education.

Andrews, Matthew; Duncombe, William; & Yinger, John. (2002). Revisiting Economies of Size in American Education: Are We Any Closer to a Consensus? *Economics of Education Review* 21(3), 245–262.

Apling, R. N., & Jones, N. L. (2005). Individuals with Disabilities Education Act (IDEA): Analysis of Changes Made by P.L. 108–446. *CRS Report for Congress RL32716*. Washington, DC: Council for Exceptional Children. Retrieved from www.cec.sped.org/pp/docs/CRS-AnalysisofNewIDEAPL108–446.pdf.

Archambault Jr., F. X.; Westberg, K. L.; Brown, S.; Hallmark, B. W.; Zhang, W.; & Emmons, C. (1993). "Regular Classroom Practices with Gifted Students: Findings from the Classroom Practices Survey." *Journal for the Education of the Gifted* 16, 103–119.

Archer, J. (2000). The Link to Higher Scores. In R. Pea (ed.), *The Jossey-Bass Reader on Technology and Learning* (pp. 112–123). San Francisco: Jossey-Bass.

Archibald, Sarah. (2006). Narrowing In on Educational Resources That Do Affect Student Achievement. *Peabody Journal of Education* 81(4), 23–42.

Archibald, S., & Gallagher, H. A. (2002). A Case Study of Professional Development Expenditures at a Restructured High School. *Education Policy Analysis Archives* 10(29), 1–24.

Arsen, D.; Clay, T.; Davis, T.; Devaney, T.; Fulcher-Dawson, R.; & Plank, D. (May 2005). *Adequacy, Equity and Capital Spending in Michigan Schools: The Unfinished Business of Proposal A*. (Michigan State University, Education Policy Center, Lansing MI). Retrieved August 15, 2006, from www.epc.msu.edu/publications/publications.htm.

Ascher, C. (1998). Summer School, Extended School Year, and Year-Round Schooling for Disadvantaged Students. *ERIC Clearinghouse on Urban Education Digest* 42, 1–2.

Augenblick, John. (1991). *Report Concerning the SEEK Program*. Mimeo.

Augenblick, John. (1997). *Recommendations for a Base Figure and Pupil-Weighted Adjustments to the Base Figure for Use in a New School Finance System in Ohio*. Columbus: Ohio Department of Education.

Augenblick, John, & Adams, E. Kathleen. (1979). *An Analysis of the Impact of Changes in the Funding of Elementary/Secondary Education in Texas: 1974/75 to 1977/78*. Denver: Education Commission of the States.

Augenblick, John, & DeCesare, D. (2006, March). *A Review of the "Support Education Excellence in Kentucky" (SEEK) System*. Denver: Augenblick, Palaich.

Augenblick and Myers, Inc. (2001a). *Calculation of the Cost of an Adequate Education in Maryland in 1999–2000 Using Two Different Analytic Approaches*. Report prepared for the Maryland Commission on Education Finance, Equity and Excellence.

Augenblick and Myers, Inc. (2001b). *A Procedure for Calculating a Base Cost Figure and an Adjustment for At-Risk Pupils That Could Be Used in the Illinois School Finance System*. Report prepared for the Education Funding Advisory Board.

Austin, G. R.; Roger, B. G.; & Walbesser, H. H. (1972). The Effectiveness of Summer Compensatory Education: A Review of the Research. *Review of Educational Research* 42, 171–181.

Baker, B.; Taylor, L.; & Vedlitz, A. (2004). *Measuring educational adequacy in public schools*. Report prepared for the Texas Legislature Joint Committee on Public School Finance, The Texas School Finance Project. Retrieved from www.capitol.state.tx.us/psf/reports/htm.

Baker, Bruce. (2005). *Development of an Hedonic Wage Index for the Wyoming School Funding Model*. Analysis prepared for the Wyoming legislature under the auspices of Lawrence O. Picus and Associates.

Baker, Bruce; Taylor, Lori; & Vedlitz, Arnold. (2004). *Measuring Educational Adequacy in Public Schools*. Report prepared for the Texas Legislature Joint Committee on Public School Finance, Texas School Finance Project. Available at www.capitol.state.tx.us/psf/reports.htm.

Baker, D., & Witt, P. (1996). Evaluation of the Impact of Two After-School Recreation Programs. *Journal of Park and Recreation Administration* 14(3), 23–44.

Baker, E. L.; Gearhart, M.; & Herman, J. L. (1994). Evaluating the Apple Classrooms of Tomorrow. In E. L. Baker & J. F. O'Neil, Jr. (eds.), *Technology Assessment in Education and Training*. Hillsdale, NJ: Lawrence Erlbaum.

Bangert-Drowns, R. L. (1993). The Word Processor as an Instructional Tool: A Meta-Analysis of Word Processing in Writing Instruction. *Review of Educational Research* 63(1), 69–93.

Barnett, W. Steven. (1995). Long-Term Effects of Early Childhood Programs on Cognitive and School Outcomes. *The Future of Children: Long-Term Outcomes of Early Childhood Programs* 5(3), 25–50.

Barnett, W. Steven. (1996). *Lives in the Balance: Age-27 Benefit-Cost Analysis of the High/Scope Perry Preschool Program*. Yspilanti, MI: High/Scope Press.

Barnett, W. Steven. (1998). Long-term Effects on Cognitive Development and School Success. In W. S. Barnett & S. S. Boocock (eds.), *Early Care and Education for Children in Poverty: Promises Programs and Long-Term Outcomes* (pp. 11–44). Buffalo: SUNY Press.

Barnett, W. Steven. (2000). Economics of Early Childhood Intervention. In Jack Shonkoff & Samuel Meisels (eds.), *Handbook of Early Childhood Intervention* (2d ed.). Cambridge: Cambridge University Press.

Barnett, W. S.; Brown, K.; & Shore, R. (April 2004). The Universal vs. Targeted Debate: Should the United States Have Preschool for All? *Preschool Policy Matters, Issue 6*. New Brunswick, NJ: Rutgers University, National Institute for Early Education Research.

Barro, Stephen. (1989). Fund Distribution Issues in School Finance: Priorities for the Next Round of Research. *Journal of Education Finance* 11(1), 17–30.

Barro, Stephen M. (1992). *What Does the Education Dollar Buy? Relationships of Staffing, Staff Characteristics, and Staff Salaries to State per-Pupil Spending*. Los Angeles: Finance Center of CPRE, working paper.

Barro, Stephen M., & Carroll, Stephen J. (1975). *Budget Allocation by School Districts: An Analysis of Spending for Teachers and Other Resources*. Santa Monica, CA: RAND Corporation.

Baum, S. M.; Owen, S. V.; & Oreck, B. A. (1996). Talent beyond Words: Identification of Potential Talent in Dance and Music in Elementary Students. *Gifted Child Quarterly* 40, 93–101.

Becker, Henry J. (2000). *Pedagogical Motivations for Student Computer Use That Lead to Student Engagement*. Retrieved May 5, 2005, from www.crito.uci.edu/TLC/FINDINGS/spec_rpt_pedegogical/.

Bell, Michael E., & Bowman, John H. (1986). Direct Property Tax Relief. In *Final Report of the Minnesota Tax Study Commission, Volume 1* (pp. 291–326). St. Paul and Boston: Butterworth.

Bennett, R.; Hall, K.; & Berg, C. (2006). *Budgets, School Finance and the Finance of Bargaining* (PowerPoint presentation). Sacramento: School Services of California.

Berke, Joel. (1974). *Answers to Inequity: An Analysis of the New School Finance*. New York: Russell Sage Foundation.

Berne, Robert, & Stiefel, Leanna. (1979). Taxpayer Equity in School Finance Reform: The School Finance and Public Finance Perspective. *Journal of Education Finance* 5(1), 36–54.

Berne, Robert, & Stiefel, Leanna. (1984). *The Measurement of Equity in School Finance*. Baltimore: Johns Hopkins University Press.

Berne, Robert, & Stiefel, Leanna. (1999). Concepts of School Finance Equity: 1970 to Present. In Helen Ladd, Rosemary Chalk, & Janet Hansen (eds.), *Equity and Adequacy in Education Finance: Issues and Perspectives*. Washington, DC: National Academy Press.

Berne, Robert; Stiefel, Leanna; & Moser, Michelle. (1997). The Coming of Age of School-Level Finance Data. *Journal of Education Finance* 22(3), 246–254.

Berner, Maureen M. (1993). Building Conditions, Parental Involvement, and Student Achievement in the District of Columbia Public School System. *Urban Education* 28(1), 6–29.

Betts, J. R., & Shkolnik, J. L. (1999). The Behavioral Effects of Variations in Class Size: The Case of Math Teachers. *Educational Evaluation and Policy Analysis* 21, 193–215.

Birman, Bea F.; Desimone, Laura; Porter, Andrew C.; & Garet, Michael. S. (2000). Designing Professional Development That Works. *Educational Leadership* 57(8), 28–33.

Black, D. E.; Lewis, K. A.; & Link, C. K. (1979). Wealth Neutrality and the Demand for Education. *National Tax Journal* 32(2), 157–164.

Bleske-Rechek, A.; Lubinski, D.; & Benbow, C. P. (2004). Meeting the Educational Needs of Special Populations: Advanced Placement's Role in Developing Exceptional Human Capital. *Psychological Science* 15(4), 217–224.

Bolton, Denny G., & Harmer, W. Gary. (2000). *Standards of Excellence in Budget Presentation*. Reston, VA: Association of School Business Officers International.

Borg, Mary O.; Mason, Paul M.; & Schapiro, Stephen L. (1991). *The Economic Consequences of State Lotteries*. New York: Praeger.

Borland, J. H., & Wright, L. (1994). Identifying Young Potentially Gifted, Economically Disadvantaged Students. *Gifted Child Quarterly* 38, 164–171.

Borman, Geoffrey D. (2001). Summers Are for Learning. *Principal* 80(3), 26–29.

Borman, Geoffrey D., & Boulay, M. (eds.). (2004). *Summer Learning: Research, Policies and Programs*. Mahwah, NJ: Lawrence Erlbaum.

Borman, Geoffrey, & D'Agostino, Jerome. (2001). Title I and Student Achievement: A Quantitative Analysis. In Geoffrey Borman, Samuel Stringfield, & Robert Slavin (eds.), *Title I: Compensatory Education at the Crossroads* (pp. 25–27). Mahwah, NJ: Lawrence Erlbaum.

Borman, Geoffrey D.; Hewes, Gina; Overman, Laura; & Brown, Shelly (2003). Comprehensive School Reform and Achievement: A Meta-Analysis. *Review of Educational Research* 73(2), 125–230.

Borman, G.; Rachuba, L.; Hewes, G.; Boulay, M.; & Kaplan, J. (2001). Can a Summer Intervention Program Using Trained Volunteer Teachers Narrow the Achievement Gap? First-Year Results from a Multi-Year Study. *ERS Spectrum* 19(2), 19–30.

Borman, Geoffrey; Stringfield, Samuel; & Slavin, Robert (eds). (2001). *Title I: Compensatory Education at the Crossroads*. Mahwah, NJ: Lawrence Erlbaum.

Bossert, S.; Dwyer, D.; Rowan, B.; & Lee, G. (1982). The Instructional Management Role of the Principal. *Educational Administration Quarterly* 18, 34–64.

Bowman, John H. (1974). Tax Exportability, Intergovernmental Aid, and School Finance Reform. *National Tax Journal* 27(2), 163–173.

Brabeck, M. M.; Walsh, M. E.; & Latta, R. (2003). *Meeting at the Hyphen: Schools-Universities-Professions in Collaboration for Student Achievement and Well-Being. The One-Hundred and Second Yearbook of the National Society for the Study of Education, Part II*. Chicago: National Society for the Study of Education.

Bransford, John; Brown, Ann; & Cocking, Rodney. (1999). *How People Learn*. Washington, DC: National Academy Press.

Brazer, Harvey E. (1974). Adjusting for Differences among School Districts in the Costs of Educational Inputs: A Feasibility Report. In Ester Tron (ed.), *Selected Papers in School Finance: 1974*. Washington, DC: U.S. Office of Education.

Break, George F. (1980). *Financing Government in a Federal System*. Washington, DC: Brookings Institution.

Brown, Lawrence L., et al. (1977). *School Finance Reform in the Seventies: Achievements and Failures*. Washington, DC: U.S. Department of Health, Education and Welfare, Office of the Assistant Secretary for Planning and Evaluation, and Killalea Associates.

Bruer, John. (1993). *Schools for Thought*. Cambridge, MA: MIT Press.

Bryk, Anthony; Lee, Valerie E.; & Holland, P. (1993). *Catholic Schools and the Common Good*. Cambridge, MA: Harvard University Press.

Buday, Mary, & Kelly, James. (1996, November). National Board Certification and the Teaching Profession's Commitment to Quality Assurance. *Phi Delta Kappan* 78(3), 215–219.

Budget of the U.S. (2006). *Historical Tables, Budget of the United States Government, Fiscal Year 2006*. Retrieved from frwebgate2.access.gpo.gov/cgi-bin/waisgate.cgi?WAISdocID=05720239515+36+0+0&WAISaction=retrieve.

Burtless, Gary (ed.). (1996). *Does Money Matter?* Washington, DC: Brookings Institution.

Busch, Carolyn; Kucharz, Karen; & Odden, Allan. (1996). Recognizing Additional Student Need in Wisconsin: A Re-Examination of Equity and Equity Analysis. In Barbara LaCost (ed.), *School Finance Policy Issues in the States and Provinces* (pp. 109–126). Lincoln: University of Nebraska and American Education Finance Association.

Busch, Carolyn, & Odden, Allan. (1997). Special Issue: Collection of School-Level Finance Data. *Journal of Education Finance* 22(3).

Capizzano, J.; Adelman, S.; & Stagner, M. (2002). *What Happens When the School Year Is Over? The Use and Costs of Child Care for School-Age Children during the Summer Months*. (Assessing the New Federalism, Occasional Paper, No. 58.) Washington, DC: Urban Institute.

Cardenas, Jose; Bernal, J. J.; & Kean, N. (1976). *Bilingual Education Cost Analysis: Texas*. San Antonio: Intercultural Development Research Association.

Carey, Kevin. (2002). *State Poverty-Based Education Funding: A Survey of Current Programs and Options for Improvement*. Washington, DC: Center on Budget and Policy Priorities.

Carpenter-Huffman, P., & Samulon, S. M. (1981). *Case Studies of Delivery and Cost of Bilingual Education Programs*. Santa Monica, CA: RAND Corporation.

Cavin, E.; Murnane, R.; & Brown, R. (1985). School District Response to Enrollment Changes: The Direction of Change Matters. *Journal of Education Finance* 10(4), 426–440.

Chaikind, Steve; Danielson, Charlotte; & Braven, Marsha L. (1993). What Do We Know about the Costs of Special Education? A Selected Review. *Journal of Special Education* 26(4), 344–370.

Chambers, Jay G. (1978). *Educational Cost Differentials across School Districts in California*. Denver: Education Commission of the States.

Chambers, Jay G. (1980). *The Development of a Cost of Education Index for the State of California, Final Reports, Parts 1 and 2*. Prepared for the California State Department of Education.

Chambers, Jay G. (1981). Cost and Price Level Adjustments to State Aid for Education: A Theoretical and Empirical View. In K. Forbis Jordan & Nelda Cambron-McCabe (eds.), *Perspectives in State School Support Programs*. Cambridge, MA: Ballinger.

Chambers, Jay G. (1995). Public School Teacher Cost Differences across the United States: Introduction to a Teacher Cost Index (TCI). In *Developments in School Finance*. Available at www.ed.gov/NCES/pubs/96344cha.html.

Chambers, Jay G.; Odden, Allan; & Vincent, Phillip E. (1976). *Cost of Education Indices among School Districts*. Denver: Education Commission of the States.

Chambers, Jay, & Parrish, Thomas. (1983). *The Development of a Resource Cost Model Funding Base for Education Finance in Illinois*. Stanford, CA: Associates for Education Finance and Planning.

Chambers, Jay, & Parrish, Thomas. (1994). State-Level Education Finance. In *Advances in Educational Productivity* (pp. 45–74). Greenwich, CT: JAI Press.

Chambers, Jay; Parrish, Thomas; & Guarino, Cassandra (eds.). (1999). *Funding Special Education*. Thousand Oaks, CA: Corwin Press.

Chambers, Jay G.; Parrish, Thomas B.; & Harr, Jennifer J. (2002). *What Are We Spending on Special Education Services in the United States, 1999–2000?* (Report 02-01.) Palo Alto, CA: American Institutes for Research, Center for Special Education Finance.

Chambers, Jay G.; Parrish, Thomas; Levin, J.; Smith, J.; Guthrie, J.; & Seder, R. (2004). *The New York Adequacy Study: Determining the Cost of Providing All Children in New York an Adequate Education: Volume 1–Final Report*. Report submitted to the Campaign for Fiscal Equity by AIR/MAP. Available at www.cfequity.org/FINALCOSTINGOUT3-27-04.pdf.

Clotfelter, Charles, & Ladd, Helen. (1996). Recognizing and Rewarding Success in Public Schools. In Helen Ladd (ed.), *Holding School Accountable* (pp. 23–64). Washington, DC: Brookings Institution.

Clune, William. (1994a). The Shift from Equity to Adequacy in School Finance. *Educational Policy* 8(4), 376–394.

Clune, William. (1994b). The Cost and Management of Program Adequacy: An Emerging Issue in Education Policy and Finance. *Educational Policy* 8(4).

Clune, William. (1995). Adequacy Litigation in School Finance Symposium. *University of Michigan Journal of Law Reform* 28(3).

Clune, William, & White, Paula. (1992). Education Reform in the Trenches: Increased Academic Course Taking in High Schools with Lower Achieving Students in States with Higher Graduation Requirements. *Educational Evaluation & Policy Analysis* 14(1), 2–20.

Cochrane-Smith, M. (1991). Word Processing and Writing in Elementary Classrooms: A Critical Review of Related Literature. *Review of Educational Research* 61(1), 107–155.

Coeyman, Marjorie. (November 1998). Small-Town Schools: Changing Times and Budgets Put the Squeeze On. *Christian Science Monitor* 90(252), 15.

Cohen, David K., & Hill, Heather C. (2001). *Learning Policy: When State Education Reform Works*. New Haven, CT: Yale University Press.

Cohen, David K.; Raudenbush, Steve W.; & Ball, Deborah L. (2002). Resources, Instruction, and Research. In R. Boruch & F. Mosteller (eds.), *Evidence Matters: Randomized Trials in Education Research* (pp. 80–119). Washington, DC: Brookings Institution.

Cohen, P.; Kulik, J.; & Kulik, C. (1982). Educational Outcomes of Tutoring: A Meta-Analysis of Findings. *American Educational Research Journal* 19(2), 237–248.

Cohen, Matthew C. (1997). Issues in School-Level Analysis of Education Expenditure Data. *Journal of Education Finance* 22(3), 255–279.

Cohn, Elchanan. (1974). *Economics of State Aid to Education*. Lexington, MA: Heath Lexington Books.

Cohn, Elchanan, & Geske, Terry G. (1990). *The Economics of Education* (3d ed.). Oxford: Pergamon Press.

Committee on Increasing High School Students' Engagement and Motivation to Learn. (2004). *Engaging Schools: Fostering High School Students' Motivation to Learn*. Washington, DC: National Academies Press.

Consortium for School Networking [COSN] (2004). *Taking TCO to the Classroom*. Retrieved May 5, 2005, from classroomtco.cosn.org/gartner_intro.html.

Coons, John; Clune, William; & Sugarman, Stephen. (1970). *Private Wealth and Public Education*. Cambridge, MA: Belknap Press of Harvard University Press.

Cooper, Bruce. (March 1993). School Site Cost Allocations: Testing a Microfinancial Model in 23 Districts in Ten States. Paper presented at the annual meeting of the American Education Finance Association, Albuquerque, NM.

Cooper, H.; Charlton, K.; Valentine, J. C.; & Muhlenbruck, L. (2000). Making the Most of Summer School: A Meta-Analytic and Narrative Review. *Monographs of the Society for Research in Child Development* 65(1, serial no. 260).

Cooper, H.; Nye, B.; Charlton, K.; Lindsay, J.; & Greathouse, S. (1996). The Effects of Summer Vacation on Achievement Test Scores: A Narrative and Meta-Analytic Review. *Review of Educational Research* 66, 227–268.

Corcoran, Thomas B. (1995). *Helping Teachers Teach Well: Transforming Professional Development.* (RB-16). Philadelphia: Consortium for Policy Research in Education, University of Pennsylvania.

Cosden, M.; Morrison, G.; Albanese, A. L.; & Macias, S. (2001). When Homework Is No Home work: After School Programs for Homework Assistance. *Journal of Educational Psychology* 36, 211–221.

Cubberly, Elwood Patterson. (1905). *School Funds and Their Apportionment.* New York: Teachers College Press.

Cubberly, Elwood Patterson. (1906). *School Funds and Their Apportionment* (2d ed.), New York: Teachers College Press.

Cummins, James. (1980). The Exit and Entry Fallacy in Bilingual Education. *NABE Journal* 4, 25–60.

Cunningham, P., & Allington, R. (1994). *Classrooms That Work: They Can All Read and Write.* New York: HarperCollins.

D'Agostino, J. V. (2000). Instructional and School Effects on Students' Longitudinal Reading and Mathematics Achievements. *School Effectiveness and School Improvement* 11, 197–235.

Danielson, Charlotte. (1996). *Enhancing Professional Practice: A Framework for Teaching.* Arlington, VA: Association for Supervision and Curriculum Development.

Darling-Hammond, Linda. (1997). *The Right to Learn.* San Francisco: Jossey-Bass.

Dede, C. (2000a). Implications of Emerging Information Technologies for States' Education Policies. In Council of Chief State School Officers, *2000 State Educational Technology Conference Papers.*

Dede, C. (2000b). Rethinking How to Invest in Technology. In Jossey-Bass (ed.), *The Jossey-Bass Reader on Technology and Learning* (pp. 181–194). San Francisco: Jossey-Bass.

Delcourt, M. A. B.; Loyd, B. H.; Cornell, D. G.; & Golderberg, M.C. (1994). *Evaluation of the Effects of Programming Arrangements on Student Learning Outcomes.* Storrs, CT: National Research Center on the Gifted and Talented.

Denton, K.; West, J.; & Walston, J. (2003). *Reading—Young Children's Achievement and Classroom Experiences: Findings from the Condition of Education 2003.* Washington, DC: National Center for Education Statistics.

Desimone, L. M.; Porter, A. C.; Garet, M. S.; Yoon, K. S.; & Birman, B. F. (2002). Effects of Professional Development on Teachers' Instruction: Results From a Three-Year Longitudinal Study. *Educational Evaluation and Policy Analysis* 24(2), 81–112.

Desimone, L.; Porter, A. C.; Birman, B. F.; Garet, M. S.; & Yoon, K. S. (2002). How Do District Management and Implementation Strategies Relate to the Quality of Professional Development That Districts Provide to Teachers? *Teachers College Record* 104(7), 1265–1312.

Dishion, T. J.; McCord, J.; & Poulin, F. (1999). When Interventions Harm: Peer Groups and Problem Behavior. *American Psychologist* 54(9), 755–764.

Dobbs, Michael. (2003, November 28). Big Schools Reborn in Small World. *Washington Post.*

Donovan, Suzanne, & Bransford, John. (2005a). *How Students Learn—History in the Classroom.* Washington, DC: National Research Council.

Donovan, Suzanne, & Bransford, John. (2005b). *How Students Learn—Mathematics in the Classroom.* Washington, DC: National Research Council.

Donovan, Suzanne, & Bransford, John. (2005c). *How Students Learn—Science in the Classroom.* Washington, DC: National Research Council.

Dooley, Robert W. (2004). Creating a District-Wide Energy Management Program. In David A. Ritchey (ed.), *Innovative Ideas for School Business Officials: Best Practices from ASBO's Pinnacle Awards* (pp. 19–23). Lanham, MD: Scarecrow Education.

Doyle, Denis, & Hartle, Terry. (1985). *Excellence in Education: The States Take Charge.* Washington, DC: American Enterprise Institute.

Due, John F., & Mikesell, John L. (1994). *Sales Taxation: State and Local Structure and Administration.* (2d ed.). Washington, DC: Urban Institute.

Duncombe, William; Ruggiero, John; & Yinger, John. (1996). Alternative Approaches to Measuring the Cost of Education. In Helen F. Ladd (ed.), *Holding Schools Accountable: Performance-Based Reform in Education* (pp. 327–356). Washington, DC: Brookings Institution.

Dye, Robert F., & McGuire, Teresa I. (1991). Growth and Variability of State Individual Income and Sales Taxes. *National Tax Journal* 44, 55–66.

Dynarski, M.; Moore, M.; Mullens, J.; Gleason, P.; James-Burdumy, S.; Rosenberg, L.; et al. (2003). *When Schools Stay Open Late: The National Evaluation of the 21st Century Community Learning Centers Program.* Princeton, NJ: Mathematica Policy Research.

Earle, R. S. (2002). The Integration of Instructional Technology into Public Education: Promises and Challenges. *Educational Technology* 42(1), 5–11.

Earthman, G., & LeMasters, Linda. (1996). *Review of Research on the Relationship between School Buildings, Student Achievement, and Student Behavior.* Paper presented at the annual meeting of the Council of Educational Facility Planners, International, Santa Fe, NM.

Ebel, Robert D., & Ortbal, James. (1989). Direct Residential Property Tax Relief. *Intergovernmental Perspective* 16, 9–14.

Education Trust. (2003). *Zap the Gap: Gap Closing Strategies in High-Performing Classrooms, Schools, Districts and Colleges.* Washington, DC: Author.

Elbaum, B.; Vaughn, S.; Hughes, M. T.; & Moody, S. W. (1999). Grouping Practices and Reading Outcomes for Students with Disabilities. *Exceptional Children* 65, 399–415.

Elmore, Richard. (1990). *School Restructuring: The Next Generation of Educational Reform.* San Francisco: Jossey-Bass.

Elmore, Richard F. (2002). *Bridging the Gap between Standards and Achievement: The Imperative for Professional Development in Education.* Washington, DC: Albert Shanker Institute.

Elmore, Richard F., & Burney, Deanna. (1999). Investing in Teacher Learning: Staff Development and Instructional Improvement. In Linda Darling-Hammond & Gary Sykes (eds.), *Teaching as the Learning Profession: Handbook of Policy and Practice* (pp. 263–291). San Francisco: Jossey-Bass.

Enrich, Paul. (1995). Leaving Equality Behind: New Directions in School Finance Reform. *Vanderbilt Law Review* 48, 100–194.

Erlichson, Bari Anhalt, & Goertz, Margaret. (2001). *Implementing Whole School Reform in New Jersey, Year Two.* New Brunswick: Rutgers, the State University of New Jersey, Bloustein School of Planning and Public Policy.

Erlichson, Bari Anhalt; Goertz, Margaret; & Turnbull, Barbara. (1999). *Implementing Whole School Reform in New Jersey, Year One in the First Cohort Schools.* New Brunswick: Rutgers, the State University of New Jersey, Bloustein School of Planning and Public Policy.

Evans, William; Murray; Sheila; & Schwab, Robert. (1997). *State Education Finance Policy after Court Mandated Reform: The Legacy of Serrano*. 1996 Proceedings of the Eighty-Ninth Annual Conference on Taxation. Washington, DC: National Tax Association, Tax Institute of America.

Evertson, C. M., & Randolph, C. H. (1989). Teaching Practices and Class Size: A New Look at an Old Issue. *Peabody Journal of Education* 67, 85–105.

Farkas, George. (1998). Reading One-to-One: An Intensive Program Serving a Great Many Students While Still Achieving. In Jonathan Crane (ed.), *Social Programs That Work* (75–109). New York: Russell Sage Foundation.

Farland, Gary. (1997). Collection of Fiscal and Staffing Data at the School Site Level. *Journal of Education Finance* 22(3), 280–290.

Fashola, Olatokunbo S. (1998). *Review of Extended-Day and After-School Programs and Their Effectiveness*. Washington, DC: Center for Research on the Education of Students Placed at Risk (CRESPAR), Howard University.

Feldman, A. F., & Matjasko, J. L. (2005). The Role of School-Based Extracurricular Activities in Adolescent Development: A Comprehensive Review and Future Directions. *Review of Educational Research* 75(2), 159–210.

Feldstein, Martin. (1975). Wealth Neutrality and Local Choice in Public Education. *American Economic Review* 64, 75–89.

Ferguson, Ronald F. (Summer 1991). Paying for Public Education: New Evidence on How and Why Money Matters. *Harvard Journal on Legislation* 28, 465–497.

Fermanich, Mark. (2002). School Spending for Professional Development: A Cross Case Analysis of Seven Schools in One Urban District. *Elementary School Journal* 103(1), 27–50.

Fermanich, Mark. (2003). *School Resources and Student Achievement: The Effect of School-Level Resources on Instructional Practices and Student Outcomes in Minneapolis Public Schools*. Ph.D. dissertation, University of Wisconsin–Madison.

Fermanich, Mark; Picus, Lawrence O.; & Odden, Allan. (2006). *A Successful-Districts Approach to School Finance Adequacy in Washington*. Analysis prepared for the K–12 Advisory Committee of Washington Learns. Available at www.washingtonlearns.wa.gov/materials/Tab1Doc1Evidence-BasedReportforAC7-18-06_02.pdd.

Finkelstein, Neil; Furry, William; & Huerta, Luis. (2000). School Finance in California: Does History Provide a Sufficient Policy Standard? In Elizabeth Burr, Gerald C. Hayward, Bruce Fuller, and Michael W. Kirst (eds.), *Crucial Issues in California Education 2000: Are the Reform Pieces, Fitting Together?* (pp. 45–78). Berkeley: Policy Analysis for California Education.

Finn, Jeremy. (1996). Class Size and Students at Risk: What Is Known? What Next? Paper prepared for the National Institute on the Education of At-Risk Students, Office of Educational Research and Improvement, U.S. Department of Education.

Finn, Jeremy. (2002). Small Classes in America: Research, Practice, and Politics. *Phi Delta Kappan* 83(7), 551–560.

Finn, J. D., & Achilles, C. M. (1999). Tennessee's Class Size Study: Findings, Implications, Misconceptions. *Educational Evaluation and Policy Analysis* 21, 97–109.

Finn, Jeremy D.; Gerber, Susan B.; Achilles, Charles M.; & Boyd-Zaharias, Jane. (2001). The Enduring Effects of Small Classes. *Teachers College Record* 103(2), 145–183.

Finn, J. D.; Pannozzo, G. M.; & Achilles, C. M. (2003). The "Why's" of Class Size: Student Behavior in Small Classes. *Review of Educational Research* 73(3), 321–368.

Firestone, William A.; Goertz, Margaret E.; Nagle, Brianna; & Smelkinson, Marcy F. (1994). Where Did the $800 Million Go? The First Years of New Jersey's Quality Education Act. *Educational Evaluation and Policy Analysis* 16(4), 359–374.

Fordham Institute. (2006). *Fund the Child: Tackling Inequity and Antiquity in School Finance*. Washington, DC: Author.

Fortune. (2006, April 17). Fortune 500 Largest U.S. Corporations. *Fortune* 153(7).

Fowler, William Jr., & Monk, David. (2001). *A Primer for Making Cost Adjustments in Education*. Washington, DC: U.S. Department of Education, National Center for Education Statistics.

Fox, William F. (1981). Reviewing Economics of Size in Education. *Journal of Education Finance* 6(3), 273–296.

Fuhrman, Susan H. (ed.). (1993). *Designing Coherent Education Policy: Improving the System*. San Francisco: Jossey-Bass.

Fusaro, J. A. (1997). The Effect of Full-Day Kindergarten on Student Achievement: A Meta-Analysis. *Child Study Journal* 27(4), 269–277.

Gallagher, H. Alix. (2004). Vaughn Elementary's Innovative Teacher Evaluation System: Are Teacher Evaluation Scores Related to Growth in Student Achievement? *Peabody Journal of Education* 79(4), 79–107.

Gallagher, J. (1996). The Strange Case of Acceleration. In C. Benbow & D. Lubinski (eds.), *Intellectual Talent* (pp. 83–92). Baltimore: Johns Hopkins University Press.

Gallagher, J. (2002). *Society's Role in Educating Gifted Students: The Role of Public Policy* (RM02162). Storrs: National Research Center on the Gifted and Talented, University of Connecticut.

Gallagher, J., & Coleman, M. R. (1992). *State Policies on the Identification of Gifted Students from Special Populations: Three States in Profile*. Chapel Hill: University of North Carolina Gifted Education Policy Studies Program.

Gallagher, S., & Stepien, W. (1996). Content Acquisition in Problem-Based Learning: Depth versus Breadth in American Studies. *Journal for the Education of the Gifted* 19, 257–275.

Gallagher, S.; Stepien, W.; & Rosenthal, H. (1992). The Effects of Problem-Based Learning on Problem Solving. *Gifted Child Quarterly* 36, 195–200.

Gandara, P.; Rumberger, R.; Maxwell-Jolly, J.; & Callahan, R. (2003). English Learners in California Schools: Unequal Resources, Unequal Outcomes. *Education Policy Analysis Archives* 11(3).

Garcia, O. (1977). Analyzing Bilingual Education Costs. In G. Banco et al. (eds.), *Bilingual Education: Current Perspectives* (90–107). Arlington, VA: Education Center for Applied Linguistics.

Garet, M. S.; Birman, B.; Porter, A.; Desimone, L.; & Herman, R. (1999). *Designing Effective Professional Development: Lessons from the Eisenhower Program*. Washington, DC: Department of Education.

Garet, Michael S.; Porter, Andrew; Desimone, Laura; Birman, Beatrice; & Yoon, Kwang. (2001). What Makes Professional Development Effective? Results from a National Sample of Teachers. *American Educational Research Journal* 38(4), 915–945.

Garms, Walter I. (1979). Measuring the Equity of School Finance Systems. *Journal of Education Finance* 4(4), 415–435.

General Accounting Office. (1995a). *School Facilities: Conditions of America's Schools*. Washington, DC: Author. (GAO/HEHS-95-61.)

General Accounting Office. (1995b). *School Facilities: American's School Not Designed or Equipped for 21st Century*. Washington, DC: Author (GAO/HEHS-95-95.)

General Accounting Office. (1995c). *School Facilities: State's Financial and Technical Support Varies*. Washington, DC: Author. (GAO/HEHS-96-27.)

General Accounting Office. (1996). *School Facilities: America's Schools Report Differing Conditions*. Washington, DC: Author. (GAO/HEHS-96-103.)

General Accounting Office. (1998). *School Finance: State Efforts to Reduce Funding Gaps between Poor and Wealthy Districts*. Washington, DC: Author. (Chapter Report, 06/16/1998, GAO/HEHS-98-92.)

General Accounting Office. (2000). *School Facilities: Construction Expenditures Have Grown Significantly in Recent Years*. Washington, DC: Author. (GAO/HEHS-00-41.)

Gerber, Susan; Finn, Jeremy; Achilles, Charles; & Boyd-Zaharias, Jane. (2001). Teacher Aides and Students' Academic Achievement. *Educational Evaluation and Policy Analysis* 23(2), 123–143.

Gilster, P. (2000). Digital Literacy. In R. Pea (ed.), *The Jossey-Bass Reader on Technology and Learning* (pp. 215–225). San Francisco: Jossey-Bass.

Glass, G. V., & Smith. M. L. (1979). Meta-Analysis of Research on Class Size and Achievement. *Educational Evaluation and Policy Analysis.?* 1(1), 2–16.

Glenn, William; Picus, L. O.; Marion, S. F.; & Calvo, N. (May 2006). School Facilities Quality and Student Achievement in Wyoming. *School Business Affairs* 72(5), 12–16.

Glenn, W.; Picus, L. O.; Odden, A.; & Aportela, A. (2006). *An Analysis of the Equity of School Facilities Funding in Kentucky*. Prepared for the Kentucky Department of Education. North Hollywood, CA: Lawrence O. Picus and Associates.

Goertz, Margaret. (1983). School Finance in New Jersey: A Decade after *Robinson v. Cahill*. *Journal of Education Finance* 8(4), 475–489.

Goertz, Margaret. (1988). *School District's Allocation of Chapter 1 Resources*. Princeton, NJ: Educational Testing Service.

Goertz, Margaret. (1997). The Challenges of Collecting School-Based Data. *Journal of Education Finance* 22(3), 291–302.

Goertz, Margaret; McLauglin, Margaret; Roach, Virginia; & Raber, Suzanne. (1999). What Will It Take: Including Students with Disabilities in Standards-Based Education Reform. In Jay Chambers, Thomas Parrish, & Cassandra Guarino (eds.), *Funding Special Education* (pp. 41–62). Thousand Oaks, CA: Corwin Press.

Goertz, Margaret, & Odden Allan (eds.). (1999). *School-Based Financing*. Thousand Oaks, CA: Corwin Press.

Gold, Steven. (1994). *Tax Options for States Needing More School Revenue*. Washington, DC: National Education Association.

Gold, Steven D.; Smith, David M.; & Lawton, Stephen B. (1995). *Public School Finance Programs of the United States and Canada: 1993–94*. New York: American Education Finance Association of Center for the Study of the States, Nelson A. Rockefeller Institute of Government.

Gold, Stephen D.; Smith, David M.; Lawton, Stephen B.; & Hyary, Andrea C (eds.). (1992). *Public School Finance Programs in the United States and Canada, 1990–1991*. Albany: State University of New York, Center for the Study of the States.

Goldhaber, Dan. (2002). Teacher Quality and Teacher Pay Structure: What Do We Know and What Are the Options? *Georgetown Public Policy Review* 7(2), 81–94.

Goldhaber, Dan, & Callahan, Karen. (2001). Impact of the Basic Education Program on Educational Spending and Equity in Tennessee. *Journal of Education Finance* 26(4), 415–436.

Goldhaber, Dan, & Player, Dan. (2005). What Different Benchmarks Suggest about How Financially Attractive It Is to Teach in Public Schools. *Journal of Education Finance* 30(3), 211–230.

Greenwald, Rob; Hedges, Larry V.; & Laine, Richard D. (1996a). The Effect of School Resources on Student Achievement. *Review of Educational Research* 66(3), 361–396.

Greenwald, Rob; Hedges, Larry V.; & Laine, Richard D. (1996b). Interpreting Research on School Resources and Student Achievement: A Rejoinder to Hanushek. *Review of Educational Research* 66(3), 411–416.

Grissmer, David. (1999). Class Size: Issues and New Findings. *Educational Evaluation and Policy Analysis* 21(2). (Entire issue.)

Gronberg, Timothy J.; Jansen, Dennis W.; Taylor, Lori L.; & Booker, Kevin. (2004). *School Outcomes and School Costs: The Cost Function Approach*. Report prepared for the Texas Legislature Joint Committee on Public School Finance, Texas School Finance Project. Available at capitol2.tlc.state.tx.us/psf/Reports/school%20outcomes%20an%20school%20costs.doc2.pdf.

Grubb, W. Norton, & Michelson, Stephan. (1974). *States and Schools: The Political Economy of Public School Finance*. Lexington, MA: Lexington Books.

Grubb, W. Norton, & Osman, J. (1977). The Causes of School Finance Inequalities: Serrano and the Case of California. *Public Finance Quarterly* 5(3), 373–392.

Gullo, D. (2000). The Long-Term Effects of Full-School-Day Kindergarten on Student Achievement: A Meta-Analysis. *Early Child Development and Care* 160(1), 17–24.

Guskey, T. R. (1986). Staff Development and the Process of Change. *Educational Researcher* 15(5), 5–12.

Guss-Zamora, M.; Zarate, R.; Robledo, M.; & Cardenas, Jose. (1979). *Bilingual Education Cost Analysis: Utah*. San Antonio: Intercultural Development Research Association.

Guthrie, James W. (1979). Organizational Scale and School Success. *Educational Evaluation and Policy Analysis* 1(1), 17–27.

Guthrie, James; Garms, Walter; & Pierce, Lawrence. (1988). *School Finance and Education Policy*. Englewood Cliffs, NJ: Prentice-Hall.

Guthrie, James W., & Rothstein, Richard. (1999). Enabling "Adequacy" to Achieve Reality: Translating Adequacy into State School Finance Distribution Arrangements. In Helen Ladd, Rosemary Chalk, & Janet Hansen (eds.), *Equity and Adequacy in Education Finance: Issues and Perspectives* (pp. 209–259). Washington, DC: National Academy Press.

Guthrie, James, et al. (1997). *A Proposed Cost-Based Block Grant Model for Wyoming School Finance*. Davis, CA: Management Analysis and Planning Associates. Available at legisweb.state.wy.us/school/cost/apr7/apr7.htm.

Gutierrez, Roberto, & Slavin, Robert. (1992). Achievement Effects of the Nongraded Elementary School: A Best Evidence Synthesis. *Review of Educational Research* 62(4), 333–376.

Hahn, A.; Leavitt, T.; & Aaron, P. (1994). *Evaluation of the Quantum Opportunities Program: Did the Program Work?* Waltham, MA: Brandeis University.

Haller, Emil; Monk, David H.; Spotted Bear, Alyce; Griffith, Julie; & Moss, Pamela. (1990). School Size and Program Comprehensiveness: Evidence from High School and Beyond. *Educational Evaluation and Policy Analysis* 12(2), 109–120.

Hallinger, P., & Heck, R. H. (1996). Reassessing the Principal's Role in School Effectiveness: A Review of Empirical Research, 1980–1995. *Educational Administration Quarterly* 32(1), 5–45.

Hallinger, P., & Heck, R. H. (2002). What Do You Call People with Visions? The Role of Vision, Mission and Goals in School Leadership and Improvement. In K. Leithwood, P. Hallinger, & Colleagues (eds.), *The Handbook of Educational Leadership and Administration* (2d ed.) Dordrecht: Kluwer.

Hallinger, P., & Heck, R. H. (2003). Understanding the Principal's Contribution to School Improvement. In M. Wallace & L. Poulson (eds.), *Learning to Read Critically in Educational Leadership and Management*. London: Sage.

Halverson, Richard. (2003). Systems of Practice: How Leaders Use Artifacts to Create Professional Community in Schools. *Educational Policy and Analysis Archives* 11(37). Available at http://epaa.asu.edu/epaa/v11n37.

Hamilton, Stephen F. (1983). The Social Side of Schooling: Ecological Studies of Classrooms and Schools. *Elementary School Journal* 83(4), 313–334.

Hansen, J., & Feldhusen, J. F. (1994). Comparison of Trained and Untrained Teachers. *Gifted Child Quarterly* 38(3), 115–121.

Hanushek, Eric A. (1981). Throwing Money at Schools. *Journal of Policy Analysis and Management* 1(1), 19–41.

Hanushek, Eric. (1986). The Economics of Schooling: Production and Efficiency in Public Schools. *Journal of Economic Literature* 24(3), 1141–1177.

Hanushek, Eric. (1989). The Impact of Differential Expenditures on Student Performance. *Educational Researcher* 18(4), 45–52.

Hanushek, Eric A. (1994). Money Might Matter Somewhere: A Response to Hedges, Laine, and Greenwald. *Educational Researcher* 23(3), 5–8.

Hanushek, Eric A. (1997). Assessing the Effects of School Resources on Student Performance: An Update. *Educational Evaluation and Policy Analysis* 19(2), 141–164.

Hanushek, Eric. (2002). Evidence, Politics and the Class Size Debate. In Lawrence Mishel & Richard Rothstein (eds.), *The Class Size Debate* (pp. 37–65). Washington, DC: Economic Policy Institute.

Hanushek, Eric, and Associates. (1994). *Making Schools Work: Improving Performance and Controlling Costs*. Washington, DC: Brookings Institution.

Hanushek, Eric; Kain, J. F.; & Rivkin, S. G. (2004). The Revolving Door: Factors Effecting Teacher Turnover. In W. J. Fowler (ed.), *Developments in School Finance: 2003* (pp. 5–16): Washington, DC: U.S. Department of Education, National Center for Education Statistics.

Hanushek, Eric, & Rivkin, Steven. (1997). Understanding the Twentieth-Century Growth in U.S. School Spending. *Journal of Human Resources* 32(1), 35–68.

Hartman, William. (1980). Policy Effects of Special Education Funding Formulas. *Journal of Education Finance* 6(2), 135–139.

Hartman, William T. (1988). *School District Budgeting*. Englewood Cliffs, NJ: Prentice-Hall.

Hartman, William T. (1994). District Spending Disparities Revisited. *Journal of Education Finance* 20(1), 88–106.

Hartman, William. (2002). *School District Budgeting* (2d ed.). Reston, VA: Association of School Business Officers International.

Hayward, Gerald C. (1988). *The Two Million Dollar School*. Berkeley: University of California, School of Education, Policy Analysis for California Education.

Heck, R. H.; Larsen, T. J.; & Marcoulides, G. A. (1990). Instructional Leadership and School Achievement: Validation of a Causal Model. *Educational Administration Quarterly* 26(2), 94–125.

Hedges, Larry. V.; Laine, Richard D.; & Greenwald, Rob. (1994a). Does Money Matter? A Meta-Analysis of Studies of the Effects of Differential School Inputs on Student Outcomes. *Educational Researcher* 23(3), 5–14.

Hedges, Larry V.; Laine, Richard D.; & Greenwald, Rob. (1994b). Money Does Matter Somewhere: A Reply to Hanushek. *Educational Researcher* 23(3), 9–10.

Heise, Michael. (1995). State Constitutions, School Finance Litigation and the "Third Wave": From Equity to Adequacy. *Temple Law Review* 68(3), 1151–1176.

Hentschke, Guilbert C. (1986). *School Business Administration: A Comparative Perspective*. Berkeley, CA: McCutchan.

Hertert, Linda. (1996). Does Equal Funding for Districts Mean Equal Funding for Classroom Students? Evidence from California. In Lawrence O. Picus & James L. Wattenbarger (eds.), *Where Does the Money Go? Resource Allocation in Elementary and Secondary Schools* (pp. 71–84). 1995 Yearbook of the American Education Finance Association. Newbury Park, CA: Corwin Press.

Hertert, Linda; Busch, Carolyn A.; & Odden, Allan R. (1994). School Financing Inequities among the States: The Problem from a National Perspective. *Journal of Education Finance* 19(3), 231–255.

Heyns, B. (1978). *Summer Learning and the Effects of Schooling*. New York: Academic Press.

Hickrod, G. Alan; Chaudhari, Ramesh B.; & Hubbard, Ben C. (1981). *Reformation and Counter-Reformation in Illinois School Finance: 1973–1981*. Normal, IL: Center for the Study of Education Finance.

Hightower, Amy M. (2002). San Diego's Big Boom: Systemic Instructional Change in the Central Office and Schools. In Amy H. Hightower, Michael S. Knapp, Julie A. Marsh, & Milbrey W. McLaughlin (eds.), *School Districts and Instructional Renewal* (pp. 76–93). New York: Teacher's College Press.

Hinrichs, William L., & Laine, Richard D. (1996). *Adequacy: Building Quality and Efficiency into the Cost of Education*. Springfield: Illinois Board of Education.

Hirth, Marilyn. (1994). A Multistate Analysis of School Finance Issues and Equity Trends in Indiana, Illinois, and Michigan, 1982–1992. *Journal of Education Finance* 20(2), 163–190.

Hodge, Michael. (1981). Improving Finance and Governance of Education for Special Populations. In K. Forbis Jordan & Nelda Cambron-McCabe (eds.), *Perspectives in State School Support Programs*. Cambridge, MA: Ballinger.

House Committee on Education and the Workforce (2004). *Reforming and Reauthorizing IDEA*. Washington, DC: Author. Retrieved November 11, 2004, from edworkforce.house.gov/issues/108th/education/idea/idea.htm.

Hughes, M. F. (2000). *Financing Facilities in Rural School Districts: Variations among the States and the Case of Arkansas*. (ERIC Document Reproductive Service no. 445857.)

Iatarola, Patrice. (2005). Learning from Experience: New York City's Small High Schools. *PEA Bulletin* 30(1), 1–2, 3–5.

Imazeki, Jennifer. (2005). Assessing the Use of Econometric Analysis in Estimating the Costs of Meeting State Education Accountability Standards: Lessons from Texas. *Peabody Journal of Education* 80(3), 96–125.

Imazeki, Jennifer. (2006). Regional Adjustments for Washington State. Paper prepared for the K–12 Advisory Committee of Washington Learns under the auspices of Lawrence O. Picus and Associates.

Imazeki, Jennifer; & Reschovsky, Andrew. (2004). *Estimating the Costs of Meeting the Texas Educational Accountability Standards*. Retrieved September 16, 2006, from www.investintexas-schools.org/schoolfinancelibrary/studies/files/2005/january/reschovsky_coststudy.doc.

Imazeki, Jennifer, & Reschovsky, Andrew. (2006). Does No Child Left Behind Place a Fiscal Burden on States? Evidence from Texas. *Education Finance and Policy* 1(2), 217–246.

Jacobson, Linda. (2003). State-Financed Pre-K Shows Positive Effect, New Research Says. *Education* Week, November 19.

Johns, Roe; Alexander, Kern; & Jordan, K. Forbis (eds.). (1971). *Planning to Finance Education, Vol. 3*. Gainesville, FL: National Education Finance Project.

Johnson, Gary, & Pillianayagam, George. (1991). A Longitudinal Equity Study of Ohio's School Finance System: 1980–89. *Journal of Education Finance* 17(1), 60–82.

Johnson, Nicholas. (2000). State Low-Income Tax Relief: Recent Trends. *National Tax Journal* 53(3, Part I), 403–416.

Joyce, Bruce, & Calhoun, E. (1996). *Learning Experiences in School Renewal: An Exploration of Five Successful Programs*. Eugene, OR: ERIC Clearinghouse on Educational Management.

Joyce, Bruce, & Showers, B. (2002). *Student Achievement through Staff Development* (3d ed.). Alexandria, VA: Association for Supervision and Curriculum Development.

Karoly, L.; Greenwood, P.; Everingham, S.; Hoube, J.; Kilburn, M. R.; Rydell, C. P.; Sanders, M.; & Chiesa, J. (1998). *Investing in Our Children: What We Know and Don't Know about the Costs and Benefits of Early Childhood Interventions*. Santa Monica, CA: RAND Corporation.

Kauerz, Kristie. (2005). *Full Day Kindergarten: A Study of State Policies in the United States*. Denver: Education Commission of the States.

Kearney, Phillip; Chen, Li-Ju; & Checkoway, Marjorie. (1988). *Measuring Equity in Michigan School Finance: A Further Look*. Ann Arbor: University of Michigan, School of Education.

Kelley, Carolyn. (1998). The Kentucky School-Based Performance Award Program: School-Level Effects. *Educational Policy* 12(3), 305–324.

Kelley, Carolyn; Heneman III, Herbert, G.; & Milanowski, Anthony. (2002). Teacher Motivation and School-Based Performance Award Programs. *Educational Administration Quarterly* 38(3), 372–401.

Kelley, Carolyn, & Protsik, Jean. (1997). Risk and Reward: Perspectives on the Implementation of Kentucky's School-Based Performance Award Program. *Educational Administration Quarterly* 33(4), 474–505.

Kenny, L.; Denslow, D.; & Goffman, I. (1975). Determination of Teacher Cost Differentials among School Districts in the State of Florida. In Ester Tron (ed.), *Selected Papers in School Finance*. Washington, DC: U.S. Office of Education.

Kirst, Michael. (1977). What Happens at the Local Level after School Finance Reform? *Policy Analysis* 3(1), 302–324.

Kleiner, B.; Nolin, M. J.; & Chapman, C. (2004). *Before and After School Care Programs, and Activities through Eighth Grade: 2001*. Washington, DC: U.S. Department of Education, National Center for Education Statistics.

Kozol, Jonathan. (1992). *Savage Inequalities: Children in America's Schools*. New York: Harper Perennial.

Krashen, Steve, & Biber, Douglas. (1988). *On Course: Bilingual Education's Success in California*. Sacramento: California Association for Bilingual Education.

Krueger, Alan. (2002). Understanding the Magnitude and Effect of Class Size on Student Achievement. In Lawrence Mishel & Richard Rothstein (eds.), *The Class Size Debate* (pp. 7–35). Washington, DC: Economic Policy Institute.

Krueger, A. B., & Whitmore, D. M. (2001). *Would Smaller Classes Help Close the Black-White Achievement Gap?* (Working paper #451.) Princeton, NJ: Princeton University. Available at www.irs.princeton.edu/pubs/pdfs/451.pdf.

Kulik, J. (1994). Meta-Analytical Studies of Findings on Computer-Based Instruction. In E. Baker & H. O'Neil, Jr. (eds.), *Technology Assessment in Education and Training* (pp. 9–34). Hillsdale, NJ: Erlbaum.

Kulik, J. (2003). *Effects of Using Instructional Technology in Elementary and Secondary Schools: What Controlled Evaluation Studies Say*. SRI Project no. P10446.001. Arlington, TX:. SRI International.

Kulik, James. A., & Kulik, Chen-Lin C. (1984). The Effects of Accelerated Instruction. *Review of Educational Research* 54(3), 409–425.

Kulik, James. A., & Kulik, Chen-Lin C. (1992). Meta-Analytic Findings on Grouping Programs. *Gifted Child Quarterly* 36(2), 73–77.

Ladd, Helen. (1975). Local Education Expenditures, Fiscal Capacity and the Composition of the Property Tax Base. *National Tax Journal* 28(2), 145–158.

Ladd, Helen; Chalk, R.; & Hansen, Janet (eds.). (1999a). *Equity and Adequacy in Education Finance: Issues and Perspectives*. Washington, DC: National Academy Press.

Ladd, Helen F., & Hansen, Janet S. (eds). (1999b). *Making Money Matter: Financing America's Schools*. Washington, DC: National Academy Press.

Laine, Richard D.; Greenwald, Rob; & Hedges, Larry V. (1996). Money Does Matter: A Research Synthesis of a New Universe of Education Production Function Studies. In Lawrence O. Picus & James L. Wattenbarger (eds.), *Where Does the Money Go? Resource Allocation in Elementary and Secondary Schools* (pp. 44–70). Thousand Oaks, CA: Corwin Press.

Landry, S. H. (1999). Issues in Developing Effective Interventions for Children with Developmental Disorders. In S. Broman & M. Fletcher (eds.), *The Changing Nervous System: Neurobehavioral Consequences of Early Brain Disorders* (pp. 341–364). New York: Oxford University Press.

Lankford, Hamilton; Loeb, Susanna; & Wyckoff, James. (2002). Teaching Sorting and the Plight of Urban Schools. *Educational Evaluation and Policy Analysis* 24(61), 37–62.

Lankford, Hamilton, & Wyckoff, James H. (1995). Where Has the Money Gone? An Analysis of School Spending in New York. *Educational Evaluation and Policy Analysis* 17(2), 195–218.

Lattimore, C. B.; Grotpeter, J. K.; & Taggart, R. (1998). *Blueprints for Violence Prevention, Book Four: Quantum Opportunities Program.* Boulder, CO: Center for the Study and Prevention of Violence.

Lawler, Edward E. (1990). *Strategic Pay: Aligning Organizational Strategies and Pay Systems.* San Francisco: Jossey-Bass.

Lawler III, Edward E. (2000). *Rewarding Excellence: Pay Strategies for the New Economy.* San Francisco: Jossey-Bass.

Lee, V.; Croninger, R.; & Smith, J. (1997). Course Taking, Equity and Mathematics Learning: Testing the Constrained Curriculum Hypothesis in U.S. Secondary Schools. *Educational Evaluation and Policy Analysis* 19(2), 99–122.

Lee, Valerie, & Smith, Julia. (1997). High School Size: Which Works Best, and for Whom? *Educational Evaluation and Policy Analysis* 19(3), 205–228.

Levacic, Rosalind. (1999). Case Study 2: United Kingdom. In Kenneth Ross & Rosalind Levacic (eds.), *Needs-Based Resource Allocation in Schools via Formula-Based Funding.* Paris: UNESCO, International Institute for Educational Planning.

Levin, Betsy. (1977). New Legal Challenges in Educational Finance. *Journal of Education Finance* 3(1), 53–69.

Lewis, A.; Bednarek, D.; Chion-Kenney, L.; Harrison, C.; Kolodzy, J.; McCormick, K.; Smith, J.; Speich, D.; & Walker, L. (1989). *Wolves at the Schoolhouse Door: An Investigation of the Condition of Public School Buildings.* Washington, DC: Education Writers Association.

Lewis, L. (June, 2002). Teaching with Technology: Creating the Student-Centered Classroom. From *Now On* (electronic journal). Retrieved on May 5, 2005, from www.fno.org/jun02/teachingreview.html.

Lewis, L.; Snow, K.; Farris, E.; Smerdon, B.; Cronen, S.; & Kaplan, J. (2000). *Condition of America's Public School Facilities: 1999* (NCES 2000-032). Washington, DC: U.S. Department of Education, National Center for Education Statistics.

Linn, Robert L.; Baker, Eva L.; & Betebenner, Damian W. (2002). Accountability Systems: Implications of Requirements of the No Child Left Behind Act of 2001. *Educational Researcher* 31(6), 3–16.

Little, J. W. (1993). Teachers' Professional Development in a Climate of Educational Reform. *Educational Analysis and Policy Analysis* 15(2), 129–151.

Liu, Goodwin. (2006). *Interstate Inequality in Educational Opportunity.* New York: New York University Law Review.

Loucks-Horsley, Susan; Love, Nancy; Stiles, Katherine; Mundry, S.; & Hewson, Peter. (2003). *Designing Professional Development for Teachers of Science and Mathematics.* Thousand Oaks, CA: Corwin Press.

Louis, Karen S.; Kruse, Sharon D.; & Marks, Helen. M. (1996). Schoolwide Professional Community. In Fred Newmann and Associates (eds.), *Authentic Achievement: Restructuring Schools for Intellectual Quality* (pp. 179–203). San Francisco: Jossey-Bass.

Louis, Karen; Marks, Helen; & Kruse, Sharon D. (1996). Teachers' Professional Community in Restructured Schools. *American Educational Research Journal* 33(4), 757–798.

Louis, Karen S., & Marks, Helen M. (1998). Does Professional Community Affect the Classroom? Teachers' Work and Student Experiences in Restructuring Schools. *American Journal of Education* 106, 532–575.

Lowe, D. D. (1996). *School Facilities Equity in California: An Empirical Study.* (ERIC Document Reproductive Service no. 425613.)

Madigan, Timothy. (1997). *Science Proficiency and Course Taking in High School: The Relationship of Science Course-Taking Patterns to Increases in Science Proficiency Between 8th and 12th Grades.* Washington, DC: National Center for Education Statistics.

Mahoney, J. L.; Stattin, H.; & Magnusson, D. (2001). Youth Recreation Center Participation and Criminal Offending: A 20-Year Longitudinal Study of Swedish Boys. *International Journal of Behavioral Development* 25(6), 509–520.

Maker, C. J. (1996). Identification of Gifted Minority Students: A National Problem, Needed Changes and a Promising Solution. *Gifted Child Quarterly* 40, 41–50.

Malhoit, Gregory C. (2005). *Providing Rural Students with a High Quality Education: The Rural Perspective on the Concept of Educational Adequacy*. Raleigh, NC: Rural School and Community Trust, Rural Education Finance Center.

Management Analysis and Planning, Inc. (2002). *A Professional Judgment Approach to Determining Adequate Education Funding in Wyoming*. Davis, CA: Author.

Mangan, Michelle Turner; Odden, Allan; & Picus, Lawrence O (2006). *School Uses of Resources in Arkansas after Increased Funding from an Adequacy Mandate*.

Mann, D.; Shakeshaft, C.; Becker, J.; & Kottkamp, R. (1999). *West Virginia's Basic Skills/Computer Education Program: An Analysis of Student Achievement*. Santa Monica, CA: Milken Family Foundation.

Mantzicopoulos, P.; Morrison, D.; Stone, E.; & Setrakian, W. (1992). Use of the SEARCH/TEACH Tutoring Approach with Middle-class Students at Risk for Reading Failure. *Elementary School Journal* 92, 573–586.

Mason, DeWayne & Burns, Robert. (1996). "Simply No Worse and Simply No Better" May Simply be Wrong: A Critique of Veenman's Conclusion about Multigrade Classes. *Review of Educational Research* 66(3), 307–322.

Mason, D. A., & Stimson, J. (1996). Combination and Non-Graded Classes: Definitions and Frequency in Twelve States. *Elementary School Journal* 96(4), 439–452.

Massell, Diane; Hoppe, Margaret; & Kirst, Michael. (1997). *Persistence and Change: Standards-Based Reform in Nine States*. Philadelphia: University of Pennsylvania, Graduate School of Education, Consortium for Policy Research in Education.

Mathes, P. G., & Fuchs, L. S. (1994). The Efficacy of Peer Tutoring in Reading for Students with Mild Disabilities: A Best-Evidence Synthesis. *School Psychology Review* 23, 59–80.

McCaffrey, Daniel R.; Lockwood, J. R.; Koretz, Daniel; Louis, Thomas A.; & Hamilton, Laura. (2004). Models for value-added modeling of teacher effects. *Journal of Educational and Behavioral Statistics* 29(1), 67–101.

McDonnell, Lorraine M.; McLaughlin, Margaret J.; & Morison, P. (eds.). (1997). *Educating One and All: Students with Disabilities and Standards-Based Reform*. Report by the National Research Council Committee on Goals 2000 and the Inclusion of Students with Disabilities. Washington, DC: National Academy Press.

McGuffey, C., & Brown, C. (1978). The Impact of School Building Age on School Achievement in Georgia. *Educational Facility Planner* 2, 78.

McGuire, C. Kent. (1982). *State and Federal Programs for Special Student Populations*. Denver: Education Commission of the States.

McLauglin, Margaret. (1999). Consolidating Categorical Educational Programs at the Local Level. In Jay Chambers, Thomas Parrish, & Cassandra Guarino (eds.), *Funding Special Education* (pp. 22–40). Thousand Oaks, CA: Corwin Press.

McLaughlin, W. Milbrey, & Yee, Sylvia. (1988). School as a Place to Have a Career. In Ann Lieberman (ed.), *Building a Professional Culture in Schools* (23–44). New York: Teachers College Press.

McMahon, Walter W. (1994). Intrastate Cost Adjustment. In *Selected Papers in School Finance*. Available at www.ed.gov/NCES/pubs/96068ica.

McUsic, M. (1991). The Use of Education Clauses in School Finance Reform Litigation. *Harvard Journal on Legislation* 28(2), 307–340.

Michie, J., & Holton, B. (2005). *Fifty Years of Supporting Children's Learning: A History of Public School Libraries and Federal Legislation from 1953 to 2000* (NCES 2005-311). U.S. Department of Education. National Center for Education Statistics. Washington, DC: U.S. Government Printing Office.

Mieszkowski, Peter. (1972). The Property Tax: An Excise Tax or Profits Tax? *Journal of Public Economics* 1, 73–96.

Mikesell, John L. (1986). *Fiscal Administration: Analysis and Application for the Public Sector.* Homewood, IL: Dorsey.

Milanowski, Anthony. (1999). Measurement Error or Meaningful Change? The Consistency of School Achievement in Two School-Based Award Programs. *Journal of Personnel Evaluation in Education* 12(4), 343–363.

Milanowski, Anthony. (2003a). An Exploration of the Pay Levels Needed to Attract Mathematics, Science and Technology Majors to a Career in K–12 Teaching. *Education Policy Analysis Archives* 11(50). Available at http://epaa.asu.edu/epaa/v11n50.

Milanowski, Anthony T. (2003b). *The Varieties of Knowledge and Skill-Based Pay Design: A Comparison of Seven New Pay Systems for K–12 Teachers.* Education Policy Analysis Archives. Retrieved from epaa.asu.edu/epaa/v11n4/.

Milanowski, Anthony. T. (2004). The Relationship between Teacher Performance Evaluation Scores and Student Achievement: Evidence from Cincinnati. *Peabody Journal of Education* 79(4), 33–53.

Milanowski, Anthony T., & Kimball, Steven M. (2005). *The Relationship between Teacher Expertise and Student Achievement: A Synthesis of Three Years of Data.* Paper presented at the American Educational Research Association, Montreal. Quebec, Canada.

Milanowski, Anthony; Kimball, Steve; & Odden, Allan. (2005). Teacher Accountability Measures and Links to Learning. In L. Stiefel, A. E. Schwartz, R. Rubenstein, & J. Zabel (eds.), *Measuring School Performance and Efficiency: Implications for Practice and Research* (pp. 137–161). Larchmont, NY: Eye on Education.

Miles, Karen Hawley. (1995). Freeing Resources for Improving Schools: A Case Study of Teacher Allocation in Boston Public Schools. *Educational Evaluation and Policy Analysis* 17(4), 476–493.

Miles, Karen Hawley, & Darling-Hammond, Linda. (1997). *Rethinking the Allocation of Teaching Resources: Some Lessons from High Performing Schools* (CPRE Research Report Series RR-38). Philadelphia: University of Pennsylvania, Graduate School of Education, Consortium for Policy Research in Education.

Miles, Karen Hawley, & Darling-Hammond, Linda. (1998). Rethinking the Allocation of Teaching Resources: Some Lessons from High-Performing Schools. *Educational Evaluation and Policy Analysis* 20(1), 9–29.

Miles, K. H.; Odden, A. R.; Fermanich, M.; & Archibald, S. (2004). Inside the Black Box of School District Spending on Professional Development: Lessons from Five Urban Districts. *Journal of Education Finance* 30(1), 1–26.

Milken Family Foundation (1999). *The Impact of Education Technology on Student Achievement: What the Latest Current Research Has to Say.* Retrieved December 26, 2001, from www.mff.org/pubs/ME161.pdf.

Miller, Samuel D. (2003). Partners in Reading: Using Classroom Assistants to Provide Tutorial Assistance to Struggling First-Grade Readers. *Journal of Education for Students Placed at Risk* 8(3), 333–349.

Miner, Jerry. (1963). *Social and Economic Factors in Spending for Public Education.* Syracuse, NY: Syracuse University Press.

Minorini, Paul, & Sugarman, Stephen. (1999a). School Finance Litigation in the Name of Educational Equity: Its Evolution, Impact and Future. In Helen Ladd, Rosemary Chalk, & Janet Hansen (eds.), *Equity and Adequacy in Education Finance: Issues and Perspectives*. Washington, DC: National Academy Press.

Minorini, Paul, & Sugarman, Stephen. (1999b). Educational Adequacy and the Courts: The Promise and Problems of Moving to a New Paradigm. In Helen Ladd, Rosemary Chalk, & Janet Hansen (eds.), *Equity and Adequacy in Education Finance: Issues and Perspectives*. Washington, DC: National Academy Press.

Mishel, L., & Rothstein, R. (2002). *The Class Size Debate*. Washington, DC: Economic Policy Institute.

Molnar, Alex. (1999). Evaluating the SAGE Program: A Pilot Program in Targeted Pupil-Teacher Reduction in Wisconsin. *Educational Evaluation and Policy Analysis* 21(2), 165–177.

Monk, David. (1987). Secondary School Size and Curriculum Comprehensiveness. *Economics of Education Review* 6(2), 137–150.

Monk, David. (1990). *Educational Finance: An Economic Approach*. New York: McGraw-Hill.

Monk, David H. (1992). Educational Productivity Research: An Update and Assessment of Its Role in Education Finance Reform. *Educational Evaluation and Policy Analysis* 14(4), 307–332.

Monk, David H. (1994). Subject Area Preparation of Secondary Math and Science Teachers and Student Achievement. *Economics of Education Review* 13(2), 125–145.

Monk, David H. (1997). Challenges Surrounding the Collection and Use of Data for the Study of Finance and Productivity. *Journal of Education Finance* 22(3), 303–316.

Monk, David H., & Brent, Brian O. (1997). *Raising Money for Schools: A Guide to the Property Tax*. Thousand Oaks, CA: Corwin Press.

Monk, D. H.; Roellke, Christopher F.; & Brent, Brian O. (1996). *What Education Dollars Buy: An Examination of Resource Allocation Patterns in New York State Public School Systems*. Madison: University of Wisconsin, Wisconsin Center for Education Research, Consortium for Policy Research in Education.

Monk, David, & Walker, Billy. (1991). The Texas Cost of Education Index. *Journal of Education Finance* 17(2), 172–192.

Moody, Scott (ed.). (2002). *Facts and Figures on Government Finance* (36th ed.). Washington, DC: Tax Foundation.

Morris, D.; Shaw, B.; & Perney, J. (1990). Helping Low Readers in Grades 2 and 3: An After-School Volunteer Tutoring Program. *The Elementary School Journal* 91(2), 133–150.

Mosteller, F. (1995). The Tennessee Study of Class Size in the Early School Grades. *The Future of Children: Critical Issues for Children and Youths* 5, 113–127.

Murnane, Richard, & Cohen, David. (1986). Merit Pay and the Evaluation Problem: Why Some Merit Pay Plans Fail and a Few Survive. *Harvard Educational Review* 56(1), 1–17.

Murnane, Richard, & Levy, Frank. (1996). *Teaching the New Basic Skills*. New York: Free Press.

Murphy, J. (1990). *The Educational Reform Movement of the 1980s*. Berkeley, CA: McCutchan.

Murphy, J.; Beck, L.; Crawford, M.; Hodges, A.; & McGaughy, C. (2001). *The Productive High School: Creating Personalized Academic Communities*. Thousand Oaks, CA: Corwin Press.

Murphy, John, & Picus, Lawrence O. (1996). Special Program Encroachment on School District General Funds in California: Implications for Serrano Equalization. *Journal of Education Finance* 21(3), 366–386.

Murphy, Joseph. (1994). Transformational Change and the Evolving Role of the Principal: Early Empirical Evidence. In Joseph Murphy & Karen Seashore Louis (eds.), *Reshaping the Principalship: Insights from Transformational Reform Efforts* (pp. 20–53). Thousand Oaks, CA: Corwin Press.

Murphy, R. F.; Penuel, W. R.; Means, B.; Korbak, C.; Whaley, A.; & Allen, J. E. (2002). *E-desk: A Review of Recent Evidence on the Effectiveness of Discrete Educational Software*. Palo Alto, CA: SRI International. Available at www.sri.com/policy/ctl/html/synthesis3.html.

Murray, Sheila E. (2001). Kentucky. In John Dayton, C. Thomas Holms, Catherine C. Sielke, & Anne L. Jefferson (eds.), *Public School Finance Programs of the United States and Canada, 1998–99* (NCES 2001-309). Washington, DC: National Center for Education Statistics.

Murray, Sheila; Evans, William; & Schwab, Robert. (1998). Education Finance Reform and the Distribution of Education Resources. *American Economic Review* 88(4), 789–812.

Musgrave, Richard, & Musgrave, Peggy. (1989). *Public Finance in Theory and Practice*. New York: McGraw-Hill.

Naglieri, J. A., & Ford, D. Y. (2003). Addressing Underrepresentation of Gifted Minority Children Using the Naglieri Nonverbal Ability Test (NNAT). *Gifted Child Quarterly* 47(2), 155–160.

Naglieri, J. A., & Ronning, M. E. (2000). Comparison of White, African-American, Hispanic, Asian Children on the Naglieri Nonverbal Ability Test. *Psychological Assessment* 12, 328–334.

Nakib, Yasser. (1995). Beyond District-Level Expenditures: Schooling Resource Allocation and Use in Florida. In Lawrence Picus & James Wattenbarger (eds.), *Where Does the Money Go?* (pp. 106–131). Thousand Oaks, CA: Corwin Press.

National Center for Education Statistics. (1990). *Financial Accounting for Local and State School Systems* (NCES 97096R). Washington, DC: U.S. Department of Education.

National Center for Education Statistics. (1998a). *Digest of Education Statistics, 1997*. Washington, DC: U.S. Department of Education.

National Center for Education Statistics. (1998b). *Federal Support for Education: Fiscal Years 1980–1998* (NCES 98-155). Washington, DC: U.S. Department of Education.

National Center for Education Statistics. (2005). *NAEP 2004 Trends in Academic Progress: Three Decades of Student Performance*. Washington, DC: U.S. Department of Education.

National Center for Education Statistics (2006). *Digest of Education Statistics, 2005*. Tables retrieved from nces.ed.gov/programs/digest/d05_tf.asp. July 25, 2006.

National Commission on Excellence and Equity in Education. (1983). *A Nation At-Risk: The Imperative of Educational Reform*. Washington, DC: U.S. Department of Education.

National Commission on Teaching and America's Future. (1996). *What Matters Most: Teaching in America*. New York: Teachers College Press.

National Education Association. (2000). *Modernizing Our Schools: What Will It Cost?* Washington, DC: Author.

National Education Association. (2005). *Rankings and Estimates: Ranking of the States 2004 and Estimates of School Statistics 2005*. Washington, DC: Author.

National Education Commission on Time and Learning. (1994). *Prisoners of Time*. Washington, DC: Author.

National Research Council. (1999). *Report of the Panel on Special Education*. Washington, DC: Author.

Nelson, F. Howard. (1984). Factors Contributing to the Cost of Programs for Limited English Proficient Students. *Journal of Education Finance* 10(1), 1–21.

Netzer, Dick. (1966). *Economics of the Property Tax*. Washington, DC: Brookings Institution.

Newmann, Fred, and Associates. (1996). *Authentic Achievement: Restructuring Schools for Intellectual Quality*. San Francisco: Jossey-Bass.

Newmann, F., & Wehlage, Gary G. (1995). *Successful School Restructuring: A Report to the Public and Educators*. Madison: University of Wisconsin, Wisconsin Center for Education Research, Center on Organization and Restructuring of Schools.

Norman, Jack. (2002). *Funding Our Future: An Adequacy Model for Wisconsin School Finance*. Milwaukee: Institute for Wisconsin's Future.

Nye, B. A.; L. V. Hedges; & S. Konstantopulos. (2001a). The Long-Term Effects of Small Classes in Early Grades: Lasting Benefits in Mathematics Achievement at Grade Nine. *Journal of Experimental Education* 69(3), 245–258.

Nye, B. A.; L. V. Hedges; & S. Konstantopulos. (2001b). Are Effects of Small Cumulative: Evidence from a Tennessee Experiment. *Journal of Educational Research* 94(6), 336–345.

Nye, B.; Hedges, L.V.; & Konstantopulos, S. (2002). Do Low-Achieving Students Benefit More from Small Classes? Evidence from the Tennessee Class Size Experiment. *Educational Evaluation and Policy Analysis* 24(3), 201–217.

Odden, Allan. (1978). Missouri's New School Finance Structure. *Journal of Education Finance* 3(3), 465–475.

Odden, Allan. (1988). How Fiscal Accountability and Program Quality Can Be Insured for Chapter I. In Denis Doyle & Bruce Cooper (eds.), *Federal Aid to the Disadvantaged: What Future for Chapter I?* New York: Falmer Press.

Odden, Allan. (1990). Class Size and Student Achievement: Research-Based Policy Alternatives. *Educational Evaluation and Policy Analysis* 12(2), 213–227.

Odden, Allan (ed.). (1991). *Education Policy Implementation*. Albany: State University of New York Press.

Odden, Allan. (1995a). *Educational Leadership for America's Schools*. New York: McGraw-Hill.

Odden, Allan. (1995b). Missouri School Finance System: Fiscal Equity after S.B. 380. Paper prepared for the Missouri Performance Commission.

Odden, Allan. (1997a). The Finance Side of Implementing New American Schools. Paper prepared for the New American Schools, Alexandria, VA.

Odden, Allan. (1997b). Having to Do More with Less: Stretching the School Budget Dollar. *School Business Affairs* 63(6), 2–10.

Odden, Allan. (1998). *Improving State School Finance Systems: New Realities Create Need to Re-Engineer School Finance Structures* (CPRE Occasional Paper Series OP-04). Philadelphia: University of Pennsylvania, Graduate School of Education, Consortium for Policy Research in Education.

Odden, Allan. (1999). Case Study 3: School Based Formula Funding in North America. In Kenneth Ross & Rosalind Levacic (eds.), *Needs-Based Resource Allocation in Schools via Formula-Based Funding* (pp. 198–227). Paris: UNESCO, International Institute for Educational Planning.

Odden, Allan. (2000). Costs of Sustaining Educational Change via Comprehensive School Reform. *Phi Delta Kappan* 81(6), 433–438.

Odden, Allan. (2003). Equity and Adequacy in School Finance Today. *Phi Delta Kappan* 85(2), 120–125.

Odden, Allan, & Archibald, Sarah. (2000). Reallocating Resources to Support Higher Student Achievement: An Empirical Look at Five Sites. *Journal of Education Finance* 25(4), 545–564.

Odden, Allan, & Archibald, Sarah. (2001a). *Reallocating Resources: How to Boost Student Achievement without Asking for More*. Thousand Oaks, CA: Corwin Press.

Odden, Allan, & Archibald, Sarah. (2001b). Committing to Class-Size Reduction and Finding the Resources to Implement It: A Case Study of Resource Reallocation in Kenosha, Wisconsin. *Education Policy Analysis Archives* 9(30). Online journal: epaa.asu.edu/epaa/v9n30.html.

Odden, Allan; Archibald, Sarah; & Tychsen, Anita. (1998). *Can Wisconsin Schools Afford Comprehensive School Reform?* Madison: University of Wisconsin, Wisconsin Center for Education Research, Consortium for Policy Research in Education.

Odden, Allan; Archibald, Sarah; Fermanich, Mark; & Gallagher, H. Alix. (2002). A Cost Framework for Professional Development. *Journal of Education Finance* 28(1), 51–74.

Odden, Allan; Archibald, Sarah; Fermanich, Mark; & Gross, Betheny. (2003). Defining School-Level Expenditure Structures That Reflect Educational Strategies. *Journal of Education Finance* 29(3), 323–356.

Odden, Allan, & Augenblick, John. (1981). *School Finance Reform in the States: 1981.* Denver: Education Commission of the States.

Odden, Allan; Berne, Robert; & Stiefel, Leanna. (1979). *Equity in School Finance.* Denver: Education Commission of the States.

Odden, Allan; Borman, Geoffrey; & Fermanich, Mark. (2004). Assessing Teacher, Classroom, and School Effects, Including Fiscal Effects. *Peabody Journal of Education* 79(4), 4–32.

Odden, Allan, & Busch, Carolyn. (1995). Costs and Impacts of Alternative Plans for Reforming Wisconsin School Finance and Providing Property Tax Relief. In Carla Edlefson (ed.), *School Finance Policy Issues in the States and Provinces* (pp. 192–203). Columbus: The Ohio State University, Policy Research for Ohio Based Education and American Educational Research Association.

Odden, Allan, & Busch, Carolyn (eds.). (1997). Special Issue: Collection of School-Level Finance Data. *Journal of Education Finance* 22(3).

Odden, Allan, & Busch, Carolyn. (1998). *Financing Schools for High Performance: Strategies for Improving the Use of Educational Resources.* San Francisco: Jossey-Bass.

Odden, Allan, & Clune, William. (1998). School Finance Systems: Aging Structures in Need of Renovation. *Educational Evaluation and Policy Analysis* 20(3), 157–177.

Odden, Allan, & Dougherty, Van. (1984). *Education Finance in the States, 1984.* Denver: Education Commission of the States.

Odden, Allan; Fermanich, Mark; & Picus, Lawrence O. (2003). *A State-of-the Art Approach to School Finance Adequacy in Kentucky.* Report prepared for the Kentucky State Department of Education.

Odden, Allan, & Kelley, Carolyn. (2002). *Paying Teachers for What They Know and Do: New and Smarter Compensation Strategies to Improve Schools* (2d ed.). Thousand Oaks, CA: Corwin Press.

Odden, Allan; Kellor, Eileen; Heneman, Herbert; & Milanowski, Anthony. (1999). *School-Based Performance Award Programs: Design and Administration Issues Synthesized from Eight Programs.* University of Wisconsin–Madison, Wisconsin Center for Education Research, Consortium for Policy Research in Education. Retrieved from www.wcer.wisc.edu/cpre/tcomp.

Odden, Allan, & Massy, William. (1992). *Education Funding for Schools and Universities: Improving Productivity and Equity.* Los Angeles: University of Southern California, Center for Research in Education Finance, Consortium for Policy Research in Education.

Odden, Allan; Palaich, Robert; & Augenblick, John. (1979). *Analysis of the New York State School Finance System, 1977–78.* Denver: Education Commission of the States.

Odden, Allan, & Picus, Lawrence O. (1992). *School Finance: A Policy Perspective.* New York: McGraw-Hill.

Odden, Allan, & Picus, Lawrence O. (2000). *School Finance: A Policy Perspective* (2d ed.). New York: McGraw-Hill.

Odden, Allan, & Picus, Lawrence O. (2004). *School Finance: A Policy Perspective* (3d ed.). New York: McGraw-Hill.

Odden, Allan; Picus, Lawrence O.; et al. (2005). *An Evidence-Based Approach to School Finance Adequacy in Wyoming.* Report prepared for the Wyoming legislature. Available at legisweb.state.wy.us/2006/interim/schoolfinance/Recalibration/WY%20RecaFinal.pdf.

Odden, Allan; Picus, Lawrence O.; Archibald, Sarah; Goetz, Michael; Mangan, Michelle Turner; & Aportela, Anabel. (2007). *Moving from Good to Great in Wisconsin: Funding Schools Adequately and Doubling Student Performance.* Madison: University of Wisconsin, Wisconsin Center for Education Research, Consortium for Policy Research in Education. See www.wcer.wisc.edu/cpre/.

Odden, Allan; Picus, Lawrence O.; & Fermanich, Mark. (2003). *An Evidenced-Based Approach to School Finance Adequacy in Arkansas*. Submitted to the Joint Committee on Educational Adequacy of the Arkansas Legislature, Little Rock.

Odden, Allan; Picus, Lawrence O.; Fermanich, Mark; & Goetz, Michael. (2004). *An Evidence-Based Approach to School Finance Adequacy in Arizona*. Report prepared for the Rodel Charitable Foundations, Phoenix.

Odden, Allan R.; Picus, Lawrence O.; & Goetz, Michael. (2006). *Recalibrating the Arkansas School Funding Structure*. Report prepared for the Adequacy Study Oversight Sub-Committee of the House and Senate Interim Committees on Education of the Arkansas General Assembly. N. Hollywood, CA: Lawrence O. Picus and Associates.

Odden, Allan; Picus, Lawrence O.; Goetz, Michael; Fermanich Mark; & Mangan, Michelle Turner. (2006). *An Evidence-Based Approach to School Finance Adequacy in Washington*. Report prepared for the K–12 Advisory Committee of Washington Learns. Available at www.washington-learns.wa.gov/materials/Tab1Doc1EvidenceBasedReportforAC7-18-06_02.pdf.

Odden, Allan, & Wallace, Marc C., Jr. (2007a). *How to Achieve World-Class Teacher Compensation*. St. Paul, MN: Freeload Press.

Odden, Allan, & Wallace, Marc C., Jr. (2007b). *Rewarding Teacher Excellence: A Teacher Compensation Handbook for State and Local Policymakers*. Madison: University of Wisconsin, Wisconsin Center for Education Research, Consortium for Policy Research in Education.

Ornstein, Allen C. (1990). How Big Should Schools and Districts Be? *Education Digest* 56(2), 44–48.

Ouchi, William G. (2003). *Making Schools Work: A Revolutionary Plan to Get Your Children the Education They Need*. New York: Simon and Schuster.

Park, Rolla Edward, & Carroll, Stephen J. (1979). *The Search for Equity in School Finance: Michigan School District Response to a Guaranteed Tax Base* (R-2393-NIE/HEW). Santa Monica, CA: RAND Corporation.

Parrish, Thomas B. (1994). A Cost Analysis of Alternative Instructional Models for Limited English Proficient Students in California. *Journal of Education Finance* 19(3), 256–278.

Parrish, Thomas. (1996). Special Education Finance: Past, Present and Future. *Journal of Education Finance* 21(4), 451–476.

Pavan, Barbara. (1992). Recent Research on Nongraded Schools: The Benefits of Nongraded Schools. *Educational Leadership* 50(2), 22–25.

Pechman, Joseph A. (1985). *Who Paid the Taxes, 1966–85*. Washington, DC: Brookings Institution.

Pechman, Joseph A. (1986). *Who Paid the Taxes, 1966–85. Revised Tables*. Washington, DC: Brookings Institution.

Perie, Marianne; Moran, Rebecca; Lutkus, Anthony D.; & Tirre, William. (2005, June). *Three Decades of Student Performance in Reading and Mathematics: Reading, 1971–2004, Mathematics, 1973–2004*. NAEP 2004 Trends in Academic Progress (NCES 2005–464). Washington, DC: National Center for Education Statistics.

Phares, Donald. (1980). *Who Pays State and Local Taxes?* Cambridge, MA: Oelgeschlager, Gunn and Hain.

Phelps, L. Allen. (2006). *Career and Technical Education in Wisconsin's New Economy: Challenges and Investment Imperatives*. Madison: University of Wisconsin, Wisconsin Center for Education Research, Consortium for Policy Research in Education.

Philliber, S.; Kaye, J. W.; & Herrling, S. (2001). *The National Evaluation of the Children's Aid Society Carrera-Model Program to Prevent Pregnancy*. Accord, NY: Philliber Research Associates.

Phillips, Robyn. (1988). Restoring Property Tax Equity. In *California Policy Choices 4* (pp. 143–169). Los Angeles: University of Southern California, School of Public Administration.

Picus, Lawrence O. (1993a). *The Allocation and Use of Educational Resources: School Level Evidence from the Schools and Staffing Survey* (Working Paper no. 37). Los Angeles: USC Center for Research in Education Finance.

Picus, Lawrence O. (1993b). *The Allocation and Use of Educational Resources: District Level Evidence from the Schools and Staffing Survey.* Paper prepared for the Consortium for Policy Research in Education Finance Center, University of Wisconsin–Madison.

Picus, Lawrence O. (1994a). Estimating the Determinants of Pupil/Teacher Ratios: Evidence from the Schools and Staffing Survey. *Educational Considerations* 21(2), 44–52.

Picus, Lawrence O. (1994b). The Local Impact of School Finance Reform in Texas. *Educational Evaluation and Policy Analysis* 16(4), 391–404.

Picus, Lawrence O. (1994c). Achieving Program Equity: Are Markets the Answer? *Educational Policy* 8(4), 568–581.

Picus, Lawrence. (1997). Using School-Level Finance Data: Endless Opportunity or Bottomless Pit? *Journal of Education Finance* 22(3), 317–330.

Picus, Lawrence O. (2000). Student Level Finance Data: Wave of the Future. *The Clearing House* 74(2), 75–80.

Picus, Lawrence O., & Bhimani, Minaz. (August 1993). Estimating the Impact of District Characteristics on Pupil/Teacher Ratios. *Journal of the American Statistical Association.* Proceedings of the annual conference of the American Statistical Association, San Francisco.

Picus, Lawrence O., & Fazal, M. (1996). Why Do We Need to Know What Money Buys? Research on Resource Allocation Patterns in Elementary and Secondary Schools. In Lawrence O. Picus & James L. Wattenbarger (eds.), *Where Does the Money Go? Resource Allocation in Elementary and Secondary Schools* (pp. 1–19) (1995 Yearbook of the American Education Finance Association). Newbury Park, CA: Corwin Press.

Picus, Lawrence O., & Hertert, Linda. (1993a). A School Finance Dilemma for Texas: Achieving Equity in a Time of Fiscal Constraint. *Texas Researcher* 4, 1–28.

Picus, Lawrence O., & Hertert, Linda. (1993b). Three Strikes and You're Out: Texas School Finance after Edgewood III. *Journal of Education Finance* 18(3), 366–389.

Picus,, Lawrence O.; Marion, S.; Calvo, N.; & Glenn, W. (2005). Understanding the Relationship between Student Achievement and the Quality of Educational Facilities: Evidence from Wyoming. *Peabody Journal of Education* 80(3), 71–95.

Picus, Lawrence O.; Odden, Allan; & Fermanich, Mark. (2003). *A Professional Judgment Approach to School Finance Adequacy in Kentucky.* North Hollywood, CA: Lawrence O. Picus and Associates.

Picus, Lawrence O.; Odden, Allan; & Fermanich, Mark. (2004). Assessing the Equity of Kentucky's SEEK Formula: A Ten Year Analysis. *Journal of Education Finance* 29(4), 315–336.

Picus, Lawrence O.; Tetreault, Donald R.; & Murphy, John. (1996). *What Money Buys: Understanding the Allocation and Use of Educational Resources in California.* Madison: University of Wisconsin, Wisconsin Center for Education Research, Consortium for Policy Research in Education.

Picus, Lawrence O., & Toenjes, L. (1994). Texas School Finance: Assessing the Impact of Multiple Reforms. *Journal of Texas Public Education* 2(3), 39–62.

Pompa, Delia. (March 26, 1998). *Testimony on the Fiscal Year 1999 Budget Requests for Bilingual and Immigrant Education.* Available at www.ed.gov/speeches.

Porter, Andrew. (1991). Creating a System of School Process Indicators. *Educational Evaluation and Policy Analysis* 13(1), 13–30.

Posner, Jill, & Vandell, Deborah L. (1994). Low-Income Children's After-School Care: Are There Beneficial Effects of After-School Programs? *Child Development* 65, 440–456.

Prince, Henry. (1997). Michigan's School Finance Reform: Initial Pupil-Equity Results. *Journal of Education Finance* 22(4), 394–409.

Public Agenda. (1997). *Getting By: What American Teenagers Really Think about Their Schools*. New York: Author.

Pulliam, John D. (1987). *History of Education in America* (4th ed.). Columbus, OH: Merrill.

Ravitch, Diane. (2004). *The Mad, Mad World of Textbook Adoption*. Fordham Institute. Maryland: District Creative Printing. Available at www.edexcellence.net.

Raywid, M. A. (1997/1998). Synthesis of Research: Small Schools: A Reform That Works. *Educational Leadership* 55(4), 34–39.

Reis, S. M., & Purcell, J. H. (1993). An Analysis of Content Elimination and Strategies Used by Elementary Classroom Teachers in the Curriculum Compacting Process. *Journal for the Education of the Gifted* 16(2), 147–170.

Reis, S. M.; Westberg, K. L.; Kulikowich, J.; Caillard, F.; Hebert, T.; Plucker, J.; Purcell, J. H.; Rogers, J. B.; & Smist, J. M. (1993). *Why Not Let High Ability Students Start School in January? The Curriculum Compacting Study* (RM93106). Storrs: National Research Center on the Gifted and Talented, University of Connecticut.

Reschovsky, Andrew. (1994). Fiscal Equalization and School Finance. *National Tax Journal* 47(1), 185–197.

Reschovsky, Andrew. (2004). *Wisconsin School Finance: A Primer*. Madison: University of Wisconsin, LaFollette Institute of Public Affairs.

Reschovsky, Andrew, & Imazeki, Jennifer. (1998). The Development of School Finance Formulas to Guarantee the Provision of Adequate Education to Low-Income Students. In William J. Fowler (ed.), *Developments in School Finance 1997* (NCES 98–212). Washington, DC: National Center for Education Statistics.

Reschovsky, Andrew, & Imazeki, Jennifer. (2001). Achieving Educational Adequacy through School Finance Reform. *Journal of Education Finance* 26(4), 373–396.

Reynolds, A. J.; Temple, J. A.; Robertson, D. L.; & Mann, E. A. (2001). Long-Term Effects of an Early Childhood Intervention on Educational Achievement and Juvenile Arrest: A 15-Year Follow-Up of Low-Income Children in Public Schools. *JAMA* 285(18), 2339–2346.

Reynolds, Arthur J., & Wolfe, Barbara. (1999). Special Education and School Achievement: An Exploratory Analysis with a Central-City Sample. *Educational Evaluation and Policy Analysis* 21(3), 249–269.

Rice, Jennifer K. (1999). The Impact of Class Size on Instructional Strategies and the Use of Time in High School Mathematics and Science Courses. *Educational Evaluation and Policy Analysis* 21, 215–229.

Riew, John. (1986). Scale Economies, Capacity Utilization and School Costs: A Comparative Analysis of Secondary and Elementary Schools. *Journal of Education Finance* 11(4), 433–446.

Rito, G. R., & Moller, B. W. (1989). Teaching Enrichment Activities for Minorities: T.E.A.M. for Success. *Journal of Negro Education* 58, 212–219.

Roberts, Greg. (2000). *Technical Evaluation Report on the Impact of Voyager Summer Programs*. Austin: University of Texas.

Robinson, A., & Clinkenbeard, P.R. (1998). Giftedness: An Exceptionality Examined. *Annual Review of Psychology* 49(1), 117–139.

Robledo, M.; Zarate, R.; Guss-Zamora, M.; & Cardenas, Jose. (1978). *Bilingual Education Cost Analysis*: Colorado. San Antonio: Intercultural Development Research Association.

Rogers, K. B. (2002). Effects of Acceleration on Gifted Learners. In M. Neihart, S. M. Reis, N. M. Robinson, & S. M. Moon (eds.), *The Social and Emotional Development of Gifted Children: What Do We Know?* (pp. 3–12). Waco, TX: Prufrock Press.

Rosen, H. S. (1992). *Public Finance* (3d ed.). Homewood, IL: Irwin.

Rosen, H. S. (2004) *Public Finance* (7th ed.). New York: Irwin.

Rossmiller, R. A.; Hale, J. A.; & Frohreich, L. E. (1979). *Educational Programs for Exceptional Children: Resource Configurations and Costs*. Madison: Department of Educational Administration, University of Wisconsin.

Rotberg, Iris; Futrell, Mary; & Lieberman, Joyce. (1998). National Board Certification: Increasing Participation and Assessing Impacts. *Phi Delta Kappan* 79(6), 462–466.

Rothstein, Richard, & Miles, Karen Hawley. (1995). *Where's the Money Gone?* Washington, DC: Economic Policy Institute.

Rowan, Brian; Correnti, R.; & Miller, R. J. (2002). What Large-Scale, Survey Research Tells Us about Teacher Effects on Student Achievement: Insights from the *Prospects* Study of Elementary Schools. *Teachers College Record* 104(8), 1525–1567.

Rubenstein, Ross. (1998). Resource Equity in the Chicago Public Schools: A School-Level Approach. *Journal of Education Finance* 23(4), 468–489.

Rubenstein, Ross. (2002). Providing Adequate Educational Funding: A State-by-State Analysis of Expenditure Needs. *Public Budgeting and Finance* 22(4), 73–98.

Rubenstein, R. (2002). Who Pays and Who Benefits? Examining the Distributional Consequences of the Georgia Lottery for Education. *National Tax Journal* 55, 223–238.

Rubenstein, Ross; Doering, Dwight; & Gess, Larry. (2000). The Equity of Public Education Funding in Georgia, 1988–1996. *Journal of Education Finance* 26(2), 187–208.

Rubenstein, R.; Schwartz, A. E.; & Stiefel, L. (2006, August 9). Weighting for Adequacy. *Education Week*. Available at www.edweek.org/ew/articles/2006/08/09/44rebenstein.h25.html.

Salmon, Richard; Dawson, Christina; Lawton, Steven; & Johns, Thomas. (1988). *Public School Finance Programs of the United States and Canada: 1986–87*. Sarasota, FL: American Education Finance Association.

Sample, Patricia Ritchey, & Hartman, William. (1990). An Equity Simulation of Pennsylvania's School Finance Simulation. *Journal of Education Finance* 16(1), 49–69.

Sanders, W. L., & Horn, S. P. (1994). The Tennessee Value-Added Assessment System (TVAAS): Mixed-Model Methodology in Educational Assessment. *Journal of Personnel Evaluation in Education* 8, 299–311.

Sanders, W. L., & Rivers, J. C. (1996). *Cumulative and Residual Effects of Teachers on Future Student Academic Achievement*. Knoxville: University of Tennessee, Value-Added Research and Assessment Center.

Sciarra, D. G.; Bell, K. L.; & Kenyon, S. (2006). *Safe and Adequate: Using Litigation to Address Inadequate K–12 School Facilities*. Newark, NJ: Education Law Center. Retrieved September 5, 2006, from www.edlawcenter.org/ELCPublic/Publications/PDF/Safe_and_Adequate.pdf.

Schinke, S. P.; Cole, K. C.; & Poulin, S. R. (2000). Enhancing the Educational Achievement of At-Risk Youth. *Prevention Science* 1(1), 51–59.

Schwartz, Myron, & Moskowitz, Jay. (1988). *Fiscal Equity in the United States: 1984–85*. Washington, DC: Decision Resources.

Schweinhart, L. J.; Montie, J.; Xiang, Z.; Barnett, W. Steven; Belfield, Clyde R.; & Nores, M. (2005). *Lifetime Effects: The High/Scope Perry Preschool Study through Age 40*. Ypsilanti, MI: High/Scope Educational Research Foundation.

Scott, L. (2004). *School Library Media Centers: Selected Results from the Longitudinal Study of 2002* (ELS 2002) (NCES 205–302). U.S. Department of Education, National Center for Education Statistics. Washington, DC: U.S. Government Printing Office.

Scott, M. S., Deuel, L. S. S., Jean-François, B., & Urbano, R. C. (1996). Identifying Cognitively Gifted Ethnic Minority Children. *Gifted Child Quarterly* 40, 147–153.

Seal, Kenna R., & Harmon, Hobart L. (1995). Realities of Rural School Reform. *Phi Delta Kappan* 77(2), 119–124.

Shanahan, Timothy. (1998). On the Effectiveness and Limitations of Tutoring in Reading. *Review of Research in Education 23*, 217–234. Washington, DC: American Educational Research Association.

Shanahan, T., & Barr, R. (1995). Reading Recovery: An Independent Evaluation of the Effects of an Early Instructional Intervention for At-Risk Learners. *Reading Research Quarterly* 30(4), 958–997.

Sher, Jonathan, & Tompkins, Rachel B. (1977). Economy, Efficiency and Equality: The Myths of Rural School and District Consolidation. In Jonathan P. Sher (ed.), *Education in Rural America*. Boulder, CO: Westview Press.

Sherman, Joel. (1992). Review of School Finance Equalization under Section 5(d) of P.L. 81–874, the Impact Aid Program. *Journal of Education Finance* 18(1).

Siegler, Robert. (1998). *Children's Thinking*. Upper Saddle River, NJ: Prentice-Hall.

Sielke, Catherine C. (1998). Fair and Adequate Funding for School Facilities. *School Business Affairs* 64(1), 24–29.

Sielke, Catherine C. (2002). Financing School Infrastructure Needs: An Overview across the 50 States. In Faith E. Crampton & David C. Thompson (eds.), *Saving America's School Infrastructure* (27–51) (Vol. II in the series Research in Education Fiscal Policy and Practice: Local, National, and Global Perspectives). Greenwich, CT: Information Age.

Sielke, Catherine; Dayton, John; Holmes, C. Thomas; & Jefferson, Ann. (eds.). (2001). *Public School Finance Programs in the U.S. and Canada: 1998–99*. Washington, DC: U.S. Department of Education, National Center for Education Statistics.

Slavin, Robert, (1992). The Nongraded Elementary School: Great Potential but Keep It Simple. *Educational Leadership* 50(2), 24.

Slavin, Robert, (1996). Neverstreaming: Preventing Learning Disabilities. *Educational Leadership* 53(4), 4–7.

Slavin, Robert, & Calderon, Margarita (eds.). (2001). *Effective Programs for Latino Students*. Mahwah, NJ: Lawrence Erlbaum.

Slavin, Robert, & Cheung, A. (2005). A Synthesis of Research on Language of Reading Instruction for English Language Learners. *Review of Educational Research* 75(2), 247–284.

Slavin, Robert, & Fashola, Olatokunbo. (1998). *Show Me the Evidence! Proven and Promising Programs for America's Schools*. Thousand Oaks, CA: Corwin Press.

Slavin, Robert; Karweit Nancy; & Wasik, Barbara (1994). *Preventing Early School Failure: Research Policy and Practice*. Boston: Allyn and Bacon.

Slavin, Robert; Madden, Nancy; Dolan, Lawrence; & Wasik, Barbara. (1996). *Every Child, Every School*. Thousand Oaks, CA: Corwin Press.

Smith, Marshall S., & O'Day, Jennifer. (1991). Systemic School Reform. In Susan Fuhrman & Betty Malen (eds.), *The Politics of Curriculum and Testing* (pp. 233–267). Bristol, PA: Falmer Press.

Smith, R. S.; Clark, T.; & Blomeyer, R. L. (2005). *A Synthesis of New Research on K–12 Online Learning*. Naperville, IL: Learning Point.

Smylie, M. (1996). From Bureaucratic Control to Building Human Capital: The Importance of Teacher Learning in Education Reform. *Educational Researcher* 25(9), 9–11.

Southern, W. T., Jones, E. D., & Stanley, J. C. (1993). Acceleration and Enrichment: The Context and Development of Program Options. In K. A. Heller, F. J. Monks, & A. H. Passow (eds.), *International Handbook of Research and Development of Giftedness and Talent* (pp. 387–410). Exeter, UK: Pergamon Press.

Sparkman, William. (1990). School Finance Challenges in State Courts. In J. Underwood & D. Verstegen (eds.), *The Impacts of Litigation and Legislation on Public School Finance* (pp. 193–224). Cambridge, MA: Ballinger.

Sparkman, William. (1994). The Legal Foundations of Public School Finance. *Boston College Law Review* 35(3), 569–595.

Speakman, Sheree; Cooper, Bruce; Holsomback, Hunt; May, Jay; Sampieri, Robert; & Maloney, Larry. (1997). The Three Rs of Education Finance Reform: Re-Thinking, Re-Tooling and Re-Evaluating School-Site Information. *Journal of Education Finance* 22(4), 337–367.

Spillane, J. P.; Halverson, R.; & Diamond, J. B. (2001). Investigating School Leadership Practice: A Distributed Perspective. *Educational Researcher* 30(3), 23–27.

Steinberg, Laurence. (1997). Standards outside the Classroom. In D. Ravitch, (ed), *The State of Student Performance in American Schools: Brookings Papers on Education Policy, Volume 1.* Washington, DC: Brookings Institution.

Stern, David. (1973). Effects of Alternative State Aid Formulas on the Distribution of Public School Expenditures in Massachusetts. *Review of Economics and Statistics* 55, 91–97.

Stringfield, Samuel; Ross, Steven; & Smith, Lana. (1996). *Bold Plans for School Restructuring: The New American School Designs.* Mahwah, NJ: Lawrence Erlbaum.

Struck, J. (2003, April). *A Study of Talent Development in a Predominantly Low Socioeconomic and/or African American Population.* Paper presented at the annual meeting of the American Educational Research Association, Chicago.

Supovitz, Jon, & Turner, Herbert M. (2000). The Effects of Professional Development on Science Teaching Practices and Classroom Culture. *Journal of Research in Science Teaching* 37(9), 963–980.

Swanson, Austin, & King, Richard. (1997). *School Finance: Its Economics and Politics.* New York: Longman.

Swiatek, M. A. (2002). A Decade of Longitudinal Research on Academic Acceleration through the Study of Mathematically Precocious Youth. *Roeper Review* 24(3), 141–144.

Tax Policy Center (2006). *Historical Number of Households, Average Pretax and After-Tax Income and Shares, and Minimum Incomes.* Retrieved August 31, 2006, from taxpolicycenter.org/TaxFacts/TFDB/TFTemplate.cfm?Docid=467.

Tax Policy Center (2006). *Household Income Quintiles 2000–2003.* Retrieved August 31, 2006, from www.taxpolicycenter.org/TaxFAct/TfdbTFTemplate.efm?Docid=467.

Taylor, Lori. (2004). *Adjusting for Geographic Variations in Teacher Compensation: Updating the Texas Cost-of-Education Index.* Report prepared for the Texas Legislature Joint Committee on Public School Finance, Texas School Finance Project, Austin. Available at www.capitol.state.tx.us/ psf/reports.htm.

Taylor, Lori L., & Fowler, William J. (2006). *A Comparative Wage Approach to Geographic Cost Adjustment.* Washington, DC: National Center for Education Statistics.

Tenopir, C. (2003). *Use and Users of Electronic Media Sources: An Overview and Analysis of Recent Research Studies.* Washington, DC: Council of Library and Information Resources. Available at www.clir.org/pubs/reports/pub120/contents.html.

Texas State Board of Education. (1986). *1985–96 Accountable Cost Study.* Austin: Texas Education Agency.

Thayer, Jennifer. (2004). *Professional Development: Costs and Effectiveness in One Rural District.* Ph.D., dissertation, University of Wisconsin–Madison.

Tiebout, Charles M. (1956). A Pure Theory of Local Expenditures. *Journal of Political Economy* 54, 416–424.

Tierney, J.; Grossman, J. B.; & Resch, N. (1995). *Making a Difference: An Impact Study of Big Brothers/Big Sisters.* Philadelphia: Public/Private Ventures.

Torgeson, J. K. (2004). Avoiding the Devastating Downward Spiral. *American Educator* 28(3), 6–19, 45–47.

Tsang, Mun C., & Levin, Henry R. (1983). The Impacts of Intergovernmental Grants on Education Spending. *Review of Educational Research* 53(3), 329–367.

Tyack, David, & Hansot, Elizabeth. (1982). *Managers of Virtue*. New York: Basic Books.

Underwood, Julie. (1995a). School Finance Litigation: Legal Theories, Judicial Activism, and Social Neglect. *Journal of Education Finance* 20(2), 143–162.

Underwood, Julie. (1995b). School Finance as Vertical Equity. *University of Michigan Journal of Law Reform* 28(3), 493–520.

Underwood, Julie, & Sparkman, W. (1991). School Finance Litigation: A New Wave of Reform. *Harvard Journal of Law and Public Policy* 14(2), 517–544.

U.S. Census Bureau. (2006). *Quarterly Summary of State and Local Government Tax Revenue, Table 1, National Totals of State and Local Government Tax Revenue for Current and Prior Quarters*, as well as 12-month calculations. Retrieved August 31, 2006, from www.census.gov/govs/www/qtax.html.

U.S. Department of Education. *The Condition of Education: 2006*. Washington, DC: Author.

U.S. Department of Education, National Center for Education Statistics. (2006). *The Condition of Education 2006* (NCES 2006–071). Washington, DC: U.S. Government Printing Office.

U.S. Department of Education, Office of Special Education Programs. *Data Analysis System* (DANS). Data based on December 1, 2001, count, updated as of August 30, 2002. Available at www.ideadata.org/tables25th/ar_aa13.htm.

U.S. Department of Labor. (2000). *A Nation of Opportunity: Building America's 21st Century Workforce*. Retrieved May 5, 2005, from www.ilr.cornell.edu/library/downloads/keyWorkplaceDocuments/21CenturyWorkforce/combined 21st century.pdf.

Valdez, McNabb; Foertsch, Anderson, Hawks, and Raack (2000). *Computer-Based Technology and Learning: Evolving Uses and Expectations*. North Central Regional Laboratory (NCREL). Retrieved May 5, 2005, from www.ncrel.org/tplan/cbtl/toc.htm.

Vandell, D. L.; Pierce, K. M.; & Dadisman, K. (2005). Out-of-School Settings as a Developmental Context for Children and Youth. In R. Kail (ed.), *Advances in Child Development and Behavior*, Vol. 33. New York: Academic Press.

VanTassel-Baska, J.; Bass, G.; Ries, R.; Poland, D.; & Avery, L. D. (1998). A National Study of Science Curriculum Effectiveness with High Ability Students. *Gifted Child Quarterly* 42(4), 200–211.

VanTassel-Baska, J.; Johnson, D. T.; & Avery, L. D. (2002). Using Performance Tasks in the Identification of Economically Disadvantaged and Minority Gifted Learners: Findings from Project STAR. *Gifted Child Quarterly* 46, 110–123.

VanTassel-Baska, J.; Johnson, D. T.; Hughes, C. E.; & Boyce, L. N. (1996). A Study of Language Arts Curriculum Effectiveness with Gifted Learners. *Journal for the Education of the Gifted* 19, 461–480.

VanTassel-Baska, J.; Zuo, L.; Avery, L. D.; & Little, C. A. (2002). A Curriculum Study of Gifted Student Learning in the Language Arts. *Gifted Child Quarterly* 46, 30–44.

Veenman, Simon. (1995). Cognitive and Noncognitive Effects of Multigrade and Multi-Age Classes: A Best Evidence Synthesis. *Review of Educational Research* 65(4), 319–381.

Verstegen, Deborah. (1996). Concepts and Measures of Fiscal Inequality: A New Approach and Effects for Five States. *Journal of Education Finance* 22(2), 145–160.

Verstegen, Deborah. (2002). Financing the New Adequacy: Towards New Models of State Education Finance Systems That Support Standards Based Reform. *Journal of Education Finance* 27(3), 749–782.

Verstegen, Deborah. (2003). *Calculation of the Cost of an Adequate Education in Kentucky*. Report prepared for the Council for Better Education, Frankfort, Kentucky.

Verstegen, Deborah, & Salmon, Richard. (1991). Assessing Fiscal Equity in Virginia: Cross-Time Comparisons. *Journal of Education Finance* 16(4), 417–430.

Vincent, Phillip E., & Adams, Kathleen. (1978). *Fiscal Response of School Districts: A Study of Two States—Colorado and Minnesota* (Report no. F78–3). Denver: Education Finance Center, Education Commission of the States.

Vornberg, J. A., & Andrews-Pool, K. (1998). *State Support of Educational Facilities Construction: A Policy Study.* (ERIC Document Reproductive Service no. 447684.)

Wasik, B., & Slavin, R. E. (1993). Preventing Early Reading Failure with One-to-One Tutoring: A Review of Five Programs. *Reading Research Quarterly* 28, 178–200.

Waxman, H. D.; Connell, M. L.; & Gray, J. (2002). *A Quantitative Synthesis of Recent Research on the Effects of Teaching and Learning with Technology on Student Outcomes.* Oak Brook, IL: North Central Regional Educational Laboratory. Available at www.ncrel.org/tech/effects.

Webster, W. J.; Mendro, R. L.; Orsak, T. H.; & Weerasinghe, D. (1998, April). An Application of Hierarchical Linear Modeling to the Estimation of School and Teacher Effect. Paper presented at the Annual Meeting of the American Educational Research Association, San Diego.

Weinstein, C. S. (1979). The Physical Environment of the School: A Review of the Research. *Review of Educational Research* 49, 577–610.

Wendling, Wayne (1981a). Capitalization: Considerations for School Finance. *Educational Evaluation and Policy Analysis* 3(2), 57–66.

Wendling, Wayne. (1981b). The Cost of Education Index: Measurement of Price Differences of Education Personnel among New York State School Districts. *Journal of Education Finance* 6(4), 485–504.

Wenglinsky, Harold. (1997). *When Money Matters.* Princeton, NJ: Education Testing Service.

Westberg, K. L.; Archambault, F. X.; Jr., Dobyns, S. M.; & Salvin, T. (1993). The Classroom Practices Observation Study. *Journal for the Education of the Gifted* 16, 120–146.

Wheldall, K.; Coleman, S.; Wenban-Smith, J.; Morgan, A.; & Quance, B. (1995). Teacher-Child Oral Reading Interactions: How Do Teachers Typically Tutor? *Educational Psychology* 12, 177–194.

White, R. N.; Reisner, E. R.; Welsh, M.; & Russell, C. (2001). *Patterns of Student-Level Change Linked to TASC Participation, Based on TASC Projects in Year 2.* Washington, DC: Policy Studies Associates.

Whitebrook, Marcy. (2004). *Bachelor's Degrees Are Best: Higher Qualifications for Pre-Kindergarten Teachers Lead to Better Learning Environments for Children.* Washington, DC: Trust for Early Education.

Wildavsky, Aaron. (1988). *The New Politics of the Budgetary Process.* Glenview, IL: Scott, Foresman.

Wise, Arthur. (1968). *Rich Schools–Poor Schools: A Study of Equal Educational Opportunity.* Chicago: University of Chicago Press.

Wise, Arthur. (1983). Educational Adequacy: A Concept in Search of Meaning. *Journal of Education Finance* 8(3), 300–315.

Wonacott, Michael. (2002). *Career Academies as Smaller Learning Communities: In Brief no. 20.* Columbus, OH: Career and Technical Education National Dissemination Center.

Wood, R. Craig; Honeyman, David; & Bryers, Verne. (1990). Equity in Indiana School Finance: A Decade of Local Levy Property Tax Restrictions. *Journal of Education Finance* 16(1), 83–92.

Wood, R. Craig; Thompson, David; Picus, Lawrence O; & Tharpe, Don I. (1995). *Principles of School Business Administration* (2d ed.). Reston, VA: Association of School Business Officials International.

Word, E.; Johnston, J.; Bain, H.; Fulton, D. B.; Boyd-Zaharias, J.; Lintz, M. N.; Achilles, C. M.; Folger, J.; & Breda, C. (1990). *Student/Teacher Achievement Ratio (STAR): Tennessee's K–3 Class-Size Study*. Nashville: Tennessee State Department of Education.

Wright, P. S.; Horn, S. P.; & Sanders, W. L. (1997). Teacher and Classroom Context Effects on Student Achievement: Implications for Teacher Evaluation. *Journal of Personnel Evaluation in Education* 11(1), 57–67.

Yinger, John. (2002). *Helping Children Left Behind: State Aid and the Pursuit of Educational Equity*. Unpublished manuscript.

Youngs, Peter; Odden, Allan; & Porter, Andrew. (2003). State Policy Related to Teacher Licensure. *Educational Policy* 17(2), 217–236.

Zodrow, George R. (2001). The Property Tax as a Capital Tax: A Room with Three Views. *National Tax Journal* 54(1), 139–156.

Name Index

Subject Index